THE ROUTLEDGE COMPANION TO ISLAMIC PHILOSOPHY

This valuable reference work synthesizes and elucidates traditional themes and issues in Islamic philosophy as well as prominent topics emerging from the last 20 years of scholarship. Written for a wide readership of students and scholars, *The Routledge Companion to Islamic Philosophy* is unique in including coverage of both perennial philosophical issues in an Islamic context and also distinct concerns that emerge from Islamic religious thought. This work constitutes a substantial affirmation that Islamic philosophy is an integral part of the Western philosophical tradition.

Featuring 33 chapters, divided into seven thematic sections, the volume explores the major areas of philosophy: logic, metaphysics, philosophy in the sciences, philosophy of mind/epistemology, and ethics/politics as well as philosophical issues salient in Islamic revelation, theology, prophecy, and mysticism.

Other features include:

- A focus on both the classical and post-classical periods
- A contributing body that includes both widely respected scholars from around the world and a handful of the very best younger scholars
- "References" and "Further Reading" sections for each chapter and a comprehensive index for the whole volume

The result is a work that captures Islamic philosophy as philosophy. In this way it serves students and scholars of philosophy and religious studies and at the same time provides valuable essays relevant to the study of Islamic thought and theology.

Richard C. Taylor is Professor of Philosophy at Marquette University, USA and is former editor of *History of Philosophy Quarterly*.

Luis Xavier López-Farjeat is Associate Professor of Philosophy at Universidad Panamericana in Mexico City, Mexico and editor of *Tópicos, Journal of Philosophy*.

ROUTLEDGE PHILOSOPHY COMPANIONS

Routledge Philosophy Companions offer thorough, high quality surveys and assessments of the major topics and periods in philosophy. Covering key problems, themes and thinkers, all entries are specially commissioned for each volume and written by leading scholars in the field. Clear, accessible and carefully edited and organised, *Routledge Philosophy Companions* are indispensable for anyone coming to a major topic or period in philosophy, as well as for the more advanced reader.

The Routledge Companion to Aesthetics, Third Edition
Edited by Berys Gaut and Dominic Lopes

The Routledge Companion to Philosophy of Religion, Second Edition
Edited by Chad Meister and Paul Copan

The Routledge Companion to Philosophy of Science, Second Edition
Edited by Martin Curd and Stathis Psillos

The Routledge Companion to Twentieth Century Philosophy
Edited by Dermot Moran

The Routledge Companion to Philosophy and Film
Edited by Paisley Livingston and Carl Plantinga

The Routledge Companion to Philosophy of Psychology
Edited by John Symons and Paco Calvo

The Routledge Companion to Metaphysics
Edited by Robin Le Poidevin, Peter Simons, Andrew McGonigal, and Ross Cameron

The Routledge Companion to Nineteenth Century Philosophy
Edited by Dean Moyar

The Routledge Companion to Ethics
Edited by John Skorupski

The Routledge Companion to Epistemology
Edited by Sven Bernecker and Duncan Pritchard

The Routledge Companion to Philosophy and Music
Edited by Theodore Gracyk and Andrew Kania

The Routledge Companion to Phenomenology
Edited by Søren Overgaard and Sebastian Luft

The Routledge Companion to Philosophy of Language
Edited by Gillian Russell and Delia Graff Fara

The Routledge Companion to Philosophy of Law
Edited by Andrei Marmor

The Routledge Companion to Social and Political Philosophy
Edited by Gerald Gaus and Fred D'Agostino

The Routledge Companion to Ancient Philosophy
Edited by Frisbee Sheffield and James Warren

The Routledge Companion to Eighteenth Century Philosophy
Edited by Aaron Garrett

The Routledge Companion to Bioethics
Edited by John Arras, Rebecca Kukla, and Elizabeth Fenton

The Routledge Companion to Virtue Ethics
Edited by Lorraine Besser-Jones and Michael Slote

The Routledge Companion to Hermeneutics
Edited by Jeff Malpas and Hans-Helmuth Gander

The Routledge Companion to Islamic Philosophy
Edited by Richard C. Taylor and Luis Xavier López-Farjeat

Forthcoming

The Routledge Companion to Sixteenth Century Philosophy
Edited by Benjamin Hill and Henrik Lagerlund

The Routledge Companion to Seventeenth Century Philosophy
Edited by Dan Kaufman

The Routledge Companion to Philosophy of Literature
Edited by Noël Carroll and John Gibson

The Routledge Companion to Medieval Philosophy
Edited by Richard Cross and J.T. Paasch

The Routledge Companion to Philosophy of Race
Edited by Paul C. Taylor, Linda Martín Alcoff, and Luvell Anderson

The Routledge Companion to Environmental Ethics
Edited by Benjamin Hale and Andrew Light

The Routledge Companion to Free Will
Edited by Meghan Griffith, Neil Levy, and Kevin Timpe

The Routledge Companion to Philosophy of Technology
Edited by Joseph Pitt and Ashley Shew Helfin

The Routledge Companion to Philosophy of Medicine
Edited by Miriam Solomon, Jeremy Simon, and Harold Kincaid

The Routledge Companion to Feminist Philosophy
Edited by Ann Garry, Serene Khader, and Alison Stone

The Routledge Companion to Philosophy of Social Science
Edited by Lee McIntyre and Alex Rosenberg

The Routledge Companion to Aesthetics
'This is an immensely useful book that belongs in every college library and on the bookshelves of all serious students of aesthetics.' - ***Journal of Aesthetics and Art Criticism***

'The succinctness and clarity of the essays will make this a source that individuals not familiar with aesthetics will find extremely helpful.' - ***The Philosophical Quarterly***

'An outstanding resource in aesthetics...this text will not only serve as a handy reference source for students and faculty alike, but it could also be used as a text for a course in the philosophy of art.' - ***Australasian Journal of Philosophy***

'Attests to the richness of modern aesthetics...the essays in central topics—many of which are written by well-known figures—succeed in being informative, balanced and intelligent without being too difficult.' - ***British Journal of Aesthetics***

'This handsome reference volume. . .belongs in every library.' - **CHOICE**

'The *Routledge Companions* to Philosophy have proved to be a useful series of high quality surveys of major philosophical topics and this volume is worthy enough to sit with the others on a reference library shelf.' - ***Philosophy and Religion***

The Routledge Companion to Philosophy of Religion
'... A very valuable resource for libraries and serious scholars.' - **CHOICE**

'The work is sure to be an academic standard for years to come... I shall heartily recommend *The Routledge Companion to Philosophy of Religion* to my students and colleagues and hope that libraries around the country add it to their collections.' - ***Philosophia Christi***

The Routledge Companion to Philosophy of Science
A **CHOICE** Outstanding Academic Title 2008

'With a distinguished list of internationally renowned contributors, an excellent choice of topics in the field, and well-written, well-edited essays throughout, this compendium is an excellent resource. Highly recommended.' - **CHOICE**

'Highly recommended for history of science and philosophy collections.' – ***Library Journal***

'This well conceived companion, which brings together an impressive collection of distinguished authors, will be invaluable to novices and experience readers alike.' - ***Metascience***

The Routledge Companion to Twentieth Century Philosophy
'To describe this volume as ambitious would be a serious understatement ... full of scholarly rigor, including detailed notes and bibliographies of interest to professional philosophers. ... Summing up: Essential.' - **CHOICE**

The Routledge Companion to Philosophy and Film
'A fascinating, rich volume offering dazzling insights and incisive commentary on every page ... Every serious student of film will want this book ... Summing Up: Highly recommended.' - **CHOICE**

The Routledge Companion to Philosophy of Psychology
'This work should serve as the standard reference for those interested in gaining a reliable overview of the burgeoning field of philosophical psychology. Summing Up: Essential.' - **CHOICE**

The Routledge Companion to Metaphysics
'The *Routledge Philosophy Companions* series has a deserved reputation for impressive scope and scholarly value. This volume is no exception ... Summing Up: Highly recommended.' - **CHOICE**

The Routledge Companion to Nineteenth Century Philosophy
A **CHOICE** Outstanding Academic Title 2010

'This is a crucial resource for advanced undergraduates and faculty of any discipline who are interested in the 19th-century roots of contemporary philosophical problems. Summing Up: Essential.' - **CHOICE**

The Routledge Companion to Ethics
'This fine collection merits a place in every university, college, and high school library for its invaluable articles covering a very broad range of topics in ethics[.] ... With its remarkable clarity of writing and its very highly qualified contributors, this volume is must reading for anyone interested in the latest developments in these important areas of thought and practice. Summing Up: Highly recommended.' - **CHOICE**

The Routledge Companion to Philosophy and Music
'Comprehensive and authoritative ... readers will discover many excellent articles in this well-organized addition to a growing interdisciplinary field. Summing Up: Highly recommended.' - **CHOICE**

'... succeeds well in catching the wide-ranging strands of musical theorising and thinking, and performance, and an understanding of the various contexts in which all this takes place.' - ***Reference Reviews***

The Routledge Companion to Phenomenology
'Sebastian Luft and Søren Overgaard, with the help of over sixty contributors, have captured the excitement of this evolving patchwork named "phenomenology". *The Routledge Companion to Phenomenology* will serve as an invaluable reference volume for students, teachers, and scholars of phenomenology, as well as an accessible introduction to phenomenology for philosophers from other specialties or scholars from other disciplines.' - ***International Journal of Philosophical Studies***

The Routledge Companion to Epistemology
A **CHOICE** Outstanding Academic Title 2011

'As a series, the *Routledge Philosophy Companions* has met with near universal acclaim. The expansive volume not only continues the trend but quite possibly sets a new standard . . . Indeed, this is a definitive resource that will continue to prove its value for a long time to come. Summing Up: Essential.'- **CHOICE**

The Routledge Companion to Philosophy of Language
'This collection presents more than 65 new essays by prominent contemporary figures working in the philosophy of language. Collectively, they represent the cutting edge of philosophical research into issues surrounding the use, understanding, and study of language. ... the book constitutes an invaluable current resource for students and scholars alike. It will appeal to anyone interested in the current state-of-play within this important area of philosophical research. Summing Up: Highly recommended.' – **CHOICE**

The Routledge Companion to Social and Political Philosophy
'This 15th book in the *Routledge Philosophy Companions* series is also the most comprehensive, both chronologically and conceptually. . . . . The polish and high quality of the essays provide a multifaceted mirror of the passions and interests of contemporary academic Anglophone philosophy. Summing Up: Highly recommended.' – **CHOICE**

The Routledge Companion to Ancient Philosophy
'This excellent reference will be useful to faculty and students alike. The essays are of uniformly high quality.' – **CHOICE**

THE ROUTLEDGE COMPANION TO ISLAMIC PHILOSOPHY

Edited by Richard C. Taylor
and Luis Xavier López-Farjeat

Routledge
Taylor & Francis Group
LONDON AND NEW YORK

First published 2016
by Routledge
711 Third Avenue, New York, NY 10017

and by Routledge
2 Park Square, Milton Park, Abingdon, Oxon, OX14 4RN

Routledge is an imprint of the Taylor & Francis Group, an informa business

British Library Cataloguing in Publication Data
A catalogue record for this book is available from the British Library

Library of Congress Cataloging in Publication Data
The Routledge companion to Islamic philosophy / [edited by] Richard C. Taylor and Luis Xavier López-Farjeat.
pages cm. -- (Routledge philosophy companions)
Includes bibliographical references and index. 1. Islamic
philosophy. I. Taylor, Richard C., 1950- editor. II. López Farjeat, Luis Xavier, editor.
B741.R68 2015
181'.07--dc23
2015004937

ISBN: 978-0-415-88160-9 (hbk)
ISBN: 978-1-315-70892-8 (ebk)

Typeset in Goudy
by Taylor & Francis Books

Printed and bound in the United States of America by Publishers Graphics, LLC on sustainably sourced paper.

CONTENTS

ACKNOWLEDGEMENTS

The editors would like to express their gratitude to the editorial team at Routledge. We are also very grateful to Jacob Andrews, Drew Dumaine, Daniel Adsett, Katja Krause, Nicholas Oschman, Venancio Ruiz, and J. Tyler Friedman.

NOTES ON THE CONTRIBUTORS

Peter Adamson is Professor of Late Ancient and Arabic Philosophy at the Ludwig Maximilians-Universität in Munich. He is the author of numerous articles on Greek and Arabic philosophy and of two monographs: *The Arabic Plotinus: a Study of the So-Called Philosophy of Aristotle* (2002) and *Al-Kindī* (2007). With P. E. Pormann he has also published *The Philosophical Works of al-Kindī* (2012).

Rumee Ahmed is Assistant Professor of Islamic Law in the Department of Classical, Near Eastern, and Religious Studies at the University of British Columbia. He is the author of *Narratives of Islamic Legal Theory* (2012).

Anna A. Akasoy is Associate Professor of Islamic Intellectual History at Hunter College, City University of New York. She is the author of *Philosophie und Mystik in der späten Almohadenzeit: Die "Sizilianischen Fragen" des Ibn-Sab'īn* (2006).

Mariam al-Attar is the Head of the Department of Ethics, Philosophy and Religion at King's Academy, Jordan. She is the author of *Islamic Ethics: Divine Command Theory in Arabo-Islamic Thought* (2010) and is currently writing a book on ethics in Arabo-Islamic thought.

Allan Bäck is Professor of Philosophy at Kutztown University. He has written widely in ancient and medieval philosophy, both Latin and Islamic. His recent books include *Aristotle's Theory of Abstraction* (2014) and two translations of parts of Avicenna's *Healing*. He has received various awards for his teaching and research, including the Humboldt Research Prize.

Catarina Belo is Associate Professor of Philosophy at the American University in Cairo. She has published several books and articles on medieval Islamic philosophy, medieval Christian philosophy, and more recently on Hegel's philosophy of religion. Her most recent work is *Averroes and Hegel on Philosophy and Religion* (2013).

Amos Bertolacci is Associate Professor of History of Islamic Philosophy at the Scuola Normale Superiore di Pisa. He is the author of *The Reception of Aristotle's Metaphysics in Avicenna's Kitāb al-Shifā': A Milestone of Western Metaphysical Thought* (2006), and of an Italian annotated translation of the metaphysics of Avicenna's *Shifā'* (2007).

Cécile Bonmariage is Chercheur qualifié at the Fond de la recherche scientifique (FNRS, Belgium) and Associate Professor of pre-modern Arabo-Islamic philosophy at the Institut supérieur de philosophie, UCLouvain (Louvain-la-Neuve). Her research focuses on post-classical Islamic philosophy, with a special interest for the study of the persistence and transformation of the Avicennian heritage in later Islamic thought.

Cristina Cerami is a senior research fellow (CR1) of the CNRS, UMR 7219. She was awarded her PhD in Scuola Normale Superiore, Pisa, Italy. She is the author of *Génération et substance. Aristote et Averroès entre physique et métaphysique* (2014).

Michael Chase is Chargé de Recherches at the Centre Jean Pépin of the French National Centre of Scientific Research, Villejuif-Paris. He has published on Greek Neoplatonism (including two volumes in the series *Ancient Commentators on Aristotle*, R. Sorabji (ed.)), Patristics, and Medieval Philosophy.

Carla Di Martino specializes in philosophical psychology, including the thought of authors of the Greek tradition in Arabic translation and the Arabic tradition in Latin translation together with their influence in Latin Europe. She works as journalist and book editor in philosophy.

Thérèse-Anne Druart is Professor of Philosophy at The Catholic University of America, Washington, DC. She is the current president of SIHSPAI (Société Internationale d'Histoire des Sciences et de la Philosophie Arabes et Islamiques). She has written some 70 articles, mainly in Arabic philosophy, and publishes annually a Brief Bibliographical Guide in Medieval and Post-Classical Philosophy and Theology.

Maha Elkaisy-Friemuth is Professor of Islamic-Religious Studies at Erlangen-Nurenberg University, Germany, and has the chair for Islamic theology. Her book *God and Humans in Islamic Thought* (2006) received the Iranian World Prize for the Book of the Year 2007.

Alexander Fidora is ICREA-Research Professor at the Department of Ancient and Medieval Studies of the Universitat Autònoma de Barcelona (UAB). He is the Executive Director of the Institute of Medieval Studies of the UAB, where he directs a research project of the European Research Council: "The Latin Talmud and its Influence on Christian-Jewish Polemic." His most recent book is *Latin-into-Hebrew: Texts in Contexts* (with H. Hames and Y. Schwartz, 2013).

Nadja Germann is Assistant Professor of Philosophy at Freiburg University (Germany). Among her recent publications are "Avicenna and Afterwards," in *The Oxford Handbook of Medieval Philosophy*, J. Marenbon (ed.) (2012), and "Imitation and Ambiguity: Some Remarks on al-Fārābī's Concept of Knowledge," in *Knowledge and Education in Classical Islam*, S. Günther (ed.) (forthcoming).

Frank Griffel is Professor of Islamic Studies at Yale University, New Haven. He has published *Apostasie und Toleranz im Islam* (2000) and *al-Ghazālī's Philosophical Theology* (2009) as well as numerous articles and book-chapters. He is also editor of two collective volumes and the translator of books from Arabic.

Rosalind Ward Gwynne is Emerita Associate Professor at the Department of Religious Studies of the University of Tennessee. She was a Fulbright Fellow in Yemen. She has published *Logic, Rhetoric, and Legal Reasoning in the Qur'ān* (2004).

Steven Harvey is Professor of Philosophy at Bar-Ilan University, and former chair of Jewish Philosophy. He is President of the Commission for Jewish Philosophy of the Société Internationale pour l'Étude de la Philosophie Médiévale. He is the author of *Falaquera's* Epistle of the Debate: *An Introduction to Jewish Philosophy* (1987) and editor of *The Medieval Hebrew Encyclopedias of Science and Philosophy* (2000) and *Anthology of the Writings of Avicenna* (2009, in Hebrew).

Rollen E. Houser is Professor at the Center for Thomistic Studies at the University of St. Thomas in Houston. He is the Bishop Wendelin J. Nold Chair in Graduate Philosophy and his research areas include Medieval and Islamic philosophy, metaphysics, and virtue theory. He has published on the influence of Avicenna and Averroes on the thought of Thomas Aquinas.

Jules Janssens is collaborator of the De Wulf-Mansion Centre for Ancient, Medieval and Early Renaissance Philosophy, KU Leuven and chercheur associé of CNRS, UPR 76 (Centre J. Pépin), Paris. His major research concerns Avicenna's thought and its reception in the Arabic and Latin world.

Terence Kleven currently teaches Philosophy and Religion at the Central College, Pella, Iowa, USA, and has taught at the Near East School of Theology in Beirut and the Memorial University of Newfoundland in St. John's, Newfoundland and Labrador. His major area of publication is on the logic and political philosophy of al-Fārābī. He has also published articles on Averroës, Ibn Daud and Maimonides as well as in Biblical and Qur'ānic Studies.

Olga Lizzini teaches at the VU University Amsterdam. She published the first Italian translation of Avicenna's *Metaphysics* (2006) and, among other essays, two monographs on Avicenna's philosophy: *Fluxus* (2011), on the theory of emanation, and *Avicenna* (2012), an introduction to Avicenna's thought.

Luis Xavier López-Farjeat is Associate Professor at the School of Philosophy at Universidad Panamericana, Mexico. He has written on Arabic Medieval Philosophy and is co-editor of the volume *Philosophical Psychology in Arabic Thought and the Latin Aristotelianism of the 13th Century* (2013). He is associate director of the Aquinas and 'The Arabs' International Working Group (www.AquinasAndTheArabs.org), and editor of *Tópicos, Journal of Philosophy*.

Toby Mayer is a Research Associate at the Institute of Ismaili Studies, London, having previously held a lectureship in Islamic Studies at London's School of Oriental and African Studies (SOAS). His current project, with Wilferd Madelung, is an edition and translation of a 6th/12th century Tayyibi Isma'ili commentary on Ibn Sina's Qasidat al-Nafs.

Jon McGinnis is Professor of Classical and Medieval Philosophy at the University of Missouri, St. Louis. In addition to numerous articles, he is the author of *Avicenna* in the Oxford University Press' Great Medieval Thinkers Series (2010), translator and editor of Avicenna's *Physics* from his encyclopedic work, *The Healing* (2009) and was co-translator with David C. Reisman of *Classical Arabic Philosophy: An Anthology of Sources* (2007).

Azim Nanji is currently Special Advisor to the Provost of the internationally based Aga Khan University. Previously he has taught at Stanford University, been Director of the Institute of Ismaili Studies in London and Professor and Chair of the Department of Religion at the University of Florida. His publications include works on Islam and Ethics.

Sarah Pessin is Associate Professor of Philosophy and Judaic Studies at the University of Denver. She is the author of a number of publications on Jewish and Islamic medieval philosophy, including *Ibn Gabirol's Theology of Desire: Matter and Method in Jewish Medieval Neoplatonism* (2013).

Mohammed Rustom is Associate Professor of Islamic Studies at Carleton University. He is the author of the award-winning book *The Triumph of Mercy: Philosophy and Scripture in Mulla Sadra* (2012), and an assistant editor of the *HarperCollins Study Qurān* (2015).

Ayman Shihadeh, of the School of Oriental and African Studies, University of London, is an intellectual historian specialized in medieval Arabic philosophy and rational Islamic theology, in particular the Ashʿarī school and the Avicennian tradition. He is the author of *The Teleological Ethics of Fakhr al-Dīn al-Rāzī* (2006), and Section Editor for Philosophy and Theology at the *Encyclopaedia of Islam*.

Richard C. Taylor teaches at Marquette University and is also a member of the De Wulf-Mansion Centre for Ancient, Medieval and Early Renaissance Philosophy, KU Leuven. He translated with Th.-A. Druart as subeditor *Averroes (Ibn Rushd) of Cordoba. Long Commentary on the* De anima (2009). He directs the Aquinas and 'The Arabs' International Working Group (www.AquinasAndTheArabs.org) which focuses on the importance of philosophy from the Arabic tradition for the development of the thought of Aquinas and other thinkers of the twelfth and thirteenth centuries.

David Twetten is Associate Professor of Philosophy at Marquette University. He works on physics, metaphysics, and natural theology in Aristotle and the Aristotelian tradition, including Arabic philosophy and its Latin inheritance, focusing on Averroes, Albert the Great and Thomas Aquinas.

Philippe Vallat is former research fellow of the Humboldt Foundation and resident researcher at the French Institute for Near East Studies (IFPO Damascus-Beirut), is associate member at the French National Center for Scientific Studies (Paris) and the author of three books on al-Fārābī.

INTRODUCTION

Richard C. Taylor and Luis Xavier López-Farjeat

Philosophy in the Arabic/Islamic tradition, commonly considered under the history of ideas as Oriental or Islamic studies, or as later developments of Greek thought, or as source study for Medieval European thought, has now reached a new stage in which it is not only studied as properly distinct from the European thinkers of the Middle Ages it influenced but also as philosophy in its own right. This consideration motivates us to present this volume, thematic in nature and focused on philosophical topics and problems, with a diversity of standpoints developed by thinkers of this tradition within the context of Islam and its history. This allows for clear focus on the innovative philosophical insights of the Islamic tradition that can be found in nearly every major area of philosophy.

Our primary focus here is on philosophical issues of the Classical period and their development in the post-Classical or fully Islamic period, in which religion and philosophy are more integrated with matters of religious revelation. The study of recent and contemporary philosophy in the lands of Islam is outside the scope of this volume. There are several reasons for this:

1 The assumption of this book is that the traditional issues of philosophy in the Islamic milieu are primarily philosophical and perennial in nature. Hence, these can be identified as such by readers of this volume and related to similar philosophical issues arising in other cultural and historical contexts.
2 Recent and contemporary philosophy is in many cases an engagement with contemporary social and political issues suitable for treatment in collections on socio-political themes and not strictly from a philosophical standpoint.
3 Philosophy in Islamic lands is undergoing further development, led by a changing and dynamic engagement with philosophical issues and discussions of the European and American traditions such as analytic philosophy, idealism, phenomenology, political philosophy, and much more. This deserves treatment at a later time in a volume specifically devoted to contemporary issues.

Hence, in this volume we seek to allow *falsafa* or philosophy in the Islamic milieu to take a place in the study of philosophy and philosophical issues currently discussed alongside the multiple methods of the study of Ancient Greek philosophy or Medieval Christian or Jewish philosophy today. The works of Plato, Aristotle, Plotinus, Augustine, Aquinas, Scotus, Maimonides and many others continue to prompt an extraordinarily wide array of philosophical discussions of fascinating issues of both historical and systematic interest in philosophy and religion, logic and science, metaphysics and epistemology, practical philosophy, and other areas. Likewise, philosophy in the Islamic tradition should be viewed in a precisely analogous way. It follows then that our intention with this volume is that philosophy in the Islamic milieu be made part of the common philosophical conversation on perennial issues without neglect of its specific content. Hence, while the philosophical writings of Plato, Aristotle, Aquinas or others offer insights into everlasting issues important today without neglect of historical or cultural context, the case is no different for philosophical teachings by thinkers of the Islamic domain, whose inputs transcend their specific context but cannot be fully understood without appealing to the historical context from which they arose. To this extent we seek to make it evident, with this volume, that there is a place for what is commonly called Islamic philosophy in both the history of philosophy and in the study of the ongoing issues of philosophy in classrooms today.

The volume is divided into seven sections. The first section, "Philosophical Issues in Islamic Revelation and Theology," consists of a group of essays devoted to selected philosophical issues insofar as these are in some fashion present in Islamic revelation and religious thought: the nature of God and how He relates to creation; the role of natural human reason (*fikr*) and intellect (*al-ʿaql*) as tools in Islamic theology or *kalām*; a philosophical analysis of normative ethics as prescribed by the Qurʾān and ḥadīth (the teachings of the Prophet Muḥammad); the physics and metaphysics of atomistic *kalām* as set forth in theological arguments; and the use of logic and reasoning in the exposition of the teachings of the Qurʾān.

The second section, "Logic, Language, and the Structure of Science," deals with human reasoning in logic, language and the discourse of science. Muslim philosophers followed a tradition in which logic was conceived as a powerful, reliable methodological tool for reason and science seeking, to the extent possible, *al-yaqīn*, what is certain. Rhetoric was also included in the *Organon* as a tool for persuasion with the certainty of demonstration clearly distinguished from the mere probability that dialectic can provide at its best. Logic was welcomed in the midst of Islamic theology by al-Ghazālī, though it had already long been functioning there without explicit reference to the Greek tradition. Key to understanding the hierarchy and relation of the sciences is the issue of the precise structure of each of the sciences and the nature of the method employed in each, a topic considered by all the major thinkers of the philosophical tradition.

The third section is devoted to "Philosophy in the Natural Sciences." Following the Greek lead, Islamic philosophers furthered and developed the investigation of natural sciences that they furthered and developed in their own right. Novel understandings of the movement of the heavens and the immaterial causes of that movement were prompted by the incompleteness of Aristotle's accounts and the philosophical, as well as theological, need to understand the natural universe as the hierarchical product of God. In this context, emanation as creation was espoused at one time or another by nearly all the philosophers in contrast to religious notions of *creatio ex nihilo*. The major philosophers also reflected upon the nature of the world as eternal, while theologians argued for a divine *creatio ex nihilo* that was also *de novo*.

Following Greek philosophy, philosophical thinkers of the Islamic tradition understood "metaphysics" as the highest and noblest science, as what Aristotle called "first philosophy." The fourth section deals precisely with "Metaphysics." The central issues of metaphysics have, at their origins, the questions of being, essence and existence, unity, the kinds of causality, and the need for a first cause of all. This section deals with the varying and diverse ways in which the philosophers understood and discussed these issues in their own contexts.

The fifth section concerns the remarkable, insightful and innovative contributions of the philosophical tradition on "Epistemology and Philosophy of Mind." These essays address the physiological accounts of perception, the development of inner senses or mental faculties (memory, imagination, the estimative faculty), the explanations of how rationality and conscious experience relate to the physical world and, of course, the theories of intellect, intellection and human understanding, issues which continue to pose philosophical challenges today.

In the sixth section, "Ethics and Political Philosophy," matters of practical philosophy and the metaphysics of responsibility are discussed in essays on divine power and human efficacy, natural and metaphysical principles for political philosophy, and how moral obligations are generated and conceived under natural and revealed religion.

Finally, the seventh section, "Philosophy, Religion, and Mysticism," contains essays related to religious issues in the developed tradition such as prophecy and mystical practices, which are part of the major philosophical topics of the tradition and addressed in a variety of ways.

As indicated, our intention with this volume is to bring the study of philosophy in the Islamic tradition into the modern classroom and into the common study of philosophy today. This collection of essays by philosophers working in the field on the great diversity of topics discussed within the Islamic philosophical tradition, displays why such contents remain appropriate for philosophical study today.

Part I

PHILOSOPHICAL ISSUES IN ISLAMIC REVELATION AND THEOLOGY

1

GOD AND CREATION IN AL-RĀZĪ'S COMMENTARY ON THE QUR'ĀN

Maha Elkaisy-Friemuth

Introduction

The concept of "the creation of the world" occupies a central place in the Qur'ān and in Islamic theological discourses. Theologians studied this issue as a division of their study on the existence and attributes of God with many arguing that the world must have a first efficient cause and that this cause must be God. Muslim philosophers, on their part, studied this issue under the study of cosmology and, though they also held that the first cause is a divine power, they argued that the world is not created in time but that the process of creation is instead eternal. Muslim theologians and philosophers had a long and bitter struggle with this issue and its central questions: how and when the world originated from God. Although the theologians sought an answer from the Qur'ān, they were strongly influenced by their Christian theologian neighbours. The concept that God created the world out of nothing, *ex nihilo*, was extensively discussed among Middle Eastern Christian theologians, among whom the most well known in Arabic were John Philoponus and John of Damascus. H. Wolfson points out that the concept of creation *ex nihilo* is not mentioned in any detail either in the Bible or in the Qur'ān, though he does refer to Maccabees 7:28 where God is said to have created heaven and earth "not from something existent." This statement was developed into the concept of "creation out of the nonexistent." However, since the Aristotelian teaching distinguishes between the essential nonexistent (absolute nothing) and possible nonexistent (potential existent), the Church Fathers adopted the term "out of nothing" instead of "out of nonexistent" in order to emphasise that God created the world out of absolute nothing, a thought expressed in Latin in the term *creatio ex nihilo* (Wolfson 1976: 355–6). Muslim theologians, on the one hand, adopted the position of their Christian neighbours and produced long argumentations for creation *ex nihilo*, considering it as an article of faith. Muslim philosophers, on the other hand, developed the concept of the eternity of the world. In this they were following the Aristotelian and Neoplatonic teachings which were taught in many intellectual circles in Baghdad and other important cities in the Islamic Empire.

Although the concept of creation *ex nihilo* was deeply rooted in medieval Islam and Christianity, here we shall ask ourselves to what extent this issue influenced their perception of God or, more precisely, whether this concept was established in order to defend a certain image of God. This is a question that gripped al-Ghazālī in his book *The Incoherence of the Philosophers* (*Tahāfut al-Falāsifa*). There he differentiated between the philosophical image of the divine produced by Ibn Sīnā and al-Farābī and the religious perception of God set out by theologians of Islam. For him, the producer of the world must forever retain certain connections to his production. He emphasises that God made the world through his eternal knowledge (*'ilm*), power (*qudra*) and will (*irāda*). These three qualities produced the world with certain definite intentions and wisdom (*ḥikma*). This wisdom protects and guides the world through revelation. Al-Ghazālī claims that the philosophers, conversely, interpret the production of the world as a necessary process that emerged from a rational One (God) who acts through an everlasting productive nature. God, for the philosophers, is also endowed with eternal knowledge and power, such that there is no period when He was not acting and using these qualities. Thus, the world has existed for as long as God has; that is, from eternity. Al-Ghazālī argues here that the existence of the world, according to the philosophers, happened through a necessary process and as a result of God's divine ability and knowledge. In his analysis, excluding the divine will from the process of creation distorts the relationship between God and the world and denies that creation is truly an expression of divine wisdom.

In this way, the different interpretations of the existence of the world caused a lengthy dispute between the philosophers and the theologians regarding which characteristics must be attributed to God in presenting the image of the Divinity. For the theologians, God wills, knows and has omnipotent power, and also acts wisely and in a perfect fashion. This wisdom not only creates but also protects creation through divine guidance. The philosophers, alternatively, believed that God is a rational intellect whose eternally productive action follows from his eternal contemplation of himself. According to al-Ghazālī, the philosophers hold that God's knowledge of his production comes out of his knowledge of himself rather than any direct connection to the actual world. This connection would seem to imply that as the world changes, God changes with it.

Here we will consider these issues through the Qur'ān's perspective and examine how some key verses convey the concept of "creation" and how this concept relates to God. This will be done through the interpretation of *The Long Commentary* (*al-Tafsīr al-Kabīr*, also called *Keys to the Unknown, Mafātīḥ al-Ghayb*) written by Fakhr al-Dīn al-Rāzī (d. 1209). This choice of al-Rāzī is based on the fact that he mastered both theology and philosophy, an achievement that broadens his discussion of some key verses and demonstrates the ability of some Muslim thinkers to engage their philosophical acumen with their own religious beliefs. For the sake of clarity, it is valuable to initiate this exploration with a brief explanation of al-Rāzī's understanding of this issue in his last work (*The Higher Issues, al-Maṭālib al-'Ālya*), and how he connects it to the study of the attributes of God. This will provide some basic knowledge of his view important for understanding his discussion in the *al-Tafsīr*. It is also germane to mention that al-Rāzī wrote *al-Maṭālib* during his writing of *al-Tafsīr* and he died before finishing both works.

Al-Rāzī and His Conception of the Creation of the World

Fakhr al-Dīn al-Rāzī, one of the most prominent scholars of Islamic Theology, was strongly influenced by philosophy and followed the footsteps of the philosophically astute theologian Abū Ḥāmid al-Ghazālī. Born in Rayy in 1149 C.E., he died in Herat in 1207 C.E. He left a very rich corpus of philosophical and theological works that reveals influence from the works of Ibn Sīnā (d. 1037 C.E.), Abū al-Barakāt al-Baghdādī (d. 1168 C.E.) and Abū Ḥāmid al-Ghazālī (d. 1111 C.E.). *Eastern Studies in Metaphysics and Physics* (*Al-Mabāḥith al-Mashriqiyya fi 'ilm al-Ilahiyyat wa-l-ṭabi'iyyāt*) and his last work *al-Maṭālib al-'Ālya* are usually regarded as his most important philosophical works. Al-Rāzī changed his theological and philosophical views during his intellectual life and the *Maṭālib* is commonly considered his full and last opinion on the issues discussed here. In this work, his views are very close to the opinion of the philosophers. Moreover, he often employed many philosophical concepts explained in the *Maṭālib* in his great work the *al-Tafsīr*, one of the most detailed works on the commentary on the Qur'ān (al-Zurkān 1963: 15–25).

His discussion on the creation of the world is closely connected to his study on the attributes of God, which will assist us in understanding how the world originated from Him. Al-Rāzī ascribes to God different attributes, both positive (such as ability, knowledge and will) and negative (such as His not being subject to space, and not being incarnate). The positive attributes constitute the basis for his discussion on the creation of the world in volume four of the *Maṭālib*. Here I will mainly concentrate on some of the positive attributes that are connected to his concept of creation.

In the *Maṭālib*, al-Rāzī starts by presenting some arguments for the existence of a divine power that is necessary for the existence of the world. This divine power is, in itself, necessarily existent (*wājib al-wujūd*), which means it necessitates its own existence. He argues here that being necessary is describing the manner in which a thing exists, not the fact that it exists. Therefore, the necessity of existence cannot be applied to every existing thing because obviously there is a time when a given created thing ceases to exist and thereby loses the necessity of its existence. Thus, the thing can exist either by its own power or by another. If it exists by itself, then it is necessary (*wājib*), but when it exists by another, then it is contingent (*mumkin*) even if it exists eternally. Since the only entity that exists through its own power is God, al-Rāzī applies to God the term "necessary existence," a term that is familiar in the philosophy of al-Fārābī and Ibn Sīnā. Since God is the only being whose existence is necessary, God is therefore the source of all existence and the first cause of all things (al-Rāzī 1999: 1, 90–4).

After establishing the concept that the only giver of existence is the Necessary Existent, al-Rāzī considers the attribution of different qualities to God. He reasons that whatever is necessarily existent is consequently eternal and everlasting since God never ceases to exist. In this manner, al-Rāzī continues assigning to God many positive attributes such as power (*qādir*) and knowledge (*'ilm*), and holds that He has will, life, hearing and seeing. For my purpose, I shall henceforth focus exclusively on three attributes: power (*qudra*), knowledge (*'ilm*), and will (*irāda*) and explain their connection to al-Rāzī's concept of the creation of the world.

These three attributes form the basis for the concept of the creation of the world in al-Rāzī's philosophical theology because they are connected to God's activities. In order for God to bring the world into existence, He must possess the power and ability for this act and must also know what He will achieve and produce. This production must also be in accordance with what the producer intends from this production. Thus al-Rāzī devotes long discussions to these three attributes. He does so mainly in the third volume of the *Maṭālib*, but also deals with them extensively in the fourth volume where he discusses whether the world existed eternally or was created in time. While explaining these attributes in the third volume, he starts by giving a definition of each of them. He realizes that his aim here is to correct our understanding of these qualities and to show the difficulty of grasping the reality of the divine power, the divine knowledge and the divine will.

In defining "power," al-Rāzī indicates that this simply refers to the ability to act or not to act (*al-fi'l wa al-tark*), which is the ability to do an act and its opposite. He shows the weakness of this definition since, as he points out, if the powerful agent (God) did not act, the nonexistent would remain in this position, while when God acts the nonexistent would exist. Hence, the existence of all things depends on the act of God. Thus, the conception of God as a capable agent that can act or refrain from acting is an unsound concept. This is because, for al-Rāzī, God cannot refrain from acting; refraining from the act would mean letting the nonexistent remain in its possible destiny. A wise agent would not choose this (al-Rāzī 1999: 3, 102).

Here it is clear that al-Rāzī accepts the opinion of the philosophers that God is always acting; however, he does not consider this quality to be part of God's nature but rather a logical consequence of God's wisdom.

Next, when defining the attribute of "knowledge," al-Rāzī explains that knowledge means a connection between the knower and the object of knowledge. This connection is not only the imprinting of the image of the thing or its essence on the mind of the knower, but also a certain connection between known and knower. Al-Rāzī explains that it is possible to apply to God the philosophical concepts of *taṣṣawur* and *taṣdīq*. *Taṣṣawur* means that the image of the thing or its essence will be imprinted in the mind, while *taṣdīq* is giving a judgment about this thing as to its relation to others and whether, for example, it is a cause or an effect. This is a very important point because it leads al-Rāzī to the position that God knows particulars through *tasdīq* since, in this process, God must be aware of the relationship between the particular thing and other things. This explanation enables him to argue against the philosophical concept that God does not know particulars. God must also know nonexistent things because this is an important condition for producing a perfect act, that is, an act that is known to the knower before the knower produces it. It is important for each of us, he explains, to engage in much thinking and analysis before producing a wise act. Thus al-Rāzī argues that God must know the nonexistent thing in order to be able to bring it into existence and in connection with other existent things (al-Rāzī 1999: 3, 102–3).

Now, when defining the reality of a willing act of God (*irāda*), al-Rāzī explains that it is an act which brings benefit or prevents injury. He argues in many places of the third volume of the *Maṭālib* that the choice between two possibilities (i.e. one brings benefit and the other injury) can only happen when a third option (*al-murajiḥ*) appears in order to produce the conviction for one's choice. He argues, however, that this should not be applicable to God, because God knows all three options before acting since God, as explained above, knows all possible options before He brings an act into existence. Thus, al-Rāzī believes that whether God's act comes out of necessity or out of choice, this does not make a great difference, because God acts according to His omniscient knowledge. In many places in the *Maṭālib*, al-Rāzī confidently refers to God as a "willing Agent" (*fā'il mukhtār*). God is willing on the basis of knowledge of the thing in all its stages: before it exists, when it exists and throughout all its changes. The important difference between attributing to God an act of necessity or an act of will, though, is that the latter is produced because the agent knows the importance of his/her act and therefore it deserves praise, while the former act is produced by the productive nature of the agent, and can neither be blamed nor praised (al-Rāzī 1999: 3, 49).

From the discussion above we see that God, for al-Rāzī, is a powerful, knowing and willing agent who, according to these qualities, has the power to bring the world into existence either in a certain time or from eternity. In the fourth volume, al-Rāzī provides a long argument for these two possibilities based on the three qualities, without showing his own decisive view on this issue. İskenderoğlu concludes in his book *Fakhr-al-Dīn al-Rāzī and Thomas Aquinas on the Question of the Eternity of the World* that:

> [F]or Rāzī, the arguments produced either for the eternity of the world or for its temporal creation are inconclusive. In his discussion of these arguments Rāzī tried to show the weakness of these arguments. However, his evaluation of the arguments for the eternity of the world, especially those taken from the nature and the attributes of God is more serious. … In most cases Rāzī tries to leave the discussion at this point without indicating clearly his own view.
>
> (İskenderoğlu 2002: 123)

Creation in al-Rāzī's *al-Tafsīr al-Kabīr*

The *al-Tafsīr* is one of the most detailed works on the Qur'ān. It enjoys a good reputation and proved to have popularity among theologians. However, it is not clear when al-Rāzī started writing this work, though it seems likely that he wrote it when he was working on his *Maṭālib* because he left both works unfinished. The most problematic issue about it, still, is that many historians like Ibn Khilkān, Ibn Shahba and al-Dhahabī inform us that al-Rāzī died before finishing *Mafātīḥ*, and that there is no reliable information as to where al-Rāzī stopped. Ḥāji Khalīfa, in his *The Unveiling of Suppositions* (*al-Kashf 'an al-Ẓunūn*), mentions that two students of al-Rāzī completed this work: Shams al-Dīn al-Khīūbī and Nijm al-Dīn al-Qumūlī. Thus, for the accuracy of the thought of al-Rāzī, I have tried here to refer to those verses that al-Rāzī mentioned in the *Maṭālib* (al-Zurkān 1963: 65–6).

Al Rāzī's methodology in the *al-Tafsīr* is similar to his main system in *Maṭālib*, where he usually divides his arguments into different issues, *masā'il*, and produces for each *mas'ala* several arguments: first he gives the differing opinions of the various theological groups or theologians and then concludes by adding his own view.

After this brief introduction to the *al-Tafsīr*, in what follows I will discuss some of al-Rāzī's views on the question of creation by examining some key verses regarding this issue. We start our study by examining several divine attributes that are mentioned in some key verses regarding the concept of creation. These qualities are: powerful (*qādir*), knowledge (*'ilm*), and creator (using the verb *khalq* or the substantive *fāṭir*).

Qādir *(powerful)*

Qur'ān 67:1 "Blessed be He in Whose hands is Dominion; and He over all things hath Power."

Al-Rāzī here divides his discussion into different issues and deals with each separately. The importance of this verse lies in its common usage among different theologians. Many theologians argue that this verse refers to God's ability and power over the *nonexistent* things. They claim that the sentence "and He over all things hath Power" refers mainly to power over the nonexistent things. This also seems to be the opinion of al-Rāzī because he argues that divine *qudra* is an effective power that changes the status of things from nonexistence to existence or from existence to nonexistence, and this is the meaning of "to have power over all things." On the other hand, the Ash'arite theologians use this verse in order to argue that God has power not only over his own ability but also over the ability of others (humans), while the Mu'tazilites reject this understanding and hold instead that God's power is limited to existent things and, therefore, God has no power over humans' nonexistent deeds. Further, al-Rāzī displays here his understanding of the discussions of several theologians concerning other understandings of God's ability. He finally expresses clearly that, for him, this verse provides a justification for concluding that God has power over the nonexistent thing that is necessary for the act of creation (al-Zurkān 2003: 30, 47–9).

'Ālim *and* Qayūm *(knowledgeable)*

Qur'ān 2:255 "Allah. There is no god but He,— the Living, the Self-subsisting (*qayūm*) Eternal. No slumber can seize Him nor sleep. His are all things in the heavens and on earth. Who is there can intercede in His presence except as He permitteth? He knoweth what (appeareth to His creatures as) before or after or behind them. Nor shall they compass aught of His knowledge except as He willeth. His Throne doth extend over the heavens and the earth, and He feeleth no fatigue in guarding and preserving them for He is the Most High, the Supreme (in glory)."

For this magnificent verse, al-Rāzī gives a long commentary including the opinion of the most important theologians from both Mu'tazilī and 'Ash'arī circles. At the beginning, he gives a summary of his own understanding of the whole verse and considers it to reveal the secrets of this verse. He focuses on the term *qayūm* in the first part of the verse, which occupies a considerable portion of the discussion. He renders the second part of the verse as if it unveiled the reality about the knowledge of God that is beyond the understanding of the human mind, as shown in his discussion below.

Here he presents both theologians who interpret the term *qayūm* as self-subsisting, *qā'im*, and others who interpret it as *qawwām*, subsisting others. *Qā'im* means "he who stands alone without the need or support of others" while *qawwām* means "he who *gives* support to others." Al-Rázī finds the second meaning more appropriate for understanding *qayūm* but he also includes the meaning of the first in it. God is by nature self-subsisting and precisely the only self-subsistent and therefore the only one who can make the others subsist by bringing them into existence. Thus the term *qayūm* is a quality that is included in the act of creation. *Qayūm*, thus, unveils the divine reality and power, explains al-Rázī. He further discusses in this context the division between the possible beings that cannot exist by their own power because they consist of parts, none of which can bring the other into existence. This possibility of existence needs, certainly, an effective cause to bring the thing with its parts into existence. This cause is the self-subsisting, which al-Rázī also calls here the Necessary Existence (*wājib al-wujūd*) as he calls God also in the *Maṭālib*. The meaning of "self-subsisting" indicates that God is the only one who can make the others subsist. The description of God in this verse as the living self-subsistent reveals the ability of giving life to everything. This ability is implied in the fact that God is the only being that possesses existence *per se* and consequently is the only entity capable of giving existence and life to others. Thus, for al-Rázī, the giving of life is the actual meaning of self-subsistence.

This quality of being *qayūm* is linked to God's ability to know which is before or which lies behind everything. What is self-subsistent is not in need of others and God's knowledge of them comes from within Himself, for He has a complete knowledge of each thing before bringing it into existence. Therefore, "No slumber can seize Him nor sleep," which means His knowledge of all things is endless and therefore His productive acts never stop nor take a rest in sleep. Al-Rázī unveils here the core of this verse as indicating the connection between the endless divine knowledge of all things and the endless divine power that does not rest. Indeed, for Al-Rázī, this is the mystery of creation that brings together the omniscience and the omnipotence in effective activities (al-Zurkān 2003: 7, 3–24). We will, however, come back to divine knowledge when we discuss how God created the world.

Now we move to the other two terms which are directly connected with creation: *khalq* and *fāṭir* both refering to the creator.

khalq *(to create)*

Qur'ān 7:54 "Your Guardian-Lord is Allah, Who created the heavens and the earth;" and: 3:49 [Jesus said] "I have come to you, with a Sign from your Lord, in that I create for you out of clay, as it were, the figure of a bird, and breathe into it, and it becomes a bird by Allah's leave [permission]."

Al-Rázī refers to these two verses also in his *Maṭālib* in order to explain the meaning of creation (*khalq*). However, his full explanation of this term is to be found here in his *al-Tafsīr*. The meaning of *khalaqa* in these two verses is forming or determining the form of a thing since it is impossible to attribute creation to Jesus in the sense of creating new life. In this case, al-Rāzī insists that creation must be understood as *taqdīr*, determining the form, the shape and the place of the thing before its actual existence. He explains at length in 7:54 that the things exist mainly within a certain shape, place and function. Creation of heaven and earth can happen only after having all knowledge of their shape, place and function. For example, day and night happen through the movement of the heavenly bodies, and therefore their creation in a certain shape and place influences the whole life of the universe. Thus the words of Jesus "I create for you" in 3:49 are in the context of his forming the bird out of clay. This formation is what is meant by "I create," while breathing into it to bring the actual life happens by God's permission and not through Jesus, as al-Rāzī explains. He also considers here the possibility of creation from a certain matter, just as Jesus' shaping of the bird out of clay. Hence, creation as expressed in these two verses is to be understood as decreeing and forming of the thing either from a matter or in the mind of God. Al-Rāzī is consistent in his understanding of the term "create" in his *al-Tafsīr*: it means for him decreeing the form of the thing and its relation to others. Since creation, for al-Rāzī, does not mean the actual appearing of the thing, but rather the preparation for its existence, it is closely connected to the willingness of the agent to bring the thing into a certain context and a precise position. Thus the divine wisdom behind the existence of things plays a very important role in Rāzī's understanding of the concept of creation. He explains in exhaustive detail the creation of heaven with all its spheres and planets, showing great precision and perfection of their formation, *takwīn*, that can only be created through a willing and wise agent (al-Zurkān 2003: 7, 52–6).

fāṭir *(creator)*

Qur'ān 12:101 "O Thou Creator (*fāṭir*) of the heavens and the earth!"

Al-Rāzī explains that *fāṭir* is a word which is used in many places in the Qur'ān to mean create. Here and elsewhere in his *al-Tafsīr*, al-Rāzī shows that this word in Arabic is attributed not only to God but is also used to express the act of formation or building. He provides the example of two Arabs fighting for the right to use a well of water since each claims that it was he who made it *faṭarahā* (from *faṭara*, *fāṭir*). This again proves for him that *fāṭir* does not mean creation in the sense of creating all at once, nor does it indicate creation out nothing (*ex nihilo*) (al-Zurkān 2003: 18, 178–83). Thus neither the word "create" (*khalq*) nor *fāṭir* are used in the Qur'ān, according to al-Rāzī, to mean creation *ex nihilo*.

To conclude, al-Rāzī holds that the terms *khalq* and *fāṭir* do not necessarily prove creation *ex nihilo* but rather describe God as the originator of the world and indicate that this creation happened in a process of different levels. The word *khalq* refers to the level of decreeing the formation of the thing and its connection to other existing things. At this level, things have a sort of semi-existence, while the word *fāṭir* indicates the actual bringing of things into existence. Both terms do not specify the exact way in which the things move from non-existence to existence, that is, whether this happens through a pre-existing matter or *ex nihilo*. In the *Maṭālib*, al-Rāzī supposes that it is possible that God could have first created a light and from this light the world was created.

How Did God Create the World?

Let us now move to al-Rāzī's explanation of how the world was originated from God. In this section we will focus on two main forms of creation: creation through the word "*kun*" ("Be"), and the creation which took place in six days. I will mainly examine Qur'ān 3:59 and 7:54. The next section will discuss how God created human beings. 3:59 "The similitude of Jesus before Allah is as that of Adam; He created him from dust, then said to him: 'Be' (*kun*). And he was." A fascination with the word "*kun*" is widespread among Muslims. Many wonder how this word can be a cause of existence and why God mentioned it in more than ten different and decisive places in the Qur'ān. Al-Rāzī gives much attention to this word and displays the theories of the theologians who viewed it as evidence of creation *ex nihilo*. Al-Rāzī explains that advocates of the view that God's speech in the Qur'ān is eternal hold that the phrase "Be and it is" (*kun fa-yakun*) means that God created everything through the reality of this word *kun*, which in turn proves that God's speech in the Qur'ān is eternal. Al-Rāzī does not accept this interpretation and shows its weakness. In this verse and those like it, creation is decreed or even formed and prepared for existence before the uttering of "Be," as 3:59 declares "He created him from dust, *then* said to him: 'Be.' And he was." Thus the word "*kun*" in itself is as contingent as the created thing, both originated from God in the process of creation. He argues further that if in the process of creation the word "*kun*" is necessary for creating, but in itself is contingent, then it must need another "*kun*" to bring it into existence, since creation according to orthodox theologians can happen only through this word, yet this would lead to a chain of "*kuns*," which is absurd. Therefore, al-Rāzī decides, the word "*kun*" is neither contingent nor eternal. It also cannot have in itself any power because when we utter it we do not experience any change. It is also absurd to think that God is speaking to the nonexistent things through the word "*kun*." However, if we believe that God is all-powerful and is able to bring everything into existence, then it is obvious that God does not need this word for the act of creation to take place. Al-Rāzī reaches the conclusion that this word is a metaphor for the speed of God's creation, which takes neither time nor effort (al-Zurkān 2003: 7, 70–2).

The next verse, in contrast, shows that creation took six days but for al-Rāzī this expresses the mode of wisdom rather than time. 7: 54 "Your Guardian-Lord is Allah, Who created the heavens and the earth in six days, and is firmly established on the throne: He draweth the night as a veil o'er the day, each seeking the other in rapid succession: He created the sun, the moon, and the stars, (all) governed by laws under His command. Is it not His to create and to govern? Blessed be Allah, the Cherisher and Sustainer of the worlds!"

This verse includes many important issues: the timing of creation, the establishing of or sitting on the throne, and the details of what God created. I shall concentrate on the question of timing and the relationship between the different created things mentioned in this verse.

When interpreting this verse al-Rāzī devotes more than 25 pages, going into great detail in order to: (1) demonstrate that the number "six" should not be taken literally here; (2) show that *Istiwā'* on the throne cannot have the meaning of actual sitting but mainly establishing and governing through it; and (3) explain the existence of the heavenly bodies and their relations to God and the angels.

First, according to al-Rāzī, the word "create," as we saw above, means decreeing specific forms and sizes, which demonstrates a willing agent who works according to a specific and wise plan. Further, he argues that the phrase "in six days" should not be taken literally because the days are connected to the movement of the sun and the moon (as it was believed in Medieval Islamic sciences). But, how could this be counted when the sun and the moon were not yet created? Thus, the mentioning of the six days here and elsewhere is, according to al-Rāzī, related to the biblical tradition that God created the world in six days and rested on the seventh. The Qur'ān, in his opinion, refers to it as a confirmation of what the Arabs heard from the Jews and Christians in Arabia. It also can be understood as a metaphor for creation according to a specific plan, which once again emphasizes a willing agent whose act is perfectly planned.

Al-Rāzī also demonstrates that the heavenly bodies could not have been moving from eternity because movement, in his opinion, is temporal, since motion takes place from one point to the next. Thus, either these bodies were eternally static and then were moved by the power of an agent, or they were created with their movements. In both cases the agent must have specified the time of its movement or its creation. He concludes that this efficient cause must be a willing agent who specified all these things: their time of existence, their form of movement, and their shape and size. Perfection can be experienced while each reality keeps its own role without changing its place or movement: we cannot expect that the sun suddenly rises from the west and sets in the east, al-Rāzī argues. Here he goes into details to explain the movement of each planet and the role that the sun and the moon play in our sphere. Again and again he comes to the conclusion that all this unveils the wisdom and precise perfection of a willing agent (*fā'il mukhtār*).

Next, he discusses at length the concept of the throne and God being seated on it. Al-Rāzī argues that God cannot be limited to any throne, nor can there be a throne which could encompass His infinity. He reasons that the throne is a metaphor for the furthest heaven or sphere, which is the fastest of all other spheres and the cause of the movements of all of them. This is the meaning of "He draweth the night as a veil over the day, each seeking the other in rapid succession."

"The sun, moon and the stars are constrained under God's command" could mean, according to al-Rāzī, that: (1) each of these bodies has its specific function in the world; or (2) that they have a special relationship to the furthest sphere or "the throne," which symbolizes God's power. Al-Rāzī believes the second meaning to be more likely since, as we have seen above, the furthest sphere is the cause of the movement of all heavenly bodies. Thus, al-Rāzī conceives the constraining to God's dominion as the power of the furthest sphere, the throne. Further, he proposes that the throne is governed by one of the highest ranks of angels. This means that God's dominion over the heavenly bodies is mediated through the throne, which symbolizes the dominion of the angels or the intellects over the spheres. Al-Rāzī here explains that the movements of the heavenly bodies and their relation to the angels are constructed for the welfare of the world (al-Zurkān 2003: 14, 79–114).

All these statements, according to al-Rāzī, prove over and over again that God is a willing wise agent (*fā'il mukhtār*) who knows all the particulars and how they relate to each other for the welfare of this universe. Thus the dominion of God over everything in this world aims towards its best function and welfare.

The Creation of Human Beings

Al-Rāzī reflects here on the creation of human beings through the interpretation of different verses, the most important of which are: 2:30, 23:14, 38:71–2, 15:28 and 17:85. We will look here at 38:71: "Behold, thy Lord said to the angels: 'I am about to create man from clay: When I have fashioned him (in due proportion) and breathed into him of My spirit, fall ye down in obeisance unto him.'"

From this verse it seems that human beings were created in the last phase of creation. The fact that the angels are referred to in the creation of human beings here, shows that they have existed long before the existence of humans. Al-Rāzī narrates here a story that enjoyed wide circulation in his time: "it is widely known that 'the jinni' were living first on earth and they caused a lot of evil so that God sent the angels under the leadership of Iblīs to fight them, and finally expelled them from there." This explains the mistrust of the angels concerning the creation of humans. Al-Rāzī takes the opportunity here to consider the nature of the angels and their hierarchy in the divine kingdom. He describes them as immaterial beings similar to God, though he considers them contingent beings. He also affirms that the human soul belongs to this category as we will see below (al-Zurkān 2003: 26, 207–12).

There are two versions in the Qur'ān regarding the way humans are created. They are created out of clay and from the development of the foetus in the womb of mothers: 23:12–14 "Man We did create from a quintessence (of clay). Then We placed him as (a drop of) sperm in a place of rest, firmly fixed. Then We made the sperm into a clot of congealed blood; then of that clot We made a (foetus) lump; then we made out of that lump bones and clothed the bones with flesh; then we developed out of it another creature. So blessed be Allah, the best to create!"

Al Rāzī interprets both forms of creation as the formation of the body and the shape of the human being. He argues that the clay and the sperm are very closely related since the sperm is developed, in his opinion, from the nourishing of the body through foodstuff that comes from earth. Al-Rāzī here is convinced that this verse is explaining the development of the foetus until it is born as a baby. When explaining "We developed out of it another creature," he argues that the "another creature" emerges when the breathing of the soul into the human body takes place and it starts moving. This again shows that creation means only the preparation and forming of the body to receive the soul that bestows the actual life (al-Zurkān 2003: 23, 79–83).

To understand the mystery of the human soul and its reality we move to 17:85: "They ask thee concerning the Spirit (*al-ruh*). Say: 'The Spirit (cometh) by command of my Lord: of knowledge it is only a little that is communicated to you (O men!).'"

In the explanation of this verse al-Rāzī gives his latest and final opinion on the nature of the human soul. He argues first against some of the theologians and the

Mu'tazilites who deny that being human refers to certain power in the body. They believe that nothing exists beyond this body. The body in itself possesses the power to act and think through accidental attributes that come to inhere in the body and cause different activities. Both here and in the *Maṭālib* al-Rāzī builds lengthy arguments to prove that humanity is not reduced to the body, rather it is identified with the soul that inheres in the body and causes its identity and its activities. Some of his arguments are drawn from Ibn Sīnā such as when al-Rāzī affirms that the loss of any bodily sense organ does not change the knowledge of the person of him/herself and although the human being consists of parts, s/he recognizes himself/herself as the unity of one identity. Al-Rāzī here brings many arguments and proofs in order to defend the unity of the human soul and its nature, opposite to that of the body. He also states here that the soul is the power in the body that can understand, feel, see and hear at the same time while the different organs are concerned exclusively with one single activity. But since the soul is one entity and does not consist of parts, then it is not material because all material entities consist of parts. Al-Rāzī also recalls many other verses that prove that the soul is not a material substance but rather immaterial such as 76:2, 15:29, and 91:7–8. He also argues that theologians are mistaken when they reject the existence of immaterial beings out of concern that such immateriality would make them equivalent to God. Al-Rāzī explains that having an immaterial nature does not automatically correspond to being equivalent to God, because sharing a negative attribute with God (such as having no material body) does not mean sharing all His other positive attributes, such as omnipotence or omniscience. Moreover, every two species under one genus share many attributes, but nevertheless they are not totally identical. Since this is evidently true, then there is no obvious reason why it should not be possible to share immateriality with God without sharing His divinity (al-Zurkān 2003: 21, 33–49).

To sum up, al-Rāzī considers the existence of the human being in the same terms he considers the existence of all other things, that is, taking place in different stages, starting with the formation of the body until reaching the actual creation, which takes place when the soul joins the body to form the person.

Conclusion

The concept of creation, according to al-Rāzī, consists of different levels. Creation should be understood, in the first sense, as the decreeing (*taqdīr*) of the existence of each thing according to a plan in order to constitute a unified universe. Second, there is an arrangement of all things so they exist in relation to each other, while on the third level the actual existence of things happens. Finally, the last level takes place when angels are entrusted to govern and control the world according to a divine system. The most important point for al-Rāzī is that at the core of the universe stands a willing and wise God whose knowledge, power and wisdom are beyond the understanding of the human mind and therefore, no matter how much we may understand the concept of creation, it will always remain a mystery.

In this short study, I have worked to uncover al-Rāzī's understanding of the concept of creation in the *al-Tafsīr* with reference to his last work, the *Maṭālib*. We have noticed that his thoughts in both works are very similar, though in the *al-Tafsīr* he tends to demonstrate that the Qur'ān is in agreement with the rational understanding of the concept of creation and in line with many philosophical concepts. Nevertheless, he insists that God must be conceived as a willing and wise agent and that most philosophical concepts should be interpreted with this in mind. Al-Rāzī thus reconciles philosophy with the Qur'ān in such a way that it can be said that, rather than philosophizing the Qur'ān, he Islamized philosophy.

Further Reading

Abrahamov, B. (2002) "Fakhr al-Dīn al-Rāzī On the Knowability of God's Essence and Attributes," *Arabica* 49: 204–30.
Fakhry, M. (1983) *A History of Islamic Philosophy*, London: Longman.
Kafrawi, S. (2004) "The notion of necessary being in Fakhr al-Dīn al-Rāzī's philosophical theology," *Islam and Christian–Muslim Relations* 15: 125–33.
Muhibbu-Din, M. A. (1994) "Imām Fakhr al-Dīn al-Rāzī: philosophical theology in *Al-tafsīr al-kabīr*," *Hamdard Islamicus* 17: 55–84.

References

Ali, A. Y. (ed. and tr.) (1977) *The Holy Qur'ān*, USA: American Trust Publications.
al-Rāzī, Fakhr al-Dīn (1999) *al-Maṭālib al-'Āliya*, Beirut: Dār al-Kutub al-'Ilmiyya.
al-Zurkān, M. S. (1963) *Fakhr-al-Din al-Rāzī wa Ārāuhū al-kalāmiyya wa'l-Falsafiyya*, Cairo: Dār al-Fikr.
——. (2003) *al-Tafsīr al-Kabīr or Mafatīḥ al-Ghayb*, Cairo: al-Maktaba al-Tawfiqiyya.
İskenderoğlu, M. (2002) *Fakhr-al-Din al-Rāzī and Thomas Aquinas on the Question of the Eternity of the World*, Leiden: Brill.
Wolfson, H. A. (1976) *The Philosophy of Kalām*, Cambridge & London: Harvard University Press.

2
REASONING IN THE QUR'ĀN

Rosalind Ward Gwynne

Introduction

Muslims consider the Qur'ān to be the revealed speech of God—sublime, inimitable and containing information that only God knows. It has been analyzed in every possible way—theologically, linguistically, legally, metaphorically—and some of these analyses have presented their results as the conclusions of reasoning in the Qur'ān itself, whether explicit or implicit. For example, nearly 500 years after the Prophet's death, the theologian and anti-Batini mystic al-Ghazālī (d. 505/1111) presented five types of Qur'ānic arguments as the "Just Balance" (*al-Qisṭās al-Mustaqīm*) by which the truth or falsehood of earthly [sc. human] reasoning on the same schemata could be ascertained. These forms of reasoning are the equivalents of the first, second and third figures of the Aristotelian categorical syllogism, and the Stoic conditional and disjunctive syllogisms. In all, I have identified ten broad categories, which, when counted along with their subcategories (not all of which appear in this article), produce some 30 identifiable forms of reasoning (Gwynne 2004). Here I treat eight major categories: commands, rules, legal arguments, comparison, contrast, categorical syllogisms, conditional syllogisms, and disjunctive syllogisms.

Commands

It is a matter of consensus in Islam that the first word of the Qur'ān to be revealed to the Prophet Muḥammad was a command: "*Iqra*" ("read" or "recite") (Qur'ān 96:1). Commands, commandments and orders, especially from the strong to the weak, are often not considered to be reasoned arguments but threats, arguments *ad baculum*: "Do this or I will hit you with a stick!" However, when the reasons for the command are given, when the authority of the source of the command is made clear, when the one given the command benefits from it, its identity as an argument—a reasoned consequence—is much clearer. Usually these elements precede the command; indeed, some authorities maintain that the command is invalid if not so worded.

Explanations do not precede "*iqra*" but they follow it immediately. The command is issued in the name of the One God, Who created human beings, Who is the most Generous, Who taught human beings by the Pen what they did not know (Qur'ān 96:1-5).

Rules

The principles that are the bases for Qur'ānic commands can be called "rules," and there is a branch of logic/rhetoric known as "rule-based reasoning." This body of rules for appropriate and pious human action constitutes the Covenant (*'ahd*; cf. Qur'ān 7:172; 2:27, 80; 3:81, 187). In the Qur'ān, God's unswerving adherence to the Covenant and his various ways of doing that over millennia are called "the sunna of God" (*sunnat Allah*). Concerning the struggles with the Quraysh—the Prophet's tribe—and regarding the authority of the *sunna*, the Qur'ān says, "Are they looking at anything other than the *sunna* of the ancients? You will not find any change to God's *sunna* and you will not find that God's *sunna* is ever turned aside" (Qur'ān 35:43).

But does the omnipotent Deity see all choices as equal? For example, two verses (Qur'ān 6:12, 54) state that God has written mercy [sc. as a condition binding] upon Himself. While these do not occur in the verses citing *sunnat Allah*, they show God limiting his actions in certain ways; and although they constituted an element in later theological arguments over predestination and the omnipotence of God, that does not detract from their role as rules in Qur'ānic rule-based reasoning.

Gidon Gottlieb's indispensable *The Logic of Choice* explains that rule-based reasoning is neither deductive nor inductive: conclusions in legal or moral decisions are based on legal or moral rules, not on empirical evidence or probability. The original declaration of the rule must be restatable as follows: "In circumstances X, Y is required/permitted" (Gottlieb 1968: 40). This seemingly simple form includes: the circumstances in which the rule is applied; an indication of the necessary, possible, or impossible conclusion or decision; whether the inference used to extract the rule is permitted, required, or prohibited; and an indication that the statement is in fact meant to be a rule.

Imperative verbs in the Qur'ān are not in fact always commands, and those that are may cover very minor points of conduct. But its hierarchy of rules does not negate the fact that the Covenant is a single rule and is treated as such in the Qur'ān:

1 Circumstances: The Covenant governs relations between humans and God, with corresponding implications for humans' relations with each other.
2 Conclusion: Humans shall observe the Covenant.
3 Type of inference: Adherence to the Covenant is mandatory, with some sub-rules for those who have never heard the Word (Qur'ān 9:11) or are temporarily unable to observe one or more of its conditions (Qur'ān 2:173). Ultimately, however, the Covenant will apply to all, as expressed in the key verse Qur'ān 2:172: "Am I not your Lord? (*a-lastu bi-rabbikum?*)."
4 Proof that it is a rule: Those who follow it will be rewarded; those who do not will not be.

Legal Arguments

Rules are not laws, but the elements of rules as laid out above shape arguments that are the basis of legal thinking. Thus we shall examine legal arguments based upon the principles that form them (e.g. reciprocity or recompense), not the legal questions they address, such as property ownership, inheritance, or criminal acts. We shall also look at Aristotle's "non-artistic proofs" (e.g. contracts and oaths), and the very interesting class known as "performative utterances"—words that are themselves deeds.

The Covenant is based upon reciprocity, the relation between one agent (divine or human) and another: "O Children of Israel! Remember My favor which I bestowed upon you, and keep My Covenant as I keep yours. And fear Me" (Qur'ān 2:40). The same words are used for each party despite the fact that the actions and words described are far from identical: "We have granted you abundance. Therefore worship God and sacrifice" (Qur'ān 108:1–2). Charity, one of the pillars of the faith, is also based upon recompense, but it is a three-sided relationship: the first person provides help for God's sake, the second person who is in need receives the help, and God rewards the helper (e.g. Qur'ān 2:272, 8:60). In this way, God protected the orphaned Prophet, and humans must do the same for orphans and the poor (Qur'ān 93:6–11).

Recompense refers to the relation between an action and its result: reward or punishment. "Whatever you spend in the cause of God will be repaid, and you will not be wronged" (Qur'ān 8:60). "Whoever performs a good deed will have ten like it; whoever performs an evil deed will be punished only with its equivalent; and they shall not be wronged" (Qur'ān 6:160, cf. Qur'ān 27:89–90, 28:84).

The rhetorical devices of comparison and contrast (to be discussed below) also appear as forms of legal arguments that prescribe priority, equivalence, and limitation. God is to be feared more than humans (Qur'ān 9:13); God and His Apostle are to be preferred even above one's family, if they are not believers (Qur'ān 9:23–4). "The Prophet is closer to the believers than they are to each other (or 'to their own souls'), and his wives are their mothers" (Qur'ān 33:6). Family over friends (Qur'ān 8:75, 33:6), Muslims over non-Muslims as friends and allies (Qur'ān 3:28), obedience over fear when fighting is necessary (Qur'ān 47:20–1)—the examples are endless but often nuanced (cf. Qur'ān 33:6) and not always easy to observe. Even the Prophet is chided for fearing the people more than God (Qur'ān 33:37) and preferring the rich to the poor (Qur'ān 80:1–10).

A necessary counterpart to priority is equivalence, particularly when one is physically, financially or otherwise unable to fulfill an obligation. "Whoever obeys the Apostle has obeyed God" (Qur'ān 4:80) contains perhaps the most common equivalence, one that is made 26 times. Equivalences that compensate for inabilities include such acts as: compensatory fasting if the Muslim is traveling or ill during Ramadan; feeding the poor, though fasting is preferable (Qur'ān 2:184–185); and equal punishment for murder, though forgoing revenge in favor of charity atones for one's sins (Qur'ān 5:45). A woman's inheritance (Qur'ān 4:11) and contract testimony (Qur'ān 2:282) are *legal* equivalents to those of men despite being only half of the actual quantity. And civil legal matters such as marriage, divorce and inheritance will always provide livings for lawyers.

God puts limits (*ḥudūd*) on such things as proper conduct during Ramadan (Qur'ān 2:187); marriage, divorce, and remarriage (Qur'ān 2:229–30); inheritance (Qur'ān 4:12–14); and He makes clear the differences between those who do not know God's limits (Qur'ān 9:97) and those who do (Qur'ān 9:112). Later the word became synonymous with severe punishments.

Further legal ramifications can be classed as distinctions and exceptions. A distinction differentiates between two apparently similar actions or entities on the basis of source, motive, or circumstance. "The good that reaches you is from God, while the evil that reaches you is from yourself" (Qur'ān 4:79). "Those who extort usury … say 'Selling is like usury', whereas God has permitted selling and forbidden usury" (Qur'ān 2:275). An exception cites things of the same genus but bans one or more on the basis of some other rule. "Know that there is no deity except God" (Qur'ān 47:19; cf. Qur'ān 3:62 and the *shahāda* or Islamic creed). Clearly the legal ramifications of the exceptive construction are potentially enormous, such as exemption from divine punishment if forced to deny Islam publicly while keeping the faith in one's heart (e.g. Qur'ān 16:106), or learning to observe the ban on marriage with daughters, sisters, and nieces (among others) while accepting the legality of such unions if they existed prior to the revelation (Qur'ān 4:22–3).

A useful supplement to our list can be found in Book One of Aristotle's *Rhetoric*, which lists what he calls "non-artistic proofs": laws, witnesses, contracts, evidence taken under torture (of slaves), and oaths (Aristotle 1991: 109, n. 247). In the Qur'ān, the only real law is, of course, the Law of God (e.g. Qur'ān 7:185, 45:6, 77:50). Human laws are usually referred to as "opinion" (*ẓann* e.g. Qur'ān 6:116) or "desires" (*ahwa'* e.g. Qur'ān 5:49–50). Aristotle places actual human witnesses in third place after literary wisdom (e.g. poetry and proverbs) and the opinions of persons who are "well-known." The Qur'ānic concept of "witness" is more complex (Mir 1987), in that it includes components of both the Covenant, to which God is a witness (e.g. Qur'ān 6:19), and law among human beings, in which a witness may know the facts first-hand (e.g. Qur'ān 12:26), or the character of the accused (Qur'ān 5:107), or fill any of a number of other slots.

As for contracts, one of the longest verses in the Qur'ān (2:282) is a virtual tutorial for believers in the matters of debts, record-keeping, and contracts. "O you who believe, when you contract a debt for a designated period of time, write it down. Let a scribe write it fairly." The verse includes the concepts of sale, debt, record, witness, legal competency, guardianship and immunity, and it clearly forms a framework for the vast complexity of Islamic law, commerce, and social cohesion.

Oaths are important in the Qur'ān and their terms, in places, are quite nuanced. First, they are part of the Covenant. God commands people to keep their oaths but allows for certain compensations (e.g. feeding the poor, freeing a slave, fasting) if the oaths were made in good faith but cannot be kept (Qur'ān 5:89). Those who swear falsely to the Prophet or break their oaths are to be fought (Qur'ān 9:95–6; 58:14–18), but rash or inadvertent oaths will not bring punishment (Qur'ān 2:225, 5:89).

And contrary to Aristotle's inclusion of torture as a method of extracting truth, the Qur'ān does not validate or even mention torture.

Speech acts, "performative utterances," are not themselves forms of reasoning, but they may well serve to end arguments or totally transform the circumstances.

Such utterances are not descriptions of acts but are themselves acts with legal, moral, and/or religious consequences. "You're under arrest!" "I accept your offer." "I do." "I now pronounce you husband and wife." The Qur'ānic distinction between *muslimun* (i.e. "submitters") and *mu'minun* ("believers") dramatizes the difference between the two groups. The former are those whose visible acts appear to other humans to be Islamically acceptable but whose inner motives may or may not be. The latter are those whose hearts are also true, something known only to God. The clearest distinction between the two comes in Qur'ān 49:14–15; there are, however, passages that seem to equate them (e.g. Qur'ān 5:111, 27:81, 33:35). Most significantly, the word *mu'minun* is used over six times more often than *muslimun*.

Comparison

Comparison and contrast will clearly be important figures in any speech that deals with God and humanity, with good and evil, with this world and the next. Both appear in numerous distinguishable forms. Comparison includes similarity (Corbett 1971: 116), analogy, parable, and degree. Contrast covers difference, inequality, opposition, opposites and contraries, contradictions, reversal, and antithesis (Corbett 1971: 129). Many of these can be subdivided as well. Thus "similarity" in "comparison" includes similarity of genus (e.g. rewards earthly and divine, cf. Qur'ān 8:28 and Qur'ān 29:10); similarity of action (e.g. the same word *i'tadā* used for aggression by the enemy and just retaliation against it, cf. Qur'ān 2:194); and similarity of consequence (e.g. unbelievers who continue as such whether warned of the consequences or not, cf. Qur'ān 36:10, 7:193).

Analogy and parable are often based on the messages of the earlier scriptures. Thus many jurists rejected the use of analogy because the first to use it was Satan, who refused to prostrate himself to Adam. "I am better than he: You created me from fire, and you created him from clay" (Qur'ān 7:12, 38:75–6) (Ibn Hazm 1960: 70). But "analogy" here is a technical term in logic, not the equivalent of *qiyās*, which is only a partial synonym. People of the Book who argue knowledgeably about some things argue about others of which only God has knowledge (Qur'ān 3:66, 45:24) and study the scriptures anachronistically (Qur'ān 3:65). Parables and shorter examples abound in the Qur'ān, from the tiniest creature, the gnat, (Qur'ān 2:26) to charity like a seed (Qur'ān 2:261), to truth and falsehood like metal and "the scum that rises from what they smelt to make jewelry and tools" (Qur'ān 13:17). The Qur'ān often points out to its audience that these *are* parables or analogies: the word *mathal* (likeness) and its plural *amthal* occur 88 times; but humans may not make up their own. "Do not coin *amthal* for God: God knows and you do not" (Qur'ān 16:74).

Some arguments based on degree—"good, better, best"—are types of comparison; others—"better" and "worse"—are contrasts and will appear in the next section, but there are constructions that fit both. While many of God's attributes are positive and non-comparative, others use the elative (*af'al*) form to the same effect; that is, they suggest God's action. "Whose word is truer than God's?" (Qur'ān 4:122). "Who is better than God in judging a people whose faith is certain?" (Qur'ān 9:111).

Some of the Divine Names are in elative form: *arham al-rahimin* (Most Merciful of those who have mercy: Qur'ān 7:151, 12:64 et. al.). One appeared in the very first revelation: Most Generous (*al-akram*) (Qur'ān 96:3). Muslims must learn to rank other humans according to their beliefs, not worldly criteria: "Do not marry polytheist women until they believe: a believing slave woman is better than a [free] polytheist woman, even though she pleases you" (Qur'ān 2:221). One's own treatment of others must also be considered: extra charity (*sadaqat*) is better given secretly than openly (Qur'ān 2:271). One should not collect a debt until the debtor can repay it easily; better still, forgive it as charity (Qur'ān 2:180).

Comparisons between evils begin at the negative end of the scale. "God does not forgive that anything should be associated with Him, but He forgives whom He will for what is less than that" (Qur'ān 4:48). "Who is more evil than one who forges the lie against God even as he is being called to Islam? (.)" (Qur'ān 61:7; cf. 6:21, 6:157 et al.).

Contrast

Because it shows God to be the Unique, Incomparable Reality, the Qur'ān is in many ways a single, huge contrast. "There is nothing like Him" (Qur'ān 42:11). "No one is equal to Him" (Qur'ān 112:4). In the first of the aforementioned subcategories, the multiplicity and variety of Creation will be reduced to three broad categories of difference: genus, motive, and action. As to genus, a prophet, for example, is a mortal man with a divine connection, whereas his audiences think he should be an angel (Qur'ān 25:7) or an important person (Qur'ān 43:31). If not, he must be a madman, poet, soothsayer, or forger (Qur'ān 52:29–33), or a lying sorcerer (Qur'ān 38:4).

A well-known *ḥadīth*—the sayings of the Prophet—states that "Actions are judged [only] by motives." Thus unbelievers who build mosques are not equal to Muslims who do the same (Qur'ān 9:17–19), as their motives damage and divide the believers (Qur'ān 9:107). But most hypocrites may not be known until the Day of Judgment, and therefore it is far easier to determine who they are by their public declarations and visible actions that are contrary to Islam. "We deny [the Message] with which you have been sent, and we are in serious doubt about that to which you call us (...)" (Qur'ān 14:9–10). Inequality is far more often a contrast and not a comparison. "Is the blind equal to the sighted, or is the darkness equal to the light?" (Qur'ān 13:16, cf. 6:50, 35:19). "Are they equal, those who know and those who do not?" (Qur'ān 39:9). And in the final irony, "Inhabitants of the Fire and inhabitants of the Garden are not equal. It is the inhabitants of the Garden who are triumphant" (Qur'ān 59:20).

Opposites, contraries, and contradictories are difficult to distinguish, not least because their forms in theology and in rhetoric/logic often differ. We shall confine ourselves to a few examples. God controls opposites: death and life, laughter and tears (Qur'ān 53:43–4), day and night (Qur'ān 17:12), heaven and earth (Qur'ān 2:164), land and sea (Qur'ān 6:59). Some of His names *are* opposites: "He is the First and the Last, the Evident and the Hidden" (Qur'ān 57:3). The damned and the saved are constantly compared. The former are on the left, the latter on the right (Qur'ān 90:18–19) and receive their Books of Deeds in the corresponding hands (Qur'ān 69:19, 25). The faces of the saved will be bright, those of the damned covered with dust (Qur'ān 80:38–41).

Contraries can exist in a single person or group: good and evil deeds (Qur'ān 46:16), good and evil people among People of the Book (Qur'ān 46:16), and among the *jinn* (Qur'ān 72:14–15); and there is a possibility of there being intermediate positions (Qur'ān 11:12, 3:167). Contradictories, on the other hand, do not contain intermediate positions and are most clearly seen in an affirmation and denial of the same word: "Any to whom God does not give light has no light" (Qur'ān 24:40). "Reversal" is complete transformation, whether of repentant sinners (Qur'ān 25:69–70), former enemies now friends (Qur'ān 41:34), or the earth and heavens on the Day of Judgment (Qur'ān 14:48, and *suras* 81, 82, and 84). "Antithesis," as I use the term, is an extended contrast, such as occurs in Qur'ān 38:49–64: the righteous have gardens of Paradise, rest, fruit and drink on call, and attentive companions; the wrongdoers have an evil place in which they will fry, boiling and bitterly cold, stinking drinks, no greeting from the Lord, and no opportunity to see those at whom they used to laugh.

Categorical Syllogisms

As mentioned in the introduction, the inspiration for my study of reasoning in the Qur'ān was a logical treatise of al-Ghazālī, *al-Qisṭās al-Mustaqīm* (*The Just Balance*), which analyzes passages in the Qur'ān to produce categorical, conditional, and disjunctive syllogisms. Ghazālī wrote the book after his spiritual retreat, so it contains more Qur'ānic and fewer scholarly technical terms than his earlier works on logic. For example, it uses the Qur'ānic word *mizan* instead of *qiyās* for "syllogism" and is presented in the form of a dialogue with a Batini. The title of the book is taken from Qur'ān 17:35: "Weigh by the Just Balance" and much of the clarification from Qur'ān 55:1–9: "Do not cause the scale to give short weight."

The first figure of the Aristotelian categorical syllogism ("Barbara," in which all propositions are universal affirmatives = A) comes from Qur'ān 2:258, where Abraham shows Nimrod that he is not a god by asking him to make the sun rise in the west. The usual form of such a proof is as follows:

> [Whoever has power over the sunrise is God.]
> My god is the one who has power over the sunrise.
> Therefore, my god is God.

Ghazālī clarifies the reasoning by using some examples from daily life and from Islamic law:

> All wine is intoxicating.
> All intoxicants are forbidden.
> Therefore, all wine is forbidden.

Other first-figure syllogisms can be constructed from, for example, Qur'ān 39:71–2, 50:3–5, 17:27, and 22:52. Other moods of the first figure can also be found: Darii in

Qur'ān 4:162 and 5:83–5; Celarent in Qur'ān 9:44–5 and 43:15–18; and Ferio in Qur'ān 26:224–7.

In the second figure, one premise must be negative and the major premise must be universal. Ghazālī uses another example from the life of Abraham, when he mistook the moon, sun, and stars for God until he saw them set.

The moon sets.
The Deity does not "set."
Therefore, the moon is not a deity.

Other modes of this figure are based upon Qur'ān 6:76–9, 5:18, and 62:6–7.

Ghazālī takes the third figure of the categorical syllogism from Qur'ān 6:91, when Moses' enemies deny that he or any other human received revelation.

[Moses was a human being].
God sent a book to Moses.
Therefore, God sends books to some humans.

Of the 19 modes of the categorical syllogism, Ghazālī uses only four. Conditional and disjunctive syllogisms as analyzed in Stoic logic are treated even less analytically, largely because the language of the Qur'ān, and Arabic as a whole, contain so many gradations of condition, consequence, and distinction. What appears to be a conditional particle may not be serving as such in its particular context, whereas a conditional argument may be indicated only by syntax and grammar. "Keep your covenant and We will keep Ours" (Qur'ān 2:40) is a conditional; "Do not fear them but fear Me, if (*in*) you are believers!" (Qur'ān 3:175) is a categorical despite the presence of the word "if." In addition, sound and fallacious forms of the arguments are easily confused, especially when parts of them are left unstated, to be grasped by the audience.

Conditional Syllogisms

There are two types of conditional syllogism. **Type 1** conditionals ("constructive mood"), in which the conclusion is reached by affirming the antecedent, are rather scarce in the Qur'ān. "Say: Do you see that if [the Revelation] is from God and you reject it, who is in greater error than one who has split off far away?" (Qur'ān 41:52, cf. 46:10). Supplying what is missing, we complete the argument as follows:

If the Revelation is from God and you reject it, [then you are in error (*dalal*)].
[The Revelation is from God and you reject it].
[Therefore, you are in error].

As seen from the bracketing, only the antecedent is explicitly stated. It is up to the listener or the reader to complete the argument correctly by switching the consequent from the third person—"one who has split off"—back to the second— "you."

The content of a longer verse, Qur'ān 2:120, regarding the attitude of Jews and Christians to Islam, can be schematized as follows:

If you do not follow their religion, the Jews and Christians will never accept you.
You do not follow their religion.
Therefore, the Jews and Christians will never accept you.

The fallacious form of the type 1 conditional denies the antecedent. Ghazālī's simple illustration is:

If Zayd's prayer is valid, then he is ritually pure.
His prayer is not valid.
Therefore, he is not ritually pure. [Fallacious]
Prayers, of course, are invalidated by a number of conditions.

Type 2 conditionals (destructive mood) work by denial of the consequent. Ghazālī's everyday example of the unsound form is as follows, fallacious because it does *not* deny the consequent:

If Zayd's prayer is valid, then he is ritually pure.
Zayd is ritually pure.
Therefore, his prayer is valid. [Fallacious]

Ghazālī constructs two Qur'ānic examples from three verses: Qur'ān 21:22, 17:42, and 21:99.

If there were two gods in the world, it would be ruined.
It has not been ruined.
Therefore there are not two gods.
If there were other gods than the Lord of the Throne, they would have sought a way to get to the Lord of the Throne.
It is known that they did not seek such a thing.
Therefore, there are no gods except the Lord of the Throne.

Many Qur'ānic conditionals of this type have the consequent in the form of a command, as in Qur'ān 2:94–5, cf. 62:6–7. Schematized, it is as follows:

"If you (Jews) are assured of heaven, then wish for death!"
They will never wish for death.
Therefore, they are not assured of heaven.

Disjunctive Syllogisms

Just as contrast is the key rhetorical construction in the Qur'ān, disjunction is the key distinction between true belief and error. There are three forms of the disjunctive syllogism, which we schematize below. The numbering signals that they follow the two conditional syllogisms, according to the system of the Stoics.

Type 3—Not both A and B (or Either A or B ... or C or D)

This establishes that two things cannot co-exist but does not deny the possibility of intermediate positions. The Stoic example says:

Not both: it is day and it is night.
It is day.
Therefore, it is not night.
But this does not eliminate intermediate positions such as twilight.

A Qur'ānic example can be made from Qur'ān 2:91: "Why did you kill God's prophets in the past if you are believers?" When schematized:

Not both: you kill God's prophets and you believe in God.
You kill God's prophets.
Therefore you do not believe in God.

Countless verses in the Qur'ān are so concise that they can be expanded into both of the either-or disjunctions, the first affirmative, the second negative. Ghazālī calls this pair of disjunctions "the scale of mutual opposition" (*mīzān al-ta'ānud*). "Say: Do you know best or does God?" (Qur'ān 2:140).

Type 4—Either the first or the second. The first. Therefore, not the second.

Either you or God knows best.
[God knows best].
[Therefore you do not know best].

Type 5—Either the first or the second. Not the first. Therefore, the second.

Either you or God knows best.
[You do not know best].
[Therefore God knows best].

Clearly, type 5, which ends with the affirmation of God's knowledge, is rhetorically and theologically more effective than the anticlimactic type 4. The only Qur'ānic example Ghazālī uses is Qur'ān 34:24: "And surely we or you are rightly guided (*'alā hudā*) or in clear error (*fī ḍalāl mubīn*)."

Either we or you are in clear error.
[It is known that we are not in error].
[Therefore you are in error].

But often there are more than two alternatives, so one must detect when a disjunctive argument omits the only valid choice: They say: "Be Jews or Christians and you will be guided!" Say: "Rather the religion (*milla*) of Abraham—a monotheist (*ḥanīf*), not one of the polytheists!" (Qur'ān 2:135).

Conclusion

As can be seen from this brief treatment, reasoning is an integral part of the Qur'ān and has shaped the thoughts of Qur'ānic scholars. Muslims have remarked to me that the first appeal of the Qur'ān is to human reason and that an unbiased reading will bear that out. God has given most human beings the capacity to understand and fulfill the commands, recommendations, and abstentions contained therein. To those who cannot do so, through mental or physical incapacity, duress or imprisonment, God has given compensation, alternatives, and forgiveness. And charity may be material or spiritual, thus proceeding equally—though not identically—from the rich to the poor and from the poor to the rich.

Further Reading

Fischer, M. J. & Abedi, M. (1990) *Debating Muslims: Cultural Dialogues In Postmodernity and Tradition*, Madison: University of Wisconsin Press.
Gwynne, R. W. (1990) "The *a fortiori* argument in *fiqh*, *naḥw*, and *kalām*," in K. Versteegh & M. Carter (eds.), *Studies in the History of Arabic Grammar II*, Philadelphia: John Benjamins.
——. (2004) *Logic, Rhetoric, and Legal Reasoning in the Qur'ān: God's Arguments*, London and New York: RoutledgeCurzon.
Hawting, G. R. & Shareef, A. A. (eds.) (1993) *Approaches to the Qur'ān*, New York: Routledge.
Jeffery, A. (1937) *Materials for the History of the Text of the Qur'ān*, Leiden: Brill (repr. AMS Press, 1975).
Rippin, A. (2001) *The Qur'ān and Its Interpretive Tradition*, Aldershot: Ashgate Variorum.

References

al-Ahram al-Tijariya (1392/1972) *al-Qur'ān al-Karim*, Cairo: Maktabat.
al-Ghazālī (1392/1973) *al-Qisṭās al-Mustaqīm*, M. 'Afif al-Zu'bi (ed.), Beirut: Mu'assasat al-Zu'bi.
——. (1406/1986) *al-Qisṭās al-Mustaqīm*, R. M. 'Abd Allah (ed.), Damascus: Dar al-Hikma.
Ali, A. Y. (ed. and tr.) (1977) *The Holy Qur'ān*, USA: American Trust Publications.
Aristotle (1991) *Aristotle on Rhetoric: A Theory of Civic Discourse*, G. A. Kennedy (ed. and tr.), New York: Oxford University Press.
Corbett, E. P. J. (1971) *Classical Rhetoric for the Modern Student*, New York: Oxford University Press.
Gottlieb, G. (1968) *The Logic of Choice: An Investigation of the Concepts of Rule and Rationality*, London: Allen and Unwin.
Gwynne, R. W. (2004) *Logic, Rhetoric, and Legal Reasoning in the Qur'ān: God's Arguments*, London & New York: RoutledgeCurzon.
Ibn Hazm (1379/1960) *Mulakhkhaṣ Ibṭāl al-Qiyās wa-al-Ra'y wa-al-'Istiḥsān wa-al-Taqlīd wa-al-Ta'līl*, S. al-Afghani (ed.), Damascus: Damascus University Press.
Mir, M. (1987) *Dictionary of Qur'ānic Terms and Concepts*, New York: Garland.
Pickthall, M. M. (trans.) (1953) *The Meaning of the Glorious Koran*, New York: New American Library.
Rescher, N. (1966) *The Logic of Commands*, London: Routledge & Kegan Paul.
Searle, J. (1991) "How Performatives Work," *Tennessee Law Review* 58: 371–392.

3
ETHICAL ISSUES IN THE QUR'ĀN AND ḤADĪTH

Azim Nanji

Introduction

Ethics concerns human action and practices and occupies the realm of religion and philosophy. In the medieval European tradition prior to the availability of translations from Greek and Arabic in the twelfth and thirteenth centuries, philosophy from the Greek and Latin traditions played an integral yet subsidiary role in the formation of reasoning about right and wrong actions. The primary guiding source for morality and ethical action was the Hebrew Bible and the New Testament as interpreted by leading figures of the Christian church. In the Islamic milieu, while the science of philosophy influenced ethical thinking among philosophers and theologians, it did not significantly affect the development of ethical definitions grounded in religious texts and interpretations. While philosophers such as al-Fārābī, Ibn Miskawayh, Ibn Sīnā, Ibn Rushd and others wrote on practical philosophy from the Greek tradition, most Muslims used the Qur'ān and *ḥadīth*, as religious scholars interpreted them, as guides for everyday ethical action. The present essay concerns the ethical grounds of human actions in religious texts and their interpretation. What follows here can be philosophically characterized as an account of ethical practice and the religious doctrines that formed the common mores of human right action.

Qur'ān and Ḥadīth

Muslims regard themselves as the last in a line of a family of revealed faith traditions, whose messages originate from one God. The revelations given to Prophet Muḥammad, through divine inspiration, are believed by Muslims to be recorded in the Qur'ān, literally "recitation." The Muslim concept of revelation encompasses previous revelations: "We have inspired you [Muḥammad] as We inspired Noah and the prophets after him, as we inspired Abraham, Ishmael, Isaac, Jacob and the tribes; and Jesus, Job, Jonah, Aaron and Solomon; and we gave to David the Psalms. [These are] messengers of whom we have spoken to you and others that we have not mentioned" (Qur'ān 4:163–4). Thus the Prophet Muḥammad can be situated within the line of prophetic figures who, while seeking to reform their respective societies, were inspired by an experience of transcendence.

The actions and sayings of the prophet Muḥammad complemented the divinely revealed message of the Qur'ān and embodied a paradigm, constituting a source for establishing norms for Muslim conduct. These actions and sayings are known as *ḥadīth* and collectively represent the *sunna*, the Prophetic model. Early Islamic scholars further developed and elaborated the concept of the *sunna* in their search to recapture as complete a picture of the Prophet's exemplary life as they could authenticate on the basis of the *ḥadīth*, accounts of his words and deeds transmitted by his companions and others from the first generation of Muslims. This quest to memorialize the life of the Prophet and ground it in a historically verifiable process also led to a type of literary reconstruction of the narrative of the Prophet's life. All these forms of enactment acted as reference points that would subsequently inform and inspire various Muslim communities of interpretation as they sought to ground their own ethical, judicial, doctrinal, and historical identities in what they perceive to be the normative *sunna*.

Recent scholarship, such as the writings of William Graham (1977) and Hashim Kamali (2005), building on epistemological and hermeneutical stances prevalent in current comparative studies, has attempted to widen the basis for studying the *ḥadīth*. They tend to emphasize questions of how oral traditions and written texts are produced, transmitted, and interpreted, and they have further attempted to relate these interpretations to specific communities of scholars, social boundaries, and political contexts. In this wider view the *sunna* appears as a multivalent concept, illustrating how different kinds of Muslim orientations and institutions have found through *ḥadīth* literary formulation, expression and codification in law, ethics, theology, and mysticism. The *sunna* serves as a common template for all these Muslim groups and individuals, connecting them to the beginnings of Islam and acting as a common referent in the religious discourse of community formation and identity.

The revelation the Prophet experienced and communicated to his fellow Meccans is not to be understood, according to the Qur'ān, as removed from the day-to-day reality of life in society. In fact "revelation" took on significance immediately because it spoke to the need to transform the moral and social world of the time. The noted Muslim scholar and academic, F. Rahman, has argued that: "What emerges most clearly from the entire drift of the Qur'ān and the Prophet's actions ... is that no moral or spiritual welfare is possible without a sound and just socio-economic base. Indeed one may correctly assert that the rectitude of moral life in Islam is to be tested by, and is finally realized in, this society-building activity" (Rahman 1967: 106). Moreover, he asserted that the perspective of the Qur'ān was underpinned by moral and ethical rather than purely prescriptive and legal considerations.

Humanity: Moral Reasoning and Choice

While God's will is revealed in the Qur'ān and complemented in the *sunna*, Muslims are also urged to exercise reason in understanding revelation and reflecting on human choice. In the account of the creation of humanity as narrated in the Qur'ān,

Adam is shaped from clay, enlivened by divine spirit and endowed with the capacity to "name things" (Qur'ān 2:31). This suggests a layered and multi-dimensional being, in whom material, spiritual and intellectual orientations are combined. Adam is referred to as a *khalīfah* (caliph) or vicegerent, granted custody of the earth and guided by God to create conditions that enable life to be lived in dignity and according to an ethical and moral purpose. Being human, in this broad sense, thus has a special, even privileged, status in creation according to the Qur'ān (95:4) and brings with it accountability for the choices that are made, as illustrated in the story of creation.

According to the Qur'ānic account of creation, humanity was also endowed with the capacity to distinguish between right and wrong. God has also provided additional guidance through Messengers and Prophets to complement and build further on the human capacity for moral reasoning. In one of the chapters of the Qur'ān, entitled the "Criterion" (*Furqān*: *sura* 25), revelation—to all humanity—becomes the point of reference for distinguishing right from wrong. The same chapter goes on to cite examples of past biblical prophets and their role as mediators of God's word to their respective societies. Like Judaism and Christianity, Islam's beginnings are thus rooted in the idea of the divine command as a basis for establishing moral order through human endeavor. By grounding a moral code in divine will, an opportunity is afforded to human beings to respond by creating a rational awareness that sustains the validity of revelation. If revelation enables human reason to elaborate criteria for the totality of human actions and decisions, a wider basis for human action is possible. These themes are played out in the Qur'ānic telling of the story of Adam's creation and trespass.

Adam, the first human, is distinguished from existing angels who are asked to bow down to him by virtue of his divinely endowed capacity to "name things," that is, to conceive of knowledge capable of being described linguistically and thereby codified, a capacity not possessed by angels who are seen as one-dimensional beings. This creative capacity carries with it, however, an obligation not to exceed set limits. Satan in the Qur'ān exemplifies excess because he disobeys God's command to honor and bow before Adam, thus denying his own innate nature and limits. In time, Adam too fails to live within the limits set by God and loses his honorable status but without any connotation that this implies a doctrine of original sin. This he will have to recover subsequently by struggling with and overcoming his indiscretions on earth, which is the new arena of life that allows for choice and action. Ultimately, he does recover his former status, attesting to his capacity to return to the right course of action through an awareness of his error. Adam's story, therefore, reflects all of the potential for good and evil that has been built into the human condition and the unfolding saga of human response to a continuous divine revelation in history. Moreover, it exemplifies the ongoing struggle within humanity to discover the moral equilibrium that allows for balanced action.

Personal Ethics

The ideal of a moral and ethical consciousness based on belief and faith in God and His revelation as well as on human commitment and personal responsibility frame the model of human behavior in Islam. The Prophet Muḥammad, like the great prophetic figures before him, serves as the example of these qualities as they translate into daily life. These Qur'ānic values are complemented by the sayings of the Prophet relating to personal qualities, such as:

- Let those who believe in God and the Day of Judgment refrain from harming their neighbors, let them honor their guests and speak well of others or hold their tongues.
- The one who shows concern for widows and the disadvantaged is like the one who struggles in the way of God or fasts by day and rises at night for prayer.
- Adore God as though you see Him, if you do not see Him, He nonetheless sees you.

(*Mishkat* 1973)

Ethics and Learning

Among the earliest revelations received by the Prophet Muḥammad are verses emphasizing learning and knowledge: "Your Lord is full of generosity, instructing by the Pen, educating humanity about that which they did not know" (Qur'ān 96:3–5). Adam is distinguished in the creation story from other created beings by virtue of the divinely given capacity to "name things" (Qur'ān 2:31). One of the prayers in the Qur'ān is "Increase me O Lord, in knowledge" (Qur'ān 20:114). Complementing the Qur'ān's emphasis are the *ḥadīth* of the Prophet urging the pursuit of knowledge: "Seek knowledge, even into China" and "The pursuit of knowledge is obligatory on every Muslim, men and women" (*Mishkat* 1973). Muslim philosophers, such as al-Kindī (d. 866), argued strongly on the basis of such verses that philosophy and the Qur'ānic message were entirely compatible and that the Prophet was the highest example of a rational philosophic mind (Nasr 1996: 27–39).

Wealth and its Ethical Purposes

Mecca had grown in the Prophet's time as a major centre of trade and gave rise to the emergence of a merchant class with some wealth. The Qur'ān is, however, critical of the use to which some of them put their wealth. They are accused of being fraudulent, unjust, niggardly and exploitative: "Woe to those who deal in fraud, those who when they receive from others, extract the right measure, but when they give, are deceitful and give less. Are they not aware that they will be accountable on the Day of Judgment, when all humankind will stand before the Lord of the Worlds?" (Qur'ān 83:1–6). They are also criticized for hoarding and circulating wealth amongst themselves (Qur'ān 3:180). They are further accused of usurious practices through which they hold hostage those to whom they have lent money so as to exploit their dependence on them. The Qur'ān regards wealth as a blessing and a trust. Individuals should use their wealth responsibly to meet their own needs but are urged to spend the surplus in socially beneficial and ethical ways: "Believe in

God and His Messenger and give out of that which you have acquired. For those who have faith and give to others for them there is a great reward. And why do you not wish to spend in the way of God? To God belongs the heritage of the heavens and the earth" (Qur'ān 57:7–10). The specific notion of setting aside a portion of one's wealth for others or of recognizing the necessity and value of giving are articulated in the Qur'ān through a number of terms that are often used interchangeably. The most significant of these are *zakāt* and *sadaqah*.

Sadaqah and *zakāt* offer a very textured and multivalent conception of giving that draws upon the ideals of compassion, social justice, sharing, and strengthening the community. This act aims at being both socially corrective and of spiritual benefit, while reflecting the ethical and spiritual values that are associated with wealth, property, resources and voluntary efforts in personal as well as communal contexts. It is in this broader sense that Muslims understand the use of wealth and apply it in their daily life.

The perspective of the Qur'ān on sharing wealth and individual resources through acts of giving is rooted in specific essential ideals such as the absence of a dichotomy between spiritual and material endeavors in human life. Acts sanctioned as a part of faith are also linked to the daily conditions of life in this world and the nature, purpose and function of the Muslim community as "the best of communities created to do good and to struggle against evil" (Qur'ān 3:110). The notion of trusteeship of wealth and property carries with it the responsibility to be accountable for the ways in which it is spent. The Prophet organized the collection and distribution of alms. This process of institutionalization and accountability was later incorporated into the rules of the *sharī'a*, thus giving it legal form and purpose. This turn towards systematization and formalization did not preclude acts of voluntary almsgiving outside of what was deemed obligatory. Based again on Qur'ānic precedents and Prophetic practice, almsgiving was also translated into endowments known as *waqf*. These charitable trusts were used to endow mosques, schools, hospitals, water fountains and other useful public structures and they played an important role throughout history. Notable Muslims, descendants of the Prophet, and many women played noteworthy roles in generating such philanthropic works. These acts were not restricted to benefiting Muslims alone. The Prophet himself specified that non-Muslims could also be beneficiaries of charity and encouraged non-Muslims to establish charitable foundations for the benefit of their own coreligionists. Wealth however was not to be gained by unethical or unlawful means, such as stealing, gambling, or fraud.

The Elderly

The Qur'ān is very explicit about the treatment of the elderly. With regards to those within the family, its guidance is very clear. "Your Lord has commanded that you worship none but Him and that you be kind to your parents. If either of them becomes elderly, do not show disrespect to them or be angry with them but be compassionate towards them and act with humility and display kindness. Say: My Lord have mercy on them, since they looked after me when I was a child" (Qur'ān 17:23–4). There is a saying attributed to the Prophet which says that Paradise lies at the feet of mothers.

Other guidance, based on the Prophet's example, indicates that the elderly who are unable to carry out the performance of fasting are to be excused and may instead feed the poor. Muslim societies, like those of many other traditions, accord great respect to the elderly and their literature and practice reflects how the wisdom and experience associated with age is honored.

Those in Need

The Qur'ān identifies those in need broadly. They include orphans, the unfortunate and the very poor, those who are neither able to help themselves or have been struck down by disability or natural disasters and calamities, and those rendered homeless, refugees or living rough as wayfarers. It specifically obligates the assistance of those in need by insisting that the needy and the deprived have an acknowledged right to the wealth of those possessing it (Qur'ān 70:24 and 51:19). The *ḥadīth* tradition offers a broad range of voluntary and institutionalized practices to fulfill the right of the needy to assistance. Particular attention is paid to the vulnerable, such as orphans, the sick and the very poor. The Qur'ān and *ḥadīth* encourage guardianship of orphans, and in various Muslim societies special institutions have been established through endowments to care for and educate orphans as well as to create hospitals to care for the sick.

Right and Wrong

The moral underpinning of issues of right and wrong is best expressed through the idea of Law (*sharī'a*) as developed from the Qur'ān and the *ḥadīth*. Yet it is important to get a sense of the historical development of law in Islam, to help dispel two false assumptions. The first is that Muslim law is a fixed and unchanging seventh-century system and the second that it is highly restrictive and "medieval" in its outlook and antithetical to the needs of modern society.

The term used to refer to the idea of law is *sharī'a*. The connotation behind this concept is that God intends human beings to follow a divinely ordained path, but that such a path had also been revealed to others in the past. The Qur'ān is explicit in stating: "To each of you we have granted a path and a way of life. Had God wished he could have made you into a single community. But God's purpose is to test you in what He has granted to each of you, so strive in pursuing virtue and be aware that to God you will all return and He will clarify for you your differences" (Qur'ān 5:48).

Muslim schools of law developed over a period of centuries in response to questions that arose as the *umma* or Muslim community expanded and encountered other peoples and cultures with established systems of belief and law. There developed over time a methodology of analysis and application through which answers could be obtained. The methodology is known as *fiqh* (science of jurisprudence), its foundational principles are known as *usūl al-fiqh*, and the body of law it produced is collectively called the *sharī'a*. In a certain sense, however, the *sharī'a* encompasses more than the Western understanding of the sum total of its case law. It represents norms for living in accordance with ethical precepts. Different schools of jurisprudence emerged around geographic centers of the Islamic empire and out of sectarian differences, achieving a systematization that had many common features. These schools attempted to create procedures for framing human action, classifying ethical terms into five categories:

1 *fard* (obligatory) as in actions such as prayer;
2 *sunna* (recommended) such as supererogatory acts of virtue and charity;
3 *mubāḥ* (neutral);
4 *makrūh* (reprehensible) such as acts of pollution and overindulgence; and
5 *ḥarām* (forbidden) such as murder and adultery.

These categories assimilated traditionally established customary laws that were not superseded in the conversion process.

Muslim scholars, when elaborating the *sharī'a*, sought to ground it in the Qur'ān and the example and actions of the Prophet, but it was for human beings through the exercise of moral reasoning to discover and develop the details of the law. In fact, it was the speedy growth of Islamic lands in the first centuries of history that ensured a common legal culture. The difference in approaches helped create a pluralistic legal tradition among Muslims, with differing emphases on the methodology for deriving legal and ethical systems.

Differences between People

The Qur'ān sees humankind as having been made as a single community (Qur'ān 2:213) and all human beings as created from one soul (Qur'ān 4:1). However, God has also created diversity to reflect the inherent pluralism of human society (Qur'ān 49:13). A common shared identity as well as historical difference is therefore built into the human condition. As indicated earlier, this difference is reflected not only in the outward appearance of people but is also found in the way they govern the conduct of their daily lives: "And among His signs is the creation of the heavens the earth and the diversity in your language and color" (Qur'ān 30:22).

Religious Pluralism

Muslims believe that God has communicated to humanity from the beginning of time by way of revelations and messengers. None has been neglected, though not all religions or messengers are always known to us. Those to whom God has communicated are therefore referred to as the "People of the Book" (*Aḥl-al-Kitāb*). According to the Qur'ān, Muslims are urged: "Call to the way of your Lord with wise and gentle words and argue with them in the best of ways" (Qur'ān 16:25). It also states that: "There is no compulsion in Religion" (Qur'ān 33:33). It is this broad spirit of inclusiveness and mutual acceptance that has generally guided Muslims in the preaching of their faith and their relations with other religions, though in the course of history this has not necessarily prevented conflict between Muslims and people of differing religious background. In the history of Islam such conflict has often been political in nature but disguised as religious.

The principle of pluralism and peaceful coexistence is also based on the Prophet's own early efforts to build common ground with Jews and Christians, through an agreement sometimes referred to as the "Constitution of Medina" (Haykal 1976), affording status and rights to them. It laid out the ground rules for permitting non-Muslims to practice their faith freely, retain their religious organization and maintain their places of worship and local authority.

The Qur'ān also teaches that God's grace and salvation are for all: "Those who believe in God and His revelations, Jews, Christians, Sabeans, whosoever believes in God and the Day of Judgment and does good, will have their reward from God, they should have no fear nor should they grieve" (Qur'ān 2:62).

Women and Men

The Qur'ān declares that God created humankind as male and female (Qur'ān 46:13). The accounts of Creation (Qur'ān 4:1 and 7:189) give no priority to the male over the female and the Qur'ān, in the course of its guidance to people, addresses both 'believing men' and 'believing women' (Qur'ān 33:35). Its ethical teachings on the responsibility of women and men were developed further and are reflected in the legal and social practices of diverse Muslim communities across the world, which have also been much influenced by local custom and Arab cultural traditions.

The immediate context of pre-Islamic Arabia is relevant in understanding the changes that the Qur'ān and the Prophet's mission brought about in gender relations. The primary changes enhanced and provided new rights for women. They were accorded inheritance rights, a share in the estate of their parents and husbands, in addition to the agreed gift or dowry. Men proportionally inherited more because in the context of the time their role was to head the family and have custodial responsibility for the household, including the extended family. In a similar fashion, some Muslim scholars also believe that polygamy was permitted out of historical necessity particularly when men were killed in battle and women needed the legal protection of marriage.

Both men and women are urged to comport themselves with modesty. This has influenced how Muslims dress, as well as their outward appearance. In various Muslim cultures this is reflected in the way women wear a cloak over their clothes as well as a head covering known as *hijāb*. There is, however, considerable diversity in the modes by which modesty is expressed and, as with inter-personal contact and relationships, such modes are generally governed by how such cultural norms have become established in different parts of the Muslim world, urban and rural.

Ultimate Values and Global Responsibility

For that reason, the ethical language of the Qur'ān that addresses issues of poverty, also speaks to issues that have legal, social and economic implications. The community and its leaders are to be seen as custodians of these values endowed with the responsibility of ensuring that the state and key segments of society oversee the needs of the poor. This compassion and care on the part of leaders or the state as urged by several Muslim thinkers and leaders, is seen as a key to fostering a just and beneficial order in their societies.

Muslims have often sought inspiration from a Qur'ānic chapter entitled, "Al-Balad" (Qur'ān 90) which can stand for "city," "community," "village," and "place" and even, by extension, "the earth." The verses are addressed to the Prophet and witness to his right to be a free individual in that space, likening it to the ties binding child and parent (i.e. as heir and as custodian). The revelation reminds him that human beings are created to be in a state of struggle, but that they are empowered with choices that God has offered. Of these choices, the verses go on to state the most difficult path is the one that involves "freeing the oppressed and relieving the hunger of those uncared for and those so destitute as to be reduced to grinding poverty." Those who choose this path are called "the Companions of the Right Hand," deserving of their exalted status because they embody in their actions the qualities of "compassion and caring." Among the ethical writings of one of the earliest Muslim philosophers, al-Fārābī (d. 970 C.E.), there is a work entitled *The Excellent City*. The excellence embodied in such cities, according to al-Fārābī, rests on the balanced connection between the virtues of the citizens, the character of the ruler, and a moral grounding in society. The issues of human happiness involve for al-Fārābī civil, political, social and ethical/religious dimensions. They are all part of the moral universe of excellence and, if sought as an ultimate goal in each of these realms, then the conditions of the excellent city become possible (al-Fārābī 1985).

Planet Earth and Ecology

Although God communicates primarily through messengers and revelations, the universe as a whole is also a sign from God. The Qur'ānic universe unfolds in a harmonious pattern, each element in balance with the others, and it is this sense of natural order and equilibrium that is pointed out as a sign of God's creative power and unity. His power extends also to other created things in nature that are endowed with qualities that enable them to function in an ordered way. A good example cited in the Qur'ān is the bee. "And your Lord gave inspiration to saying: 'Build your hives in the hills and the trees' (…) there comes from the (bees) a finely colored drink, with the power to heal. Indeed here is a sign for those who ponder" (Qur'ān 16:68–9).

The whole of nature is created to conform to God's will. In this sense all of creation can be understood to be paying homage to and worshiping God. "The seven heavens and the earth and all that is in them glorify Him; there is nothing that does not praise Him but you do not understand their praise" (Qur'ān 17:44). A parallel is thus established between human beings, nature, and other creatures that act in accord with the will of God. In that sense, all are "Muslim," for they participate in a universal act of submission implied in the word *islām*. However, it is only persons, because of their God-given capacity to know and respond to his message, who can attain through their own intelligence the highest state of being Muslim. Human action can discover and conform to the Divine Will, thus actualizing "*islām*" as the harmonious order that results when all creation works in harmony rather than conflicting with divine purpose.

There is a sense of harmony in the cosmos and in this world. The custodial role of human beings is to sustain it rather than disrupt it through environmental protection, including respect for living creatures of all types. The need to respect the intrinsic balance in the natural order as many Muslim scholars point out is, as already mentioned, referred to throughout the Qur'ān. Furthermore, humans are reminded that their co-inhabitants on this planet are to be treated as members of communities like themselves. The systematic destruction of species would be indefensible in this scheme of things: "There is not an animal (that lives) on the earth nor a being that flies on its wings, but (forms part of) communities like you" (Qur'ān 6:38). Thus, conservation of other species is part of our human responsibility on this earth. However, these resources are available for the benefit of humanity: "Say: Who has forbidden the beautiful (gifts) of God, which He has produced for His servants, and the things, clean and pure (which He has provided) for sustenance?" (Qur'ān 7:32).

The majority of Muslims have lived, and continue to live, in rural areas. As this environment becomes increasingly neglected and people are forced to move to crowded cities, the balance between the two becomes severely disrupted. The Qur'ān points to agriculture and farming as important needs in society. "It is He who produces gardens, with and without trellises, and dates, and cultivated land with produce of all kinds, and olives and pomegranates, similar and different: Eat of their fruit in their season, but render the dues that are proper on the day that the harvest is gathered. But waste not by excess: for God loves not the wasteful" (Qur'ān 6:141). Similarly it advocates proper care of animals. "And cattle He has created for you: from them ye derive warmth and numerous benefits, and of their (meat) ye eat" (Qur'ān 16:5); "And you have a sense of pride and beauty in them" (Qur'ān 16:5); "And (He has created) horses, mules, and donkeys for you to ride and use for show, and He has created (other) things of which you have no knowledge" (Qur'ān 16:5, 6, 8).

Conclusion

A great number of *ḥadīth* make reference to the Prophet's Farewell Pilgrimage and his last sermon (Haykal 1976). Some of the traditions highlight the guidance he gave. He declared that the safety of the lives and property of the people was to be regarded as inviolate and that men and women have rights over each other and that women are partners to men and are to be treated with kindness. He declared usury to be unacceptable. It is also said that it was on this occasion that the following verse was revealed: "This day I have fulfilled your Religion and given you my blessing and chosen Islam as your Religion" (Qur'ān 5:4).

If there is an overriding factor that constantly highlights the moral concern of the Qur'ān in this fulfillment of its core ethical message, it is best reflected in the following verse:

> It is not righteousness that you turn your faces towards East and West. The righteous are those who believe in God, the last Day, the Angels, the Book,

the Prophets and who give from what they have to: relatives, orphans, those in need, those away from their homes, those who ask (when in need) and to free the enslaved. They observe prayer and give in charity and support and keep their word when they make a commitment, preserving with patience when faced with difficulty, adversity and hardship. Such are the firmly committed and the morally conscious.

(Qur'ān 2:177)

Further Reading

Fakhry, M. (1994) *Ethical Theories in Islam*, Leiden: Brill.

Hashmi, S. (2002) *Islamic Political Ethics, Civil Society, Pluralism and Conflict*, Princeton: Princeton University Press.

Izutsu, T. (1966) *Ethico-Religious Concepts in the Qur'ān*, Montreal: McGill University Press.

Lings, M. (1993) *Muḥammad: His Life: Based on the Earliest Sources*, London: Allen Unwin/ Islamic Texts Society.

Nanji, A. (2007) "Islam," in P. Morgan & C. Lawton (eds.), *Ethical Issues in Six Religious Traditions*, Edinburgh: Edinburgh University Press, pp. 283–333.

Sajoo, A. (ed.) (2004) *Muslim Ethics: Emerging Vistas*, London: I.B. Tautis/Institute of Ismaili Studies.

References

al-Fārābī (1985) *Al-Farabi on the Perfect State: Abu Nasr al-Farabi's Mabadi' Ara' Ahl al-Madinah al-Fadilah*, R. Walzer (ed. and tr.), New York: Oxford University Press.

Ali, A. Y. (tr.) (1946) *The Glorious Qur'ān*, Lahore: Muḥammad Ashraf.

Graham, W. (1977) *Divine Word and Prophetic Word in Early Islam*, The Hague: Walter De Gruyter.

Haykal, M. (1976) *The Life of Muḥammad*, I. Faruqui (tr.), Indianapolis: North American Trust Publications.

Kamali, M. H. (2005) *A Textbook on Hadith Studies*, Leicester: Islamic Foundation.

Nasr, S. (1996) "The Qur'ān and the Ḥadīth as Source and Inspiration of Islamic Philosophy," in S. Nasr & O. Leaman (eds.), *History of Islamic Philosophy*, London: Routledge, pp. 27–39.

Rahman, F. (1967) "Some Reflections on the Reconstruction of Muslim Society in Pakistan," *Journal of Islamic Studies* 6, 9: 103–20.

——. (1980) *Major Themes in the Qur'ān*, Minneapolis: Bibliotheca Islamica.

Reinhart, K. (2002) "Ethics and The Qur'ān," in J. Dammen (ed.), *Encyclopaedia of the Qur'ān*, vol. II, Leiden: Brill, pp. 55–79.

Robson, J. (trans.) (1973) Mishkāt ul Masābīh (Collection of Ḥadīth), Lahore: Muḥammad Ashraf.

4
HUMAN REASON IN ISLAMIC THEOLOGY

Toby Mayer

Introduction

The transfer to Islam of certain accepted theological categories, in particular the tripartite division into *theologia revelata*, *theologia naturalis*, and *theologia mystica*, may suffice as a heuristic point of departure. This typology's transfer seems oddly neat. The self-representational locutions of the divine, solidified into the text of the Qur'ān, are the pre-eminent revealed theology of Islam. To varying degrees, these are supplemented by theological locutions authoritatively transmitted from the Islamic *theopneustos* (inspired by God) *par excellence*, Muḥammad, "the Prophet" (d. 11/632). Indeed, the expansive corpus of prophetic sayings (*ḥadīth*) itself also contains certain statements with God Himself as interlocutor despite their being extra-Qur'ānic, within the sub-class known as "holy locutions" (*al-aḥādīth al-qudsiyya*). Moreover, in Shī'ism, *theologia revelata's* grounds are, notionally, further widened by the teaching that the "Muḥammadan light" (*al-nūr al-Muḥammadī*) passes down into the Prophet's lineage, the imāms, whose authoritative sayings (*aḥādīth walawiyya* versus *aḥādīth nabawiyya*) are thereby radically valorized, thereby gaining a quasi-prophetic character. In Shī'ī nomenclature, the imām is even sometimes termed "the Speaking Qur'ān" (*al-Qur'ān al-nāṭiq*).

Islamic intellectual culture in turn boasts a potent range of natural theology. Most fit for the title, undoubtedly, are the *ilāhiyyāt* systems of the thinkers within the Graeco-Arabic philosophical tradition. These were fundamentally rational theologies that claim to bring out God's existence, unicity, nature, etc., without any recourse to revealed authority, on the grounds of syllogisms and pure deductive thought. The project was in practice strongly historically contextual—the Muslim development of a long-accumulating tradition descending ultimately from the Academy and the Lyceum. Indeed, the most influential of all Muslim philosophers, Ibn Sīnā (Avicenna, d. 428/1037), traditionally known as "the Chief Sheikh," has been configured in recent Western scholarship as basically a late "Ammonian commentator"; that is, his positions have been shown to reflect a hermeneutical context directly resulting from Aristotle's Late Antique commentator Ammonius (Wisnovsky 2005). While being a commendable stride towards a more precise historical evaluation of Ibn Sīnā, the focus on context and transmission should not blunt us to his stature as a systematic thinker in his own right, and such terms might indeed seem dispensable for engaging with a comparable modern thinker.

At any rate, more noteworthy for the present discussion is a current traceable to the second/eighth century or even earlier, distinct from this Graeco-Arabic tradition, with some traits definitely qualifying it as a natural theology, namely Muʿtazilism. Though partly a religious apologetics, consistently negotiating the revealed text and using its *loci probantes* (*nuṣūṣ*), this school nevertheless took human reason as its formal starting point, striving to find, and then interpret, religious truth strictly on its basis. It in fact insisted that assent to certain judgements of unguided reason was necessary *before* drawing any instruction from Scripture. The Muʿtazilite edifice thus rests on purely reason-based arguments for God's existence and His nature—as powerful, wise, living, etc. Moreover, humans may not initially admit prophetic authority simply through its *own* insistence that they do so. That would be absurd, the Muʿtazilites claimed. They instead argued for prophecy through a theodicy of optimism, proposing God's inherent motive to meet the conditions of human welfare (*maṣlaḥa*), guidance being fundamental to the latter. Again, grasping that lying is evil cannot, logically, simply derive from Qurʾānic texts which condemn lying and speak of God's abandonment of liars, like 39:33 and 40:28. Lying's wrongness, as in the case of other basic ethical judgements, should be knowable free of revelation—the grounds, precisely, for reasoning that the omnibenevolent promulgator of Scripture is *not* lying to us in it. Hence, Muʿtazilite ethics are primarily "objectivist" (Hourani 1971; Vasalou 2008), or as the dictum reads: "Acts are intrinsically ascribed with rightness and wrongness" (*al-afʿāl tūṣafu bi'l-ḥusni wa'l-qubḥi li-dhawātihā*). In ways such as these, reason was given a certain priority in the school, which moreover employed a wider system of physics and cosmology that owed nothing *per se* to Scripture. As an aside, the Fall was not generally viewed in Islam as impairing the human intellect or leaving it in need of regeneration. Though the Fall (*al-hubūṭ*) is referred to in the Qurʾān and is certainly a powerful motif in Islamic spirituality, it did not *per se* yield to a subordination or mistrust of the human intellect, or any functional distinction in Muslim thought between intelligence *post lapsum* and intelligence *ante lapsum*. Instead the Qurʾān and *ḥadīth* stress the continuing presence and accessibility in humanity of a sound, original disposition. The disputed point was not so much whether the intellect's function was yet intact but its intrinsic scope.

Finally, an ample Muslim mystical theology is found in Ṣūfism. The texts of this theology strive to express the relation, interaction and ecstatic experiences claimed by the Ṣūfi mystics with God, or rather, with God's epiphanies. While radically transcendental, this God of mysticism was by no means the "hyperbolic Beyond" posited by schools based on sheer ratiocination—a Beyond merely "ventriloquized" by religion, in some provocative readings (Villani 2007). Ṣūfi theology was instead deeply rooted in the mystics' intimate experience (*dhawq*/tasting) of a living, personal deity. It consequently stressed the paradoxical interplay of the eternal and the temporal, of transcendence and immanence, of the infinite and the finite. A prime task of mystical theologies seems to be to try to elucidate how the divine might, without debasement, be projected into objective contact with the creaturely or become a real percept in the mystic's experience, whether through some theory of divine self-finitisation, epiphany, or "energies." The Ṣūfī tradition from as early as the fourth/tenth century began to articulate its theology in increasingly intellectual terms. Comparable to, say, the *Corpus Areopagiticum* and the Christian mystical tradition flowing from it, this voluble discourse was uninterested in Aristotelian strictures and logical constants like the Law of Non-Contradiction. Instead, it has been suggested that a consistent pattern emerging from study of the (similarly, *hyper*-intellectual) writings of the Andalusian mystic, the so-called "Greatest Master" Ibn 'Arabī (d. 638/1240), is his bid to rupture linear thought and engender a state of perplexity (*al-ḥayra*) by "a constant circular movement round a point mentally incomprehensible" (Burckhardt & Culme-Seymour 1975: 3). Alternatively, the underlying model of his thought has been compared to a Möbius band, where there is a baffling identity of outer and inner surfaces (Chodkewicz 1993: 24–5). Such a theology, with its "deviant logic" and defiantly dialetheic texture, responds of course to a God apprehended as the great *coincidentia oppositorum* (*jam' al-ḍiddayn*). However, under the influence of the Avicennian tradition, Ṣūfī expositors of Ibn 'Arabī's world-view, such as Ṣadr al-Dīn al-Qūnawī (d. 673/1274) and 'Abd al-Raḥmān al-Jāmī (d. 898/1492), increasingly tried to present it in a manner more conformable—terminologically and even logically—with the Islamic Peripatetic heritage.

Reason, Revelation, and the *Kalām*

It would be unchallenging, and also uncandid, to broach the subject of human reason's role in Islamic theology as *other* than a question or a problematic. A restive, fascinatingly complex relationship between reason and revelation seems one of the principal dynamics of Muslim intellectual history. So in terms of this triad of theologies the following will focus on the *frontier* between revealed and natural theologies: the vital, disputed borderland between prophetic and rational discourse. This was, of course, a realm largely inhabited by the *mutakallimūn*, literally, "the speakers" or "discoursers," mentioned as *loquentes* in Latin sources, i.e. the exponents of "the science of *kalām*." These were Muslim thinkers who, with roots as far back as the period of the early Umayyad caliphate, set about exploring and defending the faith through rational arguments, and assumed the feasibility of some synergy of reason and revelation.

This assumption followed naturally from the profound "philosophical" dimensions and possibilities of the prophetic canon *itself*. For instance, the *locus classicus* for the standard *kalām* argument for divine unicity from "reciprocal hindrance" (*tamānu'*) is Qur'ān 21:22 which reasons from the unity of the divine will that makes of our world a cosmos, rather than a chaos, to the unity of the divine willer. Again, *ḥadīth* literature itself addresses that major *topos* of *kalām*, the seeming conflict of freedom and predestination. The Prophet is said to have referred his companions Abū Bakr al-Ṣiddīq and 'Umar ibn al-Khaṭṭāb, who were hotly discussing the issue, to the symbolic figure of a mighty angel. He explained that this angel is of highly paradoxical constitution, being half fire and half ice, yet praises its Maker for maintaining it in existence. It is correspondingly necessary to co-affirm that the course of events is unfolding from our vantage point and is ever accomplished from God's vantage point. The major sixth/twelth-century theologian Sharastānī drew from this *ḥadīth* his own solution to the antinomy of free will and determinism, and adopted its terminology (Mayer 2009). Thought-provoking leads of this sort may be found in Islam's canonical sources, surprisingly extending even to realms like mathematics—as in the case of a saying on the authority of the Prophet's wife, Abū Bakr's daughter 'Ā'isha, according to which the surd, or irrational, root (*jadhr aṣamm* versus *jadhr nāṭiq*) is knowable only to God, and not to His creatures (Lane 1984: 1724).

Though it was axiomatic for *kalām* thinkers to be able to trace their ideas to such dimensions of the canonical sources and these ideas emerged through pondering pregnant texts of the kind, especially those in the Qur'ān itself, such seeds cannot by themselves explain how *kalām* arose. A highly specific, very early stimulus for the emergence of what would become *kalām* was the Battle of Ṣiffīn (37/657), in the caliphate of 'Alī ibn Abī Ṭālib, among the first ever occasions when Muslims fought among themselves. This battle led to the movement of "Seceders" (*al-Khawārij*) from 'Alī's army and a raging debate over what became a formative issue in *kalām*: the criteria for the status of being a "believer" (*mu'min*), a status which, it was ruled, the legitimate leader of Muslims must possess. The *Khawārij* asserted that the previous caliph, 'Uthmān, had forfeited this standing through his wrongdoing, as presently had 'Alī himself through giving way to an arbitration process concerning 'Uthmān's assassination. In reaction to the obvious potential for civil strife in the judgemental and intransigent position of the *Khawārij*, a latitudinarian position developed known as Murji'ism, in which the need was put forward for a suspension or postponement (*irjā'*) of judgement on the precise status of the believer compromised by wrongdoing, and even grave sins *per se* were held *not* to annul the formal status of being a believer. Transparently theological issues were implicated in what began as a discussion about the ruler's legitimacy, notably the Muslim individual's responsibility, or absence of responsibility, for his acts. At any rate, the issue of the status of the sinful Muslim shortly became *the* decisive point for the supposed founder of the Mu'tazilite school, Wāṣil ibn 'Aṭā' (d. 131/748), who marked himself out from his peers by advocating a *tertium quid*, according to which the grave sinner was neither an unbeliever nor a believer in status, but required a special, separate classification. This became a definitive, core teaching of the emergent Mu'tazilite school.

A more general original stimulus for the growth of *kalām* seems to have been the Muslim encounter with pre-Islamic intellectual cultures in the Near East, including the gradual adoption of Islam by parts of the population. By these imponderable, as yet non-textual processes of transmission and interpenetration, early *kalām* readily absorbed cosmological ideas like atomism (strongly theistic, unlike the older atomisms of Leucippus, Democritus and Epicurus) and even the assumption (less assimilable to theism) of an infinite extra-cosmic void as the context of the atomic substances from which our world has in turn been generated. It also inherited various elements from Stoic logic, like "the proof based on an indicative sign" (*qiyās al-ghā'ib 'ala 'l-shāhid*). Such Stoic traces in particular are discernible, yet awkward to account for precisely. The Stoic hypothetical syllogism, built on one premise only (as distinct from the two-premise syllogism of Aristotelian philosophy), was widespread, and was later defended by Pseudo-Qudāma in *Naqd al-Nathr*. *Kalām* definition shared with the Stoics a concern with individual facts and with concrete being, without raising individual phenomena to any higher generic category, as in the case of formal Aristotelian definition. It has even been argued that the Stoic notion of the *lekton* (the concept, subsisting in the mind, of an object indicated) is perhaps reflected in the typical *kalām* use of the term *ma'nā* (literally, "meaning") (van Ess 1970). Particularly thought-provoking in relation to the Stoics is the presence of some sort of trivalent logic in *kalām*. In due course a major Mu'tazilite figure like al-Jāḥiẓ (d. 255/868) tried solving the famous liar paradox via such a logic, precisely as had certain Stoics long before (Bochenski 1956: 152 ff; van Ess 1970: 31); and indeed, such an implicit trivalent logical paradigm had, in a sense, incepted the *entire* Mu'tazilite movement: Wāṣil's aforementioned *manzila bayn al-manzilatayn* (belief and unbelief). A major modern Arab thinker, Jabiri, has argued that this kind of triple-value logic is a mark of wider rational thought in Islam, and can be observed in a series of breakthrough solutions by Muslim thinkers in different fields (Jabiri 1986).

It was Syriac, however, not Greek, that was the language through which any Greek elements were initially mediated. Texts from the period of Christological schism characterising sixth and seventh century Syria, demonstrably offer the closest immediate precedents for vital aspects of *kalām* discourse. From as early as the anti-libertarian polemic "Questions against the Qadarites" (al-Ḥanafiyya, hence, arguably dating from only 60 years after the Prophet's death), *kalām* discourse was framed in terms of a stereotyped question-answer format known as *istinqāl*, = the 10th form gerund (*maṣdar*) from *in qāla*, "if he says ... (then we reply ...)." It has been proposed that the phraseology was directly drawn from pre-Islamic Syriac precedents, as was the routine use of destructive dilemmas and the odd absence of any introductory phrases that address the reader in the said format (Cook 1980).

The *istinqāl* formula also points to how the religious debate typified *kalām*'s formative milieu. Such debates are recorded even under the Umayyad caliphs, and the *Disputatio Chrisitiani et Saraceni* of St. John of Damascus (d. circa 131/748) has the institution in question for its backdrop. The discussion would be held before a silent audience in the presence of the ruler or his vizier, and in principle the party deemed to have lost was expected to renounce their teaching and convert to the winner's—though this was generally avoided through the formal claim of "parity in arguments." The spontaneous exchange of arguments (often *ad hominem*), and adversarial structure of the public debate, left their traces on many *kalām* texts and patterns of thought. In the absence of formal logics, early theologians spoke instead of the proper etiquettes of debating, and it is known that Wāṣil's student Ḍirār ibn 'Amr composed a manual (sadly not extant) on the subject: *Kitāb Ādāb al-Mutakallimīn* (*Protocols of the theologians*). Notwithstanding the potential dynamism and excitement of this original intellectual context, it doubtless made *kalām* more suspect for the morally influential, pious-minded grouping which, in coming generations, would elaborate the "traditionary disciplines" as distinct from the "rational disciplines." This group viewed unanimity as the gauge of the health and authenticity of wider Muslim society. From its beginnings, *kalām* faced their opposition as a spiritually injurious, innovatory (*mubtada'*), and disputatious (*jadalī*) approach to the sacrosanct truths of God and religion. The Qur'ān after all declares its own absolute sufficiency: "We have left nothing out of the Scripture" (Qur'ān 6:38), and in many verses it disapproves of divergence in opinion (Qur'ān 3:105, 4:82, 8:46). It also employs reasoned argumentation and strongly enjoins intellectual reflection (e.g. Qur'ān 7:185)—as emphasised in the later polemical literature defending speculative reason against its critics, such as the *Excellence of Delving into* kalām (*Istiḥsān al-Khawḍ fī 'Ilm al-Kalām*) by Ash'arī, the fourth/tenth century architect of the major *kalām* school which was named after him, and the *Decisive Treatise* (*Faṣl al-Maqāl*) by the great sixth/twelth century philosopher of Cordoba, Ibn Rushd. How, exactly, the *mujādala/munāẓara* paradigm implicit in *kalām* discourse marked relations between reason and revelation is obscure, but it surely did not smooth them over.

Mu'tazilite Monotheism and Theodicy

Though early *kalām* thinkers had a surprising variety, even randomness, in their views, the Mu'tazila formed round a stable core of positions. Even more primary than the five-fold agenda put forward by Abu'l-Hudhayl al-'Allāf (226/840), the deepest basis of the self-styled People of [God's] Unity and Justice (*Ahl al-Tawḥīd wa'l-'Adl*) lay in their strongly rationalised monotheism and their theodicy. Their whole doctrine, with all its minutiae, sprouted from these two deepest concerns. Mu'tazilite rationalism could here be said to have led in oddly divergent directions—generating a view of God's identity that was as strictly *de*-anthropomorphic as their view of God's justice was anthropomorphic. The problem of "monotheism," for its part, amounted for them to the challenge of resolving a multiplicity of qualificatives into their subject, given the radical singularity of the latter in God's case. This was a challenge of scriptural hermeneutics only secondarily; it was, in the first place, a free-standing, rational task since the Mu'tazilites claimed to discover God's main attributes through reason not revelation. Yet from their reasoning there definitely emerged a richly qualified God, to this extent corresponding with the Qur'ānic God. The Mu'tazilites did not adopt the more uncompromising philosophical stances which traced multiplicity to a level quite *beneath* God's oneness, and spoke of Him in terms of sheer conceptual simplicity or even His transcendence of *all* predicates (as in Muslim Peripateticism or Ismā'īlism, respectively). In such systems, the reduction of multiplicity to unity was deflected, becoming a cosmological problem, subordinate to God's identity.

But for the Mu'tazila the enigma was not consigned to a cosmological discussion beneath God—it was *in* God Himself, and was thus the problem par excellence addressed in their theology. The general Mu'tazilite solution was as follows: to start with, a careful differentiation was drawn between what is extrinsically and is intrinsically said of God. The former, termed adjectives of action (*al-ṣifāt al-fi'liyya*), are said of God on the basis of His time-bound works and productions, such as the description of Him as *rāziq* ("Provider"), which assumes the existence of creatures provided for. The real problem instead concerned adjectives eternally and intrinsically applicable to God, the so-called essential adjectives (*al-ṣifāt al-dhātiyya*). But these divine qualificatives, the Mu'tazilites insisted, did not amount to substantive attributes, or separate "entitative determinants" within Him. Certain linguistic positions were tied in to this claim. The Mu'tazilites tended towards a conventionalist theory (*muwāḍa'a*) of the origins of language (*aṣl al-lugha*) as opposed to a revelationist theory (*tawqīf al-lugha*). For these thinkers, then, all human languages, including Arabic, are historically generated by human societies, and modified by processes of transmission and derivation. Qāḍī

'Abd al-Jabbār (d. 415/1025), the last major Sunnī Mu'tazilite, puts it with a boldness that unwittingly highlights its secular quality: before God could address Adam and impart to him the names of all things (Qur'ān 2:31), Adam and the angels *themselves* had to have invented some language (McDermott 1978: 135). Ultimately, the ascription of such and such a series of phonemes to such and such a referent is a matter of pure convention (*istilāḥa*), and is not an objective linkage. Mu'tazilites, moreover, resisted interpreting divine qualificatives (*ṣifāt*) as nouns or substantives, and maintained the strict adjectival sense of *ṣifa* given it by the Arabic grammarians. A Mu'tazilite trend to nominalism on the divine attributes partly stood on such linguistic views as these.

The classic stance of the school was then framed by the aforementioned Abu'l-Hudhayl: "God is a knower through a 'knowledge' which is the *same as* Him." In this cautious formulation, then, God's internal unity is kept despite His being predicable in various ways. The descriptions are not referred back to any substantives in Him, introducing complexity and multiplicity into Him. They are, rather, just ways that human intellects apprehend God's own, intrinsically abundant essence, a "super-rich" undifferentiated singularity. As Ḥillī would later state it, the attributes are extra to the divine essence [only] in human ratiocination (Schmidtke 1991: 169). Some Mu'tazilites like Qāḍī 'Abd al-Jabbār tried to dissolve the qualifications even further into the divine essence, by ellipting any, even nominal, grounds *in divinis* for the adjectives: "He is a knower through Himself (or: by Himself)" (*bi-nafsihi/li-nafsihi*) (McDermott 1978: 137). In this formula, there is no longer any reified "knowledge" at all. The modalism of Abū Hāshim al-Jubbā'ī (d. 321/933) was another well-known bid to frame divine predication to fit with divine unity, controversial because viewed by some as re-introducing quasi-substantives or crypto-attributes. According to this, attribute such and such is simply a state or modalisation (*ḥāl*) of the one, divine essence as *being* so and so. The terminology, it is argued, was drawn from Arabic grammar, and when this is grasped its allegedly substantival character dissolves. In certain sentences the verb *kāna* (Arabic: "to be") is complete yet takes its complement in the accusative. The accusative complement in this instance is not understood as the predicate of *kāna* (as it would be if *kāna* were incomplete), but as a *ḥāl* of the subject. Thus God's attribute of knowledge, say, is simply the fact of God *being* knowing (*kawnuhu 'āliman*)—it does not involve a substantive "knowledge" that God's nature operates through, notwithstanding the human inclination to discern it and express it as though it did (Schmitdke 1991: 171; Frank 1971).

This strongly philosophical understanding of Islamic monotheism, of which the Mu'tazilites saw themselves as the arch-custodians, clashed with vital features of wider Muslim belief and Islam as a living faith. The Visio Beatifica (*al-ru'ya*), for instance, was a galvanic focus for pious hope and indeed had a climactic place in the practice of eschatological visualisation referred to in certain Ṣūfī texts of the period, notably in the *Kitāb al-Tawahhum* (*Book of Contemplation*) by Muḥāsibī (d. 243/837). The prospect that, in the future existence of the saved, they would actually see the Lord is explicitly mentioned in the Qu'rān (75:2–3) and in the *ḥadīth*. Yet "seeing" presupposes some kind of form, embodiment, or directionality for God, obviously unacceptable in Mu'tazilite theology. Mu'tazilites moreover pointed out that another Qur'ānic verse unequivocally states: "Vision does not grasp Him, but He grasps vision!" (Qur'ān 6:103).

They therefore resorted, as often, to a de-anthropomorphic interpretation of Qur'ān 75:2: "Faces that day will beam, gazing at their Lord." They drew attention to the fact that the word for "gazing" (*nāẓira*) also has a viable meaning, "awaiting," in Arabic lexicology, and they suggested that its complement should be read as a metonymy: "their Lord" really means "*the reward* of their Lord" (*thawāb rabbihā*). Here, the rich development of Arabic grammar, lexicology, and rhetoric, was indispensable to the Mu'tazilites as providing authoritative grounds for different kinds of de-anthropomorphic interpretations. Mu'tazilite interpretations frequently evoked metonymy (*kināya*), along with other rhetorical figures. The Qur'ān, for example, refers to the "face" of God in such verses as: "Wherever you turn, there is the face of God!" (2:115), and "All in [heaven and on earth] is passing away, and the face of your Lord endures, in its majesty and splendour" (55:27). Yet there were clear precedents in Arabic poetry and usage for "face" to refer metonymically to the "self," or total identity, of the person in question—the idiom *li-wajhika* (literally, "for your face") simply means "for you," as in "I did it *for you*." In the same vein, figuration was evoked in interpreting God's "hand" or "eye," which were deciphered by the Mu'tazilites as God's grace and knowledge, respectively.

The rationalisation of theologemes by the Mu'tazilites was part of their self-appointed task of safeguarding Islam's monotheistic purity, as they understood it. The most dramatic clash of their programme with popular pietistic currents was over the problem of the Qur'ān's theological status. A latent activism was built into al-'Allāf's original Mu'tazilite agenda under the heading "Enjoining right and condemning wrong." This led the Mu'tazlite school in Baghdad to collude with the 'Abbāsid caliphs in their official policy during part of the third/nineth century, of suppressing belief in a Qur'ān which was (in some sense) pre-eternal or uncreated. In the caliph al-Ma'mūn's edicts al-'Allāf clearly identified his motive, in common with the Mu'tazilites, behind unleashing this notorious "Inquisition" (*miḥna*) as being to fight the offensive, popular idea that the Qur'ān and God Himself are equivalent in level, like the Christian belief about Jesus Christ. This, at any rate, was a moment of decision for Mu'tazilism, the high-water mark of its authority as the semi-official doctrine of the whole caliphate, the high noon of its ambition to configure the faith in terms of its own models of reason. The *miḥna* puts paid to some older, naive notions of the Mu'tazilites, the anachronism that they were Islam's "free thinkers." Instead it seems precisely to enshrine that same pointed problematic of rationality, seen in any historical movement that seeks control through a presumed identity with sheer reason. Such episodes often presage some kind of *un*reason that lurks within the so-called "reason" that dominates, but also conversely, a kind of reason hidden in the "unreason" dominated. Doubtless the *miḥna*'s most famous victim, the great Aḥmad ibn Ḥanbal (d. 241/855), who was beaten and detained for up to two and a half years by the 'Abbāsid authorities for refusing to acknowledge that the Qur'ān is created, was hardly a proponent of rationality in any definition. He is instead depicted as an unreconstructed traditionist, moulding himself to the point of obsession on the model of the Prophet, and freely advocating the formula of "unquestioning assent" (*bi-lā kayf*, "without [asking] how") in many points of doctrine. Yet later defenders of the Qur'ān's uncreated status, principally in the Ash'arite school of *kalām*, elaborated a theology of the Qur'ān quite as sophisticated as that of the Mu'tazilites, in which the instrumentality of reason was deeply in evidence. Ash'arism, when it presently emerged through a renegade from the Baṣran school of Mu'tazilism, cannot simply be dismissed as a reflex of tradition against reason; it instead resulted, in some part, from the self-critical application of reason *to* reason, thereby uncovering the limits of rationality as conceived by the Mu'tazilites (compare Leaman & Rizvi 2008: 85–6).

Mu'tazilite theodicy shows the same ambiguity in their rationalistic aspiration—God's justice being the second of their identifying emblems. Here it was proposed that an objective ethical rationale could be worked out, applicable both to God and humanity. The anthropocentric vantage-point of these ethics is clear in its grounding in human introspection, and epitomises the Mu'tazilite analogy from the apparent to the hidden. This theodicy was a direct outgrowth of the original moral concern and high-mindedness of the group in second/eighth century Baṣra around al-Ḥasan al-Baṣrī (d. 110/728), from which Wāṣil first emerged. It was understood that God must be "just" in a humanly understandable way for us to place full confidence in the religious economy of effortful inputs and commuted outputs. There was a suppressed epistemic motive too for the optimist theodicy of Mu'tazilism. God's root concern with our welfare (*maṣlaḥa*) justified trust in the God-given channels of knowledge, i.e. the senses, reason, and revelation. God's benevolent justice, then, was established thus: to say "God" would be to say an omniscient and omnipotent being. Now such a being would only do good, since, as omniscient, He would know, in full, good from evil, and that good is to be done and evil *not* to be done; and as omnipotent, He would have no impediment to actually carrying through what is to be done. So God must be just in every circumstance. In their philosophy of action, on the grounds of God's absolute justice, the Mu'tazilites accommodated human free will. Since God is innately just, He would not punish beings for what He Himself *made* them do. If it would be unjust for a human being to demand something of someone incapable of fulfilling it, then it would a fortiori be unjust for God to do that. The Mu'tazilites therefore proposed that God in His omnipotence, by "delegation" (*tafwīḍ*), empowers human beings to act. That is: they must have a genuine potential or capacity to act *before* the act itself and through the subsequent act there is an objective engendering of some effect on their part.

In this way the Mu'tazilites formulated a philosophy of action systematically opposed to the notion of God's determination of our behaviour, such that the reward and punishment of that behaviour remained fully intelligible. Awkward Qur'ānic references to God guiding *and* misguiding whom He wills (e.g. 14:4) were interpreted, implausibly, to mean God *judging* some to be guided and others misguided. Whatever the worthiness of this reason-driven commitment to divine probity, it may be sincerely asked whether the rich, sometimes exultantly paradoxical, texture of *theologia revelata* is honoured or served with sensitivity in such an exegesis. Moreover, even in terms of its intrinsic criteria of rational coherence, Mu'tazilite thought arguably breaks down. To begin, there is the spectre of vicious circularity in the concealed grounds for trust in matters of human intellect, namely, God's benign justice, and then, the discovery of God's benign justice *through* human intellect. Grounding intellect in God's guaranteed welfare and on-going assistance seems a mark of 'Abd al-Jabbār's thought and the Baṣran school (e.g. Vasalou 2008: 48–9; Martin, Woodward & Atmaja 1997: 63).

The Ash'arites and the Problem of the Three Brothers

Moreover, the failure of the theodicean dogma that God's ethics were conformable with human notions of optimal benefit was devastatingly highlighted in a well-known problem, crucial to the Ash'arite narrative: the problem of the three brothers. According to the famous story, the first brother died in early childhood, the second lived out his term of life but as a man of unbelief, and the third lived out his life as a man of faith. After all had died, each found himself in a situation appropriate to the conditions of his earthly life: the infant in a lower heaven, the second, faithless brother in hell, and the third, faithful brother in a high station of heaven. The child, seeing his oldest brother's higher station, begged God for the same. But God replied that his oldest brother had earned his high place through his life of good deeds, whereupon the child asked: "Why did you not allow me a life as long as his so I could also have earned a high place for myself?" God replied that, in line with His concern with best interests, He knew full well that if He had let him live, he would have become an unbeliever, bound for hell. Hearing this, the middle brother called out of the depth of hell: "Why, then, did You not also make me die as a child, since You also knew I would grow up to become a disbeliever?"

The middle brother's fate, it seems, is not reconcilable with the rationale of *al-aṣlaḥ* (optimal benefit), i.e. God's necessary selection of optimal benefit, and the story is already being used in the works of the Ash'arite theologian al-Baghdādī (d. 429/1037) to get across this doctrine's incoherence. But in the narrative of the school's origins which post-date Fakhr al-Dīn al-Rāzī (d. 606/1209), the "three brothers" problem is raised to become the very point of intellectual fission, the historic moment of disillusion (Gwynne 1985). For it was supposedly on the basis of the problem that the decisive doubt over his earlier doctrinaire Mu'tazilite worldview entered the mind of al-Ash'arī (d. 324/936), eponym and founder of the Ash'arite school. As he found that his great Mu'tazilite teacher Abū 'Alī al-Jubbā'ī simply could not answer the problem, he repudiated the entire Mu'tazilite system.

Whether or not the second brother's howl from the beyond literally roused Ash'arī from the torpor of his own prior allegiance, it has real symbolic force. That the thought experiment was not confined to this world made it a more telling problematic of Mu'tazilite attempts to submit God's ethics to human scrutiny. Following through the postulates of their a priori theodicean system, the Mu'tazilites freely inferred the necessity of divine compensation (*'iwaḍ*) in the next world for provisional injustices in this world—theirs was not an optimism confutable on the mere grounds of the inequities and moral absurdities of life as observed in this lower world. Rather than outrage at the human propensity for smug rationalisation, the story amounts to a seeming discovery, *through* reason, of the limited scope of human rationalisation in theodicy. That is not to say that outrage was quite absent either. Its main focus, however, was God's dignity, not man's: the blasphemous imposition of human ethical norms on the divine enigma and all the Mu'tazilite talk of God's "obligations." And implicit here, after all, *was* a pathos on the human level too, a foreshadowing of the "pious skepticism" marking Kant's disquisition on Job (Ormsby 1984). Ash'arism's pious skepticism seems no less to hover on the very brink of pessimism than Kant's—at any rate, this way of reading it seems the least unsatisfying. How else does Ash'arī's poignant insistence on calling God *al-'ādil*, "the Just One," despite the ultimate inscrutability of His justice, strike us? It is a "bearing witness" (*shahāda*) to God which carries some trace of that other, painful, sense of the Arabic word—"martyrdom," a testimony to God even to one's own grave hurt. It is perhaps in this spirit that Ash'arī's intentionally, deeply shocking statement is to be taken, that God might inflict pain on infants in the afterlife, give an infinite punishment for a finite sin, or damn believers and save unbelievers, but in doing that He would still be called "just" (McCarthy 1953: 99).

Ash'arī likewise revolted against the ingenious Mu'tazilite contraction of divine predicates, yielding a highly impersonal, denuded concept of God in the name of His rational unity. The problem here can be directly framed in terms of the aforementioned negotiation between *theologia naturalis* and *theologia revelata*. Ash'arī deemed that Mu'tazilism had failed in this vital but elusive negotiation, doing violence to the latter on behalf of the former. On the one hand, scripture laid down a whole set of graphic theologemes, giving the strong sense of a divine personhood. On the other hand, reason ruled that God's transcendence be strictly affirmed. The approach pressed (at least according to the cliché) by a Ḥanbalite fringe, insisted on not questioning scriptural descriptions, seemingly at the price of God's transcendence. The stance offered by Mu'tazilism instead stressed a rationalistic defence of God's transcendence at the price of taking scriptural descriptions literally. So whereas Ḥanbalite theology sacrificed reason to revelation, Mu'tazilite theology sacrificed revelation to reason. Ash'arism, however, seemed to satisfy both concerns—discovering a true *tertium quid*. Its stance on divine predication was framed in the dictum "affirmation without anthropomorphism." It thus embraced the divine person revealed in scripture, resisting the Mu'tazilite trend to interpretation, lexical reduction, etc., even in the case of anatomical references. It however stressed that these words were equivoques, and were *unlike* their non-divine senses or anthropomorphic equivalents, in this way fully preserving God's transcendence: the Ash'arite God has a real face, but unlike any humanly conceivable one. There was indeed an emphatic Ash'arite apophasis, but one focused on purging each divine attribute of human associations, not focused on purging the divine essence of the divine attributes. Ash'arism's highly nuanced approach was partly disguised by its use of the Ḥanbalite formula "without [asking] how" (*bi-lā kayf*) on divine attributes in scripture. In the context of Ash'arism, *bi-lā kayf* or *bi-ghayr al-takyīf* did not betoken an assent without question, but an assent without *reduction*: i.e. an assent without trace of anthropomorphic distortion. Although one can see this as a merging of the imperative of revelation and of reason, the Qur'ān of course *itself* warns against anthropomorphism in its very delivery of theologemes: "There is nothing like unto Him, [yet] He is the One Who hears and sees!" (Qur'ān 42:11).

Al-Ghazālī's Contributions

The staunch Ash'arite reification of attributes saw a shift from the idea of God as an eternal simplex to the idea of Him as an eternal complex. Ash'arite theology took God as a coeval combination of the self-subsistent essence and the attributes subsisting through the essence. It urged the (admittedly, highly paradoxical) formula to explain their relationship, "He/not He" (*huwa lā huwa*), that is: the attributes are at one with the essence, but also distinct from it. Defence of a complex divine "person" was a keynote of Ash'arism, even ingeniously reformulated after it encountered Avicennism and came to adopt some of its panoply of philosophical assumptions and terms, while refusing to draw the same theological conclusions. The result is, certainly, philosophically *avant garde*. For instance, al-Ghazālī (d. 505/1111) quips that the very term "Necessary of Existence" involves what is "possible of confusion," begging, as it does, the question of whether all types of causal chain end at the divine identity as such, or some might still regress deeper *into* it. He thus accepts that the divine person is the first efficient cause (*'illa fā'iliyya*) but stresses that it need not be the first "receptive" cause (*'illa qābiliyya*). The latter could turn out to be the divine essence, whereas the wider divine person, encompassing the divine attributes contingent on the essence, is the first efficient cause (Marmura 1997: 99). Al-Ghazālī hereby took up the Avicennian idea of different kinds of causal regress terminating at God, but questioned the need to conclude with divine simplicity.

Al-Ghazālī is an epochal, if ambiguous, representative of Ash'arism. Though a prime contributor to the school through crucial testaments such as his Just Mean of Belief, he yet gives a stark context to doctrinaire Ash'arite elements in his *oeuvre* when he appears to relativise the utility of *kalām* in his autobiography and *Iljām* (*Restraining [the Common People from Studying Kalām]*). It is impossible, however, to neglect the deep Ash'arite subtext of his critique of Avicennian philosophy, the *Tahāfut al-Falāsifa* (*Incoherence of the Philosophers*), or to miss the Ash'arite undercurrents in his Ṣūfism and *theologia acroamatica*. Al-Ghazālī is even, perhaps, the epitomic Ash'arite if a defining trait of the school was indeed, as proposed earlier, the defence of scriptural tradition through a reason-based problematic *of* reason. Though Fakhr al-Dīn al-Rāzī (d. 606/1209), the so-called "Leading Sceptic" (*Imām al-Mushakkikīn*), later emerged as the paragon of this Ash'arite trend, some of the best known episodes in Ghazālī's thought are classic expressions of the same reflex. His autobiography, for example, opens with a crisis of scepticism (*safsaṭa*) in which he takes his reader, step by step, through a period of hyperbolic doubt undergone in his youth, in many ways foreshadowing that of Descartes. The critical question which, as al-Ghazālī explains, confronted him at that time was how to free himself from the void in which he had placed himself through doubting the viability of discursive reason itself, *without* in turn depending on it. Again, in the famous Seventeenth Discourse of his *Tahāfut*, al-Ghazālī brilliantly problematizes the confidence placed by reason in cause-effect sequences. He insists (in this case, foreshadowing Hume) that the maximum that observation allows us to infer is that the so-called effect *goes with* the so-called cause, not that it occurs *through* it.

Al-Ghazālī's rare skill lay not only in rationally "imagining" and bodying forth nethermost problems like those just mentioned; he also had a vehement drive to break through to their solution, though this might be through a final "leap" outside reason, into a mystical synthesis. One of his greatest achievements lay in resolving the very radical Ash'arite causal framework with an epistemology (seemingly hopelessly at odds with it) which could support the full panoply of Avicennian science. He was, whatever his polemical posture in the *Tahāfut*, deeply enamoured of Avicennian thought (at least, from an instrumental point of view) and to the extent possible strove to make it available to his fellow religious scholars. For instance, he finally ushered into Shāfiʿite law and Ashʿarite *kalām* a fully Aristotelian logic—demonstrating in his *Correct Balance* (*al-Qisṭās al-Mustaqīm*) various kinds of syllogisms, using the text of the Qurʾān to bring home the utter religious respectability of this logic. Aspects of "philosophical" psychology and cosmology, let alone mathematics and applied sciences such as medicine and astronomy, were endorsed in the Ghazalian synthesis. Yet the entire causal premises of this encyclopaedic Avicennian system of knowledge, the very underpinning of its inferential reasoning, was the objective operation of cause-effect sequences and "natures" in the world, discoverable by induction. These were precisely *denied* in Ashʿarite causal theory.

In its philosophy of action, Ashʿarism was defined from the beginning against Muʿtazilism, by a divine omnipotence/human impotence equation. Whereas the Muʿtazilites had based their libertarianism on the ruling that capacity preceded the act, the Ashʿarites ruled that it was simultaneous with the act. Humans act, they claimed, by a lent power at the very time of acting, thus negating the possibility of real choice to do or *not* do the act, by the Law of Non-Contradiction. We only imagine, *ex post facto*, that we chose what we did. Following the same "formalism" which made them affirm divine justice but largely strip it of human coherence, the Ashʿarites formally endorsed the idea of the acquisition (*kasb*) of merit and demerit through these acts of ours, which have God as their subject in every respect *except* in having any moral responsibility for them. Extended from the realm of human action into the world at large, this causal theory became a theistic occasionalism of the most radical kind. "Causes" and "effects" are concomitant events, without an intrinsic "active power" (*quwwa fāʿiliyya*) in the former and passive power (*quwwa munfaʿila*) in the latter. This can also be formulated in terms of the problem of "incomplete induction": only an infinity of observed instances would justify an *absolute* conclusion about the respective "natures" of cause and effect. The occasionalist worldview of Ashʿarism drew its own uncompromising consequences from the old atomism of *kalām* physics. For, said the Ashʿarites, we might view endurance itself as an accident lent the atoms that constitute physical reality, such that the atoms themselves lack any intrinsic power to subsist. Thus their very subsisting from moment to moment would be an input from God. Again, this could also be formulated in terms of a philosophy of time in which time was constituted of discrete atoms (*ānāt*, "nows"), forming an apparent, though not real, continuum. Everything in each moment is in a total gestalt, uncaused by anything the moment before, but directly caused by God Himself. This, then, is a doctrine of *continuata creatio*, with a new creation every moment. Such an unconventional worldview might be thought more appropriate to the altered states of mysticism than rational discourse. But al-Ghazālī, a mystic who was steeped in reason, craved to find the deeper compatibility of this occasionalist worldview with the philosophical sciences.

He ventured ways to take up an Avicennian cosmological framework in practice, while still cleaving to the occasionalist worldview in principle. His most important expedient was to take over, and press to the hilt, the old Ashʿarite notion of divine custom. This corresponds closely with the Christian scholastic distinction of *potentia absoluta* and *potentia ordinata*. The world of nature is as much a manifestation of God's power as any miracle, but it manifests specifically God's *ordained* power, his "habitual" recreation of things from moment to moment according to a certain determinate pattern. In principle, God's absolute power makes many quite different sequences of events possible. But the world tends always to have predictable cause-effect patterns, based not on any intrinsic necessity, but through God's choice to recreate it in that way. This creational *habitus* has a direct epistemic aspect: it is by God's custom, not otherwise, that acquired knowledge arises within us through discursive reason—as al-Ghazālī's teacher Juwaynī himself had affirmed (Juwayni 2000: 9). In this way both the objective and subjective underpinning of a "rational" cosmos were provided by the Ash'arite idea of God's custom. Al-Ghazālī also found other routes, offered by Ṣūfism, to re-instate a rational cosmos. In his monumental *Revival of the Religious Sciences* (*Iḥyā 'Ulūm al-Dīn*), he takes up the Ṣūfī virtue (and mystical station) of "trust in God," and applies it to the cause-effect patterning of our world. An epistemic "reliance on God" places confidence in the circumstantial natural sequences observed in the universe, which depend on God; a yet higher level of trust is focused on the supra-temporal ground of these patterns, which al-Ghazālī refers to as the Well-Guarded Tablet, mentioned in the Qur'ān—a kind of epiphany of divine knowledge (Griffel 2009: 194).

Conclusion

The initially attractive prospect in Mu'tazilism of a free-standing rationality, externally confirming and interpreting revealed religion, was challenged through Ash'arism. This challenge, as was proposed above, itself used reason to try to show the limits of the Mu'tazilite model of reason—a significant, self-critical form of rationality which opened up new scope for epistemic "humility" towards the revealed forms of knowledge. But its quasi-sceptical caution on human reason, and its occasionalist worldview, seemed to isolate it from the vast possibilities of the philosophical sciences. These had taken deep root in Islamic culture as a result of the Graeco-Arabic translation movement and the contribution of towering figures like Ibn Sīnā. In the narrative of the exacting negotiation of reason and revelation in Islam, al-Ghazālī marks a culmination and a new threshold. Al-Ghazālī pointed out new ways to "re-activate" human reason, opening links with the project of philosophy and its worldview (though he himself never seriously addressed certain glaring conflicts of detail, notably, the incompatibility of Ash'arism's atomistic physics with the anti-atomistic physics of Peripateticism). Perhaps most importantly, how al-Ghazālī achieved this was not *in spite of* the Ash'arite emphasis on divine voluntarism and omnipotence, but *because* of it.

Further Reading

Montgomery, W. (1962) *Islamic Philosophy and Theology*, Edinburgh: Edinburgh University Press.
——. (1973) *The Formative Period of Islamic Thought*, Edinburgh: Edinburgh University Press.
Winter, T. (ed.) (2008) *The Cambridge Companion to Classical Islamic Theology*, Cambridge: Cambridge University Press.
Wolfson, H. A. (1976) *The Philosophy of the Kalam*, Harvard: Harvard University Press.

References

Bochenski, I. M. (1956) *Formale Logik*, Freiburg: Karl Alber.

Burckhardt, T. & Culme-Seymour, A. (tr.) (1975) *Muhyi-d-din Ibn 'Arabi: The Wisdom of the Prophets (Fusus al-Hikam)*, Aldsworth: Beshara.

Chodkewicz, M. (1993) *An Ocean Without Shore: Ibn 'Arabi, The Book, and the Law*, D. Streight (tr.), Albany: State University of New York Press.

Cook, M. (1980) "The Origins of 'kalām'," *Bulletin of the School of Oriental and African Studies* 43, 1: 32–43.

Frank, R. (1971) "Abu Hashim's Theory of 'States': its Structure and Function," in *Actas do IV Congresso de Estudos Árabes e Islâmicos (Coimbra, Lisboa 1 a 8 setembro de 1968)*, Leiden: Brill, pp. 85–100.

Griffel, F. (2009) *Al-Ghazālī's Philosophical Theology*, New York: Oxford University Press.

Gwynne, R. (1985) "Al-Jubbā'ī, al-Ash'arī and the Three Brothers: The Uses of Fiction," *The Muslim World* 75: 132–61.

Hourani, G. (1971) *Islamic Rationalism*, Oxford: Oxford University Press.

Jābirī, Muḥammad al- (1986) *Naḥnu wa'l-Turāth*, Casablanca: Arab Cultural Center.

Juwayni, Imām al-Ḥaramayn al- (2000) *A Guide to Conclusive Proofs for the Principles Of Belief (Kitāb al-irshād ilā qawāṭi' al-adilla fi uṣūl al-i'tiqād)*, P. Walker (tr.), Reading: Garnet Publishing.

Lane, E. W. (1984) *Arabic–English Lexicon*, Cambridge: Islamic Texts Society.

Leaman, O. & Rizvi, S. (2008) "The developed kalām tradition," in T. Winter (ed.), *The Cambridge Companion to Classical Islamic Theology*, Cambridge: Cambridge University Press, pp. 77–96.

Marmura, M. (tr.) (1997) *Al-Ghazālī: The Incoherence of the Philosophers*, Provo, UT: Brigham Young University Press.

Martin, R., Woodward, M., & Atmaja, D. (1997) *Defenders of Reason in Islam: Mu'tazilism from Medieval School to Modern Symbol*, Oxford: One World Publications.

Mayer, T. (tr.) (2009) *Keys to the Arcana: Shahrastānī's esoteric commentary on the Qur'ān*, Oxford & London: Oxford University Press/Institute of Ismaili Studies.

McCarthy, R. (tr.) (1953) *The Theology of al-Ash'arī*, Beirut: Imprimerie Catholique.

McDermott, M. (1978) *The Theology of al-Shaikh al-Mufīd (d. 413/1022)*, Beirut: Dar al-Machreq Ïditeurs.

Ormsby, E. (1984) *Theodicy in Islamic Thought: The Dispute over al-Ghazālī's "Best of All Possible Worlds,"* Princeton: Princeton University Press.

Schmidtke, S. (1991) *The Theology of al-'Allāma al-Ḥillī (d. 726/1325)*, Berlin: Klaus Schwarz Verlag.

van Ess, J. (1970) "The Logical Structure of Islamic Theology," in G. E. von Grunebaum (ed.), *Logic in Classical Islamic Culture*, Wiesbaden: Otto Harrassowitz, pp. 21–50.

Vasalou, S. (2008) *Moral Agents and Their Deserts: The Character of Mu'tazilite Ethics*, Princeton & Oxford: Princeton University Press.

Villani, A. (2007) "'I Feel Like I Am a Pure Metaphysician': The Consequences of Deleuze's Affirmation," in *Collapse: Philosophical Research and Development*, vol. III, Falmouth: Urbanomic, pp. 45–62.

Wisnovsky, R. (2005) "Avicenna and the Avicennian Tradition," in P. Adamson & R. C. Taylor (eds.), *The Cambridge Companion to Arabic Philosophy*, Cambridge: Cambridge University Press, pp. 92–136.

5
JURISPRUDENCE AND POLITICAL PHILOSOPHY IN MEDIEVAL ISLAM

Rumee Ahmed

Introduction

Islamic political philosophy has a long and illustrious history, growing and evolving from its first mature expositions in the thought of Abū Naṣr al-Fārābī (d. 950). Al-Fārābī authored several works that outlined the characteristics of a virtuous city, a just ruler, and a properly functioning polity, depicting a city whose inhabitants worked together to achieve mankind's perfection, and representing the pinnacle of human capabilities. Throughout the medieval period, various Islamic philosophers have expanded upon, agreed or disagreed with, and modified al-Fārābī's initial vision, each presenting distinct conceptions of the perfect society. What is immediately apparent to any student of Islamic history is that none of these visions were ever actualized, nor has there been any serious attempt to establish them as a social reality. Several reasons have been offered for this disconnection between theory and practice, but the most oft-repeated is that political philosophy had a marginal role in medieval Islamic society. Islamic societies are characterized as having neglected philosophy due to a preoccupation with Islamic law, which is derived, at least theoretically, from textual sources—primarily the Qur'ān and the sayings of Muḥammad—and demands acceptance and application by citizens of the Islamic state. The application of Islamic law, it is argued, makes political philosophy unnecessary, and undermines any attempt to re-conceive society on purely theoretical principles. All of this suggests that Islamic political philosophy was a futile exercise, doomed from the start.

The basis of the above argument is that jurisprudence and political philosophy cannot both serve as a foundation for a society. If a society were founded on political philosophy, then it would create jurisprudence based on the needs of logic and circumstance. Conversely, if a society were founded on jurisprudence, then political philosophy would have no room to question or subvert jurisprudence without destroying the society. Some researchers have therefore concluded that since Islamic jurisprudence had pride of place in medieval Islamic discourse and society, Islamic political philosophy failed as a project and was never adopted on a societal level. This explanation of the role of political philosophy in medieval Muslim society, however, stems from a misunderstanding of how both Islamic jurisprudence and Islamic political philosophy were intended to function. The two are much closer to each other than it might appear, and they were written with similar goals in mind. In order to understand how medieval Islamic political philosophers intended their works to be received, it is helpful first to understand how their presumed counterparts—Muslim jurists—intended their own works.

Islamic Jurisprudence in Medieval Muslim Society

Medieval Muslim jurists wrote expansive tracts on the subject of Islamic jurisprudence that detailed myriad aspects of individual and communal life. These works, which bloomed and proliferated after the third century of Islam, enumerated the intricate technicalities of religious rituals—including prayer, fasting, pilgrimage, and the like—as well as social regulations about diverse activities such as trade, taxes, war, and just governance. These works claimed to be comprehensive compendiums that covered all the necessary regulations for a just society, leading to the perception that Islamic laws governed all aspects of life in the Islamic state. Moreover, Muslim jurists formed guilds that were patronized by the state and/or wealthy individuals who subsidized their work and practice. This suggests that the project of Islamic jurisprudence had broad support from the ruling class and the social elite. Yet, the claims of Muslim jurists did not necessarily reflect the reality of life in the medieval Islamic state, and there is evidence to suggest that even the jurists knew that this was the case.

Although Islamic jurisprudence detailed the minutiae of private and public life, it should not be read as positive law. That is because jurists wrote their treatises with the full understanding that they would not directly affect social practice and that they did not necessarily reflect contemporary concerns (Moosa 1998: 20). Instead, jurists were contributing to a jurist's law: a rarified discussion amongst legal scholars who took as their starting points ancient doctrines laid down by Muslim scholars in the first few centuries of Islam. Medieval Muslim jurists were not coming up with laws that would be applied; they were justifying the historical opinions of their predecessors and arguing for how they should be applied in an ideal world.

A quick look at a juridical argument in all its complexity will, after intimidating the reader with its detail, expose the disconnection between jurisprudence in theory and actual practice. For example, some Muslim jurists argued about whether, after a battle, Muslims were allowed to capture an enemy's lynx—as opposed to, say, a wild boar—and distribute it as a spoil of war. First, it is highly unlikely that Muslims would find themselves having to contend with a lynx on the battlefield, let alone dealing with the attendant problems of its capture and distribution. However, the issue of the lynx affects several other issues that are important in Islamic jurisprudence, among them being the role of precedent, the legitimacy of certain prophetic sayings, the ritual cleanliness of various animals, and the discretion of officers in war. Thus, Muslim jurists struggled with issues like that of the lynx, justifying historical opinions through sophisticated argumentation to come to a definitive conclusion.

These jurists would look to the precedent of the legal guild with which they were affiliated, and justify their guild's historical opinion through proof texts from the

Qur'ān and prophetic practice. Sometimes jurists might disagree with the historical precedent, but more likely they would simply justify the precedent so that it would lend itself to a particular application. The way that jurists justified these positions is of paramount importance. If a jurist's legal guild historically held that an enemy's lynx might be captured and distributed when found on the battlefield, that jurist might cite from the Qur'ān and prophetic practice to prove that his legal guild has a strong textual foundation for its position. The jurist might additionally cite slightly different sources, however, that suggest that even though you can capture and distribute a lynx, you really should not do so. Or the jurist might cite still other sources to suggest that there was a time when a lynx might be captured and distributed, but that time is now gone. All of these justifications uphold the historical position of the legal guild that, in theory, it is permissible to capture a lynx on the battlefield and distribute it, but the way that the historical position is justified affects how that legal precedent would be applied in the future.

Now, if an officer in a Muslim army actually found himself in the position of having to deal with a lynx captured on the battlefield, it would be impracticable for him to consult the books of Islamic jurisprudence or a coterie of Muslim jurists when deciding on the best course of action. More than likely, he would simply use his best judgment to rule on the lynx and move on to more pressing matters. This reality was not lost on jurists, who nevertheless argued about the laws of war at great length. Their theoretical discourses were a product of the way in which medieval Islamic society worked in relation to law. Whereas we now think of a polity having a rule of law that is applied within the boundaries of a state, medieval Islamic jurisprudence was often confined to case-based rule in the judiciary; and even then judicial rulings did not create an authoritative precedent and could always be overruled by the executive. Thus, Islamic jurisprudence was a recondite genre of Islamic literature that had a limited relationship to governance.

That is not to suggest that Islamic jurisprudence was disingenuous or useless. Rather, it should be read as describing an ideal that leads to a virtuous life for the individual and for society. It is almost impossible for any society to abide by all the rules outlined in works of Islamic jurisprudence, but the actualization of all the rules is not their most important function. The works were aspirational: they described a vision of the good life through practical rules and regulations. This is crucial to understanding medieval Islamic jurisprudence—even though jurists argued about the correct application of the law, citizens of a polity did not actually have to apply the law in order to be virtuous. Whether or not an individual or society implemented its rules or not was largely irrelevant—that individual could live a virtuous life by acknowledging the importance of living according to Islamic law. Islamic jurisprudence in the medieval tradition, therefore, succeeded as a project by laying out a vision for virtuous life through the discourse of law that the Muslim community upheld as an ideal, regardless of whether or not that vision was ever actualized.

Islamic Political Philosophy in Light of Jurisprudence

If we examine the context in which Muslim jurists wrote their works of jurisprudence, we see three essential elements that are analogous to Muslim philosophers writing works of political philosophy. First, Muslim political philosophers relied on the patronage of ruling and wealthy individuals, forming guilds similar to, if smaller than, those formed by Muslim jurists. Second, Muslim political philosophers were not trying to refashion Islamic society from scratch; rather, they worked within the existing religious framework and dominant discourse of their time to articulate a philosophic vision that encompassed, but did not overturn, that reality. Similarly, Muslim jurists, rather than deriving new laws, inferred a dominant framework through which the existing laws could be properly applied. Third, just as jurists recognized a disconnect between their jurisprudential writings and social practice, so too did political philosophers recognize that their systems were not necessarily meant to be realized in practice. Instead, Muslim political philosophers composed works that were aspirational, and this aspiration itself was viewed as a success, whether or not the object of aspiration was ever realized. Each of these three features requires some elaboration in order to appreciate the structure and function of medieval Islamic political philosophy.

With regard to the first element, that of patronage, we find that Muslim political philosophers often enjoyed widespread support. The most prominent medieval political philosophers—al-Fārābī, Ibn Sīnā (d. 1037), al-Māwardī (d. 1050), al-Ghazālī (d. 1111), Ibn Bājjah (d. 1138), Ibn Ṭufayl (d. 1185), and Ibn Rushd (d. 1198)—all enjoyed patronage from wealthy and politically-connected individuals. They were celebrated in their own time by both the ruling class and the laity and, if they were persecuted by a local leader for some reason, they were sure to find safe harbor in a community elsewhere. To be sure, these philosophers were writing within, and to, a socio-political structure in which they were part and parcel. Medieval Muslim political philosophers were, on the whole, neither freethinkers nor renegade firebrands; they were not advocating revolution, but rather re-conceiving life within their own privileged social context.

This leads to the second element of Muslim political philosophy with regard to law and society: the philosophers were in fact affirming the contexts in which they lived while presenting an idealized version of political life. This affirmation is easier to see in the works of some philosophers as opposed to others. For the sake of clarity, we will divide medieval Islamic political philosophers into two camps, which we will call "Pragmatic Political Philosophers" and "Idealist Political Philosophers." Pragmatic Political Philosophers—like al-Māwardī, al-Ghazālī, Ibn Ṭufayl, and Ibn Bājjah—upheld the importance of Islamic jurisprudence and the need to follow the political leaders of their time, even if those leaders were deeply flawed (al-Māwardī 1996: 3; Hillenbrand 1988: 87–8; Cornell 1996: 134; Pavalko 2008). These philosophers were themselves celebrated jurists who wished for the moral rectitude of political leaders but, recognizing that a perfect political state is a virtual impossibility, suggested only small changes in actual methods of governance (Leaman 1980: 110). These thinkers asserted the primacy of religious knowledge, and encouraged their leaders to consult Muslim jurists when making their policies, yet did not bind leaders to do so. In effect, this made the political elite above the law, meaning that they needed the jurists to define the boundaries of virtue, but did not have to stay within those boundaries themselves.

One might read works of Pragmatic Political Philosophers and suppose that they were granting their political leaders unlimited power. The reality, however, was that the political leaders of their time already had relative autonomy and were not constrained by any jurist class. In fact, what Pragmatic Political Philosophers were doing was making space for Muslim jurists as an indispensable resource without whom the political class could have no claim to virtue. Whether or not the political class actually acted virtuously was somewhat irrelevant; Pragmatic Political Philosophers were arguing that jurists needed to be supported and patronized in order to establish the scope and limits of virtue itself (Feldman 2008: 39). Jurists, under the patronage of the political regime, would reflect on historical legal opinions and justify how they should be applied and understood in their contemporaneous context, and all in an aspirational mode. You will remember that writing in an aspirational mode means that jurisprudence achieves its objective so long as it is upheld as an ideal, not if it is actually applied. In that spirit, Pragmatic Political Philosophers were applying the logic of jurisprudence to the political regime; just as jurisprudence achieves its objective by being upheld as an ideal, regardless of whether it is actually applied, so does Pragmatic Political Philosophy achieve its objective when the political regime patronizes a jurist class to describe ideal virtuosity through jurisprudence, whether or not the regime acts according to that jurisprudence. Thus, Pragmatic Political Philosophers were describing a society in which a scholarly, jurist class could define an ideal virtuous person and society, without requiring any substantial change to either governance or historical Islamic jurisprudence. This effectively shifted the burden of virtue to the individual, so that citizens of such a society might focus on their own virtue as defined in large part by the jurist class regardless of or in spite of the relative virtue of the political elite.

Pragmatic Political Philosophers offer a helpful lens through which to view Idealist Political Philosophers because the difference in their approaches is only in degree, not in kind. Idealist Political Philosophers—like al-Fārābī, Ibn Sīnā, and Ibn Rushd—were articulating grand visions of a virtuous society that upended neither the political class nor the tenets of Islamic jurisprudence, though their approach to the subject was somewhat different. Whereas Pragmatic Political Philosophers described how an imperfect political regime might be made virtuous through the jurist class, and thus turned the focus to the individual, Idealist Political Philosophers started by describing the perfect society and then explained how the jurists and jurisprudence functioned within it. Nevertheless, both Pragmatic and Idealist Political Philosophers concluded that the virtuous city could include the current political regime as well as Islamic jurisprudence.

This allegiance to the current regime and Islamic jurisprudence is sometimes obvious. Ibn Rushd, for instance, was a celebrated Mālikī jurist and held a government post as a judge. He actively touted the superiority of Islamic law and the need to adhere to it in order to be virtuous. At other times the allegiance is less obvious. Al-Fārābī and Ibn Sīnā, though they were themselves patronized by Muslim rulers and celebrated in their own time, did not make obvious overtures to Islamic law or to the ruling class. However, a closer look reveals that though they often espoused heterodox views on Islamic theology, neither philosopher controverted law or society. Instead, they justified established legal beliefs and principles through philosophy. Ibn Sīnā, for example, said that God—a necessary existent—sent prophets to guide mankind, the best of whom happens to have borne a striking resemblance to

Muḥammad. This prophet must have been sent by God in order to tell humans how to properly engage in obligations that lead them to virtue. The most central of these obligations, according to Ibn Sīnā, happen to be what are commonly referred to as the "five pillars of Islam"—the testimony of faith, regular prayer, prescribed charity, fasting, and the *ḥajj* pilgrimage (McGinnis 2010: 217). Ibn Sīnā validated the laws prescribed in the Qur'ān, and happened to describe law in a way that was congruent with his Ḥanafī legal education and milieu (Gutas 1987–88: 332–3). However, he accomplished this through theoretical discourses about virtue in the abstract, such that following the logical consequents of virtue would result in a virtuous person enacting the dictates enshrined in historical Islamic jurisprudence. Of course, someone reading between the lines would find Ibn Sīnā's more radical ideas (Morris 1992: 163), but his political philosophy did not require him to explicitly subvert the positions of his legal school.

While one might be able to see how Idealist Political Philosophers were upholding the dominant legal narrative of their time, it is harder to see how they supported the regimes in which they lived. Idealist Political Philosophers provided grand theories about a virtuous society that most certainly did not accord with their political surroundings. How, then, can they be sincere in their overtures toward the virtuous city and yet uninterested in regime change? Should they not have had the most fervent desire to change and mold their societies to fit their theoretical conceptions of virtue, unless they were hypocrites? Here it is helpful to remember the Pragmatic Political Philosophers' conception of virtue: the political class does not need to enact Islamic jurisprudence in order to be virtuous, it needs only to articulate jurisprudence as an aspirational ideal. Idealist Political Philosophers engaged in a similar logic, and to fully grasp how this was articulated, we will turn to the work of al-Fārābī.

Al-Fārābī on Virtuosity and the Virtuous City

Al-Fārābī was of the opinion that the virtuous city was one in which the actions of the rulers and the laity were directed toward achieving happiness. This required a philosopher or philosopher-class that would first determine how to achieve happiness and would then assume a governing role so as to mold the society into a happy one. That would be a perfect society, one constantly aimed at the highest end in life, and well-positioned to achieve the perfect happiness that can only be had outside the world of corporeality. In essence, the happy society would be geared toward cultivating virtues that lead its citizens to happiness so that they might achieve the ultimate happiness after their deaths.

For society to be virtuous, therefore, there must exist individuals who know true happiness and know how to achieve it; al-Fārābī identifies these individuals as "philosophers." In an ideal society, the philosophers would have a governing role and direct the masses to happiness. That means that they must understand happiness in its entirety; not only in theory, but in practice. That is, they must know how to achieve happiness through action and implementation as well as through intellection. This melding of the theoretical and the practical should keep us from assuming that al-Fārābī was advocating a purely Platonic, unprejudiced reflection on the reality that underlies all of observed creation. Rather, the philosopher must know how to produce happiness in non-philosophers, which requires knowledge of ethics and politics. A philosopher is thus not perfected in knowledge of happiness until she (1) knows true happiness in theory; (2) acts in a way that is consistent with happiness; and (3) is able to produce happiness in others.

All three of these levels were intertwined such that a philosopher's happiness, both theoretical and practical, required interaction with her society. This interaction was meant to be mutually beneficial and generate happiness in both the philosopher and society; a philosopher could not simply bend society to her will or subvert societal norms, lest she be a tyrant or be branded a deviant. She had to articulate his thought inside the boundaries of what her society considered to be virtuous. Hence, working within societal customs, history, and religious traditions, was essential. If such work is essential to happiness, then a philosopher cannot be truly happy until and unless she acts according to conventional morality such that her society recognizes her virtue and she embodies the higher principles of virtue through her moral conduct. Al-Fārābī coined an example of two hypothetical individuals to demonstrate the centrality of societal norms: the first has mastered all the works of Aristotle, and the second has no knowledge of philosophy, but always acts in accordance with conventional morality. The second person, he says, is closer to being a philosopher than the first, for the second's practical knowledge allows her to understand and properly contextualize the knowledge learned by the first (Galston 1992: 110). The direction of knowledge, then, flows from practice to theory, and al-Fārābī repeatedly required philosophers to adhere to conventional morality, which was provided in large part by religious jurisprudence. The philosopher must enact religious jurisprudence in her own life, and hypothesize about the intent behind that jurisprudence (Mahdi 2001: 40). By properly inferring the intent behind the law, the philosopher can apply the law so that it leads to happiness. Once the law is applied so that it reflects the original intent, the laity can follow the law and be happy.

Such a vision of philosopher as interpreter of laws as opposed to generator of ethics might seem overly prudent, if not anti-philosophical, especially in light of the philosophers upon whom al-Fārābī was commenting; that is, Plato and Aristotle. While al-Fārābī's thought is firmly ensconced in the Alexandrian tradition (Vallat 2004), it is precisely this prudence that makes al-Fārābī's political philosophy "Islamic." He was not encouraging a re-creation of jurisprudence along philosophic lines, but rather a re-assessment of jurisprudence according to the hypothesized intent of the law. The philosopher is not law-giver—except in the extremely rare case in which a prophet receives revelation—but rather a kind of jurist-philosopher. This description of the philosopher closely resembles that of Islamic jurists mentioned above, as inferring the intent and proper application of the law through reflection on received jurisprudence. The jurist and the jurist-philosopher are not exactly the same, but their functions are remarkably similar.

What, then, of the virtuous city that Idealist Political Philosophers believed would lead society and its citizens to happiness? Should not the philosopher rule a polity in order to attain practical perfection and virtuously guide the society? If citizens can be truly happy only in a virtuous city, is happiness even possible unless the philosopher is in charge? Al-Fārābī acknowledges that it would be best to live in a polity ruled by a prophet-philosopher, but makes it clear that the age of prophets has passed. In the absence of the prophet, the jurist-philosopher should rule in a way that is best described as progressive-conservative. The ideal jurist-philosopher-ruler governs according to the body of laws and customs established by the "true princes" and possesses

> a combination of new qualities ... that make him proficient in the 'art of jurisprudence,' that is, in knowledge of laws and customs of his predecessors; willingness on his part to follow these laws and customs rather than change them; the capacity to apply them to new conditions by the deduction of new decisions from, or the discovery of new applications for, established laws and customs; and the capacity to meet every new situation (for which no specific decisions are available) through understanding the intention of previous legislators rather than by the legislation of new laws or by any formal change of old ones.
>
> (Mahdi 2001: 138)

One might easily mistake such a description of "ruler as philosopher" for a description of "ruler as jurist."

But even that would be too radical a reading of al-Fārābī. He believed that if a society were not ruled by a jurist-philosopher, that society could still achieve a state of happiness through a hybrid setup. In this system, the jurist-philosopher, or groups of jurist-philosophers, would advise a ruler whose only qualification was having the nebulous attribute of "wisdom." Al-Fārābī was not clear about what made a person—other than a prophet—"wise" (Mahdi 2001: 168). He left the door open about who such a person might be, but insisted that this wise ruler consult the jurist-philosophers in his decision-making. It could even be argued that a ruler would be considered "wise" if he consulted with the philosopher-jurists. In this way, al-Fārābī can be seen as creating an indispensable role for a jurist class in political life, a project very similar to that of the Pragmatic Political Philosophers. Virtuous politics, in this conception, is not so much about instituting a particular ruling order or set of laws as ensuring that a process of governance is enacted in which there are open lines of communication between the ruling class and the jurist-philosopher class; and happiness is achieved when the jurist class is engaged in the kind of philosophical inquiry that uses the intent behind received jurisprudence to determine how law should be applied. The process of philosophical-*cum*-juridical investigation is, therefore, the foundation of virtuous government, such that "philosophic activity is the archetype of governance and political rule is the metaphor" (Galston 1992: 146).

Conclusion

Islamic political philosophers, whether Pragmatic or Idealist, were engaged in a kind of theoretical speculation that closely aligns with the project of Islamic jurisprudence, and both could succeed while maintaining the status quo. Yet the two projects are not one and the same. Islamic jurisprudence was a project that made inferences about how legal dictates should be ideally applied to lead one to virtue, though as long as one upheld jurisprudence as an ideal, one did not need to apply all of its dictates to be virtuous. Islamic political philosophers developed theories for how a virtuous regime should function through a jurist class that defined the boundaries of virtue, though the regime could be virtuous even if it was not ruled by the findings of that jurist class. The two genres have a similar logic, and both succeed when they are upheld as aspirational but, because they have different starting points, Islamic political philosophy can be seen in a far more pluralist light. Whereas Islamic jurisprudence can never transcend the bounds of its religious particularity, Islamic political philosophy, because it claims to describe the ideal virtuous society in the abstract, might be brought to bear beyond its Islamic context. Political philosophers often described theoretical regimes that could lead the world to virtue in a way that rises above theological and juridical affiliations. They imagined a government that re-inscribed religious doctrines in the language of philosophy, and thus might be understood in diverse contexts. This is something that could never be accomplished by jurists working only within the genre of Islamic jurisprudence.

Yet political philosophers acknowledged that their grander visions of a perfect society were highly theoretical, requiring a type of prophetic character who would not be found after Muḥammad. Thus, their task was not to describe how a prophet would lead a virtuous regime in the future, but how jurist-philosophers should understand the words and deeds of the Prophet and apply them in their milieu. This is not, in itself, a radical view of Islamic principles, nor of Islamic governance, and has a strong cognate in jurisprudential literature. It should be no surprise, then, that Islamic political philosophers were celebrated in Islamic societies throughout the medieval period, were patronized by the political elite, and had their works studied in religious seminaries throughout the Muslim world. If anything, Islamic political philosophy valorized the Islamic juridical tradition and the prevailing governance structure, and, in that light, should be seen as a resounding success in its ability to mold philosophy to the contours of both religious jurisprudence and the state.

Further Reading

Calder, N. (2010) *Islamic Jurisprudence in the Classical Era*, Cambridge: Cambridge University Press.

Crone, P. (2004) *God's Rule: Government and Islam*, New York: Columbia University Press.

Emon, E. (2010) *Islamic Natural Law Theories*, Oxford: Oxford University Press.

Gleave, R. & Kermeli, E. (1997) *Islamic Law: Theory and Practice*, New York: I. B. Tauris.

Mahdi, M. (2001) *Alfarabi and the Foundation of Islamic Political Philosophy*, Chicago: University of Chicago Press.

References

al-Māwardī (1996) *al-Ahkam al-Sultaniyya (The Ordinances of Government)*, W. Wahba (tr.), Reading, UK: Garnet Publishing.

Cornell, V. (1996) "Ḥayy in the Land of Absāl: Ibn Ṭufayl and Ṣūfism in the Western Maghrib during the Muwaḥḥid Era," in L. Conrad (ed.), *The World of Ibn Ṭufayl: Interdisciplinary Perspectives on Ḥayy ibn Yaqẓān*, Leiden: Brill, pp. 133–64.

Feldman, N. (2008) *The Fall and Rise of the Islamic State*, Princeton: Princeton University Press.
Galston, M. (1992) "The Theoretical and Practical Dimensions of Happiness as Portrayed in the Political Treatises of al-Fārābī," in C. Butterworth (ed.), *The Political Aspects of Islamic Philosophy: Essays in Honor of Muhsin S. Mahdi*, Cambridge: Harvard University Press, pp. 95–151.
Gutas, D. (1987–88) "Avicenna's Maḏhab' With an Appendix on the Question of His Date of Birth," *Quaderni di Studi Arabi* 5, 6: 323–36.
Hillenbrand, C. (1988) "Islamic Orthodoxy of Realpolitik? Al-Ghazali's Views on Government," *Journal of Persian Studies* 26: 81–94.
Leaman, O. (1980) "Ibn Bajja on Society and Philosophy," *Der Islam* 57, 1: 109–19.
Mahdi, M. (2001) *Alfarabi and the Foundation of Islamic Political Philosophy*, Chicago: University of Chicago Press.
McGinnis, J. (2010) *Avicenna*, New York: Oxford University Press.
Moosa, E. (1998) "Allegory of the Rule (*Ḥukm*): Law as Simulacrum in Islam?" *History of Religions* 38, 1: 1–24.
Morris, J. (1992) "The Philosopher-Prophet in Avicenna's Political Philosophy," in C. Butterworth (ed.), *The Political Aspects of Islamic Philosophy: Essays in Honor of Muhsin S. Mahdi*, Cambridge: Harvard University Press, pp. 152–98.
Pavalko, R. (2008) *The Political Foundations of Ibn Bajjah's "Governance of the Solitary,"* PhD Dissertation, University of Maryland, College Park, MD.
Vallat, P. (2004) *Farabi et l'École d' Alexandrie: Des prémisses de la connaissance à la philosophie politique*, Paris: Vrin.

Part II

LOGIC, LANGUAGE, AND THE STRUCTURE OF SCIENCE

6
LOGIC AND LANGUAGE

Thérèse-Anne Druart

Introduction

In Greek *logos*, word or discourse, gave rise to *logike techne* or craft of reasoning, i.e. logic. Further, the basic type of reasoning studied in logic is called the *syllogismos*, a word deriving from *logos*. These etymologies reveal a link between language and logic, particularly since symbolic logic was not yet invented. Classical Arabic too manifests a link between word or speech and logic as the word for logic *mantiq* derives from *nutq*, which means articulated speech. Yet, logic claims to be universal, whereas there is a great multiplicity of languages. Distinguishing logic from linguistic arts, as well as articulating their relationship, is a complex and difficult endeavor that philosophers in Islamic lands faced in various ways. They had to take into account not only the Greek philosophical tradition but also some theological positions. In the first section I look at logic as essentially an autonomous discipline focusing on syllogisms. In the second I explore how some philosophers either emphasize their relationship or try to articulate better logic's autonomy. The last and final section deals with some of the philosophers' reflections on various aspects of language in general.

Logic

For a long time the pioneering work of N. Rescher (1963, 1964) was our main source of information for the History of Arabic logic during the classical period. More recently the edition of various logical texts has led to interesting developments. Detailed studies on Arabic syllogistic in the Aristotelian tradition have come out (Black 1990; Lameer 1994, 1996; and Street 2004, 2008). In addition, Street & El-Rouayheb (2004, 2005, 2010) have begun to explore developments beyond the classical period, particularly those occurring in the *madrasa* or mosque school setting, where the teaching of logic remains very much alive. Most of what I shall say on logic owes much to Street's work.

First, in the footsteps of the Alexandrian tradition, the Arabic tradition includes both the *Rhetoric* and the *Poetics* in Aristotle's *Organon* and, therefore, considers these two texts as integral parts of logic proper rather than of practical philosophy. This inclusion of the *Poetics* and the *Rhetoric* among the logical works reinforces the link between logic and the linguistic arts. As the classical period gave rise to many commentaries or quasi commentaries on Aristotle's *Organon* so construed, one may wonder whether in Islamic lands the whole history of logic is dominated by Aristotelian influences. The answer is clearly no. Galen's logic, particularly his treatise *On Demonstration*, seems to have transmitted some aspects of Stoic logic and has influenced modal logic. So the Arabic logical tradition moves from being essentially Aristotelian with al-Fārābī (d. 950) to being Avicennian at least in the East. In the West it remained more Aristotelian, as Ibn Bājja (Avempace, d. 1138) and Ibn Rushd (d. 1198) followed al-Fārābī. Despite the many editions and translations of al-Fārābī's numerous logical texts, evaluating his contribution is not easy. He is not always consistent in his views and the chronology of his works is mostly uncertain, but his logical works clearly remain Aristotelian. On the other hand, Ibn Sīnā makes great changes in logic and develops a modal syllogistic quite different from that of Aristotle. Soon, in the East, Aristotle's logical texts will no longer be read much and Ibn Sīnā's texts will take precedence.

Second, as is well known, originally Muslim religious authorities did not welcome logic and doubted its usefulness for Arabic speakers. The famous debate ca. 932 in front of the Vizier between the Christian translator and logician Abū Bishr Mattā (d. 940), whose Arabic was not the best, and the brilliant young grammarian al-Sīrāfī turns around whether logic is a universal discipline useful for speakers of any language or simply Greek grammar and, therefore, useless to Arabic speakers. The amusing report of the dispute highlights Abū Bishr's defeat and, therefore, logic's defeat. Later on, al-Ghazālī's (d. 1111) adoption of Avicennian logic for the *madrasas* and its application to Islamic Law in particular will give rise to lively debates and refinements, even if the relationship between *kalām* and logic will remain tense. Ibn Taymiyyah (1993) (d. 1328) may write at length against the logicians but cannot afford to ignore their importance. The traditional *madrasa* training of leading religious elites or *'ulamā'* will always include a serious grounding in logic leading to lively disputes and innovative developments. Street (2005) informs us about al-Kātibī's (d. 1276) Avicennian *al-Risāla al-shamsiyya*, which for many centuries commonly was the first substantial logical textbook a Sunnī Muslim would study in the *madrasa*.

Street (2008) indicates that in the East, post-Avicennian logic develops its own autonomy and, therefore, at some stage will leave aside texts and topics that were part of the Aristotelian *Organon*, such as the *Categories*, as they become part of metaphysics. Yet a tendency to distinguish more clearly what pertains to logic from what pertains to metaphysics was already observable in Ibn Sīnā, as Bertolacci indicates in his article "The 'Ontologization' of Logic. Metaphysical Themes in Ibn Sīnā's Reworking of the *Organon*" (2011). Moreover, Diebler (2005), Menn (2008), and Druart (2007a) have shown that such a phenomenon was already present in al-Fārābī, particularly, in his so-called *Book of Letters*, which is highly metaphysical and reminds one of Aristotle's *Metaphysics* Delta, or book 5, in its first and third parts, but mostly quotes the *Categories*. For Ibn Sīnā the categories deal with first intention words and, therefore, become quasi-ontological "species," as being is not a genus (a view adopted in the Latin world by John Duns Scotus), rather than logical concepts (Avicenna 2005: 10).

Logic and Language

The famous early dispute whether logic is a universal discipline or simply Greek grammar indicates that the question of the relation between logic and grammar was far from clear. Logic certainly uses language and early on a lack of technical Aristotelian vocabulary in Arabic led to awkward translations and usages. A need to articulate better the relation between a particular language and logic led to interesting developments.

As Street (2008) explains so well, definitions of logic change. These definitions reveal different views about the relationship between logic and language. In his *Enumeration of the Sciences* al-Fārābī speaks at length of logic and defines it in the following way: "The subject matters of logic for which it gives rules are 1. the intelligibles in as much as utterances signify them and 2. the utterances in as much as they signify the intelligibles" (al-Fārābī 1949: 59). Further, being well aware of the Arabic grammarians' contempt for logic, al-Fārābī follows this definition of the two subject matters of logic, intelligibles and utterances, with an explanation of the distinction between grammar and logic. "Logic shares some common ground with grammar by the rules it gives for utterances, but it differs from it in so far as the science of grammar gives the rules for the utterances of a certain nation, whereas the science of logic gives *shared* rules which are *common* to the utterances of *all* nations" (al-Fārābī 1949: 60; the italics for emphasis are mine). The particularity of grammar for each language is strongly contrasted to the universality of logic. In the West, in his *Remarks* on al-Fārābī's *On Interpretation*, Ibn Bājja offers views similar to those of al-Fārābī (1994: 140).

Ibn Sīnā (d. 1037), on the other hand, makes two moves distancing him from al-Fārābī's definition: (1) he qualifies which kind of intelligibles is meant and (2) he limits the subject matter of logic to intelligibles and, therefore, no longer claims that logic studies utterances, not even in so far as they signify intelligibles. He accomplishes the first move in the *Metaphysics* of the *Shifā'* where he says "The subject matter of logic, as you have known, was the secondary intelligibles that depend on the primary intelligibles" (Avicenna 2005: 7, tr. mod.). This discreet qualification allows Ibn Sīnā to better distinguish logic from ontology. The second move, this time in the *Isagoge* of the *Shifā'*, is highly critical of al-Fārābī's views, even if it does not name him: "There is no merit in what some say, that the subject matter of logic is speculation concerning the utterances insofar as they signify intelligibles … . And since the subject matter of logic is not in fact distinguished by these things, and there is no way in which they are its subject matter, [such people] are only babbling and showing themselves to be stupid" (Avicenna 1952:23–4; Street 2008 tr. mod.).

These two moves render logic more removed from the particularity of any specific language. In her interesting examination of the relation between logic and the linguistic arts in both Medieval Latin and Arabic Philosophy, D. Black wryly remarks that, despite his stated views on the autonomy of logic, in fact Ibn Sīnā often still applies the technical terminology of the logicians to utterances (Black 1992: 60–1). Yet, with time, utterances will become less and less a concern of the logician and the philosopher will more and more focus on intelligibles or "intentions." This focus on intelligibles, independently of their linguistic expression, may explain why, in his famous philosophical tale, *Ḥay ibn Yaqẓan*, Ibn Tufayl (d. 1185) claims that his hero, raised by a doe on a deserted island, discovered the whole of philosophy before having even learned to talk. For Ibn Tufayl the intelligibles bestowed by the single agent Intellect are language neutral and common to all human beings.

In contrast, the original link between language and logic remains strong in a more popular type of philosophical work, *The Epistles of the Brethren of Purity*. The *Ikhwān as-Safā'* or Brethren of Purity were the anonymous members of a tenth-century esoteric fraternity, centered around Basra. Though in *Epistles* ten to fourteen they follow the traditional order of *Isagoge, Categories, On Interpretation, Prior Analytics,* and *Posterior Analytics*, they moved the reflections on the definition of logic from the *De Interpretatione* to the very beginning of the *Isagoge*. There in Chapter 2 they tell us:

> Know that the word *mantiq* ('speech', 'logic') derives from [the forms of the verb] *nataqa, yantuqu, nutqan, mantiqan*; that language is one of the acts of the human soul; and that this act is of two species, mental and spoken. Spoken language is a physical, sensible object, and mental language is a spiritual, intelligible object. In fact, spoken language consists of sounds that can be heard, expressed through an alphabet ... . The study and investigation of this language and the discourse on how it is transformed and of the concepts indicated by it is called the 'science of linguistic logic'. As to mental language, that is a spiritual, intelligible object, it consists of the soul's representation of the concepts of things in themselves ... . By such a language is man distinguished from the other animals.
>
> (Brethren of Purity 2010: 67, Baffioni tr.; Arabic 9–10)

Earlier this *Epistle* had indicated that logic was "the noblest among human arts ... . For through logic man is distinguished from the other animals" (2010: 65; Arabic 5). For them logic includes both a study of the intelligibles and of the utterances. Since they deny that animals can speak—though their longest epistle, n. 22, *The Case of the Animals versus Man Before the King of the Jinn*, is a fable in which various animals denounce human beings for their inhumane treatment of animals—the Brethren claim that logic in both its aspects, i.e. the one dealing with utterances and the one dealing with intelligibles, is what distinguishes human beings from animals. Notice that the Brethren seem to include all utterances without qualification under one of the two divisions of logic, while al-Fārābī more cautiously had specified that the utterances are part of the subject matter of logic, only in so far as they signify the intelligibles.

Language

As logic and its relation to the linguistic arts and language are now getting more scholarly study, I shall give more attention to philosophy of language, which up to now has not fared so well. Already in Ancient philosophy various questions had been raised about language as such: (1) Is language a natural or conventional phenomenon? In the *Cratylus*, Plato already wonders whether names signify by convention or by nature. Aristotle claims language is conventional but the Epicureans, for instance, hold it is natural. (2) Is language a purely human characteristic, as Aristotle claims, or do animals—or at least some animals—which indubitably communicate by sound, use language too, as Plutarch and Porphyry argue? (Sorabji 2004: 213–19; Newmyer 2011: 62–9). (3) While languages vary from one nation to another, are all intelligibles nevertheless the same for all human beings? (4) Do animals have at least some level of rationality, as Plutarch and Porphyry think (Newmyer 2011: 15–21) and do they have some grasp of the universal, a view the Arabic tradition attributes to Galen? (Sorabji 1993: 62–4). To these questions raised in late Antiquity one needs to add issues arising from the Islamic context. In the Bible God tells Adam to name the animals (Genesis 2:19–20) and so language seems to be a product of human convention. But some Christian authors, such as Origen, as well as some Greek commentators, claim that names have a divine origin which implies that names are natural (Sorabji 2004: 220–6). On the other hand, the Qur'ān emphatically declares that God taught Adam all the names (Qur'ān 2:31). Interpretations of this sentence vary widely but often seem to imply that names are by imposition and have a divine origin and, therefore, do not arise by human convention. Some theologians, therefore, infer that names are not by convention because human beings, to establish convention, would already need to use the language the convention is supposed to establish. This circularity leads them to reject the view that language rises by human convention and to claim it is posited by God (Hasnaoui 1988). Besides, does the acceptance of the uncreatedness and inimitability of the Qur'ān give a special status to one unique language, namely, Arabic? (Druart 2007b). Furthermore, Qur'ān 6:38 says that animals will be gathered to their Lord and several theologians hold that not only human beings but also animals will be revived on the day of resurrection. The Mu'tazilites seem to grant a high status to animals. 'Abd al-Jabbār (d. 995) claims that children, insane adults and animals cannot be blamed for pain they inflict as they are without complete minds, and so no obligation is imposed on them. Yet, if animals did not receive proper compensation in this life, they will receive it in the afterlife (Heemskerk 2000).

The first philosopher to focus on language, its origin, and development and to give them their most extensive treatment is al-Fārābī. His *Long Commentary on Aristotle's De Interpretatione* and his *Book of Letters* focus much attention to language because he is very aware of cultural and linguistic differences. Let us begin with his *Long Commentary on Aristotle's De Interpretatione*, before moving to his more independent and more personal *Book of Letters*. First, this commentary indicates that al-Fārābī is fully aware of the Ancient discussions about whether language is by convention or by nature as is clear in his commentary on 17a1–2: "Every sentence is significant (not as a tool but, as we said, by convention)" (Aristotle 1984). He begins his very long commentary to this very short lemma by indicating that

> This is Aristotle's opinion regarding sentences and single utterances (i.e. words) alike. [The reason why he makes this point is that] some people hold that single significant utterances are not *by convention*. Some of them believe that they are by nature, others that they are tools formed by human will, just as the craftsman's tools are formed.
>
> (al-Fārābī 1981: 41–2, Zimmermann tr. mod.; Arabic al-Fārābī 1960: 50)

He then explains that those who adopt a naturalist position hold that all names must imitate what they signify, that is to say, their essence or some important accident, such as the word "*hudhud*" [hoopoe] that imitates the cry of this bird. This claim seems, as

Zimmermann points out, to be inspired by some synopsis of Plato's *Cratylus*. Some other thinkers hold the view that single utterances were agreed upon by convention but compound utterances were not. Al-Fārābī then adds: "Aristotle holds that all of these [single utterances and sentences] have been agreed by convention" and argues this point for both sentences and single utterances (al-Fārābī 1981:43, Zimmermann tr.).

In his commentary on 16a5–67 ("just as written marks are not the same for all men, neither are spoken sounds," Aristotle 1984, Ackrill tr.) al-Fārābī's reasoning for claiming that single utterances are by convention is interesting:

> Aristotle wishes to explain how things are with utterances: that their signification is by convention. Script, where this is more evident than in utterances, resembles utterances in matters of signification. *And just as* scripts are *not the same for all* nations, their scripts being in fact different, *so too* the utterances signifying intelligibles are *not the same* with all nations, their languages differing just like their scripts. If human beings had been given their utterances by nature they would be the same for all nations, just as the intelligibles signified by different languages are the same with all nations, and just as the sense-objects which these intelligibles are intelligibles of are also common to all nations ... . The relation of the intelligibles within the soul to the beings outside the soul is by nature. By contrast, the relation of the intelligibles to the utterances, i.e. the relation which the utterances signify, is by convention and by plain legislation.
>
> (al-Fārābī 1981: 12, Zimmermann tr. mod.)

Al-Fārābī here introduces a political theme in Aristotle's text. Aristotle claimed that language is by convention but did not explain how the convention arose. Al-Fārābī compares utterances giving to law giving and indicates that either representatives of a nation or city or one or several rulers impose utterances and scripts just as they impose law. There is no doubt that, for al-Fārābī, imposing and forming language is an exercise in power.

The text we have just commented upon also indicates that words may differ from one language to another but the intelligibles are common to all human beings and so are by nature. Al-Fārābī will make this same point once again a few lines further down:

> The intelligibles all human beings understand in their various languages are one and the same. The sense-objects which these intelligibles are intelligibles of are also common to all human beings. For whatever is a sense-object for an Indian, if the same thing is observed by an Arab, he will have the same grasp of it as the Indian.
>
> (al-Fārābī 1981: Arabic 27.25–28.2, my translation)

This position goes far to ensure a realist theory of knowledge for first intelligibles, but may not apply to secondary intelligibles that do not correspond directly to a sense-object that can be pointed to. It also does not fit experience very well. Anyone who has learned a foreign language and done translations does know that some words do not have a real equivalent in the target language. This is puzzling as al-Fārābī was not a native speaker of Arabic and so was at least bilingual. Moreover, in *The Book of Letters* he gives detailed rules for the translation of philosophical technical terms that show his awareness that intelligibles do not always match from one culture to another (Druart 2010), since distinctions and connotations at times are not the same.

Al-Fārābī also tackles the issue of whether animals really have speech since they communicate with each other. In *De interpetatione* 1, 16a3–8 & 27–29, Aristotle states:

> A *name* is a spoken sound significant by convention, without time, none of whose parts is significant in separation … . I say 'by convention' because no name is a name naturally but only when it has become a symbol. Even inarticulate noises (of beasts, for instance) do indeed reveal something, yet none of them is a name.
>
> (Aristotle 1984, Ackrill tr.)

In *Parts of Animals*, a text on which al-Fārābī wrote in a little known treatise in which he criticizes some of Galen's criticisms of Aristotle's views (al-Fārābī 1983), Aristotle himself had acknowledged that "All birds use their tongues to communicate with each other. But some do this in a greater degree than the rest; so that in some cases it even seems as though actual instruction were imparted from one to another" (II, 17, 660a36–660b2; Aristotle 1984, Ogle tr.). So al-Fārābī is rather troubled by differences he perceives between Aristotle's refusal to grant any articulate communicative sounds to animals in *De interpretatione* and his more generous views in *On the Parts of Animals*, particularly as he wishes to attribute articulate sounds or utterances to at least some animals. Al-Fārābī, therefore, emends the lemma and, as a good philosopher, makes distinctions. This allows him to claim that (1) mere vocal sound or voice is distinct from articulate sound or utterance and so grants utterances at least to some animals; and (2) utterance or articulate sound is distinct from a name or noun. So utterances may be common to both human beings and some animals but speech proper requires naming and animals are not capable of naming. He grounds his emendation and interpretation on *Parts of Animals* 660a2 where

> Aristotle says that many birds and other animals occasionally produce sounds composed of letters. And if utterances are composed of letters, the sounds these animals produce are utterances, even if [composed of] letters we do not happen to know. At the same time, we observe that many of the animals which live around us, such as goats and others, produce sounds—sounds they have been endowed by nature—which are composed of letters we do know. I am not thinking of birds like parrots and the magpie, which can be taught utterances, but of those that produce sounds which they have been given by nature. Such sounds are utterances though they are not by convention.
>
> (al-Fārābī 1981: 19–20, Arabic 31, Zimmermann tr. mod.)

Animals' utterances signify as they indicate to each other fear, pleasure, or aggression. Al-Fārābī has divided vocal sounds into the articulate or utterances and the inarticulate.

Some animals, birds in particular and even goats, by nature produce utterances that allow them to communicate with each other and in some cases can be easily transcribed in the phonetic system of a certain language. As such utterances are by nature, they are common to all the members of the same species. By contrast, human beings, who also produce utterances, produce them by convention and so develop various languages. Birds that simply parrot human utterances do not really have speech because they do not really use names or nouns.

Though in this text al-Fārābī follows Aristotle fairly closely, particularly in defending the view that language is by convention, in other, more personal texts he moves some distance from Aristotle or, more exactly, qualifies this view. In *The Political Regime* he nuances it in claiming that, though language is conventional, it has some basis in natural things (al-Fārābī 1964: 70). It suggests that he holds the ability to speak as natural to human beings but that the various languages develop by convention. In *The Book of Letters* he explains that various groups of human beings naturally develop different "letters" in the sense of "phonemes" because in each ethnic group the vocal organs are slightly different and so articulating some sounds is easier for one group than for another (al-Fārābī 1969: 135 n. 115). Though phonemes may be ethnically and at least partially naturally determined, from then on language develops by convention.

In *The Book of Letters* al-Fārābī dedicates many pages to explain the development of language in a group of human beings because he wishes to present an account that can rival that of some of the theologians, who had argued that language cannot develop by human convention as the establishment of a convention presupposes the use of language. Though he never refers to children, his account closely parallels the steps of language acquisition in children. In *The Book of Letters* he explains in detail how ostension or pointing gives rise to linguistic conventions as gestures too can be a mode of communication. Gestures originally indicate whom one is addressing and pointing to sensible things indicates the objects of the communication. At some stages gestures get linked to specific articulate sounds. Al-Fārābī explains how steps in the development of a specific language lead to parallel steps in the development of the linguistic arts and logical disciplines (Druart 2010: 8–12). Al-Fārābī's explanation of the development of language clearly implies that language is not of divine origin.

On the other hand, in the first chapter of his *De interpretatione of the Shifā'* Ibn Sīnā speaks of the dispute about whether language develops by human convention or results from divine teaching but does not take a position. I. Madkour thinks that maybe he favors the human conventional origin since even if we postulate that language is taught by a first teacher, this teacher will need a convention and an agreement from those who will use the language he is teaching (Avicenna 1970: 10). In this chapter, Ibn Sīnā also speaks of the relation between sensible things, intelligibles or intentions, utterances, and script. In the footsteps of Aristotle and al-Fārābī he considers that intelligibles are common to all human beings, as are the sensible objects, but utterances and scripts vary. Ibn Sīnā was Persian and, therefore, bilingual, so one may well find this view rather puzzling. Yet, Ibn Sīnā is one of the few philosophers at the time to reflect on what he calls "vain" intelligibles, i.e. intelligibles of non-existent beings, such as the phoenix, which do not correspond to any sensible object (Michot 1985, 1987), but he limits his reflections to their epistemic and ontological status without addressing how they fit his views on language (Black 1997; Druart 2012).

The far ranging influence of the philosophers and logicians on some theologians is particularly striking in al-Ghazālī's treatise on *The Ninety-Nine Beautiful Names of God*, as in this text al-Ghazālī wishes to convince believers to meditate on the traditional ninety-nine beautiful names of God. Philosophical views on logic arise even in his spiritual texts. The first three chapters are dedicated to philosophical reflections on naming and are followed by a detailed analysis of each of the ninety-nine names. In the introductory chapters al-Ghazālī indicates that the utterances or words are posited by human choice to signify concrete particulars (al-Ghazālī 1971: 19) and, therefore, does not hesitate to adopt the philosophers' view that languages originate in human convention. Though bilingual he too follows rather uncritically the position that not only the concrete individuals but also the intelligibles or universals are common to all human beings whereas the utterances differ from language to language. He integrates this view into his presentation of three levels of existence which help him to argue against various other positions that the name, the thing named, and the act of naming are distinct. "Things have existence in individuals, in language, or in minds." He applies this claim to "man":

> How could these beings fail to be distinguished from one another, given the properties associated with each of them which are not connected with the other? Insofar as man, for example, exists as an individual, sleeping and waking, living and dead ... are all associated with him. But in so far as man exists in minds, subject and predicate, general and specific, universal and particular ... are associated with it. And insofar as man exists in language, Arabic or Persian or Turkish are associated with it ... whether it be a noun, a verb, or a particle, and the like. This existence is something which can differ from time to time, and also vary according to the usage of countries, whereas existence in individuals and in the mind never varies with time or with nations.
>
> (al-Ghazālī 1992: 7, Burrell & Daher tr. mod.)

Al-Ghazālī also suggests that one could add to the traditional distinction between words posited by first imposition and those by second imposition a class of words posited by third imposition if nouns may be identified as either definite or indefinite. Al-Ghazālī's detailed study of naming, very peripatetic in its approach to semantics, surprises the reader. Not only is it a preface to a spiritual practical guidebook for meditation on God's ninety-nine names but it goes far beyond what is needed for treating divine names. Further, in a recent article T. Kukkonen (2010) argues that it is ill suited to treat of the divine names and so is not even very helpful for al-Ghazālī's purpose in this treatise.

Since philosophy of language was not yet a specific philosophical discipline, interesting reflections on language crop up in unusual contexts. The issue of the undesignated individual is explored by Ibn Sīnā reflecting on language acquisition in children in the *Physics* of the *Shifā'* as he expands on Aristotle's famous statement in *Physics* I, 1, 184b11–12 "a child begins by calling all men father, and all women mother, but later on distinguishes each of them" (Aristotle 1984, Hardie & Gaye tr.). Ibn Bājja addresses this same issue in non-logical texts but this time as it was raised by Galen reflecting on animal behavior. The generality of the undesignated individual puts it in some way in the uncharted territory of the borderline between universal and designated individual and may explain why Aristotle raises it in using a feature of still childish and undeveloped speech while Galen, as understood by Ibn Bájja, raises it in reflecting on the behavior of an animal looking for water.

Ibn Sīná explains that "What is understood from the utterance 'vague individual' in the primary meaning is that it is some individual from among individuals of the species to which it belongs, without it being specified what condition it is in or which individual it is—and 'some man' and 'some woman' are [utterances] of this sort" (Black 2012; her tr. mod.; Arabic Avicenna 2009: 9.9). For Ibn Sīná, in its epistemological function, the vague individual explains how the senses chronologically move from an indeterminate grasp of their objects to greater precision. As Black puts it, "For Avicenna, then, the vague individual is an *image* which represents a random token of a determinate type or species without differentiating it from other individuals sharing the same specific form" (Black 2012: 264).

The same description of the undetermined individual applies to the phenomenon Ibn Bájja refers to in one of his main works, *The Regime of the Solitary*. He points out that any being that is very thirsty does not desire a designated quantity of water but any quantity of water—or, more accurately, simply water—and so focuses on the species rather than on the designated particular. According to him, this explains why Galen claimed that beasts grasp the species and, therefore, the universals (Ibn Bájja 2010: 170, n. 187, pp. 334–5). He develops this view in his very brief *Treatise on the Agent Intellect* in the third way to establish the existence of the agent intellect. There he tells us the following:

> the imaginative faculty by means of which an animal desires neither looks for one and the same water nor for one and the same food as it happens in the case of a friend looking for his friend or a father for his child. Rather the animal searches for what is universal to any bit of water. This explains why Galen mistakenly thought that donkeys grasp in a universal manner, according to what he says at the beginning of his *De methodo medendi*. Galen and anyone who is not well educated thinks that imagination is part of the intellect.
>
> (Ibn Bájja 1968: 108)

Clearly Ibn Bájja is contrasting the undesignated particular, which is more general, with the designated particular. As he knows Aristotle's *Physics* well, one may wonder whether the example of the father fully aware of the individuality of his child is not a deliberate contrast to Aristotle's example of the child not yet able to distinguish his own father from all other male human beings. Ibn Bájja refers to a specific passage in Galen—which in fact he does not fully understand—in order to claim that Galen makes of imagination a part of intellect. His second criticism of Galen's view is rather amusing:

> Besides, we should consider what we find in any animal which does not live in isolation, such as cranes, pigeons, ganga cata birds, and those that resemble them as in some way they grasp the universal. Such grasp is not possible for

> this domestic animal [the donkey], but is more clear and evident in the case of these [birds living in groups].
>
> (Ibn Bájja 1968: 108)

Clearly for Ibn Bájjá social life is sign of a greater cognitive ability and, therefore, a grasp of something more akin to the universal, even if it does not really reach its level. Ibn Sīná had argued that perception of the undesignated particular was a poor grasp of the individual, whereas Ibn Bájja considers it as a progress towards the universal. In his psychology, Ibn Bájja gives great importance to the inner senses and, therefore, introduces spiritual forms which are an intermediary between the sensible forms grasped by direct sensory perception and the intelligible forms grasped by the intellect. There are different species of spiritual forms ordered hierarchically and, therefore, some are closer to intelligible forms that can be grasped only universally.

Conclusion

Much work still remains to be done in the study of Arabic logic and its development, particularly in its non-Aristotelian and post-classical aspects. There also is still much more to be done in philosophy of language, but what is already known shows that innovative thinking went on well beyond the classical period.

Further Reading

El-Rouayheb, K. (2011) "Logic in the Arabic and Islamic World," in H. Lagerlund (ed.), *Encyclopedia of Medieval Philosophy. Philosophy Between 500 and 1500*, vol. I, Dordrecht: Springer, pp. 686–92.

——. (2012) "Post-Avicennan Logicians on the Subject Matter of Logic: Some Thirteenth- and Fourteenth-Century Discussions," *Arabic Sciences and Philosophy* 22: 69–90.

Ighbariah, A. (2012) "Between Logic and Mathematics: Al-Kindī's Approach to the Aristotelian Categories," *Arabic Sciences and Philosophy* 22: 51–68.

Roccaro, G. (2012) "Universabilità e analogia: metafisica e logica nel pensiero islamico," in A. Musco (ed.), *Universabilità della Ragione. Plurabilità delle Filosofie nel Medioevo*, vol. III, *Orientalia*, Palermo: Officina di Studi Medievali.

Street, T. (2013) "Avicenna on the syllogism," in P. Adamson (ed.), *Interpreting Avicenna: Critical Essays*, Cambridge: Cambridge University Press.

Thom, P. (2011) "On Formalizing the Logics of the Past," in M. Cameron & J. Marenbon (eds.), *Methods and Methodologies: Aristotelian Logic East and West, 500–1500*, Leiden: Brill, pp. 191–206.

References

al-Fārābī (1949) *Ihsā' al'ulūm. La statistique des sciences*, O. Amine (ed.), Cairo: Dar El-Fikr El-Arabi.

——. (1960) *Alfarabi's Commentary on Aristotle's Peri Hermeneias (De interpretatione)*, W. Kutsch & S. Marrow (eds.), Beirut: Imprimerie Catholique.

——. (1964) *Al-Farabi's The Political Regime*, F. Najjar (ed.), Beirut: Imprimerie Catholique.

——. (1969) *Alfarabi's Book of Letters*, M. Mahdi (ed.), Beirut: Dar el-Mashreq.

——. (1981) *Al-Farabi's Commentary and Short Treatise on Aristotle's De interpretatione*, F. W. Zimmermann (tr.), London: The British Academy.
——. (1983) "Treatise of refutation of Galen about what is missing from Aristotle's *Parts of the Human Beings*," in A. Badawi (ed.), *Traités philosophiques par al-Kindī, al-Fārābī, Ibn Bājjah, Ibn 'Adyy*, Beirut: Dār Al-Andalus.
al-Ghazālī (1971) *Al-Maqsad al-Asnā fī sharh ma'ānī asmā' Allāh al-husnā*, F. Shehadi (ed.), Beirut: Dar el-Machreq.
——. (1992) *The Ninety-Nine Beautiful Names of God*, D. Burrell & N. Daher (tr.), Cambridge: The Islamic Texts Society.
Aristotle (1984) *The Complete Works of Aristotle: The Revised Oxford Translation*, J. Barnes (ed.), Princeton: Princeton University Press.
Avicenna (1952) *Al-Shifā'. La logique, 1. L'Isagoge*, I. Madkour, M. El-Khodeiri, G. Anawati & F. El-Ahwani (eds.), Cairo: Imprimerie Nationale.
——. (1970) *Al-Shifā'. La logique, 3. De l'Interprétation*, N. El-Khodeiri (ed.) & I. Madkour (intro.), Cairo: Dar el-katib al-'arabi.
——. (2005) *The Metaphysics of The Healing*, M. Marmura (tr.), Provo, UT: Brigham Young University.
——. (2009) *The Physics of the Healing*, 2 vols., J. McGinnis (tr.), Provo, UT: Brigham Young University.
Bertolacci, A. (2011) "The 'Ontoligization' of Logic. Metaphysical Themes in Avicenna's Reworking of the *Organon*," in M. Cameron & J. Marenbon (eds.), *Methods and Methodologies: Aristotelian Logic East and West, 500–1500*, Leiden: Brill, pp. 27–51.
Black, D. (1990) *Logic and Aristotle's* Rhetoric *and* Poetics *in Medieval Arabic Philosophy*, Leiden: Brill.
——. (1992) "Aristotle's 'Peri hermeneias' in Medieval Latin and Arabic Philosophy: Logic and the Linguistic Arts," *Canadian Journal of Philosophy* Supplementary 17: 25–83.
——. (1997) "Avicenna on the Ontological and Epistemic Status of Fictional Beings," *Documenti e Studi* 8: 425–53.
——. (2012) "Avicenna's 'Vague Individual' and Its Impact on Medieval Latin Philosophy," in R. Wisnovsky, F. Wallis, J. C. Fumo & C. Fraenkel (eds.), *Vehicles of Transmission, Translation, and Transformation in Medieval Textual Culture*, Turnhout: Brepols, pp. 259–92.
Brethren of Purity (2010) *On Logic, Epistles 10–14*, C. Baffioni (ed. and tr.), Oxford: Oxford University Press.
Diebler, S. (2005) "Catégories, conversation et philosophie chez al-Fārābī," in O. Bruun & L. Corti (eds.), *Les catégories et leur histoire*, Paris: Vrin, pp. 275–305.
Druart, T-A. (2007a) "Al-Fārābī, the Categories, Metaphysics, and *The Book of Letters*," *Medioevo* 32: 15–37.
——. (2007b) "Islam and Christianity: One Divine and Human Language or Many Human Languages," *Journal of Religion and Society* 9: 1–13.
——. (2010) "Al-Fārābī: An Arabic Account of the Origin of Language and of Philosophical Vocabulary," *Proceedings of the American Catholic Philosophical Association* 84: 1–17.
——. (2012) "Avicennan Troubles: The Mysteries of the Heptagonal House and of the Phoenix," *Tópicos, Revista de Filosofía* 42: 51–73.
El-Rouayheb, K. (2004) "Sunni Muslim Scholars on the Status of Logic, 1500–1800," *Islamic Law and Society* 11, 2: 213–32.
——. (2005) "Was There a Revival of Logical Studies in Eighteenth-Century Egypt?," *Die Welt des Islam* 45, 1: 1–19.
——. (2010) *Relational Syllogisms and the History of Arabic Logic, 900–1900*, Leiden: Brill.
Hasnaoui, A. (1988) "Les théories du langage dans la pensée arabo-musulmane," in M. A. Sinaceur (ed.), *Aristote aujourd'hui*, Paris: Erès.

Heemskerk, M. (2000) *Suffering in the Muʿtazilite Theology: ʿAbd al-Jabbār's Teaching on Pain and Divine Justice*, Brill: Leiden.
Ibn Bājja (Avempace) (1968) *Opera metaphysica*, M. Fakhry (ed.), Beirut: Dar an-Nahar.
——. (1994) *Taʿālīq ʿalā mantiq al-Fārābī*, M. Fakhry (ed.), Beirut: Dār al-Mashriq.
——. (2010) *La conduit de l'isolé et deux autres épîtres*, C. Genequand (tr.), Paris: Vrin.
Ibn Taymiyya (1993) *Against the Greek Logicians*, W. B. Hallaq (tr.), Oxford: Clarendon Press.
Kukkonen, T. (2010) "Al-Ghazālī on the Signification of Names," *Vivarium* 48: 55–74.
Lameer, J. (1994) *Al-Fārābī and Aristotelian Syllogistics: Greek Theory and Islamic Practice*, Leiden: Brill.
——. (1996) "The *Organon* of Aristotle in the Medieval Oriental and Occidental Tradition," *Journal of the American Oriental Society* 116: 90–8.
Menn, S. (2008) "Al-Fārābī's *Kitāb al-Hurūf* and his Analysis of the Senses of Being," *Arabic Sciences and Philosophy* 18: 59–97.
Michot, Y. (J.) (1985) "Avicenna's 'Letter on the Disappearance of the Vain Intelligibles after Death'," *Bulletin de Philosophie médiévale* 27: 94–102.
——. (1987) "'L'Epître sur la disparition des formes intelligibles vaines après la mort' d'Avicenne," *Bulletin de Philosophie médiévale* 29: 152–65.
Newmyer, S. (2011) *Animals in Greek and Roman Thought: A Source Book*, London: Routledge.
Rescher, N. (1963) *Studies in the History of Arabic Logic*, Pittsburgh: University of Pittsburgh Press.
——. (1964) *The Development of Arabic Logic*, Pittsburgh: University of Pittsburgh Press.
Sorabji, R. (1993) *Animal Minds & Human Morals*, Ithaca, NY: Cornell University Press.
——. (2004) *The Philosophy of the Commentators, 200–600 AD: A Sourcebook*, vol. 3, *Logic and Metaphysics*, London: Duckworth.
Street, T. (2004) "Arabic Logic," in D. Gabbay & J. Woods (eds.), *Handbook of the History of Logic, vol. 1: Greek, Indian and Arabic Logic*, Amsterdam: Elsevier, pp. 471–556.
——. (2005) "Logic," in P. Adamson & R. C. Taylor (eds.), *The Cambridge Companion to Arabic Philosophy*, Cambridge: Cambridge University Press, pp. 247–65.
——. (2008) "Arabic and Islamic Philosophy of Language and Logic," in *Stanford Encyclopedia of Philosophy*, http://plato.standford.edu/entries/arabic-islamic-language/

7
RHETORIC, POETICS, AND THE *ORGANON*

Terence Kleven

Introduction

The Prophet of Islam had given his followers a book and it was their responsibility to learn its teachings and to determine how these teachings were to be practiced in the various political and religious contexts into which they were introduced. The internal conversations within the Islamic community regarding what constituted right teaching and right law led to the development of various schools of thought, both theological and legal. Therefore, within the community there was need for rigorous learning if one was to persuade others of the best understanding of Islam. Moreover, by the time of the emergence of Islam, the Hindus, the Persians and the Greeks, to name the most prominent peoples for the Middle East, had long-standing philosophic traditions, and the wisdom they provided in the study of medicine, physics, and logic, amongst other subjects, could not easily be avoided if scholars of Islam were to articulate Islam's unique teachings with credibility. The Greeks, in particular, had been the most vigorous source of philosophic and scientific learning for the Middle East, especially the books of Plato and Aristotle. Thus, scholars of the Islamic community turned to various sciences in Greek philosophy for assistance, whether it was rhetoric to articulate the meaning of the Qur'ān and *ḥadīth*, poetry to praise or blame an action, idea, or person, dialectic to refute false teaching, physics to understand natural laws, or medicine to cure the ill. To be sure, there was much debate over what subjects of Greek philosophy were legally acceptable within Islam. Among the sciences, logic, as articulated in Aristotle's *Organon* or "instrument" of knowledge, occupied a key position because it was, or at least claimed to be, the instrument of all the sciences and of all knowledge. As an instrument it was not obviously controversial, if used for the right purposes, and it could be helpful in distinguishing true from false opinions. It was necessary, however, to know what logic was, and there was more than one opinion on the matter. One particular question that emerged in this inquiry of the nature and scope of logic was which books of Aristotle actually constituted his "instrument" of study. Aristotle's *Rhetoric* and *Poetics* were included as two of the syllogistic arts by some ancient and medieval scholars and excluded by others. Classical Islamic philosophy devoted considerable attention to the place of these two books among the logical arts, and thus the title of this chapter introduces a topic for inquiry that is forcefully present in Islamic philosophy. The purpose of this chapter is to articulate the reasoning on the basis of which two of the finest Arabic philosophers—al-Fārābī and Ibn Rushd (Averroes)—included rhetoric and poetry in the corpus of logical arts in the Islamic world.

The Inclusion of the *Rhetoric* and the *Poetics* in the *Organon*

In his introductory book, the *Letter with Which the Book Begins* (*Risāla ṣudira bi-hā al-kitāb*), to his series of commentaries on Aristotle's *Organon*, al-Fārābī presents the art of logic as composed of five syllogistic arts. These five arts are philosophy, dialectic, sophistry, rhetoric and poetry. He says that although practical arts such as medicine and farming may use syllogisms to bring out some of their parts, they are not syllogistic arts because their actions and ends are the doing of physical actions and not the use of syllogisms alone. The syllogistic arts have as their action and end an intellectual activity, not the movement of limbs as in the practical or political arts. Key in this is that syllogisms are used in discoursing with one another or in an individual's bringing out something to philosophical clarity in one's own mind. Thus, philosophy is distinguished from the other syllogistic arts because it uses syllogisms in both ways, while the four remaining arts use syllogisms only in discoursing with others (al-Fārābī 1957: 225.13–226.8).

In this introductory *Letter*, al-Fārābī describes these five arts as five species of discourse; the actual word he uses is *mukhāṭaba*, "rhetoric," which is from the same root as the word used for the name of the fourth syllogistic art. "Philosophical discourse" seeks to teach and to make known the things about which there is certitude (*yaqīn*); it is also known as "demonstration" (*burhān*). Dialectical discourse seeks to persuade or overcome the interlocutor in the things that are generally accepted opinions. Sophistical discourse seeks to overcome the interlocutor in things by way of making him think that something is true when it is not. Rhetorical discourse (literally "rhetorical rhetoric") seeks to persuade by satisfying the soul of the hearer in what generally accepted opinions may be true but which have not been proven to be the case. Poetical discourse seeks to imitate a thing and to imagine it in speech, and, although the imitation is not true, it must be probable and must resemble life. Thus, al-Fārābī formulates on the basis of Aristotle's eight books of the longer *Organon* his own account of the syllogistic arts; in al-Fārābī's series of 11 books, including two introductory books and a commentary on Porphyry's *Eisagoge*, he presents a unity of purpose in Aristotle's *Organon*. Rhetorical and poetical syllogisms are presented as two of the five syllogistic arts and therefore are parts of logic (al-Fārābī 1957: 226.6–24).

But what is a syllogism and why does it matter if the arts of rhetoric and poetry are syllogistic or not? Al-Fārābī writes, "The syllogism is a discourse in which more than one thing is posited, and if they are conjoined, then another different thing follows from them necessarily, that is, essentially and not by accident" (al-Fārābī 1986: 19.8–9). The two premises need a connection, a middle term, which creates what follows and causes the two premises to be productive of knowledge. The achievement of

Aristotle's logic is the analysis of the connection between two premises, and logic is the varied interplay that can exist between two premises and the ways in which knowledge follows necessarily. The Arabic word for "syllogism" is *qiyās*; it also means "analogy" because it draws an analogy between two things. The study of the five syllogistic arts is, thus, a study of the range of coherent connections or analogies between two premises which produce a necessary conclusion. These connections and analogies exist in all coherent thought whether we are aware of them or not. Al-Fārābī argues that rhetoric and poetry participate in the production of these necessary conclusions. The same definition of syllogism is also found in Ibn Sīnā (Avicenna 1964: 54) and Ibn Rushd (Averroes 1983: 65).

Al-Fārābī rearticulates his account of the five syllogistic arts in his book *The Utterances Employed in Logic*. We quote only one of several formulations of the five arts of logic in this book, a formulation in which he calls each of them a "guidance of the mind" in respect to truth. He writes:

> The types of guidance of the mind are several. One [type] of guidance of the mind is for the thing by which a certain method causes guidance by poetical things. Another [type] of the guidance is for the thing with respect to its guidance by generally accepted statements and the statements by which man is praised or blamed. Examples of these are those in which there is guidance by disputatious speeches, and rebukes, and accusation and apology, and what is of this genus. This type is the rhetorical guidance. Another [type] of the guidance of the mind is for the sophistical things which are mentioned in it. Another [type] of guidance is for the thing according to the way of dialectic. And there is the [type of] guidance for what is certain truth.
>
> (al-Fārābī 1968: 96.7–13)

This "guidance" of the mind, or the "governance" the mind receives, derives from the five logical or syllogistic arts. Each is an intellectual activity. Although al-Fārābī says that "The highest intention of the art of logic is the discernment of demonstrations" (al-Fārābī 1968: 99.13–14), this demonstration is only obtained through the mastery of all five syllogistic arts which entails the identification of the arguments, that is, the syllogisms pertaining to each. Therefore, al-Fārābī speaks definitively of the common purpose of all the five syllogistic arts in defense of the unity of the expanded *Organon*. Thus as we see in this text, the emphasis on the five syllogistic arts is found in more than one of his books. Along with the *Rhetoric* and the *Poetics*, al-Fārābī includes Porphyry's *Eisagoge* as one of the introductory books of the *Organon*, even if two of his own books precede it.

To be sure, this seemingly novel inclusion of the books of *Rhetoric* and *Poetry*, as well as Porphyry's *Eisagoge*, with Aristotle's logical writings is not the only account of Aristotle's *Organon*. European and North American publications of Aristotle's *Organon* have, for some time, only incorporated six books as essential to logic proper: the *Categories*, *De Interpretatione*, the *Prior* and *Posterior Analytics*, the *Topics* and the *Sophistical Refutations*. However, Walzer has shown that certain Alexandrian Greek writers such as Ammonius also included the *Rhetoric* and *Poetics* (Walzer 1934, republished in 1962; and Black 1990: 17–51). This expanded *Organon* is also found throughout the major figures of the Islamic philosophic tradition, al-Kindī, Ibn Sīnā, Ibn Bājja, and Ibn Rushd.

So why did al-Fārābī and Ibn Rushd, among others, include rhetoric and poetry as two of the five syllogistic arts constituting the art of logic? There are at least three *aporia* or questions that must be addressed in reply to this question.

1 Are the actions and ends of the arts of rhetoric and poetry knowledge rather than political or practical action? Or, to reformulate the question slightly, since the Greek as well as the Arabic-speaking philosophers were aware that nothing ever comes from nothing, and, thus, the art of demonstration could not emerge from nothing, are these two arts essential parts of logic and of demonstration because their actions and ends are the same as demonstration? Or in contrast, if rhetoric and poetry are separate from logic, would these arts be vacuous, that is, nothing, if they seek some supposed "eloquent" or "creative" end while their expressions are incoherent?
2 In regard to the specific nature of rhetoric with its premises taken from the generally accepted opinions of a people, is it a necessary art to which the philosopher must attend because of the power of opinions of the public to govern thought and action for either good or ill?
3 In regard to the specific nature of poetry, is poetry, with its imaginative imitation of the good, true and beautiful in likely stories and probable myths, also necessary in order to distinguish between truth and falsity?

Here we focus on two of the most important figures in the Arabic philosophical tradition, al-Fārābī and Ibn Rushd. In our examination of their texts, our intention is to explain the cogency of arguments to include rhetoric and poetry as syllogistic arts because of the intellectual content of these arts. Furthermore, although these scholars write in Arabic and are Muslims, their aim is to show that the rules of rhetoric and poetry which were articulated by Classical Greek philosophy in general and by Aristotle in particular are transferable to the practice of these arts in an Arabic-speaking and Islamic world.

Rhetoric

Rhetoric is, according to al-Fārābī in *The Book of Rhetoric* (*Kitāb al-Khaṭāba*), "a syllogistic art, whose aim is persuasion in all the ten genera, and that which is obtained in these things is in the soul of the hearer and whose persuasion is the ultimate aim of the actions of rhetoric" (al-Fārābī 1971: 31.3–5). Persuasion is a particular supposition (*ẓann*) and supposition is, in general, the belief (*'i'tiqād*) that a thing is such and not otherwise, but it is possible that it is otherwise in its essence (al-Fārābī 1971: 31.6–8). "Persuasion" here means "contentment," contentment caused in the hearer (al-Fārābī 1971: 33.1–6). In order to clarify the nature of rhetorical supposition, he explains that supposition is a species of opinion.

> Supposition and certainty have in common that each of them is an opinion, and opinion is the belief in a thing that it is such and not otherwise. This

> [opinion] is like the genus for them and they are its species. And the propositions which are in this genus are opinions and they are rhetorical, some of them are necessary and some of them are possible.
>
> (al-Fárábī 1971: 33.7–9)

Thus, the rhetorician identifies generally accepted opinions which are unexamined and he seeks to cause satisfaction or assent (*taṣdīq*) to certain opinions over other opinions. The causes of certainty of a topic are such that the public may not understand them, and thus for the public true and certain opinions are indistinguishable from those which are less certain or even fanciful. Rhetoric properly employed seeks to cause the acceptance of opinions which are known to be certain or which are nearer to certainty than other opinions, even if the public does not initially assent to them. Thus rhetoric is a rationalizing of the opinions for the public, even if only in a moderate and limited way.

According to al-Fárābī, the two methods of reasoning in rhetoric are enthymemes and comparisons, both types of syllogisms. "The enthymeme (*ḍamīr*) is a statement composed of two combined premises which is used by the omission of one of the two combined premises, and it is called an enthymeme because it is used by hiding (*yuḍmiru*) some of its premises and not declaring them" (al-Fárābī 1971: 62.4–6). Even more than the Greek term *enthumēma*, which means "a thought, piece of reasoning, or argument" (Liddell and Scott 1889), the Arabic indicates that a premise needed for a complete syllogism is hidden. It is not missing because of neglect nor because it is self-evident, but because the public would not apprehend the premise. The enthymeme is persuasive because a premise is hidden and the syllogism is not demonstrative, but the syllogism is not formulated with complete disregard for the demonstrative syllogism because the relation between the hidden premise and a demonstrative premise is known at least by the philosophical rhetorician.

The comparison (*tamthīl*) seeks to verify the existence of one thing by the existence of another thing because the two resemble each other in some way (al-Fárābī 1971: 63.10–11). Al-Fárābī says that the public call the comparison a "syllogism" (*qiyās*) or "analogy" and al-Fárābī accepts the syllogistic nature of the comparison. The comparison is less persuasive than the enthymeme because the comparison compares only two individual things and therefore the comparison is limited because it may not apply to anything other than to the specific things. The enthymeme possesses at least a measure of universality in its premises and therefore is more persuasive than comparison. Elsewhere, al-Fárābī explains that "The rank of the enthymeme in rhetoric is like the rank of the demonstration in the sciences and the rank of syllogisms in dialectic" (al-Fárābī 1971: 68.8–9). Although in this statement there is no indication that the ranks of the three arts are identical, the comparison shows the similarity of the enthymeme to dialectical and demonstrative syllogisms, thus indicating that rhetoric participates in the syllogistic arts.

Both religious and political life is governed by "beliefs" or "opinions" of what is good. Rhetoric is the syllogistic art which examines these beliefs and which seeks to persuade the hearers that some opinions are more satisfying than other opinions. Rhetoric can argue either side of a position and for this reason rhetoric may be sophistical. This sophistry takes place if the purpose of the rhetoric is undetermined and rhetoric is deliberately used for obfuscation, for the promotion of ideology, or for tyrannical control. Moreover, if rhetoric is purposefully limited only to political discourse, the question of the justice of one argument over another may not be asked and the art becomes a technique which may not serve a just end. If, on the other hand, the rhetoric is syllogistic and therefore the philosophical rhetorician is aware of what is hidden in the enthymeme, and the rhetoric is used for just or reasonable purposes, then rhetoric is not simply a technique. Religion manifests itself publicly as opinion, as does politics, and this leads to the conclusion that rhetoric is the art that is most appropriate to the study of theology (*kalām*), tradition (*ḥadīth*), jurisprudence (*fiqh*), and Qur'ān, even if it is the art which is often neglected by *kalām* but which would be immediately salutary to the improvements of its arguments. In neither politics nor religion does al-Fārābī limit rhetoric to the practical order for the regulation of the actions of the body. The art of rhetoric examines opinions, even if in the form of belief, in order to encourage opinions that lead to knowledge. Thus, despite rhetoric's usefulness in the improvement of the life of the community of the city, it never loses its place as a logical or intellectual art.

Ibn Rushd's account of rhetoric is similar to al-Fārābī's; Ibn Rushd includes the arts of rhetoric and poetry in the *Organon*. In his *Short Commentary on Aristotle's Rhetoric*, Ibn Rushd defines rhetoric in the following way: "Since we have finished speaking about dialectical syllogisms and the extent of assent they provide, let us speak about persuasive things and the extent of assent they provide. It is apparent that persuasion is a kind of probable supposition which the soul trusts, despite its awareness of an opposing consideration" (Averroes 1977: 164.4–7; Butterworth tr. 63). The purpose of the rhetorical art is a persuasion which produces a kind of probable supposition (*ẓann*). Although Ibn Rushd includes in this commentary a discussion of what he calls "external things" which influence persuasion, for example, oaths and testimonies, he focuses most of his attention on "arguments used in public speaking" which fall into two classes: examples and proofs. Of these, the latter are enthymemes, that is, they are a type of syllogism. The enthymeme actually is of higher rank than examples because with examples each of the two entities being compared may not be more universal than the other. Thus, because there is no mental movement between universal and particular, and there is no knowledge produced, it is not a demonstratively conclusive speech. The enthymeme, in contrast, may be conclusive because one or more of the terms may be universal.

For Ibn Rushd, "the enthymeme is a syllogism leading to a conclusion which corresponds to unexamined opinion previously existing among all or most people. Unexamined common opinion is opinion which strikes a man as a probable supposition and which he trusts as soon as it occurs to him" (Averroes 1977: 63–4). This unexamined opinion (*bādī' al-ra'y*) is an opinion which strikes one as a probable supposition (*ẓann*) once the rhetorical argument is heard. In this formulation, probable supposition is a species of the genus "opinion" and thus Ibn Rushd's philosophical terminology is identical to al-Fārābī's (Butterworth 1997). The public hold generally accepted opinions about which the rhetorician needs to be aware. These opinions are of various kinds: some are actually certain and knowable, although as yet they are unrecognized as such. Others are probable and the rhetorician constructs his speech to affirm this probability and to make the opinion a probable supposition. Yet other species of opinions are false or uncertain. In order to cause assent to probable suppositions, the rhetorician may use either the forms or the matter of an argument, that is, either a particular figure of the syllogism or the premises. Thus, his argument is syllogistic and causes an intellectual assent to a supposition.

This account is reiterated and expanded in Ibn Rushd's *Middle Commentary on the* Rhetoric *of Aristotle*. The enthymeme is the pillar of this art. He writes:

> Any of those who have spoken of this art from amongst our predecessors have not spoken concerning a thing which takes place in this art as the necessary part and the matter by which it is more properly an art. And this is the matter by which rhetorical assent takes place, particularly the syllogisms which are called in this art enthymeme and are the pillar of the assent fostered by this art, I mean that which is first and by essence.
>
> (Averroes 2002: II, 2.16–21)

Lest we make a mistake about the nature of this syllogism, Ibn Rushd clarifies the place of the enthymeme among the logical arts: "The enthymeme is a species of syllogism and the cognizance of syllogism is part of the art of logic. It is necessary therefore that the logician investigates this art, either in totality or parts of it" (Averroes 2002: II, 7.13–15). Examples, as well as the external things, are included in his discussion in this substantial commentary, but they are of secondary place in relation to the syllogism. Ibn Rushd continues in the tradition of al-Fārābī in arguing that rhetoric is a syllogistic art.

In conclusion, according to both al-Fārābī and Ibn Rushd rhetoric is the art that is used in persuasion of the public. The rhetorician uses one or more premises that are generally accepted opinions, even though they are unexamined and unproven, at least not yet, in order to persuade the public that certain opinions are more reasonable than others. As a logical art, rhetoric is a rationalization, even if only partial, of the common opinions of a people. It may also be an elucidation of what is rational in opinions but which is not identified as such. Rhetoric is useful for instruction and harmonization of the political order inasmuch as it is used in public address, legal matters and in conversation with others. Rhetoric is also useful for the clarification of religious truths and for the instruction of the public in religious teaching through sermons, prayers and conversation. At the same time, rhetoric is a philosophical art because the careful selection of terms and premises is necessary for the discovery through syllogisms of right conclusions. These two representatives of Arabic philosophy, al-Fārābī and Ibn Rushd, show the significance of the rhetorical art for all aspects of Islamic civilization.

Poetry

"Poetical rhetoric (*al-mukhāṭaba al-shi'riya*) seeks the representation (*muḥākāh*) of a thing and the imitation (*takhyīl*) of it in speech," according to al-Fārābī in his introductory *Letter* (al-Fārābī 1957: 226.17–18). As noted earlier, he says all of the other four syllogistic arts—philosophical, dialectical, sophistical and rhetorical—are types of rhetoric, and now he states that the fifth syllogistic art is poetical rhetoric (al-Fārābī 1957: 226.17–18). Moreover, although the art of poetry is a syllogistic art, it occupies a unique relation to the other syllogistic arts. He writes: "The relation of the art of poetry to the rest of the syllogistic arts is like the relation of the action of sculpture to the rest of the practical arts, and like the relation of the playing of chess to the skillful conduct of armies" (al-Fārābī 1957: 226.19–21). The art of poetry is unique in relation to the other arts because it is analogical with them, that is, it imitates the actions and ends of the other syllogistic arts. Still, the imitation of these actions and ends in poetry is neither less serious nor less important than the learning of the actions and ends in the other syllogistic arts.

In the context of discerning truth and falsity in his *A Letter on the Canons of the Art of Poetry* (*Risāla fī Quwānīn Ṣanā'a al-Shu'arā'*) (al-Fārābī 1938), al-Fārābī carefully distinguishes between sophistry and imaginative imitation by stating that the intentions of the two arts are different. Whereas sophistry seeks to delude the hearer into thinking that he is listening to a contrary proposition when in fact he is not, imitation seeks to cause the hearer to imagine a similar though not a contrary proposition (al-Fārābī 1938: 267–8). That poetry is an imitative art does not make it any less an intellectual art. In another passage, he goes on to show the relation of the syllogistic arts to each other.

> Statements are either absolutely true, or absolutely false, or mainly true and partly false, or the reverse of this, or true and false in equal proportions. The absolutely true statement is called demonstrative; that which is mainly true dialectical; that which is equally true and false, rhetorical; that which has truth in a small part, sophistical; that which is wholly false, poetical. It is proved from this division that poetical discourse is neither demonstration, nor dialectic, nor rhetoric, nor sophistry, but for all this it belongs to one of the species of syllogism or what follows from a syllogism. By my statement that it follows [the syllogism], I mean that induction, examples, intuition and what resembles them have their power as the power of a syllogism.
>
> (Averroes 1938: 268.11–18; Arberry tr. mod. 274)

Here al-Fārābī articulates the nature of the five syllogistic arts in relation to true and false statements, and although poetry is composed of false statements, because it has the force of a syllogism or analogy, it still is one of the syllogistic arts.

Al-Fārābī clarifies his intention in this book by explaining that there are three types of poets. The first type possesses a natural gift for composing and reciting poetry. These poets are not acquainted with the art of poetry, but are confined to their natural dispositions. They are not called "syllogizing" poets because, as he says, "they lack the perfection of vision and the grounding in the art" (Averroes 1938: 271.4; Arberry tr. 277). The second type of poet is one who knows the art fully and who excels in similes and images; he is properly said to be "syllogizing." The third class consists in those poets who imitate either one of the first two types of poets without having any poetical disposition or understanding of the canons of the art. Errors are frequent in this third type. It is also possible that a poet is good at a certain type of poetry, either by disposition or by studying the art, but he is required to write a different type of poetry. Yet the finest type of poetry is what is composed with a natural disposition (*ṭab'*) and is not written by compulsion. Although al-Fārābī recognizes the place of natural disposition in good poetry, the best poets are those who also know the art (al-Fārābī 1938: 271).

The imitation is called syllogizing because it compares two objects which are similar to one another. In al-Fārābī's vocabulary, "syllogism" (*qiyās*) is the same word as "analogy" (*qiyās*). The poet will compare A with B and B with C and in this sequence he impresses on the hearer the idea that there is knowledge to be learned about A and C. The imitation produces in the senses and the imagination the nature of the resemblance between two objects. Al-Fārābī acknowledges, however, that this resemblance in the hands of a skillful poet may not be as close as what first appears, for the intention may be to compare two objects which are different from one another and the striking comparison causes us to see the objects differently. In a recent formulation by T. S. Eliot on the use of metaphor in the metaphysical English poets, he says: "But a degree of heterogeneity of material compelled into unity by the operation of the poet's mind is omnipresent in poetry" (Eliot 1932: 243). And to reinforce the significance of this heterogeneity Eliot quotes S. Johnson's criticism of the "metaphysical" poets: Johnson says "the most heterogeneous ideas are yoked by violence together" (Eliot 1932: 243); but in so doing, the poetry awakens our minds to a characteristic of a thing that we had not recognized earlier. Al-Fārābī, too, many centuries earlier noted that the difference between the two objects may be as important as their resemblance in causing this recognition. The metaphor produces knowledge and thus the poetic art is syllogistic.

In similar fashion, Ibn Rushd in his *Short Commentary on Aristotle's "Poetics"* writes: "With them [poetical speeches], one strives for an imaginary representation (*takhyīl*) or exemplification (*tamthīl*) of something in speech so as to move the soul to flee from the thing, or to long for it, or simply to wonder because of the delightfulness which issues from the imaginary representation" (Averroes 1977: 203.3–5; Butterworth tr. 83). Imagination is central to poetic representation, as it was for al-Fārābī. Yet the representation is, as Ibn Rushd explains in the next paragraph, not the thing itself, and there are many errors because there is confusion regarding this. Ibn Rushd says that the art is syllogistic, even though no syllogism is actually used in it and, if the syllogism were used, it would be a deceit, that is, part of the sophistical art (Averroes 1977: 205.4–6; Butterworth tr. 84). He concludes that Aristotle came to the opinion that the art was highly useful because by it the souls of individuals could be moved to believe (*'i'tiqād*) or not to believe in a certain thing or to do or to abandon a certain thing. It is the art of poetics, not personal inspiration, which makes it possible for a man to make an imaginary representation in the most complete manner possible.

In Ibn Rushd's *Middle Commentary on Aristotle's "Poetics,"* he explains further the nature of poetic art. He writes: "With respect to poetical statements, imitation (*takhyīl*) and representation (*muḥākāh*) come about by means of three things: harmonious tune, rhythm, and comparison (*tashbīh*) itself" (Averroes 2000: 62–3). As Butterworth notes regarding this passage, Ibn Rushd uses *takhyīl* here and elsewhere in the generic sense of Aristotle's *mimēsis*, of which "representation" (*muḥākāh*) and "comparison" (*tashbīh*) are species (Averroes 2000: 63, n. 18). Thus, at the heart of the poetic art is Aristotle's complex notion of *mimēsis*, to make a thing in the imagination which may be at least as real as physical beings. Of the three arts of imitation, melody, meter and representation, the third, "representative statements," is the logical art (Averroes 2000: 64).

Ibn Rushd's *Middle Commentary on Aristotle's "Poetics"* is an extensive exploration of the rules that can be gleaned from Aristotle's *Poetics* and used in other contexts. Ibn Rushd seeks to determine what is universal in Aristotle's account and to show its significance for Arabic-speaking Islamic culture. That Ibn Rushd thinks Aristotle's art has a substantial contribution to make is confirmed in his last paragraph where he says: "When you have grasped what we have written here, you will discover—as Abū Naṣr [al-Fārābī] said—that in comparison with what is in this book of Aristotle and in the *Rhetoric* what the people of our tongue know about poetical rules is a mere trifle" (Averroes 2000: 141–2). Despite critical remarks about many Arabic poets, he claims they have technical strengths, especially if and when they rely upon the Qur'ān. Ibn Rushd is more consistently critical of them, however, in his presentation of an initially puzzling theme that runs throughout his commentary. He says that the "Arabs," by which he means primarily the pre-Islamic Arabs, are not a "natural nation" as are the Greeks and the Andalusians. Through a careful argument ruling out the possible explanation of this theme, Butterworth argues that what is meant by Ibn Rushd is that the Arabs are nomadic, in contrast to the Greeks and Andalusians, and therefore they do not care for living together in harmony and do not think of themselves as a nation and a people (Averroes 2000: 44–6). Rather, the nomadic Arabs seek to sing the glories of fighting with one another. For this reason, Butterworth argues, Ibn Rushd stresses all the more the need that poetry is written for moral education and for the unification of the political order (Averroes 2000: 45). In Ibn Rushd's *Middle Commentary*, the logical and poetic are brought together for the improvement of the political order.

Conclusion

We may now return to the three *aporia* that we posed, at the end of the section on the inclusion of the *Rhetoric* and the *Poetics* in the *Organon*. In regard to the question whether rhetoric and poetry are rational arts in Islamic philosophy, as formulated in *aporia* (1), the writings of al-Fārābī and Ibn Rushd reveal their agreement that these two arts are syllogistic; these arts need to be included with the other three syllogistic arts, demonstration, dialectic and sophistry. We have cited enough evidence from each of these two writers to show that their interests in the arts of rhetoric and poetry are neither accidental lapses from philosophic concerns nor simply concessions to political causes, however significant the harmonization of the political regime is. In regard to the specific nature of rhetoric, *aporia* (2), inasmuch as the enthymeme is a syllogism with a deliberately-hidden premise, it is used by the philosophical rhetorician to communicate with others to convince them that certain generally accepted and unexamined opinions are more rational than others. In regard to poetry, *aporia* (3), inasmuch as the imagination makes an imitation or resemblance of one thing with another, certain imitations may be so perfectly chosen by the philosophical poet that they cause us to recognize a significant characteristic of a thing even if this characteristic cannot be shown through imitation alone to be its essence. Thus, al-Fārābī and Ibn Rushd explain the syllogistic or logical nature of the arts of rhetoric and poetry and show why they are useful to the Islamic community.

Further Reading

Blaustein, M. (1992) "The Scope and Methods of Rhetoric in Averroes' *Middle Commentary on Aristotle's Rhetoric*," in C. E. Butterworth (ed.), *The Political Aspects of Islamic Philosophy. Essays in Honor of Muhsin Mahdi*, Cambridge, MA: Harvard University Press, pp. 262–303.
Butterworth, C. E. (1966) *Rhetoric and Reason: A Study of Averroes' Commentary on Aristotle's Rhetoric*, University of Chicago, UMI Dissertation Services.
——. (1984) "The Rhetorician and His Relationship to the Community: Three Accounts of Aristotle's *Rhetoric*," in M. Marmura (ed.), *Islamic Theology and Philosophy. Studies in Honor of George F. Hourani*, Albany, NY: University of Toronto Press, pp. 111–36.
Kemal, S. (2003) *The Philosophical Poetics of Alfarabi, Avicenna and Averroes: the Aristotelian Reception*, London & New York: Routledge.

References

al-Fārābī (1938) "Fārābī's Canons of Poetry," A. J. Arberry (ed. and tr.), *Rivista degli Studi Orientali* XVII: 266–78.
——. (1957) "Al-Farabi's Introductory Risālah on Logic," D. M. Dunlop (ed. and tr.), *Islamic Quarterly* 3: 224–35.
——. (1968) *Kitāb al-Alfāẓ al-Musta'mala fī al-Manṭiq*, M. Mahdi (ed.), Beirut: Dar El-Mashreq.
——. (1971) *Deux ouvrages inédits sur la Réthorique: I. Kitāb al-Ḥaṭāba and II. Didascalia in Rethoricam Aristotelis ex Glosa Alpharabi*, J. Langhade & M. Grignaschi (eds.), Beirut: Dar El-Mashreq.
——. (1986) *Al-Manṭiq 'inda al-Fārābī*, Rafīq al-'Ajam (ed.), Beirut: Dar El-Mashreq.
Averroes (1977) *Averroës' Three Short Commentaries on Aristotle's "Topics," "Rhetoric," and "Poetics,"* C. E. Butterworth (ed. and tr.), Albany: State University of New York Press.
——. (1983) *Talkhīṣ Kitāb al-Qiyāṣ*, M. Qāsim, C. E. Butterworth, & A. Haridi (eds.), Cairo: al-Hay'a al-Miṣriyya al-'Āmma li-l-Kitāb.
——. (2000) *Averroes' Middle Commentary on Aristotle's "Poetics,"* C. E. Butterworth (tr.), South Bend, Indiana: St. Augustine's Press.
——. (2001) *The Book of the Decisive Treatise*, C. E. Butterworth (tr.), Provo, UT: Brigham Young University Press.
——. (2002) *Commentaire moyen à la* Rhétorique *d'Aristote*, vol. II, M. Aouad (ed. and tr.), Paris: Librarie Philosophique J. Vrin.
Avicenna (1964) *Al-Shifā': al-Qiyaṣ*, S. Zāyid & I. Madkour (eds.), Cairo: Wizārat al-Thaqāfa.
Black, D. (1990) *Logic and Aristotle's* Rhetoric *and* Poetics *in Medieval Arabic Philosophy*, Leiden: E. J. Brill.
Butterworth, C. E. (1997) "De l'opinion, le point de vue, la croyance, et la supposition," in A. Hasnawi, A. Elamrani-Jamal & M. Aouad (eds.), *Perspectives arabes et médiévales sur la tradition scientific et philosophique*, Leuven: Peeters, pp. 453–64.
Eliot, T. S. (1932) "The Metaphysical Poets," *Selected Essays of T. S. Eliot*, San Diego, New York & London: Harcourt Brace Jovanovich, pp. 241–50.
Liddell, H. G. & Scott, R. (1889) *Greek–English Lexicon*, Oxford: Clarendon Press.
Walzer, R. (1934, reprinted 1962) "Zur Traditionsgeschichte der Aristotelischen Poetik," in *Greek into Arabic*, Oriental Studies I, Oxford: Bruno Cassirer, pp. 129–36.

8

DEMONSTRATION AND DIALECTIC IN ISLAMIC PHILOSOPHY

Allan Bäck

Introduction

Plato had seen in dialectic a way to justify the first principles of philosophy, from which the demonstration of universal truths could proceed (e.g. *Republic* VI). Likewise, Aristotle uses dialectic to arrive at an intuitive grasp of the first principles on which demonstrative syllogisms are based (e.g. *Metaphysics* IV). Islamic philosophers inherited and developed these doctrines on demonstration and dialectic from the Greeks. In what follows I will sketch the Greek background and then examine some important developments in the Islamic context, in particular how dialectic became more removed from demonstration in the thought of Ibn Sīnā, if not in Islamic philosophy as a whole. I conclude by considering how intuition grew in importance and why this view deserves serious consideration even in philosophy today.

Plato and Aristotle

For Plato, and perhaps even more for Socrates, dialectic lies at the heart of philosophizing. It constitutes the very method leading the philosopher from merely assuming the axioms of the sciences to the apprehension and grounding of those first principles. Presumably, Plato illustrates one sort of dialectic in the dialogues where Socrates questions someone's opinion and shows it to be inconsistent. Thereby it has a refutation (*elenchos*). Those opinions that withstand repeated dialectical attacks have a strong claim to truth. Socrates' elenchic questioning seems to be just this sort of dialectic, which Plato describes when he says, "To rob us of discourse is to rob us of philosophy" (*Sophist* 260a). Another sort of dialectic is that found in *Republic* VI where Plato explains, through the image of the Divided Line, that there is a dialectic of a more metaphysical sort that can be used to establish the Ideas that are the unchanging principles above the realm of becoming, the visible natural world (511b–d).

Despite his metaphysical disagreements with Plato, Aristotle has a similar view of dialectic. Aristotle lists three uses for it: intellectual training, casual encounters, and the philosophical sciences (*Topics* 101a26–8). The first use pertains to education, even for potential philosophers; the second use is for winning arguments; while the third has a strictly philosophical use. Aristotle says that this dialectic has to be used in discussing the principles of the sciences "because the ability to puzzle on both sides of a subject will make us detect more easily the truth and error" about them (*Topics* 101a34–6; cf. Alexander, in *Topics* 19, 23–4; 26, 30–27, 4). Dialectic here becomes "a process of criticism wherein lies the path to the principles of all inquiries" (*Topics* 101b3–4). Like Plato, Aristotle uses dialectic to ground the axioms of all the sciences including first philosophy (Irwin 1988; Bäck 1999). However, the grounding itself comes from an act of intuition (*noûs*); likewise, Plato talks about such knowledge (*noûs*) being grounded on the intuition of the Forms and their principles. Accordingly, in his practice Aristotle regularly goes through the reputable opinions (*endoxa*) and standing puzzles in the various sciences dialectically. He brings together dialectic with induction, opinions with phenomena, persuasion with truth. This strand of Aristotle's thought gives dialectic considerable philosophical respectability. On the other hand, Aristotle agrees with Plato that we can have a simple act of apprehension of first principles via *noûs* after a laborious process involving induction and perhaps dialectic. This other strand implies that philosophy has no need for dialectic, which has use here perhaps only for the philosopher in training.

Thus, the problem arose for those after Aristotle as to just how to practice philosophy: by dialectic or via induction (*epagōgē*) and intellectual intuition (*noûs* in the sense of "advancing to the first principles and grasping them intuitively") and demonstration? Do we debate with each other to get at the best explanation, or do we purify our minds, via intellectual discipline, to somehow intuit the truth? Dialectic may purify it but cannot replace intellectual intuition. As Sally Raphael says, "dialectic becomes a necessary means to the end of grasping universal truths by intuitive induction" (1974: 155; cf. Le Blond 1939: c. 1). That is, here there is induction by means of intellectual intuition. It brings us from what is evident to us but not in itself, to what is evident in itself but not at first to us (Philoponus, *in Prior Analytics* 474, 14–15). If dialectic serves only as a means, then it may be of little use once we have attained the end.

The founder of Neoplatonism, Plotinus, claims to follow Plato. Still, he stresses intellectual intuition far more than dialectic in having knowledge. Only the ascent to apprehension of the Forms yields true knowledge. We may start with sense perception so as to be reminded of the Forms. Dialectic may assist in the ascent but the key lies in intellectual intuition. His follower Proclus accordingly insists that definitions cannot be grasped via induction and abstraction from sense perception. The abstraction itself requires already knowing the Forms. He insists that abstracting provides no way to avoid extraneous elements in definitions (*In Parmenides* iv, 893, 11–7; cf. Helmig 2010: 36). Ibn Sīnā will agree with this last point though he will reject the Neoplatonic metaphysics of Forms.

To sum up, Plato and Aristotle treat dialectic and demonstration as intertwined; practicing the former can produce the insight of the latter. The Neoplatonists tended to stress the insight of *noûs* more than the dialectical exercises preparing the philosopher for the ascent to the apprehension of the Forms and the One or Good of the Platonic tradition.

Greek Teachings on Dialectic and Intuition (*noûs*) in the Islamic Philosophical Tradition

Philosophers of the Islamic tradition received all these teachings, along with the Neoplatonist presumption that Aristotle and Plato could be made consistent (Fakhry 1965). In addition they had native traditions of disputation, based upon Islamic jurisprudence and *kalām* (Madkour 1969: 234; Maróth 1984: 34). With Ibn Sīnā and Ibn Rushd there arose a fairly uniform, comprehensive synthesis.

The Greek doctrines on dialectic and demonstration came with Alexandrian interpretations from the late Greek period. Two have particular importance: (1) the *Organon*, the corpus of the logical works of Aristotle, was taken to include the *Poetics* and the *Rhetoric*; and (2) a treatise on the analysis of materials so as to yield syllogistic premises was sometimes inserted into presentations of the *Organon*, between the syllogisms of the *Prior Analytics* and the demonstrations of the *Posterior Analytics* (Black 1990: 1–18). This treatise consisted of selected materials from Aristotle's *Topics*, chiefly Book II.

Aristotle himself had offered some justification for both points. On the first, he too talks of enthymemes as rhetorical syllogisms (*Rhe*toric I.2). Although he does not mention syllogisms in his *Poetics*, Ibn Sīnā and Ibn Rushd in their commentaries managed to find syllogistic structures there. Perhaps this is not too silly: Aristotle employs the practical syllogism to explain motion, and the *Poetics* is concerned with one type: *e*motion. Yet, even so, these syllogisms are not demonstrations; after all, Aristotelians recognize sophistical syllogisms as well (*Topics* I.1).

Second, this insertion of a dialectical treatise between the two *Analytics* would make demonstration and dialectic intertwined. Aristotle himself says at *Prior Analytics* 46a28–30 to look at his *Topics* for pointers on how to select premises. The Greek commentators then took appropriate materials from there to explain this remark (Hasnaoui 2001: 40). Alexander (in *Prior Analytics* 332, 37–333, 6) restricted his reference to *Topics* 1.14 and 8.1, while Philoponus vaguely referenced the whole *Topics* (in *Prior Analytics* 306, 25–8).

Yet these comments are cursory; these writers composed no treatises or analyses on the topic. Al-Fārābī and Ibn Rushd each gave such a treatise only in a preliminary work; Ibn Rushd omits it even in his *Epitome of Logic*. At most the treatise on analysis constituted not part of philosophical dialectic but only a dialectic for philosophers in training—something fitting the Neoplatonist background—and tended, as was usual, to keep dialectic away from demonstration and intuition.

Accordingly, in his *Philosophy of Plato and Aristotle*, al-Fārābī reserves scientific demonstration for the ruling class, the philosophers. He says that the first cause, the creation of the world, and the good for human beings may be known in two ways: by apprehension through *noûs* (intellect) or by the use of metaphors (1964a: 69, 19–22; 1926: 40, 2–13). As Lameer (1994: 261, 269, 276–7) remarks, this reflects Plato's view, where the philosopher has strict knowledge of the first principles while the common people have only images, presented to them perhaps in religious Scriptures. For al-Fārābī, strict philosophical knowledge takes the form of Aristotelian demonstrative science, with deductions from necessarily true first principles apprehended by *noûs* (1964b: 85, 2–87, 4).

Al-Fārābī seems to have inherited this tradition also from a late Greek understanding of Aristotle. Andronicus of Rhodes had separated Aristotle's teachings into the esoteric technical doctrines and the exoteric, popular teachings on ethics and politics (Lameer 1994: 276–7). Philoponus and Simplicius make the same distinction in their commentaries on Aristotle's *Physics* (Philoponus, in *Physics* 705, 22–4; Simplicius, in *Physics* 695, 34–696, 1). Likewise, in *The Book of Letters*, al-Fārābī advocates teaching the elite philosophers with demonstrations while using only the persuasive methods of rhetoric and poetry for the people incapable of grasping proof (1969: 151, 17–153, 9; 131, 4–133, 13). He distinguishes various senses of philosophical terms along the lines of Aristotle's *Metaphysics* V. Here al-Fārābī follows Aristotle and admits that various expressions are used in many ways, though, again perhaps like Aristotle, he focuses on making the language precise so as to disambiguate it (Bäck 2000: 90–6). In this way the goal becomes not merely to recognize the various meanings of expressions but to select out the key ones. Thereafter only these intellectually purified senses are allowed into the ideal language of the philosophers. The method there is the demonstrative one, from first principles stated rigorously via valid syllogisms.

Nevertheless, al-Fārābī still allows dialectic to have a philosophical use. He advises us to use dialectic in the natural sciences in order to get at the axioms and principles for demonstration as well as to hit upon the middle terms so as to complete syllogisms (1961: 91, 20–92, 8). He advises this not on account of the superiority of dialectic but on account of the inferiority of human ability. Because we must start from ignorance and the confusion of sense perception, we have to grope towards the truth, and dialectic aids in that groping (Vallat 2004: 193–4). Even aside from our failings, al-Fārābī holds that the conclusions of natural science can be probable but not certain, because of the imperfections and vagaries of matter. The subject of metaphysics allows for the higher standard of truth, absolute certainty, although, once again, we infirm human beings might not be able to attain that. So even there we may have to use dialectic as a crutch (Vallat 2004: 200–201).

In this way al-Fārābī is able to accommodate Plato's position that even after the philosopher has made the ascent and attained the intuitive knowledge of the Form of the Good, the philosopher should still continue to engage in dialectical practice (*Republic* 509b; 534b–c). In principle, though, al-Fārābī makes dialectic dispensable. As we shall see next, Ibn Sīnā has a more sanguine view about human ability and, accordingly, gives dialectic less status and demonstration more adequacy.

When dealing with ordinary discourse, al-Fārābī allows for local custom and tradition, vagueness and speaker intention. Analyzing such discourse requires clarifying it. Once this is done, from the strict, philosophical point of view, its inadequacies become apparent. In the ideal language, al-Fārābī tends to seek a proper meaning for each expression used, fully explicit reasoning, necessarily true premises, and valid inferences. Common people have metaphor, vagueness, and mere opinion in their language; philosophers have precision, proof, and truth in theirs.

Ibn Sīnā on Dialectic and Demonstration

For Ibn Sīnā, dialectic likewise has no function in philosophy proper. Instead, the philosopher acquires knowledge of the first principles via activating a connection with the separately existing active intellect. Perhaps dialectic has some use in the activation process, yet, like the games of childhood, we should put dialectic aside once we have attained intellectual maturity. Dialectic applies to popular concerns and customs; philosophy consists in demonstration.

Like al-Fārābī, Ibn Sīnā tends to stick to a single meaning for the experts; he allows for vagaries and ambiguities in common usage (Avicenna 1965: 86, 4–15). His theory of homonymy reflects this with a range of uses from a single, strictly synonymous meaning of the expert to the hopelessly ambiguous prattling of the many (Bäck 2008). Ibn Sīnā distinguishes a common meaning from an expert meaning for many expressions. He too generally fixes on a strict, scientific meaning for the philosopher and a looser, metaphorical meaning for the common people in such a way that in his philosophical practice he has little patience with Aristotle's doctrine that expressions are said in many ways, so as to accommodate common usage.

With this attitude, Ibn Sīnā rejects some of Aristotle's specific doctrines—more so than do al-Fārābī and Ibn Rushd, or, at any rate, more explicitly. He claims that Aristotle is wrong, or at least hasty, in some of the inferences that he allows in his logic. For instance, commenting on *Categories* II, Ibn Sīnā rejects the fourfold division of being, known as the ontological square, as inadequate and useless for philosophers. He thinks it is at best useful only for beginners starting out from popular belief and instead offers a fivefold division of being, depending heavily on Aristotle's *Metaphysics* (Bäck 1999a). More generally, Ibn Sīnā sees little philosophical use for the *topoi*. He does mention what Aristotle says but does not himself use dialectic to advance to first principles. Demonstration and intellectual insight or intuition (*noûs*, *'aql*) suffice for the truth; the *topoi* have use only for dealing with those who cannot do philosophy.

Thus, Ibn Sīnā starts his *Topics* (*al-Jadal*) by affirming that knowledge comes from demonstrative science. There the ultimate goal for the philosopher is "to perfect his individual essence and then to be concerned with what benefits or preserves his species" (Avicenna 1965: 7, 8–9). Perfecting the individual human essence amounts to perfecting the noblest part of the individual human soul, the human intellect in its connection with the active intellect. This is the theorizing (*theoria*) recommended by Aristotle in his ethics as the ultimate goal for a human being. The concern with the species amounts to a concern with society: the practical moral activity to which Aristotle gives second place in his account of *eudaimonia* (Avicenna 1965: 13, 12–15).

The theorizing consists in constructing and apprehending demonstrations, valid syllogisms based on necessarily true premises. Ibn Sīnā says that the soul acquires the most fundamental principles when it is united to the divine effluence, while it acquires the less fundamental ones from the middle terms of demonstration and from experience (1956: 255, 5–8; cf. Bäck 2009). By means of intellectual purification, using dialectic perhaps, it is possible for us to come to have intuitions of essences. Somehow, the intellect in us thereby gains direct contact with the "storehouse" of universals, the quiddities in themselves in the active intellect (Avicenna 1975: 58, 4; Hasse 2001: 48; Gutas 2001: 12). This storehouse constitutes the content of the celestial active intellect, the "giver of forms" (*dator formarum*), perhaps Itself emanating from the Divine Intellect (Hasse 2012: 225–6). Acquaintance with it makes it possible for us to separate the essential, necessary attributes from the merely necessary and from the merely concomitant attributes:

> When the soul has reached a sublime stage, acquired the excellent [sacred] faculty, and separated from the body, it attains whatever is attained. There, where all distractions are vanished, faster than through intuition, the intellectual world presents itself to the soul according to the order of the terms of propositions and according to the essential, not temporal order of the intelligibles.
>
> (*Mubāḥathāt* §467, tr. Gutas 1988: 166)

In this way, the enlightened soul can grasp and validate the real definitions, giving the formulae of the essences of things, like "rational animal" for human beings. It can also distinguish the constituents of an essence from those accidents that are necessary to it, the *propria* (essential characteristics), and from those that belong to it always but not necessarily. Thus, in the first case the *propria* like risibility are eliminated from the human essence; in the second those like being terrestrial are.

After someone has acquired philosophical wisdom, Ibn Sīnā, the self-taught philosopher, sees little need for dialectic, disputation, or interpretation of the speech of others. Alone he can prevail; he can construct demonstrative syllogisms by himself (Avicenna 1965: 11, 6–7; 11, 13–14). In contrast, Plato had Socrates say that the philosopher needs dialectic even after apprehending the Form of the Good (*Republic* 511b-d).

Ibn Sīnā recognizes the utility of other sorts of syllogisms in practical affairs: the dialectical and the fallacious (Avicenna 1965: 8, 3–4). Knowing the dialectical has its use in dealing with common affairs; knowing the fallacious has its in preventing mistakes (11, 13–14; 8, 7–8). For Ibn Sīnā, these syllogisms have the same logical form (or, in the case of the fallacious: appear to) but differ in the matter of their premises (9, 3–5). Like Aristotle, he has the premises of dialectical syllogisms come about from particular posits and assumptions made by those in the context of their discussions (9, 6–10, 4). More common dialectical premises come from the endoxic (*mašhūr*), what is widely accepted among the experts or in the culture (Avicenna 1965: 20, 8–9; 43, 7–8; 47, 3–48, 6; 1959: 21, 19–22, 7; 35, 13–19). Such syllogisms have no function for a philosopher who already has wisdom, though they may have some use in educating someone coming to be a philosopher (1965: 12, 9–13, 3). Still, Ibn Sīnā advises: "Know that the intelligent (person) does not deviate from what is widely accepted when it is avoidable" (Avicenna 1959: 18, 5–6).

Dialectical premises are justified by a different standard than are demonstrative ones. (Avicenna 1965: 47, 3–48, 6; 245, 7–10). They can look the same as demonstrative premises—make the same universal claims about the world and imply the same conclusions—but do not come from the apprehension of necessarily true principles (34, 5–12). Other dialectical premises concern matters not dealt with in theoretical science, notably those in social and political affairs. Unlike the demonstrative ones, dialectical propositions will often be singular in form, as they deal with the contingencies of human affairs (37, 6–17). For Ibn Sīnā, philosophical demonstration looks at the sentence meaning of the statements used, whereas dialectic focuses on their speaker meaning (78, 14–16). In understanding the reputable opinions, Ibn Sīnā advises focusing on the intention of the speaker (Avicenna 1959: 10, 17–11, 2).

Ibn Sīnā concludes that dialectic has no use in philosophy proper (Avicenna 1965: 50, 15–51, 7). *Topoi* have little claim to truth or often even to plausibility. Dialectic has its main use not for the philosopher but for the political leader to persuade the masses (14, 6–7; 48, 7–9). "The scientific way is long, and not every soul is receptive to it" (14, 12). So instead, like al-Fārābī, Ibn Sīnā advises using persuasive arguments, especially for inculcating religious doctrines useful for the state into those incapable of apprehending the truth (14, 13–15; 50, 1–2). The rulers may make up some *topoi* just to control or distract the masses; for instance, they may discuss silly questions like whether Saturn is good or bad and whether the number of stars is odd or even (77, 4–8).

Ibn Sīnā even goes so far as to say that when Aristotle discusses *topoi* in *On Interpretation* he does not mean the dialectical *topoi* of the *Topics*. Rather those are *topoi* in a related, philosophical sense (Avicenna 1965: 77, 8–9; 233, 8–10; Hasnaoui 2001: 37). So perhaps Ibn Sīnā does see some use for *topoi* as Aristotle did. In his actual practice Ibn Sīnā likewise regularly brings up objections and puzzles, works through them, and then reaches his own conclusions. This resembles the type of dialectic recommended by Plato and Aristotle for the philosopher, even once enlightened. Still, this dialectic does not ground the principles.

For Ibn Sīnā, intuition (*ḥads*) on the part of intellect provides the key to demonstration. Demonstration has an axiomatic structure, reasoning from first principles like the principle of non-contradiction and then proceeding to prove theorems via chains of syllogisms, each with a middle term. Success comes from apprehending the first principles and from seizing upon the correct middle terms. Some people have stronger powers of intuition than others for doing this. Those with the strongest have philosophical, demonstrative knowledge immediately; they have no need for instruction or study. Ordinary people think them to be prophets. Other people, having weaker intuition, require study and instruction (Avicenna 1975: 272, 3–274, 4; tr. Gutas 1988: 161–2).

According to Ibn Sīnā we rational beings can come to have a kind of intuition of the one, the existent, and the necessary (*ḍarūrī*) (Avicenna 1960: I.6; 1956: 256, 2–4). From such notions we can grasp axioms like "it is not possible for something to exist and not to exist." Once philosophizing has awakened our intellects, we can have direct acquaintance with essences, quiddities in themselves (Avicenna 1975: 39, 3–40,16; 209, 1–8). This connection made with the active intellect enables us to grasp the real definitions, the formulae of the essences of things (as Aristotle had put it in his *Metaphysics*, 1029b25ff.). We can then separate those features belonging to these quiddities in themselves stated in these definitions, from those features that quiddities always have when they exist. Ibn Sīnā gives the following example: suppose all the human beings whom you know came from the Sudan. Then, for you, all human beings would have black skin. Yet even so you would know that being black is not essential to a human being and does not belong to the definition, on account of being acquainted with humanity, the quiddity in itself (Avicenna 1956: 46, 11–16; 1952: 70, 1–20). In gaining knowledge of the real definitions and distinguishing them from those attributes necessarily or always accompanying constituents of the definitions, we then become able to construct syllogisms, where the middle terms are elements of those definitions, and the major terms, the predicates in the conclusions, are those concomitant features.

The intuitive power of the intellect then suffices for us to attain philosophical wisdom, embodied in demonstration (Avicenna 1956: 257, 2–12). Ibn Sīnā thinks that "the structure of reality is ... syllogistical" (Gutas 1988: 174). For the truly elite, those having outstanding intuition, discussion and dialectic have no use. They can intuit the syllogisms directly.

Later Islamic philosophy in the tradition of Ibn Sīnā emphasized this apprehension, this leap of intuition (Karabela 2011). Those who had such an ability could apprehend the truth; others could not. Such an approach was congenial to doctrines of revelation and the prophetic power. Philosophy came to take a mystical turn away from the demonstrative syllogisms of Aristotelian science; some scholars claim that it changed into "theosophy" (Ziai 1996: 466–7). An actualized active intellect enables you to have contact with the storehouse of wisdom, with the active intellect as "giver of forms" (*dator formarum*). It is as if one has been given the password to access a divinely ordained source, containing no longer work and wisdom in progress but now the perfection of knowledge. Later thinkers took this connection to the active intellect more religiously, in the popular sense, than Ibn Sīnā did. Thus, those like Suhrawardī discussed extraordinary phenomena like reviving the dead and personal revelations and an "imaginal world" (as Henri Corbin 1964 puts it), a separate world of angelic intelligences in space and time.

Ibn Rushd on Dialectic and Demonstration

Despite his polemical differences with Ibn Sīnā, especially in his *Incoherence of the Incoherence of the Philosophers*, the Andalusian Ibn Rushd has an analogous approach, albeit considerably closer to the thought of al-Fārābī. People are found to align themselves into three natural classes with some persuaded by rhetoric (the mass of humanity moved by emotion), others persuaded by dialectic (theologians who ground their thinking on literal understandings of religious texts), and lastly philosophers persuaded by scientific philosophical demonstration that grasps truth *per se*. With these distinctions of modes of assent, Ibn Rushd dismissed this sort of dialectic as a valuable foundation for the attainment of scientific knowledge.

In his doctrine of intellect, Ibn Rushd follows Aristotle and allows dialectical thinking drawn from common beliefs (*endoxa*) and observations to guide his account in its preliminary stages of the discussion of intellect. Human beings are observed to have intellectual knowledge and so are asserted to have the potential to be actively rational through a connection with the separately existing agent intellect and material intellect (Taylor 2009: lxii ff.). Those who actualize the sensory powers and their internal powers of imagination, cogitation, and memory are able to achieve intellectual fulfillment through a conjoining with those intellects which abstract intelligibles (agent intellect) and retain them (material intellect) in a way accessible in an ongoing way to the individual human knower. The scientific intelligibles apprehended in this way provide knowledge for the philosopher, who now has no need for dialectic, a result that does not differ much from Ibn Sīnā's in the assertion of separate intelligibles in act outside the individual human being. In this, as with Ibn Sīnā, dialectic—aside from its part in Aristotle's establishment of the principle of contradiction—has no role in the establishment of intellectual principles for the abstraction by which the individual may ascend to a knowledge attained by the few who are able to function at the highest level of intellect. Both thinkers found the intellect's apprehension of intelligibles in one way or another to be the foundation for the premises of scientific demonstration.

For Ibn Rushd too then, dialectic does not play a positive, direct or ongoing role in establishing the truths of science and philosophy where demonstration is the proper method. It is useful for students who are just beginning the path of philosophy, as well as for those who never take that path but who can still follow reasoning. Only in mundane affairs, dealing with particulars for which there can be no science, does dialectic have first place (Maróth 1994: 181–3; 195).

The method for gaining philosophic wisdom bequeathed by the Greeks, then, retains the two strands of demonstration and dialectic. Perhaps these two strands themselves are found interwoven in the writings and thought of Plato and Aristotle, but in philosophy in the lands of Islam the two strands unravel as a result of deeper philosophical reflection. With al-Fārābī and Ibn Rushd, and especially with Ibn Sīnā, the dialectical strand loses its philosophical luster; at best, it offers preliminary training for the student of philosophy. An active *noûs* is argued to suffice instead. Dialectic then becomes the method for dealing with ordinary, non-philosophical discourse. Understanding the intention of the speaker and the customs of the speakers, the *usus loquendi*, here become crucial in interpreting such discourse. However, philosophical insight and wisdom come much better from the technical discourse of the philosopher and the invocation of the powers of separate intellect.

Conclusion

We may be inclined to dismiss as unphilosophical the intuitive and mystical turn in the later Avicennian tradition or even the appeal to the absolute certification and confirmation of abstractive powers in Ibn Sīnā or Ibn Rushd. Nevertheless, if we consider what other options there are, perhaps we should not be so smug when considering the ideal of attaining to real definitions. Let us consider how this position functions as it did for Ibn Sīnā in philosophy today.

Even aside from the doctrine of an imaginal world, scientific talk of apprehending the real essences of physical objects via pure intuition seems out of place today, indeed, almost "metaphysical" in the pejorative sense. Yet, once we update the terminology, perhaps we can see that modern science has some similarities.

Today, scientists and even philosophers often describe their work as providing mere models, functioning as useful for us. They say that they are avoiding the pretension of describing reality itself. Instead, on a functional level they act *as if* many well-entrenched models and theoretical constructs can be taken to describe reality accurately. Science at the basic level is often taught thus, and much real money is invested in developing technologies such as electricity, nanotechnology, quantum computers, and supercolliders. If we take the pragmatic standpoint, it seems that, given that we act *as if* these models and theories are real and uncontestedly established, we talk about them as foundational and we commit ourselves to acting accordingly with full confidence.

In this, modern scientists do not admit or seek out real definitions, the formulae of the essences, of quiddities in themselves. Still, consider current scientific practice.

Chemists think that they understand what it is to be copper: an element with 29 protons. This captures the true nature of copper—even though, if something is copper, it has many other necessary features: conducting electricity and being ductile under certain conditions of temperature, pressure, etc. Somehow they are able to isolate this atomic description of the nature of copper as privileged, as if the other necessary properties could be inferred from it. How? In developing their theoretical constructs, they have found it more practical and perhaps more economical if the atomic number of copper is taken as more fundamental. Like Aristotle and Ibn Sīnā, they are groping towards the real definitions, the constituents of the quiddities in themselves, and are distinguishing these from their other necessary features, their essential properties. In the contemporary effort to think beyond the models and constructs to the realities themselves, something analogous to Ibn Sīnā's intuitions of quiddities in themselves seems to be at work. We make theoretical leaps and intellectually intuit realities to ground them.

Further Reading

Bäck, A. (2009) "Insights of Avicenna," in A. Storck (ed.), *Aristotelis analytica posteriora: estudos acerca da recepção medieval dos segundos analíticos*, Porto Alegre: Linus Editores, pp. 111–48.

——. (2014) *Aristotle's Theory of Abstraction*, Berlin: Springer.

Black, D. (1990) *Logic and Aristotle's Rhetoric and Poetics in Medieval Arabic Philosophy*, Leiden: Brill.

Lameer, J. (1994) *Al-Fārābī and Aristotelian Syllogistics*, Leiden: Brill.

Taylor, R. C. (2005) "Averroes. Religious Dialectic and Aristotelian Philosophical Thought," in P. Adamson & R. C. Taylor (eds.), *The Cambridge Companion to Arabic Philosophy*, Cambridge: Cambridge University Press, pp. 180–200.

References

Alexander of Aphrodisias (1883) *Commentary on Prior Analytics (Commentaria in Analyticorum Priorum)*, M. Wallies (ed.), *Commentaria in Aristotelem Graeca* vol. 2.1, Berlin: Reimer.

——. (1891) *Commentary on Topics (Commentaria in Aristotelis Topica)*, M. Wallies (ed.), *Commentaria in Aristotelem Graeca* vol. 2.2, Berlin: Reimer.

al-Fārābī (1926) *Tāḥṣīl al-saʿāda [The Attainment of Happiness]*, Hyderabad.

——. (1961) *Falsafat Arisṭūṭālīs [Philosophy of Aristotle]*, M. Mahdi (ed.), Beirut: Dār Majallat Shi'r.

——. (1964a) *Kitāb (Mabādi') ārā' ahl al-madīna al-fāḍila [The Perfect State]*, in F. Dieterici (ed.), *Al-Fārābī's Abhandlung der Musterstaat*, Leiden: Brill.

——. (1964b) *Kitāb al-Siyāsa al-Madaniyya [The Political Regime]*, Najjār (ed.), Beirut: Imprimerie Catholique.

——. (1969) *Kitāb al-Ḥurūf [Book of Letters]*, M. Mahdi (ed.), Beirut: Dār al-Mashriq.

Avicenna (1952) *Al-Madkhal, al-Shifā'*, vol. I.1, G. Anawati et al. (eds.), Cairo: Organisme Général des Imprimeries Gouvernementales.

——. (1956) *al-Burhān, al-Shifā'*, vol. I.4, A. Affifi (ed.), Cairo: Organisme Général des Imprimeries Gouvernementales.

——. (1959) *Al-Maqūlāt, al- Shifā'*, vol. I.2, G. Anawati, A. El-Ehwani, M. El-Khodeiri, & S. Zayed (eds.), Cairo: Organisme Général des Imprimeries Gouvernementales.

——. (1960) *Al-Ilāhiyyāt, al-Shifā'*, vol. 2.1, M. Y. Moussa, S. Dunya, & S. Zayed (eds.), Cairo: Organisme Général des Imprimeries Gouvernementales.
——. (1965) *al-Jadal, al-Shifā'*, vol. I.7, A. F. Al-Ehwany (ed.), Cairo: Organisme Général des Imprimeries Gouvernementales.
——. (1975) *Nafs, al-Shifā'*, vol. I.1, G. C. Anawati & S. Zayed (eds.), Cairo: Organisme Général des Imprimeries Gouvernementales.
Bäck, A. (1999) "Aristotle's Discovery of First Principles," in M. Sim (ed.), *From Puzzles to Principles*, Lanham, MD: Lexington Books, pp. 163–82.
——. (1999a) "Avicenna's Ontological Pentagon," *Journal of Neoplatonic Studies* 7: 87–109.
——. (2000) *Aristotle's Theory of Predication*, Leiden: Brill.
——. (2008) "Avicenna The Commentator," in L. A. Newton (ed.), *Medieval Commentaries on Aristotle's Categories*, Leiden: Brill, pp. 31–71.
——. (2009) "Insights of Avicenna," in A. Storck (ed.), *Aristotelis analytica posteriora: estudos acerca da recepção medieval dos segundos analíticos*, Porto Alegre: Linus Editores, pp. 111–48.
Black, D. (1990) *Logic and Aristotle's Rhetoric and Poetics in Medieval Arabic Philosophy*, Leiden: Brill.
Corbin, H. (1964) "Mundus imaginalis ou l'imaginaire et l'imaginal," *Cahiers internationaux du symbolisme* 6: 3–26.
Fakhry, M. (1965) "Al-Farabi and the Reconciliation of Plato and Aristotle," *Journal of the History of Ideas* 26, 4: 469–78.
Gutas, D. (1988) *Avicenna and the Aristotelian Tradition*, Leiden: Brill.
——. (2001) "Intuition and Thinking: The Evolving Structure of Avicenna's Epistemology," in R. Wisnovsky (ed.), *Aspects of Avicenna*, Princeton: Markus Wiener Publishers, pp. 1–39.
Hasnaoui, A. (2001) "Topic and Analysis: The Arabic tradition," in R. W. Sharples (ed.), *Whose Aristotle? Whose Aristotelianism?* Aldershot: Ashgate, pp. 28–62.
Hasse, D. N. (2012) "Avicenna's 'Giver of Forms' in Latin Philosophy," in D. N. Hasse & A. Bertolacci (eds.), *The Arabic, Hebrew and Latin Reception of Avicenna's Metaphysics* (Scientia Graeco-Arabica), Berlin: De Gruyter, pp. 225–50.
Helmig, C. (2010) "Proclus' Critique of Aristotle's Theory of Abstraction and Concept Formation in *Analytica Posteriora* II.19," in F. de Haas et al. (eds.), *Interpreting Aristotle's Posterior Analytics in Late Antiquity and Beyond*, Leiden: Brill, pp. 27–54.
Irwin, T. (1988) *Aristotle's First Principles*, Oxford: Oxford University Press.
Karabela, M. K. (2011) *The Development of Dialectic and* Argumentation Theory in Post-classical Islamic Intellectual History, dissertation, Canada: McGill University.
Lameer, J. (1994) *Al-Fārābī and Aristotelian Syllogistics*, Leiden: Brill.
Le Blond, J. M. (1939) *Logique et méthode chez Aristote*, Paris: J. Vrin.
Madkour, I. (1969) *L'Organon d'Aristote dans le monde arabe*, Paris: J. Vrin.
Maróth, M. (1984) "Die Topik Avicennas und ihre Rolle in den arabischen Wissenschaften," *Acta Antiqua Academiae Scientiarum Hungaricae* 29: 33–41.
——. (1994) *Die Araber und die antike Wissenschaftstheorie*, Leiden: Brill.
Philoponus, J. (1887) *Commentary on the Physics of Aristotle (Commentaria in Aristotelis Physica)*, H. Vitelli (ed.), *Commentaria in Aristotelem Graeca*, vols. XVI–XVII, Berlin: Felix Reimer.
——. (1905) *Commentary on the Prior Analytics of Aristotle (In Aristotelis Analytica priora commentaria)*, M. Wallies (ed.), *Commentaria in Aristotelem Graeca*, vol. XIII.2, Berlin: Felix Reimer.
Proclus (1864) *In Parmenides*, in Procli *philosophi Platonici opera inedita*, V. Cousin (ed.), Paris: Durand.
Raphael, S. (1974) "Rhetoric, Dialectical and Syllogistic Argument," *Phronesis* 19, 2: 153–67.
Simplicius (1882) *In Physics (In Aristotelis Physicorum libros (1–4))*, H. Diels (ed.), *Commentaria in Aristotelem Graeca*, vol. IX, Berlin: Felix Reimer.

Taylor, R. C. (ed. and tr.) (2009) *Averroes (Ibn Rushd) of Cordoba, Long Commentary on the De Anima of Aristotle*, New Haven: Yale University Press.
Vallat, P. (2004) *Farabi et l'école d'Alexandre*, Paris: J. Vrin.
Ziai, H. (1996) "The Illuminationist Tradition," in S. H. Nasr & O. Leaman (eds.), *History of Islamic Philosophy*, London: Routledge, pp. 465–96.

9
THE STRUCTURE AND METHODS OF THE SCIENCES

Anna A. Akasoy and Alexander Fidora

Introduction

"What can I know?" From its very beginning, philosophical reflection has been concerned with the objects and methods of certain knowledge. Plato and Aristotle divided the realm of what is knowable and assigned different epistemological principles to the individual parts. As a result of their deliberations, they developed divisions of philosophy (i.e. science) in which they also discussed the methodological requirements for its different branches.

Plato in his *Republic* (VII, 521c–531c) proposed a model in which four propaedeutic sciences (arithmetic, geometry, astronomy and harmony) lead to the highest form of scientific knowledge (dialectic). Later authors also credited him with the division of philosophy into ethics, physics and logic, a division that became very popular among the Stoics. Aristotle formulated a more complex division with several subdivisions: thus, he distinguished practical, poietical (or technical, productive) and theoretical knowledge, the latter of which was divided into physics, mathematics and theology or metaphysics (*Metaphysics* VI, 1, 1025b 25 and 1026a 6–13).

In Late Antiquity, Neoplatonists such as the sixth-century Aristotelian commentators Elias and David made use of these divisions of philosophy in their attempts to create a comprehensive outline of Aristotle's philosophy in the form of a bibliographical survey. Three centuries later, Arabic authors studied these divisions in a much more systematic fashion and took into consideration their epistemological implications (Hein 1985). Their interpretation, which applied the theory of science from the *Posterior Analytics* to the division of philosophy, is not only philosophically interesting, but also of historical significance. Incorporating Greek epistemology, Arabic philosophy determined for centuries the standards of epistemic practice in general and had a crucial impact on the organization of learning in religious schools (*madrasa*) (Biesterfeldt 2000) and, later on, in the universities.

From Late Antique Prolegomena to Classifications of the Sciences

The interest of Arabic philosophers in the structure of science begins with al-Kindī, "the philosopher of the Arabs." Of several works concerned with the structure of philosophy, only his *On the Quantity of Aristotle's Books* (*Risāla fī kammiyyat kutub Arisṭūṭālīs*) has come down to us (Adamson 2007). While the author shows familiarity with the contents of some of Aristotle's texts, the summaries of others, notably the *Posterior Analytics*, are probably simply derived from an otherwise unknown Greek source. Al-Kindī ultimately drew on the tradition of the Prolegomena to Aristotle's works associated with the School of Alexandria and commentators such as Elias and David.

Taking up the Neoplatonic approach, al-Kindī compiled a catalogue of writings of Aristotle and organized them according to the subjects of the (theoretical) sciences: logic, physics, psychology and metaphysics/theology. The books on logic are: *Categories*, *On Interpretation*, *Topics*, *Prior Analytics*, *Posterior Analytics*, *Sophistical Refutations* and, following the Alexandrian tradition, *Rhetoric* and *Poetics*; those on physics: *Physics*, *On the Heavens*, *On Generation and Corruption*, *Meteorology*, the pseudo-Aristotelian works *On Minerals* and *On Plants*, and *On Animals*; those on psychology (which al-Kindī lists separately from physics, following the Neoplatonic tradition): *On the Soul*, *On Sense and the Sensible*, *On Sleep and Sleeplessness* and *On Longevity and Shortness of Life*; theology is contained in *Metaphysics*. In addition, reference is also made to the *Ethics* and *Politics* as practical sciences.

While this catalogue obviously represents an Aristotelian streak in al-Kindī's division of the sciences, other elements can be attributed to Plato's influence. A general feature of al-Kindī's philosophy that distinguishes him and his circle from the Aristotelians of tenth-century Baghdad is the significance he attributed to mathematics. Thus, in his *Quantity*, he explains that every student of philosophy has to begin with sciences that study quantity and quality (i.e. the mathematical sciences) before tackling knowledge of secondary substances (i.e. the universals). Al-Kindī even wrote a treatise, now lost, about *How Philosophy Can Only be Acquired through Knowledge of the Mathematical Sciences*. Reminiscent of the above-mentioned model from Plato's *Republic*, this view of mathematics is nowadays often connected with Proclus. However, al-Kindī did more than simply perpetuate the late antique Neoplatonist tradition. With his discussion of quantity, quality and secondary substances he introduced a metaphysical criterion for his division of the sciences.

Al-Kindī's work also reveals that the place of Greek philosophy within the canon of the sciences was controversial in the Islamic world. In his *Quantity*, al-Kindī insisted there was no conflict between prophetic and philosophical knowledge, and in his *First Philosophy* he famously defended the study of foreign sciences. From al-Kindī's time onwards, Muslim authors held differing views as to how the different sciences of foreign provenance related to those associated with the Islamic religion and the Arabic language. This distinction was to underlie many medieval Arabic classifications of the sciences. In addition to classifying sciences according to their subject matter or their method in this way, there was also a tradition of assessing them according to the cultural contexts in which they had originated. A well-known reflection of this conflict is the debate between the grammarian al-Sīrāfī and the philosopher Abū Bishr Mattā about the merits of their respective disciplines.

Throughout the tenth century, Arabic philosophers such as Qusṭā ibn Lūqā or the mathematician al-Khwārizmī continued to present divisions of the sciences as they were known in the Greek philosophical tradition (Biesterfeldt 2000). The most prominent interpretation is al-Fārābī's *Enumeration of the Sciences* (*Kitāb iḥṣā' al-'ulūm*). Though its title may evoke a simple list rather than a systematic presentation of the sciences, this treatise was a decisive step towards a complex classification of the sciences and deserves a more detailed discussion (Jolivet 2006).

Al-Fārābī's treatise is marked by the ambition to integrate Greek philosophy and the Arabo-Islamic disciplines into one single account and to demonstrate that both are compatible and that philosophy may even be superior. Adopting a late antique introduction to the sciences originally composed by Paul the Persian (Gutas 1983), he included the Arabo-Islamic disciplines theology (*kalām*), jurisprudence (*fiqh*) and grammar (*naḥw*) into his treatise. The result is a sixfold division: al-Fārābī's *Enumeration* starts with the language sciences, including grammar, followed by logic (which also follows the structure of the books of Aristotle's *Organon*), mathematics, natural philosophy (using again the Aristotelian works as a model), and divine science or metaphysics, with Aristotle's homonymous work at its centre. Finally there is a section on ethics and politics, which includes a discussion of the autochthonous disciplines *fiqh* and *kalām*.

Like al-Kindī's *Quantity*, al-Fārābī's *Enumeration* owes a lot of its underlying structure to the late antique interpretation of Aristotle's *oeuvre*. Both texts combine genuinely Aristotelian models (such as the threefold division of theoretical philosophy) with Neoplatonic concepts (such as the propaedeutic character of mathematics). At the same time, however, al-Fārābī's treatise is clearly marked by the effort to arrive at a more general and comprehensive classification of human epistemic practices. This ambition led the author not only to include Islamic theology and jurisprudence and Arabic grammar, but also to devote particular attention to a large number of "new" sciences such as statics or optics. He discusses these so-called intermediate sciences (the Latin *scientiae mediae*) as part of the chapter on mathematics.

The innovative character of al-Fārābī's *Enumeration* is mostly obvious in the structure of the text. Thus, while it may seem that the author merely describes the individual sciences and refrains from establishing an explicit hierarchy between them, he places the *Posterior Analytics* at the very centre of the architecture of his work. He makes a revealing statement in Chapter II, where he claims that all parts of logic are ultimately directed towards the *Posterior Analytics* as their end. It seems that demonstrative science, as defined by Aristotle in this work, is al-Fārābī's guideline for assessing all the different disciplines, even though he never discusses this explicitly.

In the years following al-Fārābī, the interest in classifications of sciences persisted among Arabic authors. Some, such as the Brethren of Purity (*Ikhwān al-Ṣafā'*) (Callataÿ 2008) with their Neoplatonic encyclopaedia, Ibn Ḥazm with his *The Categories of the Sciences* (*Marātib al-'ulūm*) or Fakhr al-Dīn al-Rāzī with several treatises, adapted the philosophical tradition of dividing the sciences. Unlike al-Fārābī, however, they did not try to integrate Greek and Arabo-Islamic sciences into one single framework. They rather all agreed on a fundamental separation between "foreign" and indigenous sciences (Rosenthal 1975: 52–70).

At the same time, the influence of al-Fārābī's *Enumeration* unfolded in the medieval world across linguistic boundaries. It was translated twice into Latin in the twelfth century (Burnett 2001) and turned into an important reference for the curricular design of the University of Paris in its early years (Lafleur 1988).

There can be no doubt that the classifications of the sciences developed in the ninth and tenth centuries, primarily by al-Kindī and al-Fārābī, are a milestone in the history of epistemology. They substantially enlarge the scope of the late antique Prolegomena so as to embrace different and new forms of knowledge. Yet, these classificatory schemes alone yield a static view of the sciences that does not go into explaining their proper logic and their interdependences.

Construing the System: First Principles, Subject Matter and Subordination

From the eleventh century onwards, Arabic philosophers interpreted the dynamic structure of the sciences in a more systematic fashion. Within this tradition, Ibn Sīnā's *Book of the Healing* (*Kitāb al-Shifā'*) deserves a special place. The very structure of this philosophical compendium reveals just how influential Aristotle's division of the sciences was. The *Kitāb al-Shifā'* comprises books on logic, physics, mathematics and metaphysics (Gutas 1988: 102–3).

In this work Ibn Sīnā tried to provide metaphysical criteria for the division of the sciences. Thus, in the part of the *Shifā'* which corresponds to the *Isagoge* we encounter a division of the sciences clearly based on a metaphysical distinction: the subject of theoretical philosophy includes those things "whose existence is not by our choice and action," whereas the subject of practical philosophy is comprised of those which are. As for Aristotle, the subjects of these two categories are further divided according to whether, for example, they mix with motion (Marmura 1980: 240–1).

At the same time, philosophers such as Ibn Sīnā and Ibn Rushd succeeded in methodically implementing a series of concepts from Aristotle's theory of science in his *Posterior Analytics* in the epistemological discourse. Thus, they took up Aristotle's very dense and complex remarks concerning the principles and distinctive features of the individual sciences, as well as the possible relations between them.

In his *Posterior Analytics*, Aristotle had presented two different ways of how to describe the first principles of a science. While in Chapter 2 of Book I he proposed three categories to distinguish the different principles of demonstrative science, in Chapter 10, he divided them into two. Thus, in the first passage, he says that the first principles of every science consist of "axioms," which everybody grasps intuitively, and of "theses," which are not immediately clear to everybody, but which can also not be demonstrated. The latter fall into "hypotheses," which concern the existence (*hoti*) of a given object, and "definitions," which concern its quiddity (*ti*). In contrast, in Chapter 10 Aristotle divides the first principles into those that are common (*koina*) to all the sciences, e.g. logical rules, and those that are specific (*idia*) to a particular science.

Faced with these two different approaches, Aristotle's commentators developed, from late antique until modern times, various models of how to conceive of the first principles of the sciences. In the *Book of Demonstration* (*Kitāb al-burhān*), i.e. the part of the *Kitāb al-Shifā'* that corresponds to the *Posterior Analytics*, Ibn Sīnā discusses the first principles of the sciences (Maróth 1994: 144–6). In Chapter 12 of Book I (Ibn Sīnā 1954: 58–9), he distinguishes the principles of the demonstrative proof for science absolutely speaking and those for any particular science. The former, also presented as "evident knowledge" (*al-'ilm al-muta'āraf*), consists of propositions in which the predicate is connected with its subject in a self-evident manner and excludes a middle term. Like Aristotle's axioms, they thus allow no demonstration at all. The latter, also referred to as relative (*waḍ'*), correspond to Aristotle's theses. Ibn Sīnā describes them as propositions which cannot be demonstrated within the science in which they are applied. Their truth, however, can be demonstrated by means of another science. It is thus appropriate to refer to the relative principles, which correspond to Aristotle's theses, as the first principles of a particular science, since within that specific science they are assumed to be true without further demonstration. This view is a very original interpretation of Aristotle's theory and developed a significant impact on later writers. Thus, two centuries after Ibn Sīnā, Ibn Rushd was to take up this distinction in his commentary (*Talkhīṣ*) on Aristotle's logic (Maróth 1994: 146). While Aristotle, *Posterior Analytics* II, 19, indicates that the theses must be acquired through a certain form of induction (*epagôgê*), Ibn Sīnā and Ibn Rushd understand the first principles of the particular sciences in the context of a general division of labour among the sciences. Ultimately, metaphysics validates the theses of both physics and mathematics and thus provides their methodological foundation.

While developing such an integrated view of the sciences, which stressed their interconnectedness, Arabic philosophers also emphasized the autonomy of the individual sciences. Thus, in his *Kitāb al-burhān*, Ibn Sīnā repeatedly insists on the proper genus or subject matter of each science, which grants its distinctness. In order to resolve the tension between this independence of the sciences and the complex relations which Arabic philosophers recognized between the different and occasionally overlapping branches of knowledge, Ibn Sīnā set out to identify a criterion which explains the various connections between the sciences.

Once more, his starting point was Aristotle, in particular his attempt in *Posterior Analytics* to explain how two disciplines can share the same subject matter without being identical. Aristotle tackled the question by proposing his model of subordinate sciences. As in the case of the first principles, he offered two different models in his explanation. In *Posterior Analytics* I, 7, he maintains that two sciences can consider the same subject matter differently, namely in an absolute (*haplôs*) or in a relative (*ê pê*) manner. While the absolute consideration belongs to the superior science, the relative consideration is characteristic of the subordinate science. In Chapter 9, however, he develops another argument explaining that harmonics is subordinate to arithmetic because the former only knows the *hoti* (i.e. that it is), while the latter also knows the *dioti* (i.e. why it is) of the phenomenon in question.

Like the two different ways of describing the first principles of a science mentioned above, these passages from *Posterior Analytics* I, 7 and 9 have given rise to an extensive and ongoing debate. Again, Ibn Sīnā's views on the issue had a crucial impact on the discussion (Maróth 1994: 156–8). In addition to shaping the Arabic tradition, they influenced developments in Latin philosophy, since Dominicus Gundissalinus (fl. ca. 1150) translated Chapter 7 of Book II (Ibn Sīnā 1954: 104–11) of the *Kitāb al-burhān* into Latin and included it in his *De divisione philosophiae*.

In this brilliant interpretation, Ibn Sīnā claims that it can be the case that one science considers a subject matter *x*, while another science considers a subject matter *x'* which relates to *x* as a species relates to its genus. This relation between the subject matter *x* and the derivative subject matter *x'* establishes a hierarchy between the two sciences, insofar as the science concerned with *x* will be more comprehensive than the one that considers *x'*. In a second step, Ibn Sīnā distinguishes two cases of what it means for a science to consider the derivative subject matter *x'*. The first case is that it considers the derivative subject matter *x'* in an absolute manner, in which case this science will be part of the science concerned with *x*. An example for this is biology and its relation to physics. Both are concerned with the body, but physics is concerned with the genus "body," while biology considers its species "living body." The second case is that a science considers only certain accidents of the derivative subject matter *x'*, in which case it will be subordinate to the science concerned with *x*. Medicine, for example, is subordinate to physics, for both are concerned with the genus "body," but medicine considers the species "living body" with respect to some of its proper accidents, namely illness and health (unlike biology, which considers it in an absolute way). Therefore, Ibn Sīnā concludes, there are at least two basic manners in which one science can be contained in another, either as a part (Arabic *juz'*—Latin *pars*) of it or as a subordinate science (Arabic *naw'* —Latin *species*).

With these explanations, Ibn Sīnā draws an extremely complex picture of the relations that can obtain between different sciences. For although his starting point is Aristotle, especially the reflections in *Posterior Analytics* I, 7 concerning the distinction between an absolute and a relative way of considering the genus, his interpretation introduces a new element. In addition to elucidating the subordination of the sciences, it explains that one science may fall into different constitutive parts, which are located not on a vertical, but on a horizontal line.

Thus, Ibn Sīnā provides a solid theoretical foundation for any attempt to classify the sciences. It explains in a coherent manner how disciplines such as logic or natural philosophy have different parts (in the classifications outlined above, the Aristotelian works), and how one has to conceive of those disciplines which al-Fārābī inserted as "intermediate sciences" into his division.

These reflections on the first principles of the sciences, on their particular subject matters as well as on their internal differentiation and subordination make up an extremely attractive epistemological theory. It accounts for the methodological primacy of metaphysics and offers an original and lucid solution for the difficulty of how to reconcile the autonomy of the individual sciences with their patent interdependences. This approach developed—probably for the first time in the history of Aristotelian Neoplatonism—a genuinely consistent and clear-cut *system of the sciences*. Apart from covering a considerable variety of epistemic practices, it also allowed an understanding of their proper dynamics.

Innovating Methods: Induction vs. Experimentation

As mentioned above, Ibn Sīnā took a critical stance on Aristotelian induction, or *epagôgê*, i.e. the idea that the observation of particular instances can lead to a universal judgment.

Of course, Ibn Sīnā was not the first to tackle this difficult issue, which is at the core of Aristotle's scientific methodology; several Greek philosophers had already pointed to some of the weaknesses of Aristotle's concept of induction. They primarily objected that one can hardly ever be certain to have considered all the particular instances which are relevant to the judgement in question, and that an incomplete induction cannot generate universal knowledge.

Ibn Sīnā, however, went further in his critical analysis of induction, showing in his *Kitāb al-burhān* that even supposedly complete induction is ultimately a deficient mode of knowledge and cannot by any means lead to a universal and necessary proposition. His criticism of *epagôgê* or *istiqrā'* may be best explained by drawing on an inductive syllogism which Jon McGinnis (2003: 312) extrapolates from Chapter 1 of Book IV of the *Kitāb al-burhān*: "Socrates, Plato, Aristotle and so on are rational animals; the species 'humans' applies to Socrates, Plato, Aristotle and so on; therefore 'human' is identical with being a rational animal." The crucial point which Ibn Sīnā is making against this form of argument is that such an inductive syllogism presupposes what it is meant to show. Thus, the minor premise (i.e. that the species "human" applies to the given individuals) obviously implies a definition of "human." We can only subsume the different individuals under the species if we already know what humans are. But of course this definition is nothing else than the definition given in the conclusion, namely that humans are rational animals. Thus, identifying the relevant set of instances whose characteristic similarities one wishes to observe in the process of induction, requires knowing beforehand the essential formula of these instances. This is not only true for inductive syllogisms which infer a definition, as is the case of our example. According to Ibn Sīnā, it also holds for inductions which are meant to establish a universal relationship between a subject and a necessary accident (or property), since the latter can only be necessary insofar as it is related to the subject's essential formula. On this view, every kind of scientific induction presupposes knowledge of the subject's definition or of its essential formula, and therefore becomes circular or, at least, mediated.

What is at stake here is not so much the practical viability of induction, namely the problem of the actual limits of observation. Rather, Ibn Sīnā's criticism addresses the theoretical foundations of induction, which on his account proves to be extremely weak and unable to provide universal and necessary knowledge on its own. Ibn Sīnā's objections may not do justice to the complex role of *epagôgê* in Aristotle's scientific methodology, but there can be no doubt that the Arabic philosopher is one of the finest critics of induction such as it was commonly understood in the Aristotelian tradition.

His critical attitude notwithstanding, Ibn Sīnā was well aware of the need for a scientific method that allowed drawing necessary conclusions from observation. Therefore, once he refuted induction (*istiqrā'*), he set out to develop a new, more modest approach in his important theory of experimentation (*tajriba*) (see again

McGinnis 2003). Unlike induction, experimentation does not intend to establish absolute necessary knowledge, but it contents itself with conditional necessary knowledge. An example Ibn Sīnā gives in the *Kitāb al-burhān* illustrates this concept well. He discusses here the case of scammony necessarily purging bile (Ibn Sīnā 1954: 45–6). The philosopher develops his argument in two steps. Having shown that scammony has the power to purge the bile, he uses the resulting proposition as a minor premise in a syllogism which concludes that scammony necessarily causes the purging of the bile.

Ibn Sīnā realizes the first of these steps through multiple observations. When two phenomena usually occur together, we may assume that they do so not just by chance or due to an accidental relationship, but that this regularity arises from the subject's nature. The second option can be explained in two ways: either our assumption (i.e. that they are bound by a non-accidental, essential relationship) is based on numerous positive repetitions of our observation, or we reach this assumption because we do not observe any falsifying instances. While at first glance these seem to be merely two sides of the same coin, the two alternatives differ considerably regarding their implications for the scientific methodology and practice. Ibn Sīnā clearly supported the latter explanation. In fact, in the *Kitāb al-burhān* he states that the essential difference between induction (*istiqrā'*) and experimentation (*tajriba*) lies precisely here: the former supposedly provides absolute knowledge through the acquaintance with a number of positive cases, whereas the latter endeavours to obtain knowledge which is not absolute, but conditional, since it is subject to falsification. Returning to the example of scammony, this means for Ibn Sīnā that as long as we do not come across any counterexample, we are entitled to affirm that scammony has the power to purge the bile, and we know that it does so by reason of its nature, even though we do not grasp the exact causal relations.

The second step in Ibn Sīnā's model is meant to address this gap and to render judgments based on experimentation formally necessary. Thus, one can formulate the following syllogism: "The power to purge causes purging, scammony has the power to purge the bile, ergo, scammony necessarily causes purging the bile" (McGinnis 2003: 321). Yet, as is obvious from step one, this necessity cannot be absolute, but only conditional.

To these deliberations, Ibn Sīnā adds the important caveat nowadays known as the *caeteris-paribus* condition. For the first step to work properly, the experimenter has to record all the surrounding or background conditions which determine his or her observations. For only when the different observations are repeated under comparable circumstances will they offer reliable results.

One can hardly overestimate the importance of experimentation (*tajriba*) as it was developed by Ibn Sīnā and his contemporaries such as Ibn al-Haytham for the history of scientific method. When Ibn al-Haytham's optics became known in the Latin West to authors such as Robert Grosseteste or Roger Bacon, experimentation turned into a key ingredient in the scientific discourse (see Tachau 1988). It maintained this important position in the following centuries and up until modern times.

Conclusion

The various ideas presented in this chapter concerning the structure and methods of the sciences presuppose an understanding of these as a complex network. This network of the sciences is the result of a consistent re-interpretation of Aristotle's philosophy in the light of his theory of science.

As has been shown, this approach is original, both in its critical reconstruction of Aristotle's work as well as with regard to the new concepts it puts forward, such as the distinction between parts and species of a science or the notion of experimentation. Hence, Arabic theory of science represents not only an important chapter in the history of the Aristotelian tradition, but it constitutes a significant contribution to the systematic exploration of the foundations of science where it provides manifold insights into the proper dynamics of science and the logic of discovery. It is therefore no surprise that this idea of the sciences as a highly differentiated network was eagerly picked up by Latin scholars during the Middle Ages (see Fidora 2011). Thus it became an integral part of the universal philosophical discourse which continues to underlie our institutional organization of knowledge and science today.

Further Reading

Bin Bakar, O. (1989) *Classification of the Sciences in Islamic Intellectual History. A Study in Islamic Philosophies of Science*, Philadelphia: Thesis Temple University.

Bosworth, C. E. (1963) "A Pioneer Arabic Encyclopedia of the Sciences: al-Khwārizmī's Keys of the Sciences," *Isis* 54: 97–111.

Forcada, M. (2006) "Ibn Bājja and the Classification of the Sciences in al-Andalus," *Arabic Sciences and Philosophy* 16: 287–307.

Gutas, D. (2002) "Certainty, Doubt, Error: Comments on the Epistemological Foundations of Medieval Arabic Science," *Early Science and Medicine* 7, 3: 276–89.

Witkam, J. J. (1987) "Ibn al-Akfānī (d. 749/1348) and his Bibliography of the Sciences," *Manuscripts of the Middle East* 2: 37–41.

References

Adamson, P. (2007) *Al-Kindī*, Oxford: Oxford University Press.

al-Kindī (1950) *Risāla fī kammīyat kutub Arisṭūṭālīs*, in M. Abū Rīda (ed.), *Rasā'il al-Kindī al-falsafiyya*, vol. 1, Cairo: Dār al-Fikr al-'Arabī, pp. 363–84.

Biesterfeldt, H. H. (2000) "Medieval Arabic Encyclopedias of Science and Philosophy," in S. Harvey (ed.), *The Medieval Hebrew Encyclopedias of Science and Philosophy*, Dordrecht: Kluwer Academic Publishers, pp. 77–98.

Burnett, C. (2001) "The Coherence of the Arabic–Latin Translation Program in Toledo in the Twelfth Century," *Science in Context* 14: 249–88.

Callataÿ, G. de (2008) "The Classification of Knowledge in the *Rasā'il*," in N. El-Bizri (ed.), *The Ikhwān al-Ṣafā' and their Rasā'il. An Introduction*, Oxford: University Press, pp. 58–82.

Fidora, A. (2011) "Aristotelische Wissenschaft als Netzwerk von Wissenschaften: Die Rezeption der aristotelischen Wissenschaftstheorie bei al-Fārābī und Dominicus Gundissalinus," in L. Honnefelder (ed.), *Albertus Magnus und der Ursprung der Universitätsidee. Die Begegnung der Wissenschaftskulturen im 13. Jahrhundert und die Entdeckung des Konzepts der Bildung durch Wissenschaft*, Berlin: Berlin University Press, pp. 77–96.

Gutas, D. (1983) "Paul the Persian on the Classification of the Parts of Aristotle's Philosophy: A Milestone Between Alexandria and Baghdad," *Der Islam* 60, 2: 231–67.

——. (1988) *Avicenna and the Aristotelian Tradition*, Leiden: Brill.
Hein, C. (1985) *Definition und Einteilung der Philosophie. Von der spätantiken Einleitungsliteratur zur arabischen Enzyklopädie*, Frankfurt: Peter Lang.
Ibn Sīnā (1954) *Kitāb al-burhān*, A. Badawī (ed.), Cairo: Maktabat al-nahḍa al-miṣriyya.
Jolivet, J. (2006) "Classifications des sciences arabes et médiévales," in *Perspectives médiévales et arabes*, Paris: Vrin, pp. 175–94.
Lafleur, C. (1988) *Quatre Introductions à la philosophie au XIIIe siècle. Textes critiques et étude historique*, Montréal & Paris: Institut d'Études Médiévales/Vrin.
Marmura, M. (1980) "Avicenna on the Division of the Sciences in the *Isagoge* of his *Shifa*," *Journal of the History of Arabic Science* 4: 239–51.
Maróth, M. (1994) *Die Araber und die antike Wissenschaftstheorie*, Leiden & New York: Brill.
McGinnis, J. (2003) "Scientific Methodologies in Medieval Islam," *Journal of the History of Philosophy* 41, 3: 307–27.
Rosenthal, F. (1975) *The Classical Heritage in Islam*, London: Routledge & Kegan Paul.
Tachau, K. (1988) *Vision and Certitude in the Age of Ockham. Optics, Epistemology and the Functions of Semantics 1250–1345*, Leiden & New York: Brill.

Part III

PHILOSOPHY IN THE NATURAL SCIENCES

10
THE ESTABLISHMENT OF THE PRINCIPLES OF NATURAL PHILOSOPHY

Jon McGinnis

Introduction

As with physicists today, natural philosophers in the medieval Islamic milieu frequently differed significantly with respect to various aspects of their physical theory while sharing roughly the same scientific paradigm or research project. In the medieval Islamic world there were two such dominant paradigms for thinking about natural phenomena: *falsafa* (whose proponents are the *falāsifa*) and *kalām* (whose proponents are the *mutakallimūn*). *Falsafa* is that philosophical tradition that sees itself as the continuation of classical Greek scientific thought (whether as found in the physical works of Aristotle and his later Neoplatonic commentators, the astronomical works of Ptolemy or the medical works of Galen). *Kalām* in contrast more closely aligned itself with the traditional Islamic sciences, such as Qur'ānic exegesis, Islamic law and Arabic grammar. Despite the animosity between the *falāsifa* and *mutakallimūn*, they in fact adopted many of the same starting points, addressed most of the same questions and shared numerous common intuitions (Rashed 2005: 287–8). While this study focuses primarily on the *falsafa* tradition of natural philosophy, it also occasionally considers *kalām* arguments particularly as they relate to or offer trenchant criticisms of various doctrines of the *falāsifa*.

This study begins with the ancient and medieval topography of the cosmos, both its size and shape, and the various kinds of motion it was thought to undergo. Next it turns to the concept of "nature" itself: what is a nature, whether one can prove that there are natures and a criticism of the idea that nature is a cause. Sections on the principles of nature follow. These principles include privation, matter, and form. Included in the section on matter is an extended discussion of physical bodies and the medieval Islamic debate over whether they have a continuous or discrete structure. The final two sections treat the formal principle: how form is to be understood and whether the generation of form can result from natural causal processes.

The Cosmos of Ancient and Medieval Natural Philosophy

Medieval thinkers were fairly unanimous in their belief that the physical universe must be finite in spatial extent. Aristotle had argued as much in both his *Physics* I, 5 and *De caelo* I, 5–6, using what is best described as "physical-style" arguments. In contrast with the physical-style arguments preferred by Aristotle and his Greek commentators, Arab natural philosophers preferred what might be called a "mathematical-style" proof (McGinnis 2010). Their general strategy was to imagine, as part of a *reductio*-style argument, an infinitely extended magnitude from which some finite amount is removed and then compare the original magnitude with the reduced magnitude. The goal was to show that no matter how one conceived the remaining magnitude, whether as finite or infinite, the comparison with the original would always end in contradiction.

Here is a simplified version of the argument: imagine two rigid beams, which cannot give way so as to stretch. Moreover, suppose that these beams extend from the earth infinitely into space. Next, imagine that some finite length, *x*, is removed from one of the beams, for instance, the distance between the earth and the end of our galaxy; call that beam from which *x* has been removed *R*. Now imagine that *R* is pulled toward the earth, and then is compared with the beam from which nothing had been removed. Call that original beam O. In this case, since the beams are rigid, *R* could not have stretched so as to extend the extra length *x*. Consequently, *R* must be less than O by a length equal to *x*. Now imagine the two beams lying side-by-side and compare them. Since they are side-by-side, either *R* corresponds exactly with O and so is equal to O in spatial extent, or *R* falls short of O. On the one hand, if *R* does not fall short of O but exactly corresponds with, and so is equal to, O, then *R* is not less than O, but it was posited that *R* is less than O by the length *x*, and so there is a contradiction. If, on the other hand, *R* falls short of O on the side extending into space, then where it falls short of O is a limit of *R*, in which case *R* is limited on both the side extending into space and on the earth side. In that case, *R* is finite, but it was assumed to be infinite, another contradiction. In short, if an actually infinite extension could exist and can be shortened by some finite amount (which is assumed as given), then the shortened amount must be either equal to or less than the original infinite extension; however, either case leads to contradiction. Therefore, the premise that gave rise to the contradictions—namely that an actually infinite extension could exist—must be rejected.

A quite sophisticated version of this proof is found as early as al-Kindī (ca. 800–870), the first Arab philosopher, who also seems to be its originator. Variations of it can also be found in Ibn Sīnā (980–1037), Ibn Bājja, that is, the Latin Avempace (ca. 1085–1139), Ibn Ṭufayl (ca. 1110–1185) and Suhrawardī (1154–1191). While there was disagreement among these philosophers as to what sort of magnitudes the proof applies—al-Kindī thought it applies equally to temporal magnitudes, whereas most others thought it has application only to spatial and/or material magnitudes—there was agreement that it demonstrated the finitude of the sensible universe.

As for the shape of the universe, most medieval natural philosophers envisioned it as a finite sphere that roughly centered on the earth. Unfortunately, the issue of whether the earth truly was at the center of the universe was a bit of a scientific embarrassment. For according to the best physics of the day (Aristotle's), the earth should be exactly at the center of the universe, but according to the best astronomy of the day (Ptolemy's), the earth needs to be slightly off center (Sabra 1984).

Additionally, they believed that within the cosmos there were two distinct types of motion—the perfectly uniform circular rotations of the heavens and the seemingly erratic rectilinear motions of the elements. These two types of motion formed part of the subject matter for two distinct physical sciences: celestial physics and terrestrial physics. Celestial physics—namely, astronomy—concerned itself with the supra-lunar realm: the supra-lunar realm extends from the orbit of the moon outward toward the sphere of the fixed stars and the outermost celestial sphere. The sphere of the fixed stars had embedded within it the stars of the various constellations of the zodiac and the like and was thought to rotate from east to west roughly once every 24 hours, sweeping everything below them with it. Below the sphere of the fixed stars were additional spheres that slowly and with unique rates rotated uniformly from west to east and bore along the visible planets: Mercury, Venus, Mars, Jupiter and Saturn as well as the sun and moon. To account for the apparent "wandering" of these planets, additional uniformly rotating spheres were posited as required to make the astronomical models empirically adequate (helpful overviews include Kuhn 1957; Saliba 1994).

In addition to heavenly motion, there is the motion of the sub-lunar realm. For the *falāsifa* the sub-lunar realm consisted of four elements: earth, water, air and fire. Unlike the perfectly uniform circular rotations of heavenly bodies, the elements exhibit rectilinear motion, naturally moving either up or down. Absolute down was identified with the center of the universe, with earth and water naturally moving downward, whereas away from the center was identified with absolute up, with air and fire naturally moving upward as far as the moon. In a (hypothetical) state of absolute equilibrium, the elements would settle into four layers with earth forming a sphere at the center of the universe, followed by a surrounding sphere of water and then air and finally fire forming the highest terrestrial sphere.

The elements, however, are not in a state of absolute equilibrium; rather, they are in constant motion mixing with one another and, in so doing, providing the underlying material for all the various composite substances that we experience around us like the flesh, blood and bone that make up animals and the wood, leaves and seeds that make up plants (along with their composite motions). According to ancient science, this constant mixing of the elements is due to the circular motion of the heavens, which affects the elements by causing their deviation from pure rectilinear motion. Consequently, the heavens were believed to have a definite effect upon the mixing of the elements and the formation of composite substances. It was this theory that underwrote many medieval natural philosophers' belief in astrology.

The Concept of Nature

While heavenly influences were of interest to ancient and medieval natural philosophers, it was the various substances' natures that was the real focus of physics; it was by appeal to a composite substance's nature that the natural philosophers explained the various motions and actions proper to that substance. In Arabic, the term for nature was most frequently *ṭabīʿa*, and the etymologically linked terms *ṭabʿ* and *ṭibāʿ*; additionally, *ḥaqīqa* ("reality or truth") was also sometimes used (Pingree & al-Haq 1998). Aristotle at *Physics* II, 1, 192b21–3 gave what became the standard definition of nature for centuries to come. The Arabic version runs thus: "Nature is a certain principle and cause on account of which the thing in which it is primarily is essentially, not accidentally, moved and at rest" (Arisṭūṭālīs 1964–1965). Arabic natural philosophers, physicians and alchemists alike adopted this definition. Thus, one sees it repeated virtually verbatim by Yaḥyā ibn ʿAdī (d. 974), Ibn al-Samḥ (d. 1027), Ibn Sīnā, Ibn Bājja and Ibn Rushd (1126–1198). Variations closely dependent upon Aristotle's definition are also found in the works of al-Kindī, al-Fārābī (ca. 870–950) and Ibn Ṭufayl (McGinnis 2011: 60–4).

What all these thinkers held in common is that a nature is in some way a cause of the motion and actions that belong to a substance on account of what that substance is. Aristotle himself had identified two ways that natures are causes: either as form or as matter (although see Macierowski & Hassing 1988 for how later Hellenistic thinkers understood nature as cause). While the technical understanding of form and matter varied from thinker to thinker, in general they stand to one another as *what structures* to *what can be structured*. Form is the active (structuring) principle or cause and matter is the passive (structured) principle.

Aristotle and many working within the *falsafa* tradition took the existence of natures, understood as causes, as self evident and so in need of no proof. Indeed, Aristotle went so far as to write, "Trying to prove that there is nature is ridiculous, for it is obvious that there are many such things, whereas proving obvious things through what is not obvious belongs to one who is incapable of distinguishing between what is known in itself and what is not" (*Physics* II, 1, 193a3–6). In this vein, al-Kindī felt that the regular movements of the elements, whether away from or toward the center, gave ample witness to the existence of natures (1953a: vol. 2, 40–4). Similarly, other philosophers point to the regularity of fire's burning, alcohol's intoxicating, and scammony's purging as evidence that these substances have certain innate causal powers, identified with their natures.

Despite Aristotle's insistence that the existence of natures was obvious, not all agreed. For example, the Ashʿarite theologian al-Bāqillānī (d. 1013) railed against the purportedly self-evident character of natures:

> Concerning that over which [the philosophers] are in such a stir, namely that, they know by sense perception and necessarily that burning occurs from fire's heat and intoxication from excessive drink, it is tremendous ignorance. That is because what we observe and perceive sensibly when one drinks and fire comes into contact is only a change of the body's state from what it was, namely, one's being intoxicated or burnt, no more. As for the knowledge that this newly occurring state is from the action of whatever, it is not observed.
>
> (al-Bāqillānī 1957: 43 [77])

Bāqillānī's complaint, which al-Ghazālī (1058–1111) also repeats (1997: 171), is that although one might observe the constant conjunction of two types of events—like fire's contacting cotton and the cotton's burning—one does not observe the causal connection or mechanism that explains such regularities, which is supposedly the thing's nature. Based solely on sense perception, one could equally explain the regularity of one's observations by appealing to a divine habit to bring about one type of event on the occasion of another type of event. For example, it might be that when fire is placed in contact with cotton, God, not the fire, causes the burning of the cotton. Both interpretations of the cause of the burning are underdetermined, should one appeal solely to sense perception.

In fact, Bâqillânī went on and argued that natures alone are not sufficient to account for the varying and non-constant actions of sensible substances. For if the natures act in a constant, uniform way, why do the actions and motions that result from them vary? If the variations in the nature's actions are explained by appeal to other natures, one is quickly on the road to infinite regress. To stop the regress, Bâqillânī argued that one must appeal to a cause outside the natural order, namely, God. Thus, the purported series of natural causes must terminate with God. While one might claim that God acts through a finite series of intermediary natural causes, Bâqillânī's earlier argument indicated that there is no empirical reason for assuming such causal relations. Simplicity suggests that one needs only a single cause, God. In fact, many Muslim *mutakallimūn* did adopt a theory of occasionalism—the position that God causally determines everything in the world at every instant—and rejected the suggestion that natures were causes (Fakhry 1958; McGinnis 2006; Perler & Rudolph 2000).

Even within the *falsafa* tradition, there were detractors of Aristotle's position concerning the epistemic status of natures. Thus, Ibn Sīnâ in his *Physics* criticized Aristotle and the suggestion that the existence of natures is self-evident, for, complained Ibn Sīnâ, one should not simply accept but must demonstrate that every action or motion has a cause (Avicenna 2009: I.5 [4]). Like Bâqillânī, Ibn Sīnâ too believed that natural causes must terminate at a cause outside the natural order, but unlike Bâqillânī he argued that the intermediary series of natural causes cannot be eliminated, if one is to give an empirically adequate account of our world. Admittedly, continued Ibn Sīnâ, such a demonstration does not take place in the science of physics itself but in metaphysics (e.g. Avicenna 2005: II.2 [all bodies have formal and material causes] & VI.5 [all things act owing to some final cause]).

Principles of Nature: Privation, Matter, and Physical Bodies

As for the causal interactions within the physical world around us, Aristotelians identified four natural causes: material, formal, efficient and final. Additionally, medieval natural philosophers further divided these causes into internal causes—form and matter—and the external causes—the final and efficient causes (or end and agent respectively).

That form and matter should be identified with internal principles is no surprise, for form and matter, as already noted, correspond with a thing's active and passive natures, and natures are causes inherent within a thing. In addition to form and matter, Aristotle identified privation as a third "accidental" principle of nature (*Physics* I, 7). The reason for positing privation as a principle of change is simple enough: something cannot become what it already is but can only become what it is not. So, for example, if a quantity of water becomes hot, there must be the water, which is the underlying matter that undergoes the change. Additionally, there must be the form, that is to say, the heat that comes to be in the water. Finally, if there is to be a change or becoming, there must be the initial privation of the heat that will come to be; for if the water were already hot it could not become hot any more than you or I, who are presently human, can at this moment come to be human.

In general, natural philosophers in the medieval Islamic milieu wanted to distinguish the privation necessary for generation (*ʿadam*) from mere non-being or nonexistence (*lā wujūd*) (Lizzini 2009; Wolfson 1976: 359–72). One way they did this was by identifying privation with "the nonexistence of what possibly will exist" (al-Fārābī 1964: 56) or, to be more exact, with a relative absence in some matter. The privation is relative inasmuch as the matter is directed toward some specific natural form or perfection, in which case one can speak of a potentiality (*qūwa*) for that form or perfection in the matter. So, for example, while it is true that an acorn *is not* granite, an elephant or even a pine tree, neither does it stand in any essential relation to these substances; that is, it is not in proximate potentiality to any of these. In contrast, the acorn also *is not* an oak tree but it does stand in a special relation to an oak, namely, it is potentially an oak, for under the right condition the acorn will become an oak.

Matter (*mādda* or *hayūlā*, as well as *ʿunṣur*, "element" or "constituent," and the Greek loanword *usṭuqiss* [Gk. *stoicheion*] for element) was the subject of varying descriptions and numerous controversies. These concerns arose, no doubt, because there is something obscure about matter. Matter's obscurity is due, at least in part, to its association with privation, potentiality or possibility, for there is something indeterminate about all of these. Moreover, prime or first matter is supposedly independent of any form, and yet a thing is known through its form. Thus, there is very little in matter to get one's mind around conceptually. The Andalusian peripatetic Ibn Bājja, thus, had this to say about matter's elusive nature:

> Prime matter is that whose existence is essentially without a form and that indeed privation always accompanies its existence—not a single privation, but privations that replace one another. Moreover, possibility is not its form, for one possibility after another occurs successively in it just like the privations occur successively in it. Here, then, one understands prime matter itself. The conception preferred before this investigation was only by way of analogy, but there is no [exact] analogue [for prime matter] that can take place in the analogy, for [prime matter] is conceived as something whose relation to the elements is like the relation of wood to a wardrobe, but the latter relation is between two actually existing things, whereas the former relation is between something existing potentially and something existing actually. Thus, when the one is substituted for the other, the relation of [prime] matter to the wood is not like the relation of the wardrobe to the <elements>*.
>
> (Ibn Bājja 1978: 20, *reading the marginal correction *isṭaqisāt* in place of *al-mādda*/matter)

Because of the difficulty associated with matter *qua* pure potency or wholly indeterminate, this study limits itself to a consideration of matter insofar as it has the most basic determination of three-dimensionality and so is a natural body.

Understanding natural bodies gave rise to one of the more heated scientific debates in the Islamic medieval world, namely, whether bodies have an atomic or continuous structure. An atom is something indivisible, in Arabic, a part that itself has no parts (*juz' lā yatajazzu'*). There are at least two senses, however, that something can be indivisible: one, physically indivisible and two, conceptually and physically indivisible. *Kalām* physics, which for the most part was atomistic in its orientation, favored atoms that, while occupying space (*ḥayyiz*), were nonetheless *both* physically *and* conceptually indivisible (Dhanani 1994; Pines 1936; Sabra 2006).

It was the idea that atoms were *conceptually* indivisible that drew the greatest fire. The criticisms generally fell into two camps: those arguments that attempted to show a physical absurdity about a conceptually indivisible part (e.g. Avicenna 2009: III.4 (4); Averroes 1562–1574: 247v–48r), and those that attempted to show that conceptually indivisible parts were incompatible with the best mathematics of the time (e.g. Avicenna 2009: III.4 (5); Maimonides 1963: I 73, "third premise"). As an example of the first kind of criticism consider a sheet of atoms one atom thick between yourself and the sun. Surely, the philosophers complained, it is absurd to think that the side of the sheet in front of you is the very same side that is facing the sun; however, if there are two sides to the sheet, then the atom can be conceptually divided into the side facing you and the side facing the sun.

A progenitor to the modern "Weyl tile" argument (Salmon 1980: 62–6; Weyl 1949: 43) provides an example of a mathematical-style critique. Moses Maimonides, in his *Guide of the Perplexed*, presented a version of the tile argument, which runs thus. The Muslim atomists envisioned atoms as cuboidal in shape and yet again physically and conceptually indivisible. Given this premise Maimonides retorts:

> By virtue of [this *kalām*] premise all geometrical demonstrations become invalid … . Some of them would be absolutely invalid, as, for instance, those referring to the properties of incommensurability and commensurability of lines and planes and the existence of rational and irrational lines and all that are included in the tenth book of Euclid and what is similar.
>
> (Maimonides 1963: 198; after Pines)

To give one a sense of Maimonides' concern, imagine, for example, a three-by-three checkerboard square of space. Next, upon the space transcribe a right triangle, the base and height of which are three units each. Applying the Pythagorean theorem, $A^2 + B^2 = C^2$, the hypotenuse should be $\sqrt{18} \asymp 4.2426$; however, if the atomic theory is correct, the hypotenuse can only be 3 units long, since there are only three squares making up the diagonal of our atomic triangle. It does no good to say that the diagonal of the cuboidal atom is longer than its side, for the atom supposedly occupies the smallest conceptually indivisible space. Thus, set the side of the atom at unit-length 1. In that case, the diagonal of our atom turns out to be $\sqrt{2} \asymp 1.4142$, but 0.4142 is an amount of space *less than* the smallest conceptually possible space, which is absurd.

Viewing matter as a continuum, which was the preferred view of natural philosophers in the Graeco-Arabic scientific tradition, had its own set of problems. At least one way that Aristotle typified continua was in terms of potentially infinite divisibility (*Physics* VI, 2, 232b24–5). A body is continuous, then, if one can take indefinitely smaller divisions, as, for example, in increments of 1, 1/2, 1/4, 1/8, 1/16 … 1/2n. While medieval Aristotelians were virtually unanimous that an actual infinity is impossible, they felt potential infinities were not only possible but even necessary, particularly if material bodies are continuous.

It was just this appeal to the potentially infinite divisibility of bodies that the *mutakallimūn* found objectionable. They criticized thus: if something truly is potential, then its existence must be at least possible. A thing is possible, however, just in case some agent has the power to bring about the given effect. Consequently, something is truly possible if it falls within the power of an omnipotent deity. In that case, then, let God bring about the potentially infinite number of divisions that purportedly can be made in some continuous body. If there truly were a potentially infinite number of divisions, then God would have brought about an *actual infinity*; however, both philosopher and theologian alike conceded that an *actual* infinity was impossible and so outside the scope of any agent, even God. The mere possibility of a potential infinity implies an impossibility and so the reality of a potential infinity must *a fortiori* be rejected. Thus, concluded the atomists, matter is not continuous but made up of discrete parts or atoms.

While both sides had stratagems for responding to their opponent's criticisms, by far one of the true scientific contributions of medieval Islamic natural philosophy was a sort of compromise theory, namely, the doctrine of *minima naturalia*. The idea of natural minimums is that although bodies are conceptually divisible *ad infinitum*, there nonetheless are physical limits beyond which they cannot be divided. The idea is most closely linked with the great Spanish Muslim philosopher, Ibn Rushd (Glasner 2001, 2009: Chapter 8), although Ibn Sīnā too had a theory of natural minima even if less well known (Avicenna 2009: III.12).

One version of the theory begins with the basic assumption that natural substances, for example, flesh and blood, are a composite of matter—or more precisely some elemental mixture—and a species form by which the substance acts. In order for the form to produce the activities specific to the substance, the analysis continues, the material must have a qualitative disposition suitable to the given form; that is, the matter must be of the right hotness or coolness, wetness or dryness. If the matter loses the qualitative disposition required for the form, the form can no longer be preserved. The qualitative disposition of any matter, however, is affected by the hotness, coolness, wetness and dryness of the surrounding bodies. Furthermore, the smaller the body is, the more forcefully those surrounding bodies and their qualities affect it. Beyond a certain minimal size, the body's own qualities are insufficient to counter the qualitative affect of the surrounding bodies. The body, then, becomes qualitatively identical to that of the surrounding bodies. At that point the reduced body receives the species form of the surrounding bodies and so loses its previous species form.

So, for example, imagine a cup of water that is surrounded by hot, dry summer air. Now imagine half that amount of water, and then keep taking halves. At some point the amount of water is so small that the water simply evaporates as it were instantaneously. Medieval natural philosophers would say that the form of water in that minuscule physical quantity was immediately replaced with the form of air. In other words, there are natural minima less than which a given form cannot be sustained. While the theory of *minima naturalia* is in many ways thoroughly Aristotelian, it is also decidedly influenced by *kalām* atomism and shows the fruitful cross-pollination of these two physical theories.

Principles of Nature: Form

In discussing *minima naturalia* the notion of form is introduced. While the most common Arabic term for form was *ṣūra*, one also occasionally sees *ṣīgha* and *hay'a*. Aristotelian natural philosophers divided forms into artificial and natural forms. Artificial forms are the forms of manmade things, such as beds, swords or coins. Natural forms are the forms of naturally occurring things, like the elements and composite substances, such as flesh, blood, human, as well as the forms of, for example, green, hot, wet and other features consequential upon substances. Natural forms were sometimes additionally divided into species forms, which correspond with the forms of things in the category of substance, and accidental forms, which correspond with the forms of things falling under one of Aristotle's nine categories of accidents—quantity, quality, relation, where, when, position, possession, action and passion.

Natural philosophers were most interested in the natural forms of substances, for the substantial form explains the various actions proper to a given species. As for how to understand the substantial form, there were at least two accounts in the medieval Islamic world: one that identified forms with certain primary qualities, namely, the pairs hot/cold and wet/dry, and another that took forms to be unanalyzable powers.

Concerning the first account, ancient and medieval physicists associated the primary qualities, hot, cold, wet and dry, with the four basic elements. For example, associated with fire are the qualities hot–dry, with air, the qualities hot–wet, with water, the qualities cold–wet and with earth the qualities cold–dry. Aristotle had argued that a thing's substantial form in a sense is just its primary qualities (*On Generation and Corruption* II, 2–3), or what Porphyry and certain Neoplatonic commentators dubbed its "substantial qualities" (De Haas 1997: 180–250; Stone 2008). Thus, for example, the element fire is matter at the extreme degrees of hotness and dryness. Simply put, the substantial form of a thing, for many Aristotelians, was identical with the proportionality of its primary qualities. Al-Kindī suggests such a theory in a number of treatises (e.g. 1953b: 23–24). Ibn Rushd is explicit: "the forms of [the elements] are the four simple qualities, which are at the extreme. (I mean the two of them that are active and passive, for example, the hot and dry that are in fire and the cold and wet that are in water)" (Averroes 1987: 55). The alchemist, Jābir ibn Hayyān, took this position to its extreme and reified these primary qualities, making hot, cold, wet and dry themselves the first elements (al-Haq 1994: 57–62).

Such a theory was advantageous from a scientific point of view because it provided a simple account of generation and corruption; that is, of substantial change. In substantial change, one kind of substance becomes another kind when the underlying matter throws off one substantial form and acquires a new one. An example is self-nourishment, for in self-nourishment the animal or plant takes in one kind of substance and converts it into a new kind that it can use. Now if a thing's substantial form is nothing more than its (primary) qualitative constitution, then substantial change is a straightforward matter of altering the primary qualities. So, for example, heat the substance water, which again is a cool–wet mixture. When the level of heat no longer corresponds with the cool–wet substantial form of water, there comes to be the substantial form of air, a hot–wet mixture, and so a new substance. In short, the explanation of how substantial change occurs comes down to such basic and well-understood operations as heating/cooling and moistening/drying.

Still, not all were happy with this account of natural substantial forms, which leads to the second view of substantial forms. Al-Fārābī recognized that the forms of natural things and even certain artifacts are not sensible features such as hot and cold. "The forms and materials of most natural bodies are insensible," asserts al-Fārābī, "and their existence is confirmed for us only through syllogisms and apodictic demonstrations" (al-Fārābī 1968: 114–15). Thus, for example, the power of wine by which it intoxicates—a power that al-Fārābī identifies with its form—is not something sensible but is recognized only through the wine's actions. Such a conclusion follows all the more clearly for natural substances such as eyes with respect to sight and other bodily organs and their functions.

In addition to al-Fārābī's inductive argument, Ibn Sīnā offers a theoretically based objection against the identification of substantial forms and primary qualities (Avicenna 1969: 122–132; Stone 2008). He complains that the theory fails to distinguish between species forms and accidental forms, such as of qualities. Accidents are essentially dependent upon the actual existence of the substances in which they inhere, while the actual existence of a substance is essentially dependent upon its form, which actualizes the matter. For Ibn Sīnā, it is simply ad hoc to say that hot, cold, wet and dry are "special substantial qualities" different from other accidents. In short, the theory that identifies substantial forms with primary qualities, protests Ibn Sīnā, commits itself to circular causation. Qualities exist because the substances in which they inhere exist, and substances exist because their substantial forms exist, and the substantial forms of the elements (at least according to the theory being rejected) exist because the qualities that constitute them exist, and one finds oneself at the beginning, since qualities are again accidents. In the end, Ibn Sīnā, like al-Fārābī, held that substantial forms must be non-sensible, occult things, which are ultimately known only through the operations that they allow a natural substance to do.

Natural Causation

Because of the supposed "metaphysical" nature of forms, as opposed to a physical one, certain medieval natural philosophers distinguished between physical and metaphysical causation. Physical causation involves basic physical processes—moving an object from one place or position to another, altering its sensible qualities and increasing or decreasing its bulk—operations that ancient and medieval natural philosophers ultimately traced back to the motion of the heavens. For certain medieval thinkers, these processes merely prepare the underlying matter so as to make it suitable for some new substantial form. Such processes, however, do not create forms. Instead, concluded this group, forms are produced as a result of metaphysical causation, and as such require an agent working outside of the natural order.

For a number of reasons, proponents of this view identified the immediate producer of forms not with God—even though God was viewed as the ultimate cause—but with an intermediary immaterial agent. Thus, al-Fārābī suggested that the active intellect infuses properly disposed matter with its suitable form, and Ibn Bājja, at least in one place, followed al-Fārābī (al-Fārābī 1961: 129–130 & 1964: 54–5; Ibn Bājja 1968: 107). Ibn Sīnā developed this notion further and introduced a "giver of forms" (*wāhib al-ṣuwar*), which is frequently identified with the active intellect, as the needed metaphysical agent (Avicenna 1969: XIV & 2005: IX.5). Al-Suhrawardī adopted a similar theory, albeit recast in his preferred light imagery:

> Lights become the cause of motions and heat, where both motion and heat obviously belong to light, not that they are its cause, rather, they prepare the recipient so that [a light] occurs in it from the dominating light that emanates through its substance onto the recipients properly prepared for it.
> (Al-Suhrawardī 1999: 129)

Here "light" is a trope for "form" or "nature," and "dominating light" is al-Suhrawardī's terminology for a separate, immaterial substance, such as al-Fārābī's "active intellect" or Ibn Sīnā's "giver of forms." Even the *mutakallim* and critic of *falsafa*, al-Ghazālī, seems to have thought that the forms and natures of things here in the terrestrial realm are preserved and maintained by an angelic agent (1986: 119–22).

Despite its appeal to many, the idea of metaphysical causation and a separate, immaterial agent imparting forms was not without its critics. Perhaps the most vehement was Ibn Rushd (Averroes 1938–1952: 878–86). Ibn Rushd argued that the introduction of a "giver of forms" indicates a fundamental misunderstanding of the relation between matter and form. That is because if the matter's being prepared were different from the form impressed onto it, then one must assume that matter and form are really distinct, when in fact they are merely conceptually distinct. For example, if one considers an actually existing bed, one might conceive of the shape of the bed as different from the stuff that has that shape, but the shape and stuff of the bed are not really distinct such that there could be both a self-subsisting shape and self-subsisting matter. Yet such a view, objected Ibn Rushd, seems to be exactly what is assumed when one maintains that the "giver of forms" has certain forms that it impresses into prepared matter. In the end, Ibn Rushd complained that both al-Fārābī and Ibn Sīnā were misled about the generation of form "because it was an opinion very much like the account upon which *mutakallimūn* in our religion rely, namely that, the agent of all [generated] things is one and that some of the [generated] things do not bring about an effect in others" (Averroes 1938–1952: 885).

Conclusion

No single work can possibly do justice to the full array and richness of medieval Arabic natural philosophy. In the present study the focus has been on the *falsafa* tradition, and yet we have also had glimpses of how the *mutakallimūn* engaged with that tradition in creative ways, in ways that pushed natural philosophy forward; and, of course, much more can be said about *kalām* physics itself. Moreover, the present study has been limited exclusively to the so-called classical period of Islamic natural philosophy (ca. 850–1200), and yet recent research on the post-classical period suggests that exciting innovations were still continuing beyond this small window of time. Finally, only a small handful of topics central to medieval Arabic physics have been canvassed, and these only scratch the surface. Still, despite its limitations, hopefully this study has provided the reader with a basic framework to appreciate the concerns and the significance of a number of the physical doctrines and arguments used by the medieval natural philosophers working in Arabic, as well as how these thinkers viewed and established the most basic principles of nature.

Further Reading

al-Kindi (2007) "The Explanation of the Proximate Efficient Cause for Generation and Corruption," J. McGinnis & D. C. Reisman (tr.), *Classical Arabic Philosophy: An Anthology of Sources*, Indianapolis & Cambridge: Hackett Publishing Company, Inc., pp. 1–35.

Averroes (1958) *Averroes on Aristotle's* De Generatione et Corruptione, *Middle Commentary and Epitome*, S. Kurland (tr.), Cambridge, MA: The Mediaeval Academy of America.

Bakar, O. (1996) "Science," in S. H. Nasr & O. Leaman (eds.), *History of Islamic Philosophy*, London & New York: Routledge, pp. 926–46.

Dhanani, A. (2002) "Problems in Eleventh-Century *Kalām* Physics," *Bulletin of the Royal Institute for Inter-Faith Studies* 4, 1: 73–96.

Lettinck, P. (1994) *Aristotle's* Physics *and Its Reception in the Arabic World*, Leiden: Brill.

McGinnis, J. (2006) "Arabic and Islamic Natural Philosophy and Natural Science," in *Stanford Encyclopedia of Philosophy*, http://plato.stanford.edu/entries/arabic-islamic-natural/

Setia, 'Adī (2004) "Fakhr al-Dīn al-Rāzī on Physics and the Nature of the Physical World: A Preliminary Survey," *Islam & Science* 2: 61.

References

al-Bāqillānī (1957) *Tamhīd*, R. J. McCarthy (ed.), Beirut: Libraire Orientale.

al-Fārābī (1961) *Falsafat Arisṭūṭālīs*, M. Mahdi (ed.), Beirut: Dār Majallat Shi'r.

——. (1964) *al-Siyāsa al-Madaniyya*, F. M. Najjar (ed.), Beirut: Imprimerie Catholique.

——. (1968) *Iḥṣā' al-'ulūm*, 'U. Amin (ed.), Cairo: Maktaba l-Anglo l-Miṣriyya.

al-Ghazālī (1986) *al-Maqṣad al-asnā fī sharḥ asmā'Allāh al-ḥusnā*, F. A. Shehadi (ed.), Beirut: Dār Al-Mashriq.

——. (1997) *The Incoherence of the Philosophers*, M. E. Marmura (ed. and tr.), Provo, UT: Brigham Young University Press.

al-Haq, S. N. (1994) *Names, Natures and Things*, Dordrecht: Kluwer Academic Publishers.

al-Kindī (1953a) *Ṭabī'at al-falak*, M. Abū Rīda (ed.), *Rasā'il al-Kindī l-Falsafiyya*, Cairo: Dār al-Fikr al-'Arabī.

——. (1953b) *Liber de quinque essentiis*, M. Abū Rīda (ed.), *Rasā'il al-Kindī l-Falsafiyya*, Cairo: Dār al-Fikr al-'Arabī.

al-Suhrawardī (1999) *The Philosophy of Illumination*, J. Walbridge & H. Ziai (eds. and tr.), Provo, UT: Brigham Young University Press.

Arisṭūṭālīs (1964–1965) *al-Ṭabī'a*, A. Badawī (ed.), Cairo: al-Dār al-Qawmiyya lil-Ṭibā'a wa l-Nashr.
Averroes (1562–1574) *Aristotelis opera cum Averrois commentariis*, vol. 4, Venetiis apud Junctas; reprint (1962), Frankfurt: Minerva G.m.b.h.
——. (1938–1952) *Tafsīr mā ba'd al-ṭabī'īyāt*, 3 vols., M. Bouyges (ed.), Beirut: Imprimerie Catholique.
——. (1987) *Talkhīṣ kitāb al-usṭuqissāt li-Jālīnūs*, G. Anawati & S. Zayed (eds.), Cairo: The General Egyptian Book Organization.
Avicenna (1969) *al-Kawn wa-l-fasād*, M. Qasim (ed.), Cairo: General Egyptian Book Organization.
——. (2005) *The Metaphysics of The Healing*, M. E. Marmura (ed. and tr.), Provo, UT: Brigham Young University Press.
——. (2009) *The Physics of The Healing*, 2 vols., J. McGinnis (ed. and tr.), Provo, UT: Brigham Young University Press.
De Haas, F. A. J. (1997) *John Philoponus' New Definition of Prime Matter: Aspects of Its Background in Neoplatonism and the Ancient Commentary Tradition*, Leiden: Brill.
Dhanani, A. (1994) *The Physical Theory of Kalām: Atoms, Space, and Void in Basrian Mu'tazilī Cosmology*, Leiden: Brill.
Fakhry, M. (1958) *Islamic Occasionalism and Its Critique by Averroës and Aquinas*, London: Allen & Unwin.
Glasner, R. (2001) "Ibn Rushd's Theory of *Minima Naturalia*," *Arabic Science and Philosophy* 11, 1: 2–26.
——. (2009) *Averroes' Physics: A Turning Point in Medieval Natural Philosophy*, Oxford: Oxford University Press.
Ibn Bājja (1968) "al-Wuqūf 'alā l-'aql al-fa''āl," M. Fakhry (ed.), *Rasā'il ibn Bājja al-ilāhīya*, Beirut: Dār al-Nahār lil-Nashr.
——. (1978) *Shurūḥāt al-samā' al-ṭabī'ī*, M. Ziyāda (ed.), Beirut: Dār al-Kindī.
Kuhn, T. S. (1957) *The Copernican Revolution: Planetary Astronomy in the Development of Western Thought*, Cambridge, MA: Harvard University Press.
Lizzini, O. (2009) "Il nulla, l'inesistente, la cosa: note intorno alla terminologia e alla dottrina derl Nulla e della creazione dal nulla nel pensiero islamico," in M. Lenzi & A. Maierù (eds.), *Discussioni sul nulla tra Medioevo ed età moderna*, Firenze: Olschki, pp. 63–103.
Macierowski, E. M. & Hassing, R. F. (1988) "John Philoponus on Aristotle's Definition of Nature: A translation from the Greek with Introduction and Notes," *Ancient Philosophy* 8, 1: 73–100.
Maimonides (1963) *The Guide of the Perplexed*, S. Pines (tr.), Chicago: University of Chicago Press.
McGinnis, J. (2006) "Occasionalism, Natural Causation and Science in al-Ghazālī," in J. E. Montgomery (ed.), *Arabic Theology, Arabic Philosophy, From the Many to the One: Essays in Celebration of Richard M. Frank*, Leuven: Peeters, pp. 441–63.
——. (2010) "Avicennan Infinity: A Select History of the Infinite through Avicenna," *Documenti e Studi sulla Tradizione Filosofica Medievale* 21: 199–221.
——. (2011) "Natural Knowledge in the Arabic Middle Ages," in P. Harrison, R. L. Numbers, & M. H. Shank (eds.), *Wrestling with Nature: From Omens to Science*, Chicago: University of Chicago Press, pp. 59–82.
Perler, D. & Rudolph, U. (2000) *Occasionalismus: Theorien der Kausalität im arabisch-islamischen und im europäischen Denken*, Göttingen: Vandenhoeck & Ruprecht.
Pines, S. (1936) *Beiträge zur islamischen Atomenlehre*, Berlin: A. Heine G.m.b.H.; English translation (1997), *Studies in Islamic Atomism*, Jerusalem: The Hebrew University Magnes Press.
Pingree, D. E. & al-Haq, S. N. (1998) "Ṭabī'a," Th. Bianquis *et al.* (eds.), *The Encyclopedia of Islam*, New Edition, Leiden: Brill.

Rashed, M. (2005) "Natural Philosophy," in P. Adamson and R. C. Taylor (eds.), *The Cambridge Companion to Arabic Philosophy*, Cambridge: Cambridge University Press, pp. 287–307.

Sabra, A. I. (1984) "The Andalusian Revolt Against Ptolemaic Astronomy: Averroes and al-Bitrûjî," E. Mendelsohn (ed.), *Transformation and Tradition in the Sciences: Essays in honor of I. Bernard Cohen*, Cambridge: Cambridge University Press, pp. 133–52.

——. (2006) "*Kalām* Atomism as an Alternative Philosophy to Hellenizing *Falsafa*," in J. E. Montgomery (ed.), *Arabic Theology, Arabic Philosophy, From the Many to the One: Essays in Celebration of Richard M. Frank*, Leuven: Peeters, pp. 199–272.

Saliba, G. (1994) *A History of Arabic Astronomy: Planetary Theories During the Golden Age of Islam*, New York: New York University Press.

Salmon, W. C. (1980) *Space, Time, and Motion*, Minneapolis: University of Minnesota Press.

Stone, A. (2008) "Avicenna's Theory of Primary Mixture," *Arabic Sciences and Philosophy* 18, 1: 99–119.

Weyl, H. (1949) *Philosophy of Mathematics and Natural Science*, Princeton: Princeton University Press.

Wolfson, H. A. (1976) *The Philosophy of the Kalam*, Cambridge, MA: Harvard University Press.

11
CAUSALITY IN ISLAMIC PHILOSOPHY

Luis Xavier López-Farjeat

Introduction

Islamic discussions on causality are frequently related to two main philosophical issues, namely, the nature of God as the causal agent *par excellence* and the creation or origination of the world. Islamic theologians and philosophers both built their different conceptions of causality upon Greek sources, mainly Neoplatonic—such as the Arabic version of the *Liber de causis* (Taylor 2012), some texts derived from Plotinus's *Enneads* known as the *Plotiniana arabica* (d'Ancona 2010), and some Neoplatonic commentators on Aristotle's works (Wisnovsky 2002). From the Neoplatonic sources, metaphysicians such as al-Kindī, al-Fārābī, and Ibn Sīnā developed the notion of primary causality which was essential to argue for the existence of a First Cause (*al-'illa al-ūlā*) or God as responsible for the origination or creation of being (Taylor 2012). Nevertheless, the Aristotelian tradition was also quite influential: from Aristotle's *Physics* and *Metaphysics* the Islamic tradition took the characterization of the four causes as something essential for their comprehension of the natural world and of the moving heavens. Aristotle's conception of causality, however, was controversial for some theologians, mainly al-Ghazālī and the Ash'arites, given that it explained natural phenomena without appealing to the necessity of a creator.

In *Physics* II, 3 Aristotle explains four ways in which the term "cause" (Greek: *aitia*/ Arabic: *'illa*) is used: (1) that out of which a thing comes to be and which persists; (2) the form or archetype which determines the essence of a thing; (3) the primary source of change and rest; and, (4) the end or that for the sake of which a thing is done. These four causes are known traditionally as material, formal, efficient, and final causes, respectively, and they are central in Aristotelian physics and metaphysics. Islamic philosophers inherited this depiction of the four causes, but they amplified and even transformed Aristotle in this matter. The best example of this sort of transformation is found in the insightful innovations of Ibn Sīnā: although he drew deeply on the Aristotelian theory of causality, his understanding of the four causes, especially the efficient cause, is significantly different from Aristotle's: Ibn Sīnā holds the need for a permanent efficient cause that is responsible for the existence of the world. Yet it is important to note that neither the Aristotelian nor the

Avicennian theories of causality were accepted by some of the most important Islamic theologians. For instance, in his *Incoherence of the Philosophers* (*Tahāfut al-Falāsifa*) al-Ghazālī provides several powerful objections against the philosophical understanding of causality. In what follows, in the first section I focus on Ibn Sīnā's notion of causality and the way in which he transformed the understanding of the four Aristotelian causes; in the second section I present al-Ghazālī's account of causality in the *Tahāfut* as an example of a radical rejection of the plurality of causes and as a thoughtfully argued account of God being the sole causal agent. Finally, I conclude by highlighting the main differences between these two approaches.

Ibn Sīnā on Causality

Ibn Sīnā's theory of causality is one of the richest in the Islamic philosophical tradition. In several treatises, but mainly in the *Physics* (*Kitāb al-Samāʿ al-ṭabīʿī*) and the *Metaphysics* (*al-Ilāhiyyāt*) of the encyclopedic work *The Healing* (*al-Shifāʾ*), Ibn Sīnā reworks the Aristotelian account of causality to present his own penetrating conception. Although at first glance the proximity to Aristotle seems obvious, Ibn Sīnā's development of the four causes is original and differs from Aristotle's in several key aspects. While most modern interpreters dealing with Ibn Sīnā's conception of causality have focused on his important metaphysical account of the efficient cause (Gilson 1960; Marmura 1981a, 1984: 172–87; Richardson 2013), relatively little has been said on the importance of final causality and even less on his conception of material and formal causes. In *Samāʿ al-ṭabīʿī* 1.10 and *Ilāhiyyāt* 6.1, Ibn Sīnā explains that the causes are four: formal, elemental or material, agent or efficient, and purpose or final cause (Avicenna 2009: 64; 2005: 194). He refers to the formal cause as that part of a subsisting thing whereby a thing is what it is in actuality; the elemental or material cause is that part of a subsisting thing through which that thing is what it is in potency; the agent or efficient cause is that which brings about some existence which is essentially other than itself; and the purpose or final cause is that for the sake of which the existence of something is realized (Avicenna 2005: 194–5).

Ibn Sīnā's amplification and transformation of Aristotle is not obvious and has been given scant attention, particularly the formal and material causes (Bertolacci 2002). According to Bertolacci, it is difficult to capture Ibn Sīnā's conception of material and formal causality using rigid schemes and, as he observes, a careful reading of the *Ilāhiyyāt* would enable us to detect a variety of nuances (Bertolacci 2002: 153–4). Despite the complexity of systematizing Ibn Sīnā's understanding of the formal and material causes, something can be said at the risk of being simplistic. In *Ilāhiyyāt* 2.4 and *Samāʿ al-ṭabīʿī* 1.2, Ibn Sīnā stresses that, given the potentiality of matter, form must be the cause of matter. Nevertheless, in light of his emanationist cosmological model, which will be explained below, the form is not the only cause of matter when it comes to corruptible substances because another cause would have to be determined in order to account for the form that is received by a given corruptible substance. This cause is that which in *Ilāhiyyāt* 9.5 Ibn Sīnā describes precisely as the "giver of forms," identified as the tenth celestial intelligence within his cosmological model (Bertolacci 2002: 133). Ibn Sīnā explains that both formal and material causes are different because matter is receptive of the form and is the cause of potentiality, while the form is responsible for the actuality. Given that the relationship between matter and form is a causal one, form is the cause of matter acting in the compound but not the cause of the existence of matter. Matter is the cause of change and privation and in view of its receptive character, the form needs to be prior because it is the cause of matter being something specific and not merely formless or amorphous matter: a piece of wood is the material cause, but what makes it to be a table or a chair is the formal cause.

As mentioned above, out of the four causes treated by Ibn Sīnā, the one that has received most attention has been the agent or efficient cause with which Ibn Sīnā deals the most in the *Ilāhiyyāt*. His treatment clearly shows Ibn Sīnā's Neoplatonic imprint. The common Neoplatonic account held that the One or First Efficient Cause is not only responsible for all existence—that is, existence itself—but also for sustaining existence. In *Ilāhiyyāt* 6.1, Ibn Sīnā advances beyond Aristotle and explains that metaphysicians do not mean by agent or efficient cause only the principle of motion, as naturalists do, but "the principle that gives existence, as in the case of God with respect to the world" (Avicenna 2005: 195). However, when defining the four kinds of causes in *Samā' al-ṭabī'ī*, Ibn Sīnā explains in that context of natural philosophy that in natural things "agent" is usually understood as being the principle of the motion of another insofar as it is other, confining the agent-efficient cause to the realm of motion, that is, to the transition from potency to act (Avicenna 2009: 64). Yet, if efficient causality is considered from the perspective of the metaphysician, then it takes on a broader sense—namely, as the cause of existence. Certainly, Ibn Sīnā's doctrine of efficient causality is devised to show that God is the cause of the existence of the world and that in this sense God is the Primary or First Cause. As a consequence, a crucial subject in Ibn Sīnā's position is the relation between God as Primary Cause and His effect. God as the efficient cause, and the world as His effect, must be understood in light of Ibn Sīnā's emanative model. This model can be traced back to Plotinus, who propounded a paradigm where the physical universe and all beings that inhabit it derive from the One through a series of emanations.

In *Ilāhiyāt* 9, Ibn Sīnā describes the origin of the world as an eternal and necessary emanation. There he depicts the emanative process as coming from the self-contemplation of God that originates the first immaterial intellect, from which the multiplicity of the immaterial intellectual world and eventually the celestial and physical worlds of the visible cosmos proceed (Avicenna 2005: 326–38). Even though that first created intellect is incorruptibly and immaterially eternal, the distinction between God and His effects is that, while God is the Necessary Being (simple, perfect, immutable, one, single, unique, and in Him existence and essence coincide), all of His creation, that is, His effects individually and collectively, is made up of possible beings that are possible *in se* (*mumkin al-wujūd bi dhātihi*) and necessary by another (*min ghairihi*), that is, made necessary by God (Avicenna 2005: 30). Hence, there is a sort of causal necessity required to ground the existence of the world. According to Ibn Sīnā, the first intellect "emanates" from the Necessary Being in a process he hierarchically depicts as the origin of possible beings by an eternal and necessary emanation of the first created intellect—the source of multiplicity—which contemplates God and itself. Though possible in itself, but grounded or made necessary by God, this first created entity is intellectual in nature because it comes from the pure immaterial intellect which is the Necessary Being or God who is simultaneously an intellect, intelligent, and an object of intellection. Then, in accordance with the different ways in which the first intellect knows (1) itself as necessary by another, (2) itself as a possibility, and (3) that from which it proceeds (that is, the Necessary Being), this first created intellectual entity engenders three distinct things respectively: (1) the soul of the first celestial sphere, (2) the body of the first celestial sphere, and (3) the second intellect from which a third intellect, its soul, and its body will in like fashion proceed. According to *Ilāhiyāt* 9.3–4, all further emanations follow the same process, until the completion of all the remaining heavenly spheres that compose the Avicennian cosmos (Avicenna 2005: 318–34). Finally, at the tenth and last link of the process the active intellect or "giver of forms" (Avicenna 2005: 325–6; 334–8) brings to completion the emanation of separate intellects, and from it the sublunary world emanates.

Such an emanative process reveals a robust relationship between God and the world, where God is causally responsible for the actuality of existence or necessity of every cause-effect relation as primary cause of all. However, this does not lead to a substantial coincidence between God and the world, which would make of Ibn Sīnā some sort of pantheist. The Necessary Being and the possible beings are clearly and precisely differentiated and, although the essence of the world depends on God's essence, as stated in *Ilāhiyāt* 9.1, God and the world are different existents (Avicenna 2005: 299–307). That is, all creation depends not on the divine substance as such but rather on the efficient creative metaphysical causal act that originates the first created intellect as an entity outside the divine substance. Such intellect and all the possible beings that follow from reality outside the Divine are an outcome of God's emanative action. In *Ilāhiyāt* 1.6, Ibn Sīnā makes use of the term "creation" (*ibdā'*) in a metaphysical sense; that is, conceiving God as the Primary Cause of every being, where the term "creation" implies that God perpetually originates the possible beings which are also made necessary by Him. In the eternal emanative process, the Primary Cause is the proximate cause of the first intellect, and such causation becomes much more distant when it comes to the creatures of the sublunary world. This means that, although God is the Primary Cause, between Him and creatures there is a multiplicity of efficient causes and effects. As we shall see, this is precisely one of the problematic metaphysical assertions in Ibn Sīnā that the Ash'arite theologians like al-Ghazālī criticized.

The centrality of the efficient cause in Ibn Sīnā's metaphysics has led most scholars to overlook the Avicennian treatment of the other causes, final causality included. Wisnovsky's approach has pertinently turned the attention of scholars towards these neglected deficiencies, arguing in different places that God does not operate solely as efficient cause, but also as final cause (Wisnovsky 1994: 97–99, 2002, 2003: 49–68). According to him, Ibn Sīnā followed the Neoplatonic commentators who tried to harmonize Plato with Aristotle (Plutarch, Syrianus, Proclus, Ammonius, Asclepius, namely, what he calls the "Ammonian synthesis") in holding that, although efficient and final causes are distinct, there is a link between them: while the final cause is prior to the efficient cause in terms of essence, the efficient cause is prior to the final cause in terms of existence (Avicenna 2005: 228–9).

To sum up, Avicennian metaphysics regards God as both final and efficient cause. Moreover, God as Primary Cause is responsible in proximate or remote ways for all the causal links that take place in the world. This is clear from *Ilāhiyyāt* 9.6, where Ibn Sīnā argues that the marvelous manifestations of worldly creatures, from the heavens to the humblest beings, in their perfect array and constitution, do not proceed out of chance, but depend on the guidance and governance of God (Avicenna 2005: 339). In other words, the order and goodness in all the different levels of the world overflow from God, and this is what is meant by divine providence. Providence, then, does not describe a divine intentionality on the part of God for the sake of the world, but rather providence is the very structure and nature of the world consequent upon the nature of God's goodness. However, if all causal links proceed from and are related to the Primary Cause, which is good and perfect, the Highest Good, then how is the presence of evil in the world possible? This very peculiar issue of evil and causality arises when considering the sublunary level of the Avicennian emanationist model.

According to Ibn Sīnā's approach, evil exists only at the sublunary level of the world and affects all individual realities which entail potency and are related to matter, that is, to those things that are subject to generation and corruption. Hence, we notice that the world is subject to a process of continuous change in order to come to be and to remain. In this respect, what we understand as evil, a privation of some [proper] existence, is a necessary byproduct of divine goodness. Therefore, Ibn Sīnā concludes that the created world is both good and perfect, and absolute evil is not possible, because it would be an absolute privation, that is, the non-existence of things (Avicenna 2005: 339–47).

Still, we could question the existence of another kind of evil, that is, moral evil. If we were to assume a strict determinism where divine providence governed over every occurrence, then there would be no room at all for human freedom—that is, human volitional causation—and, consequently, this would lead to the preclusion of human moral responsibility. Ibn Sīnā did not deal with this matter in detail, and this absence has not gone unnoticed. For instance, as Janssens has noted, the modern reader of Ibn Sīnā is perplexed when learning about the lack of any explicit reference to human freedom within his works (Janssens 1996: 112–18). However, Janssens asserts that this does not mean that Ibn Sīnā overlooked or was not interested in practical wisdom. The Islamic doctrine on punishment and reward was not alien to him. Ibn Sīnā holds that human beings are responsible for their acts through the use of reason, whose role is to harmonize human potencies—namely, intellect, imagination, desire, passions—and the natural dispositions that intervene in our moral decisions. Reason is unable to achieve its guiding purpose when it is vanquished by the natural desires of individual humans, which in turn drive humans to misguided decisions. Given the directing role of reason, Ibn Sīnā seems to hold an intellectualist stance, while it also looks like he leaves some room for "free causality" (Janssens 1996: 117–18). We could suspect, as McGinnis has noticed, that Ibn Sīnā adopts some sort of problematic compatibilism: it appears that while he accepts moral responsibility on the part of human beings, he also appears to endorse a causal determinism in which the ultimate cause of every event is God or the Necessary Existent. Although from such a stance, as we have explained, God is the efficient and final cause of all events, including the existence and constitution of human beings, according to Ibn Sīnā, this does not mean that God is responsible for their moral decisions (McGinnis 2010: 225).

Al-Ghazālī and the Criticism of Causality

Al-Ghazālī is the best known critic of Ibn Sīnā's theory of causality. Given his Ash'arīte background, it seems that he rejects natural efficient causality and makes of God the only agent, the absolute and sole Primary Cause of all. However, al-Ghazālī's proximity to the Ash'arītes has been a matter of debate (Frank 1994; Marmura 2002). According to Ash'arīte theologians, every event and phenomenon is distinctly and particularly caused by the divine will. God has arranged a causal network that explains every particular event in the world only through a direct link to God's willing causal agency. Certainly, these theologians face the problem of whether the causal determinism that stems from God eliminates the moral responsibility of human beings. If so, then how can the Islamic doctrine on punishment and reward make any sense? In order to deal with this question, in this section I explain first the Ash'arītes' rejection of natural causality, followed by al-Ghazālī's own intricate position concerning causality, and I expound al-Ghazālī's criticism of Ibn Sīnā. This will enable us to deal with the question of moral responsibility and the role of human freedom.

For Ash'arīte theologians, God's absolute omnipotence implies the impossibility of any creaturely causality. Such a stance leads them, unlike Ibn Sīnā, to maintain that there cannot be a plurality of efficient causes, i.e. secondary causes. In contrast, Ibn Sīnā, though holding the doctrine of primary causality that traces all things and actions back to God, couched the relationship between God and His creatures in the doctrine of secondary causality that recognizes real causal efficacy by creatures, be it in a proximate or remote fashion. Ash'arīte theology dismisses secondary causes and instead affirms an absolute determinism on the part of God, while strengthening this divine causal exclusivity through an atomistic conception of the world. Ash'arītes think that every material body is made out of transitory atoms, arranged in order to fashion the wide variety of bodies that compose reality. Hence, bodies are but a whole set of ever-changing atoms, which are created and annihilated according to God's spontaneous will. Thus, while appealing to an atomistic philosophy of nature, Ash'arītes argue that the world is not ruled by intrinsic natural causes, but depends absolutely and utterly on God in every way. This stance is compatible neither with the Aristotelian theory of causality (though Aristotle's first mover is not an efficient cause, natural causality is fundamental to his natural philosophy), nor with that of Ibn Sīnā (even if Ibn Sīnā admits that the Necessary Existent is an efficient cause, secondary causes are by no means discarded). Given that for the Ash'arītes there is no natural efficient causality, they thought (as Hume later did) that it is our mind that perceives natural phenomena as displaying regularity and attributes causality to them. This is very close to what al-Ghazālī argues in the seventeenth discussion of the *Tahāfut* (al-Ghazālī 2000: 166–7; Marmura 1981b: 85–112).

In this discussion, al-Ghazālī addresses the natural phenomenon of combustion and explains that, although some philosophers would argue that fire is the natural efficient cause of combustion, fire is in fact an entity that is in itself incapable of action, and that the true cause of burning cannot be other than the First, i.e. God. All natural processes are governed by the divine will, which is responsible for any connection between events. This particular discussion from the *Tahāfut* is one of the places where al-Ghazālī clearly adheres firmly to Ash'arīte occasionalism. God, as Primary Cause as well as sole cause, is responsible for every entity, change, and accident that takes place in the world. Thus, al-Ghazālī and Ibn Sīnā agree in conceiving God as the Primary Cause of all; yet, whereas al-Ghazālī seems to ascribe all causality to the Primary Cause, Ibn Sīnā admits the presence of real secondary causes. However, although in the *Tahāfut* al-Ghazālī seems to reject natural causality, his position has been a matter of considerable dispute. On the one hand, some scholars have argued that in fact al-Ghazālī rejects causality (Fakhry 1958: 56–82; Wolfson 1976: 549). On the other hand, some hold that al-Ghazālī does not reject the existence of causality itself, but the apparent necessary nexus between the causes and their effects. In this respect, God grants every cause its nature, so that every cause is able to produce its effect (Courtenay 1973: 77). Still, there is a tendency within the secondary literature to maintain that al-Ghazālī does in fact acknowledge an ontological notion of causality (Goodman 1978; Alon 1980; Abrahamov 1998; Druart 2006: 425–40). Nonetheless, we can assume that, at least in the *Tahāfut*, al-Ghazālī is rejecting the notion of causality associated with the philosophers, that is, the necessary natural causal link between cause and effect. That would render God's absolute freedom and omnipotence philosophically questionable, since such causality would imply that God's action is in some way limited by the natures or essences of the things of which God is the cause. However, al-Ghazālī's subtle stance points in a novel direction: although God is the First Cause that explains all other subsequent causes, God is not bound to these causes or the essential natures which He creates as if there were a necessary link between the cause and its effect, because in His own mind and will the possible effect that will precede the cause could be otherwise, no matter how often we have witnessed the succession from a given cause to a given effect. For instance, going back to the example of the combustion caused by fire, al-Ghazālī holds that if God commanded fire not to cause combustion, it would not do so.

This emphasis on God's omnipotence and absolute governance over the world in all its minutiae is distinctive of al-Ghazālī's position and contrasts with Ibn Sīnā's view. For Ibn Sīnā, God is Himself the determining cause of the necessary causal relationship between fire and combustion, making it necessary for fire to cause combustion and not otherwise. In contrast, in the case of al-Ghazālī, although God is responsible for every causal relation, in virtue of His absolute governance God can freely break the apparently necessary cause–effect nexus. In other words, while al-Ghazālī conceives God as a completely free agent in regard to all things, Ibn Sīnā identifies God with eternal unchanging and determinate efficient causality. Actually, in the third discussion of the *Tahāfut*, al-Ghazālī discusses the meaning of the term "agent," and argues against the philosophers, claiming they have erroneously identified the notion of "agent" with that of a natural "efficient cause." According to al-Ghazālī, not every efficient cause is an agent because in a strict sense "agent is an expression [referring] to one from whom the act proceeds, together with the will to act by way of choice and the knowledge of what is willed" (al-Ghazālī 2000: 56). This is why the philosophers have erred when conceiving the world as an effect proceeding from God as a necessary consequence and in this sense as something He is not able to avert. Al-Ghazālī points out that an agent is not called an agent by simply being a cause, but a true agent must comply with the characteristics mentioned previously: (1) the agent produces the act; (2) the agent is capable of willing and of free choice, even acting in a different way than expected; and (3) the agent knows what he wills and the result of his action. In this sense, in contrast to what occurs in an emanationist model such as Ibn Sīnā's, where events take place according to a necessary causal succession, al-Ghazālī holds that God is an agent who creates the world freely and is thus responsible for every act that takes place (or does not take place) in the world. This is precisely why al-Ghazālī portrays God as the sole agent and absolute ruler who can choose at any time whether or not fire is to burn, hence removing strict necessity from the causal relationship between fire and combustion and making it depend solely on God's will.

Now, given God's omnipotence and His governance over the natural world, we must consider whether God directs the realm of human actions. In other words, given this notion of agent, the question arises whether human beings themselves can be considered to be fully agents and, consequently, whether they are morally responsible for their actions. Let us remember that the religious doctrine that is here at stake is the Islamic teaching on punishment and reward for human actions. Apparently, al-Ghazālī sympathizes with the notion of *kasb*, the acquisition doctrine of the Ash'arītes, according to which human actions are originated by God and then made to be acquired by human beings. In a similar way, al-Ghazālī does not deny the existence of human free will, but he holds that God originates every act for each individual human being. In other words, every human decision, freely made by each individual will, matches God's origination of these individual actions. This position seems to be in accord with what is said in Qur'ān 37:96: "Allah has created [both] you and what you do." When dealing with this issue in his theological masterpiece, *The Revival of the Religious Sciences* (*Ihyā' 'ulūm al-dīn*), al-Ghazālī emphasizes that everything stems from God, including choices, and the fact that there is free will does not contradict the fact that God is the ultimate cause that originates every act (al-Ghazālī 1990: 36). However, this is not to be conceived as the philosophical position on primary causality that allowed for the actions of real secondary causes. Rather, God Himself originates in particular and determinate fashion the exact succession of each and every cause that will bring about human choice. Furthermore, free will is not a human faculty but a disposition provided by God. As is evident, al-Ghazālī's main concern is to argue for God's absolute omnipotence, which includes His preeminence over every cause and action, hence making of Him both the ultimate cause and ultimate agent of all events that take place in the world.

Conclusion

Ibn Sīnā and al-Ghazālī exemplify the philosophical and theological controversies surrounding the notion of causality within the Islamic context. I have shown that Ibn Sīnā drew from Aristotelian and Neoplatonic sources. However, he transformed these sources and formulated an original theory of causality that would subsequently become influential within Latin Scholasticism. In contrast with Ibn Sīnā's assimilation of Greek sources, al-Ghazālī's argumentation in the *Tahāfut* regarding this issue could be considered as an attack on the philosophical notion of "causality." Since he is concerned with Ibn Sīnā's restrictive notion of causality that seems to undermine God's omnipotence and freedom, he argues that the connection between a cause and an effect is completely contingent and dependent on God's immediate governance.

The Avicennian philosophical approach stresses the robust relationship between God and the world to the point that, according to his emanationist model, every event and cause-effect relationship stems in a proximate or remote way from God as a primary efficient cause. Although both Ibn Sīnā and al-Ghazālī agree on the fact that God has total governance over the world, al-Ghazālī rejects Ibn Sīnā's view of God as an efficient cause that necessarily produces the world and argues instead for God's absolute omnipotence—that is, for God as a free agent who even has the power to intervene in natural causality. Therefore, al-Ghazālī's position in the *Tahāfut* would suggest some sort of occasionalism, although such conclusion remains a matter of debate (Perler & Rudolph 2000: 57–124; Lizzini 2002: 155–83).

The contrasting approaches between these two thinkers belonging to the Islamic tradition reveal the complexity of dealing with such a broad subject as causality and its philosophical and theological consequences.

Further Reading

Acar, R. (2005) *Talking about God and Talking about Creation*, Leiden & Boston: Brill.
Belo, C. (2007) *Chance and Determinism in Avicenna and Averroes*, Leiden & Boston: Brill.
Esposito, C. & Porro, P. (eds.) (2002) *Quaestio* 2 (La causalità), pp. 96–183.
Griffel, F. (2009) *al-Ghazālī's Philosophical Theology*, Oxford: Oxford University Press, pp. 123–234.
Yasrebi, Y. (2007) "A Critique of Causality in Islamic Philosophy," *Topoi* 26: 255–65.

References

Abrahamov, B. (1998) "al-Ghazālī's Theory of Causality," *Studia Islamica* 67: 75–98.
al-Ghazālī (1990) *On Repentence (being the translation of book XXXI of the Ihyā' 'ulūm al-dīn)*, S. M. Stern (tr.), New Delhi: Sterling Publishers Private Limited.
——. (2000) *The Incoherence of the Philosophers*, M. Marmura (tr.), Provo, UT: Brigham Young University Press.
Alon, I. (1980) "al-Ghazālī on Causality," *Journal of the American Oriental Society* 100: 397–205.
Aristotle (1984) *The Complete Works*, J. Barnes (ed.), 2 vols., Princeton: Princeton University Press.
Avicenna (2005) *The Metaphysics of the Healing*, M. Marmura (tr.), Provo, UT: Brigham Young University Press.
——. (2009) *The Physics of the Healing*, 2 vols., J. McGinnis (tr.), Provo, UT: Brigham Young University Press.
Bertolacci, A. (2002) "The Doctrine of Material and Formal Causality in the 'Ilāhiyyāt' of Avicenna's 'Kitāb al-Šifā'," *Quaestio* 2: 125–54.
Courtenay, W. (1973) "The Critique on Natural Causality in the Mutakallimun and Nominalism," *Harvard Theological Review* 66: 77–94.

d'Ancona, C. (2010) "The Origins of Islamic Philosophy," in L. P. Gerson (ed.), *The Cambridge History of Philosophy in Late Antiquity*, vol. II, Cambridge: Cambridge University Press, pp. 869–93.
Druart, T-A. (2006) "al-Ghazālī's Conception of the Agent in the *Tahāfut* and the Iqtisād: Are People Really Agents?," in J. E. Montgomery (ed.), *Arabic Theology, Arabic Philosophy. From the Many to the One: Essays in Celebration of Richard M. Frank*, Leuven; Peeters, pp. 425–40.
Fakhry, M. (1958) *Islamic Occasionalism*, London: George Allen & Unwin Ltd.
Frank, R. M. (1994) *Al-Ghazālī and the Ash'arite School*, Durham & London: Duke University Press.
Gilson, E. (1960) "Avicenne et la notion de cause efficiente," *Atti del Congreso Internazionale di Filosofia XII*, Firenze: Sansoni, pp. 121–30.
Goodman, L. E. (1978) "Did al-Ghazālī Deny Causality?," *Studia Islamica* 47: 83–120.
Janssens, J. (1996) "The Problem of Human Freedom in Ibn Sīnā," in P. Llorente et al. (eds.), *Actes del Simposi Internacional de Filosofia de l'Edat Mitjana. El pensament antropològic medieval en els ambit islàmic, hebreu i cristià*, Vic: Patronat d'Estudis Osonencs, pp. 112–18.
Lizzini, O. (2002) "Occasionalismo e causalità filosofica: la discussione della causalità in al-Ġazālī," *Quaestio* 2: 155–83.
Marmura, M. E. (1981a) "Avicenna on Causal Priority," in P. Morewedge (ed.), *Islamic Philosophy and Mysticism*, New York: Caravan Books, pp. 65–83.
——. (1981b) "al-Ghazālī's Second Causal Theory in the 17th Discussion of his *Tahāfut*," in P. Morewedge (ed.), *Islamic Philosophy and Mysticism*, New York: Caravan Books, pp. 85–112.
——. (1984) "The Metaphysics of Efficient Causality in Avicenna," in M. Marmura (ed.), *Islamic Theology and Philosophy*, Albany: SUNY Press, pp. 172–3.
——. (2002) "Ghazālī and Ash'arism Revisited," *Arabic Sciences and Philosophy* 12: 91–110.
McGinnis, J. (2010) *Avicenna*, Oxford: Oxford University Press.
Perler, D. & Rudolph, U. (2000) *Occasionalismus, Theorien der Kausalität im arabisch-islamischen und im europäischen Denken*, Göttingen: Vandenhoeck & Ruprecht.
Richardson, K. (2013) "Avicenna's Conception of the Efficient Cause," *British Journal of the History of Philosophy* 21, 2: 220–9.
Taylor, R. C. (2012) "Primary Causality and *ibdā'* (*creare*) in the *Liber de causis*," in A. Mensching-Estakhr & M. Städtler (eds.), *Wahrheit und Geschichte. Die gebrochene Tradition metaphysichen Denkens. Festschrift zum 70 Geburtstag von Günther Mensching*, Würzburg: Königshausen & Neumann, pp. 115–36.
Wisnovsky, R. (1994) *Avicenna on Final Causality*, PhD Dissertation, Princeton University.
——. (2002) "Final and Efficient Causality in Avicenna's Cosmology and Theology," *Quaestio* 2: 97–123.
——. (2003) *Avicenna's Metaphysics in Context*, New York: Cornell University Press.
Wolfson, H. A. (1976) *The Philosophy of the Kalam*, Cambridge: Harvard University Press.

12
THE ETERNITY OF THE WORLD

Cristina Cerami

Introduction

The question of knowing whether or not the world is eternal undoubtedly constitutes one of the most debated controversies in the history of philosophy. In Classical Antiquity this debate comes powerfully to the forefront with Aristotle. If no philosopher of the Ancient world had conceived the possibility of a creation *ex nihilo*, holding the preexistence of absolute nothingness to be inconceivable, all were in agreement in maintaining that the universe, such as it appears, did not always exist. While Plato in many ways literally revolutionized the philosophy of his predecessors, he does not seem to have contradicted them on this point. In the *Timaeus*, in fact, he affirms that, if the world as a whole endures as it is forever, it had to have been forged by the work of a divine demiurge who organized a pre-existing chaotic matter. Opposing all his predecessors in this, Aristotle was the first philosopher in the history of philosophy in the Mediterranean to affirm that *our* world has always existed and will exist forever. To use terminology which will be introduced later, to a world conceived by Plato as eternal *a parte post*, but not *a parte ante*, Aristotle opposes a world that is eternal both *a parte post* and with one *a parte ante*. He explains in this way that the universe as a whole was not generated and will not be corrupted, even if it is constituted of one region that is eternal in and by itself, that is, that of the celestial spheres endowed with a purely local movement, and another region necessarily subject to generation and corruption which lies beneath the final celestial sphere, that is, the sublunary world.

It is around this antinomy that the Greek philosophers of the first centuries before and after Christ pursued the debate on the eternity of the world. It was not a question of arguing for or against the possibility of a creation from nothing but of comprehending how the world with its supralunary and sublunary regions ought to be made so as to enjoy an eternal life. In this context, one of the greatest difficulties for the defenders of the eternalist theory of Aristotle was that of proving the eternity of a world whose main part was not only inaccessible to human beings but also ontologically different from the one human beings inhabit. It is precisely to this difficulty that is grafted the other side of the debate concerning the eternity of the world that will be tackled by later philosophers: Can one truly demonstrate that the world is or is not eternal? And, if so, how? Galen (second to third century C.E.)—who affirmed that it cannot be demonstrated apodictically that the world is eternal—situated at the heart of the debate the question of knowing whether human beings can determine scientifically the eternal character of the world. This question rests at the heart of the debate even after the arrival of monotheistic religions because it constitutes the background for all the philosophical theories which were opposed to the idea of a creation *ex nihilo* or which proposed to defend it. This is found notably in the *Guide of the Perplexed* by Maimonides (1135–1204) who, after having reviewed the collection of arguments in favor of the eternity of the world, affirms that this question does not admit of demonstration and concludes that the Holy Scriptures do not lie in affirming that the world was created from nothing (Maimonides 1974: 348ff).

The question of the demonstrable or indemonstrable character of the theory which affirms the eternity of the universe traverses the Greek, Arabic and Latin worlds, but the debate concerning the eternity of the world is enriched by the new questions and challenges that the three monotheistic religions faced. In Judaism and Christianity as well as in Islam, the notion of an all powerful God seems to be opposed to that of an eternal world. In fact, regardless of the exegetical problem of reconciling Qur'ānic passages in favor of a divine creation, the principal question for all the authors of Classical Islam is to understand whether and how the eternal character of the world still leaves room for real divine efficacy. In this sense the question of knowing whether or not the world is eternal is intimately connected to that of understanding the kind of relationship the world maintains with God is conceived as its ultimate principle. If the world is eternal and if we admit the existence of God—which was never questioned—then the relationship of God to the universe must also be eternal. If we admit from an Aristotelian point of view that eternity and necessity mutually imply one another, we are compelled to conclude that this relationship belongs to the order of necessity and not that of will. On the contrary, the notion of creation (*ibdā'*), whether or not implying innovation (*ḥudūth*), seems to convey the attribution of a real will to God, at least according to some theories. In so doing, the antinomy opposing the created or eternal character of the world is joined to that opposing a willing God to a God who is not endowed with a will in a strict sense (Sorabji 1983: 318 ff.).

The arguments for or against the eternity of the world constitute, in this sense, one step in one single reasoning toward defining, in addition to the existence of God and the modality of his causal relation to the world, the very nature of the Divinity. Whether this questioning falls to a single science or several (Cerami 2014), it remains that these two moments are considered by all the Arabic thinkers involved in this debate as absolutely inseparable (Davidson 1987: 149–51, 188–90, 387). These must be considered as linked in a relationship of strong implication where the attribution of certain attributes to God follows directly upon the system of the world that we accept. It is precisely in this conceptual framework that al-Ghazālī (d. 1111) placed his invective against the Muslim philosophers who defended the eternity of the world. If, as al-Fārābī and Ibn Sīnā maintained, the world is not the product of an instantaneous voluntary act but of an ontological necessity, God will not be a true agent and will not be strictly speaking God. This is why, al-Ghazālī affirms, we must conclude that the arguments of the *falāsifa* are not only heretical but also contradictory. Indeed, the so-called god of the philosophers is not a true Deity, particularly as He is not even free to create when He wishes to do so. It is to this charge, and in order to ensure the necessity of a divine causality in an eternal world, that Ibn Rushd will respond.

Eternal Movement and the Eternity of the World: Aristotle's Three Demonstrations

Even if in Classical Islam the philosophical discussion of the eternity of the world engages issues unknown to Greek philosophers—notably that of the possibility of a creation *ex nihilo* and that associated with the existence of a divine will and providence—Aristotle's eternalist paradigm, his arguments, and the critiques that later philosophers set forth in opposition surely constitute the starting points and the background of the debate.

The reasoning that led Aristotle to establish the eternity of his *cosmos* unfolds in stages. In the eighth and final book of his *Physics* he devotes himself first of all to the establishment of the eternity of natural movement. He shows that movement is necessarily eternal because we cannot conceive of a movement which is not preceded by another movement. In this way he is able to assert the necessary existence of an eternal and continuous circular movement, i.e. that of the celestial sphere which encompasses the world and of an absolutely immobile and incorporeal mover, i.e. the separate intellect of the last celestial body.

In his *De Caelo* Aristotle deduces the eternity of these celestial bodies from the existence of a continuous and eternal circular movement. He explains that if one simple body cannot have more than one natural movement, there must exist one body which moves itself in a circle by its own proper nature. This body differs for this same reason from the four sublunary bodies (i.e. fire, air, water, and earth) of which every body subject to generation and corruption is constituted. For, the four sublunary bodies move themselves by nature upward or downward and are necessarily subject to reciprocal transformation. In the same work, Aristotle demonstrates the ungenerated and incorruptible character of the *cosmos* considered as a whole (*De Caelo* I, 10–11). He concludes that it is contradictory to say that one eternal thing passesses eternally the possibility of not existing forever (*De Caelo* I, 12).

In the *De Generatione et Corruptione* Aristotle considers the sublunary world and affirms that "God assures the completeness of the All, making generation perpetual" (*GC* II, 10, 336b26). He demonstrates in this way that in the world of generation the sole necessity is that of the cyclic coming into being of things (i.e. the rhythm of the seasons as well as the reproduction of species with their biological cycles) caused by the eternal movements of the last sphere and the ecliptic. Thus, the cycle of generations and corruptions based on the continuous and reciprocal transformation of the elements is sempiternal but not infinite by essence. As for the species, the "rectilinear" infinity of the generation of their members one after another is made necessary by this same circular principle. Indeed, affirms Aristotle, there is no necessity in the generation of one individual A by one individual B (*GC* II, 11, 337b7–9) because matter always retains a part of indetermination. The eternity of sublunary generation derives its necessity from the circular movement of the heavens but remains a necessity belonging to the species and not the individuals.

The world, then, is as a whole and in its celestial part eternal *a parte ante* and *a parte post*, just as is its movement and the mutual generation of the four sublunary elements. However, due to the fact that the world does not constitute a unique and unified being (Falcon 2005), there cannot be for Aristotle one single demonstration which applies by itself to every part of the world and to both supralunary and sublunary movements. This is why the three demonstrations exhibited in these three treatises must be considered as irreducible to one another.

It is well known that by supporting the eternity of the world and the existence of incorruptible celestial bodies Aristotle carried on a polemic against all his predecessors and notably against his master, Plato. Still, it must also be emphasized that his eternalist theories from the beginning were widely criticized not only by members of rival schools but even within the *peripatos*, his own school (Rashed 2007; Falcon 2011). The Neoplatonic commentator Simplicius (sixth century C.E.) reports on this debate and also bears witness to the fact that in his time it was far from over. The doctrine of the eternity of the world was attacked by John Philoponus, a Christian Neoplatonic commentator who in his *Contra Aristotelem* had formulated a series of arguments to refute not only the incorruptibility of celestial body but also the eternity of movement and of the world in its entirety (Davidson 1987).

The arguments by Philoponus against the eternalist theory of Aristotle as well as the arguments that he elaborated in the *Contra Proclum* against the theory of an eternal emanation became known in the Arabic-speaking world from the beginning of the translation movement supported by the Abbassid caliphate (Gannagé 2011). These arguments came to be frequently utilized by the theologians of *kalām* who held that God had created the world *ex nihilo* by a voluntary act (Wolfson 1976: 410–34; Davidson 1987: 91 ff.; Sorabji 1983: 196 ff.) as well as by the philosopher al-Kindī (d. ca. 866) who interpreted this creation in terms of an emanation (Walzer 1962; Davidson 1969, 1987; Adamson 2003, 2007). They were also criticized by philosophers who defended the eternity of the world by integrating it into an emanationist ontology (al-Fārābī and Ibn Sīnā) or by reading it in the light of a Neo-Aristotelian ontology (Ibn Rushd). For that reason, we cannot fully understand the eternalist theories defended by those authors without placing them in their polemical context.

Eternity of the World and Eternal Movement According to al-Fārābī

The question of knowing whether the emanationist ontology that al-Fārābī defends can be reconciled with the affirmation of the eternity of the world or necessarily implies creation *ex nihilo* is a question presently much debated. The sole text attributed to al-Fārābī which provides explicit support in favor of an instantaneous creation is the *Harmony between the Opinions of Plato and Aristotle*. For that reason some specialists have questioned the authenticity of that work (Lameer 1994: 23–39; Rashed 2008: 55–8; 2009) while others have attributed it to a first phase of Farabian reflection (Endress in al-Fārābī 2008; Janos 2012: 235–82).

In the great majority of his treatises, however, specifically in *The Attainment of Happiness* (*Kitāb Taḥṣīl al-sa'ādah*), *Aphorisms of the Statesman* (*Fuṣūl munṭaza'ah*), *Opinions of the Inhabitants of the Virtuous City* (*Kitāb ārā' ahl al-madīnah al-fāḍilah*), *Political Regime* (*al-Siyāsah al-madaniyyah*) and the *Treatise on the Intellect* (*Risālah fi-l-'aql*), al-Fārābī maintains an eternalist position and defends a notion of emanation as continuous creation opposed to the reading that al-Kindī sets forth. The notion of emanation conceived as continuous creation excludes the possibility of conceiving the causal action of God in terms of a true temporal creation from nothing. According to this reading, the priority of the cause in relation to the effect that emanates from it is not chronological but ontological. Al-Fārābī explains that the First Cause, i.e. God, is the "cause of the existence" and "cause of coming to be" of the first emanated intellect and each of the later intellects is in the same way cause of its soul and its celestial body (al-Fārābī 1981: 63, 1938: 34–5). It is in understanding the first that each separate intellect determines the existence of the intellect that follows and in understanding its own essence that it determines the existence of its orb and its soul. It is from the Agent Intellect, the tenth and last cosmic intelligence, that the substantial forms of the sublunary world finally emanate. This intellect in this sense governs and determines the existence of sensible species while the celestial bodies determine the continuous existence of prime matter and render continuous the process of multiple generations and corruptions. Unlike the Aristotelian system in which God, conceived as an unmoved mover, is only the final cause of the movement of the first heavens and indirectly of everything else, the Farabian system seems in this sense to imply that God and the celestial intellects are not simply final causes but also efficient causes (Janos 2012; Vallat 2011). It is the same type of causality that acts at all levels of the cosmos and which determines its interconnection (al-Fārābī 1985: 94–7) as well as its eternity. This relationship of causality however does not imply the precedent non-existence of the effect in relation to the cause because the action of the latter, insofar as it is necessary, is eternally simultaneous in relation to the effect (al-Fārābī 1993: 47, lines 11–12).

By reasoning this way from cause to effect, al-Fārābī concludes that the world as a whole is necessarily eternal because of the emanative procession which supports it (Rashed 2008). The world has always existed as an infinite temporal extension *a parte ante* (*azaliyy*) and *a parte post* (*abadiyy*). From the Aristotelian point of view, al-Fārābī admits that what has no beginning can have no end, and vice versa. If the celestial bodies with their intellects and souls have always existed from forever and for forever in virtue of a necessary relation which links them to the First Cause, then they are in a strict sense co-eternal with this cause even if they do not enjoy the same necessary existence that It has. As al-Fārābī explains, they belong to the sort of being which, while being possible, cannot not exist, while sublunary beings belong to the sort of possible being that is at once both opposed to and accompanied by privation and always mixed with non-being (al-Fārābī 1993: 57). But what type of eternity, according to this "eternalist" paradigm, can be attributed to sublunary generation?

The texts cited give us a clear response: the sublunary movements are not continuous and eternal in their own right but they are so in virtue of the movement of the celestial spheres and the formal action of the Agent Intellect which endows the sublunary matter with the forms of natural species. According to the testimony of Ibn Rushd, the reading that al-Fārābī proposes in his lost treatise *On Changing Beings*

(*Fī al-mawjūdāt al-mutaghayyira*) concerning the eternalist argument of *Physics* VIII seems to confirm this conclusion.

Ibn Rushd says he first shared the account of al-Fārābī before dismissing it, judging it unsatisfactory (Puig Montada 1999; Glasner 2010; Twetten 1995, 2007). He explains that, according to al-Fārābī, the argument of Aristotle consists in establishing the continuity and eternity of movement by inductive reasoning. The aim was to show that in every kind of movement there is "a movement before any movement," in order to conclude that movement in general and celestial movement are eternal and. Al-Fārābī, in other words, proved the eternity of movement by an argument going from effect to cause, which is in a sense complementary to the argument based on emanation (Rashed 2008).

Ibn Rushd also tells us that al-Fārābī completed the argument of Aristotle with what he had done in the second book of *On Generation and Corruption* (Averroes 1962a: 345–6). At the end of this book (GC II, 10–11) Aristotle explains that only the continuous movements of the celestial spheres are truly continuous and that only the concomitance of the movements of the sphere of the fixed stars and of the ecliptic can make continuous the movements of the sublunary world continuous and the living species eternal. The sublunary transformations, in other words, would not be continuous and without stop if there were not two continuous and opposed movements which act on them. Thus, we can reasonably assume that if al-Fārābī in his treatise does something similar to what Aristotle does in his *On Generation and Corruption*, as Ibn Rushd tells us, it is that he points out the non-essential and continuous character of sublunary movements to be able then to infer the necessary existence of the truly continuous motion of the celestial spheres (Cerami 2015b, 2015c). This reconstruction of the argument of al-Fārābī confirms the idea, expressed in his other treatises, according to which eternity and continuity belong to the sublunary world not by an intrinsic necessity but in virtue of the action of the heavens, a causality at once both efficient and final.

The insistence upon the non-essential continuous character of the cycle of generation and corruption was also not a novelty in the discussion of the eternity of the world. We find this same idea in the treatise of Alexander of Aphrodisias translated into Arabic under the title, *On the Principles of the All*. There Alexander affirms that the sublunary movements are not of themselves eternal and continuous but that they are so in virtue of the celestial movements which are the sole movements continuous in themselves (Alexander of Aphrodisias 2001: 73). In this treatise as well as in his *De providentia* Alexander tries to lessen the role of sublunary causes and to accentuate that of the celestial principles. As a result, he develops an explanation of the way in which the generable and corruptible things depend on the heavens for their existence and form (Freudenthal 2006, 2009; Rashed 2007: 277–85). There are many elements which prove that these two treatises, translated into Arabic during the first phase of the translation movement, exercised a decisive influence on the cosmology of al-Fārābī (Maróth 1995; Fazzo & Wiesner 1993; Hasnawi 1994; Alexander of Aphrodisias 2001: 21 ff.; Janos 2012: 133–7, 151ff.). Thus, we would like to suggest that these works and the theories which are revealed in them on the eternity of sublunary generation also played a crucial role in the elaboration of the eternalist paradigm of al-Fārābī.

But for what reason, we may ask, did Ibn Rushd reject the reasoning of al-Fārābī? The reason is essentially epistemological. Not, as has been suggested, because of its possible determinist implications (Glasner 2010: 62 ff.), but because the argument of al-Fārābī assumes that the continuity of the eternal movement of celestial bodies can be shown by way of the derived continuity of sublunary movements. If the movements, as well as the different regions of the cosmos, are not homogeneous because the sublunary movements are not essentially continuous and eternal, then their "accidental" continuity cannot be "transferred" to the movement of the sphere of the fixed bodies, which is continuous "in itself" (Averroes 1962a: 339 B13–F7). The two demonstrations of *Physics* VIII and *On Generation and Corruption* II, 10–11 must be considered as distinct and necessary displayed in two different treatises. They cannot be mixed or interchanged because the demonstration which would result from it will not be truly universal. In other words, the epistemological conditions that Aristotle set in place in *Posterior Analytics* I, 4–5 would be contravened. It is for this reason that Ibn Rushd formulates another interpretation of the argument for the eternity of motion in *Physics* VIII, 1. Aristotle does not want to show at the outset that any movement whatsoever is eternal and continuous. After having shown in *Physics* VII the existence of a first moved mover, namely the first heaven, he wants to show in *Physics* VIII, 1 that the movement of this latter is eternal (Averroes 1962a: 341 M14–342 B5). It is then only on the basis of this preliminary demonstration that Aristotle may establish in *On Generation and Corruption* II, 10–11 the eternity of sublunary generation (Cerami 2015b).

Radical Eternalism: Ibn Rushd against Ibn Sīnā on Natural Necessity and Providence

It was concluded in the preceding section that al-Fārābī and Ibn Rushd did not diverge with respect to the idea that the sublunary movements are continuous and eternal in virtue of a superior movement and a superior cause. According to both of them, the eternity of the sublunary world depends on the existence of a system of causes capable in some measure of filling the ontological gap between the individually eternal celestial bodies and the sublunary world which is eternal through species. The readings of the two philosophers differed, however, regarding the possibility of establishing the continuity of celestial movement by way of sublunary movements. We will now see that they diverge also regarding the type of causal action in play in the relationship between the heavens and the earth. If in the first phase of his reflection Ibn Rushd, along with al-Fārābī and Ibn Sīnā, conceived this action in terms of an emanation, he subsequently abandons this theory in order to explain that the notion of emanation cannot guarantee a true eternity for the sublunary world (Davidson 1992).

As with al-Fārābī, we find in the thought of Ibn Sīnā the idea that emanation (*fayḍ*) must not be conceived in terms of a creation *ex nihilo* in time, but in terms of an ontological dependence which implies the co-eternity of the cause and the effect (Hasnawi 1990a; McGinnis 2010; Lizzini 2011). The greatest effort of Ibn Sīnā in this sense is to better define a modal ontology capable of combining a metaphysics of necessity proper to the notion of emanation as he sets forth with a metaphysics of contingency proper to the notion of creation *ex nihilo* (Janssens 1997: 455). God, conceived as the first of all the causes, is the source from which emanates all being to the exclusion of God himself. Emanated being in this sense is conceived as what is caused, an effect immediate and concomitant with the will and knowledge of God. Thus, God is not identified with the emanation itself, nor with His will and His knowing, for the characterizations are not part of His essence. Nonetheless, they must be considered as His concomitants (Avicenna 1960: 403). Caused being, fruit of emanation, is not posterior to the cause from a chronological point of view. Its posteriority, explains Ibn Sīnā, is "essential." Caused being, as contingent, implies in itself a connection with non-being and possesses being in virtue of its relation to the ultimate source of the emanation which is necessary in itself and by essence. Ibn Sīnā affirms in this way that "not being belongs to caused being, while being belongs to it thanks to its cause" (Avicenna 1960: 266, 12–15). The non-existence of caused being is "prior" to its existence and its existence is "posterior," although it is an issue of a priority and of a posteriority "by essence" and not temporal. The causality of the First is comparable, explains Ibn Sīnā, to that of the hand which moves the key in the lock of a door: the hand, conceived as the cause and the key which turns conceived as the effect are distinguished by intellect but operate simultaneously. It is in this sense that the priority of one in relation to the other is not temporal but essential (Avicenna 1960: 165). Every caused being is contingent in itself. Even the heavens which are individually incorruptible, as emanated, retain a part of possibility and are necessary exclusively in virtue of something other than themselves, namely the sole being necessary in itself, i.e. God. They will be in this sense "contingent in themselves" and in this sense, necessary by another, while the beings of the sublunary world will be, strictly speaking, necessary neither in themselves nor by another. By this distinction Ibn Sīnā introduces into the Aristotelian cosmos a new schema which allows him to conclude that the world as a whole is eternal, even while safeguarding the incommensurability which separates the First Principle from the caused, whether it be of the sublunary world or of eternal caused beings.

Ibn Sīnā explains in this sense that we must consider two types of eternity. The eternity of the celestial bodies must be conceived in terms of a perpetuity (*dahr*) because their existence, from the fact of being related to movement without being *in* time, is necessarily *with* time (Avicenna 1973: 143). Only those beings which are not at all related to movement, such as the intellects of celestial bodies, exist eternally without reference to time. Their persistence in being is in this sense of the order of absolute eternity (*sarmad*). This distinction between two types of eternity will be later criticized by the Eastern followers of Ibn Sīnā. Abū al-Barakāt al-Baghdādī (ninth to tenth century) asserts against this distinction that time does not measure only motion but being as a whole. God, as well as the emanated intellects and celestial bodies, are all related to time and they are all for this same reason both in perpetuity (*dahr*) and in eternity (*sarmad*) (Hasnawi 1990b; Kukkonen 2012).

Necessity and true eternity therefore belong only to the First Cause, according to Ibn Sīnā. The celestial bodies, although incorruptible, are necessary only in virtue of the relation to the sole being which is necessary in itself. Their eternity, we could say, is only a sempi-eternity. But what of the species of the sublunary world?

Following the emanationist schema, Ibn Sīnā affirms that every ontological determination in the sublunary world is the fruit of the last emanation which proceeds from the intellect of the last sphere. This intellect, which Ibn Sīnā seems to identify with what he calls the "giver of forms" and with the Agent Intellect (Janssens 2006) guarantees the existence of the forms of the sensible realm as well as the matter which receives them and delimits the horizon of the emanation. The form of a composed substance, a member of this or that species, is only an intermediary cause to the extent that it is the cause of the subsistence (*qiwām*) of the composed individual; but it is, in turn, the product of the emanative action of this external principle, i.e. the Agent Intellect. The form, then, is not the agent cause and formal cause of the matter but rather of its composition with matter. It is the Agent Intellect which is the agent and formal cause of both the matter and the form. Matter and form are in this sense dependent on one another but their union is guaranteed and ultimately caused by the agent intellect as the last celestial intelligence and separate form (Lizzini 2004). Ibn Sīnā explains also that even if the final substrate of the forms is matter absolutely free of determination, each substantial form has its own substrate: the from can be received only in a particular matter predisposed for receiving it. This "predisposition" (*isti'dād*) for receiving the form is both through the qualitative modifications which are caused by the elements and their qualities and through natural agents. But the occurrence of the substantial form depends directly on the Agent Intellect which makes the form exist in determinate particular matter previously predisposed to receive it. From this point of view, the instances of substantial generation—but more generally nature as a whole—depends on a principle which, as separate form, is not subject to movement and transcends nature as a whole.

Although at the beginning of his career Ibn Rushd endorses the doctrine of emanation and the Avicennian distinction between the being necessary in itself and the being possible in itself but necessary by another, he later rejects these two theories and provides to the heavens a necessity in a strict sense. The sole possibility with which the heavens are endowed, explains Ibn Rushd, is not related to their essence/existence but to the type of matter with which they are endowed. Following the Aristotelian text, Ibn Rushd affirms that this incorruptible celestial matter only has a "topological" potency, i.e. a potency in virtue of which the celestial body can change place by moving in a circular way, but not changing in substantial form. The celestial bodies are in this sense constituted by a matter, says Ibn Rushd, that is "self-subsistent," meaning that their celestial intellects are not immanent forms belonging to these bodies but immobile and separate movers which move them as end and object of desire. For this reason, we could say that the celestial spheres have the possibility of moving and being moved or, if we accept a distinction between souls and intellects, that their souls have the possibility for causing motion or not (Twetten 2007). In any case, this cosmological theory permits Ibn Rushd to deny the Avicennian distinction between eternity (*sarmad*) and perpetuity (*dahr*) and return to the Aristotelian equivalence between necessity and eternity. Actually, even if heavens have "topological" potency, they have no possibility in being, since according to Aristotle's ontology their essence cannot be reduced to their movement.

The world of the heavens is eternal not by an extrinsic necessity but by its own essence. Again is the status of the sublunary world? Is Ibn Rushd inclined to deny this equivalence in the case of sublunary species and to agree that they are not eternal by essence? It seems not to be so. In the wake of Alexander and also Ibn Rushd's Arabic predecessors, Ibn Rushd affirms on the one hand that substantial generations, those of the elements and also those of complete substances, depend on the movements of the celestial spheres that are in a way true efficient causes (Freudenthal 2002). Still, he contends against al-Fārābī and Ibn Sīnā that celestial souls are only in a remote way agent causes of sublunary beings. Sublunary agents must act by their form, even if celestial spheres contribute to their generation. To admit, as al-Fārābī and Ibn Sīnā do, that it is the Agent Intellect that provides substantial forms to matter amounts to admitting a form of creationist Platonism comparable to the creationist theories of *kalām* (Cerami 2010). If each type of matter does not already have (even if it is only in potency) the substantial form that a sublunary agent actualizes and if it were sufficient to admit the existence of a separate form to explain the generation of the individual, nothing could guarantee the perpetuity of species, concludes Ibn Rushd, and, as we shall see, the possibility to arrive at a first mover.

This is most evident in the case of species which reproduce by sexual generation. But it is also true in the case of species which seem to be generated spontaneously, as is the case with insects generated from putrefying materials. Ibn Rushd tells us, in fact, that the existence of this sort of generation was used as an argument in favor of the existence of an Agent Intellect as "giver of forms." In fact, explains Ibn Rushd, one might think that in the case of animals which are generated by putrefaction it is not an individual of the same species or same genus which gives the form to the matter but instead the Agent Intellect. We could then extend the same conclusion to sexual reproduction and admit that in this sort of generation as well it is the Agent Intellect which introduces the form into the matter. Against this hypothesis, Ibn Rushd responds that the form of animals that have come from putrefaction do not proceed by emanation from the Agent Intellect but rather that their form is actualized in the matter by the action of the celestial bodies and of the heat which proceeds from them. These latter play the role of the synonymous efficient cause while the heat which proceeds from them due to an "informing" power plays a role analogous to that of semen. Following then the line Alexander opens, Ibn Rushd affirms that this motive causality is also, in a sense, formal. Not because there is a separate form which creates the form of the species in the sensible thing, but in a remote way to the extent that the celestial spheres, moved by the desire for the unmoved mover, possess a universal knowledge of the effects produced by their movement. As for the species which reproduce by sexual generation, celestial bodies cannot trigger the generation without the concomitant efficient agency of the male on the female (Allard 1952–1954; Freudenthal 2002; Cerami 2010, 2015a). If it is affirmed that the individuals in these species are generated in virtue of the direct action of the Agent Intellect, we will be required to conclude that the existence of the generators, male and female, are not necessary. And so in this case we must admit that nature and God have done something in vain. It must then be admitted that celestial spheres are causes of generation *per se* and in a primary way, and not in an immediate and proximate way and that the relation of the generated substances to their proximate efficient causes as well as the relationship of their form to their matter is of the order of necessity. It is in this sense that Ibn Rushd affirms that "the relation of each thing to its four causes is a necessary relationship" (Averroes 1962b: 44–5). The relationship between the matter, the form, the end and the agent in living species must be necessary. One species can have only one proximate agent, as well as one material, formal and final causes. That is why the definitions of sensible species mention necessarily their form and matter. If the relationship that involves a being with these four causes were not of the order of necessity but of sempiternity, concludes Ibn Rushd against Ibn Sīnā, one could no longer infer that nature acts in a necessary way. The world order as we know it would no longer have any necessity. As a result, our knowledge, which for Ibn Rushd proceeds from the effect to the cause, would no longer have any foundation. And for the same reason we could no longer arrive to a first motive cause.

Thus, to deny true causal efficacy to sensible agents and to eliminate the necessity of a relationship of the thing to these four causes would have a doubly disastrous consequence for Ibn Rushd: (1) if the relationship of the effect to the cause were not necessary, we could no longer establish the existence of God, given that the sole demonstration of the existence of God, conceived as the ultimate unmoved mover, proceeds from the effect to the cause; (2) we could not prove that the world is the fruit of a divine providence, because we could no longer infer that there is a teleological causality in the sublunar world (Cerami 2015a, 2015b). The sole conclusion which we can and must draw is that the eternal universe is necessary in all respects.

Conclusion

The question of the eternity of the world which had marked the debate between the two great philosophers of Greek Antiquity, Plato and Aristotle, is found to be reinstated in the Arabic-speaking world with new challenges and new implications that only the confrontation with a new creationist theory could provide. To affirm that the world that we see has always existed and will exist forever either in an emanationist fashion or in a fundamentally hylomorphic Neo-Aristotelian system is to commit oneself to the type of causality and the type of necessity which binds that eternity to God.

The three philosophers we have considered here all deal with this dual challenge. Despite the profound differences which mark their systems, they all strive to develop an ontology which permits divine action to encompass the entire universe, all the while safeguarding the gap which separates the different modalities of being and nature. Even if it would be in part misleading to attribute to the three philosophers one single project, we find in all a common strategy: the unification of a causal system which permits a uniform conception of an irremediably heterogenous world and the inference of its eternity. If one must at the same time maintain the separation between an incorruptible region nevertheless endowed with eternal movement and a region subject to generation and corruption, with the ultimate end of connecting them to the First Cause, the sole possibility is to postulate a unified causal network. Unlike that of Aristotle, these three systems imply that the causes which govern the supralunary world and the sublunary world are not the same by analogy but the same numerically. For our three philosophers, in fact, the eternity of the sublunary world is "caused" by the eternity of the celestial bodies and their separate intellects.

But if in the Farabian and Avicennian systems the agent causality of these separate forms can guarantee the relative necessity of the celestial bodies, it cannot do so for the sublunary world according to Ibn Rushd. This is the true point of disaccord with the Cordoban for whom the sole true eternity is that of necessity in the strict sense. In the world of the celestial spheres this necessity and this eternity belong to individuals (even if they have a possibility in the genus of motion), in the world of living mortals, to the species. Their eternity can be guaranteed only by the necessity of their four proximate causes: each species has a single form, a single end, a single matter and a single agent. The vertical causality between the sky and the earth assures the continuity of horizontal causality in the sublunary world, but it cannot do without the formal action of sensible agents nor the necessary relationship which links these to their effects. No necessity and no eternity would belong to the sublunary world if the necessity of these two causal orders were not postulated at once.

Acknowledgement

The author would like to thank Richard Taylor for translating and improving this text and David Twetten for his precise and insightful remarks.

Further Reading

Frank, R.M. (1992) *Creation and the Cosmic System: Al-Ghazālī & Avicenna*, Heidelberg: C. Winter.

Kukkonen, T. (2000) "Possible Worlds in the *Tahāfut al-Tahāfut*. Averroes on Plenitude and Possibility," *Journal of the History of Philosophy* 38: 329–47.

Lettinck, P. (1994) *Aristotle's Physics and Its Reception in the Arabic World*, Leiden: E. J. Brill.

Marmura, M. (1984) "The Metaphysics of Efficient Causality in Avicenna," in M. Marmura (ed.), *Islamic Theology and Philosophy*, New York: State University of New York Press, pp. 172–88.

Pines, S. (1979) "The Limits of Human Knowledge according to al-Farabi, Ibn Bajja and Maimonides," in I. Twersky (ed.), *Studies in Medieval Jewish History and Literature*, vol. 1, Cambridge: Harvard University Press, pp. 82–109.

Sorabji, R. (ed.) (1987) *Philoponus and the Rejection of Aristotelian Science*, London: Duckworth.

Wolfson, H. A. (1929) *Crescas' Critique of Aristotle: Problems of Aristotle's Physics in Jewish and Arabic Philosophy*, Cambridge: Harvard University Press.

References

Adamson, P. (2003) "Al-Kindī and the Mu'tazila: Divine Attributes, Creation and Freedom," *Arabic Sciences and Philosophy* 13: 45–9.

——. (2007) *al-Kindī*, Oxford: Oxford University Press.

Alexander of Aphrodisias (2001) *Alexander of Aphrodisias on the Cosmos*, C. Genequand (ed. and tr.), Leiden: Brill.

al-Fārābī (1938) *Risālah fī l-'aql*, M. Bouyges (ed.), Beirut: Bibliotheca Arabica Scholasticorum.

——. (1981) *Kitāb taḥṣīl al-sa'ādah*, J. Al-Yāsīn (ed.), Beirut: Dār al-Andalus.

——. (1985) *Kitāb ārā' ahl al-madīnah al-fāḍilah*, A. N. Nādir (ed.), Beirut: Dār al-Mashriq.

——. (1993) *al-Farabi's The Political Regime. Al-Siyasa al-Madaniyya also Known as the Treatise on the Principle of Beings*, Fawzi M. Najjar (ed.), Beirut: Dār al-Mashriq.

——. (2001) *The Political Writings: Selected Aphorisms and Other Texts*, C. E. Butterworth (tr.), Ithaca, New York & London: Cornell University Press.

——. (2008) *L'armonia delle opinioni dei due sapienti, il divino Platone e Aristotele*, C. Martini Bonadeo (tr.), Pisa: Edizione Plus/Pisa University Press (Greco, arabo, latino. Le vie del sapere, 3).

al-Ghazālī (2000) *The Incoherence of the Philosophers*, M. E. Marmura (tr.), Provo, UT: Brigham Young University Press.

Allard, M. (1952–1954) "Le rationalisme d'Averroès d'après une étude sur la création," *Bulletin d'études orientales* 14: 7–59.

Averroes (1962a) *Averrois Cordubensis Commentarium Magnum In Aristotelis De Physico Audito libri octo*, in *Aristotelis Opera cum Averrois Commentariis*, vol. IV, Venetiis apud Junctas, 1562–1574.

——. (1962b) *Aristotelis de Generatione Animalium cum Averrois Cordubensis Paraphrasi. Iacob Mantino Hispano Hebraeo, Medico interprete* (vol. VI, part 2, ff. 43v–144r), in *Aristotelis Opera cum Averrois Commentariis*, vol. VI, Venetiis apud Junctas, 1562.

Avicenna (1960) *Al-Shifā', kitāb al-Ilāhiyyāt (La Metaphysique)*, 2 vols., G. C. Anawātī, S. Zāyed, M. Y. Mousa, & S. Dunya (eds.), Cairo: Ministère de la Culture et de l'Orientation.

——. (1973) *Kitāb al-Ta'līqāt*, 'A. Badawī (ed.), Cairo: al-Hay'ah al-Miṣrīyah al-'Āmmah lil-Kitāb.

Cerami, C. (2010) "Generazione verticale, generazione orizzontale : il principio di sinonimia nel *Commento Grande* di Averroès al libro Z della *Metafisica* di Aristotele," *Chôra, Revue d'études anciennes et médiévales* 7, 8: 131–60.

——. (2014) "Signe physique, Signe métaphysique. Averroès contre Avicenne sur le statut épistémologique des sciences de l'être," in C. Cerami (ed.), *Nature et Sagesse. Les rapports entre physique et métaphysique dans la tradition aristotélicienne. Recveil de textes on hommage à Pierre Pellegrin*, Louvain: Peeters: 429–495.

——. (2015a) *Génération et Substance. Aristote et Averroès entre physique et métaphysique*, Berlin: W. de Gruyter.

——. (2015b) "L'eternel par soi. Averroès contre Al-Farabi sur les Enjeux épistémologiques de *Phys*. VIII 1," in P. Bakker (ed.), *Averroes' Natural Philosophy and Its European Reception*, Leuven: Leuven University Press.

Chase, M. (2011) "Discussions on the Eternity of the world in Late Antiquity," *ΣΧΟΛΗ, A Journal of the Centre for Ancient Philosophy and the Classical Tradition* 5, 2: 111–73.

Davidson, H. A. (1969) "John Philoponus as a Source of Medieval Islamic and Jewish Proofs of Creation," *Journal of the American Oriental Society* 89: 357–91.

——. (1987) *Proofs for Eternity, Creation and the Existence of God in Medieval Islamic and Jewish Philosophy*, Oxford: Oxford University Press.

——. (1992) *Alfarabi, Avicenna & Averroes on Intellect, Their Cosmologies, Theories of Active Intellect and Theories of human intellect*, New York & Oxford: Oxford University Press.

Falcon, A. (2005) *Aristotle and the Science of Nature. Unity without Uniformity*, Cambridge: Cambridge University Press.

——. (2011) *Xenarchus of Seleucia: Aristotelianism in the First Century BCE*, Cambridge: Cambridge University Press.

Fazzo, S. & Wiesner, H. (1993) "Alexander of Aphrodisias in the Kindī-circle and al-Kindī's Cosmology," *Arabic Sciences and Philosophy* 3: 119–53.

Freudenthal, G. (2002) "The Medieval Astrologization of Aristotle's Biology: Averroes on the Role of the Celestial Bodies in the Generation of Animate Bodies," *Arabic Sciences and Philosophy* 12: 111–37.

——. (2006) "The Medieval Astrologization of The Aristotelian Cosmos: From Alexander of Aphrodisias to Averroes," *Mélanges de l'Université Saint-Joseph* (MUSJ) 59: 29–68.

——. (2009) "The Astrologization of the Aristotelian Cosmos: Celestial Influences on the Sublunary World in Aristotle, Alexander of Aphrodisias, and Averroes," in A. C. Bowen & C. Wildberg (eds.), *A Companion to Aristotle's Cosmology: Collected Papers on* De Caelo, Leiden: Brill, pp. 239–81.

Gannagé, E. (2011) "Philopon (Jean-). Tradition arabe," in R. Goulet (dir.), *Dictionnaire des Philosophes Antiques*, t. V, *De Paccius à Rutilius Rufus*. Va, *De Paccius à Plotin*, Paris, pp. 503–63.

Glasner, R. (2010) *Averroes' physics: a turning point in medieval natural philosophy*, Oxford: Oxford University Press.

Hasnawi, A. (1990a) *Fayd* (épanchement, émanation), in A. Jacob (dir.), *Encyclopédie philosophique universelle, vol. II: Les notions philosophiques*, PUF: Paris.

——. (1990b) *Dahr* (éternité, perpétuité), in A. Jacob (dir.), *l'Encyclopédie philosophique universelle, vol. II: Les notions philosophiques*, PUF: Paris.

——. (1994) "Alexandre d'Aphrodise vs. Jean Philopon: notes sur quelques traites d'Alexandre 'perdus' en grec, conservés en arabe," *Arabic Sciences and Philosophy* 4: 53–109.

Janos, D. (2012) *Method, structure, and development in al-Fārābi's Cosmology*, Leiden & Boston: Brill.

Janssens, J. (1997) "Creation and emanation in Ibn Sīnā," *Documenti e Studi sulla Tradizione Filosofica Medievale* 8: 455–77.

——. (2006) "The Notions of Wāhib al-ṣuwar (Giver of Forms) and Wāhib al-'aql (Bestower of Intelligence) in Ibn Sīnā," in C. Pacheco & F. Meirinhos (eds.), *Intellect et imagination dans la Philosophie médiévale. Intellect and Imagination in Medieval Philosophy. Intellecto e imaginação na Filosofia Medieval*, Actes de XIe Congrès International de Philosophie Médiévale, Porto, 26 au 30 août 2002 organisé par la Société Internationale pour l'Étude de la Philosophie Médiévale, 3 vol., Turnhout: Brepols, pp. 551–62.

Kukkonen, T. (2012) "Eternity," in J. Marenbon (ed.), *The Oxford Handbook of Medieval Philosophy*, pp. 525–46.

Lameer, J. (1994) *Al-Fārābī and Aristotelian Syllogistics: Greek theory and Islamic practice*, Leiden, New York & Köln: Brill.

Lizzini, O. (2004) "The relation between Form and Matter: some brief observations on the 'homology argument' (*Ilāhiyyāt*, II, 4) and the deduction of fluxus," in J. McGinnis & D. Reisman (eds.), *Interpreting Avicenna. Proceedings of the Second Conference of the Avicenna Study Group*, Leiden & Boston: Brill, pp. 175–85.

——. (2011) *Fluxus (fayḍ). Indagine sui fondamenti della Metafisica e della Fisica di Avicenna*, Bari: Edizioni di Pagina.

Maimonides (1974) *The Guide for the Perplexed*, vol. II, S. Pines (tr.), Chicago & London: The University of Chicago Press.

Maróth, M. (1995) "The Ten Intellects Cosmology and its Origin," *The Arabist* 13–14: 103–113.

McGinnis, J. (2010) *Avicenna*, Oxford: Oxford University Press.

Puig Montada, J. (1999) "Zur Bewegungs-definition im VIII Buch der Physik," in G. Endress & J. A. Aertsen (eds.), *Averroes and the Aristotelian Tradition. Sources, Constitution and Reception of the Philosophy of Ibn Rushd (1126–1198)*, Leiden: Brill, pp. 145–59.

Rashed, M. (2007) *Essentialisme, Alexandre d'Aphrodise entre logique, physique et cosmologie*, Berlin: De Gruyter.

——. (2008) "Al-Fārābī's lost treatise *On changing beings* and the possibility of a demonstration of the eternity of the world," *Arabic Sciences and Philosophy* 18: 19–58.

——. (2009) "On the Authorship of the Treatise *On The Harmonization of the Opinions of the Two Sages* Attributed to Al-Fārābī," *Arabic Sciences and Philosophy* 19: 43–82.

Sorabji, R. (1983) *Time, Creation and the Continuum. Theories in Antiquity and the Early Middle Ages*, London & Ithaca: Cornell University Press.

Twetten, D. (1995) "Averroes on the Prime Mover Proved in the Physics," *Viator* 26: 107–34.

——. (2007) "Averroes' prime mover argument," in J.-B. Brenet (ed.), *Averroès et les averroïsmes juif et latin. Actes du colloque international, Paris 16–18 juin 2005*, Turnhout: Brepols, pp. 9–75.
Vallat, P. (2011) "Al-Fārābī's arguments for the eternity of the world and the contingency of natural phenomena," in J. Watt & J. Lössl (eds.), *Interpreting the Bible and Aristotle: the Alexandrian commentary tradition between Rome and Baghdad*, Aldershot: Ashgate, pp. 259–86.
Walzer, R. (1962) "New Studies on al-Kindī," in R. Walzer (ed.), *Greek into Arabic. Essays on Islamic Philosophy*, Cambridge: Harvard University Press, pp. 175–205 (first published in *Oriens* 10 (1957): 203–32).
Wolfson, H. A. (1976) *The Philosophy of the Kalam*, Cambridge, MA: Harvard University Press.

13
ARABIC COSMOLOGY AND THE PHYSICS OF COSMIC MOTION

David Twetten

Introduction

One of the hallmarks of the philosophical versus the religious outlook in classical antiquity was the explanation of cosmic change in terms of simple, universal principles and unchanging first causes. This article focuses on the Aristotelian account of cosmic change and its metamorphosis in classical Arabic philosophy under the influence of Neoplatonism and monotheism. In effect, as monotheist philosophers in the wake of al-Kindī focus on Neoplatonic argumentation for a first "agent cause" of all being, "the true One," they come to reject change as providing access to the primary and universal efficient cause of all things. Thus, Ibn Sīnā denies that the argument from motion proves the unique God and cause of all being. Subsequently, however, Ibn Rushd gives an elaborate account of Aristotle's reasoning such that the prime mover, even if it is improperly called an efficient cause, is nevertheless the one, divine cause of all being. Presenting Ibn Rushd's account in some detail will allow us to set forth the Aristotelian philosophy of cosmic change in its fullest development within an Islamic context. The issue of the First Cause, however, must not blind us to the degree to which the thought of Ibn Rushd arises out of sophisticated use of Aristotelian cosmology by al-Fārābī, Ibn Sīnā, and Ibn Bājja, whose work itself has surprising continuity with, even while it represents a departure from, al-Kindī's affirmation of a Neoplatonic triad of primary causes (God, intellect and soul).

Classical Greek Cosmology and the Questions it Raises for Arabic Philosophy

According to the best science in late antiquity, the science inherited by the Arabic thinkers, the earth stands at the center of the universe, around which perpetually revolve the sun, moon, and the planets Mercury, Venus, Mars, Jupiter and Saturn. In the cosmology developed by Aristotle based on Plato, Eudoxus, and Callippus, each of these visible bodies is embedded on its own invisible sphere, which is itself the lowest in a "nest" of concentric spheres that communicate to it the motion by which it stands out against the background of the outermost, daily rotating "sphere of the fixed stars" (see Beere 2003). Two important qualifications to this cosmology were introduced by Ptolemy and Hipparchus: (1) the planetary motions are better explained by spheres not centered on the earth (eccentrics), together with mini-spheres that rotate on the circumference of the main spheres (epicycles); and (2) the discovery of the precession of the equinoxes is explained by adding an outermost starless sphere (Pedersen 1993). But what causes the 40 or 50 spheres to be moved? Even though they are made of an invisible, imperishable "fifth" element, which has a nature to be rotated in some direction and at some velocity, they require a distinct efficient mover to cause this rotation. Books 7 and 8 of Aristotle's *Physics* present arguments against an infinite regress of movers each of which is moved by another, affirming instead a first unmoved mover that appears to be an efficient cause, whereas *Metaphysics* 12 or Lambda affirms in Chapter 7 a first unmoved mover that moves as an object of desire.

The Arabic philosophers received an understanding of Aristotle's cosmology heavily influenced by the intermediate Greek thought. First, the Greek commentators on Aristotle proposed interpretations that, in effect, harmonized the accounts of the prime mover in the *Physics* and *Metaphysics* (Sharples 2002: 4–22). Alexander of Aphrodisias' *On the Principles of the Whole*, which, with *On Providence* (both extant only in Arabic or Syriac), was translated (and adapted) perhaps by the Kindī circle, presents the celestial spheres as ensouled and as moved by the first cause as by an intelligible object of desire (Endress 2002). Alexander appears to affirm a plurality of final causes, differing from one another according to prior and posterior, so that the first is superior in nobility to the rest (Alexander of Aphrodisias 2001: 48, 52, 88–96, 140–2).

A second main influence is Platonic. For Plotinus, the cosmic Soul is the cause of motion as such, whereas prior to it is the ultimate source of all, the One, as well as the source of intelligible forms as such, intellect, which he identifies with Being. Subsequently, Proclus expressly criticizes Aristotle for affirming intellect as the highest principle of all, especially since it is an exclusively final cause, and he mounts an argument, starting from Aristotelian principles, for a first efficient cause that bestows upon the cosmos everlasting motion and therefore also being. Ammonius Hermeiou, Proclus' student, identifies Aristotle's prime mover with a demiurgic efficient cause of being; and Ammonius' students, Simplicius and Philoponus, while disagreeing as to whether philosophy proves or disproves a temporal beginning, articulate this position within full-fledged commentaries on Aristotle's text. Hence, early Arabic thought is a continuation of late Greek cosmology, which combined the three primary causes in the Neoplatonic scheme—soul, intellect, and the One—with an Aristotelian/Ptolemaic cosmology of multiple ensouled spheres and separate subordinate intellects (hereafter "Intelligences") (Bodnar 1997: 196–9).

Given the best available science and cosmology, then, four sorts of questions arise for us in reading the Arabic philosophers.

Q. 1 As regards the God of monotheism, (a) how can Aristotle's prime unmoved mover be identified with God, and (b) how, if at all, can Aristotle's cosmological argument concluding to an unmoved mover be used to defend the existence of God? If God, for example, is to be identified with the first Neoplatonic emanative cause of being, (c) in what way is God also a cause of motion, properly speaking?

Q. 2 As regards the cosmic Intelligence, (a) is it an efficient cause of being, as in Neoplatonism, and if so, what causality is proper to God? Or, (b) if an Intelligence is an exclusively final cause, as in Aristotelianism, then can the first Intelligence, the mover of the outermost sphere, be the God of monotheism? If, instead, God is beyond the Intelligences that move the spheres, (c) what argument arrives at the God beyond?

Q. 3 As regards the celestial soul, if the first—*efficiently*-moving cause of cosmic motion is a soul that is moved by a *finally*-moving Intelligence as its object of desire, (a) how can the celestial soul be affirmed in the first place as a first unmoved mover? And, (b) what argument arrives at a separate Intelligence as a cause of the celestial soul? As we shall see, the more sophisticated the arguments for distinct cosmic causes (God, Intelligences, celestial souls) become, as in Ibn Sīnā, the greater becomes the need to weigh such arguments against a close reading of Aristotle's text, as in Ibn Rushd.

Q. 4 As regards Aristotle's text, then, how can the entire cosmic system of celestial souls and Intelligences be squared with the argumentation in *Physics* 8 and *Metaphysics* Lambda? In particular, (a) how does *Physics* 7.1 and 8.5–6 conclude to "movable" celestial souls in the very place where these chapters conclude to an "unmoved mover"? (b) How does the mover of infinite power proved in *Physics* 8.10, which appears to be introduced as an efficient cause, turn out to be a final cause only?

Al-Kindī and the *Neoplatonica Arabica*

As befits the "philosopher of the Arabs," al-Kindī inherits and furthers late Greek cosmology, namely, that of the "Ammonian" or "Alexandrian school," in which Plato and Aristotle were harmonized against a monotheist background. Al-Kindī's answers to the aforementioned questions form the horizon against which Islamic *falsafa* is developed. Despite his appreciation of Aristotle, al-Kindī does not adopt, at least in extant works, Aristotle's argumentation for a prime mover (Q. 1b). Siding with the theologians (*mutakallimūn*) on the non-eternity of the world, he develops a metaphysics of the First Cause that creatively appropriates styles of reasoning evident in two works apparently translated by the Kindī circle: the *Theology of Aristotle* and the *Book on the Pure Good* (*Liber de causis*), adaptations based on portions of *Enneads* IV–VI of Plotinus and of the *Elements of Theology* of Proclus. In his most important work, *On First Philosophy*, al-Kindī, after giving a Proclean argument for the One as first cause of all unity and multiplicity (Chapter 3), argues in Chapter 4 that since the multiplicity of things would not *be* without the One, their "being-ification" (*tahawwin*) is also from the One (al-Kindī 1998: 97). The One thereby makes them *be* through its very being; that is, it creates them. Precisely at this point, al-Kindī discloses his Alexandrian Aristotelianism by identifying the creator (*mubdi'*) as also, in the

Aristotelian formula, "a cause from which is the beginning (*mabda'*) of motion," or, in other words, an "agent" or efficient cause. Similarly, the author of the Prologue to the *Theology of Aristotle* (al-Kindī himself or some member of the Kindī circle) affirms that the *motion* of all things is from, because of, and for the sake of the First, from which First come intellect and "the universal celestial soul" (Badawī 1955: 6). In the paraphrase of Ptolemy's *Almagest* 1.1 (and of Theon of Alexandria's commentary on the same), al-Kindī even identifies God with the prime mover (al-Kindī 1987: 124, 131). On the other hand, the proximate mover of the motion of the heavenly bodies—bodies al-Kindī argues that must be alive, must possess the senses of sight and hearing (alone) in order to achieve virtue, and must possess rationality since they are the cause of other living, rational beings—is therefore their soul (al-Kindī 1998: 181–91).

How is it, we may ask, that the pagan theology of prime movers can be acceptable in a Muslim world (Q. 1a)? In a monotheist context, God cannot be identified as the first among equals, as merely one among the many proximate unmoved movers of the celestial spheres, especially if these movers are celestial souls. But such a consequence apparently ensues if God is identified with Aristotle's prime mover. Although al-Kindī, for whom the *Theology of Aristotle* is authentic, does not raise these questions, his thought contains an answer. He explicitly identifies the "being-ification" of the First Agent as a kind of "motion" (*ḥaraka*), since it involves passing from non-being to being, which is generation (*kawn*; al-Kindī 1950: ch. 2, 118). In a fragment quoted by al-Tawḥīdī, al-Kindī calls this motion "creation" (*ibdā'*) and distinguishes it from other motions since it involves no preexisting substrate (Altmann & Stern 2009: 69–70). Thus, al-Kindī's First Agent is a mover in the sense that it brings all things into being from non-being (al-Kindī 2012: Chapter 4, 55). And so, al-Kindī has the resources to distinguish between two kinds of "prime mover" corresponding to two kinds of "motion": God versus the unmoved proximate efficient mover that is the soul of the heavenly spheres in the Aristotelian cosmos (Q. 1c). Many questions still remain, of course. What is the role of a subordinate Intelligence in this system (Q. 2)? This, as well as questions regarding the celestial souls (Q. 3), will receive rich answers in the next three centuries of philosophical reflection.

Al-Fārābī and the Baghdad School

With the "emanation scheme" by which all things flow from the First Cause, the "Second Teacher" al-Fārābī reaps the harvest, for example in *Political Regime* (*al-Siyāsa*) 1, of taking the *Theology of Aristotle* as the completion of Aristotle's metaphysics. The same Neoplatonic strata for which there is good evidence in al-Kindī (albeit without a clear or systematic account of their causal roles), namely, God, Intellect, and Soul (Adamson 2002: 186–91), overlie in al-Fārābī a Ptolemaic cosmology of ensouled spheres moving for the sake of the Intelligences as objects of desire. Just as from the First Cause there emanates by natural necessity (1) the first Intelligence, so from the latter as "intellecting" the First Cause there emanates (2) the second Intelligence, and from the first Intelligence as intellecting itself there emanates (3) the celestial "body" or substance (which terms, as often in al-Fārābī and subsequent thinkers, include both celestial soul and its corporeal "substrate"). The emanation continues until there emerge: (4) nine Intelligences (also to be called "angels"); (5) the nine main spheres (the seven bodies of the visible solar system are embedded on eccentric and epicyclic spheres that, taken together in seven groups, resemble the organs of an ensouled animal); and (6) the agent intellect (Janos 2012: 123–6, 162–7, 356–68). From the heavens and their soul emanate prime matter, according to the account of the *Perfect State* (*al-Madīna al-fāḍila*), as well as all corporeal forms, so that together they emanate and maintain the existence of all natural terrestrial things.

In blending together this emanation scheme and the cosmology of *Alexander Arabus*, al-Fārābī also, in effect, addresses some of our questions. The souls of the celestial spheres can only be called "forms of bodies" and "souls" in a special sense of the terms (al-Fārābī 1993: 31–4, 37, 53). Though they are incorporeal intellects (lacking imaginative powers), rather than forms actualizing matter, they are said to resemble forms by being in a sense "in" bodies with which they form composites, and by requiring a subject that they in a sense "substantify." That is how they manage to be both efficient movers and also unmoved along with their spheres (Q. 3a). The incorporeal souls are not moved from potency to act as they cause motion, but are always actually intellecting the higher causes for the sake of which they cause motion. The Intelligences that are their final causes also emanate being (Q. 2b), yet they themselves are composite and emanated, unlike the First Being, God, which is absolutely simple and uncaused (Q. 2a).

In general, al-Fārābī's extant non-logical works are systematizing compendia rather than exhaustive commentaries or scientific treatments that follow Aristotle closely, such as were common in the "Baghdad school" begun by Abū Bishr Mattā. Two other authors are worth mentioning because their extant works present creative argumentation defending, in essence, the cosmology of *Alexander Arabus*, while also apparently using Themistius' paraphrase of *Metaphysics* Lambda: the great Sabean astronomer Thābit ibn Qurra, who may be considered as a precursor of the Baghdad school; and Abū Sulaymān as-Sijistānī, who taught in Baghdad between 939 and 985 C.E.

Ibn Sīnā

Ibn Sīnā's most important contributions to cosmology arise from his concern, unlike what we find in al-Fārābī, for giving *arguments* defending each of the Fārābīan cosmic causes. He introduces the principle "from one comes only one" to justify the emanation scheme, thereby giving grounds for al-Fārābī's answer to Q. 2a: what causality is proper to God if other Intelligences also emanate being? And Ibn Sīnā creates the proof, exclusive to metaphysics, of the existence of God as a being that, unlike all other beings, is necessary through itself. With this proof he answers the questions regarding God that are directly raised by the following reading of Aristotle's "prime mover argument" (Qq. 1a, b and 2c). Motion, he insists, cannot be used to arrive at the One as the source of all beings (Ibn Sīnā 1978: 23–4). The natural sciences, instead, give (only) an idea of God's existence insofar as they prove a cause of motion that is *one* and that is *neither a body nor a power of a body* (i.e. the conclusion of Aristotle's *Physics* 8.10; Ibn Sīnā 2005: 4). According to *Notes* (*al-Ta'līqāt*), a work containing Avicennian material, an infinitely powerful "prime mover" is proved in physics, whereas the First is known to be a cause of being and a final cause of celestial motion in metaphysics (Gutas 1988: 263), once we see that the "prime mover" in the *Physics* need be no more than an Intelligence that is below the First (Q. 2b). In fact, Ibn Sīnā apparently does not, when speaking formally, use the term "prime mover" as such of the First. Even in the early *Origin and Destination* (*al-Mabda' wa al-ma'ād*) 1.24–45, where, after giving his "necessary being argument," he apparently for the last time presents a proof of God's existence from motion: "prime mover" refers to the multiple, infinitely powerful celestial final causes, the Intelligences (see especially the passage copied into the *Najāt*, Ibn Sīnā 1985: 634). Nonetheless, Ibn Sīnā continues to see the First as providing a unique role as a cause of motion (Q. 1c). A distinct Intelligence is required to serve as a final cause for the *eternity* of each particular celestial motion. By contrast, "first mover of the whole of heaven"—or simply "the mover of the whole"—is the final cause of the perpetual circulation of all (Ibn Sīnā 2005: 317.2–22, 325, 333).

This last conclusion points to the problem with Ibn Sīnā's—and, in general, with the Neoplatonic—reading of Aristotle in Arabic monotheism. For, neither Ibn Sīnā, nor Aristotle, nor Alexander and Themistius, whom Ibn Sīnā uses, offer a proof that there must be a "mover of the whole" separate from and beyond the prime movers of each sphere. Why must God, the Necessary Being, be other than the Intelligence that is the final cause of the outermost sphere (Q. 2c)? At the same time, Ibn Sīnā does enter into the details of Aristotelian cosmology, thereby addressing Qq. 3 and 4. He displays close knowledge of the text of Aristotle and his commentators, so we are on good grounds to say that in Ibn Sīnā's view Aristotle's *Physics* 8.4–5 concludes to a celestial soul, *Physics* 8.10 concludes to an infinitely powerful separate Intelligence (Ibn Sīnā 1984: 29–35, 52–3, 57–61), and *Metaphysics* 12.7 proves that the infinitely powerful mover causes *motion* proper (only) as an object of desire. Ibn Sīnā (2005: 311–12, 314) develops an argument for Intelligences that had been alluded to by Alexander and Themistius: celestial souls as corporeal (Q. 3a) are in themselves only *finitely* powerful; in order to cause an infinite, everlasting motion, they must be moved by something that is *infinitely* powerful insofar as it is separate from any body (Q. 3b). Similarly, Ibn Sīnā develops elaborate reasoning to justify celestial souls as opposed to their mere nature as movers of the heavens. Each celestial soul, desiring to imitate the object of its intellection, uses reason, choice, and, contrary to al-Fārābī, also *imagination* to bring about the *particular* direction and velocity of its sphere; for, the sphere souls are, says Ibn Sīnā, corporeal, changeable, not denuded of matter, and cognizant of changeable particulars (Janos 2011: 180, 202–11). As a result, Intelligence stands to celestial soul just as agent intellect to the human soul, from which latter *emanate* the *motions* of the human body.

Such novel argumentation for primary causes nevertheless raises new questions regarding the Aristotelian character of Ibn Sīnā's enterprise. How is it that Aristotle's *Physics* concludes to changeable celestial souls in the very place where it concludes to an "unmoved mover" (Q. 4a)? Celestial souls, if they are forms, perfections of the body, and corporeal, are therefore changed with what they move, as insists Ibn Sīnā (2005: 307, 310–12), especially as regards their constantly renewed particular imagination and volition. Furthermore, how is it that the mover of infinite power, which appears to be introduced by Aristotle as well as by Themistius as an efficient cause, can turn out to be an exclusively final cause without also threatening the very proof in *Physics* 8.10 of a separate mover that "gives" infinite, everlasting motion to the heavens in the first place (Q. 4b)? Of course, these worries about "causes of motion" are minimized within a cosmology, borrowed from al-Fārābī and the *Theology of Aristotle*, of emanative, efficient "causes of being" at each level of the primary causes. Still, the worries return if the late Ibn Sīnā as can appear (although not for the best recent scholarship), questions the authenticity of the *Theology of Aristotle*, despite this work's continuing influence in his thought. We turn next to the first Arabic philosopher who pursues an Aristotelian cosmology uninfluenced by this work.

Ibn Rushd

These last questions for Ibn Sīnā's cosmology lead us naturally to the great inheritor in Andalusia of Baghdad Aristotelianism, Ibn Rushd. We now know that he engaged in a project of cleansing his thought (and his own early writings) of emanationism, which we associate with Neoplatonism, but which he regards as a theological accretion—poor dialectical arguments that are contrary to "the Philosopher" (Aristotle). Thus, his early "short commentaries," prior to his revisions, espouse an emanation scheme (yet, he already prefers a purely Aristotelian over a Ptolemaic astronomy, he rejects a starless outermost sphere, and he affirms no efficient cause of prime matter) (Davidson 1992: 223–49). His middle and long commentaries adopt, instead, an Aristotelian cosmology that returns to that of *Alexander Arabus*, comprising efficiently-moving celestial souls and finally-moving Intelligences. These works also criticize the following doctrines of Ibn Sīnā: agent and emanative causality, an agent intellect as "giver of forms," a First Cause beyond the final movers proper to each sphere, and the metaphysical proof of this God's existence through the "necessary and the possible."

Most noteworthy for present purposes is that Ibn Rushd offers one of the greatest harmonizing accounts of Aristotle's cosmological treatises ever offered, one that rivals that of his great Greek predecessors Alexander and Simplicius. The key to the correct interpretation of this account lies in works extant only in Latin and Hebrew. Put differently, the key is to use the extensive discussion in *Physics* 7–8 as the basis for understanding the comparatively thin but memorable discussion of *Metaphysics* Lambda. Though scholars disagree, this strategy is arguably the best for interpreting Aristotle's own account of the prime mover, but in Ibn Rushd it is a strategy required by an over-arching principle that he defends contra Ibn Sīnā: only natural philosophy, not metaphysics, proves the existence of God, the prime mover (Bertolacci 2007: 84–96). Notice immediately in this principle the interpretative lens of monotheism, common to the Arabic philosophical tradition, through which Ibn Rushd reads his (purportedly) "purified" Aristotle. In light of this hermeneutic principle, the Commentator's breakthroughs lie in three areas, which we shall examine successively: (A) how *Physics* 8.1–6 arrives at the first celestial soul as an absolutely unmoved mover (Qq. 3a and 4a); (B) how natural philosophy arrives at a separate Intelligence as a moving cause of each celestial sphere (Q. 3b); and (C) how *Physics* 8.10 proves the existence of God as the first Intelligence of the first sphere (Q. 1b).

A second hermeneutic principle lies behind (A) Aristotle's arrival at the first celestial soul: Averroes takes *Physics* 7 and 8 to form a single, continuous argument, each part of which builds on what came before. Accordingly, he takes the famous proof in *Physics* 8.1 of eternal or everlasting motion to be the "second" such proof, concluding to everlasting motion, not in general as in *Physics* 7.1, but specifically of the first (outermost) sphere. All subsequent discussion in Book 8 "of the first thing moved," then, refers to the celestial sphere. Thanks to this hermeneutic principle, a key interpretation of Book 7's reasoning, which Ibn Rushd borrows from the detailed commentary of his great Andalusian predecessor Ibn Bājja (Lettinck 1994: 615–22), also applies to all subsequent conclusions: "everything moved, *if* it is moved by something other than itself, must be moved *by a body* in corporeal contact with it" (Twetten 1995: 11–17). This interpretation provides grounds, in turn, for what the best Aristotle scholars have noticed, along with Ibn Rushd, about *Physics* 8.5–6's reasoning: Aristotle's presumption throughout is that the first mover, arrived at by rejecting an infinite regress of per se efficient causes, is self-moved rather than moved by another (Paulus 1933: 267–77, 293). The question of Book 8.5–6 subsequently becomes: can a first *self-moving sphere* move itself without having a moving part that is absolutely unmoved, that lacks even the *per accidens* local motion of animals' souls? Since Aristotle's arguments answer no, contra Ibn Sīnā, Ibn Rushd is compelled to develop the notion, at best only hinted at in the commentary tradition (Alexander of Aphrodisias 2001: 48, 52–4), of a (Platonic) celestial soul that is incorporeal (with al-Fārābī) and non-hylomorphic, that lacks "subsistence" (*qiwām*) through the sphere with which it forms a "self-moving" whole. By contrast, its sphere serves, as for al-Fārābī, as a prime-matter-less "substrate" for its soul. Ibn Rushd, in the "treatise" *On the Substance of the Sphere*, explains, again contra Ibn Sīnā, that such celestial souls are absolutely immobile and, though characterized by intellect and desire, they lack any corporeal power of imagination (Qq. 3a and 4a).

Since the celestial soul is fundamentally characterized as an intellect, some passages in Ibn Rushd, such as those presenting his famous "analogy of the baths" (see below), appear to identify the celestial souls and Intelligences. This identification, with its consequence that the first of these is the prime mover or God, constitutes the Standard Reading of the Averroean cosmos, rooted in the Middle Ages and Renaissance (Ibn Rushd 1986: 33–5, 113–115, n18–19). This reading receives confirmation from the fact that Ibn Rushd can speak, as can Alexander and al-Fārābī, of the heavenly *bodies* themselves as moved by the separate Intelligence as an object of desire. Nevertheless, an equally old interpretative tradition takes as foundational a key passage in the *Long Commentary on the Metaphysics* that affirms an *infinitely* powerful mover "not in matter," *as well as* a *finitely* powerful mover that is "in" the heavens (Ibn Rushd 1973: 1630). In support of this as the Revised Reading, it is possible to find at least two (paradoxically Avicennian) arguments for (B) the arrival at a separate Intelligence "moving" each celestial soul (Q. 3b): (1) there must be a celestial soul causing motion with a power that is finite *in velocity* to account for the determinate motions of the heavens (Q. 3a), whereas for *Physics* 8.10 there must (also) be a power that is *infinite in duration* to account for everlasting motion, a power that is "not a body or 'in' a body," as is Ibn Rushd's celestial soul (Twetten 2007: 28–53); and (2) although the heavens and their proximate movers have no unactualized *potency*, that is, no potency for not undergoing or causing motion, they each are in themselves *possible* (*mumkin*) with respect to their causing and undergoing motion in the sense that *without what causes them*, left to themselves, it is *possible* that their causing or undergoing motion not occur. Therefore, since it is necessary that there be everlasting motion, there must be a cause other than themselves that makes them necessarily cause or undergo motion. In several places Ibn Rushd accepts Ibn Sīnā's "possible in itself, necessary through another," but only in the case of motion, not in the case of existence.

Since the aforementioned reasoning for (B) is not found in Aristotle's extant works, Ibn Rushd fills it in within his own account of the natural science of the heavens (astrophysics). With this established, it is easy to understand (C) the arrival at the existence of the absolutely first cause, God. What Ibn Rushd finds in *Physics* 8.10 is simply the proof of a prime mover that, since it must be infinitely powerful in duration, is neither a body nor a power of a body. As in Ibn Sīnā, this is an Intelligence that is separate from the heavens (and from the celestial soul). But unlike in Ibn Sīnā (and al-Fārābī), since it is otiose to affirm a cause without evident effects, the first Intelligence is identifiable with the first Being, God. Here we see how Ibn Rushd addresses Qq. 1b and 2b: how can the "prime mover argument" arrive at God, not a subordinate Intelligence? Thus, whereas *Physics* 8.6 for Ibn Rushd proves the existence of the first immobile celestial soul, *Physics* 8.10 arrives at the first Intelligence or God, which is known in astrophysics, as we have seen, to be other than the first celestial soul. Within metaphysics, Ibn Rushd insists that the first being alone is simple, although apparently there is nothing in his cosmology that explains how the other incorporeal Intelligences, although they must be composite and formally diverse from each other, are receptive of anything from the First. Why must subordinate finally-moving Intelligences be moved by desire to contemplate the First Intelligence or God? Intelligences appear to be hierarchized on extrinsic grounds alone: because of the rank of the sphere that each moves, not because of the objects of their contemplation. And, the cosmology requires that all celestial souls, not subordinate Intelligences, contemplate the mover of the outermost sphere. Thus, Q. 1a remains somewhat incompletely answered: can Aristotle's prime unmoved mover be identified with the God of monotheism if it cannot in any scientifically acceptable sense be the "cause" of *all* things, that is, if it is in no non-metaphorical sense the cause of other separate Intelligences?

As in Ibn Sīnā, metaphysics shows that the infinitely powerful mover proved to exist in physics moves as an object of desire. Does God, then, for Ibn Rushd, move *only* as a final cause (Q. 4b)? According to what appears to be the fullest statement by the Cordoban master, the separate Intelligence moves the heavens (only) as formal and final cause (Ibn Rushd 1869: 3–4). Just as the active intellect is both form and end for the material intellect, so God for the outermost celestial soul is the form intellectually conceived for the sake of which it moves. It is through God as formal and final cause that the celestial soul and the heavenly bodies are the *efficient* cause of the coming to be from potency to act of all sublunar substances. This is the point of the bath analogy: unlike in the material order, such as in the case of our desire for the spa, in things separate from matter, there is no dichotomy between the agent that desires (namely, the celestial soul) and the end desired, as though desire could cease once the end is attained. Accordingly, Ibn Rushd writes: "Insofar as these intelligibles are [the heavens] forms, they are motive after the manner of the agent, and insofar as these are their ends, they [the heavens] are moved by them through desire" (Ibn

Rushd 1973: 1594–5). The Commentator does not give up on the claim that God as first being is the cause and source of all other beings (albeit indirectly), as for the entire Arabic philosophical tradition. In language that resembles Thābit's and probably has a common source in Alexander, he argues as follows. The very being of the heavens is for the sake of their motion (Ibn Rushd 1986: 49.30–8). Therefore, if, *per impossibile*, they were to cease to be moved, they would cease to be, and all of their effects, namely, generable and corruptible substances, would likewise cease to be. In this sense, God is the cause of the being of all things (Qq. 2b and 4b) (though this explanation would not seem to apply to the Intelligences). Thus, Ibn Rushd discovers in the "argument from motion" precisely the dependence of all in being that Ibn Sīnā explicitly finds absent there. This dependence of all of the heavens and their proximate movers on the First does not violate the principle "from one comes only one," which Ibn Rushd accepts, since that principle applies only to efficient causes in the proper sense, which actualize potencies (Wolfson 1973: 421–8), whereas God moves as form and end, or, in short, moves as object of desire, *all* of the proximate movers of the heavens (Ibn Rushd 1973: 1648–50). Consequently, every sphere shares in the diurnal motion caused by the first intellect, God, so that the proximate movers of all *subordinate* spheres conceptualize and are moved by two formal/final causes.

Conclusion

In Ibn Rushd we find arguably the most sophisticated presentation of Aristotelian cosmology ever offered, the fruit of over 300 years of cutting-edge scientific reflection in the Arabic world. The fact that the Aristotelian/Ptolemaic cosmology has been proved false by scientific advances should not prevent us from recognizing its significance for the history of science, as well as for our own reflections on causality and cosmology. Still, from the standpoint of contemporary Aristotle scholarship, the presence of monotheism, possible v. necessary beings, and the overlapping formal causality of Intelligences upon subordinate celestial souls seem quite remote from the Stagyrite's thought. These are the remnants in Ibn Rushd of the Neoplatonic reading of Aristotle in Greco-Arabic philosophy, a reading spawned in the Islamic world by al-Kindī and nourished on the *Theology of Aristotle*. We have traced the development of this reading, showing how, even as it addresses questions as to how Aristotle's prime mover can be God, it raises new questions regarding the role of Intelligences and celestial souls. At the same time that the Baghdad school begins to develop a close textual reading of Aristotle in the context of a full-bodied philosophical curriculum, al-Fārābī embeds the Aristotelian/Ptolemaic cosmology within a novel "emanation scheme" that begins to answer such cosmological questions. Ibn Sīnā with great ingenuity gives a complete argumentative justification for the main elements of the Fārābīan scheme, while at the same time subordinating the "logic" of the prime mover to that of the Necessary Being. Only against the background of al-Fārābī and Ibn Sīnā, then, can Ibn Rushd's renewed defense of Aristotelianism be understood. Our findings confirm the observation of d'Ancona (2005: 24) regarding *falsafa* in general: the key to Arabic Aristotelian cosmology is Neoplatonism.

Further Reading

Adamson, P. (2007) *Al-Kindī*, New York: Oxford University Press.
Davidson, H. A. (1987) *Proofs for Eternity, Creation and the Existence of God in Medieval Islamic and Jewish Philosophy*, Oxford: Oxford University Press.
Freudenthal, G. (2006) "The Medieval Astrologization of the Aristotelian Cosmos: From Alexander of Aphrodisias to Averroes," *Mélanges de l'Université Saint-Joseph* 59: 29–68.
Kogan, B. (1985) *Averroes and the Metaphysics of Causation*, Albany, New York: SUNY Press.
Themistius (1999) *Paraphrase de la* Métaphysique *d'Aristote (livre Lambda)*, R. Brague (tr.), Paris: Vrin (background important especially for Ibn Sīnā and Ibn Rushd).

References

Adamson, P. (2002) *The Arabic Plotinus: A Philosophical Study of the* Theology of Aristotle, London: Duckworth.
Alexander of Aphrodisias (2001) *On the Cosmos*, C. Genequand (ed. and tr.), Leiden: Brill.
al-Fārābī (1993) *The Political Regime* (al-Siyāsa al-madaniyya, also known as *The Treatise on the Principles of Beings*), F. Najjar (ed.), Beirut: Dar El-Mashreq.
al-Kindī (1950) *Rasā'il al-falsafiyya (Philosophical Treatises)*, vol. 1, M. 'A. H. Abū Ridā (ed.), Cairo: Dār al-Fikr al-'Arabī.
——. (1987) *Kitāb fī l-Ṣinā'at al-'uẓmā (On the Greatest Art (Almagest))*, 'A. Ṭḍḥ A. al-Sayyid (ed.), Cyprus: Dar al-Shabab.
——. (1998) *Oeuvres philosophiques et scientifiques d'al-Kindī*, vol. 2: Métaphysique et cosmologie, R. Rashed & J. Jolivet (ed. and tr.), Leiden: Brill.
——. (2012) *The Philosophical Works of al-Kindī*, P. Adamson & P. E. Pormann (tr.), Karachi: Oxford University Press.
Altmann, A. & Stern, S. M. (2009) *Isaac Israeli: A Neoplatonic Philosopher of the Early Tenth Century*, Chicago: University of Chicago Press (repr. Oxford: Oxford University Press, 1958).
Badawī, 'A. (1955) *Plotinus apud Arabes:* Theologia Aristotelis *et fragmenta quae supersunt (Aflūṭīn 'inda l-'arab)*, Cairo: Dirasat Islamiyya.
Beere, J. (2003) "Counting the Unmoved Movers: Astronomy and Explanation in Aristotle's Metaphysics XII.8," *Archiv für Geschichte der Philosophie* 85: 1–20.
Bertolacci, A. (2007) "Avicenna and Averroes on the Proof of God's Existence and the Subject-Matter of Metaphysics," *Medioevo* 32: 61–97.
Bodnar, I. M. (1997) "Alexander of Aphrodisias on Celestial Motions," *Phronesis* 42: 190–205.
d'Ancona, C. (2005) "Greek into Arabic: Neoplatonism in Translation," in P. Adamson & R. C. Taylor (eds.), *Cambridge Companion to Arabic Philosophy*, Cambridge: Cambridge University Press, pp. 10–31.
Davidson, H. A. (1992) *Alfarabi, Avicenna, and Averroes on Intellect: Their Cosmologies, Theories of the Active Intellect, and Theories of Human Intellect*, Oxford: Oxford University Press.
Endress, G. (2002) "Alexander Arabus on the First Cause: Aristotle's First Mover in an Arabic Treatise attributed to Alexander of Aphrodisias," in C. d'Ancona & G. Serra (eds.), *Aristotele e Alessandro di Afrodisia nella tradizione Araba: Atti del colloquio "La ricezione araba ed ebraica della filosofia e della scienza greche,"* Padova, 14–15 maggio 1999, Padua: Il Poligrafo, pp. 19–74.
Gutas, D. (1988) *Avicenna and the Aristotelian Tradition: Introduction to Reading Avicenna's Philosophical Works*, Leiden: Brill.
Ibn Rushd (1869) *Treatise 1 on the Conjunction of the Separate Intellect with Man*, in *Drei Abhandlungen über die Conjunction des separaten Intellects mit dem Menschen von Averroes*

(Vater und Sohn), aus dem Arabischen übersetzt von Samuel Ibn Tibbon, zum ersten Male herausgegeben, übersetzt und erlaütert von Dr. J. Hercz, Berlin: H. G. Hermann, pp. 3–10 [Hebrew].

——. (1973) *Tafsīr Mā ba'd aṭ-Ṭabī'at ("Grand Commentaire" de la* Métaphysique*)*, vol. 3, M. Bouyges (ed.), Beirut: Dar el-Machreq.

——. (1986) *Averroes'* De substantia orbis, A. Hyman (ed. and tr.), Cambridge, MA: Medieval Academy of America and Israel Academy of Sciences and Humanities.

Ibn Sīnā (1978) *Sharḥ Kitāb Ḥarf al-Lām (Commentary on* Metaphysics *Lam* 6–10, from the *Book of Fair Judgment)*, in 'A. Badawī (ed.), *Ariṣṭū 'inda l-'arab (Aristotle amidst the Arabs)*, 2nd edition, Kuwait: Wakālat al-Maṭbū'āt, pp. 22–33.

——. (1984) *al-Mabda' wa al-ma'ād (The Origin and Destination)*, A. al-Nūrānī (ed.), Tehran: Institute of Islamic Studies.

——. (1985) *Kitāb al-najāt (The Salvation)*, M. Fakhry (ed.), Beirut: Dār al-afāq al-jadīdah.

——. (2005) *Metaphysics of the Healing (al-Shifā': Ilāhiyyāt)*, M. E. Marmura (tr.), Provo, UT: Brigham Young University Press.

Janos, D. (2011) "Moving the Orbs: Astronomy, Physics, and Metaphysics and the Problem of Celestial Motion according to Ibn Sīnā," *Arabic Sciences and Philosophy* 21: 165–214.

——. (2012) *Method, Structure, and Development in al-Fārābī's Cosmology*, Leiden: Brill.

Lettinck, P. (1994) *Aristotle's* Physics *and Its Reception in the Arabic World: With an Edition of the Unpublished Parts of Ibn Bājja's* Commentary on the Physics, Leiden: Brill.

Paulus, J. (1933) "La Théorie du premier moteur chez Aristote," *Revue de philosophie* 33: 259–94, 394–424.

Pedersen, O. (1993) *Early Physics and Astronomy: A Historical Introduction*, Cambridge: Cambridge University Press.

Sharples, R. (2002) "Aristotelian Theology after Aristotle," in D. Frede & A. Laks (eds.), *Traditions of Theology: Studies in Hellenistic Theology, Its Background and Aftermath*, Leiden: Brill, pp. 1–40.

Twetten, D. (1995) "Averroes on the Prime Mover Proved in the *Physics*," *Viator* 26: 107–34.

——. (2007) "Averroes' Prime Mover Argument," in J.-B. Brenet (ed.), *Averroès et les averroïsmes juif et latin*, Turnhout, Belgium: Brepols, pp. 9–75.

Wolfson, H. A. (1973) "Averroes' Lost Treatise on the Prime Mover," in his *Studies in the History of Philosophy*, vol. 1, I. Twersky & G. H. Williams (eds.), Cambridge, MA: Harvard University Press, pp. 402–29.

14
BODY, SOUL, AND SENSE IN NATURE

Luis Xavier López-Farjeat

Introduction

Aristotle's well-known definition of the soul is found in *On the Soul* 2.1, 412a19: the soul is the form or actualization (*entelekheia*) of a natural or organic body which potentially has life. In other words, the soul is the principle through which living beings are alive and have different capacities such as nutrition, reproduction, perception, desire, and thinking. Non-human animals and plants share the most basic capacities, i.e. nutrition and reproduction. Perception and desire, however, are powers that pertain to non-human and human animals. Within his biological treatises Aristotle conceived a sort of phylogenetic scale, according to which inferior non-human animals possess at least the sense of touch while higher forms of life, for instance mammals, have five external senses and more complex capacities such as common sense, memory, and imagination. Human animals share the capacities performed by plants and non-human animals, but in the particular case of humans an exclusive and unique capacity is added: thinking.

When dealing with those capacities shared by human and non-human animals, i.e. perception, it is not clear whether Aristotle is explaining this capacity and others related to it (appetite, desire, pleasure and pain, etc.) through the soul, or if, on the contrary, the soul is explained by means of perceptive operations. Aristotle's standard position is that these capacities are common to both body and soul. However, as some scholars have shown (Morel 2006: 121; Sharples 2006: 165; Rapp 2006: 187), this alternative is problematic since it is not clear in which sense "common" should be understood. My intention here is not to go into this discussion in the Aristotelian corpus. This problem, however, serves to contextualize some issues that were at the heart of Arabic-Islamic medieval philosophical psychology: the relationship between body and soul, the cognitive capacities of the soul, the immortality of the human soul, and the knowledge of the self.

The understanding of these issues had a strong Aristotelian background. Arabic-Islamic philosophers were influenced by Aristotelian treatises such as *On the Soul* (*Kitāb al-Nafs*), related treatises known collectively as the *Parva Naturalia*, and also by Aristotle's writings on animals (*History of Animals*, *Parts of Animals*, *Movement of*

Animals, Progression of Animals, and *Generation of Animals*), all of which were gathered under the name of *Book of Animals* (*Kitāb al-hayāwān*). In these main treatises devoted to the investigation of living beings it becomes quite evident that Aristotle considers the study of the soul as part of the natural sciences. Although this kind of approach was very influential to Arabic-Islamic philosophers, it was somewhat problematic: Aristotle held the unity of body and soul but he also described the body as an instrument of the soul, as though the two were different substances. Furthermore, given his definition of the soul as the substantial form of the body, he claimed that this relationship ceases when the body perishes and seems to have left little or no room for human individual immortality. Islamic philosophers were concerned about these issues and discussed different matters in depth—such as the origination of the soul and its relationship to the body, the distinction between the cognitive operations that rely on the body and those intellective operations that do not depend on it—and they tried to define the ontological status of the soul in efforts to determine whether it is immortal.

The relationship between body and soul in Aristotle's philosophical psychology is difficult to grasp. Modern and contemporary discussions on philosophy of mind have put aside Aristotle and those traditions that built their views on these matters upon Aristotelian foundations, and hence have treated the question of the relationship between body and soul as if it were exclusively a modern problem. In fact, it is a commonplace to attribute the beginning of philosophy of mind to Descartes and his distinction between *res cogitans* and *res extensa*. There are, however, reasons to hold that it actually started with Ibn Sīnā and his understanding of Aristotle's *On the Soul* (Lagerlund 2007a: 1–16, 2007b: 11–32; Kaukua & Kukkonen 2007: 95–119). In what follows, I shall explain the way in which Ibn Sīnā (d. 1037) and Ibn Rushd (d. 1198) understood the relationship between body and soul and some related issues such as perception, self-awareness, intellection, and the immortality of the soul.

There were different approaches to the Aristotelian philosophical psychology in the Arabic-Islamic context. For example, there are several treatises where al-Kindī (d. 870) deals with psychological matters displaying a strong Aristotelian and Neoplatonic background, but it is difficult to integrate his ideas into a coherent theory (Adamson 2007: 106–43). Al-Fārābī (d. 950) also wrote the *Epistle on the Intellect* (*Risālat fi al 'aql*), which envince quite clearly the influence of Aristotle's doctrine of the soul and its interpretation by Alexander of Aphrodisias. Although both philosophers made early valuable contributions to the understanding of the soul and its relationship with the body, Ibn Sīnā's and Ibn Rushd's approaches to this matter were more highly systematic.

In his psychological writings Ibn Sīnā did not intend to expound and clarify Aristotle's standpoint. Rather, as a result of his reading of the pseudo-Aristotelian work *Theology of Aristotle*, and some Neoplatonic writings on the soul, he somewhat distanced himself from Aristotle's doctrine of the soul. This led him to a different and original perspective wherein the soul is conceived as an independent, individuated, and immortal substance. In contrast, in his three commentaries on Aristotle's *On the Soul*, Ibn Rushd went through Aristotle's text in detail, trying to establish its correct understanding and mend some of the misunderstandings of his predecessors (al-Fārābī, Ibn Sīnā, Ibn Bājja). Ibn Rushd's commentaries are different from each other but they also have something in common: as Aristotle before him, in all three commentaries, Ibn Rushd considered the study of the soul as related to the natural sciences. What both Ibn Sīnā and Ibn Rushd have in common is their conception of intellectual understanding as something that goes beyond the bodily powers.

Ibn Sīnā's Conception of the Soul and its Relationship to the Body

Ibn Sīnā deals with the ontological status of the soul in several writings but mainly in the psychology of *The Healing* (*Shifā'*) and in the psychological section of a shorter work entitled *The Salvation* (*Najāt*). Ibn Sīnā's treatment of the soul, as mentioned before, is not entirely Aristotelian; although he also considers the soul to be the form of a natural organic body, at the same time he conceives the soul in Neoplatonic terms, as a whole substance distinct and independent from the body. In fact, Ibn Sīnā identifies the soul with the essence or the self in human beings. Ibn Sīnā also somewhat distances himself from Aristotle insofar as he takes a dualistic approach which requires him to resolve at least two key issues concerning body and soul in *Shifā': al-Nafs* 5.2: (1) the origination and individuation of the soul; and (2) the interaction between soul and body (Avicenna 1959: 209–21). The first issue can be stated in the following terms: in *Shifā': al-Nafs* 5.3 Ibn Sīnā holds that the soul originates simultaneously with the body and that the body is necessary for the soul's individuation (Avicenna 1959: 221–7), but later in *Shifā': al-Nafs* 5.4 he asserts that the soul is a complete and independent substance that remains individuated after the body perishes (Avicenna 1959: 227–34). The second issue is clearly related to the first: following Aristotle, Ibn Sīnā considers the soul to be the principle of operation of the body and, in this sense, the body to be an instrument of the soul; therefore, it is necessary to clarify the causal relationship between body and soul.

Ibn Sīnā explains that the soul comes forth from the active or agent intellect that, as we shall see, is responsible for an emanative process where the form, i.e. the soul, originates concurrently with matter. In other words, the origination of the soul happens simultaneously with a natural process, i.e. the harmonic mixture of the elements (earth, water, air, and fire) that give rise to different bodies with the potentiality to perform a diversity of operations (Avicenna 1952: 24–5; 1959: 227–34). The more harmonious or balanced this mixture is, the more complete are the operations a body is able to perform. While explaining the way natural bodies come to exist, Ibn Sīnā upholds the unity of the body-soul composite: the soul perfects the body but the soul needs the body in order to exist. The soul is not a pre-existent substance independent from the body; it actually depends on the body in order for some of its operations to take place. The soul is neither the cause of the body nor is the body the cause of the soul: the soul just happens to have a natural disposition to be "with" (Arabic: *ma'a*; Latin: *cum*) the body (Druart 2000: 263). Following Aristotle, Ibn Sīnā considers three kinds of soul according to the capacities that living beings can perform: at the lowest level there is the vegetative soul in living beings with capacities such as nutrition, reproduction, and growth (the latter is present in some plants); these capacities are shared with animals that in addition have motive and perceptive capacities; finally, in the case of the human rational soul the exclusive and unique capacity (at least among animals) of thought is added (Avicenna 1952: 25).

Perception is one of the operations shared by human and non-human animals where the interaction between body and soul is displayed. Ibn Sīnā deals with this in detail and makes a distinction between various kinds of perception depending on the degree of abstraction or separation from matter: the form (*ṣūrah*), intentions/connotational attributes (*ma'ni*), or intelligibles (sing. *ma'qūl*) can be extracted from matter. The bodily faculties are necessary for the attainment of forms, intentions, and intelligibles. In the case of human beings, bodily faculties are necessary to acquire primary intelligibles but at a certain point they become no longer necessary. Ibn Sīnā conceives the human intellect as an immaterial substance that needs the body for its origination and also to acquire primary intelligibles. However, once the human intellect has attained the intelligibles, the body becomes an obstacle for perfect knowledge. The fact that the human rational intellect distances itself from the body confirms Ibn Sīnā's conception of the body and the soul as two different substances. Although Ibn Sīnā insists on the differentiation between body and soul, he also claims that the origination of the soul happens with the body and that perception in human and non-human animals is only possible through the body. Still, his account of the relationship of soul and body is thoughtfully grounded in reasoning which respects the multiple relevant issues at stake.

Ibn Sīnā defines perception as the extraction of the form of a perceptible object (Avicenna 1952: 25–6, 1959: 58–74). The perceptive faculty is divided into two parts: external and internal. The external senses perceive forms and, according to Ibn Sīnā's account, they encompass the sense of sight (which perceives the image of the forms of colored bodies), the sense of hearing (which perceives the vibration of the air when two solid bodies strike each other, i.e. sound), the sense of smell (which perceives the odor of the bodies transmitted by the air), the sense of taste (which perceives the sensible forms of tastes when these are mingled with the saliva), and the sense of touch (which distributed over the nerves of the skin has four different faculties for four different kinds of sensations: hot and cold, dry and moist, hard and soft, rough and smooth). Considering this division of touch into four faculties, Ibn Sīnā lists eight external senses (Avicenna 1952: 26–7). In all these cases, external sensation consists in the attainment of the sensible forms of perceptual objects through a sense organ. Ibn Sīnā himself admits that this is almost evident in every case except for sight, because some people have argued what in the theories of visual perception has been called "the extramission theory," namely that vision happens because the eye emits light (Avicenna 1952: 27). Ibn Sīnā's position, in contrast, is quite Aristotelian since he holds the mediation of light as necessary for vision; he therefore rejects the extramission theory (McGinnis 2010: 103–10; Lindberg 1976: 43–52).

Regarding internal perception, Ibn Sīnā lists the following internal faculties as "powers of the mind" (*dhihn*): common sense (*ḥiss al-mushtarak*) receives the forms provided by the external senses; retentive imagination (*al-khayāl*) retains images; the estimative power (*wahm*) receives the intentions that are retained by memory (*dhikr*); the compositive imagination (*mutakhayyilah*), a permanently active faculty, composes and divides forms as well as intentions; and what Ibn Sīnā calls the "cogitative" (*mufakkirah*) faculty, when the human rational intellect takes control of the compositive imagination.

All these faculties have a location in the brain; hence, even internal perception needs a bodily basis. The internal faculties are indispensable for the attainment of intelligibles, since they provide forms and intentions or connotational attributes. Ibn Sīnā's account of these capacities leads to a relevant philosophical issue: the cognitive value of non-conceptual content.

Aside from the cogitative power, the remaining internal faculties are common to human and non-human animals. .This means that non-human animals have some cognitive capacities, that is, they are able to direct mental states towards objects and through their estimative power—the highest faculty in non-human animals—to attain non-material properties that are perceived from perceptible objects. And this is precisely what Ibn Sīnā calls "intentions" (*ma'ni*), i.e. properties perceived by the soul from the sensible object that the external senses did not perceive previously, as for example, when the sheep perceives "enmity" in the wolf and as a consequence experiences fear and runs away (Avicenna 1952: 30). This well-known example suggests that non-human animals are able to go beyond the information provided by external sensation and grasp some meanings that are non-conceptual. In other words, the lack of a propositional-conceptual knowledge does not prevent non-human animals from recognizing, discerning, and associating some state of affairs in the world and reacting as a consequence.

The estimative faculty helps to understand non-human animal behavior, which involves the recognition of some meanings that are commonly linked to their survival in such a way that they react to the world because they have an impulse for self-preservation. Ibn Sīnā's observations on non-human animal cognition lead to another issue: if non-human animals are aware of the state of affairs in the world, do they then have a self? Ibn Sīnā is ambivalent on this point, but as several scholars have pointed out it seems that he suggests a sort of primitive self-awareness for non-human animals (Black 2008: 63–87; 1993: 219–58; Kaukua 2007; López-Farjeat 2012: 121–40). Although it is true that there are passages where Ibn Sīnā accepts this primitive self-awareness, there are also a number of texts where he affirms that cognitive capacities in non-human animals are limited to sense perception and that this is what distinguishes them from human animals: the latter are not only capable of a higher degree of abstraction and the attainment of intelligibles, but they are also capable of reflection. This last capacity, which is proper to the human rational soul, allows humans to be aware of themselves and confirms the existence of the individual human soul or self. In *Shifā': al-Nafs* 1.1 and 5.7 Ibn Sīnā formulates an experiment or admonition (*tanabbahah*) known as the "floating man argument" (Avicenna 1959, 4–16, 250–62; Marmura 1986: 383–95) that precisely serves as an indication of the individuation of the human soul/self (*nafs/dhāt*).

The floating man thought experiment invites us to imagine ourselves as created in a perfect fashion (i.e. with the perfect operation of all our faculties) but having our sight veiled so it is impossible to look at external things; we shall imagine ourselves as suspended in midair and with our limbs separated from one another in such a way that we are not able to feel them. In other words, if we could suspend the perception of our own body and anything external to it, we would be able, according to Ibn Sīnā, to affirm that our own essence exists. Whoever follows this admonition would conclude

> the essence whose existence has been affirmed is particular to him, since it is himself (*huwa bi-'ayni-hi*), different from his body and his body parts, which were not affirmed. Therefore, he who has been instructed (*mutanabbih*), does have a way to affirm the existence of the soul (*nafs*) as something different from the body or, better said, without body.
>
> (Avicenna 1959: 16)

Ibn Sīnā thinks that the former thought experiment manages to indicate the existence of the individual human soul as something evident and primary. In several passages Aristotle states that it is impossible to talk about self-awareness unless the intellect has been previously actualized by an object (*On the Soul* 417a18–20; 429b29–30a1); Ibn Sīnā argues the contrary: we need to prove the existence of the soul/self if we want to be sure that we are able to perceive objects. This is why the floating man argument does without both external and internal perceptions.

From the experiment of the floating man Ibn Sīnā concludes several things: (1) the soul is different from the body; (2) the body is an instrument of the soul; (3) if the soul were identical to the body, it would be impossible to be aware of our own perceptions because the body itself would not be able to perceive by itself what it feels (Avicenna 1959: 250–3). Now, the soul is distinct from the body, it acts through the body and in this sense the body is an instrument of the soul. With this dualistic position Ibn Sīnā confirms that the soul is an independent and subsisting substance that should not be confused with the body; in fact, the organization and coordination of the body depends on and comes from the soul. In the case of human beings, the soul is responsible for two operations: (1) a theoretical operation, which consists in the intellection of intelligibles; and (2) a practical operation, which is related to rational choices, deliberations, and human actions.

Ibn Sīnā's explanation of the rational or intellective soul is quite complex and should be understood from a cosmological, metaphysical, and epistemological stance (Gutas 2012: 418). In his cosmology, Ibn Sīnā presents an emanationist scheme where God, the necessary being (*wājib al-wujūd*), through its self-contemplation conceives a first intellect which generates through an emanative and successive hierarchy several intellects and their respective souls and bodies. From the self-contemplation of the first intellect emanates a second intellect and the soul and the body of each heavenly sphere (Avicenna 2005: 318–26). At the last stage of this process there is the active or agent intellect (*al-'aql al-fa''āl*) from which, as mentioned earlier, the human intellect originates. I have already referred to the cognitive capacities of human beings, to their external and internal senses, and I also mentioned that the body becomes an obstacle for the perfect attainment of intelligibles. Thus, in order for perfect intellection or separation/abstraction (*tajrīd*) of intelligibles to take place, a conjunction (*ittiṣāl*) between the human intellect and the active intellect needs to take place.

Ibn Sīnā distinguishes four kinds of intellects or, in other words, four different modes of interaction between the human intellect and intelligibles. He refers to the material intellect (*'aql hayūlānī*) as a capacity of the rational soul to receive immaterial intelligible forms. He does not refer here—as Aristotle does—to intelligible forms separate from matter, but to the attainment of separate intelligible forms contained in the agent intellect. According to Ibn Sīnā, to abstract a form from a material object is proper to perception; in contrast, to apprehend abstract or separate intelligible forms from the agent intellect is an immaterial operation proper to intellection. When we have the primary principles provided by the agent intellect, the human intellect becomes dispositional intellect (*'aql bi-l-malakah*); when we have attained intelligibles but they are not actively thought, Ibn Sīnā uses the term actual intellect (*'aql bi-l-fi'l, intellectus in effectu*). Finally, when we have attained intelligibles and we are actively thinking them, Ibn Sīnā refers to our intellect as the acquired intellect (*'aql mustafād, intellectus adeptus*). In light of this explanation, it is clear that the pre-noetic levels of abstraction and the formation of images involving bodily powers both external and internal work only as a preparation for the human intellectual apprehension of intelligible forms in the active or agent intellect (Hasse 2001: 39–72). That is, the apprehension of intelligible forms is prompted by perception but comes about through a conjoining with the separate active or agent intellect.

To sum up, intellectual understanding involves the reception of an emanation from the agent or active intellect and a conjoining with it because it is the receptacle of all the intelligible forms and the source of the forms of the world (Avicenna 1959: 246–7). Through this conception of intellectual understanding we can see how important is the interaction between soul and body for the acquisition of primary intelligibles; Ibn Sīnā, however, thinks that in order to attain perfect knowledge it is necessary to go beyond bodily powers, i.e. beyond the pure naturalistic explanation of human knowledge.

Ibn Rushd's Conception of the Soul and its Relationship to the Body

As mentioned earlier, Ibn Rushd wrote three commentaries on Aristotle's *De anima*: the *Epitome* or *Short Commentary on the De anima* (*Mukhtaṣarāt* or *Jawāmi'*) (Averroes 1985, 1987), the *Middle Commentary on the De anima* (*Talkhīṣ Kitāb al-nafs*) (Averroes 2002) and the *Long Commentary on the De anima* (*Sharḥ*) (Averroes 1953, 2009). Although there are developments and relevant differences from one commentary to another, especially in regard to the doctrine of the intellect, the description of the nature and capacities of the soul is similar, and the definition of the soul in the three commentaries is the same as that of Aristotle in *On the Soul* 2.1, namely, the first form or actualization of a natural or organic body.

In the *Epitome* or *Short Commentary*, Ibn Rushd gives an account of Aristotle's *On the Soul*, emphasizing the naturalistic character of the science of the soul. There, Ibn Rushd explains the generation of the soul as part of a physical and biological process as described in Aristotle's natural philosophy. According to Ibn Rushd, in the *Book of Animals* Aristotle holds that plants and animals receive their shape (*al-shakl*) or external form through a natural heat existing in the seed and the semen. Those plants and animals that do not reproduce are generated through the heavenly bodies. This natural heat, which is suitable for informing and creating, does not have in itself what would be required in order to give shape and natural dispositions to plants and animals unless there is an informing power of the genus of the nutritive soul (Averroes 1985: 7–8). In other words, the presence of the primary nutritive faculty is necessary in order for higher faculties such as sensation and reasoning to take place. According to Ibn Rushd's account,

> It is evident that according to its capacities, there are five species of soul: the first of them in temporal, that is, material priority, is the vegetative soul; then the sensitive soul; then the imaginative; then the rational; and finally the appetitive, which is like something concomitant to these powers, namely, the imaginative and the sensitive.
>
> (Averroes 1985: 19)

All these capacities are biological or organic, i.e. they happen through the body, although Ibn Rushd's conception of the rational soul needs, as we shall see, a more complex explanation given its conjunction with the separate intellects, namely, the material and the agent intellects (Black 1999: 159–84).

There is thus a set of operations and affections that happen through the body but which are also common to the soul. When commenting *On the Soul* 403a3–10 in the *Long Commentary* Ibn Rushd says that it is quite obvious that most of the capacities and affections alluded to involve the body, with the exception of thinking or understanding:

> Understanding, however, is altogether unclear and involves a great deal of uncertainty. For it has been thought that its proper affection does not involve the body. But as he [Aristotle] said, if to understand is to imagine, or it involves imagining, then it is impossible that it exist without the body, i.e. that it exist outside something in a body.
>
> (Averroes 2009: 15)

Ibn Rushd will resolve this uncertainty by explaining that understanding is proper to the intellectual soul and, thereafter, arguing that the intellect can be neither in a body nor be a power of a body, because otherwise it would not be capable of apprehending intelligibles in act. If thinking or understanding properly speaking is an act that is not restricted to bodily operations, then what is the role of the body and how is it united to the soul?

As mentioned before, most of the capacities and affections we experience as human beings are common to the body and to the soul. Ibn Rushd, like Aristotle, gives a detailed account of these capacities starting from nutrition and sensation (sight, hearing, smell, taste, touch) to common sense, imagination, appetite, and understanding at the pre-noetic level. These capacities, especially perception, make it clear that Ibn Rushd, unlike Ibn Sīnā but like Aristotle, holds that our perceptive acts are common to the body and the soul. In other words, the body is not an instrument of the soul, as Ibn Sīnā thought, but there is a substantial, hylomorphic relationship between body and soul. Ibn Rushd's explanation of external sensation is quite close to the Aristotelian version but they also differ somewhat, since Ibn Rushd, unlike Aristotle, is acquainted with the role of the brain and the nervous system. Therefore, although Aristotle and Ibn Rushd agree that the heart is the center of natural heat and the brain is its moderator, Ibn Rushd assumes the contributions of the medical science of his time and takes into account the nervous system and its connection to the brain to explain the function of the five external senses; furthermore, as Ibn Sīnā did, he locates the so-called internal senses in the brain.

Ibn Rushd's analysis of the external senses within the three commentaries is quite similar: very detailed and very Aristotelian indeed. The primary external sense is touch and it can exist without the rest of the senses—as happens according to Aristotle and Ibn Rushd himself with the sponge and those animals located in the phylogenetic scale between plants and animals—but the other senses cannot exist without touch. Touch is the most necessary sense for the existence of animal life given that it is necessary for the reactions to the external stimuli and for locomotion (Averroes 1985: 40). After touch there is the sense of taste, which is a kind of touch that allows the animal to discern between desirable and undesirable food. The sense of smell enables the animal to detect food. These three senses are necessary for the survival of animals, whereas the remaining senses—hearing and sight—exist in animals for the sake of excellence and not because they are necessary, as is the case, for instance, with the mole, which lacks vision (Averroes 1985: 40–1). Sight will be described as the sense that receives the intentions of colors abstracted from matter, and this abstraction depends on the mediation of light (Averroes 1985: 43); hearing is the sense that apprehends the sound produced when two solid bodies hit each other, and in this case the mediation of air or water becomes necessary to transmit the vibrations that we call "sound" (Averroes 1985: 43–5).

Ibn Rushd makes the well-known Aristotelian distinction between proper and common sensibles, i.e. those sensibles that are proper to a particular sense—as is the case of colors for vision, sounds for hearing, flavors for taste, odors for smell, warmth and cold for touch—and those that are common to more than one sense—motion, rest, number, shape, magnitude (Averroes 1985: 41–2). He also distinguishes between those sensibles that make contact with the senses, as is the case with touch and taste, and those that need a medium—light, air, or water—for otherwise perception would not happen, as in the case of sight, hearing, and smell (Averroes 1985: 43–5).

After his account of the five external senses, Ibn Rushd contends that, given that we are able to discern the characteristic sensibles of each sense, it is necessary to explain this capacity through an internal power common to all of the senses. According to Ibn Rushd:

> this faculty is one in number and multiple in extremities and organs, in the manner of the point which is the center of the circle when more than one line extends from it to the circumference. For, just as this point is multiple in respect of the radii which extend from it, and single and indivisible in respect of being the terminus of all of them, so, too, this faculty (that is, the common sense) is one in respect of being that at which all the sensibles terminate, and it is multiple in respect to the organs (that is, the senses [which comprise it]). As resembling the point, this faculty determines that different things are different, while it resembles the radii in the aspect of the senses, so structured as to conduct the sensibilia to it and enable it to apprehend different things via the sense.
>
> (Averroes 2002: 100–1)

Within his three commentaries on the *De anima*, Ibn Rushd does not describe in detail the organic location of the common sense and the other internal powers (imagination, memory, and cogitative). In the *Long Commentary* (Averroes 2009: 331, 379), however, he mentions a couple of times that these powers are in the brain and refers to what he has explained in *Sense and Sensibilia* (*al-Ḥiss wa al-Maḥsūs*), that is, his *Epitome of Parva Naturalia*, where he states that the common sense and the imagination are in the sensory region (the front area), the cogitative in the middle region, and the memory in the back part of the brain (Averroes 1961: 26). Regarding imagination, Ibn Rushd mentions that it is easy to confuse it with sensation. Certainly, there are some animals that seem to lack imagination—worms, flies and mollusks (Averroes 1985: 82). Imagination, however, is not the same as sensation. Led by Aristotle, Ibn Rushd holds that when the external senses are healthy and work properly there can be no error in what we perceive through them, especially in the case of proper sensibles, while we frequently judge falsely (*nakdhibu*) through imagination. Furthermore, imagination is able to compose things which have no real existence and are products of this faculty; moreover, we are able to imagine things that are no longer present; therefore, imagination is different from sensation. Imagination is also different from opinion given that this is always accompanied by assent, which is not the case with imagination, especially when we imagine things whose truth or falsehood we do not yet know. Imagination should not be mistaken for the intellect either, given that we can only imagine individual and material things, whereas through the intellect we can abstract universal and immaterial intentions (Averroes 1985: 83–4).

In the case of non-human animals, the role of the imagination is essential for perceiving what is pleasant or painful. Thus it is a faculty that is linked to the appetitive faculty. Ibn Rushd discards the necessity of what Ibn Sīnā called the "estimative faculty" in both human and non-human animals, and he thinks that the imagination is sufficient for explaining the behavior of non-human animals; hence, he replaces the estimative with the cogitative in the case of human animals (Black 2000: 62–3). In the *Long Commentary* Ibn Rushd lists the inner powers according to the ascending level of spirituality and, following the common sense and the imagination, he places the cogitative and the memory. The imagination presents and retains the image of perceived objects whereas the cogitative power discerns individual intentions and sets them into the memory (Averroes 2009: 331–2; Taylor 1999: 217–55, 2000: 111–46). Ibn Rushd's account of the memory is different from that of Aristotle: while for Aristotle it is a faculty that is aware of past perceptions, for Ibn Rushd this faculty is aware of the intention of individuality (Black 1996: 161–87), that is, through the memory we are able to recognize this human being as Zayd. Only human animals possess the cogitative power and its interaction with the other inner powers is already a cognitive act that nevertheless is limited to the attainment of individual intentions but not of intelligibles. In other words, intentions are potential intelligibles that need to be transformed into active intelligibles. This transformation is possible only through an active intellect.

Ibn Rushd distinguishes six different meanings of intellect: agent, material, acquired, dispositional, theoretical, and passible. The acquired, the dispositional, and the theoretical intellects are part of the soul and consist in different moments of the intellective act, whereas passible intellect refers to the role of the internal powers in the cognitive act. Therefore, according to Ibn Rushd, it is called "intellect" equivocally since these powers, as mentioned above, provide images and intentions but not intelligibles. Ibn Rushd's mature conception of the so-called "material intellect" is found in the *Long Commentary*, where he holds that it is a unique and separate entity shared by all human beings whose function is to receive from the passible intellect the intentions of the images in potency, without their contraction into particulars (Averroes 2009: 300–29); at the same time this intellect receives the intelligibles in act thanks to the intervention of the agent intellect. In this sense, the material intellect is the depository of the intelligibles in act to which all our knowledge of particulars refers (Taylor 2004: 289–309). Summarizing, the material intellect understands both the material particular forms (images and intentions) and the intelligibles in act through the mediation of the agent intellect, whose role is analogous to that of light when we perceive colors (Averroes 2009: 398).

The agent intellect is described as an eternal, separately existing substance (Averroes 2009: 349–63; Taylor 2005: 18–32). Ibn Rushd claims that

> it will necessarily happen that the intellect which is in us in act be composed of theoretical intelligibles and the agent intellect in such a way that the agent intellect is as it were the form of the theoretical intelligibles and the theoretical intelligibles are as it were matter. In this way we will be able to generate intelligibles when we wish. Because that in virtue of which something carries out its proper activity is the form, and we carry out our proper activity in virtue of the agent intellect, it is [therefore] necessary that the agent intellect be form for us.
>
> (Averroes 2009: 398–99)

To clarify the act of understanding, Ibn Rushd adds that

> when the theoretical intelligibles are united with us through forms of the imagination and the agent intellect is united with the theoretical intelligibles (for that which apprehends [theoretical intelligibles] is the same, namely the material intellect), it is necessary that the agent intellect be united with us through the conjoining of the theoretical intelligibles.
>
> (Averroes 2009: 399)

In other words, human understanding occurs when the two separate intellects, material and agent, are intrinsically united with the human soul understood as the first form of an organic body. With this Aristotelian conception of the soul and the necessity of a certain sort of collaboration of two separate intellects in order to explain the act of thinking or understanding, it is clear that for Ibn Rushd the "rational part" of the soul, i.e. the intellect, is different from the soul as form of an organic body: this latter is called "soul" equivocally (Averroes 2009: 128). The intellect is not part of the hylomorphic body-soul composite and in this regard Ibn Rushd seems to be faithful to Aristotle, who believed that intellect (*nous*) remains after death, as opposed to the individual soul which, according to Ibn Rushd's account and in contrast with that of Ibn Sīnā, perishes with the body (Taylor 2012: 580–96).

Conclusion

Ibn Sīnā's and Ibn Rushd's conceptions of body and soul were quite influential, particularly in the Jewish and Latin Christian contexts. Both philosophers were controversial in the Islamic world: central Islamic thinkers as al-Ghazālī and as Suhrawardī were strongly influenced by Ibn Sīnā's philosophical psychology, while Ibn Rushd's views, though known to some, were largely neglected. In contrast, both were essential sources for several Jewish philosophers, such as Maimonides (Harvey 2003: 258–80, 2005: 349–69). The contributions of these two philosophers, however, definitely received more attention within the Latin Christian context. Dominicus Gundissalinus, in collaboration with Ibn Daud, translated Ibn Sīnā's *De anima* into Latin in the second half of the twelfth century (Avicenna 1972, 1968). Gundissalinus also wrote a treatise on the soul that is clearly dependent on that of Ibn Sīnā. In the Latin tradition there are numerous treatises on the soul that draw significantly on Ibn Sīnā, for instance, that of John Blund or Jean de la Rochelle, among others (Hasse 2000: 13–69), and, of course, Albert the Great and Thomas Aquinas. The Avicennian doctrines which received more consideration were the floating man argument, his conception of the inner senses and their location in the brain, the estimative as an inner power whose object are the intentions, and his account of intellectual understanding.

Ibn Rushd's commentaries were also well known within Jewish and Christian traditions: whereas the *Epitome* was known to both traditions and the *Middle Commentary* in its Hebrew translation was studied by Jewish scholars, the Christian tradition only knew the Latin translation of the *Long Commentary* (Ivry 1999: 199–216). This latter was carefully studied in the thirteenth century with much of the doctrine of the material intellect that Ibn Rushd explains there adopted by Siger of Brabant and the so-called Latin Averroists. The Bishop of Paris condemned this doctrine in 1270 and 1277, and Aquinas wrote a treatise entitled *On the Unity of the Intellect against the Averroists*, where he refuted the conception of the material intellect as a separate entity. This doctrine had its critics, to be sure, but Ibn Rushd's influence was positive in many other respects, especially for philosophers such as Albert the Great and Thomas Aquinas himself, who delved deeply into the Averroistic interpretation of Aristotle's *On the Soul*, adopting and in some cases reformulating his views on the intellect, the role of the imagination and the cogitative powers, and his theory of vision. Albert's, Aquinas's, and even Roger Bacon's philosophical psychology must be treated as a "hybridization" of Ibn Sīnā and Ibn Rushd. The presence of these two Islamic philosophers within the philosophical psychology of the Latin Middle Ages and the Renaissance is a good example of the constant intellectual dialogue between different traditions that are nourished from the same source: Aristotle and the Greek tradition.

Further Reading

Black, D. (2004) "Models of the Mind: Metaphysical Presuppositions of the Averroist and Thomistic Account of Intellection," *Documenti e studi sulla tradizione filosofica medievale* 15: 319–52.

——. (2005) "Psychology: soul and intellect," in P. Adamson & R. Taylor (eds.), *The Cambridge Companion to Arabic Philosophy*, Cambridge: Cambridge University Press, pp. 308–26.

Davidson, H. A. (1992) *Alfarabi, Avicenna & Averroes,* On Intellect, New York & Oxford: Oxford University Press.
Hasse, D. (2000) *Avicenna's De anima in the Latin West. The Formation of a Peripatetic Philosophy of the Soul 1160–1300*, London/Turin: The Warburg Institute/Nino Aragno Editore.
Kaukua, J. (2015) *Self-awareness in Islamic Philosophy*, Cambridge: Cambridge University Press.
Knuutila, S. (2008) "Aristotle's Theory of Perception and Medieval Aristotelianism," in S. Knuutila & P. Kärkkäinen (eds.), *Theories of Perception in Medieval and Early Modern Philosophy*, Dordrecht: Springer, pp. 1–22.
Wolfson, H. A. (1935) "The Internal Senses in Latin, Arabic, and Hebrew Philosophic Texts," *The Harvard Theological Review* 28, 2: 69–133.

References

Adamson, P. (2007) *Al-Kindī*, Oxford: Oxford University Press.
Averroes (1953) *Averrois Cordubensis Commentarium Magnum in Aristotelis De Anima Libros*, F. S. Crawford (ed.), Cambridge: The Mediaeval Academy of America.
——. (1961) *Epitome of Parva Naturalia*, H. Blumberg (tr.), Cambridge: The Mediaeval Academy of America.
——. (1985) *Epitome De Anima*, S. Gómez Nogales (ed.), Madrid: Consejo Superior de Investigaciones Científicas.
——. (1987) *La psicología de Averroes. Comentario al libro sobre el alma de Aristóteles*, S. Gómez Nogales (tr.), Madrid: Universidad Nacional de Educación a Distancia.
——. (2002) *Middle Commentary on Aristotle's De anima*, A. L. Ivry (ed. and tr.), Provo, UT: Brigham Young University Press.
——. (2009) *Long Commentary on the* De anima *of Aristotle*, R. C. Taylor (tr.), New Haven & London: Yale University Press.
Avicenna (1952) *Avicenna's Psychology*, F. Rahman (tr.), London: Oxford University Press.
——. (1959) *Avicenna's De anima, being the Psychological Part of Kitāb al-Shifā'*, F. Rahman (ed.), London: Oxford University Press.
——. (1972; 1968) *Liber de anima seu Sextus de naturalibus*, 2 vols., S. Van Riet (ed.), Louvain/ Leiden: E. Peeters/E. J. Brill.
——. (2005) *The Metaphysics of the Healing*, M. E. Marmura (tr.), Provo, UT: Brigham Young University Press.
Black, D. (1993) "Estimation in Avicenna: The Logical and Psychological Dimensions," *Dialogue* 32: 219–58.
——. (1996) "Memory, Individuals, and the Past in Averroes's Psychology," *Medieval Philosophy and Theology* 5: 161–87.
——. (1999) "Conjunction and the Identity of Knower and Known in Averroes," *American Catholic Philosophical Quarterly* 73: 159–84.
——. (2000) "Imagination and Estimation: Arabic Paradigms and Western Transformations," *Topoi* 19, 1: 59–75.
——. (2008) "Avicenna on Self-Awareness and Knowing that One Knows," in S. Rahman et al. (eds.), *The Unity of Science in the Arabic Tradition*, Dordrecht: Springer, pp. 63–87.
Druart, T-A. (2000) "The Human Soul's Individuation and its Survival after the Body's Death: Avicenna on the Causal Relation between Body and Soul," *Arabic Sciences and Philosophy* 10: 259–73.
Gutas, D. (2012) "Avicenna: The Metaphysics of the Rational Soul," *Muslim World* 102: 417–25.

Harvey, S. (2003) "Arabic into Hebrew: The Hebrew Translation Movement and the Influence of Averroes upon Medieval Jewish Thought," in D. H. Frank & O. Leaman (eds.), *The Cambridge Companion to Medieval Jewish Philosophy*, Cambridge: Cambridge University Press, pp. 258–80.

——. (2005) "Islamic Philosophy and Jewish Philosophy," in P. Adamson & R. C. Taylor (eds.), *The Cambridge Companion to Arabic Philosophy*, Cambridge: Cambridge University Press, pp. 349–69.

Hasse, D. (2000) *Avicenna's De anima in the Latin West. The Formation of a Peripatetic Philosophy of the Soul 1160–1300*, London/Turin: The Warburg Institute/Nino Aragno Editore.

——. (2001) "Avicenna on Abstraction," in R. Wisnovsky (ed.), *Aspects of Avicenna*, Princeton: Markus Wiener, pp. 39–72.

Ivry, A. L. (1999) "Averroes' Three Commentaries on *De Anima*," in G. Endress & J. Aersten (eds.), *Averroes and the Aristotelian Tradition. Sources, Constitution and Reception of the Philosophy of Ibn Rushd (1126–1198). Proceedings of the Fourth Symposium Averroicum (Cologne, 1996)*, Leiden: Brill, pp. 199–216.

Kaukua, J. (2007) *Avicenna on Subjectivity*, Jyväskylä: University of Jyväskylä.

Kaukua, J. & Kukkonen, T. (2007) "Sense-Perception and Self-Awareness: Before and After Avicenna," in S. Heinämaa et al. (eds.), *Consciousness. From Perception to Reflection in the History of Philosophy*, Dordrecht: Springer, pp. 95–119.

Lagerlund, H. (2007a) "The Mind/Body Problem and Late Medieval Conceptions of the Soul," in H. Lagerlund (ed.), *Forming the Mind. Essays on the Internal Senses and the Mind/Body Problem from Avicenna to the Medical Enlightenment*, Dordrecht: Springer, pp. 1–16.

——. (2007b) "The Terminological and Conceptual Roots of Representation in the Soul in the Late Ancient and Medieval Philosophy," in H. Lagerlund (ed.), *Representation and Objects of Thought in Medieval Philosophy*, Aldershot: Ashgate, pp. 11–32.

Lindberg, D. (1976) *Theories of Vision from Al-Kindi to Kepler*, Chicago: University of Chicago Press.

López-Farjeat, L. X. (2012) "Self-awareness (*al-shu'ūr bi-al-dhāt*) in Human and Non-human Animals in Avicenna's Psychological Writings," in A. Vigo (ed.), *Oikeiosis and the Natural Bases of Morality*, Hildesheim: Georg Olms Verlag, pp. 121–40.

Marmura, M. E. (1986) "Avicenna's 'Flying Man' in Context," *The Monist* 69: 383–95.

McGinnis, J. (2010) *Avicenna*, Oxford: Oxford University Press.

Morel, P-M. (2006) "Common to Soul and Body," in R. A. H. King (ed.), *Common to Body and Soul. Philosophical Approaches to Explaining Living Behaviour in Greco-Roman Antiquity*, Berlin & New York: Walter de Gruyter, pp. 121–39.

Rapp, C. (2006) "Interaction of Body and Soul: What Hellenistic Philosophers Saw and Aristotle Avoided," in R. A. H. King (ed.), *Common to Body and Soul. Philosophical Approaches to Explaining Living Behaviour in Greco-Roman Antiquity*, Berlin & New York: Walter de Gruyter, pp. 187–208.

Sharples, R. W. (2006) "Common to Body and Soul: Peripatetic Approaches After Aristotle," in R. A. H. King (ed.), *Common to Body and Soul. Philosophical Approaches to Explaining Living Behaviour in Greco-Roman Antiquity*, Berlin & New York: Walter de Gruyter, pp. 165–86.

Taylor, R. C. (1999) "Remarks on Cogitation in Averroes' Commentarium Magnum in Aristotelis De Anima Libros," in G. Endress & J. Aersten (eds.), *Averroes and the Aristotelian Tradition. Sources, Constitution and Reception of the Philosophy of Ibn Rushd (1126–1198). Proceedings of the Fourth Symposium Averroicum (Cologne, 1996)*, Leiden: Brill, pp. 217–55.

——. (2000) "Cogitatio, Cogitativus and Cogitare: Remarks on the Cogitative Power in Averroes," in J. Hamesse & C. Steel (eds.), *L'elaboration du vocabulaire philosophique au Moyen Age*, Louvain-la-Neuve: Peeters, pp. 111–46.

——. (2004) "Separate Material Intellect in Averroes' Mature Philosophy," in R. Arnzen & J. Thielmann (eds.), *Words, Texts and Concepts Cruising the Mediterranean Sea: Studies on the Sources, Contents and Influences of Islamic Civilization and Arabic Philosophy and Science, dedicated to Gerhard Endress on his sixty-fifth birthday*, Leuven: Peeters, pp. 289–309.
——. (2005) "The Agent Intellect as 'Form for Us' and Averroes Critique of al-Fārābī," *Tópicos, Revista de Filosofía* 29: 29–51, reprinted in *Proceedings of the Society for Medieval Logic and Metaphysics* 5: 18–32.
——. (2012) "Averroes on the Ontology of the Human Soul," *Muslim World* 102, 3/4: 580–96.

Part IV
METAPHYSICS

15
ESTABLISHING THE SCIENCE OF METAPHYSICS

Amos Bertolacci

Introduction

The Islamic philosophers of the Middle Ages did not share the radical doubts expressed by their modern European colleagues about the scientific character of metaphysics. Although they often adopted positions that we tend now to regard as "empirical," and anticipated key concerns of the so-called "Scientific Revolution" of the sixteenth century that ultimately led to the expulsion of metaphysics from the family of the exact sciences, they regarded metaphysics, to all intents and purposes, as a properly scientific enterprise. Without hesitation, they referred to it by means of the term they usually employed for "science" (*'ilm*), and inserted it in an overall classification of knowledge together with disciplines that have, to our eyes, much stronger credentials to be scientific, such as logic, natural philosophy, and mathematics. How could they be so optimistic? How could skepticism concerning the scientific nature of metaphysics, so convincingly formulated by a philosopher like Kant, be so alien to them? Their confidence was not due to a blind acceptance of inherited stereotypes—a commonplace still operative in contemporary interpretations of medieval thought. Their philosophical background surely played a role in their high consideration of metaphysics, namely the long and prestigious intellectual tradition, starting with Plato and Aristotle in Greek philosophy, that saw metaphysics as the culmination of the philosophical curriculum, without any sharp distinction between the respective fields of philosophy and science. But the Islamic philosophers did not simply inherit from their Greek predecessors the conviction that metaphysics is a science, nor did they merely preserve this discipline's already-established scientific profile; they also decisively contributed to the transformation of traditional metaphysics into a science in the true sense—in their opinion, at least—of the word. This transformation was possible only when, passing from the Greek to the Arabic cultural environment, reflection on metaphysics freed itself from transmitted models of interpretation and conventional ways of exposition, and experimented new possibilities of original elaboration. The resulting reshaping of the Greek heritage represents the greatest contribution of Islamic philosophy to the history of metaphysics.

This reworking of metaphysics into a scientific setting that took place in medieval *falsafa* was governed by three main assumptions. First, the idea that the *Posterior Analytics*, namely the fourth part of Aristotle's *Organon* and the section of logic in which Aristotle clarifies the conditions of the scientific enquiry, should provide the model of any science, metaphysics included. Second, the observation that Aristotle's main text on metaphysics, i.e. the eponymous work known as *Metaphysics*, did not fully respect the canons and did not completely meet the standards fixed by Aristotle in the *Posterior Analytics*; the subsequent Greek commentators, in their opinion, had been equally unable to fill this gap. Third, the persuasion that a radical effort was needed in order to remold the discipline contained in Aristotle's *Metaphysics* in accordance with the scientific parameters of the *Posterior Analytics*. Being profound connoisseurs of philosophy and well trained in logic, the Islamic metaphysicians were deeply aware of the limits, in terms of heuristic stringency and expositional cogency, that metaphysics as a science presented, even after the aforementioned reshaping. Nonetheless, the degree of consent thus obtained with the requirements of the *Posterior Analytics* was sufficient for them to maintain metaphysics within the circuit of the philosophical sciences. The adoption of the Aristotelian scientific paradigm and the focus on works of Aristotle pertaining to logic and metaphysics makes clear that metaphysics in Arabic philosophy was mainly understood as an Aristotelian product. Other influential Arabic metaphysical works—like the Plotinian *Theologia Aristotelis* and the Proclean *Liber de causis*, circulating in *falsafa* under the false ascription to Aristotle—had great doctrinal importance in so far as they helped to complement the *Metaphysics* with a doctrine of the emanation of the universe from the One more compatible with the creationism and monotheism of Islam than Aristotle's theory of the Unmoved Mover and the heavenly intellects. They did not contribute, however, in any significant way to the project of grounding metaphysics on a solid scientific basis, which remained an issue internal to the Aristotelian corpus of authentic writings and the ensuing tradition; whereas the *Theologia Aristotelis* did not evidence any particular methodological concern, the *De causis* offered an example of rigorous application to metaphysics of the axiomatic method presupposed by the *Posterior Analytics*, but did not have any visible impact on the concrete ways in which Aristotle's text was actually transformed into a full-fledged Aristotelian science.

Metaphysics as an Aristotelian Science: the Model of the *Posterior Analytics*

The *Posterior Analytics* posed to every science four basic requirements: (1) any science must deal with a well-defined genus of things (in other words: a portion of reality) that functions as its subject-matter (i.e. its scope of investigation); (2) it must possess a precise organization, given by the triad "subject-matter-properties-principles," in so far as it is charged to prove the peculiar features, or properties, of its subject-matter by relying ultimately on some undisputable proper principles (like the assumption that "the whole is greater than the part" in mathematics) and common axioms (like the two logical laws of non-contradiction and excluded-middle, valid for all sciences); (3) its arguments must have demonstrative character, assured by their syllogistic form and the certainty of the premises of these syllogisms; and (4) it must entertain a certain relation of subordination, parity, or superiority with the other sciences.

Now, Aristotle's *Metaphysics* is ostensibly at fault with respect to each of these requirements:

(1) As to the subject-matter, Aristotle does not present a consistent view of metaphysics' scope of investigation, but describes the discipline's theme in different and somehow conflicting ways. Three main perspectives (i–iii) in this regard can be distinguished. First, in book A, metaphysics is portrayed as (i) the "wisdom" dealing with the first causes and principles (A, 1, 981b28–29; A, 2, 982b9–10). Then, in book Γ Aristotle clarifies that (i) metaphysics investigates the first causes of "being *qua* being" (Γ, 1, 1003a26–32), in so far as it is (ii) the universal "science" of "being *qua* being," in distinction from the particular sciences (1003a20–26). Finally, in book E Aristotle repeats that metaphysics is (i) the research of the principles and causes of beings *qua* beings (E, 1, 1025b3–4), and (ii) the universal science of "being *qua* being," in distinction from all the other sciences (1025b7–10); but he also adds that it is (iii) the knowledge of what is eternal, immovable, and existing on its own ("separated")—as distinct from, and superior to, the type of being investigated by natural philosophy and mathematics (E, 1, 1026a13–16); accordingly, he identifies metaphysics as the "theological philosophy" dealing with the divine (E, 1, 1026a16–23).

(2) Not less problematic is the organization, or structure, of metaphysics that results from Aristotle's work, which is not only irrespective of the rules of the *Posterior Analytics*, but has always puzzled the interpreters as intrinsically incoherent. As "edited" by Andronicus of Rhodes, the *Metaphysics* is a collection of fourteen distinct books, whose order and interconnection (and, in some cases, authenticity as well) is far from clear. The very fact that the *Metaphysics* has two "first" books designed by the same Greek letter (A and α) is indicative of a certain disorder. Some books (B, Δ) break the continuity of the exposition, while others (K) are a reduplication of previous treatments. The doctrinal conclusion of the work, namely the philosophical theology of book Λ, is followed by two further books (M–N) whose relation with Λ is not manifest. The occasional statements we find in the *Metaphysics*, aimed at drawing connections between some of its books, might be in some cases later "editorial" interpolations, and the names and descriptions of metaphysics that Aristotle uses change from book to book.

(3) In a similar vein, contemporary Aristotelian scholars unanimously contend that the method of the *Metaphysics* and the other works of Aristotle is not the demonstrative (i.e. apodictic or axiomatic) method envisaged as proper to science in the *Posterior Analytics*, although they disagree on what the method of Aristotle's works positively *is*, in particular whether—and, in case, to what extent—it is dialectical, i.e. an expression of the discipline described in Aristotle's *Topics*, or not. About this issue, some scholars contend that Aristotle's method is tributary either to ordinary dialectic—the way for attaining the first principles of investigation, in every field of research, starting from "reputable opinions" (*endoxa*)—or to a stronger type of dialectic— capable of producing an absolutely certain knowledge of the first principles by relying on a special class of reputable opinions, i.e.

those without which any rational account of reality would be impossible—whereas others maintain that it does not depend on dialectic at all, since dialectic is conceived by Aristotle as a syllogistic discipline, whereas the arguments of Aristotle's works are very rarely syllogisms. Be that as it may, it seems certain that the *Metaphysics* and the other works of Aristotle, contrary to the canons of the *Posterior Analytics*, exhibit a variable methodology, which is very distant from the stability, clarity, and certainty of demonstration: the method is rather problem-oriented, in so far as it mainly consists in the piecemeal solution of doctrinal puzzles by means of argumentative procedures that change from case to case.

(4) Finally, last but not least, the relationship of metaphysics with the other sciences is not clearly expressed by Aristotle, since the *Metaphysics* overlaps with other parts of the Aristotelian *corpus*: it partially coincides, for example, with the *Organon* (substance is dealt with both in the *Categories* and in *Metaphysics* Z), and the *Physics* (the proof of the Unmoved Mover's existence is provided both in *Physics* Θ and *Metaphysics* Λ). These overlappings prompt contemporary scholars to speak of a lack of "systematization" in Aristotle's *corpus*, and raise the question of the precise way (if any) in which the *Metaphysics* relates to the other works by Aristotle.

In general, the *Metaphysics* provides a glaring example of the imperfections imputable to Aristotle's writings—a situation poignantly described by contemporary Aristotelian scholars as a contrast between "ideal" and "achievement" in Aristotle's philosophy. This regrettable state has not escaped interpreters of the *Metaphysics* throughout history, since the very first disciples of Aristotle onward. Islamic philosophers did succeed in extending the scope of the required ameliorations far beyond the level of the local emendations introduced by previous interpreters, and in bringing to completion the partial and unfinished sketch of metaphysics provided by Aristotle by means of a thorough reworking of Aristotle's authoritative text, made in compliance with the rules of the *Posterior Analytics*.

A significant example of the radical revision implied by the approach to the *Metaphysics* typical of Islamic philosophy is provided by the solution of the problem of the subject-matter of metaphysics, on which the following pages will focus. The issue of the subject-matter is pivotal in assessing the overall scientific profile of metaphysics. In so far as the subject-matter is the first and fundamental element of the triad subject-matter/properties/principles envisaged by the *Posterior Analytics*, it is the ultimate recipient of the apodictic activity of this discipline, and leads to a more or less inclusive relationship of metaphysics with the other sciences according to its greater or smaller universality. The problem posed by the text of the *Metaphysics* in this regard is particularly acute, since in this case Aristotle's position is not only fragmentary and chaotic (as in the case of the structure of metaphysics), or unstated and elliptical (as in the case of the method), or uncertain and vague (as in the case of the relationship of metaphysics with the other sciences), but even ambiguous and potentially contradictory. Ostensibly, the three perspectives that he alternatively endorses in different parts of the *Metaphysics* are not, for Aristotle, mutually exclusive. Thus, perspectives (i) and (ii) find a possible synthesis in the conception of metaphysics as a science that is both universal in scope and concerned with what is first, that recurs occasionally in the *Metaphysics* (see, for instance, A, 2, 982a19–b10; Γ, 3, 1005a34–b1). Likewise, Aristotle reconciles perspectives (i) and (iii) by identifying the realm of the first causes with that of the divine (A, 2, 982b28–983a11) and vice-versa (E, 1, 1026a16–18). Moreover, he does not regard perspectives (ii) and (iii) as mutually exclusive: on the one hand, he sees the various meanings of "being" as converging focally towards a first notion, i.e. substance, which, in its turn, presents a hierarchy of instances culminating in a first kind of substance (Γ, 2, 1003b5–19); on the other hand, he portrays metaphysics as capable of investigating also universal being *qua* being in so far as it is the first science, i.e. the study of the immovable substance (E, 1, 1026a23–32)—two passages of the *Metaphysics* on which the proverbial "rivers of ink" have been spilled. But, notwithstanding these hints towards the possibility of an overall reconciliation, it is not clear to the reader of the *Metaphysics* which of the three perspectives is the most fundamental for Aristotle and how this reconciliation should proceed. Aristotle's conception of the subject-matter of metaphysics remains highly problematic.

The Greek post-Aristotelian tradition, in a way, reinforces and amplifies the dissonance: whereas the extant commentaries on the *Metaphysics* that antedate the rise of Islamic philosophy (by Alexander of Aphrodisias, Themistius, Syrianus, and Ammonius according to the report of the disciple Asclepius) either present being *qua* being as the subject matter of metaphysics in accordance with perspective (ii) or do not deal with the issue of the subject-matter, the outlines of metaphysics that one finds in the classifications of the philosophical sciences within the Prolegomena (the introductions to philosophy in general, or Aristotle's philosophy in particular, placed at the beginning of the Neoplatonic commentaries on, respectively, Porphyry's *Isagoge* and Aristotle's *Categories*) mirror rather perspective (iii) and the overall classification of the philosophical sciences in which it is encapsulated. In spite of this, in post-Aristotelian Greek philosophy the relationship between these two perspectives—and the resulting opposition between a view of metaphysics as ontology (perspective (ii)) and a view of it as philosophical theology (perspective (iii))—was not perceived as problematic: it appears as a crucial issue neither in an independent "aporetic" treatise on metaphysics like Theophrastus' *Metaphysics*, nor in a reworking of the *Metaphysics* such as parts II and III of Nicholas of Damascus' *Philosophy of Aristotle* (at least judging from the extant portions of this latter work), nor in the aforementioned commentaries on the *Metaphysics*, nor in the Prolegomena. The Greek commentators on the *Metaphysics* (at least the ones preceding the beginning of *falsafa*) do not seem to have regarded the issue of the subject-matter of metaphysics as a question worth raising. The first signs of awareness of the antinomy determined by Aristotle's stances on ontology and philosophical theology within the *Metaphysics*, and the first specific endeavor of clarifying the relationship between these two perspectives on metaphysics, took place, as far as we know, in Islamic philosophy.

The Centrality of Ibn Sīnā's Account of Metaphysics

In Islamic philosophy the problem of the subject-matter of metaphysics emerged and became of central importance, because the two main exponents of the early phase of *falsafa*, namely al-Kindī (d. after 870) and al-Fārābī (d. 950–951), advocated the two aforementioned opposite views of metaphysics, and the clash of their standpoints brought the issue to the fore. Al-Kindī—both in his work on the arrangement of the Aristotelian corpus, and in his original treatise on metaphysics, the *Book on First Philosophy* (*Kitāb fī l-falsafa al-ūlā*), only partially extant—interpreted metaphysics as essentially a philosophical theology, relying proximately on the classifications of the sciences of Greek Late Antiquity and ultimately on Aristotle's perspective (iii) taken in isolation from the others. Al-Fārābī reacted to the view of metaphysics proposed by al-Kindī and sponsored the adoption of perspective (i): connecting himself with the commentatorial tradition of Alexander of Aphrodisias, Themistius and Ammonius, and looking at the *Metaphysics* in its entirety, in his work on the classification of the sciences and in his introduction to the *Metaphysics* entitled *On the Goals of the Sage* [= Aristotle] *in Each Treatise of the Book Marked by Means of Letters* [= *Metaphysics*] (al-Fārābī 1890, 1982), he clarifies that metaphysics is basically an ontology, one of whose parts coincides with philosophical theology. The background of the entire discussion is given by the different way of conceiving the relationship of *falsafa* and Islam: whereas al-Kindī emphasizes the theological part of metaphysics in order to introduce smoothly Aristotle's metaphysics (and Greek metaphysics in general) into the world view of Islamic religion and theology, al-Fārābī stresses the distinction of metaphysics and philosophical theology by assigning a broader scope (and, implicitly, a higher rank) to the former with regard to the latter, and is not interested in establishing a concordance between the realms of philosophy and religion. Ibn Sīnā (d. 1037) avowedly adopts al-Fārābī's point of view, but he develops the ontological perspective on metaphysics incorporating into its framework also al-Kindī's theological view of this. In this way, he presents the fullest and most articulated account of the relationship of ontology and philosophical theology within metaphysics in the history of Medieval philosophy. The work of his in which this inclusive approach to the issue is most clearly visible is the metaphysical section (*The Science of Divine Things, Ilāhiyyāt*) of his most extensive and influential *summa*, namely the philosophical encyclopedia in four parts (logic, natural philosophy, mathematics, and metaphysics, with an appendix on practical philosophy) entitled *Book of the Cure* (*Kitāb al Shifā'*).

It is noteworthy that the most important works on metaphysics written by al-Kindī, al-Fārābī, and Ibn Sīnā mentioned above are *not*, properly speaking, commentaries on the *Metaphysics*: in the case of al-Kindī, no commentary on Aristotle's work is extant; al-Fārābī might have never written a literal commentary on the *Metaphysics*; the commentaries on the *Metaphysics* by Ibn Sīnā are either lost, or indirectly and fragmentarily preserved. This switch in the expositional format from the commentary *stricto sensu* (regardless whether a literal commentary or a paraphrase) to the personal and free account is one of the most evident marks of the break of continuity of Islamic philosophy with the Greek tradition. In al-Kindī's *First Philosophy*, we find an explicit acknowledgment of Aristotle's authority, but the recourse to the text of the *Metaphysics* is scanty (it is basically limited to books Alpha elatton—the first book of the work in the Arabic tradition—and Lambda—the twelfth book and the exposition of Aristotle's philosophical theology), whereas the not yet translated *Posterior Analytics* are substantially disregarded, apart from some indirect points of contact. Al-Fārābī's *On the Goals of the Sage* consists of two main parts: the first provides a sketch of metaphysics based on the principles of the *Posterior Analytics*, whereas the second is a succinct summary of the content of each of the books of the *Metaphysics* known to the author. The two parts, however—namely the project of a scientific metaphysics in the first part and the all-encompassing recourse to the text of the *Metaphysics* in the second—remain regrettably unrelated. The metaphysics of al-Fārābī's *summae* of political philosophy does not bridge the gap, since it is still modeled on Plato, rather than Aristotle, and is not linked in any way with Aristotle's epistemology. Ibn Sīnā corrects the epistemological imprecision of al-Fārābī's model (al-Fārābī still wavers between a more strict concept of "subject-matter" of metaphysics and a looser sense of the term, occasionally used in the plural) and brings it to full implementation in the context of an encyclopedia of philosophy in which logic starts and metaphysics ends the series of the philosophical sciences, and in which therefore the doctrine of the *Posterior Analytics* coexists with that of the *Metaphysics*, being not only theoretically related to, but also materially joined with it.

Ibn Sīnā grants to the determination of the subject-matter of metaphysics a place of eminence within the *Science of Divine Things*: he adds the entry "subject-matter" (*mawḍūʿ*) to the list of preliminary questions traditionally discussed by Aristotelian commentators at the beginning of their exegesis of Aristotle's works, and starts the work with two chapters that address explicitly this issue by mentioning it in their title. At the beginning of chapter I, 1, moreover, he expressly presents the problem of the subject-matter of metaphysics as a question to be discussed. In this way, Ibn Sīnā appears to be the first thinker in the history of philosophy to have devoted to this issue a separate and articulated treatment, and his contribution in the first two chapters of the *Ilāhiyyāt* (I, 1–2) has rightly attracted the attention of scholars. In Ibn Sīnā's powerful synthesis, Aristotle's different perspectives on the topic are elucidated and harmonized. The frequent references—explicit, indeterminate, or implicit—to the *Posterior Analytics* (more precisely: to the part of the *Book of the Cure* corresponding to the *Posterior Analytics*) assure that Ibn Sīnā's accommodation is programmatically faithful to the canons of Aristotle's theory of science. Ibn Sīnā's discourse can be envisaged as a system made of five complementary elements. He starts with a classification of the parts of philosophy in which—on the footstep of the Greek Prolegomena —the notion of metaphysics is based solely on perspectives (iii) and (i) gathered together, namely on the idea that metaphysics deals with immaterial things and with the first causes and the absolute Prime Cause, i.e. God. Then, he introduces the problem and the principle of its resolution, namely the three-fold distinction, taken from the *Posterior Analytics*, of subject-matter, properties, and principles of a science. Ibn Sīnā focuses on the first two elements of this triad, speaking respectively of "subject-matter" of a science and "things searched" (*maṭālib*, sg. *maṭlūb*) by a science. In the course of the discussion, he qualifies this polarity by means of other notions reminiscent of the *Posterior Analytics*: namely the idea that every science assumes the existence of its subject-matter without proving it; that the subject-matter of a science is the common denominator of all the things searched by that science; and that the subject-matter of a science cannot be more than one. On account of these rules, Ibn Sīnā discards perspectives (iii) and (i) as not indicative of the subject-matter of metaphysics. God cannot be the subject-matter of metaphysics, since this science is deputed to prove Its existence rather than assuming it; likewise, the four ultimate causes cannot be the subject-matter of metaphysics, since this science considers them insofar as they are existents, thus indicating that existence is a notion more fundamental than causality, in which the subject-matter of metaphysics accordingly lies. The search for the only subject-matter of metaphysics leads Ibn Sīnā not only to discard the first two possible candidates to this role, but also to individuate the holder of this function, disclosed by perspective (ii): "existent *qua* existent," rather than God or the first causes, is the subject-matter of metaphysics, since all the things investigated by metaphysics refer ultimately to this notion, either as its species (basically the categories, taking the idea of the categories as "species" of "existent *qua* existent" in a broad sense, since Ibn Sīnā is aware that "existent" is not a genus and does not have, properly speaking, species) or as its properties (a series of notions including "one" and "many," "potency" and "act," "universal" and "particular," etc.); moreover, "existent" is such a fundamental notion that its existence and essence cannot be proved, not even by metaphysics, the highest of the sciences. As a third step, Ibn Sīnā brings to unity perspective (ii) and perspective (iii) by means of a peculiar notion of "existent," according to which this concept is immaterial in as much as it is not restricted to the sphere of material things. Conceived as immaterial, "existent" can be common to all the objects of research of metaphysics, including in these latter the unchangeable divine realm. In the same vein, as a fourth step, he reaches a synthesis between perspective (ii) and perspective (i) by stressing that the first causes and God are a part of "existent" and are the principles of the "existent" that is caused. Finally, Ibn Sīnā stresses that the first causes and God, despite not being the subject-matter of metaphysics, have nonetheless a fundamental function within this discipline: among the things searched by metaphysics, they are its "goal" (*ġaraḍ*), namely the things whose knowledge of which is ultimately pursued. Adopting a metaphor that Ibn Sīnā applies to metaphysics in other works of his, it can be said that, according to him, the study of "existent *qua* existent" is the "root" of metaphysics, whereas the investigation of the first causes and God is its "fruit." In this way, Ibn Sīnā shows that metaphysics is, in different respects, a study of the first causes and God, which, among the "things searched" by metaphysics, are its goal (perspective (i)); a study of "existent," which is its subject-matter (perspective (ii)); and a study of immaterial and motionless things, insofar as both the first causes and God, on the one hand, and "existent *qua* existent," on the other, are immaterial and motionless realities (perspective (iii)). In the light of its clarity and comprehensiveness, Ibn Sīnā's account is one of the most coherent and systematic explanations of Aristotle's cryptic and apparently inconsistent statements on the subject-matter of metaphysics that have ever been proposed in the history of Aristotelianism.

The same "scientific spin" can be observed in the other pivotal areas of the epistemological profile of metaphysics. Thus Ibn Sīnā recasts the structure of metaphysics in a systematic way, by dismissing the rather inconsequential order of books of the *Metaphysics*, and arranging this discipline according to a precise epistemological pattern, given by the species, properties and principles of "existent," only adumbrated in Aristotle. Likewise, he refines the method of metaphysics, by enhancing its use of demonstrations and terminological distinctions, introducing new methods of argumentation (like proofs by division and classifications), and reducing the role of procedures (like the criticism of previous philosophers' opinions, and the discussion of aporias) cognate with dialectic which have great visibility in the *Metaphysics* (let us think of the polemical character of books Alpha Meizon, Mu and Nu, and of the aporetic nature of book Beta). Finally, he elucidates the relationship of metaphysics with the other philosophical disciplines, namely logic (the instrument of all knowledge), natural philosophy and mathematics (the other two branches of theoretical philosophy), and practical philosophy (with which he deals briefly at the end of the *Science of Divine Things*): he conceives metaphysics as a science higher than all these disciplines and deputed to providing their epistemological foundation by means of the treatment of fundamental concepts, basic rules of reasoning and ultimate realities that surpass their scope of investigation. On account of this profound reworking of the epistemology of the *Metaphysics* and of the wide range of sources that it draws on, it is not far-fetched to regard the *Science of Divine Things* as a sort of second "edition" of the *Metaphysics*, after the canonical edition of the *corpus aristotelicum* by Andronicus of Rhodes in the first century BC, or as a second "beginning" of Western metaphysical speculation.

The Success of Ibn Sīnā's Model

The originality, on the one hand, and solidity, on the other, of Ibn Sīnā's doctrine of the subject-matter of metaphysics is well exemplified by the contrasting reactions that it solicited from one of the most virulent critics of Ibn Sīnā in Arabic philosophy, namely the Andalusian jurist, theologian, and Aristotelian commentator Ibn Rushd (d. 1198). Most visibly in his commentaries on Aristotle, Ibn Rushd holds an ambivalent attitude towards Ibn Sīnā's theory: an outspoken clear-cut rejection in certain passages, but also a silent acceptance in other *loci* of the same works. This oscillation suggests that Ibn Rushd perceived Ibn Sīnā's stance as a radical innovation with regard to Aristotle's authority, and therefore as a doctrine worthy to be openly criticized; but he also regarded the predecessor's position as acceptable for its own sake and in consideration of its inner consistency, and hence as a theory deserving tolerance and silent endorsement. Ibn Rushd's two-fold attitude attests that Ibn Sīnā's standpoint was strong enough to resist the most momentous objections and attacks, and was destined therefore to become the mainstream position in later Islamic philosophy. In the co-called "Long Commentary" on Aristotle's *Physics*, preserved in the Latin medieval translation, Ibn Rushd reserves to Ibn Sīnā's doctrine of the subject-matter of metaphysics—and to the related idea that metaphysics proves God's (the First Principle's) existence—one of his most disparaging attacks of the Persian master:

> Whoever contends that first philosophy tries to show the existence of separable beings, is wrong. For these beings are the subject-matter of first philosophy, and it is maintained in the *Posterior Analytics* that no science can show the existence of its own subject-matter, but takes its existence for granted, either because it is evident by itself, or because it is demonstrated in another science. Therefore Ibn Sīnā made a great mistake as he said that the first philosopher demonstrates the First Principle's existence. On this

> issue, in his book on divine science, he proceeded according to a method that he regarded as necessary and essential in this science. His mistake, however, is evident, since the most certain of the statements that he employed in this [regard] does not exceed the level of probable statements.
> (passage taken from section 83 of the commentary on the first book of the *Physics*)

In this text, Ibn Rushd endorses a position that is opposite to Ibn Sīnā's: a special class of beings, i.e. the separable beings (God included), rather than existent *qua* existent, are the subject-matter of metaphysics, so that metaphysics cannot prove God's existence and takes the proof of His existence from physics. Ibn Rushd's reference to the *Posterior Analytics* in this passage reveals an intent to defeat Ibn Sīnā on this latter's terrain: the epistemological paradigm is the same, but under the same Aristotelian umbrella the overall framework is subverted, since God—despite Ibn Sīnā's veto—replaces existent *qua* existent in the role of subject-matter of metaphysics. However, elsewhere in the same commentary on the *Physics* one finds non-polemical passages in which Ibn Sīnā is not mentioned, but an Avicennian stance on the issue (existent *qua* existent is the subject-matter of metaphysics) is *de facto* endorsed. The same type of oscillation is visible in Aristotelian commentaries by Ibn Rushd that precede the *Commentary on the Physics*, like the *Epitome on the Metaphysics* (Averroes 2010), or are coeval to it, like the *Long Commentary on the Posterior Analytics* (Averroes 1984). The Commentary deputed to treat the topic *ex professo*, namely the *Long Commentary on the Metaphysics*, remains regrettably silent on the issue. In this way, it either corroborates *e silentio* Ibn Sīnā's position, or it silently displays a view in which the antinomy fades away, in so far as existent *qua* existent coincides ultimately with the divine by means of successive "focal reductions": from existent *qua* existent to substance; from substance to form; from form to God as First form.

Latin Philosophy seems to be aware that, in passing from the *Long Commentary on the Physics* to the *Long Commentary on the Metaphysics*, the distance of Ibn Rushd's position on the subject-matter of metaphysics with respect to Ibn Sīnā's decreases, and that the two authors' respective stand-points ultimately converge. Among Latin philosophers, albeit not being the only one, Ibn Sīnā's doctrine on the subject-matter of metaphysics is certainly the most commonly adopted, and an anti-Avicennian position like that expressed by Ibn Rushd in the *Long Commentary on the Physics* did not enjoy an independent circulation. A theologian and philosopher like Albert the Great (Albert of Lauingen, d. 1280), who commented on the entire Aristotelian corpus by means of Ibn Sīnā's and Ibn Rushd's interpretations (as much as they were available to him in translation), and who sided with Ibn Sīnā on the issue at stake, is a privileged witness of the situation: whereas in his *Commentary on the Physics* (Albert the Great 1987) he defends Ibn Sīnā against the attack by Ibn Rushd reported above, which he deems wrong and unfair, in the *Commentary on the Metaphysics* (Albert the Great 1960) he propounds a more conciliatory perspective, in which Ibn Sīnā and Ibn Rushd, far from contradicting each other, contribute to the overall consensus of the Peripatetic school: "Therefore, together with all the Peripatetics who state the truth it seems right to contend that being *qua* being is the subject matter [of metaphysics]" (passage taken from the second chapter of the commentary).

Conclusion

In presenting his own *Metaphysics* after the model of the *Posterior Analytics* as a synthetic ordered account addressing the key issues concerning the questions of the subject-matter and ends of metaphysics, Ibn Sīnā crafted an account that went well beyond the Greek commentators and also responded to the concerns of al-Kindī and of al-Fārābī. In providing a systematic recasting of its very structure, he forged a new methodological approach to metaphysics and presented an account that elucidates the relationship of this science to other theoretical and practical sciences. So great was the cogency of the systematic philosophical work of Ibn Sīnā that most later thinkers in the Islamic tradition returned not to the writings of Aristotle but to those of Ibn Sīnā as ground and starting point of further philosophical development. In its twelfth-century translation into Latin, the work of Ibn Sīnā was one of the most important foundations for metaphysical and theological speculation among medieval European thinkers. Famous figures such as Aquinas, his teacher Albert the Great, Duns Scotus and many others drew heavily on the *Metaphysics* of Ibn Sīnā and brought his methods and reasoning into the heart of Western philosophical and theological discussions.

Further Reading

Aertsen, J. A. (2008) "Avicenna's Doctrine of the Primary Notions and its Impact on Medieval Philosophy," in *Islamic Thought in the Middle Ages. Studies in Text, Transmission and Translation, in Honour of Hans Daiber*, A. Akasoy & W. Raven (eds.), Leiden: Brill, pp. 21–42.

Bertolacci, A. (2006) *The Reception of Aristotle's* Metaphysics *in Avicenna's* Kitāb al-Šifā': *A Milestone of Western Metaphysical Thought*, Leiden & Boston: Brill.

——. (2007) "Avicenna and Averroes on the Proof of God's Existence and the Subject-Matter of Metaphysics," *Medioevo* 32: 61–97.

——. (2011) "The 'Ontologization' of Logic. Metaphysical Themes in Avicenna's Reworking of the *Organon*," in *Methods and Methodologies. Aristotelian Logic East and West 500–1500*, M. Cameron & J. Marenbon (eds.), Leiden & Boston: Brill, pp. 27–51.

——. (2012) "The Distinction of Essence and Existence in Avicenna's Metaphysics: The Text and Its Context," in *Islamic Philosophy, Science, Culture, and Religion: Studies in Honor of Dimitri Gutas*, F. Opwis & D. C. Reisman (eds.), Leiden: Brill, pp. 257–88.

——. (2012) "Arabic and Islamic Metaphysics," *Stanford Encyclopedia of Philosophy* (on-line), first published Jul 5, 2012, plato.stanford.edu/entries/arabic-islamic-metaphysics/

Castelli, L. M. (2011) "Greek, Arab and Latin Commentators on per se accidents of being qua being and the place of Aristotle, Met. Iota," *Documenti e studi sulla tradizione filosofica medievale* 22: 153–208.

Di Giovanni, M. (2014) "The Commentator: Averroes' Reading of the Metaphysics," in *A Companion to the Latin Medieval Commentaries on Aristotle's Metaphysics*, F. Amerini & G. Galluzzo (eds.), Leiden: Brill, pp. 59–94.

Gutas, D. (1988) *Avicenna and the Aristotelian Tradition. Introduction to Reading Avicenna's Philosophical Works (Second Revised and Enlarged Edition, Including an Inventory of Avicenna's Authentic Works)*, Leiden, New York, København & Köln: Brill.

References

Albert the Great (1960) *Metaphysica, libri quinque priores*, B. Geyer (ed.), Münster: Aschendorff; (1964) *Metaphysica, libri VI–XIII*, B. Geyer (ed.), Münster: Aschendorff.

——. (1987) *Physica, Pars I, libri 1–4*, P. Hossfeld (ed.), Münster: Aschendorff; (1993) *Physica, Pars II, libri 5–8*, P. Hossfeld (ed.), Münster: Aschendorff.

al-Fārābī (1890) *Maqāla [.] fī aġrāḍ al-ḥakīm fī kulli maqāla min al-Kitāb al-mawsūm bi-l-ḥurūf*, in *Alfārābī's Philosophische Abhandlungen*, F. Dieterici (ed.), Leiden: Brill, pp. 34–8.

——. (1982) "Le traité d'al-Fārābī sur les buts de la *Métaphysique* d'Aristote," T-A. Druart (tr.), *Bulletin de Philosophie Médiévale* 24: 38–43.

al-Kindī (1950) *Kitāb al-Kindī ilā l-Mu'taṣim bi-llāh fī l-falsafa al-ūlā*, in *Rasā'il al-Kindī al-falsafiyya*, vol. I, M. 'A. Abū Rīda (ed.), Cairo: Dār al-Fikr al-'Arabī, pp. 97–162.

——. (1974) *Al-Kindī's Metaphysics. A Translation of Ya'qūb al-Kindī's Treatise "On First Philosophy" (fī al-Falsafah al-ūlā)*, A. Ivry (tr.), Albany: State University of New York Press.

——. (1998) *Œuvres philosophiques et scientifiques d'Al-Kindī. Volume II. Métaphysique et Cosmologie*, R. Rashed & J. Jolivet (eds.), Leiden, Boston & Köln: Brill, pp. 1–117.

——. (2012) *The Philosophical Works of Al-Kindī*, P. Adamson & P. Pormann (eds.), Oxford: Oxford University Press, pp. 3–57.

Averroes (1962) *Aristotelis Opera cum Averrois Commentariis*, Venetiis apud Iunctas 1562, repr. Frankfurt am Main: Minerva.

——. (1984) *Šarḥ al-Burhān li-Arisṭū wa-Talḫīṣ al-Burhān*, 'A. Badawī (ed.), Kuwait: al-Maǧlis al-Waṭanī li-l-ṯaqāfa wa-l-funūn wa-l-adab.

——. (2010) *On Aristotle's "Metaphysics." An Annotated Translation of the So-called "Epitome,"* R. Arnzen (ed.), Berlin & New York: De Gruyter.

Avicenna (2005) *The Metaphysics of The Healing*, M. Marmura (ed. and tr.), Provo, UT: Brigham Young University Press.

16
FORMS OF HYLOMORPHISM

Sarah Pessin

Introduction

Hylomorphism—the view that substances are composed of matter (*hūlē*) and form (*morphē*)—can be found in Islamic philosophy in a variety of manners, falling under two large categories: Aristotelian hylomorphism and Pseudo-Empedoclean hylomorphism. In an effort to unpack these two trends in Islamic thought, we turn to Ibn Sīnā and Shahrastani.

Ibn Sīnā is a proponent of a doubly Neoplatonized version of the Aristotelian view. Following Aristotle, he holds that all and only corporeal substances admit of matter—plus—form composition. Additionally, revealing two different non-Aristotelian Neoplatonic impulses, he (1) theorizes a prime matter with its own special "corporeal form" in his analysis of corporeal substances, and (2) conceives of matter and form as part of a process of emanation. As we will see, Ibn Sīnā's Neoplatonic add-ons to Aristotle reveal the traces of Simplicius, Proclus and Plotinus.

Shahrastani recounts a version of the Ps. Empedoclean view according to which the ordinary Neoplatonic cosmos is supplemented with a kind of "prime matter" between God and intellect. Described as a pure supernal matter, this reality is appointed by God as the cosmic source of being and is itself composed of love and strife. While the view neither refers to Aristotle nor overtly sets out to offer a hylomorphic analysis, we might note that in emphasizing a material reality at the core of *all* substances, the Ps. Empedoclean teaching can be seen as a kind of hylomorphism that goes beyond Aristotelian hylomorphism. Whereas Aristotelian hylomorphism speaks of matter only when analyzing *corporeal* substances, the Ps. Empedoclean view envisions matter at the core of all beings, corporeal beings and spiritual beings (such as intellects and souls).

The current chapter explores these ideas through a series of inquiries in Ibn Sīnā's Neoplatonized Aristotelian Hylomorphism and Shahrastani's Ps. Empedoclean Hylomorphism.

Ibn Sīnā's Neoplatonized Aristotelian Hylomorphism: On Prime Matter, Corporeal Form and Simplicius

For Ibn Sīnā, the analysis of corporeal substances in terms of matter and form is conceptually key for making sense of a whole range of phenomena. In this regard, Ibn Sīnā reflects Aristotle's own hylomorphism which, developed in the context of Aristotle's philosophical account of change, emphasizes the matter (*hūlē*) plus form (*morphē*) composition of corporeal substances (*Physics* 1.7; *Metaphysics* 7.2).

In his hylomorphic analysis of corporeal substances, Ibn Sīnā additionally emphasizes the dual principles of prime matter and corporeity (viz. prime matter's "first form") at the foundation of all bodies. In this way, Ibn Sīnā arguably extends Aristotelian hylomorphism beyond Aristotle's own text, claiming not only that terrestrial substances are matter + form composites, but that terrestrial and celestial substances are composed of a special prime matter and a special first form.

To better understand how these arguably non-Aristotelian ideas become part of Ibn Sīnā's own approach to Aristotelian hylomorphism, we must appreciate the extent to which certain ancient commentaries on Aristotle set the stage for later ancient and medieval readings of Aristotle. Reflecting on the origin of medieval Jewish and Islamic discussions of "corporeity" (or "corporeal form") in particular, H. A. Wolfson turns our attention to Simplicius' commentary on Aristotle's *Physics* 1.7 (for Greek text, see Simplicius 1882: 229ff.; for discussion, see Wolfson 1929: 581–2). While Aristotle does not talk of "corporeal form," Simplicius introduces this notion in an attempt to help make sense of Aristotle's account of elemental change. After describing matter as completely indeterminate and as a veritable nothing, Aristotle seems on the contrary—in his account of elemental change—to envision a material substrate as a more robust body of some sort, able to take on the forms associated with water and then the forms associated with air, and so on for all the elements. According to Wolfson, Simplicius solves the difficulty by reading into Aristotle a commitment to two kinds of foundational material substrates, "prime matter" and "body," a somewhat more robust material substrate disposed through corporeal form to take on the forms associated with the elements. With these details in place, Simplicius is able to interpret Aristotle as referring to "prime matter" any time he describes a completely indeterminate material substrate, but as referring on the contrary to a more robust material substrate (viz. "body") within the context of his theory of elemental change.

For our current purposes, we need not pin down the details of Simplicius' own debated theory of corporeity (Sorabji 1988: 3–43; Sorabji 2005: 1–31, 253–73; Wolfson 1929: 99–113, 579–602; Stone 2001; see Stone 1999: 11ff. for a comparison and critique of Wolfson and Sorabji). Bearing in mind that Simplicius' commentary seems not to have even been available in Arabic (McGinnis 2004: 43, n. 2), we also need not pursue any claims about a direct Simplicius–Ibn Sīnā link. Here, we need only bear in mind that Ibn Sīnā is reading Aristotle in the general context of what we might loosely call a "Simplician commentary tradition" which introduces "corporeal form" into a reading of Aristotle, and which gives rise to a whole range of ancient and medieval interpretations of the nature of "corporeal form in Aristotle" in spite of there being no such concept in Aristotle. In such a context, we can better understand Ibn Sīnā's own reading of Aristotelian hylomorphism in terms of an unspecified, indeterminate principle of prime matter along with a principle of corporeity at the foundation of terrestrial substances, and even celestial ones (as can be seen in his commentary on book 4 of Aristotle's *De Caelo*; Wolfson 1929: 594–8).

In the context of this Simplicius-inspired form of Neoplatonized Aristotelianism, Ibn Sīnā describes all bodies first and foremost in terms of matter and corporeity. For Ibn Sīnā, corporeity is matter's first form. In terms of its own relation to matter, corporeity may be understood as a "generic form" which is "conceptually inseparable from … the 'need' (*ḥāja*) for matter" (Stone 2001: 101). In terms of its contribution to matter, corporeity is seen as the form that brings to matter its "disposition" and its "preparedness" to take on three-dimensionality. It is, in this sense, that which allows for the *ittiṣāl* ("cohesiveness," "continuity," "connection," or "continuum") of bodies. Serving as a conceptual bridge of sorts between matter and actual bodies, corporeity does not point to some additional reality beyond the actual specified bodies in the world around us; it points, rather, to a certain "aptitude by which a material substance, one *in actu*, is at the same time potentially many" (Stone 2001: 114). In his subtle conception of corporeity as an aptitude of bodies, Ibn Sīnā firmly opposes the view of corporeity as some kind of "x I know not what" quality-less body, or unspecified generic "long, wide and deep substance" (Avicenna 2005: 48).

It might be noted that in his particular conception of corporeal form, Ibn Sīnā provides an alternative to the views of al-Ghazālī and Ibn Rushd (Wolfson 1929: 100–101, 582ff.; Hyman 1977). And, in spite of being part of a broadly Simplician tradition, Ibn Sīnā's theory of prime matter and corporeity also deviates significantly from Simplicius' own view (Stone 2001). Along these lines we might note that in the *Metaphysics of the Healing* (2.2), Ibn Sīnā goes beyond the Simplician argument for "prime matter + corporeity" from a consideration of elemental change, and presents an argument for prime matter per se from a consideration of connection and separation (Avicenna 2005: 53; Lizzini 2004: 177; see Wolfson 1929: n. 22, 591–4 on the argument in the Metaphysics of *al-Najāt*). We might also note that Ibn Sīnā's *Physics of the Healing* reveals the influence of Philoponous, Simplicius' philosophical rival (see Avicenna 2009: xxiv–xxv where McGinnis addresses the influence of Philoponous' *Physics* commentary and *Contra Aristotelem*). As for other relevant backdrops to Ibn Sīnā's sense of "prime matter + corporeity" beyond the Simplician tradition, we might also consider Plotinus' own emphasis on "prime matter + quantity," a conceptual formula that makes its way into the philosophical sect known as the "Brethren of Purity" (*Ikhwān aṣ-Ṣafā'*) with possible impact on Ibn Sīnā's thinking as well (Wolfson 1929: 580, 582; see Sorabji 2005: 253–73 for texts on prime matter and body in Plotinus and other Greek sources). Possibly revealing traces of Plato, Ibn Sīnā also describes matter as form's *maḥall* (place or receptacle).

Ibn Sīnā's Neoplatonized Aristotelian Hylomorphism: On Plotinus, Proclus, and the Emanation of Bodies from Intellect

Ibn Sīnā's hylomorphism also reveals the Neoplatonic influence of the *Theology of Aristotle* (Aouad 1989) and the *Kalām fī maḥḍ al-khair* ("Discourse on the Pure Good," known in its later Latin reception as the "*Liber de Causis*," "Book of

Causes"). Thought by Ibn Sīnā and other Islamic thinkers to be parts of Aristotle's genuine body of work, the texts are summary editions of Plotinus's *Enneads* and Proclus's *Elements of Theology*, respectively. Given the influence of these textual traditions on Ibn Sīnā's thinking, we may classify his Neoplatonized Aristotelianism in overtly Plotinian and Proclean terms. And while neither the *Theology of Aristotle* nor the *Kalām fī maḥḍ al-khair* emphasizes hylomorphic ideas, the two texts do provide the context for Ibn Sīnā's commitment to emanation. Putting forth a theory of hylomorphism within his emanationist context, Ibn Sīnā theorizes an emanating Great Chain of Being (Lovejoy 1936) responsible for the flow of forms and bodies. In this context, material realities, both celestial and terrestrial bodies, flow forth as a result of the last stage of each separate intellect's tripartite process of reflecting on (1) God's necessity (2) its own necessity and (3) its own contingency. Within this emanating context, Ibn Sīnā also emphasizes that forms are not inherent in matter and that they are on the contrary introduced to matter from an outside source, viz. the active intellect, the lowest of the emanating cosmic separate intellects governing sublunar reality and identified by Ibn Sīnā as the "giver of forms."

Beyond putting forth a theory of hylomorphism in an emanationist context, Ibn Sīnā provides an argument for emanation from the very nature of the form-matter relationship itself (Lizzini 2004: 182–3).

Thinking carefully about Ibn Sīnā's Islamic Neoplatonic context, it is important to recognize that emanation is in no way seen as diminishing God's role as sovereign creator. Right alongside his theory of emanation, Ibn Sīnā argues in the *Metaphysics of the Healing* that God is Agent and First Efficient and Final Cause. Ibn Sīnā also references God's agency in his *Physics of the Healing* when he (1) emphasizes God's role as "producing the first actuality from which all other actualities follow, such as that actuality that provides prime matter with the initial corporeal form," and (2) speaks of God as in this sense providing "the initial foundation subsequent to which what comes next reaches completion" (Avicenna 2009: 1.2.8: 16). A fuller understanding of how God's sovereignty and causal agency go hand-in-hand for Ibn Sīnā with cosmic intermediaries requires a fuller consideration of Ibn Sīnā's Islamic Neoplatonic context (including the theory of intermediation outlined in the *Kalām fī maḥḍ al-khair*). Here we simply summarize and note that for Ibn Sīnā God is not simply an agent at the distant start of the Great Chain of Being. For Ibn Sīnā, God is the actively present and efficient cause of being itself. We may add that even with the role of intellect in the emanating process and in the investment of forms into matter, Ibn Sīnā sees God's own causal efficacy in the very hylomorphic structure of each and every body.

Ibn Sīnā's Neoplatonized Aristotelian Hylomorphism: On the Aristotelian Aspects of His View

Its Simplician, Plotinian and Proclean elements aside, Ibn Sīnā's ontology also reveals hylomorphic sensibilities that most readers today would identify as Aristotle's actual views. With Aristotle, Ibn Sīnā wants to ensure that a substance can stay the same across multiple accidental changes, as he also wants to ensure that sometimes a substance can cease to exist and another substance can take its place as happens in the case of elemental change. For Ibn Sīnā, the success of both philosophical analyses requires that we follow Aristotle and posit three principles: form, privation, and matter, with matter as "that which is susceptible to change or perfection" (Avicenna 2009: 1.2.14: 19; see too Avicenna 2005: 4.2.24–26: 139–40). Turning even to his more Simplician account of "Aristotelian prime matter," we might add that Ibn Sīnā is careful to uphold Aristotle's own description of elemental change as a genuine substantial change and not simply as an "accidental alteration" of a single substance from one state to another.

Following Aristotle further, Ibn Sīnā teaches that matter does not exist without form, and that matter is a principle of potency. With Aristotle, Ibn Sīnā also teaches that matter has no positive characteristics of its own. In this respect, Ibn Sīnā seems to take Aristotle's view even more seriously than Aristotle himself does: emphasizing matter's lack of active features, Ibn Sīnā critiques Aristotle for misleadingly speaking of matter's desire for form and metaphorically likening it to a woman's desire for a man. As Ibn Sīnā notes (see more at 4.1), whatever Aristotle means this metaphor to convey, its basic sentiment runs counter to Aristotle's own sense, shared by Ibn Sīnā, that matter per se does not have positive characteristics—including desires—of its own. Emphasizing in this regard that matter has no positive attributes, Ibn Sīnā speaks only of matter's "susceptibility" to receive or to be joined to forms (Avicenna 2009: 1.2.4: 14). He also reflects on matter's "receptivity," reminding us that "the existence of matter consists in its being a recipient only" (*qābila faqaṭ*; Avicenna 2005: 9.4.8: 328; see too 2.4.9: 67). In this context, Ibn Sīnā emphasizes that matter depends on form (see Lizzini 2004: 178ff. for Ibn Sīnā's dialectical arguments for the dependence of matter on form and for characterizations of Ibn Sīnā in this regard as carving out a radical position on form's relation to matter).

We end this section on Ibn Sīnā's actual Aristotelian elements by noting that even though Ibn Sīnā's principles of prime matter and corporeity arguably constitute an addition to Aristotle's conceptual scheme, they do not constitute an addition to Aristotle's parsimonious ontology. For Ibn Sīnā, neither prime matter nor body *per se* are additional items in the world; they are, rather, fundamental principles required for analyzing corporeal substance and change. Ibn Sīnā is not suggesting the real existence of indeterminate, unspecified matter or indeterminate, unspecified bodies-in-general any more than Aristotle is. For Ibn Sīnā, as for Aristotle, what actually exist in the corporeal realm are fully specified hylomorphic substances, e.g. particular horses and trees, existing as fully determined particular bodies. And yet, by conceptually engaging (1) prime matter and (2) the first composite of matter+corporeity, Ibn Sīnā is able to address a number of Aristotelian questions about substance, quantity, quality and change.

Avicennian Hylomorphism and Negative Matter Association

Indicating another point of departure from Aristotle, Ibn Sīnā does seem to mirror a more robustly Platonic or Neoplatonic sense of matter's inferiority to form. In this regard, we may consider the imagery associated with form and matter in Ibn Sīnā's

Ḥayy ibn Yaqẓān (*Alive, Son of Awake*). Whether one reads this Avicennian text as a symbolic "visionary recital" whose value and meaning exceed the bounds of philosophy and reasoning (Corbin 1960), or whether one reads this Avicennian text as an allegory whose value and meaning can be found in the philosophical teachings to which it beckons, one finds in *Ḥayy ibn Yaqẓān* a number of positive allusions to form and negative allusions to matter. Form is aligned with boundless light, the rising of the sun, the Eastern most East beyond the East, and "the permanent Spring of Life" (Corbin 1960: 141, section 11 and 157, 160–1; 321, n. 1). Matter is aligned with darkness, the Westernmost West beyond the West, the "vast sea, which in the Book of God is called the Hot (and Muddy) Sea" (Corbin 1960: 143, section 14, and 327, n. 1), and with "a place of devastation, a desert of salt, filled with troubles, wars, quarrels, tumults; there joy and beauty are but borrowed from a distant place" (Corbin 1960: 143, section 14). (Though one might also note Ibn Sīnā's elusive suggestion that an initial immersion into darkness, presumably some kind of engagement with matter, is needed on the path to purification (Corbin 1960: 142, section 12 and 151–64, 319–30).)

Hylomorphism in Shahrastani

In spite of Ibn Sīnā's many departures from Aristotle, it is still helpful to classify Ibn Sīnā's hylomorphism as an Aristotelian project framed by Aristotelian questions about corporeal substance and terrestrial change. On the contrary, Ps. Empedoclean hylomorphism is best understood as an entirely non-Aristotelian project aimed at addressing entirely non-Aristotelian questions and concerns. Leaving behind Aristotelian concerns with the corporeal world, Ps. Empedoclean hylomorphism places its focus on the spiritual world of souls and intellects. Set in a generally Neoplatonic cosmos of emanating realities along with a creator God, the Ps. Empedoclean tradition recounted by Shahrastani describes a pure spiritual prime matter "between" God and intellect in the ordinary Great Chain of Being. While not framed in terms of hylomorphism, this view can be seen as leading to the conclusion that all non-God substances—including souls and intellects—admit of a matter+form composition. We may reason as follows: in an ordinary Neoplatonic Islamic context we may speak of all things being "composed of" and essentially manifesting intellect since intellect is the emanating source of all things, created by God at the very start of the Great Chain of Being. Along these same lines, we may speak in a Ps. Empedoclean Neoplatonic context of all things being "composed of" and essentially manifesting *matter* since there is a pure matter created by God as itself the source of intellect. To the extent that all things are "filled" with intellect in an Islamic Neoplatonic context, it follows in a Ps. Empedoclean Neoplatonic context that they are also "filled" with the pure *material source* of intellect.

In the introduction to this chapter, we noted that in its teaching of a matter in all things, Ps. Empedoclean hylomorphism can be classified in contrast to Aristotelian hylomorphism which speaks of matter only in connection with corporeal substances. In its emphasis on matter in *all* things including spiritual simples, Ps. Empedoclean ontology can be classified as a kind of "universal hylomorphism." "Universal hylomorphism" is a Christian scholastic term describing a non-Aristotelian set of ontological teachings rooted in Augustine and developed in a range of Augustinian and Franciscan writings. Ps. Empedoclean traditions and Augustinian "universal hylomorphisms" share an emphasis on spiritual matter (though arguably of a different sort), as well as a subsequent sense that all things, including spiritual simples, admit of matter. However, given the root of Islamic Ps. Empedoclean teachings in a range of Islamic Neoplatonic and "Empedoclean" traditions, and given Islamic and Jewish Neoplatonic embrace of emanation and Augustinian rejection of emanation, we must be careful about drawing links between this tradition and Augustinian doctrines without further careful study.

Ps. Empedoclean Hylomorphism: Primal Matter as Love + Strife in Corporeal and Spiritual Beings

Within the context of Ps. Empedoclean traditions, the Arabic term for the supernal material principle which we have described above is *'al-'unṣur al-awwal'* which can be variously translated as *prime matter*, *first matter*, *primal matter* or "*Grounding Element*" (for this latter terminology, see Pessin 2013).

In his *Book of Religious and Philosophical Sects*, Shahrastani recounts the "view of Empedocles" according to which *'al-'unṣur al-awwal* is the first effect of God located between God and intellect in the cosmological and ontological hierarchy. Identified as a reality created by God before intellect, *'al-'unṣur al-awwal* or *primal matter* emerges as the prior cosmic source of intellect, soul, and nature. This *primal matter* is itself described as being composed of love and strife (Empedocles' own dual principles). In its emphasis on the principles of love and strife at the core of all reality and even at the core of the supernal primal matter itself, the tradition can be seen as making two different points about love. On the one hand, the tradition suggests that love is superior to strife, a point that is seen in the text's emphasis on love as the principle of the universal soul, and strife as the much less majestic principle of nature. On the other hand, the tradition also suggests that strife is just as important as love, a point that is seen in the text's also teaching that the prophet—who is the "noblest part" of the universal soul—brings to the world the dual gifts of love and strife, ministering to some through kindness and to others more harshly, depending on the nature of the human soul in question and the extent of its subjugation to corporeality. In this way the Ps. Empedoclean passages as recounted in Shahrastani emphasize a competing sense of strife as negative insofar as it is the downward tendency of nature away from soul, and as positive insofar as it is a legitimate path for the true prophet in his quest to liberate souls as part of the world's ultimate path to justice and goodness.

On this dual composition of *primal matter* in terms of love (*maḥabba*) and strife (*ghilāb*, rendered as "hate" in the following excerpt) we learn:

> Primal matter is simple in its relationship to the essence of intellect, which is below it. But it is not simple in an absolute sense, that is, it is not truly one in its relationship to the essence of cause. This is so because every effect is composite, with an ideal or perceptible composition.

> Primal matter is essentially composed of love and hate. From these two principles the spiritual simple substances and the corporeal compound substances have been produced. Love and hate, then, are two qualities or forms of primal matter and two principles of [the existence of] all beings. All spiritual beings receive the imprint or influence of pure love, as all corporeal beings that of hate. In regard to the compound beings of the spiritual and corporeal [entities], they are subject to the common influence of both principles, love and hate, even as harmony and contrariety of some beings in relation to others. The measure or quantity in which both principles have an influence upon the compound beings serves as a criterion for knowing the proportion of the influence of the spiritual beings over the corporeal beings. The same explanation applies to the concord or harmony between the various kinds and classes of beings which hold some bond or affinity among themselves, just as the diversity of contrary kinds which mutually repel each other. All affinity and love that exist in beings proceed from spiritual substances. All discrepancy and hate in them proceed from the corporeal.
>
> (tr. Asín Palacios 1978: 52; for Arabic, see Shahrastānī 2002: 261, 8–18)

In this Ps. Empedoclean account provided by Shahrastani, we find a principle composed of love and strife that God appoints as a most pure variety of spiritual matter not only at the core of corporeal reality, but at the core of the spiritual reality of souls and intellects as well. Lying at the core of the emanating intellect, the spiritual matter may on the one hand be said to introduce love and strife into intellect and into all things emanated from intellect (viz. all beings), and may on the other hand be described as investing love into all simple spirituals and strife into compound realities lower down on the chain of creation.

The Impetus Behind the View: Neoplatonic Emanation, Pure Unspecified Being, and the Dependence of Beings Upon their Source

In setting out to understand Ps. Empedoclean hylomorphism, it is important to attune oneself to the philosophical impetus behind the view and to avoid approaching it as if it were merely a misunderstanding—in the form of an erroneous over-extension—of Aristotelian hylomorphism. Thinking carefully about the meaning and implications of the Ps. Empedoclean view, we arrive at two related Neoplatonic insights:

1 Pure Unspecified Being as the Potency for All Things (and as the Potency for Love and Strife in All Things)

The first way to understand Ps. Empedoclean hylomorphism is as the deeply Neoplatonic insight that God gives rise to an unspecified Being that contains within itself the fullness of the Great Chain of Being and as such the nature of all things. In this sense, we may speak of the supernal matter as a principle of unlimited Being as an infinite potency that is the emanating source of everything other than God.

Linked to the further insight that unspecified Being generates intellect through its reflections on its own nature (related, as we will see below, to the Plotinian notion of intelligible matter), we have a set of insights about the root of all things in a potency within Being and, as such, a potency at the heart of all things, including the first intellect (and as such, all intellects and souls). In a context in which the unspecified potency of Being gives rise to intellect, and in which cosmic intellects emanate into all intellects, souls and bodies, we may speak of a "marker of potency"—theorized as a primal matter—at the core of all things other than God.

In this context, the claim that all things, even souls and intellects, are matter+form is a philosophical reflection on the ontological rootedness of all things in the potency of unspecified Being.

In light, however, of what we have seen earlier, it must also be emphasized that in this unique Islamic Ps. Empedoclean context, the very notion of "potency of Being" is identified with God-born love and strife in the universe. In this context "potency of Being" is deeply tied to the idea that God creates the world through love and justice, and to the related sense that the prophet's own defining vocation is to be found in his ability to ethically engage the hearts of humankind through these dual principles. The Islamic Ps. Empedoclean metaphysics of *primal matter* qua "potency of Being" is in this sense part of a theology, prophetology, and ethics of love and justice. Here spiritual matter qua "potency of Being" is immediately and intimately tied to questions of divine revelation and human redemption. The implications of this point within Islamic Ps. Empedoclean and Neoplatonic thought requires fuller consideration. We might here at least note that the particular theological and ethical undertones of the Islamic Ps. Empedoclean notion of "potency of Being" ought prevent us from simply reducing it to a merely Aristotelian idea of matter-as-potency.

2 Neoplatonic Descent and the Dependence of All Things Upon God

A related way to approach Ps. Empedoclean hylomorphism is as a deeply Neoplatonic set of intuitions about the failures and privations of the emanatory descent away from the divine source. In this respect, Ps. Empedoclean hylomorphism is a manifestation of the Neoplatonic insight that all non-God realities are inferior to the absolute purity, unity and goodness of God.

In this context, the claim that all things, even souls and intellects, are matter+form is a philosophical reflection on the ontological inferiority of all things to—and the utter dependence of all things on—the purity of God. Ps. Empedoclean hylomorphism in this way emerges as a sustained reflection on the falling away of all beings, corporeal and incorporeal, from the purity of the divine source.

Read in the context of the above two related insights, the Ps. Empedoclean teaching of *primal matter* is revealed to be deeply Neoplatonic in spite of what might prima facie appear to be a deviation from more standard Neoplatonic systems, which do not prima facie emphasize a material reality between God and intellect (though see the section below on the Greek background to Islamic Ps. Empedoclean hylomorphism for Plotinus' own overt reflections on intelligible matter in this regard).

Ps. Empedoclean Tradition in Jewish and Islamic Contexts

Attributed to Empedocles by various Islamic and Jewish authors, the above set of teachings about a spiritual *primal matter* has been described by scholars as part of a "Pseudo-Empedoclean" tradition or traditions in the history of philosophy. The exact origins and developments of this tradition are still uncertain, but can be found in such Islamic thinkers as Shahrastani, Shahrazuri, Ps. Ammonius, and al-Qifti (Gardet 1954; Stern 1954; Berman 2007), with the suggestion by some of Islamic roots for such a teaching in the mystical writings of Ibn Masarra (Asín Palacios 1978; Gardet 1954; Arnaldez 1971; see too Stern 1983b). This tradition can be found in such Jewish thinkers as Isaac Israeli, Ibn Gabirol, Ibn Ḥasday, and in the mystical writings of Elḥonan ben Avrohom (Kaufmann 1899; Altmann and Stern 1958; Schlanger 1968; Brunner 1954; Berman 2007; Stern 1954, 1983a; Pessin 2013). In the Hebrew versions of the Jewish Ps. Empedoclean tradition, such as the mystical writings of Elḥonan ben Avrohom and the philosophical poetry of Solomon Ibn Gabirol, the *primal matter* is referred to as *Yesōd*, "foundation," a term with strong resonances within a range of Jewish kabbalistic contexts, though not in all cases informed by or referring to those contexts.

In spite of deep similarities between medieval Islamic and Jewish philosophy in general, it does seem that Jewish Ps. Empedoclean traditions (in both Hebrew and Arabic) treat the spiritual *primal matter* as a first hypostasis that is entirely simple and coupled with a first form, while Islamic Ps. Empedoclean traditions focus instead on the *primal matter*'s own dual composition through love and strife. In this respect, we might speak of a Jewish Ps. Empedoclean focus on *primal matter* as the first cosmic component, and of an Islamic Ps. Empedoclean focus on *primal matter* as the first cosmic composite.

Greek Backgrounds to Islamic Ps. Empedoclean Hylomorphism

Teaching of love as one of *primal matter*'s key constituents, Ps. Empedoclean hylomorphism reveals a matter-love-desire link that can in some sense be seen in Aristotle (*Physics* 1.9), and more emphatically in a range of Islamic Neoplatonic texts including the *Theology of Aristotle* and Ibn Sīnā's (1891) "*Risālah fi'l 'ishq*" ("Treatise on Love") (on the idea of a "Theology of Desire" in Islamic and Jewish Neoplatonism, and on the interchangeability of terms for "love" and "desire" in such contexts, see Pessin 2013, 2014a). In further support of Neoplatonic influence, we have above suggested two Neoplatonic insights at the core of Ps. Empedoclean philosophy, including the idea that the Great Chain of Being is grounded in a pure unspecified Being that—as root of all things in love and strife—contains within itself the potential for all things (including, most significantly, the potential for all things to return to God).

We may in this latter regard consider Plotinus' own teachings on intelligible matter (see Rist 1962; Dillon 1992; Pessin 2013, A5). At times, Plotinus himself theorizes the One's giving way to intellect in terms of an "intelligible matter" (see *Enneads* 2.4.1–5; see too "indefinite dyad" at 5.4.2, 5.5.4). In this context, Plotinus describes the unfolding of the One into intellect in terms of intellect's turning inwards and upwards—a receptivity in intellect to receive the overflow from the One, followed by a grounding in intellect for all forms and for the subsequent overflow of all reality. In this sense we may point even in Plotinus, and possibly in other Greek "indefinite dyad" traditions, to a principle of spiritual primal matter at the core of intellect, and through the process of the emanation of the remainder of reality from intellect, at the core of all non-God beings.

Ps. Empedoclean Hylomorphism and Positive Matter Associations

Given its emphasis on the pure material core of all being, the Ps. Empedoclean tradition can be seen as reversing more standard negative associations with matter within a whole range of philosophical systems. This is not to say that Ps. Empedoclean contexts lack the more standard negative associations with matter when it comes to descriptions of the lower (or "secondary") corporeal matter in the world of nature (see Pessin 2014b on the relation of supernal and lower matter in Plotinus and in Ibn Gabirol's Ps. Empedoclean context). It is to say, rather, that the tradition focuses strongly on a more exalted grade of matter with decidedly positive connotations. Turning to the eleventh-century Jewish Ps. Empedoclean writings of Solomon Ibn Gabirol, one finds not only a general correlation between matter and God (as he describes both through metaphors of hiddenness), but even the express claim that pure matter arises directly from God's innermost essence with form arising secondarily from God's reality as agent (see Pessin 2013).

Ps. Empedoclean v. Avicennian Conceptions of Matter: On the Locus of Desire, and the First Reality After God

In way of more fully appreciating the diverging hylomorphisms in Shahrastani and Ibn Sīnā, we may highlight two very different ways in which each view approaches matter on the respective questions of desire and the inherent nature of what comes first after God:

1 The Locus of Desire

In its emphasis on a principle of love in the *primal matter* at the core of all non-God beings, Ps. Empedoclean hylomorphism can be seen as making of *primal matter* a locus of desire. Yet Ibn Sīnā is very careful to avoid attributing any active traits to matter. In this spirit Ibn Sīnā expresses confusion about Aristotle's own willingness to talk about matter in terms of an active desire:

> there is sometimes mentioned the material's desire for the form and its imitating the female, while the form imitates the male, but this is something I just do not understand.
>
> (Avicenna 2009: 1.2.21: 24)

He goes on to rehearse problems with this Aristotelian account, and ends:

> Had [the Peripatetics] not made this desire a desire for the forms that make [the material] subsist, which are first perfections, but rather, [made it] a desire for the secondary concomitant perfections, it would have been difficult enough understanding the sense of this desire; but how [is it possible at all] when they have made this desire a desire for the forms that cause [the material] to subsist?
>
> (Avicenna 2009: 1.2.22: 25)

One sentence later, Ibn Sīnā additionally links this critique to "the mystics":

> For these reasons, it is difficult for me to understand this talk, which is closer to the talk of mystics [*kalām aṣ-ṣūfiyya*, lit. "the talk of the Sufis] than that of philosophers.
>
> (Avicenna 2009: 1.2.23: 26; and see McGinnis 2004 n. 14)

In his critique of the Aristotelian view, Ibn Sīnā seems to be referring to *Physics* 1.9 where Aristotle likens matter's desire for form to the desire of a woman for a man. That said, it is also possible that Ibn Sīnā is referring to Islamic Neoplatonic contexts in which, following Plotinus, matter is linked with desire.

In his critique of "the mystics" for their doctrine of matter-with-desire, it is also worth considering the possibility that Ibn Sīnā has in mind the Ps. Empedoclean theory of matter. Not only is the Ps. Empedoclean theory of matter arguably found in a host of Islamic mystical traditions (Asín Palacios 1978; Gardet 1954), but in teaching of a love at the core of *primal matter*, the theory seems guilty of precisely what Ibn Sīnā is concerned to avoid, viz. ascribing active desire in the guise of an active form of love to unformed matter. Leaving aside the interesting question of whether or not Ibn Sīnā's above critique is overtly aimed at the Ps. Empedoclean view, his critique certainly can be used to argue against the Ps. Empedoclean sense that pure matter has two positive qualities, viz. love and hate as evidenced in the Ps. Empedoclean claim that "Love and hate, then, are two qualities or forms of primal matter."

2 The First Reality After God

Advancing a hylomorphism completely different from the Ps. Empedoclean variety, Ibn Sīnā forgoes ascribing desire or any active attributes to matter, as he associates all of matter's active attributes with its forms starting with corporeity, its first form. In further contrast to Ps. Empedoclean hylomorphism, Ibn Sīnā overtly denies the presence of any matter, desiring or otherwise, between God and intellect in the Great Chain of Being. Firmly committed to the rule that "from one comes only one" in his approach to Neoplatonic emanation (Avicenna 2005: 9.4.5–6: 328; 9.4.19: 333), Ibn Sīnā emphasizes that God's first creation is a single unified intellect, which he describes as "a form not in matter" (Avicenna 2005: 9.4.6: 328). In identifying intellect-as-form as the first creation, Ibn Sīnā rejects any kind of pure matter as a first creation. And in emphasizing that the first creation must be a unity so as not to violate the "from one comes only one" rule, Ibn Sīnā can also be seen as rejecting the Ps. Empedoclean sense that a first creation, matter or otherwise, could be in any way composed of dual principles, love and strife or otherwise.

Absent any sense of a Ps. Empedoclean spiritual matter, Ibn Sīnā is committed only to a prime matter that (1) has no existence without the presence of form, (2) arises not at the start (*pace* the Ps. Empedoclean view) but at the culmination of the Great Chain of Being, marking the entry into celestial and then terrestrial bodies subsequent to the spiritual overflow of intellects and souls, and (3) is part of the matter + form composition of all corporeal substances and not (*pace* the Ps. Empedoclean view) souls or intellects.

Conclusion

Avicennian hylomorphism and Ps. Empedoclean hylomorphism are not just accounts with widely divergent details about prime matter and hylomorphic reality; they are, rather, accounts with widely divergent starting points tied to widely divergent philosophical comportments. While Ibn Sīnā's view reveals a unique blend of Aristotelian, Simplician, Plotinian, and Proclean ideas, his interest in matter stems from a decidedly Aristotelian-minded set of philosophical concerns with corporeal reality and the nature of change and constancy within the realm of corporeal reality. On the contrary, the Ps. Empedoclean view is not primarily rooted in concerns about corporeal reality at all, and takes its lead instead from a set of Neoplatonic philosophical and theological insights about the nature of emanation, the rootedness of all non-God beings in the potency of Being (rooted in love and strife), and the falling away of all non-God beings from the purity and unity of the divine source. While both Islamic forms of hylomorphism are committed to the majesty of God, His purity, and His agency in the world, and while both forms of hylomorphism see the hand of God in their respective hylomorphic accounts, the two views uphold and investigate two very different kinds of prime matter with two very different senses of how God, the world, and prime matter are related. On the Avicennian account, prime matter is that which God graces with corporeity and other forms at the ontological core of corporeal substance. On the Ps. Empedoclean account, *primal matter* is that which marks the God-appointed potency at the heart of the Great Chain of Being, as well as the gap between God and all other beings, corporeal and spiritual. Each view not only results in a different kind of hylomorphic vision, but in a hylomorphic vision that stems from and leads to a very different set of overarching philosophical and theological intuitions.

Further Reading

Charles, D. (1994) "Matter and Form: Unity, Persistence, and Identity," in T. Scaltsas, D. Charles, & M. L. Gill (eds.), *Unity, Identity, and Explanation in Aristotle's Metaphysics*, Oxford: Clarendon Press, pp. 75–105.

Charlton, W. (1970) "Did Aristotle Believe in Prime Matter?," W. Charlton (tr.), *Aristotle's Physics, Books I and II*, Oxford: Clarendon Press, pp. 129–45.

Hyman, A. (1992) "From What is One and Simple Only What is One and Simple Can Come to Be," in L. E. Goodman (ed.), *Neoplatonism and Jewish Thought*, Albany: State University of New York Press, pp. 111–35.

Mathis II, C. K. (1992) "Parallel Structures in the Metaphysics of Iamblichus and Ibn Gabirol," in L. E. Goodman (ed.), *Neoplatonism and Jewish Thought*, Albany: State University of New York Press, pp. 61–76.

McGinnis, J. (2010) *Avicenna*, Oxford: Oxford University Press.

Nasr, S. H. (1993) *An Introduction to Islamic Cosmological Doctrines*, Albany: State University of New York Press.

Pessin, S. (2010) "Solomon Ibn Gabirol," in E. N. Zalta (ed.), *The Stanford Encyclopedia of Philosophy*, http://plato.stanford.edu/entries/ibn-gabirol

Stone, A. (2008) "Avicenna," in H. Gutschmidt, A. Lang-Balestra & G. Segalerba (eds.), *Substantia: sic et non: eine Geschichte des Substanzbegriffs von der Antike bis zur Gegenwart in Einzelbeiträgen*, Frankfurt: Ontos-Verlag, pp. 133–47.

References

Altmann, A. & Stern, S. M. (1958) *Isaac Israeli*, Oxford: Oxford University Press. Reprinted in 2009 by University of Chicago Press with introduction by Alfred Ivry.

Aouad, M. (1989) "*La Théologie d'Aristote et autres textes du Plotinus arabus*," in R. Goulet (ed.), *Dictionnaire des Philosophes Antiques*, Paris: *Editions du Centre national de la recherche scientifique*, pp. 541–90.

Arnaldez, R. (1971) "Ibn Masarra," in B. Lewis, V. L. Ménage, C. Pellat, & J. Schacht (eds.), *The Encyclopaedia of Islam*, vol. 3, Leiden: Brill, pp. 868–72.

Asín Palacios, M. (1978) *The Mystical Philosophy of Ibn Masarra and His Followers*, E. H. Douglas & H. W. Yoder (tr.), Leiden: Brill.

Avicenna (1891) *Risālah fi'l-'ishq (Treatise on Love)*, in A. F. Mehren (ed.), *Traités Mystiques*, Leiden: Brill, pp. 1–27; for English translation see E. Fackenheim (tr.), *Mediaeval Studies* 7 (1945): 208–28.

——. (1960) *Ḥayy ibn Yaqẓān*, H. Corbin (ed. and tr.), *Avicenna and the Visionary Recital*, Bollingen Series LXVI (66), New York: Pantheon Books, pp. 137–50.

——. (1985) *Kitāb al-najāt fi al-ḥikmah al-manṭiqīyah wa-al-ṭabī'īyah wa-al-ilāhīyah*, M. Fakhry (ed.), Beirut: Dār al-Afāq al-Jadīdah.

——. (2005) *The Metaphysics of the Healing*, M. Marmura (tr.), Provo, UT: Brigham Young University Press.

——. (2009) *The Physics of the Healing*, 2 vols., J. McGinnis (tr.), Provo, UT: Brigham Young University Press.

Berman, L. V. (2007) "Empedocles," in M. Berenbaum & F. Skolnik (eds.), *Encyclopaedia Judaica*, vol. 6, Detroit: Macmillan Reference USA, p. 397.

Brunner, F. (1954) "*La transformation des notions de matière et da forme d'Aristote à Ibn Gabirol*," *Inédit, conférence donnée en Sorbonne le 17 juillet*: 1–17. Reprinted in D. Schulthess (ed.), *Métaphysique d'Ibn Gabirol et la tradition platonicienne*, essay III (Variorum Collected Studies Series), Aldershot: Ashgate, 1997.

Corbin, H. (ed. and tr.) (1960) *Avicenna and the Visionary Recital*, Bollingen Series LXVI (66), New York: Pantheon Books.

Dillon, J. (1992) "Solomon Ibn Gabirol's Doctrine of Intelligible Matter," in L. E. Goodman (ed.), *Neoplatonism and Jewish Thought*, Albany: State University of New York Press, pp. 43–59.

Gardet, L. (1954) "hayûlâ," in H. A. R. Gibb (ed.), *The Encyclopaedia of Islam*, Leiden: Brill.

Hyman, A. (1977) "Aristotle's 'First Matter' and Avicenna's and Averroes' 'Corporeal Form'," in A. Hyman (ed.), *Essays in Medieval Jewish and Islamic Philosophy*, New York: Ktav Publishing House, pp. 335–56.

Kaufmann, D. (1899) *Studien über Salomon Ibn Gabirol* (Jahresberichte der Landes-Rabbinerschule zu Budapest für das Schuljahr 1898/99), Budapest. Reprint: New York: Arno Press, 1980.

Lizzini, O. (2004) "The Relation between Form and Matter: Some Brief Observations on the 'Homology Argument' (*Ilāhīyāt*, II.4) and the Deduction of *Fluxus*," in J. McGinnis (ed.), *Interpreting Avicenna: Science and Philosophy in Medieval Islam*, Leiden: Brill, pp. 175–85.

Lovejoy, A. O. (1936) *The Great Chain of Being: A Study of the History of an Idea*, Cambridge: Harvard University Press.

McGinnis, J. (2004) "On the Moment of Substantial Change: A Vexed Question in the History of Ideas," in J. McGinnis (ed.), *Interpreting Avicenna: Science and Philosophy in Medieval Islam*, Leiden: Brill, pp. 42–61.

Pessin, S. (2013) *Ibn Gabirol's Theology of Desire: Matter and Method in Jewish Medieval Neoplatonism*, Cambridge: Cambridge University Press.

——. (2014a, forthcoming) "Piety, Love, and Emanation in Islamic and Jewish Neoplatonism: Intermediation with Divine Presence and Other Implications of Apophatic Dialectic," in T. A. Druart (ed.), *Philosophy in Islamic Lands*, Washington: Catholic Univerisity of America Press.

——. (2014b, forthcoming) "From Universal Hylomorphism to Neoplatonic Mereology: Rethinking Prime Matter as Fundamental Part in Plotinus, Simplicius, and Ibn Gabirol," in A. Arlig (ed.), *On What There Was: Parts and Wholes*, Belgium: Brepols Publishers.

Rist, J. M. (1962) "The Indefinite Dyad and Intelligible Matter in Plotinus," *The Classical Quarterly, New Series* 12, 1: 99–107.

Schlanger, J. (1968) *Le philosophie de Salomon Ibn Gabirol*, Leiden: Brill.

Shahrastānī (2002) *Book of Religious and Philosophical Sects (Kitāb Al-Milal wal-niḥal)*, W. Cureton (ed.), Piscataway: Gorgias Press. Reprint of the 1842 Cureton edition published by the Society for the Publication of Oriental Texts, London.

Simplicius (1882) *Simplicii in Aristotelis Physicorum libros quattuor priores commentaria*, D. Hermann (ed.), Berlin: Reimer.

Sorabji, R. (1988) *Matter, Space, and Motion: Theories in Antiquity and Their Sequel*, Ithaca, NY: Cornell University Press.

——. (2005) The *Philosophy of the Commentators, 200–600* AD: *A Sourcebook*, vol. 2 (Physics), Ithaca, NY: Cornell University Press.

Stern, S. M. (1954) "Anbaduḳlīs," in H. A. R. Gibb (ed.), *The Encyclopaedia of Islam*, vol. 1, Leiden: Brill, pp. 483–84.

——. (1983a) "Ibn Ḥasday's Neoplatonist" (reprint), F. W. Zimmerman (ed.), *Medieval Arabic and Hebrew Thought*, London: Variorum Reprints, pp. 58–120.

——. (1983b) "Ibn Masarra – A Myth?" (reprint), F. W. Zimmerman (ed.), *Medieval Arabic and Hebrew Thought*, London: Variorum Reprints.

Stone, A. D. (1999) "Simplicius and Avicenna on the Nature of Body," unpublished paper available for download online at people.ucsc.edu/~abestone/papers/corpsamp.pdf

——. (2001) "Simplicius and Avicenna on the Essential Corporeity of Material Substance," in Robert Wisnovsky (ed.), *Aspects of Avicenna*, Princeton: Markus Wiener Publishers, pp. 73–130.

Wolfson, H. A. (1929) *Crescas' Critique of Aristotle: Problems of Aristotelian Physic in Jewish and Arabic Philosophy* (vol. VI, Harvard Semitic Series), Cambridge: Harvard University Press.

17
ESSENCE AND EXISTENCE IN IBN SÍNÁ

Rollen E. Houser

Introduction

Perhaps the most important and certainly famous philosophical doctrine of Ibn Sīnā (in Latin, Avicenna) is his teaching on essence (*dhāt*) or, better, quiddity (*māhiyya*) and existence (*wūjūd*). When considered metaphysically, each and every being (*mawjūd*) in the universe is one of two kinds:

1 Everything other than God, from the lowest type of material thing to the highest angel, is a being composed of two ontological principles: quiddity and existence. In such composed beings, their existence is ontologically "other" than their quiddity. Consequently, such a being must be made to exist by some external efficient cause giving it existence.
2 By contrast, God is "entirely one" and is not in any way composed of diverse ontological principles, such as quiddity and existence. His "existence is not shared by any other" being. Consequently, there can be no cause of God's existence. Rather, God is the ultimate cause of the existence of every other being (Avicenna 2005: 38; all translations in this article are mine).

By explaining the difference between God and all other things in this way, Ibn Sīnā was able to devise a philosophical explanation of creation, one that in no way involved a beginning of the created world at a first moment in time, which is how most earlier Muslims and Christians had thought of creation.

In order to understand Ibn Sīnā's doctrine of quiddity and existence, we first will look at the structure of metaphysical "science," then turn to how Ibn Sīnā explains quiddity and existence as scientific principles of metaphysics. After that, we will turn to how Ibn Sīnā used these principles to prove important conclusions about substances and accidents, the causes, and angels. (Applying the principles to God is the topic for another chapter of this book; see J. Janssens.)

Metaphysics and "Science"

Aristotle explained his theory of demonstrative "science" (we might say "discipline") in his *Posterior Analytics*. Every "science" has three components: the "subject" studied; the "conclusions" proven; and the "principles" by which they are proven. Aristotle also distinguished three kinds of principles: axioms "common" to all the disciplines; and two kinds of "proper" principles limited to a particular science, its "definitions" and "suppositions" (or "postulates") (Aristotle 1989: 72a15–24; Houser 1999: 110–14; Bertolacci 2006: 170–72). How this scheme works in the books he wrote was not always clear, but Ibn Sīnā knew a memorable example in Euclid's *Elements of Geometry*.

For Euclid, the *subject* of plane geometry is two dimensional geometrical figures. Its *principles*, laid out at the beginning of *Elements*, include: Common axiom 5, "the whole is greater than the part"; Definition 19 of triangle, "*trilateral* figures are those contained by three lines"; and Postulate 4, "all right angles are equal to one another." Definitions are attained through the first act of the mind—apprehending concepts—while postulates are grasped through the second act of the mind—making assertions. The project of a "science" is to use the third act of the mind—reasoning—in order to demonstrate conclusions, such as Book 1, Theorem 32, "triangles have three interior angles equal to two right angles."

In his *Metaphysics*, Aristotle had described its *subject* as "being as being," which is studied "universally," covering all reality; but perplexingly he also called metaphysics "theological science" (Aristotle 1958: 1003a20–5, 1026a18–22). This so confused Ibn Sīnā that he tells us "I had read the work forty times" but he still did not understand its contents, its "organizational design" (*ghārad*), or its "end" (*maqṣūd*) (Avicenna 1974: 32). But a little book by al-Fārābī showed him that metaphysics studies being because "it is *common* to all things," so he said that "the *primary subject* of this science, then, is *being as being*; and its *objects of inquiry* are the consequences of being as being, without condition" (Avicenna 2005: 9–10). This description made metaphysics an ontology, a study of "common" being presented in Books 2–7; but since God is its "perfection" (*kamāl*) metaphysics culminates in a rational theology found in Books 8–10 of Ibn Sīnā's own *Metaphysics*.

If we look backward, then, we can see that "the *usefulness* of this science [metaphysics], … is in attaining *certitude* about the *principles of the particular sciences*. … Therefore, this is like the usefulness of the *ruler* in relation to the ruled" (Avicenna 2005: 14). And looking forward, we can also see why setting out quiddity and existence as its proper principles was so important. What were principles of the physical sciences, like the categories and the causes, become "objects of enquiry" in Ibn Sīnā's metaphysics. This means they cannot be its principles, for no "science" can assume what it tries to prove; that would be arguing in a circle.

Metaphysical "Definitions": "Thing" and "Quiddity"

Ibn Sīnā begins his treatment of principles abruptly: "We say: the *being* and the *thing* and the *necessary* are those *notions* which are impressed on the soul in a *first* impression, which are not acquired from others more known than they are" (Avicenna 2005: 22).

These three notions are concepts of concrete wholes, so Ibn Sīnā's dialectical way of arguing moves from a whole to its intrinsic principles, much as Aristotle had done (Aristotle 1936: 184a9–22). The way we define things is by proceeding from more specific to more general terms (as in Porphyry's Tree, which moves from Socrates to his species "human" to his proximate genus "animal" and all the way up to the category "substance"). This shows there must be some most universal notions, for "if every notion required a higher notion, there would be an infinite regress or circularity," which would undermine knowledge by basing it on unknown terms. But why did Ibn Sīnā choose these particular trans-categorical terms—being, thing, and necessary?

His explanation points to the common axioms governing all knowledge. Just as everyone recognizes the truth of the axioms concerning contradiction and the excluded middle, so we should also recognize that the terms making up these propositions are equally fundamental. A clear statement of the axioms reveals those terms. The principle of contradiction means that "it is *impossible* that a *thing* both *be* and *not be*," while its correlative, the law of the excluded middle, says that "it is *necessary* that a *thing* either *be* or *not be*." "Thing" is the subject of both propositions, "being" is in their predicates, and their subjects and predicates are related through the modal concepts "necessary" and "impossible." So the concepts included in the common axioms are the very terms which lead to the "definitions" of metaphysics (Avicenna 2005: 22).

To explain the meaning of these notions Ibn Sīnā integrated the Islamic and philosophical traditions (Jolivet 1984: 19–28). Let us first consider "thing." This term is the most universal Qur'ānic term for a creature. When God is called "knowing" or "creating," the object of God's activity is often called a "thing" (*shay'*). The distance between God and creatures is emphasized this way: "The Originator of the heavens and the earth. … No *thing* is like a likeness of Him" (Qur'ān 42:10). But there are a few verses which seem to call God a thing, so the early Arabic grammarians said God is "a thing not like things"; and they understood "thing" to be the most universal of all *subjects* of predication (Wisnovsky 2003: 146–8).

"Those learned in *kalām*" (*Mutakallimūn*), the early Muslim theologians, also noted another Qur'ānic text: "What we [God] say to a thing, when we wish it, is just to say to it 'Be!' and then it is" (Qur'ān 16:40), which introduced the concept of "being." The Mu'tazilite school understood "thing" to be "divisible into the subcategories" of being (*mawjūd*) and non-being (*ma'dūm*). This view, however, seems to imply that "thing" is equally as primordial as God and seems to give a non-existing thing some shadowy ontological status, which undercut God being absolute creator of all things. So the Ash'arite and Maturidite schools said that "thing" and "being" are co-extensive and mutually imply each other (Wisnovsky 2005: 105–6).

But how should "thing" be understood? The theologians crafted their own version of a Greek philosophical doctrine that would highlight God's role as cause of creatures: atomism. "Ash'arite thinkers defended the view of the world as constituted of atoms and accidents, and so entirely dependent on God's grace for its continuing existence" (Leaman 2008: 84). This "atomic arrangement best displays the agency proper to the creator, which must be immediate and so cannot be identified with the causal chains which operate in the created world" (Burrell 2008: 144), so that secondary causes are but "occasions" for the action of the only true cause, God. Ibn Sīnā, however, recognized that atomism and occasionalism are inadequate.

For a better explanation of "thing," Ibn Sīnā turned to better philosophers. Socrates had concentrated on finding definitions as answers to the question "What is it?" So he introduced into philosophy the idea that individual actions and things of the same sort share a common *essence*, though this term would only be invented by Aristotle (Plato 1963: 1: 15c9–e2). Plato then took up the search for essences and uncovered a world separate from our changing world, inhabited by things he called "exemplars" (*paradeigma*) in order to emphasize their causal role on our everyday world, "forms" (*eidos*) and "ideas" (*idea*) to emphasize that they are the objects of true knowledge, and "substances" (*ousia*) to emphasize that they are permanent, unchanging, and the most perfect of beings (Plato 1963: 5: 500e3, 511a3, 511c2, 507b10; 534a3).

Aristotle then "brought the Platonic forms down to earth." From his studies of the physical world he learned to distinguish within an individual being (*on*) of our everyday experience its intrinsic nature or substance (*ousia*) from "accidents" like color and size, actions and relations. And he distinguished three kinds of substances: the whole or "composite" substance, and two senses of substance which are intrinsic principles of the whole, the "form" present in an individual thing that causes its actual nature, and the "matter" which gives it the potentiality for many kinds of change (Aristotle 1958: 1017b22–27; 1035a1).

Aristotle likened the subject of metaphysics—"being"—to "healthy," which, though attributable to food and urine, is properly said only of an animal's body. Likewise, "being" is properly and primarily attributable only to "substance," so that metaphysics studies all being by concentrating only on the highest beings: substances (Aristotle 1958: 1003a33–b23). And among the three senses of substance, form takes pride of place: "Therefore, if the form is prior to the matter and more the being, it also will be prior to the composite of both, and for the same reason" (Aristotle 1958: 1029a5–7). To expedite philosophy's search for universal definitions, he invented the technical term "essence" (*to tí ên einai*) to isolate that feature within an individual thing that is the basis for the nature it has in common with other members of its species and is the basis for universal knowledge of it (Owens 1978: 180–8).

For Aristotle, the "essence" of a being had to be substance rather than accident; but which of the three senses of substance? It could not be the composite substance, because composites come into and go out of being. And it could not be substance in the sense of matter, because that is the principle of potency and change, whereas the essence of something, say, a human or a triangle, is permanent. So the essence of a "being" had to be identical with its *substantial form*, which is permanent and unchanging in kind. Since definitions are formulae uncovering essences, in the physical sciences definitions include the substantial form, but sensible matter has to be "added" to complete the definition. And definitions in mathematics are of accidental forms, but only with the addition of "intelligible matter." In metaphysics, however, definitions are confined to the substantial form alone, for that is the essence. In metaphysics, then, "there is no definition of it [the composite substance] with its matter, for this is indefinite, but there is a definition of it with reference to its primary substance, for example, of the human the definition of the soul, for the substance is the indwelling form, from which and the matter the composite is called a substance" (Aristotle 1958: 1037a27–30; Maurer 1990: 12; Owens 1978: 335, 361–2).

So Ibn Sīnā took from the Islamic tradition the conception of "thing" as one of the most universal of terms, but for his *understanding* of "thing" he turned to Aristotelian philosophers. He did not, however, simply copy Aristotle.

Though "thing" cannot be defined by appealing to a broader genus, it can be described using two dialectical techniques: finding synonyms and dividing a concept. The synonyms Ibn Sīnā presents "indicate that each is either a 'thing' (*shay'*) or a 'matter' (*'amr*) or a 'what' (*mā*) or a 'that which [is]' (*alladhī*)" (Avicenna 2005: 23). The three synonyms of "thing" seem carefully chosen to correspond to Aristotle's three senses of substance: matter, form, and composite respectively. But rather than choosing just one of these at the expense of the other two, Ibn Sīnā focuses on what they all have in common. Each signifies essence, though with a different connotation. Ibn Sīnā then divides "thing" by offering examples. "Thing" or its equivalent in every language can be used to indicate some other concept, and for each matter there is a *truth by which* it is what it is. So the triangle has a truth by which it is a triangle, and the white thing has a truth by which it is white. The term "thing," then, points to a truth (*ḥaqīqah*)—an objective truth found in the thing, not a truth in a mind—"by which" the triangle is a triangle and the white thing is white. "By which" indicates that this "truth" functions as an intrinsic *principle* making the thing "what" it is, which is why the name Ibn Sīnā chooses for this principle is the abstract term "whatness" or "quiddity" (*māhiyya*), a term broad enough to cover accidents as well as substances, matter and form and the composite thing, and both physical composites and ontologically simple things like spirits (Avicenna 2005: 24). The *concept* of quiddity is a principle of metaphysical knowledge, but the quiddity itself is a real ontological principle found in each "thing."

Metaphysical "Definitions": "Being" and "Existence"

The reason why Ibn Sīnā reversed directions from Aristotle and espoused a broad sense of "quiddity" can be seen by turning to its twin metaphysical principle, "existence." Ibn Sīnā uncovers the notion of "existence" (*wujūd*) by analyzing the universal notion of "the being" (*mawjūd*) (sometimes translated "the existent"). "The being" is among the terms that "have the highest claim to be conceived in themselves" because, like "thing," it is "common to all matters" (Avicenna 2005: 23). This concept, as well, Ibn Sīnā divides and offers synonyms.

Dividing "being" into the ten categories, as Aristotle had done, does not produce a proper definition of it, but a more limited division into the categories of *action* and *passion* proves helpful (Avicenna 2005: 23). For if we compare two beings related to each other, the one will be active in comparison with the other, like cobbler and shoe, or light and dark. Now what is true between two full beings also should be true when we look *within* a being; for example, form is active in comparison with prime matter which is passive.

This relation then sets the stage for Ibn Sīnā's synonyms. "The meaning of 'existence' (*wujūd*) and the meaning of 'the thing' (*shay'*) are conceived in the soul and are two meanings," he notes, "but 'the being' and 'the established' (*al-muthbat*) and 'the realized' (*al-muḥaṣṣal*) are synonyms" (Avicenna 2005: 24). What is "established" or "realized" is actual or active in comparison with what is not realized. The term "being," then, conveys a note of actuality, an actuality coming from the principle Ibn Sīnā has just called "existence." Existence, then, is *actual* in comparison with "quiddity." In what does this actuality or realization consist? Aristotle had said that form is actual in comparison with matter, making something to be "what" it is. Ibn Sīnā has now added a second kind of actuality or realization, contributed by "existence" in relation to "quiddity." This must be the actuality of existence or being, in comparison with which the quiddity of the thing is passive or potential.

While Ibn Sīnā by no means abandons the actuality of "form" in relation to matter in the *quidditative* order, here he is pointing out that within the individual "thing" or "being" there is a second kind of actuality, one in the existential order, that is even more fundamental than form. If Aristotle had said that "form" is the basis for answering the question "what is it?" Ibn Sīnā has seen that "existence" is the basis for answering the prior question, "is it?"

Ibn Sīnā then summarizes his results: "The concept of 'existence' and the concept of 'thing' are conceived by the soul and are two concepts." But a distinction among concepts does not necessarily imply distinct realities. So he adds: "It is evident that each thing has a truth proper to it, namely, its quiddity. And it is known that the truth proper to each thing is something *other* than the *existence* that corresponds to what is affirmed" (Avicenna 2005: 24). So this "otherness" is a real, ontological otherness. This truth has not and cannot be demonstrated; but Ibn Sīnā's dialectical argument is designed to open our minds to insight into quiddity and existence, both as fundamental *notions* of metaphysics and as *real principles* in real things.

Metaphysical "Definitions": "Necessary," "Possible," "Impossible"

The third universal term Ibn Sīnā introduces is "necessary." We normally understand "necessary" in relation to its opposites, "possible" and "impossible," which is why definitions of these terms are normally circular, say, defining "necessary" using "possible" and then defining "possible" using "necessary." But comparing them with the other two most universal terms shows "necessary" to be primary. "But of these three, the one with most right to be first known is the necessary. This is because the necessary signifies the assuredness of existence, since existence is known in itself, while non-existence is known through existence" (Avicenna 2005: 28). The importance of these three terms rests not so much in themselves, but, since they are modal terms, how they can be combined with other terms, as Ibn Sīnā does at the beginning of his presentation of the "suppositions" of metaphysics, to which we now turn.

Metaphysical "Suppositions": "Necessary Existence" and "Possible Existence"

In the beginning of *Metaphysics* 1.6, Ibn Sīnā combines the three modal notions with "existence" in order to set out a grid of reality within which to place his "suppositions." These combinations yield three options: necessary existence, possible existence, and impossible existence. Impossible existence is a null class, made impossible by the contradictory nature of its quiddity, such as "square circle." Possible existence, when considered in itself, is possible because its quiddity is not self-contradictory; but on the other hand its quiddity does not require that it exist. So existence possible in itself, when realized, must also become necessary, but in a way, as "necessary through another," because a pure possible in no way really exists. The third option, "necessary existence" in itself, is intrinsically necessary. Its quiddity is such that it must exist; it would be self-contradictory for it not to exist. Now "there are certain properties that belong respectively to necessary existence and to possible existence." Ibn Sīnā lays down five such properties, of which the first two are the most important: "Necessary existence in itself has no cause; but possible existence has a cause" (Avicenna 2005: 29–30). The rest of c. 6–7 consists in five dialectical arguments designed to support such claims as these. The five theses for which Ibn Sīnā argues are *not* themselves the "suppositions" of metaphysics; but the dialectical arguments supporting them are designed to reveal those "suppositions," to show them to be plausible, and to open the mind of the reader to insight into the two suppositions of metaphysics.

Ibn Sīnā sets out these suppositions at the end of c. 7:

> – *Necessary existence* is *one* entirely, though not as a species under a genus, and *one* in number, though not as an individual under a species. But it is a notion whose name signifies only that whose *being is common with nothing else*. We shall add an explanation later. Therefore, it is *not multiple*. These are the properties of necessary existence.
>
> – Of *possible existence* its property is clear from what has been said, namely, that it necessarily *requires another which makes it exist in act*. For whatever is possible existence *in itself* is always possible existence. But there may *accrue* to it existence necessary through another. Now this *accrues* to it always or its necessary existence through another may not be permanent, but at some particular time. And that to which this *accrues* at some time must have matter whose being precedes it in time. That whose existence must be from another always, its truth is *not simple*, because what it has *in itself* [= its quiddity] is *other* than what it has from another [= its existence]. And from both of these [principles] it acquires its individuality in existence. Therefore, nothing is completely freed from potency and possibility in itself, except necessary existence. *It is single, all else is composite*.
>
> (Avicenna 2005: 38)

The fundamental contrast between necessary and possible existence determines the two suppositions of Ibn Sīnā's metaphysics. The *first* principle is that "necessary existence is one entirely," not composed of quiddity and existence. Ibn Sīnā does *not* here assume there really is some being that is necessary existence (or God), because he will argue for God's existence in his rational theology. What this principle means is that, should God be demonstrated to exist (as Ibn Sīnā will do later in his *Metaphysics*), he must be ontologically simple. By contrast, existence possible in itself must be ontologically composite.

So Ibn Sīnā's *second* principle is that all possible beings are ontologically composite, made up of the metaphysical principles of existence and quiddity. To emphasize that this composition of quiddity and existence is real, Ibn Sīnā uses the term *'arada*, which we have translated as "accrues to," but is also the term he uses for "accident" and was so translated into Latin. Ibn Sīnā does not mean that "existence" is a predicamental accident like "white," for that would require that the quiddity in itself already exist, a critique Ibn Rushd would level at Ibn Sīnā. Nor does it mean that "existence" is a predicable accident flowing from the quiddity, because that would make the quiddity the cause of existence and would take us back to Aristotle. Rather, "accident" here simply means that there is no intrinsic connection between quiddity and existence, which is why existence must be caused by something extrinsic to a created "being." Perhaps the best way of understanding Ibn Sīnā's "accident" language is to think of existence as like a predicable accident in being ontologically "other" than the quiddity, but different because a predicable accident is an effect of its cause, as "risibility" is an effect of already being human, whereas "existence" is a cause, since it is an act that makes the "being" to exist in the first place.

Since these two "suppositions" are *principles*, they cannot be *demonstrated*; but Ibn Sīnā does argue for them dialectically. Among those arguments, three are especially important.

1. To support his supposition concerning possible existence, Ibn Sīnā uses what can be called his "sufficiency argument," namely, that the quiddity of a possible being, what makes it a certain "kind" of thing, is not sufficient to ensure the thing exists (Avicenna 2005: 31–2).
2. He also supports this supposition using an "infinite regress argument," namely, that there cannot be an infinite regress in causes of existence (Avicenna 2005: 30).
3. Finally, to support his supposition concerning necessary existence, he uses what may be called his "predicables argument." For necessary existence, its quiddity must be identical with its existence. The reason is simply because the existence of any thing is either distinct from its quiddity or it is the same as its quiddity. If quiddity and existence are distinct, then its existence is either a property flowing from its quiddity or a predicable accident caused by an external cause. Now no thing whose quiddity is different from its existence causes that existence, because a quiddity must first exist in order to cause anything. In this reasoning it is important to note that nothing, not even God, causes itself to exist. On the other hand, if a thing's existence is caused by something else, it must be something possible in itself, not necessary. The quiddity of necessary existence, therefore, can neither cause itself nor be caused by something else, precisely because it is necessary existence. Consequently, quiddity and existence must be *one* and the same in necessary existence (Avicenna 2005: 34–7).

That Ibn Sīnā accepted these doctrines *as principles* is clear on every page of his ontology, to which we now turn.

Metaphysical Conclusions: Substances and Accidents

Aristotle had defined "substance" in opposition to the nine predicamental accidents: logically a substance, say, "Socrates," is what "is not *in* a subject," whereas an accident, like "five feet tall," is only "in a subject"; and metaphysically a substance is a "being through itself," whereas an accident is a "being through another" (Aristotle 1980: 2a11–19, 1958: 1029a7–8, 1028a29–30).

Ibn Sīnā interprets Aristotle's categories using his own metaphysical principles: "We say: *existence* belongs to a *thing* in itself, such as the existence of the human as human, or [it belongs to a thing] accidentally, as the existence of Zayd as white" (Avicenna 2005: 45). For Ibn Sīnā, existence "belongs to" a thing that is a substance differently from the way it belongs to an accident. This means that "*a being* is of two divisions." One of them, namely, accident, "is a being in another *thing*, that thing realizing the whole essence and species in itself. ... And the second is a being in this manner: that in no way is it *in* some other thing. And so it *is*, not in a subject at all. This is substance" (Avicenna 2005: 45).

By introducing his principles of quiddity and existence, Ibn Sīnā subtly re-defines both substance and accident. An accident has the kind of quiddity which requires that it exists in another—its subject. A substance has the kind of quiddity that is not present "in some other *thing*." Rather, it exists "through itself." Most importantly, the quiddity of neither accident nor substance requires that it exist in the first place. The whole being—made up of substance and accidents—must be given its existence by some other cause.

Later, when showing that knowledge is an accident, Ibn Sīnā adds to his new definition of *substance*. The claim that knowledge is an accident existing in the mind of the knower gives rise to this objection: If "knowledge is what is acquired from the forms of beings, when abstracted from their matter," then "if the forms of accidents are accidents, how can the forms of substances be accidents," which they must be if they are concepts existing in the mind? Ibn Sīnā answers that "the quiddity of a substance is substance in the sense that it is a being *in the concrete* that is *not in a subject*. ... But as for its existence *in the mind* under this description, this is not its definition in as much as it is a substance" (Avicenna 2005: 107–08). In short, the quiddity of *substance* can *exist* in two different ways, in reality as an independent substance in accord with its own nature, but also in the mind of a knower in accord with the mode of existence all mental concepts have, namely, as an accident. Such two-fold existence is possible only because in creatures quiddity is other than existence and is ontologically neutral in itself. And this two-fold existence of the quiddity is how Ibn Sīnā explains the identity between concept and real thing in human knowledge, a problem earlier Aristotelians had been unable to resolve fully.

Metaphysical Conclusions: The Causes

In order to explain causality, Ibn Sīnā again begins with Aristotle, who had recognized four kinds of causes: the intrinsic principles of matter and form; and the extrinsic principles of agent and end. Aristotle had said matter is the principle of potentiality; but when Ibn Sīnā defines matter, he again introduces his own principles: "By the elemental [cause, we mean] the cause that is part of the whole nature of the *thing*, through which the thing is what it is *in potency*, and in which the potentiality of *existence* resides" (Avicenna 2005: 194). By adding the terms *thing* and *existence*, Ibn

Sīnā makes it clear that matter in itself is *not* an internal source of the *actual* existence of a thing, but in itself it carries only a potentiality for existence. So if either of Aristotle's two intrinsic principles plays a role in causing the existence of a thing, it will be form.

Aristotle had thought of form and matter as principles only in relation to the whole, composite substance, but Ibn Sīnā also considers them directly in relation to each other. In relation to the whole, he follows Aristotle: "Form is only a *formal* cause for the *thing composed* of it and matter. Consequently, form is only a form *for* matter, not a formal cause *of* matter." Form gives the whole thing the *actual* quiddity it has; while matter gives the whole the *potency* for the quiddity it can have. Consequently, "if the form is a cause *for matter* which renders it subsistent, [this] is *not* in the manner in which form is a cause *for the composite*" (Avicenna 2005: 196).

How, then, is the form a cause of matter? When we look at the form in relation to the matter, we move away from the *quidditative* to the existential order. The form causes the *existence* of the matter. It only does so, however, "with a partner and a cause that brings into existence the cause, that is, the form." In relation to matter, then, the form acts, not as a *formal* cause, but as an *efficient* cause. "Form would be, as it were, an *efficient principle* for matter, if the existence of matter in act came about through the form alone. It seems, then, that form is a *part* of the efficient cause, as in the case of one of two movers of a boat" (Avicenna 2005: 196). So the form cannot function as the sole cause of the existence of the matter, it acts only as an *instrumental* cause, subordinate to another as yet to be named cause. The form is like an oar, subordinate to the rower of the boat.

Consideration of matter and form, then, leads inexorably to an *extrinsic* efficient cause. "The *agent* bestows from itself existence upon *another thing*, which this latter did not possess" (Avicenna 2005: 196). The agent cause of which Ibn Sīnā speaks here is not the kind of moving cause of which Aristotle spoke, a father who causes a son, a builder who causes a building, or fire which causes warmth (the examples are from Avicenna 2005: 201). For Aristotelian agents operated only in the *quidditative* order, say, the builder shaping its matter into the form of a building. But Ibn Sīnā is talking about a cause of existence: "What it [the effect] has essentially from the [external] agent is *existence*; the existence it possesses is due only to this, that the other thing [= the cause] is of a sort from which there must ensue existence for another, derived from its own existence, which belongs to it essentially" (Avicenna 2005: 197). For Ibn Sīnā, then, the form is the formal cause of the quiddity of the whole, composite substance, to be sure, but also an instrumental efficient cause of the *existence* of the matter, and thereby of the existence of the whole thing, including its accidents. (On final cause, see Druart 2005: 340–1.)

Metaphysical Conclusions: Angels or Intelligences

For Aristotle, there was no problem with the effect existing apart from its efficient cause, the son apart from the father or warmth in the water when it was taken off the fire and poured into the mixing bowl. The reason is because the Philosopher did not distinguish quiddity from existence; the human quiddity of the son—his human form—ensures that he is an actually existing human, and the quiddity "warm" ensures that the water has this accident, at least for a while. Since Ibn Sīnā has distinguished quiddity from existence, he also must distinguish the efficient causes of quiddity and existence. He does so by distinguishing how efficient causality functions in different disciplines: "the *metaphysical* philosophers do not mean by *agent* only the principle of *motion*, as the *natural philosophers* mean, but the principle and giver of *existence*, as in the case of *God* in relation to the world" (Avicenna 2005: 195). In this passage Ibn Sīnā quite clearly shows his view differs from that of Aristotle and proceeds to make it obvious that God is the *ultimate* extrinsic efficient cause of existence; but in his theory of mediated creation, God is not the only such cause.

When initially introducing the external efficient cause of the existence of all sublunar things, Ibn Sīnā does not give it a specific name: "The connection of [form and] matter in its *existence* is owing to *that thing* and a form in whatever manner it proceeds from [that thing] into [matter]" (Avicenna 2005: 67). In explaining how effects require this kind of cause after they are separated from their immediate moving cause, Ibn Sīnā emphasizes that "the *true causes* [in the plural] co-exist with the effect. As for those that are prior [in time], these are causes either accidentally or instrumentally" (Avicenna 2005: 202). A secondary cause, like the builder, educes the new accidental forms of a building from the potency of its matter, as Aristotle had seen, but "the builder, the one called the maker, is *not* the cause of the *complete nature* of the aforementioned building, nor, moreover, of its *existence*" (Avicenna 2005: 201). Rather, "the cause of the building's shape is a combination [of its form and matter], and the cause of [this combination] is the natures of the things being combined and their remaining in the way they are composed, and the cause of these is the *separate cause* that enacts the natures." Ibn Sīnā then gives the separate cause yet another name: "The cause of the son is the combination of his form and matter, through the cause that is the *giver of forms*" (Avicenna 2005: 202).

But there is more than one of these cosmic causes of sublunar things. In Ibn Sīnā's cosmology, there are ten such "intelligences"—his interpretation of Qu'rānic angels—as well as God, the one, ultimate cause:

> The separate intelligences, or rather, the *last* of them, the one closest to us, is the one from which emanates, in participation with the celestial movements, something having the configuration of the forms of the lower world, through passive receptivity to action, just as there is in that intelligence or intelligences the configuration of the forms in actuality. The forms then emanate from it through their being specified [by other factors], not singly by its essence—for the one enacts in the one, as you know, only one thing—but in association with the heavenly bodies.
>
> (Avicenna 2005: 335)

In this passage, we get a sense of the complex way Ibn Sīnā fills out his initial insight that the continued existence of creatures requires an external efficient cause. "This, then, is the meaning for the philosophers of what is called 'creation.' It is the giving of existence to a thing after absolute non-existence. For it belongs to the effect in itself," that is, in its quiddity, "to be non-existent and [then], from its cause, to be existing"

(Avicenna 2005: 203). Ibn Sīnā's philosophical understanding of creation as ontological freed him to follow Aristotle's view that the world is eternal, even though it is created and sempiternal in Ibn Sīnā's metaphysical sense of the term, while only God is properly eternal.

Conclusion

Ibn Sīnā's views about reality do exhibit some important similarities with Aristotle's, but far more striking are the differences. By replacing Aristotle's *metaphysical* principles with his own well-reasoned dialectical argumentation, Ibn Sīnā re-conceived many metaphysical doctrines, only a few of which could we cover here. In sum, Ibn Sīnā's relation to Aristotle is much like Aristotle's to Plato. And this is what made Ibn Sīnā not just the premier philosopher in the Arabic tradition, but one of the very few philosophers of truly world-historical importance.

Further Reading

Adamson, P. (ed.) (2013) *Interpreting Avicenna. Critical Essays*, Cambridge: Cambridge University Press.

Hasse, D. & Bertolacci, A. (eds.) (2012) *The Arabic, Hebrew, and Latin Reception of Avicenna's Metaphysics*, Berlin: Walter de Gruyter.

Houser, R. E. (2011) "Aristotle and Two Aristotelians on the Nature of God," *International Philosophical Quarterly* 51, 3: 355–75.

McGinnis, J. (2010) *Avicenna*, Oxford: Oxford University Press.

References

Aristotle (1936) *Physics*, W. D. Ross (ed.), Oxford: Oxford University Press.

——. (1958) *Metaphysics*, 2 vols., W. D. Ross (ed.), Oxford: Oxford University Press.

——. (1980) *Categories*, L. Minio-Paluello (ed), Oxford: Clarendon Press (originally published in 1949).

——. (1989) *Posterior Analytics*, H. Tredennick (ed. and tr.), Cambridge: Harvard University Press.

Avicenna (1974) *The Life of Ibn Sina*, W. Gohlman (ed. and tr.), New York: State University of New York Press.

——. (2005) *The Metaphysics of The Healing*, M. E. Marmura (tr.), Provo, UT: Brigham Young University Press.

Bertolacci, A. (2006) *The Reception of Aristotle's Metaphysics in Avicenna's Kitâb al-Shifâ'*, Leiden & Boston: Brill.

Burrell, D. (2008) "Creation," in T. Winter (ed.), *The Cambridge Companion to Classical Islamic Theology*, Cambridge: Cambridge University Press, pp. 141–60.

Druart, T-A. (2005) "Metaphysics," in P. Adamson & R. C. Taylor (eds.), *The Cambridge Companion to Arabic Philosophy*, Cambridge: Cambridge University Press, pp. 327–48.

Houser, R. E. (1999) "Let Them Suffer into Truth: Avicenna's Remedy for Those Denying the Axioms of Thought," *American Catholic Philosophical Quarterly* 73: 107–33.

Jolivet, J. (1984) "Aux origines de l'ontologie d'Ibn Sīnā," in J. Jolivet & R. Rashed (eds.), *Études sur Avicenne*, Paris: Les Belles Lettres, pp. 11–28.
Leaman, O. (2008) "The developed *kalām* tradition" in T. Winter (ed.), *The Cambridge Companion to Classical Islamic Theology*, Cambridge: Cambridge University Press, pp. 77–90.
Maurer, A. (1990) "Form and Essence in the Philosophy of St. Thomas," in *Being and Knowing*, Toronto: PIMS (originally published in 1951), pp. 165–76.
Owens, J. (1978) *The Doctrine of Being in the Aristotelian Metaphysics*, Toronto: Pontifical Institute of Mediaeval Studies.
Plato (1963) *Platonis opera* (5 vols.), J. Burnet (ed.), Oxford: Clarendon Press.
Wisnovsky, R. (2003) *Avicenna's Metaphysics in Context*, Ithaca, New York: Cornell University Press.
——. (2005) "Avicenna," in P. Adamson & R. C. Taylor (eds.), *The Cambridge Companion to Arabic Philosophy*, Cambridge: Cambridge University Press, pp. 92–136.

18
PRIMARY AND SECONDARY CAUSALITY

Richard C. Taylor

In the study of philosophy today, the nature of primary and secondary causality is often discussed under the headings of creation, concurrence, and conservation. Each of these involves consideration of the way God as primary cause efficiently brings about and sustains reality as a whole, and even acts through other secondary causes to sustain all individual things. Different from Deism which generally requires Divine involvement only at the start of the universe, and from Occasionalism (Lee 2014) which requires Divine immediate involvement in every action in the universe, the doctrine of primary and secondary causality takes a middle ground. It seeks to explain how the Divine first cause is both remote from lower effects arising from a plurality of intermediary causes and at the same time somehow powerfully present to those distant effects (Kvanvig 2007).

The doctrine of primary and secondary causality arose in the Arabic philosophical tradition in the ninth century C.E. as a product of the Circle of al-Kindī (Endress 1997; Adamson 2006, 2011) in a work called *Kalām fī maḥḍ al-khair* or *Discourse on the Pure Good*, a metaphysical account of emanation and creation. This short treatise is crafted carefully from selected Arabic translations of the *Elements of Theology* by Proclus (d. 485) into an important work on the mediate creation of the world by God as First Cause (d'Ancona & Taylor 2003). An important related work of this Circle was the *Theology of Aristotle*, a treatise edited by al-Kindī and constructed from materials known as the *Plotiniana Arabica*, Arabic translations of parts of the famous Greek *Enneads* by the founder of Neoplatonism, Plotinus (d'Ancona 1989, 1999, 2011). The author of the *Kalām fī maḥḍ al-khair* was quite familiar with this work and draws on it in several chapters. Though the author treats of the emanation of eternal intellects, celestial souls and celestial bodies and other metaphysical topics, its major focus is on creation. Still, strictly speaking, its famous first chapter (*bab*) does not mention creation but rather focuses on the principles and consequences of primary and secondary causality. The apparent purpose of the *Kalām fī maḥḍ al-khair* is to show how, in the origination of an ordered hierarchy of causes and effects, the primary cause has greater causal efficacy than related secondary causes inside any effect. In this way the primary cause is argued to be more present to the effect than any secondary cause. As we will see below, this reasoning, when combined with the assertion of divine creation of all reality, yields an argument for mediate creation in which it is maintained that only God acts by creation. Though this work and its doctrine played a key role in the development of medieval European theology and philosophy through its Latin translation (d'Ancona & Taylor 2003), here it will be chiefly considered in its original Arabic. Although this work has been contended to have had a profound influence on the entire Arabic philosophical tradition (d'Ancona 2010), this contribution focuses on the doctrine of primary and secondary causality in explication of creation in the *Kalām fī maḥḍ al-khair* and also in Ibn Sīnā, the greatest of the thinkers of the Classical period.

In what follows here I first provide an account of the issue of primary and secondary causality in the *Elements of Theology* of Proclus, the major source for the *Kalām fī maḥḍ al-khair*. I then explicate the meaning and import of the doctrine with respect to the notion of creation in the *Kalām fī maḥḍ al-khair*. Next I examine this doctrine as it manifests itself in the metaphysics of Ibn Sīnā. And finally I conclude with some remarks on the importance of this philosophical teaching among philosophers in both the Arabic and the Latin traditions in the medieval period.

Proclus as Source of the Doctrine of Primary and Secondary Causality

The *Elements of Theology* by Proclus (Proclus 1963) is a metaphysical treatment of the hierarchy of realities that extends from the transcendent One through levels of henads, intellects, souls, celestial bodies, and earthly things through to the exhaustion of emanation in matter. Only a small number of key texts of the *Elements of Theology* in Arabic translation are drawn upon by the unknown author of the *Kalām fī maḥḍ al-khair* to express the reasoned foundation for the teaching of primary and secondary causality which later the author calls creation (*ibdā'*, Taylor 2012). These texts are Propositions 56, 70 and probably 57 (d'Ancona 1999). They all have to do with an emanative efficient causality but can be extended to other forms of causality as well.

In Prop. 56 Proclus writes "All that is produced by secondary beings is in a greater measure produced from those prior and more determinative principles from which the secondary were themselves derived." To show this he reasons that insofar as the primary cause provides the whole being of the secondary cause, it also provides the power of operation or action belonging to the nature of the secondary cause. In this way the prior cause is also cause of the effect that the secondary brings about. Hence, that effect owes its nature as such to the first cause in the hierarchy. Further,

> it is evident that the effect is determined by the superior principle in a greater measure. For if the latter has conferred on the secondary being the causality which enabled it to produce, it must itself have possessed this causality primitively (prop. 18), and it is in virtue of this that the secondary being generates, having derived from its prior the capacity of secondary generation. But if the secondary is productive by participation, the primal primitively and by communication, the latter is causative in a greater measure, inasmuch as it has communicated to another the power of generating consequents.
>
> (Proclus 1963: 54–5)

According to this teaching which involves participation, causal origination, and production by emanation, greater causality should be attributed to the superior cause. This is because it originates the very essence as well as the powers of causality belonging to the secondary cause. For the very ability to act as a causal agent in the production of another (third) thing is provided to the second cause in its production by the prior cause. Yet to do so, the prior cause has to have had in itself the characteristic of efficacy or causal activity in a more primitive way. That passes on a sharing participation to enable the secondary thing to act and generate another.

The principles at work in Prop. 56 are summarized in a very clear way as follows in Prop. 57:

> [T]he powers which are in the consequent are present in a greater measure in the cause. For all that is produced by secondary beings is produced in a greater measure by prior and more determinative principles (prop. 56). The cause, then, is cooperative in the production of all that the consequent is capable of producing.
>
> And if it first produces the consequent itself, it is of course plain that it is operative before the latter in the activity which produces it. Thus every cause operates both prior to its consequent and in conjunction with it, and likewise gives rise to further effects posterior to it.
>
> (Proclus 1963: 54–7)

The author of the *Kalām fī maḥḍ al-khair*, however, expresses this by rephrasing and simplifying in order to form the principle, "Every primary cause emanates more abundantly on its effect than does the universal second cause" (Taylor 2012) and then goes on to draw heavily from Prop. 70.

The third text in the formation of the doctrine of primary and secondary causality in the *Elements of Theology* of Proclus is Prop. 70. This proposition upholds the priority of the primary cause and asserts that the long reach of the primary cause adheres deeply in the effect produced by the secondary cause: "All those more universal characters which inhere in the originative principles both irradiate their participants before the specific characters and are slower to withdraw from a being which has once shared in them." The example and explanation provided by Proclus makes this clear:

> [F]or example, a thing must exist before it has life, and have life before it is human. And again, when the logical faculty has failed it is no longer human, but it is still a living thing, since it breathes and feels; and when life in turn has abandoned it existence remains to it, for even when it ceases to live it still has being. So in every case. The reason is that the higher cause, being more efficacious (prop. 56), operates sooner upon the participant (for where the same thing is affected by two causes it is affected first by the more powerful); and in the activity of the secondary the higher is co-operative, because all the effects of the secondary are concomitantly generated by the more determinative cause; and where the former has withdrawn the latter is still present (for the gift of the more powerful principle is slower to abandon

> the participant, being more efficacious, and also inasmuch as through the gift of its consequent it has made its own irradiation stronger).
>
> (Proclus 1963: 66–7)

Here Proclus explains by an analysis of formalities present in a thing that they must have an ordered priority: what is a more foundational formality remains 'longer' in a thing. Here some 'earlier' formalities play the role of underlying subjects or necessary conditions for other 'later' formalities. In this way the higher cause of formality operates 'sooner' than a lower specifying formality only insofar as what it causes is a necessary condition for what some other secondary cause provides to a thing. The temporal language here is solely used to reflect levels of ontological foundations. For Proclus this means that a higher or prior productive cause is more deeply present in an effect of a secondary cause than is the secondary cause considered in its own right. Moreover, the primary cause is more causally efficacious in its productive activity and its power and thereby is more present to the effect than a secondary cause which does not act wholly in its own right. This means that the power of the One is present and acting through all intermediaries. It can thus be cogently said to be acting in each and every thing at the foundational level by providing the most universal formality which is the subject for later determinative formalities from secondary causes. This is why the primary productive cause is found causally present throughout all reality, even in that part of reality that is most remote from the primary cause itself.

Primary and Secondary Causality as Creation in the *Kalām fī maḥḍ al-khair*

Standing alone at the start of the *Kalām fī maḥḍ al-khair*, the initial chapter sets forth a simplified paraphrase of the doctrine of primary and secondary causality found in Proclus as a principle employed throughout the work. The first paragraph reflects this clearly even if in a controverted way:

> Every primary cause emanates more abundantly on its effect than does the universal second cause. And when the universal second cause removes its power from the thing, the universal first cause does not remove its power from it. For the universal first cause acts on the effect of the second cause before the universal second cause which is immediately adjacent to (the effect) acts on (the effect). So when the second cause which is immediately adjacent to the effect acts, its act is not able to do without the first cause which is above (the second cause). And when the second (cause) separates itself from the effect which is immediately adjacent to it, the first cause which is above (the second cause) does not separate itself from (the effect), because it is cause of (the effect's) cause. The first cause, therefore, is more the cause of the thing than its proximate cause which is immediately adjacent to (the thing).
>
> (Taylor 2012: 123)

This is a less complex restatement of the principle of primary and secondary causality in an ordered hierarchy found in Proclus. It explains the constitution of a thing having formalities where the lower are necessary conditions for the higher. Following Proclus's Prop. 70, the author goes on to provide his own paraphrase of the proposition's example with lower and broader formalities. The formality of *living* remains in a thing even with the removal of a higher formality for which it is a necessary condition or needed subject. *Living* cannot be present without *being* which is its necessary condition or subject. In turn, *living* is itself a necessary condition or subject for *rational*. When *rational* is removed, the formality *living* is not necessarily removed since the thing remains living even without rationality. When *living* is removed the thing still persists in existence since *being* is not necessarily removed. The context, of course, is Neoplatonic and logical, not that of a consideration of the Aristotelian philosophy of particular substances of the natural world.

The author then concludes the opening chapter with a clear account of the doctrine in his own words:

> So it has become clear and evident that the remote first cause is more encompassing and more a cause of the thing than its proximate cause. On account of that, its act has come to be more strongly adherent to the thing than the act of (the thing's) proximate cause. This came to be so only because the thing is first acted on by the remote power, then secondly it is acted on by the power which is below the first. <Moreover,> the first cause aids the second cause in its act because every act which the second cause effects, the first cause also effects, except that (the first cause) effects it in another, transcendent and more sublime manner. And when the second cause separates itself from its effect, the first cause does not separate itself from it because the act of the first cause is mightier and more strongly adherent to the thing than the act of its proximate cause. Furthermore, the effect of the second cause has been made stable only through the power of the first cause. For, when the second cause effects a thing, the first cause which is above (the second cause) emanates on that thing from its power so that it strongly adheres to that thing and conserves it. Thus, it has become clear and evident that the remote first cause is more a cause of the thing than its proximate cause which is immediately adjacent to (the thing) and that it emanates its power on it and conserves it and does not separate itself from it with the separation of its proximate cause, but rather it remains in it and strongly adheres to it in accordance with what we have made clear and evident.
>
> (Taylor 2012: 124)

It is important to highlight the key notion established here since in later parts of the *Kalām fī maḥḍ al-khair* the author connects it with the notion of creation (d'Ancona 1993–94), a term not found in this first chapter. Here the author emphasizes that any primary but remote cause in a defined hierarchy of things can rightfully be regarded as the cause bringing about all that secondary causes produced by it bring about. Further, a foundational formality, such as that of *being* used in the example, may be caused by a prior cause through secondary causes and remain in place with the removal of the secondary cause. This, however, is not merely the doctrine of primary and secondary causality but also the foundation for a doctrine of mediate creation.

This doctrine of mediate creation is set forth in Chapter 3 of the *Kalām fī maḥḍ al-khair*. There the author states that "the First Cause created the being of the soul through the mediation of the intelligence" (Taylor 1981: 148, 287), a teaching found in the *Enneads* of Plotinus and reflected in the *Plotiniana Arabica*, a work on which the author draws a number of times. Mediate creation is also set out in Chapter 8 which is based on the *Plotiniana Arabica*, not the *Elements of Theology* of Proclus (Taylor 1986, 1998; d'Ancona 1990, 1992). There the author indicates that the First Cause is the creator of intelligence without mediation and "the creator of soul, nature and all other things through the mediation of the intelligence" (Taylor 1981: 178–9, 299). And in Chapter 17 he adds, "The First Being is unmoving and is the cause of causes. If it gives all things being, it gives it to them by way of creation (*ibdā'*) … for the way of creation belongs to the First Cause alone" (Taylor 1981: 215–16, 312 tr. mod.).

For the author of the *Kalām fī maḥḍ al-khair* the sketch of primary and secondary causality in Proclus's *Elements of Theology* provided an account that permits the causality of the First Cause to be understood to permeate all reality. It also supplied the author with reasons to ground the view that the most fundamental formality of all things, being, can be traced only back to the First Cause which is pure being (Chapter 8) and the cause of being by way of creation, a causality restricted to the First Cause alone. Here being is not only the foundational formal subject or necessary condition for the reception of other formalities such as life and rationality. It is also something that is given by emanation and traced to only one thing, the First Cause. While accepting an account of mediate causality from Proclus, this author transforms that doctrine into one asserting that the sole cause of being can only be the First Cause which acts through creation. Hence, in this doctrine the name *Creator* (*al-Mubdi'*) is restricted to the First Cause alone since the activity of creation can be traced to none but God.

In contrast to early modern notions of Deism, here the Creator God is fully present to and active in all created things at all times. This is in radical contrast to later developments in the Islamic theological milieu of the doctrine of Occasionalism which assigns all action to God alone and no power of acting to secondary causes. Here through the use of Greek philosophical reasoning, the author of the *Kalām fī maḥḍ al-khair* provides a metaphysical account consonant with Divine creation and primary causality that respects the formal natures of things allowing them too to be active causes employed by God in the constitution of reality. Now it remains to see just how Ibn Sīnā accepts and explains the doctrine of primary and secondary causality.

Primary and Secondary Causality in the Metaphysics of Ibn Sīnā

Ibn Sīnā sets out his own teaching on primary and secondary causality in the *Metaphysics* of the *Shifā'*. He reasons that there is one first cause of all things, the *wājib al-wujūd* or Necessary Being, which originates all things by creation (*ibdā'*) and which remains transcendent above all created being. In his account, all things other than the First are mere possibles which for their existence require necessitation of existence though the efficient creative causality of the First. Now, it is important to note that the *Kalām fī maḥḍ al-khair* does not have the Farabian cosmological hierarchy of eternal intelligences, celestial souls and celestial bodies spelled out in a hierarchical rank as does Ibn Sīnā. Yet there is still considerable overlap: just as in the *Kalām fī maḥḍ al-khair*, Ibn Sīnā holds that what is first created is intelligence and that through the first created intelligence plurality is introduced (d'Ancona 2007). For the First Cause Itself can have only one act since it is pure unity without any distinction in its essence between its existence and its activity. This latter understanding of the identity of being and activity in the First is also found in the *Plotiniana Arabica* and the *Theology of Aristotle* (Adamson 2002) and is reflected in the *Kalām fī maḥḍ al-khair*, Chapter 19.

Ibn Sīnā is writing long past the era of al-Kindī and the initial entré of Greek philosophical thought into an Islamic milieu deeply suspicious of foreign metaphysical teachings that might undermine central religious doctrines. As in all philosophical matters, Ibn Sīnā takes his own distinctive path in agreeing with the transcendent priority of the First Cause as creator, while preferring to provide an analysis of the notion of creation (*ibdā'*) different from that of the author of the *Kalām fī maḥḍ al-khair*. In his *Metaphysics* he argues against the doctrine of the *Kalām fī maḥḍ al-khair* that creation (*ibdā'*) is something to be reserved alone to the First Cause, God, *al-Mubdi'*. Instead he holds that each of the intelligences in the cascading emanative hierarchy also creates lower intelligences, celestial souls and celestial bodies down to the level of the agent intellect.

> This, then, is the meaning that, for the philosophers, is termed 'creation (*ibdā'*).' It is the giving of existence to a thing after absolute nonexistence. For it belongs to the effect in itself to be nonexistent and [then] to be, by its cause, existing.
>
> (Avicenna 2005: 203)

Such a notion, then, also belongs to those creating intelligences since each carries out precisely the action of "giving of existence to a thing after absolute nonexistence." Yet Ibn Sīnā also makes a crucial distinction. He writes the important following remarks in his *Metaphysics* which are helpful for the interpretation of what he says of creation (*ibdā'*) in his *Book of Definitions* which will be considered later.

> This is the meaning of a thing's being created—that is, attaining existence from another. It has absolute nonexistence which it deserves in terms of itself; it is deserving of nonexistence not only in terms of its form without its matter, or in terms of its matter without its form, but in its entirety. Hence, if its entirety is not connected with the necessitation of the being that brings about its existence, and it is reckoned as being dissociated from it, then in its entirety its nonexistence becomes necessary. Hence, its coming into being at the hands of what brings about its existence does so in its entirety. No part of it, in relation to this meaning, is prior in existence—neither its matter nor its form, if it possesses matter and form.
>
> (Avicenna 2005: 272, tr. mod.)

Then he adds,

> This, then, is absolute creation. Bringing into existence [in the] absolute [sense] is not [just] any kind of bringing into existence. And everything is originated from that One, that One being the originator of it, since the originated is that which comes into being after not having been. ... Hence, in the case of everything other than the First, the One, its existence comes about after not having been, [a nonbeing] that it itself deserves.
>
> (Avicenna 2005: 272–3, tr. mod.)

In this passage from *Metaphysics* Book 9 Ibn Sīnā provides an account of the necessary and the possible which finds emanation as the installation of plurality in the world by God. He then goes on to assert that origination as *ibdāʿ* which was reserved by the earlier tradition (surely referring to the Arabic *Plotiniana Arabica* and Arabic *Liber de causis*) to God alone as creation can in fact be appropriately asserted in the description of the activity of the mediate intellects in the emanative hierarchy (Avicenna 2005: 331). Like the author of the *Kalām fī maḥḍ al-khair*, Ibn Sīnā teaches mediate creation, even though he also continues to hold the doctrine of primary causality tracing every entity back to the First Cause. In this way Ibn Sīnā allows for intelligences after the First Cause to be creators of what is below them.

This is corroborated in his *Book of Definitions* as well as in other works (Janssens 1997). In the *Book of Definitions* Ibn Sīnā insists that the meaning of *ibdāʿ* be divided into two sorts:

> Creation (*ibdāʿ*) is an equivocal term with two meanings. (1) One of them is the making of existence (*taʾyīs*) of the thing not from [another] thing and not through an intermediary thing. (2) The second meaning is absolute existence from a cause without intermediary, while of itself (*dhāti-hi*) it is not a being (*maujūdan*) and what belongs to it in its own essence (*min dhāti-hi*) is totally left lacking [from it].
>
> (Avicenna 1963: 42–3; cf. Janssens 1997: 471; Kennedy-Day 2003: 114)

The first of these, creation$_1$ (*ibdāʿ*$_1$) is predicated only of God's activity of primary causality in the origination of the first created intelligence, the first and only entity solely caused by the Divine act alone. The second, creation$_2$ (*ibdāʿ*$_2$), involves the way in which an intellect in the hierarchy efficiently causes by creation the existence of another eternal intellect, celestial soul and celestial body in what is immediately below in the emanation. This latter is true mediate creation as it takes place in a hierarchy of intellects which are both created and creating.

In the case of creation$_1$ the First Cause and True One, God, is the sole Creator, Itself uncaused and without anything prior to it. As we have seen, this doctrine is already found in the *Kalām fī maḥḍ al-khair* and in the *Plotiniana Arabica*. God is ultimately responsible for the existence of all reality, and He alone deserves the name of Creator (*Mubdiʿ*) in the view of the authors of these works. This reflects the doctrine of primary causality spelled out in the opening chapter of the *Kalām fī maḥḍ al-khair*, a doctrine found also in al-Kindī's *On the True Agent* (al-Kindī 2012). In contrast, although Ibn Sīnā too accepts that there is ultimately one Creator, he introduces a distinction of two senses for the use of the term creation (*ibdā'*). He reasons that in the emanative hierarchy each of the intelligences truly creates what is below it and so the use of the term creation (*ibdā'*) is appropriate. This is not precisely like the activity of God whose act does not presuppose anything before Him, because in this case each intelligence exists only because it is created by another intelligence prior to and above it. God, however, is an uncaused cause. This extension of the term creation (*ibdā'*) to secondary causes does not occur in the *Kalām fī maḥḍ al-khair* and *Plotiniana Arabica* but rather is an innovation by Ibn Sīnā since in his emanative hierarchy each of the intelligences truly creates what is below it.

The phraseology in the passage in the *Book of Definitions* is somewhat difficult but its meaning is clear. Creation_1 is the activity by which being is caused in something else without any presupposed subject and without intermediary by what is an uncaused cause. This is the causality of God in creating the first intelligence. In the case of creation_2 the cause does not itself have being in its essence but rather has received it from another above it. In creation_2 a caused and created being—the existence of which has come from another—is able to create_2 another thing by mediate creation. In the case of the first created intelligence, for Ibn Sīnā that intelligence does not exist in its own right—since it exists only thanks to the First Cause—yet it does create_2 what is below it in the hierarchy. The difference in these two kinds of creation is that creation_1 is an activity of the essence of an uncaused cause, while creation_2 is an activity of a caused cause, a mediate creator. This is an expression of the notion that all things except God are possible beings such that their existence is not found in their essences and so must be received from what is above. Hence, while the second highest intelligence as well is a giver of existence and a creator_2, it remains a mediator and a secondary cause simply because it is a possible being which has received its necessity of existence from God who is above it. In contrast, God as the Necessary Being is dependent upon nothing and is the primary cause of all.

Conclusion

Various versions of the doctrine of primary and secondary causality can be found in the thought of other major philosophers of the Islamic tradition. The version considered here is an explanation of creation by thinkers of the Circle of al-Kindī and the tradition's most influential philosopher, Ibn Sīnā, whose writings were widely influential if not foundational for centuries. But it is important to note that the influence of this doctrine extended well beyond its original realm to thinkers of the European philosophical and theological traditions of the twelfth century and beyond through the Latin translation of the *Kalām fī maḥḍ al-khair* known as the *Liber de causis* (*Book of Causes*). Through this translation and through the translation of Ibn Sīnā's *Metaphysics*, the reasoned doctrine of primary and secondary causality in creation developed in the Islamic milieu, later flourished in European thought and became a central issue both in philosophical metaphysics and in the theological interpretation of Scripture. In metaphysics it received new interpretations in dozens of commentaries authored by figures such as Aquinas, Albert the Great, Roger Bacon and many more (Taylor 1983). In theology it played a role in theological commentaries in the consideration of the roles of human authors as secondary causes in the communication of Divine revelation by God as primary cause. In short, this philosophical teaching from the Islamic tradition truly came to be a central part of the European tradition in philosophy and theology, as is the case for other teachings presented in this volume. This is yet another instance in which it is obvious that philosophy in the tradition of Islam is part of what today is called the Western philosophical tradition.

Further Reading

Adamson, P. (2015) "Al-Kindī," in E. N. Zalta (ed.), *The Stanford Encyclopedia of Philosophy*, http://plato.stanford.edu/archives/spr2014/entries/al-kindi/

d'Ancona, C. (2011) "The Arabic Plotinus," in H. Lagerlund (ed.), *Encyclopedia of Medieval Philosophy. Philosophy Between 500 and 1500*, Dordrecht: Springer, pp. 1030–8.

——. (2014) "The Liber de causis," in L. G. Gerson (ed.), *Interpreting Proclus*, Cambridge: Cambridge University Press, pp. 137–61.

Helmig, C. & Steel, C. (2012) "Proclus," in Edward N. Zalta (ed.), *The Stanford Encyclopedia of Philosophy*, http://plato.stanford.edu/archives/sum2012/entries/proclus/

McGinnis, J. (2010) *Avicenna*, Oxford: Oxford University Press.

References

Adamson, P. (2002) *The Arabic Plotinus. A Philosophical Study of the Theology of Aristotle*, London: Duckworth.

——. (2006) *Al-Kindi*, Oxford: Oxford University Press.

——. (2015) "Al-Kindi," in E. N. Zalta (ed.), *The Stanford Encyclopedia of Philosophy*, http://plato.stanford.edu/archives/spr2011/entries/al-kindi/

al-Kindī (2012) *The Philosophical Works of al-Kindi*, P. Adamson & P. Pormann (tr.), Oxford: Oxford University Press.

Avicenna (1963) *Avicenne. Livre des Définitions*. A.-M. Goichon (ed.), Cairo: Publications de l'Institut Français d'Archéologie Orientale du Caire.

——. (2005) *The Metaphysics of the Healing*, M. E. Marmura (tr.), Provo, UT: Brigham Young University Press.

d'Ancona, C. (1989) "Le fonti e la struttura del Liber de causis," *Medioevo. Rivista di storia della filosofia medievale* 15, pp. 1–38.

——. (1990) "'Cause prime non est yliathim'. *Liber de Causis*, prop. 8[9]: le fonti e la dottrina," *Documenti e Studi sulla tradizione filosofica medievale* 1: 327–51.

——. (1992) "La doctrine de la création 'mediante intelligentia' dans le Liber de Causis et dans ses sources," *Revue des Sciences Philosophiques et Théologiques* 76: 209–33.

——. (1993–1994) "La dottrina della creazione nel *Liber de Causis*," *Doctor Seraphicus* 40–1: 133–49.

——. (1999) "La notion de 'cause' dans les textes Néoplatoniciens arabes," in C. Chiesa & L. Freuler (eds.), *Métaphysiques Médiévales. Études en l'honneur d'Andre de Muralt*, Geneva: Cahiers de la Revue de Théologie et de Philosophie 20, pp. 47–68.

——. 2007. "Ex uno non fit nisi unum. Storia e preistoria della dottrina avicenniana della Prima Intelligenza," in E. Canone (ed.), *Per una storia del concetto di mente*, II, Florence: Olschki, pp. 29–55.

——. (2010) "Plotinus and later Platonic philosophers on the causality of the First Principle," in L. P. Gerson (ed.), *The Cambridge Companion to Plotinus*, Cambridge: Cambridge University Press, v. 2, 869–93, 1170–8.

——. (2011) "Plotinus, Arabic," in H. Lagerlund (ed.), *Encyclopedia of Medieval Philosophy. Philosophy Between 500 and 1500*, Dordrecht: Springer, pp. 1030–8.

d'Ancona, C. & Taylor, R. C. (2003) "Le Liber de causis" in Richard Goulet et al. (eds.), *Dictionnaire de Philosophes Antiques. Supplément*, Paris: CNRS Edition, pp. 599–647.

Endress, G. (1997) "The Circle of al-Kindī," in G. Endress and R. Kruk (eds.), *The Ancient Tradition in Christian and Islamic Hellenism*, Leiden: Research School CNWS, pp. 43–76.

Janssens, J. (1997) "Creation and Emanation in Ibn Sina," *Documenti e Studi sulla Tradizione Filosofica Medievale* 8: 454–77.

Kennedy-Day, K. (2003) *Books of Definition in Islamic Philosophy. The Limits of Words*, London: Routledge Curzon.

Kvanvig, Jonathan (2007) "Creation and Conservation," in Edward N. Zalta (ed.), *The Stanford Encyclopedia of Philosophy*, http://plato.stanford.edu/archives/fall2008/entries/creation-conservation/

Lee, S. (2014) "Occasionalism," in Edward N. Zalta (ed.), *The Stanford Encyclopedia of Philosophy*, http://plato.stanford.edu/archives/spr2014/entries/occasionalism/

Proclus (1963) *Elements of Theology*, E. R. Dodds (ed. & tr.), Oxford: Oxford University Press.

Taylor, R. C. (1981) *The Liber de causis (Kalām fi maḥḍ al-khair): A Study of Medieval Neoplatonism*, Doctoral Dissertation, University of Toronto, Canada.

——. (1983) "The *Liber de causis*: A Preliminary List of Extant MSS," *Bulletin de Philosophie Médiévale* 25: 63–84.

——. (1986) "The *Kalam fi mahd al-khair* (*Liber de causis*) in the Islamic Philosophical Milieu," in *Pseudo-Aristotle in the Middle Ages*, J. Kraye et al. (eds.), London: The Warburg Institute, University of London, pp. 37–52.

——. (1998) "Aquinas, the *Plotiniana Arabica*, and the Metaphysics of Being and Actuality," *Journal of the History of Ideas* 59: 217–39.

——. (2012) "Primary Causality and *ibdā'* (*creare*) in the *Liber de causis*," *Wahrheit und Geschichte. Die gebrochene Tradition metaphhyischen Denkens. Festschrift zum 70 Geburtstag von Günther Mensching*, A. Mensching-Estakhr & M. Städtler (eds.), Würzburg: Königshausen & Neumann, pp. 115–36

19
METAPHYSICS OF GOD

Jules Janssens

Introduction

When philosophy, and with it metaphysics, entered the world of Islam in the ninth century, it was certainly a current of thought that had its ultimate roots in Greece. Plato and Aristotle figured as its major founders and with late Hellenistic thinkers it was believed that there were essentially no major differences between their respective doctrines. However, partly by some challenges coming from the "new" religion, partly by further independent reflection, a new kind of philosophy, including metaphysics, was developed inside the classical Islamic world. Already in al-Kindī, the "father" of Arabic-Islamic philosophy, the development of a new metaphysics can be detected. He calls it *al-falsafa al-ūlā*, "First Philosophy," as evident from the title of his major work on this subject, and clearly defines it as a theology: "The noblest part of philosophy and the highest in rank is the First Philosophy, i.e. knowledge of the First Truth Who is the cause of all truth" (al-Kindī 1974: 56). This might at first sight look like a fundamentally Neoplatonic concept of metaphysics. However, a closer inspection shows that he no longer understands the One's causality in Neoplatonic terms of production by participation, but in rather monotheistic Islamic terms as the bringing into existence. At the same time, in a similar vein, he makes Aristotle's Unmoved Mover an explicit cause of being, not just of motion. All in all, one detects in the way he conceives and elaborates his metaphysics, a combination of Aristotelian, Neoplatonic and Islamic elements (d'Ancona-Costa 1996: 11–16; Adamson 2005). As for al-Fārābī, the "Second Master" (Aristotle being the "First"), he, at least compared to al-Kindī, reshaped the project of metaphysics fundamentally. In spite of important modifications in expression in different works, it is beyond any reasonable doubt that he distinguishes three major parts in the science of metaphysics: an ontology, i.e. the study of "being *qua* being"; an archē-ololology, i.e. the study of the foundations of the particular sciences; and a theology, i.e. the study of the divine as foundational of the universe (Martini Bonadeo 2005: 400–2). In this sense, metaphysics is for him "what (comes) after physics" (*mā ba'd aṭ-ṭabī'a*), whereas the "divine science" (*al-'ilm al-ilāhī*) is only part of it (al-Fārābī 1890: 34–5). Even when he designates by this latter expression the entirety of the discipline of metaphysics, as for example in the fourth chapter of his *Enumeration of the Sciences* (*Iḥṣā' al-'ulūm*), he still continues to distinguish the three parts (al-Fārābī 1932: 50–2 [Arabic]). Hence, it is obvious that he wants to do more justice to the entirety of Aristotle's *Metaphysics* than al-Kindī's outspoken theological approach had done. Certainly, inside metaphysics, theology remains a crucial issue, since it deals with the ultimate grounding of our world. In al-Fārābī's view this was also a major concern for Aristotle. However, the latter failed to explain the relation between the divine and the natural beings, and therefore al-Fārābī consciously introduced the Neoplatonic idea of emanation, albeit in a highly developed way that takes into account the planetary motions according to Ptolemy's astronomy (Reisman 2005: 56–60; Black 1996:187–9; Druart 1987). As to the centrality of this metaphysics of the divine for al-Fārābī, it is sufficient to look at the contents of his major work *On the Perfect State* (*Al-madīna al-fāḍila*), which starts with discussing the "First Cause." In sum, the divine is not absent in al-Fārābī's metaphysics but it is no longer its exclusive subject. Moreover, one looks in vain for typical Islamic influences: al-Fārābī's God is the God of the philosophers and his religion is "philosophy."

Ibn Sīnā's "New" Metaphysics

Metaphysics arrived at a high peak in the classical period of Islam in Ibn Sīnā, known as Avicenna in the Latin tradition. He received the honorary title of *al-shaykh al-ra'īs*, "the eminent Sheikh." Undoubtedly his elaboration of a "new" metaphysics, which became a milestone of Western metaphysical thought (Bertolacci 2006; Verbeke 1983), largely contributed to his receiving this title. With al-Fārābī, he recognizes three parts in metaphysics, but he, more than his predecessor, construes them as a unified science and thus lays the foundation of what one with Heidegger may call an onto-theology. This perspective clearly prevails in his major philosophical encyclopedia, i.e. *The Healing* (*al-Shifā'*), where—in spite of the insistence on the fact that "being *qua* being" is its proper subject—metaphysics is designated by the term *Ilāhiyyāt* (Divine things). This is also the case in most of his other minor encyclopedias, including *The Salvation* (*al-Najāt*). A major exception might constitute his most debated and partly lost work *The Easterners* (*al-Mashriqiyyūn*). There one reads in the section, entitled "On the evocation of the sciences": "It has become common practice to call … the third part [of the theoretical sciences dealing with things totally separated from matter and motion] Theology, and the fourth [dealing with things sometimes associated with matter] Universal [Science], even though this division is not one established by a long tradition" (Avicenna 1910: 7, 5–7; Gutas 1988: 254, tr. mod.). Somewhat later (8, 8–10) Ibn Sīnā affirms that he will limit himself to present only a few kinds of sciences, and mentions among these few both the universal science (*al-'ilm al-kullī*) and theology (*al-'ilm al-ilāhī*). This could indicate that he sharply distinguishes between the study of ontology and that of theology. But this is far from being sure. In fact, Ibn Sīnā mainly indicates that the division with which we are concerned was not a very old one at his time, and hence has no foundation in classical Greek thought, but rather in one of his predecessors in the Islamic world, al-Fārābī being perhaps the best candidate. But he does not explain why he uses this division, nor does he clarify in which way. In any case, theology remains a fundamental part of metaphysics and it looks doubtful that Ibn Sīnā would have profoundly dissolved the unity of metaphysics, since in the other works of almost the same period one finds no trace justifying such a move.

If metaphysics is a unified project, what is God's exact place in it? Ibn Sīnā—notwithstanding his acceptance of the Kindian appellation *al-falsafa al-ūlā* (Bertolacci 2006: 601–2) and his own preference for the designation *Ilāhiyyāt*—makes it clear from the very beginning that God cannot properly figure as its subject matter: "The existence of God—exalted be His greatness—cannot be admitted as the subject matter in this science; rather, it is [something] sought in it" (Avicenna 2005: 3). Let us for the moment allow that God is not the subject matter of metaphysics. However, what proves that His existence is something sought in it? For Ibn Sīnā this is almost self-evident because God is by definition the highest of all beings, and the study of the highest of all beings naturally belongs to the highest of all sciences, i.e. metaphysics. This looks quite reasonable, but what then about Aristotle's famous argument of the Unmoved Mover? Based on the undeniable reality of motion, as well as on the impossibility of an infinite regress, Aristotle had argued that one has to accept the existence of a First Mover who has not received motion from something else. The major development of the proof is present in his *Physics* VII–VIII, but one finds also a small allusion in his *Metaphysics, Lambda*, 7. In view of this later quotation, many commentators—or even the vast majority of them—have considered it as a genuine metaphysical proof for God's existence. Ibn Sīnā, however, sharply disagrees with this interpretation. For him it is inconceivable that one can prove God's existence based on the physical notion of motion, and, moreover, in his eyes Aristotle never intended to do so:

> He [Ibn Sīnā] said in criticism of Aristotle and (especially) the Commentators: It is inappropriate to reach the First Truth by way of motion, i.e. the one (establishing) that He is the principle of motion, and out of this to strain oneself to posit Him as a (separate) principle for the essences, for (these) people have not shown more that he [Aristotle-reading with the manuscripts *min ithbātihi*] has established that God is a mover, not that He is a principle for what is existent. How astonishing is it to think that motion is the way to establish (the existence) of the One, the True, Who is the principle of all being.
> (Avicenna 1947: 23, 21–4; 2014: 49, 47–51)

For Ibn Sīnā to prove that God is a principle of motion, even in the characterization of the Unmoved Mover, can in no way constitute a metaphysical proof for the divine existence. In fact, motion is part of the proper subject of the science of nature: "The subject matter of [physics] is the sensible body insofar it is subject to change" (Avicenna 2009: 3). Hence, the proof of the Unmoved Mover belongs properly to the science of physics. Thus, it is normal that Aristotle developed it in his work related to this science. Yet, he created an ambiguity by evoking it in the context of the theological part of his *Metaphysics*. However, he never states that it is a metaphysical proof for God's existence.

While he in all likelihood believed that the pseudo-*Theology*, which offers a paraphrase of some of Plotinus' *Enneads*, forms a genuine Aristotelian writing, or, if not by him, offers at least the real theology Aristotle had in mind, Ibn Sīnā is convinced that this latter conceived God at the metaphysical level as a principle of being rather than as a principle of motion. Therefore, Ibn Sīnā finds it a scandal that some of the

Commentators (in all likelihood Alexander of Aphrodisias, Themistius, and the like) have given the impression that the argument of the Unmoved Mover figured in Aristotle as a final metaphysical proof for God's existence, especially since motion always presupposes an already existing substratum and thus cannot be the full cause of the existence of something. In sum, the argument of the Unmoved Mover is unsuited to show God as the efficient cause of everything. At best, it can indicate He is the encompassing final cause. As final cause, God attracts everything to Him: "The First Mover moves by way of a desire to imitate Him" (Avicenna 1984: 58, 1938: 262). In the celestial spheres their motion is—although not itself in a primary intention—linked with this desire to resemble God as far as possible so that the latter becomes the very principle of their return. The basic perspective is not one of proving God's existence, but of explaining how He, in His function of *the* final cause, causes motion and thereby opens the way to the creatures to perfect themselves in coming as close as possible to Him.

It is worthwhile to note that Ibn Sīnā makes mentions of the notion of Unmoved Mover in a metaphysical section only in his *The Provenance and Destination* (*al-Mabda' wa-l-Ma'ād*), a work of his youth (Avicenna 1984: 38, § 26). However, even there he avoids presenting it as a genuine proof for God's existence. Indeed, he simply states that for each kind of moved thing there is a first unmoved mover. Strikingly, almost the same affirmation is present in the *Elements of Philosophy* (*'Uyūn al-ḥikma*) (Avicenna 1954: 19, 6–8), but this time in the section on physics—a particular stress being put on the impossibility of an infinite succession of moving bodies which move each other. Moreover, somewhat earlier in the *al-Mabda' wa-l-Ma'ād* (Avicenna 1984: 33–4, § 24), Ibn Sīnā had stressed that the present proof, which he characterizes as an evidencing proof (*istidlāl*), only follows upon the proof he had earlier established, namely the one based on the consideration of the state of being (*ḥāl al-wujūd*) and which he presents as resembling real demonstration—a proper demonstration of God being impossible because it establishes the cause of something, but God is uncaused. (We will return to this latter proof shortly.) In the same passage Ibn Sīnā affirms that regarding this proof he follows the way that Aristotle had taken in the "generalities" (*kulliyyāt*) of the sciences of physics and metaphysics, respectively in his works entitled *Physics* and *Metaphysics*. In this way it is clear that he does not consider the proof of the Unmoved Mover as belonging to Aristotle's theology, which has obviously to be sought outside the *Metaphysics*. As such, it cannot constitute a serious proof for God's existence.

Even in the *Physics* of the *Shifā'* the argument is never presented as a full proof for God's existence. It is striking that the notion of the Unmoved Mover is almost completely absent in this work; in fact, it seems to occur only once (Avicenna 2009: II, 514). Still, this does not mean that it is completely worthless regarding the establishment of God's existence. It certainly offers an indication, but as such has little in common with true knowledge that is demonstrative, or, at least, closely related to demonstration. Anyhow, physics cannot prove something that by definition belongs to metaphysics. It is limited as much in its means as in the goal it can attain:

> The "physicians" reach the establishment of the First Mover in showing by way of the necessity <of motion> (my addition) [the existence of] an

> immaterial, infinite power that moves the [uttermost] sphere, and they proceed to it [starting] from nature. As to the "metaphysicians," they follow another way than this, namely they arrive at the establishment of Him by way of the necessity of being (*wujūb al-wujūd*). They <show> (my addition) that He must be one, not multiple, and they show also that the [other] beings emanate from Him; that they are concomitants of His essence; that the spheres' motion moves toward Him by way of desire, more precisely by way of a search to resemble Him in perfection; that it is impossible that His perfection is not particular to Him; that there is no perfection above His perfection, for, if that were possible, the thing that possesses the highest perfection would be first.
>
> (Avicenna 1973: 62, 14–19, 2008: 355, § 470)

To show that God exists, one needs to establish Him as a principle of being, not just of motion. Hence, any serious proof in this sense has to start from being and therefore belongs to metaphysics, the proper subject of which is the study of "being *qua* being" (Avicenna 2005: 9).

But what is the exact meaning of "being"? How can we acquire knowledge of it? For Ibn Sīnā this latter is impossible, since "being" is the most common of all concepts and therefore is as it were inborn in man: "Reason itself knows 'being' (*hastī*) without the aid of definition or description. It has no definition because it has neither genus nor differentia since nothing is more general than it. It has no description since nothing is better known than it" (Avicenna 1952: 8, 13–9, 1), and "the ideas of 'the existent' (*al-mawjūd*), 'the thing', and 'the necessary,' are impressed in the soul in a primary way" (Avicenna 2005: 22). Hence, "being" is an all-encompassing concept that encloses both God and the creatures and the basic grasp of which is immediately accessible to reason. Its reality can therefore not be questioned: "Undoubtedly there is 'being'" (*lā shakka anna hunā wujūdan*) (Avicenna 1984: 22, § 15; Ibn Sīnā 1938: 235, 3). Given that it forms the starting point of what the later tradition has qualified as the "contingency-argument," it is obvious that this starting point has to be characterized as "a priori" and does not imply the position of any "existent" being (Mayer 2001: 23).

But before examining its significance for Ibn Sīnā's proof, or better, proofs for God's existence, it has to be stressed that Ibn Sīnā is entirely innovative—compared to Aristotle and the whole later tradition—when he adds "possible" and "necessary" among the things that belong as proper accidents to "being *qua* being" (Avicenna 2005: 10). Although he only does this in an explicit way in one single passage of the *Ilāhiyyāt* of the *Shifā'*, the distinction between both as disjunctive properties of "existent" seems to be tacitly accepted in his other writings. Most importantly, it—together with the related distinction between essence and existence—permits him to sharply distinguish between God and the possible Universe (Bertolacci 2008: 41–4; Lizzini 2003: 122) and to establish, while rewording it in causal terms, the theological distinction between what is originated and what is eternal, and, more generally, between creatures and Creator (Rudolph 1997: 342). But, at once, it situates both God and creatures inside the same realm of being. Ibn Sīnā strongly opposes the Neoplatonic idea that God is above being; rather, he defends an analogical concept of being (Verbeke 1977: 80*), or, at least, inclines in such a direction. In fact, a tension inside his system comes to the fore, mainly due his conception of the possible as necessary through another.

Given God's fullness of being, given the identity of His will with His knowledge, and of both with His essence, and given the becoming of the Universe is described in terms of an emanation through a *fluxus* (*fayḍ*) one finds a strong deterministic tendency in Ibn Sīnā's thought so that one would rather have to speak of an "analogy of necessary being" (Gardet 1951: 56) than of simply "being." But then one overlooks other affirmations such as, for example, the sharp distinction between acting by will and acting by nature or by chance, or the position of a creationist moment. It is clear that for Ibn Sīnā there is a big gap separating God from His creatures, but it is not so big that no relation whatsoever would be conceivable between them. Being both existent, they both partake in the actuality of being. Nevertheless, there exists a major difference insofar as in God there is a full identity between essence and existence, whereas in the creatures they are clearly distinguished from each other. To put it more precisely: in God there is properly speaking no essence discernible—God is no substance and therefore has no quiddity, but His reality is His "I am" (*anniyya*) (Avicenna 1973: 187, 4; Avicenna 2008: 164, § 32), whereas the possible beings need a cause to give them. In this sense one may equate the possible in itself with the necessary through another, an identification that Wisnovsky has qualified as Ibn Sīnā's big idea (2003: 199). In sum, all that is existent is necessary, but one has to distinguish between what is necessary in itself (i.e. God) and what is necessary through another (i.e. the creatures). This is the case because necessity points to the assuredness of existence, existence being better known than nonexistence (Avicenna 2005: 28). As such it is universally predicable (contrary to when it is considered together with possible as a disjunctive property of "existence"), although it remains intensionally dependent upon existent (Bertolacci 2008: 50).

There is being, but is there a divine being, i.e. God? To establish the latter's existence is the highest goal that the metaphysician at once can and has to attain. Hence, it comes as no surprise that Ibn Sīnā deals with this issue in the metaphysical sections of all his major philosophical writings. Leaving outside consideration his very early work *Philosophy for ʻArūḍī* (*al-Ḥikma al-ʻArūḍīya*), since its theological section has only partially survived, one detects in his different works two major kinds of proofs: one based on the idea of an infinite regress of causes, and one based on the concept of being (included in its basic distinction between possible and necessary being).

The former of the two arguments is preeminently present in the *Ilāhiyyāt* of the *Shifā'*, VIII, 1–3. The proof consists in demonstrating that each type of causality—Ibn Sīnā accepting with Aristotle the existence of four types, i.e. efficient, final, formal, and material—must have a principle since an infinite regress of causes in a causal chain is inconceivable; hence, there must be a first uncaused efficient cause (Davidson 1987: 339–40; Bertolacci 2007: 73–84). Ibn Sīnā insists that in a causal series one necessarily has a first term, a finite number of intermediaries and a final term. In his *Book of Guidance* (*Kitāb al-Hidāya*), the same idea of the impossibility of an infinite regress in causes is present, but this time a particular emphasis is put on the being together of cause and effect. Having emphasized that an effect always needs its appropriate cause—a moving cause not being able to guarantee the enduring existence of something, as can be illustrated by the case of the house the subsistence of which is not maintained by the builder, Ibn Sīnā says:

> The causes and the effects are together (*ma'an*) and have an order that does not extend infinitely—the reason for which you know; consequently, they result in a cause that has no (further) cause, a principle that has no (further) principle, and this is undoubtedly (*bal huwa*) the Necessary Being. It has already become obvious that the Necessary Being is one, all things return to (Him, the) "One".
> (Avicenna 1974: 265, 9–11)

A real cause is not only the cause of the coming into existence of something but also of its maintenance in existence. This idea is not absent in Ibn Sīnā's other writings, as we will see shortly, but it receives here a particular stress. God is no longer solely a giver of existence, but also the One who takes care of the conservation of His creatures. Everything indicates that Ibn Sīnā wants to present God as the ultimate cause both from the point of view of efficiency as well as finality, the *Alpha* and the *Omega* of the Universe. The idea that all creatures return to the One, is also present in his Persian philosophical encyclopedia *The Book of Science* (*Dānesh-Nāmeh*), where a proof is offered for God's existence based on the impossibility of an infinite causal series (Avicenna 1952: 81, 10–82, 8). This time, there is however a particular emphasis on the need for a cause in all that is contingent. Moreover, besides a linear series of causes, the hypothesis of a circular series is taken into account. Indeed, one could imagine a circular chain of causality at work inside a closed Universe. But for Ibn Sīnā this is an impossible hypothesis, since it either implies that something is both cause and effect (which is an absurdity), or that everything is just an effect (and then there is a clear need for a cause that is external to that totality). All this makes it doubtful that the proof can be considered as a variant of that on the impossibility of an infinite regress of causes, as Davidson claims (Davidson 1987: 340–1). Certainly, the notions of "Necessary Being" and "possible being" do not play such a crucial role as in the proof that we will present immediately hereafter, but they are nevertheless not completely absent. On the contrary, Ibn Sīnā starts his exposé with the affirmation that He (the Necessary Being) is one, and that all other beings are non-necessary, hence possible, or to put it more precisely—contingent. As such, the distinction between both kinds of beings cannot be easily dismissed as being totally insignificant in the elaboration of the proof.

The second proof which is based on the idea of being and its basic division into possible and necessary, is formulated in almost identical terms in the *al-Mabda' wa-l-Ma'ād* (Avicenna 1984: 22–7, §§ 15–19) and in the *Najāt* (Avicenna 1938: 235–9, i.e. the section *Ilāhiyyāt*, II, §§ 12–14). Before offering the proper articulation of the proof, Ibn Sīnā first develops three premises, i.e. the impossibility of an infinite linear regress of causes, the impossibility of a circular regress of causes, and the principle of causality, namely that a cause is always together with its effect, either on the level of existence, or on the level of maintenance, or on both together (Davidson 1987: 299–303). But, as already indicated above, he starts his exposé with the affirmation that "Undoubtedly there is being." *Pace* Davidson (1987: 303), Ibn Sīnā does not leave here the conceptual realm for a single empirical datum, namely that something exists. Given the actual presence of *wujūdan* in the Arabic, the reference has to be to the general concept of "being" or "existence" unless one would modify *wujūdan* into *mawjūdan*. But such a variant is nowhere attested and is clearly contradicted by the affirmation in the *al-Mabda' wa-l-Ma'ād* already referred to earlier that the present proof is based on the consideration of the state of being (*ḥāl al-wujūd*) (Avicenna 1984: 33, 20). So, there is at least an a priori moment present in the proof. This might be indicative of a move toward a kind of ontological argument. However, the proof in its totality can hardly be qualified as ontological. In fact, the basis for the whole argument seems to lie in the idea that the existence of the possible is caused—this being an a posteriori observation—and hence that it is in need of a cause for its existence, namely the necessarily existent in virtue of itself. Nevertheless, to posit "being" allows one way of considering the possible, not the impossible, as the opposite of the necessary. At once, any confusion between the logical and the ontological order is excluded. Even if Ibn Sīnā accepts a great parallelism between both orders, he clearly is aware of specific differences between them.

But let us concentrate on the way he articulates his proof. Having stressed that there is "being," he observes that it is either "necessary" or "possible." If it is necessary, then we have immediately what is looked for, i.e. the existence of the "necessary," or, in other words, God. If it is possible, it is shown by way of a long argumentation that the existence of the possible must terminate in a necessarily existent being. The switch from "possible" to the "existence of the possible" clearly implies a move from a purely ontological to a cosmological plane. On the former, the possible is completely indifferent to existence or non-existence. Hence, it does not permit one to accept the existence of the possible as a given fact since this belongs only to the concomitants of its essence (which does not mean at all that existence is downgraded to a simple accident, but that in the possible being, in sharp contrast with the necessary being, it has to be distinguished from its essence). One can only speak of an existent possible after it has been realized in existence. However, for this realization it needs a cause. This in its turn could be a possible, but then once again another cause is needed. Given that a totality of possible beings cannot be self-sufficient in such a way that it is necessary in virtue of itself (the possible being at best necessary by virtue of something else other than itself), its cause must be something outside this totality, and given the principle that an actual infinite is not given, the series of causes has to terminate at a first cause that is necessarily existent in itself. However, in Ibn Sīnā's view this does not constitute a full-fledged argument. In fact, one could imagine that there is a self-contained regress of causes inside the group of possible beings. But its absurdity comes immediately to the fore, namely as soon as one realizes that this implies that something is both cause and effect of its own existence—a logical impossibility! Based on the preceding two premises one may conclude that the existence of the entirety of possible beings results ultimately from one single efficient cause, which has to be qualified as "necessary." Still, there is need for an additional specification. If the concerned efficient cause would be only the giver of existence of the totality of the possibles, one would have to suppose a second, separate cause for its maintenance.

Ibn Sīnā insists that the possible in the present context is the possible in essence. Hence, it cannot be cause of self-conservation. In reality, insofar as every possible is something caused, its ultimate cause must be a single one that guarantees both its existence and its continuation. There is an intimate togetherness between cause and effect, as already was evident in the *Book of Guidance* as exposed before. This is most evident in these possibles that are eternal as e.g. the Higher Intelligences. In spite of their being eternal, they owe their existence not to themselves, but to the Necessary Being, who in giving them existence at once ensures their eternal preservation. Ibn Sīnā concludes that whether or not the cause of the maintenance in existence of the possibles is identical with the cause of their coming into existence, its ultimate source cannot be something else than the necessarily existent being; otherwise one would have to suppose the existence of a linear or circular infinite series of causes, the impossibility of which has been shown in the preceding premises.

One finds also shorter versions of this proof in the fourth section (*Namaṭ* 4, f. 9–15), of *Pointers and Reminders* (*al-Ishārāt wa-l-Tanbīhāt*) (Avicenna 1892: 140–2; detailed analysis in Mayer 2001) and in the first chapter of the *Treatise of the Throne* (*al-Risāla al-ʿArshiyya*) (Avicenna 1934: IV, 2–3). In both cases there is a strong emphasis on the need for an ultimate cause, which is "necessary," to explain the existence of the possible beings. Hence, it is obvious that for Ibn Sīnā a genuine metaphysical proof for God's existence has to take into account causality, not just motion. In his view Aristotle had not failed to do so: the "causality-proof," which is best expressed in the *Ilāhiyyāt* of the *Shifā'* as has been indicated earlier, has a strong basis in Aristotle's *Metaphysics* alpha minor or book 2 (Bertolacci 2007: 97). But when he develops his own argument, he clearly wants to put a particular emphasis on an a priori ontological moment, namely the pure consideration of being. This ontologization seems to reach a high peak in *al-Ishārāt wa-l-Tanbīhāt, Namaṭ* 4, faṣl 29 (Avicenna 1892: 146–7), where Ibn Sīnā strongly stresses that to show the existence of the First, i.e. God, nothing else had to be taken into consideration than the state of being, and he relies this to the Qur'ānic statement: "Does it not suffice that your Lord is witness to everything?" (Qur'ān 41:53). Hence the true philosophers, *aṣ-ṣiddīqūn*, i.e. the strictly veracious, adduce evidence through Him, not towards Him. All this makes clear that Ibn Sīnā tried to avoid as much as possible an inductive, a posteriori account—typical of the *kalām*—whereby God's existence is proven on basis of what are the results of His action, the proof by way of motion of the natural philosophers being of a similar nature. Rather, from an encompassing analysis of the very concept of "being," which in a primary way is impressed in the human soul, one cannot but conclude the existence of a necessarily existent being. Of course, this does not constitute a demonstration in the proper sense of the word, but with respect to God, Who exceeds the limits of our human understanding, this kind of demonstrative knowledge is by definition excluded. Note that it is also in the framework of being linked with the issue of causality that Ibn Sīnā shows that there can only be one necessarily existent being. For, where there to be two (or more), either, one of them would be cause of the other, but then this latter would be caused, hence possible, not necessary; or the one would reciprocally because of and caused by the other, which is an absurdity.

God exists and as such He is the First being, the First cause on which everything else depends. But since God *is* "being," i.e. His essence *is* His existence, any multiplicity is completely foreign to Him. This implies not only that all His attributes are identical with His essence, but also that only one possible being can directly come from Him, or, to put it in Ibn Sīnā's own words: "From the One inasmuch it is one, only one proceeds" (Avicenna 2005: 330). Hence, Ibn Sīnā feels obliged to explain the coming into existence of the diverse beings in the Universe by the idea of a mediated causality, expressed in terms of an emanative scheme, including two spheres: one of the Higher Intelligences and celestial spheres above the Moon and another of the this-worldly beings of generation and corruption beneath the Moon. In spite of their differences, which cannot be dealt with here, both spheres are ultimately dependent upon God. In a most significant way this latter is qualified as *musabbib al-asbāb*, i.e. not simply the "cause of causes," but the one who lends the (secondary) causes their causal activity, thus making God, and He alone, the originator and sustainer of all mediate causes (Janssens 1987: 265–6). Important as well is Ibn Sīnā's stress that God's providence encompasses the best possible order, including the existence of—be it limited—evil (Avicenna 2005: IX, 6, 339–47). With this latter idea we have entered what Gutas has labeled the "metaphysics of the rational soul" (Gutas 1988: 254–61), where Ibn Sīnā also discusses the issues of punishment and reward of the soul in the hereafter and of prophecy, to mention only the most significant ones. In all this one can detect a desire to express God's sovereignty over all beings, even the lowest of them. We have to leave here open the question whether Ibn Sīnā succeeded to do this in a coherent way. But everything indicates that at least he tried.

Conclusion

To prove God was a central issue of Ibn Sīnā's metaphysical project. He, however, could not accept al-Kindī's identification of metaphysics with "First philosophy," i.e. "theology." Rather, he considered the proper subject of metaphysics as "being *qua* being." Therefore, metaphysics is, in the first place, an ontology. But precisely in the very idea of being Ibn Sīnā discovered a genuine proof for God's existence, which was, at least partly, ontological in nature. Herewith he created a new kind of metaphysics, an onto-theological one that certainly has its point of departure in being, but has as its apex the existence of God. Precisely in this sense it can be qualified as a metaphysics of God—a new metaphysics that has a real equivalent neither in Greek thought nor in the previous Islamic times.

Further Reading

Druart, T-A. (2005) "Metaphysics," in P. Adamson & R. C. Taylor (eds.), *The Cambridge Companion to Arabic Philosophy*, Cambridge: Cambridge University Press, pp. 327–48.

Houser, R. E. (2007) "The Real Distinction and the Principles of Metaphysics: Avicenna and Aquinas," in R. E. Houser (ed.), *Laudemus viros gloriosos*, Notre Dame: University of Notre Dame Press, pp. 75–108.

Marmura, M. E. (1987) "Avicenna's Metaphysics," in *Encyclopedia Iranica*, III, 73–79 (reprinted in *Probing in Islamic Philosophy*, Binghamton, New York: Global Academic Publishers, 2005, pp. 17–32).

McGinnis, J. (2010) "Metaphysics I. Theology," in his work, *Avicenna*, Oxford: Oxford University Press, pp. 149–77.

Ramón Guerrero, R. (1996) "Sobre el objecto de la metafísica según Avicena," *Cuadernos de Pensamiento* 10: 59–75.

References

Adamson, P. (2005) "Al-Kindī and the reception of Greek Philosophy," in P. Adamson & R. C. Taylor (eds.), *The Cambridge Companion to Arabic Philosophy*, Cambridge: Cambridge University Press, pp. 32–51.

al-Fārābī (1890) *Alfārābī's philosophische Abhandlungen*, F. Dieterici (ed.), Leiden: Brill.

——. (1932) *Catálogo de las ciencias*, A. González Palencia (ed. and tr.), Madrid: Universidad de Madrid, Facultad de Filosofía y Letras.

al-Kindī (1974) *Al-Kindī's Metaphysics. A Translation of Ya'qūb ibn Isḥāq al-Kindī's Treatise 'On First Philosophy' (fī al-Falsafah al-Ūlā)*, A. L. Ivry (tr.), Albany: State University of New York Press.

Avicenna (1892) *Kitāb al-Ishārāt wa-l-Tanbīhāt*, J. Forget (ed.), Leiden: Brill.

——. (1910) *Manṭiq al-Mashriqiyyīn wa-l-qaṣīda al-muzdawija fī l-manṭiq*, M. al-Khaṭīb & 'A. al-Qatlān (eds.), Cairo: Maktaba al-Salafiyya.

——. (1934) *al-Risāla al-'Arshiyya*, in *Majmū' rasā'il al-Shaykh al-ra'īs* [treatise 4], Hayderabad: Dā'irat al-Ma'ārif al-Uthmāniyya.

——. (1938) *al-Najāt fī l-ḥikmat al-manṭiqiyya wa-l-ṭabī'iyya wa-l-ilāhiyya*, M. al-Kurdī (ed.), Cairo: al-Sa'āda.

——. (1947) *Sharḥ Ḥarf al-Lām*, A. Badawi (ed.), *Arisṭū 'inda l-'Arab*, Cairo: Maktaba al-nahḍa al-miṣriyya, pp. 22–33.

——. (1952) *Dāneshnāme-i 'Alā'ī. Al-Ilāhiyyāt*, M. Mo'īn (ed.), Tehran: Intishārāt-è Dāneshgāh.

——. (1954) *Avicennae Fontes Sapientiae*, A. Badawi (ed.), Cairo: Institut Français d'Archéologie Orientale.

——. (1973) *al-Ta'līqāt*, A. Badawi (ed.), Cairo: Al-Hay'a al-miṣriyya al-'āmma lil-kitāb.

——. (1974) *Kitāb al-Hidāya*, M. 'Abduh (ed.), Cairo: Maktaba al-Qāhira al-Ḥadītha.

——. (1984) *al-Mabda' wa-l-Ma'ād*, 'A. Nūrānī (ed.), Tehran: McGill University, Institute of Islamic Studies in collaboration with Tehran University.

——. (2005) *The Metaphysics of The Healing*, M. E. Marmura (tr.), Provo, UT: Brigham Young University Press.

——. (2008) *Kitāb al-Ta'līqāt*, Ḥ. M. al-'Ubaydī (ed.), Damascus, Aleppo: Dār al-Takwīn lil-ta'līf wa l-tarjama wa l-nashr.

——. (2009) *The Physics of The Healing*, 2 vols., J. McGinnis (tr.), Provo, UT: Brigham Young University Press.

——. (2014) *Commentaire sur le livre Lambda de la <Métaphysique d'Aristote (chapitres 6–10)*, M. Geoffroy, J. Janssens, M. Sebti (eds. & trads.), Paris: Vrin.

Bertolacci, A. (2006) *The Reception of Aristotle's* Metaphysics *in Avicenna's* Kitāb al-Šifā'. *A Milestone of Western Metaphysical Thought*, Leiden & Boston: Brill.

——. (2007) "Avicenna and Averroes on the Proof of God's Existence and the Subject-Matter of Metaphysics," *Medioevo* 32: 61–97.

——. (2008) "'Necessary' as Primary Concept in Avicenna's Metaphysics," in St. Perfetti (ed.), *Conoscenza e contingenza nella tradizione aristotelica medievale* (Philosophica 44), Pisa: Edizione ETS, pp. 31–50.

Black, D. (1996), "Al-Fārābī," in S. H. Nasr and O. Leaman (eds.), *History of Islamic Philosophy*, vol. I, London & New York: Routledge, pp. 178–97.

d'Ancona-Costa, C. (1996) *La case della Sapienza. La trasmissione della metafisica greca e la formazione della filosofia araba* (Socrates 18), Milano: Guerini e Associati.

Davidson, H. A. (1987) *Proofs for Eternity, Creation and the Existence of God in Medieval Islamic and Jewish Philosophy*, Oxford: Oxford University Press.

Druart, T-A. (1987), "Al-Farabi and Emanationism," in J. F. Wippel (ed.), *Studies in Medieval Philosophy* (Studies in Philosophy and the History of Philosophy 17), Washington: Catholic University of America Press, pp. 23–43.

Gardet, L. (1951) *La pensée religieuse d'Avicenne (Ibn Sīnā)* (Études de philosophie médievale 41), Paris: Vrin.

Gutas, D. (1988) *Avicenna and the Aristotelian Tradition. Introduction to Reading Avicenna's Philosophical Works*, Leiden, New York, København & Köln: Brill.

Janssens, J. (1987) "Ibn Sīnā's ideas of ultimate realities: Neoplatonism and the Qur'ān as problem-solving paradigms in the Avicennian system," *Ultimate Reality and Meaning* 10: 252–71 (reprinted in his *Ibn Sīnā and his Influence on the Arabic and Latin World* (CSS 843), Aldershot: Ashgate, 2006, II).

Lizzini, O. (2003) "Wujūd-Mawjūd/ Existence-Existent in Avicenna. A key ontological notion of Arabic philosophy," *Quaestio. Annuario di storia della metafisica* 3: 111–38.

Martini Bonadeo, C. (2005) "Al-Fārābī, 4. La metafisica," in C. d'Ancona (ed.), *Storia della filosofia nell'Islam medieval* (Piccola Biblioteca Einaudi. Nuova Serie Filosofia 285), Torino: G. Einaudi, pp. 400–9.

Mayer, T. (2001), "Ibn Sīnā's 'Burhān al-Ṣiddiqīn'," *Journal of Islamic Studies* 12, 1: 18–39.

Reisman, D. (2005) "Al-Fārābī and the philosophical curriculum," in P. Adamson & R. C. Taylor (eds.), *The Cambridge Companion to Arabic Philosophy*, Cambridge: Cambridge University Press, pp. 52–71.

Rudolph, U. (1997) "La preuve de l'existence de Dieu chez Avicenne et dans la théologie musulmane," in A. de Libera, A. Elamrani-Jamal & A. Galonnier (eds.), *Langages et philosophie. Hommage à Jean Jolivet*, Paris: Vrin, pp. 339–46.

Verbeke, G. (1977) "Le statut de la métaphysique," doctrinal introduction to *Avicenna Latinus. Liber de philosophia prima sive scientia divina* I-IV, S. Van Riet (ed.), Louvain/Leiden: Peeters/ Brill, pp. 1*–122*.

——. (1983) *Avicenna, Grundleger einer neuen Metaphysik* (Rheinisch-Westfälische Akademie der Wissenschaften, G 263), Opladen: Westdeutscher Verlag.

Wisnovsky, R. (2003) *Avicenna's Metaphysics in Context*, London: Duckworth.

20
CREATION IN ISLAM FROM THE QUR'ĀN TO AL-FĀRĀBĪ

Michael Chase

Introduction

This article deals with the notion of creation in general and creation *ex nihilo* in particular, in Islamic thought from the Qur'ān to al-Fārābī. Following a broadly chronological scheme, we will pay particular attention to the technical term *ibdā'* ("origination," "creation"), as it emerged and evolved in the context of the interplay between intra-Islamic debates (*falāsifa* vs. *kalām*) on the nature of creation, and as it underwent the influence of late Greek thought, particularly that of John Philoponus. Participants in the Circle of al-Kindī (Endress 1997) played a particularly important role in the tradition by developing from the thought of Philoponus a creationist metaphysics of atemporal instantaneous divine action.

Creation in the Qur'ān

There is no explicitly formulated doctrine of creation *ex nihilo* in the Qur'ān—any more than there is in the Hebrew Bible or the New Testament. Instead, God's creation of the world is generally depicted as taking place out of a primordial water, while the heavens were created out of smoke. Elsewhere, earth and heaven are conceived as a solid mass, which God separates (al-Alousī 1965: 30).

God's divine names in the Qur'ān include *Badī'* (the Originator), usually used to designate His absolute creation of heaven and earth, and *khāliq* (Creator), used primarily for creation or formation out of a pre-existent material, as when man is created from clay or some other base, earth-like material. Only two Qur'ānic passages have been considered to suggest a creation *ex nihilo*: the first is sūra 2:117 (cf. Qur'ān 3:47), where God is addressed as: "Creator of heaven and earth, when He decrees something, He merely says 'be!' (*kun*) and it is," although here, as often, it is not specified whether God creates out of some pre-existent material or not. The other occurs in the context of the creation of mankind: "I created you beforehand, when you were nothing"

(Qur'ān 19:9). In general, however, the preponderant notion of creation in the Qur'ān seems to be one of shaping, molding, vivifying or otherwise perfecting some kind of material that is already present, in however imperfect a state (al-Alousī 1965: 11–40; Peterson 2001; Lizzini 2009: 65–75).

As in Christianity, but perhaps to an even greater degree, divine creation takes place in Islam for the sake of man, or rather in order that man may praise God (Qur'ān 51:56). Yet God's motive for Creation is not His own benefit: like the Demiurge of the Platonic *Timaeus*, He creates out of pure goodness and generosity (*ikrām*, Qur'ān 55:27; 55:78; van Ess 1991–1997: 3, 280). There are, in fact, two divine creations: the primordial creation resulting in the whole of the visible world (Qur'ān 21:104; 10:4; 10:34, etc.), and the second creation, referring to the resurrection and/or the hereafter. It is the former which later theologians envisaged as taking place *ex nihilo*, from nothing (*'an al-'adam*).

As far as the exact modality and details of creation are concerned—how long did it take, what God created first, what second, etc., and above all, did it take place *ex nihilo* or out of some pre-existent material, whether eternal or not?—the Qur'ān itself was open to a variety of interpretations. In the generations following the Revelation to the Prophet, as Islam spread from the Arabian peninsula to Syria and Iraq, the practitioners of Islamic theology (*kalām*) had recourse to a variety of sources to fill in the details left imprecise in the Holy Book: oral traditions (*ḥadīth*) of the sayings of Muḥammad and his companions; scholars of the Jewish and Syriac Christian traditions; and, the traditions of Late Antique Greek religion and philosophy (Anawati 1996).

Creation in the *Kalām*: Mu'tazilites vs. Ash'arites

Several passages from the Qur'ān allowed the interpretation that God's creation of the world was not a one-time affair, but rather a continuous act of endowing being upon that which lacked it (al-Alousī 1965: 278–97; Lizzini 2009: 66ff.). This insight was to be rigorously formulated and systematized by the two great schools of *kalām*, the Mu'tazilites and the Ash'arites. Despite their considerable differences, these schools agreed that the world consists of atomic substances and their accidents, which God incessantly combines and separates, thus constantly creating and annihilating their accidental characteristics. Both considered creation to be *post nihil*, in that the world came into existence after not having existed. From God's perspective, His creative act is one of production or origination, while the world is subject to coming into being or existence. God as Creator is designated as *Muḥdith* (Creator), while the world is *muḥdath* (generated). Rather than being drawn instantaneously out of the void, however, that which is generated (maḫlūq) or created is that which is composed or compounded (*mu'allaf*).

This, however, raised a whole new set of problems. The world is created, brought into existence, or compounded, well and good: but out of what? Out of the non-existent (*al-ma'dūm*), replied the Mu'tazilites, which is not sheer nothingness, but a thing (*al-shay'*), since God must, after all, know what He is going to create before He creates it, and sheer nothingness cannot be known, simply because there is nothing to know (al-Alousī 1965: 201ff.; Frank 1980; van Ess 1991–1997: vol. 4, 445–77; Adamson 2003: 57ff.). The "non-existent" that God knows, said the Mu'tazilites, is that which is capable of existing but does not in fact exist: in other words, it is the possible. The Ash'arites disagreed: for them, only the existent is a thing, while the non-existent is mere nothingness. Creation for the Ash'arites is thus "from nothing" in the sense of being "not from a thing" (*lā min shay'*) or "from a non-thing" (*min lā shay'*).

Creation for the Mu'talizites thus takes place not so much out of nothing, but out of a thing whose name is "the non-existent." Yet this view raised further problems upon which their opponents were quick to seize: didn't this eternal "non-existent" resemble the eternally pre-existent matter of some Greek philosophers? Indeed, on some interpretations of Plato's *Timaeus*, the Demiurge creates the visible world by imposing order upon a mysterious entity known as the *khôra*, which later commentators identified with Aristotelian matter. Yet if the Mu'tazilite *ma'dūm* was already there when God set about creating, does this not make it co-eternal with Him, in clear violation of the key Islamic principle of *tawḥīd*, as epitomized in the phrase "There is no God but God" (*lā ilāha illā huwa*)? Despite these exegetical difficulties, creation for both these schools of the *kalām* implied the coming-into-being or existence of something that had previously not existed (Anawati 1971).

Since Plato's *Timaeus* has already been mentioned, perhaps a brief digression may be allowed on the Greek tradition of its interpretation (Rowson 1988: 252ff.; Chase 2011: 114–16). While it would be misleading to portray *kalām* as a mere parroting of Greek philosophy, it is hard to deny that Greek thought was influential on the thought of the practitioners of *kalām*, and the notion of creation *ex nihilo* provides a prime example of this influence.

At *Timaeus* 28b, Plato's spokesman asks the key question with regard to the world: did it always exist, having no starting point to its process of generation (Greek *arkhê geneseôs*), or did it come into being or existence (Greek *gegonen*), beginning from some starting-point? Plato's answer is laconic and unequivocal: *gegonen*, it came into being. Yet this statement was so contrary to mainstream Greek philosophical thought that Platonists and other commentators sought, as early as the generation following Plato, to explain it away: either Plato's depiction of creation in the *Timaeus* was an allegory, it was claimed, or it was said merely for pedagogical purposes. The most elaborate attempts at explaining the passage came in the Hellenistic and Late Antique period, by way of a distinction between various meanings of the Greek verb *genêtos*, the adjective derived from the verb *gignomai/genesthai*, of which Plato's *gegonen* is the aorist. The Middle Platonist Calvisius Taurus distinguished four meanings of the verb, whereupon the Neoplatonist Porphyry of Tyre added three more, for a total of seven. Of the seven, the last meaning of *genêtos*, according to Porphyry, denoted "things that have had a beginning of their being from a [point of] time after not having existed previously" (Sodano 1964: fr. 2, 36). Porphyry denies that Plato's *Timaeus* passage is to be understood in this sense. Writing some two and a half centuries after Porphyry, the Neoplatonist Simplicius (Diels 1882–1895, vol. 10, p. 1154, 2ff.) specifies that it is Aristotle who understands by "generated" (Greek *genêton*) that which comes into existence after not having existed, whereas Plato, when he uses the same term, means that which has its being in becoming and derives its existence from a source other than itself.

There seems, in short, to be a reasonably precise correspondence between, on the one hand, the *kalām* technical terms deriving from the Arabic root *ḥ-d-th* (*muḥdath*, *iḥdāth*, *ḥudūth*, etc.), and on the other hand the Greek derivatives from the verb *gignesthai/genesthai* (*gegonen*, *genêtos*, etc.). In *kalām* usage, these terms refer to the fact that the world has come to be *de novo*, i.e. it has come—or rather been brought by God—into existence after not having existed. This is precisely how the Neoplatonic commentators interpreted Aristotle's use of the Greek verbal adjective *genêtos*; and I think this is unlikely to be a coincidence.

Creation in al-Kindī

A new phase in Islamic philosophic thought about creation was inaugurated with the work of Abū Yūsuf Ya'qūb ibn Isḥāq al-Kindī (c. 796–873), usually considered the first Arab-Islamic philosopher. *Kalām* speculation on the subject was, as we have seen, characterized by reflection on the notions of "thingness" and "possibility," the re-configuration of pre-existent materials, and by terminology centering around derivatives of the Arabic root *ḥ-d-th* and formulas such as "not from a thing" or "from a non-thing." Now, the speculation of the philosophers of Greek allegiance (*falsafa*), as inaugurated by al-Kindī, features preoccupations which, while they show clear continuity in several respects with those of the Mu'tazila, nevertheless contain new emphases. These are reflected in the terminology: for instance, to denote the act of creation, al-Kindī likes to use the Arabic term *ibdā'* (Gardet 1971), which can be variously rendered as "origination," "innovation," "instauration," and denotes the instantaneous bringing-into-being of the world from no material substrate whatsoever. In his *Book of Descriptions and Definitions* (al-Kindī 1976: § 6, Arabic 15, French tr. 31), al-Kindī defines *ibdā'* as "making something appear out of not-being," while elsewhere (Rashed & Jolivet 1998: 169, 5–6) he speaks of "the existentialization of things from nothing" (*ta'yis al-aysāt 'an lays*) as the action properly called *ibdā'*. In *On the Quantity of the Books of Aristotle and What is Required for the Attainment of Philosophy*, al-Kindī, interpreting sūra 36 of the Qur'ān (non-coincidentally, one of only two Qur'ānic passages that can be interpreted as implying creation *ex nihilo* (Peterson 2001: 477)), explains how something that was previously non-existent—in this case, the fire ignited from green branches—can come into being:

> Fire is generated from not-fire, and ... all generation is from what is other than itself. So everything that is generated is generated from "not-it" (*lā huwa*).
> (Abū Rīdā 1978: 374.12–375.5; cf. Adamson 2003)

Al-Kindī goes on to explain that the non-believers portrayed in sūra 36 doubted the creation of the heavens, since in human affairs the greater something is, the longer it takes to make. Yet their analogy between human and divine creation is based on ignorance:

> So then, [God] said that He, great be His praise, needs no period [of time] to create (*li-idbā'ihi*). And this is clear, because He made "it" from "not-it." If His power is such that it can produce (*ya'malu*) bodies from not-bodies, and bring being out of non-being, then, since He is able to perform a deed from no matter, He does not need to produce in time. For, since there can

> be no act by mankind without a material substrate, the act that does not need to act upon a material substrate has no need of time. "When He wills something, His command is to say to it: 'Be!' and it is." That is, He only wills, and together with His will is generated that which He wills—great be His praise, and exalted His names above the opinions of the unbelievers!
>
> (Abū Rīdā 1978: 375.9–18)

Indeed, al-Kindī went so far as to add to the standard list of Aristotelian types of change (transportation, generation, corruption, augmentation, diminution, alteration) an additional type: the movement of creation (*al-ḥarakatu al-ibdā'*), which differs from generation precisely in that the motion of creation does not take place out of a preexistent substrate (al-Tawḥīdī 1921–1944: 3, 133; cf. Altmann & Stern 2009: 69–70).

Creation in John Philoponus

The Mu'tazilites had already made use of some of the arguments devised by the Christian Neoplatonist John Philoponus (c. 490–570) to refute Aristotle's conception of the eternity of the world, notably those based on the impossibility of actual infinity (Sorabji 1983: 193–203, 214–24; Davidson 1987). No infinite series can be traversed or increased, but a world that has no beginning implies an actually infinite number of human generations and transformations of the elements, for instance. No infinite series can be larger than another, nor can any infinite quantity be a multiple of another infinite quantity. Yet since the celestial spheres rotate at different rates, a slower sphere will have accomplished an infinite number of revolutions through infinite time, but a faster sphere will have accomplished a number of revolutions that, while also infinite, will be greater than the number of revolutions of the slower sphere, and so on. Many of these arguments were to be re-utilized by al-Ghazālī in his polemic against al-Fārābī and Ibn Sīnā.

The above-mentioned texts by al-Kindī show that the Islamic thinker made direct use of Philoponus' arguments, as set forth in his *Against Aristotle* and his *On the Eternity of the World against Proclus*, to argue for his views about the nature of divine creation itself (Rowson 1988: 252–61; Adamson 2003: 62ff.; Janos 2009: 10–12). Yet while the parallels pointed out between the views of al-Kindī and Philoponus have largely focused on the fact that such creation takes place *ex nihilo* (*min lā huwa, min laysin* ≌ *ek mê ontôn*), emphasizing al-Kindī's continuity with the Mu'tazilite view of creation as the bestowing of existence on what is possible but not yet existent, perhaps an even more striking parallel is that for both al-Kindī and Philoponus, divine creation is instantaneous. This notion thus seems to represent another instance of al-Kindī's borrowing from Greek sources in the course of his debates with contemporary *kalām*.

Late Antique commentators on Aristotle sought to show that while most changes and motions take place in time, there are some that occur instantaneously (Hasnawi 1994; Chase 2011: 133–48). This was the case, for instance, for such phenomena as sense-perception, lightning, the curdling of milk and the freezing of water (i.e. what modern physics describes as phase transitions). Several of these texts were translated into Arabic, where they circulated under the name of Alexander of Aphrodisias. Philoponus (*On the Eternity of the World against Proclus*, 4, 4, in Rabe 1899: 64, 22–65, 26) had used such instances to refute one of Proclus' arguments against creation: since Aristotle defines motion as imperfect actuality, and motion necessarily takes place in time, then if God's act of creation is a motion, it will result that He changes from an imperfect to a perfect state, and that He, who is the creator of time, will require time to create. Not so, replies Philoponus: God's act of creation is not a motion but a transformation that is instantaneous or "all-at-once" (Greek *athroon*), like sense-perception, lightning, illumination, and the various phase transitions of nature. God's act of creation, in fact, resembles the actualization of a state or *habitus* (Greek *hexis*), as when I actualize my state of literacy by reading or writing: such an actualization takes place instantaneously and without altering the subject. Thus, when God creates, He is not moved, nor is He altered, and His creation does not take place within time.

Creation in the *Neoplatonica Arabica*

Thanks to the work of a number of great scholars over the past generation or so (Endress 1997; d'Ancona 2001, 2003, 2010; Zimmermann 1986, among others), we now know that al-Kindī played a key role in the establishment of what has been called "al-Kindī's metaphysics file": a collection of paraphrastic translations, interspersed with commentaries and other interpolations, of extracts primarily from Books 4 to 6 of Plotinus' *Enneads* and from Proclus' *Elements of Theology*. The most important of these works circulated in Arabic under the titles *Theology of Aristotle* and *Book of the Pure Good*, the latter of which was hugely influential on Medieval thought thanks to its Latin translation as the *Liber de Causis*. Work on the textual constitution, sources, translation and interpretation of these treatises is still very much ongoing, but there is a consensus that they are intended to provide a kind of theological continuation of Book Lambda of Aristotle's *Metaphysics* that would explain how reality derives from the ineffable first principle, via the hypostases of intellect, soul, and nature.

What can be said, even given the current state of our knowledge, is that the notion of instantaneous creation, taken up by al-Kindī from Philoponus (who in turn may have derived it from Porphyry (Chase 2011)), plays an essential role in these writings. In a number of passages from the *Theology of Aristotle* (Badawi 1955: 31 (9 occurrences!); 41; 70; 114; cf. Vallat 2012: 95 n. 51), it is emphasized that divine action in general, and the act of creation (*ibdā'*, *ibtidā'*) in particular, take place *duf'atan wāḥidatan* (at one stroke or all in all and all at once) and/or *bi-lā zamān* (without or outside of time). In the *Neoplatonica Arabica*, it is because the Creator is beyond time, which He creates, that His creation does not require time in order to be carried out (Rashed 2008: 48). Characteristic in this regard is the following passage which is one of those that have no parallel in Plotinus' *Enneads*:

> How well and how rightly does this philosopher [probably Plato] describe the Creator when he says: "He is the creator (*khāliq*) of mind, soul, nature, and all things else," but whoever hears the philosopher's words must not

> take them literally and imagine that he said that the Creator fashioned the creation in time. If anyone imagines that of him from his mode of expression, he did but express himself through wishing to follow the custom of the ancients. The ancients were compelled to mention time in connection with the beginning of creation because they wanted to describe the genesis of things, and they were compelled to introduce time into their description of becoming and into their description of the creation—which was not in time at all—in order to distinguish between the exalted first causes and the lowly secondary causes. ... But it is not so: not every agent performs his action in time, nor is every cause prior to its effect in time.
>
> (Badawi 1955: 27)

The notion of creation all at once is usually described as Plotinian, but Zimmermann, who has provided the most detailed study of this formula in the *Theology* (1986: 202–5), notes that the anonymous author "gives much greater prominence to the Plotinian 'all at once' than does Plotinus himself." However, most of the occurrences of this formula in the *Theology* occur in passages which have no precise parallel in Plotinus: they represent what Endress (1973) has called "interpretamenta" or passages inserted by the author/compiler from an unknown source. The notion of "all at once," at least when applied to the question of creation, is thus not primarily Plotinian at all, but probably derives from Porphyry by way of Philoponus.

In fact, one of the most conspicuous features of the *Neoplatonica Arabica* is that the texts they are based on, primarily taken from Plotinus and Proclus, have been modified so that they are compatible with a creationist metaphysics. One example will suffice here (for others, Endress 1973; Chase 2013: 45–52). In proposition 45 of his *Elements of Theology*, Proclus, in the context of a discussion of what is self-subsistent (Greek *authupostaton*), declares that all that is self-subsistent is ungenerated (Greek *pan to authupostaton agenêton esti*). When paraphrasing this section of the *Elements* in the Arabic *Book of the Pure Good* (§ 28), the anonymous author writes that "Every substance subsistent through itself, i.e. its essence, has been originated atemporally" (*kull jawhar qā'im bi-nafsihi a'nī bi-ḏātihi fa-innahu mubtadi' bi lā zamān*; Taylor 1981, Arabic 248, tr. 329). Rather than a mere translation, this seems to be a deliberate adaptation, not to say a distortion of Proclus' thought. The author of the paraphrase may have believed that it is the same thing to say that something is ungenerated and that it is generated or created (the Arabic *mubtadi'* derives from the same verbal root as *ibdā'*, on which see above) timelessly. But this is not what Proclus says, and such an equivalence, designed to avoid the un-Islamic consequence that something besides God may have an eternal existence, could only have been elaborated thanks to the theory of instantaneous creation taken over by al-Kindī and the *Neoplatonica Arabica* from the thought of Philoponus and his predecessors.

Creation in Ismā'īlī Thought

As far as the notion of creation is concerned, the representatives of this branch of Shī'ite thought, elaborated in the ninth–tenth centuries C.E., took as their Qur'ānic starting point the same passages that had inspired al-Kindī: those, like 2:117, which affirm that when God wishes to create the heavens and earth, he merely says Be! and they are. Thus, for the Ismā'īlīs, the transcendent, ineffable first principle is the Originator (*Mubdi'*), who originated (*abda'a*) the intellect, which is the first created being, with all the paradigmatic forms it contains, by a creative act (*ibdā'*) that takes place "all at once" (De Smet 2012: 8ff.), whereas the generation of material entities is denoted by derivatives of the verbal root *kh-l-q* (De Smet 1989: 402 n. 34). Like its transcendent and ineffable Agent, this act of origination is completely unknowable to mortals: what we do know, however, is that it is not a case either of emanation or of causality, since either of these notions would imply a link of participation between Creator and His Creation, a possibility ruled out by the abyss of alterity between them.

Creation in the Brethren of Purity

In the late tenth century C.E., we find the same distinction between an initial creation *ex nihilo*, designated sometimes by the term *ibdā'*, and a secondary creation out of something already existent, designated by *khalq*, in the third section of the *Encyclopedia of the Brethren of Purity* (*Rasā'il Ikhwān al-Ṣafā'*; Triki 1974: 25ff.; Diwald 1975: 431–63). The Universe is not eternal (Ġālib 2006: 3.340); indeed, the realization that the world is created is the only opportunity for man to awaken from the sleep of indifference and ensure both earthly and post-mortem felicity. In the ninth *risāla* (no. 40) of the third part of the *Encyclopedia*, we read that *ibda'* and its near-synonym *ikhtirā'* ("invention") do not indicate a combination (*tarkīb*) or putting-together (*ta'līf*) of pre-existent elements, but a production (*iḥdāth*) and a bringing-forth (*ikhtirāj*) from not-being (*al-'adam*) into being (*al-wujūd*) (Ġālib 2006: 3.350.1–2); here we note echoes of the terminology of the *kalām* and of al-Kindī.

Also like al-Kindī, the Brethren invoke the Qur'ānic "be!" (*kun*) to designate instantaneous creation. Like the Ismā'īlīs (with whom they show a great deal of kinship), however, the Brethren postulate a twofold creation, with each stage characterized by a different modality. In the first instance, divine and spiritual things (the agent intellect, world Soul, Prime Matter and separate Form) were created all at once, without time, place or matter (Ġālib 2006: 3.352.9–10ff). Natural things then developed gradually over time, by a process of combination. To illustrate the first stage of non-temporal creation, the Brethren invoke, as Porphyry had done (Chase 2011: 115, 140, 142), the example of the instantaneous appearance of lightning (Ġālib 2006: 3.352.17). This creation and invention of the world, as the Brethren never tire of repeating, takes place after its non-existence, and after the Creator had not been active (Ġālib 2006: 3.346), and not, as in the case of the craftsmen whom we observe, out of a pre-existing matter, in place, in time, and by means of motion and instruments; this is what makes divine creation so difficult, not to say impossible, to conceive. Only through the divinely inspired analogy of the way the series of numbers emerges from the one can we hope to obtain a correct understanding of creation. The act of creation as *ibdā'* is like a pronounced word, while creation as *Khalq* resembles a written word (Ġālib 2006: 3: 351), a comparison which allows the Brethren to maintain that while the act of *ibdā'* is separate from God, it continues, like speech with regard to a speaker, to be ontologically dependent upon Him.

Creation in al-Fārābī

The question of creation in the thought of Abū Naṣr al-Fārābī (d. 950) is made difficult by the fact that the most significant passage on the theme in his writings occurs in a work, the *Harmony between the Opinions of Plato and Aristotle*, whose authenticity has recently been called into question (Rashed 2008, 2009; Janos 2009). The passage in question reads as follows:

> The meaning of Aristotle's discourse according to which the world has no temporal beginning is that it did not come into being bit by bit, according to a succession of parts, as happens for instance for plants and animals. This is because what comes into being bit by bit, according to a succession of parts, has some parts that precede others in time (.) the celestial sphere derives from the creation of the Creator (*ibdā' l-bārī*)—may He be praised!—at one single time, without duration in time (*duf'ata bi-lā zamān*).
>
> (Martini Bonadeo 2008: 64.2–5)

It has been argued (Rashed 2008, 2009) that this passage cannot be by al-Fārābī, because it contradicts his belief that (contrary to the Philoponan tradition) every action is a motion, and motion is continuous, thus ruling out the Kindian idea of instantaneous, timeless, or "all-at-once" action, which implies a motion that would not follow upon any previous motion as well as the creation *ex nihilo* this idea was intended to stress. For al-Fārābī, al-Kindī's notion was both un-Aristotelian and in contradiction with the principles of kinematics. Instead, al-Fārābī defended a notion of continuous creation through emanation. In response, others (Martini Bonadeo 2008: 189ff.; Vallat 2012: 93–100) have contended that there are passages elsewhere in al-Fārābī's works attesting the doctrine of instantaneous action. Yet such passages are few and far between, are susceptible of various interpretations, and refer more to epistemological issues than to the question of creation. One passage at least (Najjār 1964: 65, 8–9; Vallat 2012: 98; 2011: *passim*) does, however, seem to show that for al-Fārābī, when something is capable of producing and there is no impediment to its production, then such production does take place, and the existence of the cause is not posterior to that of the effect. If this interpretation is correct, it shows that al-Fārābī was familiar with arguments of the type Porphyry used to prove that the world was eternal by showing that a cause can be simultaneous with its effect. The existence of that which is other than the First Cause but depends on that First Cause (for instance, the world as we know it) does not presuppose a temporally previous state of non-existence (Porphyry, fr. 459 in Smith 1993: 529–531 = al-Šahrastānī 1986–1999: vol. 2, 357–58). Thus, the effects of some actions, particularly the action *par excellence*, of divine creation, can be simultaneous with their cause (cf. Augustine, *City of God*, in Dombart & Kalb 1955: 10.31, citing anonymous Platonists who probably include Porphyry; Philoponus, *On the Eternity of the World*, in Rabe 1899: 13, 12ff.). It follows that the world is generated in a causal rather than a temporal sense.

Conclusion

It would not be surprising if among the texts available to and influential upon both al-Kindī and al-Fārābī were the same series of passages of Philopono-Porphyrian inspiration that developed the doctrine of instantaneous creation. Since we know, however, that al-Fārābī devoted several works to refuting Philoponus, it seems clear that of the two philosophers, it was al-Kindī rather than al-Fārābī who had greatest recourse to this creationist tendency in late Greek thought. Ultimately, the differences between the doctrines of al-Kindī and al-Fārābī are more striking than their similarities: while al-Kindī believes, like Philoponus, that the world was created *ex nihilo* and will end at a specific point in time, al-Fārābī is convinced that the world is eternal, not created: "in reality, everything is already present, and does not proceed from higher causes, except in a logical sense" (Vallat 2012: 196).

To be sure, the Kindian notion of an instantaneous, and therefore atemporal creation *ex nihilo*, may seem to amount to much the same thing as a more standardly Neoplatonistic "emanationist" view, in which lower levels of reality emerge continuously but atemporally from the higher principles. After all, Philoponus emphasizes that creation takes place in the "now" or the present instant (Greek *en tôi nun*) (Rabe 1899: 65.14–15), that indivisible limit of time, which therefore, according to Aristotle, is not in time; while the Neoplatonists often assert that the present instant preserves a trace of divine eternity (Westerink & Combès 1997–2003: vol. 3, 189.20; Bieler 1957: 5.6.49–53). Ibn Sīnā seems to have wavered between the two conceptions of *ibda'* as instantaneous creation and as emanation or continuous creation (Janssens 1997: 470–76), while, as we saw above, the adaptor of the *Book of the Pure Good* probably thought the two more or less equivalent, when he happily translated Proclus' assertion that the self-subsistent is *uncreated* or *ungenerated* (Greek *agenêton*) into the affirmation that it is *created atemporally* (*mubtadi' bi lā zamān*). Yet the example of Ismā'īlīs and the works of the *Brethren* remind us that we should be cautious. As we saw, they take over much of the terminology of the *kalām* and especially of the al-Kindī circle, as well as the latter's doctrine of instantaneous creation. Yet they insisted on the distinction between such *ibda'*, applicable only to the intelligible world, and temporal *khalq*, as a recombination or fashioning out of pre-existent elements that characterizes the sensible world alone, and they rejected the notion of emanation, precisely because "emanation ... is the very negation of creation *ex nihilo*" (De Smet 1989: 400) as designated by the term *ibdā'* and its cognates. This alerts us to the fact that however close the Philoponan doctrine of instantaneous creation may seem to be, at least at first glance, to the more standard Neoplatonic doctrine of continuous atemporal creation or "emanation," these two notions were held, in at least some circles of 10th-century Islam, to be so different as to be incompatible, as they were in the Late Antique debate between the Christian Philoponus and his pagan opponent Simplicius, or in the Late Medieval debate between Thomas Aquinas and Bonaventure.

Further Reading

Adamson, P. (2002) *The Arabic Plotinus. A Philosophical Study of the Theology of Aristotle*, London: Duckworth.

Daiber, H. (2012) *Islamic Thought in the Dialogue of Cultures. A Historical and Bibliographical Survey*, Leiden: Brill.
Frank, R. M. (2007) *Texts and Studies on the Development and History of Kalām*, vol. 2, *Early Islamic theology: the Mu'tazilites and al-Asharī*, D. Gutas (ed.), Aldershot: Ashgate.
Sorabji, R. (1983) *Time, Creation and the Continuum. Theories in Antiquity and the Early Middle Ages*, London/Ithaca: Duckworth/Cornell University Press.
Wolfson, H. A. (1976) *The Philosophy of the Kalam*, Cambridge, MA: Harvard University Press.

References

Abū Rīdā, M. 'A. (ed.) (1978) *Rasā'il al-Kindī al-falsafiyya*, 2 vols., al-Qāhirah: Dār al-fikr al-'arabī.
Adamson, P. (2003) "Al-Kindī and the Mu'tazila: Divine Attributes, Creation and Freedom," *Arabic Sciences and Philosophy* 13: 45–79.
al-Alousī, H. E. (1965) *The Problem of Creation in Islamic Thought: Qur'an, Hadīth, Commentaries, and Kalām*, PhD Diss., King's College Cambridge.
al-Kindī (1976) *Cinq Épîtres*, Centre d'Histoire des Sciences et des Doctrines: Histoire des Sciences et la Philosophie Arabes (ed.), Paris: Éditions du Centre National de la Recherche Scientifique.
al-Šahrastānī (1986–1999) *Livre des Religions et des Sectes*, 2 vols., D. Gimaret & G. Monnot (tr., vol. I); J. Jolivet & G. Monnot (tr., vol. II), Paris: Peeters/Unesco (Collection Unesco des oeuvres représentatives. Série Arabe).
al-Tawḥīdī, Abū Ḥayyān (1921–1944) *al-Imtā' wa-l-mu'ānasa (Enjoyment and Conviviality)*, 3 vols., A. Amīn & A. al-Zayn (eds.), s.l., s.d.
Altmann, A. & Stern, S. M. (tr.) (2009) *Isaac Israeli. A Neoplatonic Philosopher of the Early Tenth Century. His works translated with comments and an outline of his Philosophy*, Chicago: University of Chicago Press.
Anawati, G. C. (1971) "Hudūṯ al-'ālam," *Encyclopédie de l'Islam*, vol. III, Leiden/Paris: Brill/ Maisonneuve & Larose, p. 567.
——. (1996) "La teologia islamica medievale," in G. d'Onofrio (ed.), *Storia della teologia nel Medioevo*, I, Piemme: Casale Monferrato.
Badawi, 'A. (ed.) (1955) *Plotinus apud Arabes. Theologia Aristotelis et fragmenta quae supersunt*, Cairo: Maktabat al-Nahḍah al-Miṣrīyah.
Bieler, L. (ed.) (1957) *Anicii Manlii Severini Boethii Philosophiae consolatio*, Turnholti: Typographi Brepols editores pontificii (Corpus Christianorum. Series Latina; 94; Anicii Manlii Severini Boethii Opera; 1).
Chase, M. (2011) "Discussions on the Eternity of the World in Late Antiquity," *ΣΧΟΛΗ, A Journal of the Centre for Ancient Philosophy and the Classical Tradition* 5, 2: 111–73.
——. (2013) "Discussions on the eternity of the world in Antiquity and contemporary cosmology, I–II," *ΣΧΟΛΗ, Ancient Philosophy and the Classical Tradition* 7, 1: 19–68.
d'Ancona, C. (2001) "Pseudo-Theology of Aristotle, Chapter I: Structure and Composition," *Oriens. Zeitschrift der internationalen Gesellschaft für Orientforschung* 36: 78–112.
——. (ed.) (2003) *Plotino, La dicesa dell'anima nei corpi (Enn. IV 8 [6]); Plotiniana arabica (Pseudo-Teologia di Aristotele, capitoli 1 e 7); "Detti del sapiente greco,"* Padova: Il Poligrapho (Subsidia Medievalia Patavina 4).
——. (2010) "La teologia neoplatonica di 'Aristotele' e gli inizi della filosofia arabomusulmana," in R. Goulet et al. (eds.), *Entre Orient et Occident: la philosophie et la science gréco-romaines dans le monde arabe*, Vandoeuvres-Genève: Fondation Hardt, pp. 1–32.
Davidson, H. A. (1987) *Proofs for Eternity, Creation and the Existence of God in Medieval Islamic and Jewish Philosophy*, Oxford: Oxford University Press.

De Smet, D. (1989) "Le verbe-impératif dans le système cosmologique de l'Ismaélisme," *Revue des Sciences Philosophiques et Théologiques* 73: 397–412.
——. (2012) *La philosophie Ismaélienne. Un ésotérisme chiite entre néoplatonisme et gnose*, Paris: Les Éditions du Cerf.
Diels, H. (ed.) (1882–1895) *Simplicii in Aristotelis physicorum libros octo commentaria*, 2 vols. (*Commentaria in Aristotelem Graeca* 9 & 10). Berlin: Reimer.
Diwald, S. (1975) *Arabische Philosophie und Wissenschaft in der Enzyklopädie. Kitāb Iḫwān aṣ-ṣafā' (III). Die Lehre von Seele und Intellekt*, Wiesbaden: Otto Harrassowitz.
Dombart, B. & Kalb. A. (eds.) (1955) *Sancti Aurelii Augustini De civitate Dei*, 2. vols., (Corpus Christianorum. Series Latina 47–18; Aurelii Augustini opera 14, 1–2), Turnholti: Brepols.
Endress, G. (1973) *Proclus Arabus. Zwanzig Abschnitte aus der Institutio Theologica in arabischer Übersetzung*, Beirut: Franz Steiner Verlag.
——. (1997) "The Circle of al-Kindi. Early Arabic Translations from the Greek and the Rise of Islamic Philosophy," in G. Endress & R. Kruk (eds.), *The ancient tradition in Christian and Islamic Hellenism: studies on the transmission of Greek philosophy and sciences dedicated to H.-J. Drossaart Lulofs on his ninetieth birthday*, Leiden: Research School CNWS (CNWS publications 50), pp. 43–76.
Frank, R. M. (1980) "*Al-ma'dūm wal-mawjūd*. The non-existent, the existent, and the possible in the teaching of Abū Hāshim and his followers," *Mélanges de l'Institut d'Études Orientales* 14: 185–210, repr. in id., 2007, study IV.
Ġālib, M. (ed.) (2006) *Rasā'il Ikhwān al-Ṣafā' wa Khullān al-Wafā'*, 4 vols., Beirut: Dāra al-ṣādir.
Gardet, L. (1971) "Ibdā'," *Encyclopédie de l'Islam*, vol. III, Leiden/Paris: Brill/Maisonneuve & Larose, pp. 685–6.
Hasnawi, A. (1994) "Alexandre d'Aphrodise vs. Jean Philopon: notes sur quelques traites d'Alexandre 'perdus' en grec, conservés en arabe," *Arabic Sciences and Philosophy* 4: 53–109.
Janos, D. (2009) "Al-Fārābī, Creation Ex Nihilo, and the Cosmological Doctrine of *K. Al-Jam'* and *Jawābāt*," *Journal of the American Oriental Society* 129, 1: 1–18.
Janssens, J. (1997) "Creation and emanation in Ibn Sīnā," *Documenti e Studi sulla Tradizione Filosofica Medievale* 8: 455–77.
Lizzini, O. (2009) "Il nulla, l'inesistente, la cosa: note intorno alla terminologia e alla dottrina del nulla e della creazione dal nulla nel pensiero islamico," in M. Lenzi & A. Maierù (eds.), *Discussioni sul nulla tra Medioevo e età moderna*, Firenze: Leo S. Olschki, pp. 63–109.
Martini Bonadeo, C. (tr.) (2008) *Al-Fārābī, L'armonia delle opinioni dei due sapienti, il divino Platone e Aristotele*, Pisa: Edizione Plus/Pisa University Press.
Najjār, F. M. (ed.) (1964) *Abū Naṣr al-Fārābī, Kitāb al-siyāsah al-madanīyah al-mullaqab bi-Mabādi' al-mawjūdāt*, Beirut: Al-Maṭba'ah al-Kathūlīkīyah.
Peterson, D. C. (2001) "Creation," in J. Dammen McAuliffe (ed.), *Encyclopedia of the Qur'ān*, vol. I, Leiden: Brill, pp. 472–80.
Rabe, H. (ed.) (1899) *Ioannes Philoponus. De aeternitate mundi contra Proclum*, Leipzig: Teubner.
Rashed, M. (2008) "Al-Fārābī's lost treatise *On changing beings* and the possibility of a demonstration of the eternity of the world," *Arabic Sciences and Philosophy* 18: 19–58.
——. (2009) "On the Authorship of the Treatise *On The Harmonization of the Opinions of the Two Sages* Attributed to Al-Fārābī," *Arabic Sciences and Philosophy* 19: 43–82.
Rashed, R. & Jolivet, J. (eds.) (1998) *Œuvres philosophiques et scientifiques d'al-Kindī*, vol. II: *Métaphysique et cosmologie*, Leiden: Brill.
Rowson, E. K. (1988) *A Muslim philosopher on the soul and its fate: Al-'Āmirī's Kitāb al-amad 'alā l-abad*, New Haven: American Oriental Society.
Smith, A. (ed.) (1993) *Porphyrii Philosophi Fragmenta*, Leipzig & Stuttgart: Teubner.
Sodano, A. R. (1964) *Porphyrii in Platonis Timaeum commentariorum fragmenta*, Napoli: Istituto della Stampa.

Sorabji, R. (1983) *Time, Creation and the Continuum. Theories in Antiquity and the Early Middle Ages*, London/Ithaca: Duckworth/Cornell University Press.
Taylor, R. C. (1981) *The Liber de Causis (Kalām fi maḥḍ al-khair): a Study of Medieval Neoplatonism*, PhD diss., U. of Toronto.
Triki, A. (1974) *Néoplatonisme et aspect mystique de la création de l'univers dans la philosophie des Iḫwān*, PhD diss., Lille III.
Vallat, P. (tr.) (2012) *Épître sur l'Intellect*, Paris: Les Belles Lettres.
van Ess, J. (1991–1997) *Theologie und Gesellschaft im 2. und 3. Jahrhundert Hidschra*, 6 vols., Berlin & New York: Walter de Gruyter.
Westerink, L. G. & Combès, J. (eds. & tr.) (1997–2003) *Damascius, Commentaire du Parménide de Platon*, 4 vols., Paris (Collection des Universités de France. Série grecque).
Zimmermann, F. W. (1986) "The Origins of the So-Called *Theology of Aristotle*," in J. Kraye, W. F. Ryan, & C. B. Schmitt (eds.), *Pseudo-Aristotle in the Middle Ages: The Theology and other texts*, London: Warburg Institute, University of London, pp. 110–240.

Part V

EPISTEMOLOGY AND PHILOSOPHY OF MIND

21
EXTERNAL AND INTERNAL HUMAN SENSES

Carla Di Martino

Translated from French by Paul Carls

Introduction

The world that we experience every day is filled with a variety of different objects. Our mental and sensory faculties are continuously appealed to and the information we receive from the outside world needs at all times to be classified, analyzed, and elaborated. In order to understand what is going on around us, to make decisions, or simply to survive (both as individuals and as a species), we need to interact with the world, and on some level, to appropriate it. In sum, we need to know the world.

From a biological point of view, humans are animals. They are rooted to the physical and material world by their body, which is composed of flesh and blood, and by the limits that are imposed upon them by their physiology. But humans do not stop at a mere classification of sensory information. They do not stop at "what appears to them," the *phenomenon*, i.e. that which is accessible to them via sight, sound, touch, taste, or smell, as it is to every other animal endowed with sense organs.

Is this basic, "animal" knowledge, which only humans are able to process and overcome, truly the same for all higher ordered animals (i.e. those physiologically endowed with the same sense organs as humans), or, rather, does human knowledge from the very beginning follow a different path? Does the superior, or ulterior, so-called "intellectual," knowledge that humans strive for originate in the sensible world? In short, do human sensory faculties and animal sensory faculties operate in the same way and provide the same results? At which point in the acquisition of knowledge do humans and animals diverge?

This is a complex subject rich with ethical, philosophical, and religious implications that are still today of significant importance to those investigating the relationship between the mind and the body or the status of humans in the world. It is a line of investigation that was pursued with precision by the principal authors of Arabic psychological science, whose texts were translated into Latin between the eleventh and thirteenth centuries (Di Martino 2008; Bazán 1998; D'Alverny 1993; Hasse 2000). Their works have structured research and reflection in various different disciplines and have forever shaped the development of Western thought.

The Extension of the Domain of Perception

In *On the Soul*, a foundational text of the Greek, Arabic, and Jewish philosophical and psychological traditions, Aristotle explains that because of our senses, we know both qualities, the sensibles "proper" to each sense, and quantities, the "common" sensibles (Aristotle, *On the Soul*, II, 6 and III, 1–3). By accident, the senses may ascertain that these qualities are inherent to an individual substance. For example, if Cleon's son is white, and if we used our sense of sight to inform us about Cleon's son, we might accidentally know Cleon's son as white, and not as a man, the son of Cleon. Our sight knows only his qualities, not his essence or his identity as Cleon's son. Aristotle also tells us that the five senses operate on the sensible object only when that object is present, and only through the use of corporeal organs. The five senses are in effect only able to grasp an individual object's particular and material characteristics. The intellect, however, is incorporeal and immaterial. Its domain is that of the universal.

Already for Aristotle, there exist, between perception and intellect, faculties with the ability to conserve and rework sensible data, even when the original sensible object is no longer present, while remaining in the domain of the particular (Aristotle, *On the Soul*, III, 4). When this is the case, we are dealing with imagination and memory, the topic of Aristotle's *Parva Naturalia*. Yet Aristotle does not explicitly give a name to these post-sensory faculties. Nevertheless, in the Arabic, Jewish, and Latin translations and commentaries of Aristotle's psychological texts, these faculties are called "internal senses" or "senses of the mind," in contradistinction to the five external or corporeal senses. Whereas the external senses use corporeal organs, the eyes for sight, the ears for sound, etc., the internal senses do not have an organ. They do, however, have a central corporeal location. This location is the brain, in conformity with the medical Galenic tradition, but in contrast with the Aristotelian tradition, which locates the origin of sensation in the heart (Wolfson 1935; Di Martino 2008).

Ibn Sīnā (or Avicenna, 980–1037), the first author to provide a systematic doctrine of the internal senses, and later Ibn Rushd (or Averroes, 1126–1198), came up with two very different theories of the internal senses (for Ibn Sīnā, Hasse 2000; for both authors Di Martino 2008). In their research on the soul, they identify, among other things, that Aristotle fails to take into account accidental perception. They make this failure the key to understanding the difference between the human soul and the animal soul, their principal interest, and also to studying the exact relationship between sensible knowledge, both internal and external, and intellectual knowledge. Both Ibn Sīnā and Ibn Rushd also ask a question that previous thinkers would never have considered and that in contrast is still today very relevant: the question of animal intelligence. Where does what we call the intellectual faculty begin? Where does it come from? Does it exist as a seed, in Aristotelian terms, "potentially," in the animal soul or not? Is humanity an animal that possesses something more than the other animals, a further added ability or an animal that is radically "other," an animal structured in a different and unique way from its very first encounter with the world?

In order to answer these questions, the philosophers of the Arabic tradition developed the notion of "*ma'nā*," or the "signification" of a thing. This term was translated into Latin as *intentio* in the Middle Ages, and profoundly marked the history of psychology, logic, and the philosophy of language (Gyekye 1971; Black 1993). By studying the signification of things, Arabic thinkers believed that they had found the key to answering the difficult question concerning the difference between human and animal knowledge. At the very least they had discovered an exceptional point of view for studying the human senses.

Human beings are animals endowed with the same organs as the other higher ordered animals, but is the knowledge both humans and other animals gain about the world through their senses the same? Do things have the same value and signification for humans as they do for other animals? Or are there important differences between the two ways of knowing?

Knowing the World: Sensible and Non-Sensible Entities

In *On the Soul*, Aristotle analyzes in succession objects, faculties, and the operations of the soul. For him, the sensible soul of humans and animals functions in the same way and to understand how, it is necessary to first study sensible objects (Aristotle, *On the Soul*: II, 6; III, 1–3; for Aristotle's text, Lories 1998; for the Greek exegesis, Di Martino 2001; for the Latin and Arabic traditions, Hasse 2000; Di Martino 2008).

As Aristotle explains, there are three ways of telling that an object is "sensible." In two of these three ways, we are dealing with the "perception by itself" of an object, and in the third way we are dealing with the "perception by accident" of an object. Of the two cases of perception by itself, one is a sensible object "proper" to each sense as an object that none of the other senses are able to perceive: color for sight, flavor for taste, etc. In the other case, there are sensible objects "common" to all or several of the senses. For example, the movement, shape, or number of an object can be perceived by sight and by touch.

Still, for Aristotle and for the entire Aristotelian tradition, psychology is a branch of physics or natural philosophy defined as the science of motion. The study of perception is thus the study of a particular type of motion. In this case it is the study of the movement of alteration produced by the sensible object on the sense organ. The proper sensible objects affect the sense organ to which they are destined, and only this one. The common sensible objects are able to alter several sense organs simultaneously. The "sensibles by accident," however, do not by themselves alter any bodily organ, but are simply associated "by accident" to a sensory alteration that is produced by a sensible object. For example, in order to say, "I see Diarès' son," it is necessary that Diarès' son is accidentally associated to the color white, a sensible object proper to sight (Sorabji 1995; Caston 2005).

The process of perception, thus, inverts the predicate relationship; Diarès' son is sensible, for example, visible, because he is an "accident" of the color white, which is the proper object of sight, while in the predication, the color white is an accident of Diarès' son.

But what kind of object of knowledge is "Diarès' son," in itself? Which faculty is devoted to knowing such an object "by itself"?

In the treatise *On the Soul*, Aristotle devotes no time to an analysis of sensibles by accident, but it is evident that "sensible by accident" and "perception by accident" are notions that cannot be superimposed. In Chapter III, 1, three examples of "perception by accident" are given: sight perceiving sweetness, sight perceiving bile, and, again, sight perceiving Cleon's son (a variant of the case of Diarès' son studied above). In the three cases, the sensible object in question, the sweetness, the bile, or Cleon's son, does not at all affect the organ of sight. The perception of the sensible object, or the awareness that the particular object is present before the sense of sight, accidentally accompanies the perception by sight of its proper object, or its color. The association of a color to an object is conserved in memory and in these cases can lead to the following associations: for yellow, yellow-sweet-honey, or yellow-bitter-bile: for white, white-Cleon's son. In this way, sight perceives by accident an object that is the proper object of another faculty, which perceives the object by itself. In the case of sweetness, the other faculty is taste.

Aristotle, thus, established:

1 that each sense perceives by itself a sensible object that is proper to itself, which is to say, suffers a movement of alteration from the action of the object, which is sensible by itself;
2 that each sense perceives by itself common sensible objects, which are not proper to any sense, which is to say that they do not affect one sense organ exclusively, but many sense organs;
3 that each sense perceives by accident sensible objects proper to other senses, of which one other sense will have perception by itself;
4 that each sense perceives by accident the sensibles by accident, such as Cleon's son. The sensibles by accident are not, in themselves, sensibles, but fall accidentally into the field of the senses because they are linked to a sensible quality.

But in the case of the bile or of Diarès or Cleon's son, which faculty is being used? Aristotle does not provide an answer. Two questions remain open:

1 What is, *in itself*, an object sensible by accident?
2 What is the proper faculty that perceives by itself the sensibles by accident?

The Value and Signification of Knowledge Gained Through the Senses

In his *Book of the Soul*, a sort of encyclopedia of comparative Aristotelian psychology including Aristotle and the principal commentators of the Neoplatonic tradition, Ibn Sīnā devotes a good deal of attention to sensible knowledge and to the internal senses (Ibn Sīnā, *Book of the Soul*, I, 5; II, 2; IV). In these pages we encounter the Aristotelian criteria that make a strict object-faculty distinction. Indeed, from the very beginning of the treatise, the first rule for the classification of the internal faculties is that "certain among them perceive the form of sensibles, while others perceive their *ma'nā* [pl. *ma'ānī*, from the Arabic root '-n-y: "to signify," "to mean"]." The sensible "forms" are Aristotle's proper and common sensible objects. They are perceived by the external senses and then transmitted to the common sense, which then reconstructs their reciprocal links. For example, an apple would be perceived in the following way: this round (object) is green and sweet. Once this initial process takes place, the "forms" of the sensibles are then kept in the imagination, where another internal faculty, the imaginative faculty, is able to retrieve them and create new associations (a square apple). In contrast, the *ma'ānī* of things, their "significations," is a new notion that is introduced by Ibn Sīnā. The *ma'ānī* are perceived by the estimative faculty (*al-qūwa al wahmiyya*), and then conserved in memory.

According to Ibn Sīnā, the existence of this object not captured by the external senses becomes obvious from the fact that sensible knowledge for animals is vaster and richer than the knowledge gained merely through the senses. For example, when a ewe perceives a wolf, the chain of perception going from external senses to common sense only identifies a four-legged-black-hairy. This information is not sufficient to make the ewe flee (a black dog would have the same attributes). The ewe flees because it perceives danger. To the ewe, the wolf signifies "danger." Hence the wolf's "signification," which the ewe perceives is due to a faculty that Ibn Sīnā calls the "estimative faculty." This faculty is responsible for "evaluating" (*w-h-m*, same root as *al-qūwa al-wahmiyya*) that the four-legged-black-hairy is a wolf and for drawing the conclusion of capital biological importance that the ewe should flee. In this way, the estimative faculty seems, at first glance, to correspond to instinct (Black 1993, 2000).

In the *Book of the Soul* Ibn Sīnā devotes a good deal of attention to *ma'nā*, the estimative faculty, and its workings in humans and other animals. He gives three definitions of *ma'nā* (*Book of the Soul* I, 5):

1 the thing that the soul perceives of the sensible world, without the external senses perceiving it first;
2 what is not material in its essence, even though it sometimes can be found accidentally within the material world;
3 what we cannot perceive by the senses, either:
3a because by its nature, it is not at all a sensible object, or,
3b because, even though it is a sensible object, we cannot perceive it at the moment of judgment [the Arabic word *ḥukm* here translates the Greek word *krisis* and "judgment by the senses" is here to be understood in Aristotelian language as perception].

The first two definitions refer back to the case of the wolf and the ewe. For the third definition there are two examples to give:

3a for things that are not, by their nature, sensibles, such as hatred, meanness, or the aversion the ewe grasps in the form of the wolf ... .

This is still an explanation of the second definition and we once again are dealing with the classic example: the ewe perceives the wolf's hostility. In Aristotelian terms, the ewe's senses would only perceive the wolf's hostility by accident, since this *ma'nā* is the proper object of a different faculty, in this case the estimative faculty, and since each sense perceives by itself the object that is proper to itself and perceives by accident the object proper to the other senses. This corresponds to Aristotle's example of sight perceiving sweetness.

Definition 3b is different:

> 3b As for things that are sensibles, we see for example a yellow thing, and thus we judge that it is honey, and that it is sweet.

It is a mixture of the two cases cited by Aristotle, sight perceiving bile/honey, or sight perceiving Cleon's/Diarès' son.

Thus, definitions 1, 2, and 3a correspond to Aristotle's "sensibles by accident," found in *On the Soul*, II, 6. Definition 3b corresponds to the two cases of "perception by accident" that are studied by Aristotle in *On the Soul*, III, 1.

Are the honey, the wolf, and Cleon's son, thus, *ma'ānī*? Or, would the honey's sweetness, the bile's bitterness, the wolf's meanness, or the whiteness of Cleon's son be *ma'ānī*?

In the end, the status of a sensible object as form or as *ma'ānī* is not absolute, but is determined by the relationship that exists during the act of perception between the subject and the perceived object. In the case involving intention and the estimative faculty, the relation between faculty and object seems reversed (Black 1996). It is no longer the faculty that is defined by its relation to its object, as Aristotle had stated. Rather, the object is defined by the faculty that apprehends it; the object is called *ma'nā* when it is perceived by the estimative faculty.

There is an ambiguity, however, that derives quite rightly from an ambiguity in Aristotle's own theory pertaining to the notions of "sensible by accident" and "perception by accident." But this slip of meaning, far from remaining a simple problem of exegesis, opens a question of capital importance. This is because for Ibn Sīnā, as for his master Aristotle, animals and humans are physiologically endowed with the same sensory apparatus, and thus able to grasp the forms and *ma'ānī* of things. Humans are certainly, like animals, endowed with instinct. Our eyes close when an object is approaching, and babies naturally look for their mother's breast. But would humans be able to perceive the singular person "Cleon's son" by a sensory faculty? And in this case, would animals be endowed with some sort of "animal intelligence"?

For Ibn Sīnā all these activities take place prior to the apprehension of intellectual knowledge and function as preparations for knowing the intelligible in act existing in the separate agent intellect. This is a knowing that comes about only thanks to a conjoining with the agent intellect or a reception of its emanation for the sake of a linking to the agent intellect where all the worldly intelligibles reside. In contrast to the apprehension of particulars, the grasped intelligible in act does not remain in the soul when this conjoining or emanation ceases simply because there is no intellectual memory in the soul itself for retention.

In his commentaries on Aristotle's works as well as in his own treatises on psychology, Ibn Rushd takes up this question. For Ibn Rushd, perception is a continuous and consequent cognitive chain in which the object is successively stripped of its material clothing and grasped by the different faculties according to different degrees of abstraction or separation (Averroes 1953, 1972). Each faculty "works" on the result of the preceding faculty, following a unique and hierarchically defined path that marks the passage of the known object from the outside, material world to the interior, "spiritual" world of the soul.

In Ibn Rushd's *Epitome of Parva Naturalia*, which is entirely devoted to human perception, three classes of sensible objects are possible. These operate on three levels of abstraction, or "spiritual input" from an object, which define for humans three internal senses, or "spiritual senses," and function according to the Aristotelian principle that the known object defines the knowing faculty (on the signification of "spiritual" *(rūhānīyy)* in Ibn Rushd, see Di Martino 2007). The form defines the senses (the five external senses and common sense). From this form that is perceived in the object by the senses, the imaginative faculty extracts and perceives the image, which defines the imaginative faculty. From this image, a third faculty, the so-called "cogitative" faculty *(al-mufakkira)*, extracts the object's *ma'nā*, the signification, and transfers it to the memory, which then perceives and preserves it.

The *ma'nā* is the most spiritual form of sensible knowledge and its faculty, human memory, not only preserves, but also knows it (Arabic root *d-r-k*. Black 1996; Di Martino 2008). The *ma'nā* is a copy of the particular object as it can exist in the soul, stripped of all material. It is the pulp of the sensible, a fruit that has been stripped of its rind by the other faculties, with the pieces of rind being sensible accidents, which are in turn the sensible qualities of an object existing in the world (Black 1996).

Each imagined form, as Ibn Rushd further explains, has a substratum, a matter (its figure) and a form (its *ma'nā*). Even though the matter and form of an image do not correspond to the material and form of the physical object (on Aristotle, cf. Black 1996), the *ma'nā* seems here to be the individual form in matter in an object of the world, where it exists enveloped by a rind of material accidents. In this case, the *ma'nā* would only be sensible because it is covered by sensible qualities. From Ibn Rushd's Aristotelian point of view, it would be "perceived by accident" by the sensory faculties, since the senses and the imagination perceive it only through its image. That is, the *ma'nā*, as an image derived from the sensed particular thing, is the subject for sensible qualities that come to be sensed in act in the soul. This is so, whereas the *ma'nā* is the proper object of another faculty, namely the faculty of memory specific to human beings.

But then what kind of faculty is memory, which knows the hidden pulp of the sensible, in a pure, spiritual way, as it is detached from every accident and all material?

Animals are not capable of the sort of memory possessed by human beings, as Ibn Rushd explains on numerous occasions. Rather, non-rational animals are capable only of the sort of memory that conserves sensible data in their imagination in the form of images, but they are never able to grasp the *ma'nā* of things. This level of abstraction is unknown to them.

For the first time, then, it is clearly stated that there are structural differences between human and animal sensibilities. Herein lies Ibn Rushd's great innovation, but also his dangerous revolution of the study of the sensible world. Humans and animals perceive sensible forms in the same way through their external senses, are both able to take stock of this sensible knowledge in the form of images that they are eventually able to manipulate as they wish. Yet only humans are able to go beyond appearances to see what there is below the sensible shell of an object, or to see what there is hidden underneath an object's sensible qualities.

Yet, what exactly is hidden underneath these qualities? What is Ibn Rushd's *ma'nā* when it is perceived by the exclusively human faculty of memory?

Humans are endowed with a special sensory apparatus that reveals to them what there is beyond the sensible world. Is this apparatus an alternative to intellectual knowledge, another path to knowledge, another form of intelligence? Thomas Aquinas would famously call this apparatus *ratio particularis* (Thomas Aquinas, *Summa Theologiae*: I, q 78, a 4) following the lead of Ibn Rushd.

This leads to a further question: do the internal human senses perceive individual substances, without the help of the intellect?

The first answer, as trivial as it might seem, is that a soul without an intellect is not endowed with memory either. Only those beings in possession of an intellectual faculty, the cogitative faculty and memory, are hence able to perceive the intentions of things and not solely their forms and images. This explanation recalls the example of the fruit/sensible, in which the sensible qualities are the rind and the *ma'nā* the pulp, leading to the analogy between the material-form pair and the image-*ma'nā* pair. All of this runs the risk of causing one to believe that the *ma'nā* is the essence of a thing, a risk that Aristotle's ambiguous text posed and of which Ibn Rushd is well aware.

In the *Long Commentary on the Soul*, where the question is explicitly asked, Ibn Rushd excludes it most clearly. He explains that the human senses are capable of grasping the *intentio* (Latin for *ma'nā*, since the *Long Commentary* exists today only in Latin translation) of this man here, or of that horse there, "and so on for the ten categories of predication" (Averroes 1953: C 63, 255), but that they are never able to go beyond the level of individuality or to void the links of individuality. Thus, following the chain sense–common sense–imagination–cogitation–human memory, humans can perceive, beyond the rind of sensible qualities that is in this case a four legged–hairy–black–loyal, that a dog is "hiding." Yet, in no case will the sensible forces alone suffice for knowing either the essence of the dog or its loyalty. The dog, or the loyalty, will be perceived only by the ewe's senses, for they fall accidentally into the domain of its senses. This data will remain linked to a particular and provisional perception, or the perception of this precise case, that is defined in time and space (i.e. the four-legged-black-hairy-loyal that is this dog here and now). Human internal senses, on the contrary, are sharper and go beyond the image of this dog in some sense to see what there is behind the image that is perceived by the senses yet still at the level of something particular. But only the intellect is able to go beyond this individual dog, which is the object of a finite, individual, and temporally unique experience.

This explanation is far from resolving the problem. But Ibn Rushd does not elaborate on this point. This is because he concludes that essence is the object of a different, non-sensory faculty. Thus, there is no reason to discuss the problem in the chapters dedicated to the senses. How to know essences is a question whose answer needs to be sought in another domain. Under the influence of Aristotle, psychology remains a branch of physics and limited to the study of the motions produced by sensible objects on the sense organs of our material body (including the brain, for the internal senses).

In addition, in his *De Anima*, Aristotle speaks of "Cleon's son," thus of this particular man and not of "Man" in universal terms. This is why Ibn Sīnā already explained that the *ma'ānī* are immaterial notions, claiming that they are anything but singularities. It is possible to know the notion of meanness in itself, of course, but what the estimative faculty of the ewe apprehends is not meanness as a universal. Rather, it is only a meanness that is incarnated in a particular wolf, or only the particular meanness that the wolf shows towards the ewe. Ibn Rushd goes even further. The *ma'nā* is what is perceived by the senses by accident, and the proper object of memory is every other individual determination of a thing (except for the proper and common sensible objects).

Why? Because here it is necessary to go from the perceptive relation back to the predicate relation. This is because "proper and common sensible objects" are merely sensible objects; they are merely accidents of the individual. Yet, animals also perceive accidents. But human sensibility is infinitely richer and more focused. It knows the individual as an individual, from all the possible points of view, before beginning to know it in its essence.

In contrast to Ibn Sīnā, for the mature Ibn Rushd in his later *Long Commentary on the De Anima* the human external and internal senses apprehend the intelligibles in potency that will be transferred from the being of intelligibles in potency in particulars to that of intelligibles in act in intellect. This takes place by a genuine abstraction or separation and not by a reception of intelligible content from the agent intellect. All that is known comes about through the senses external and internal by a separation and elevation of the intelligible intention from particularity to universality thanks to the abstractive power of the agent intellect and (uniquely for Ibn Rushd) the receptive power of a separate but shared material intellect.

Conclusion

In contradistinction to the authors in the Aristotelian philosophical tradition, Arabic philosophers asked themselves about the structural differences between the cognitive organs of humans and animals. While it is true that humans remain physiologically animals, their knowledge of the sensible world is different from the very beginning. Animals and humans both perceive the world in the same way, but they feel and live it very differently. This is what allows humans to go "beyond physical things" (in a metaphysical sense), or, better, to sense that things not perceivable by the sensory faculties do exist, be it in the great beyond, in the realm of religion, or in the mysteries of the soul and of internal life.

Further Reading

Blaustein, M. A. (1984) *Averroes on the imagination and the intellect*, Ann Arbor MI: Harvard University.

Hasse, D. (2000) *Avicenna's De anima in the Latin West. The Formation of a Peripatetic Philosophy of the Soul 1160–1300*, London/Turin: The Warburg Institute/Nino Aragno Editore.

Klubertanz, G. P. (1952) *The Discursive Power. Sources and Doctrine of Vis cogitativa according to Thomas Aquinas*, St. Louis Missouri: Modern Schoolman.

Perler, D. (2001) *Ancient and Medieval Theories of Intentionality*, Leiden: Brill.

Sorabji, R. (1991) "From Aristotle to Brentano: the development of the concept of intentionality," J. Annas (ed.), *Oxford Studies in Ancient Philosophy. Supplementary Volume: Aristotle and the Ancient Tradition*, Oxford: Clarendon Press, pp. 227–59.
Taylor, R. C. (2000) "*Cogitatio*, *Cogitativus* and *Cogitare*: Remarks on the Cogitative Power in Averroes," in J. Hamesse and C. Steel (eds.), *L'elaboration du vocabulaire philosophique au Moyen Age* (Rencontres de philosophie Médiévale Vol. 8.), Turnhout: Brepols, pp. 111–46.

References

Averroes (1953) *Commentarium Magnum in Aristotelis De Anima libros*, F. S. Crawford (ed.), Cambridge, MA: Mediaeval Academy of America.
——. (1961) *Epitome of Parva Naturalia*, H. Blumberg (tr.), Cambridge, MA: Mediaeval Academy of America.
——. (1972) *Talkhîs kitâb al-Ḥiss wa-al-maḥsûs* (*Epitome* of *Parva Naturalia*), H. A. Blumberg (ed.), Cambridge, MA: Mediaeval Academy of America.
Avicenna (1974) *al-Shifā'. 6. Kitāb al-nafs (Book of the Soul / De Anima)*, G. C. Anawati & S. Zayed (eds.), Cairo: Millénaire d'Avicenne.
Bazán, B. C. (1998) "Introduction," in B. C. Bazán (ed.), *Anonymi Magistri Artium: Sententia Super II et III De Anima*, Leuven & Paris: Peeters.
Black, D. (1993) "Estimation in Avicenna: The Logical and Psychological Dimensions," *Dialogue* 32: 219–58.
——. (1996) "Memory, Individuals, and the Past in Averroes' Psychology," *Medieval Philosophy and Theology* 5: 161–87.
——. (2000) "Imagination and Estimation: Arabic Paradigms and Western Transformations," *Topoi* 19: 59–75.
Caston, V. (2005) "The Spirit and the Letter, Aristotle on Perception," in R. Salles (ed.), *Metaphysics, Soul and Ethics in Ancient Thought. Themes from the work of Richard Sorabj*, Oxford: Oxford University Press, pp. 245–320.
D'Alverny, M. T. (1993) *Avicenne en Occident*, Paris: Vrin.
Di Martino, C. (2001) "Alle radici della percezione. Senso Comune e Sensazione Comune in Aristotele, De Anima III.1–2," *Archives d'histoire doctrinale et littérature du Moyen Age* 68: 7–26.
——. (2007) "La perception spirituelle. Perspectives de recherche pour l'histoire des *Parva Naturalia* dans la tradition arabo-latine," *Veritas* 52: 21–35.
——. (2008) *Ratio Particularis. Doctrines des sens internes d'Avicenne à Thomas d'Aquin*, Paris: Vrin.
Gyekye, K. (1971) "The terms 'prima intentio' and 'secunda intentio' in Arabic Logic," *Speculum* 46: 32–8.
Hasse, D. (2000) *Avicenna's De anima in the Latin West. The Formation of a Peripatetic Philosophy of the Soul 1160–1300*, London/Turin: The Warburg Institute/Nino Aragno Editore.
Lories, D. (1998) *Le sens commun et le jugement du phronimos. Aristote et les stoïciens*, Louvain-la-Neuve: Peeters.
Sorabji, R. (1995) "Intentionality and Physiological Processes: Aristole Theory of Sense Perception," in M. Nussbaum & A. Rorty Oksenberg (eds.), *Essays on Aristotle's De anima*, Oxford: Oxford University Press, pp. 195–225.
Taylor, R. C. (1999) "Remarks on Cogitation in Averroes' *Commentarium Magnum in Aristotelis De Anima libros*," in J. A. Aersten & G. Endress (eds.), *Averroes and the Aristotelian Tradition: Sources, Constitution and Reception of the Philosophy of Ibn Rushd (1126–1198): Proceedings of the Fourth Symposium Averroicum, Cologne, 1996*, Leiden: Brill, pp. 217–55.
Wolfson, H. A. (1935) "The Internal Senses in Latin, Arabic and Hebrew Philosophical Texts," *Harvard Theological Review* 28, 2: 69–133.

22
THE EPISTEMOLOGY OF ABSTRACTION

Richard C. Taylor

Introduction

The notion of abstraction or separation is most evidently found in Aristotle in the application of mathematical principles, as, e.g., when quantities are taken or separated off from extended objects to determine the area of plot of land in square meters or yards through a practical application of geometry. In epistemology in the medieval traditions intellectual abstraction involved the view that human knowing comes about through an apprehension of the forms of things of the world by separating or abstracting the intelligible in some sense from the formal contents of things having physical form and matter. Not just a simple issue of selective attention, this was taken to be a metaphysical process in which a special power available to human beings is understood to make possible the separation of the intelligible form or essence of a thing from its reality in the nature of a material entity and the realization of that form in the human intellect. While not altogether unrelated, this is not to be confused with the Platonic methodology of positing a one to exist over the many in the case of a sensory apprehension of a plurality of particulars found in *Republic* V (507b) which asserted there to be separately existing Forms as the essences of imperfect particular forms in things of physical reality or the realm of opinion. Rather, in intellectual abstraction the intelligible form of the thing experienced in nature in some way prompts a transference or movement of some sort whereby the human knower employs sensory experience of particulars and the power of intellect to grasp the form as intelligible through an act of the human intellect.

Though not found in an explicit way in the philosophical psychology of Aristotle (*pace* Gutas 2012: 426 ff.; cf. Burnyeat 2008), there are texts which seem to permit an abstractionist account (e.g. *De Anima* 3.5, and 3.4, 3.7, 3.8; Cleary 1985). Nevertheless, it was only many centuries after Aristotle (d. fifth century B.C.E.) that the doctrine of intellectual abstraction for the formation of intelligibles in act by the human rational soul or intellect was first unambiguously set forth by Alexander of Aphrodisias (second century C.E.). His work was important for Porphyry and influential in both the Latin and the Arabic philosophical traditions (Tweedale 1984). In Alexander's *On the*

Intellect which was very important in Isḥāq Ibn Ḥunayn's Arabic translation (Finnegan in Alexander of Aphrodisias 1956) we find the following:

> [E]nmattered forms are made intelligible by the intellect, being intelligible potentially. The intellect separates them (*chōrizōn/yufridu-hā*) from the matter with which they have their being, and itself makes them intelligible in actuality, and each of them, when it is thought, then comes to be intelligible in actuality and intellect; [but] they are not like this previously or by their own nature.
> (Alexander of Aphrodisias 1887: 108.4–7, tr. 2004: 28, Arabic 1956: 185.1–6, 1971: 34.4–7)

> For intellect, apprehending the form of the thing that is thought and separating it (*chōrizōn/faṣala-hā*) from the matter, both makes it intelligible in actuality and itself comes to be intellect in actuality.
> (Alexander of Aphrodisias 1887: 111.15–16, tr. 2004: 29, Arabic 1956: 185.1–6, 1971: 34.4–7)

> First it [the intellect] produces by abstraction (*aphairesei/ifrād*) [something] intelligible, and then in this way it apprehends some one of these things which it thinks and defines as a this-something. Even if it separates and apprehends at the same time, nevertheless the separating is conceptually prior; for this is what it is for it to be able to apprehend the form.
> (Alexander of Aphrodisias 1887: 108.14–16, tr. 2004: 36, Arabic 1956: 193.2–4, 1971: 38.16–18)

While this last quotation from *On the Intellect* is based on Alexander's account of Aristotle of Mytilene (Sharples 1987: 1211–12), the teaching on abstraction is also found in his treatise *On the Soul* (e.g. Alexander of Aphrodisias 1897: 90.9 *ex aphaireseōs*), a work known in Arabic but no longer extant in that language.

For Alexander the enabling assistance of a separate immaterial intellect ultimately identified as the active principle of intellect mentioned by Aristotle in *De Anima* 3.5—and also identified by Alexander as the First Cause and Unmoved Mover—is required for human intellectual thinking, though Alexander does not detail precisely how this takes place. Through that principle the human intellect performs the process of abstraction and comes to be the abstracted intelligible in a noetic identity, though it should be noted that in Alexander's *On the Soul* the disposition for abstraction is developed through maturation and personal effort while in his *On the Intellect* the disposition is acquired from the Agent Intellect (Sharples 1987: 206–8, 1213). However, it is important to note that, while Aristotle himself did not have notion of intellectual abstraction outside of mathematical contexts (Cleary 1985), Alexander's abstractionist interpretation of Aristotle was read into the texts of Aristotle by the translators and philosophers of the Arabic/Islamic tradition and developed in much greater detail. As we shall see below, while the three major thinkers of the classical rationalist tradition in Arabic/Islamic philosophy—al-Fārābī, Ibn Sīnā and Ibn Rushd—declined to follow Alexander in identifying that separate assisting principle of intellect with the First Cause or God, each held for an essential role for a separate Agent Intellect (or Active Intellect: *al-'aql al-fa''āl*) in abstraction while still providing distinctively different accounts of the nature and process of abstraction (Davidson 1992).

al-Fārābī (d. 950/951)

The consideration of abstraction in al-Fārābī provided here draws on selected works to construct a coherent account of his view. Yet it has to be acknowledged that we do not have a sufficiently firm understanding of the chronology of his works to allow a hard and fast rendering of the development of his thought generally and of his teaching on abstraction in particular. Further, various works sometimes offer partial or unclear accounts of his thought requiring controversial interpretations which are contested with vigor and conviction by several of the best scholars of his thought today (see, for example, Rashed 2009). What follows here does not reflect all the ambiguities of his conception of abstraction, but it still provides an interpretation coherently grounded in key texts of al-Fārābī. While the works of al-Fārābī are not always clear and definitive regarding the use and meaning of abstraction, it is still possible to set out a coherent account from careful consideration of several key writings.

In his *Treatise on the Intellect*, al-Fārābī holds that composite material things of the natural world have forms or essences brought to reality by the lowest of the hierarchy of emanated intellects, the agent intellect (*al-'aql al-fa''āl*), in cooperation with celestial bodies. As such, they are considered intelligibles in potency insofar as they are able to be received into an intellect as intelligibles in act. According to al-Fārābī in this treatise on the meaning of intellect (*al-'aql*) there are three additional Aristotelian senses of intellect involved in the process of human understanding. These are the acquired intellect (*al-'aql al-mustafāḍ*) which constitutes the highest level of existence for human beings, the intellect in act (*al-'aql bi-l-fi'l*) which is the human intellect as it is in the process of knowing an intelligible in act, and the intellect in potency (*al-'aql bi-l-quwah*). For human beings the abstractive reception of intelligibles takes place only thanks to a special power of receptivity provided to the human soul by the agent intellect by emanation: "[T]he Agent Intellect provides this thing to it so by it it becomes a principle for which the intelligibles which were in potentiality become intelligibles in actuality for [the intellect]" (al-Fārābī 1983: 27.2–3; tr. al-Fārābī 1973: 218, tr. mod.). He writes that this power is "something the essence of which is ready and disposed for abstracting (*tantazi'u*) the essences (*mahiyāt*) and forms (*ṣuwar-hā*) of all existents from their matters so as to make all of them a form or forms for it" (al-Fārābī 1983: 12.7–9; tr. al-Fārābī 1973: 215, tr. mod.).

For al-Fārābī, then, the power of abstraction or separation is characterized as a human being's potency for transferring—*naqala*, the term used for this in his work, *The Perfect State* (al-Fārābī 1985: 198–200; see de Vaulx d'Aracy 2010)—and receiving the intelligibles into itself by its own action. That is, human beings must individually strive by their own personal efforts at education and scientific learning, employing this power emanated from the agent intellect together with the powers of the sensation and image-formation, to come to be intelligent knowers of the intelligible content of the natural world. According to this account of abstraction, abstract intelligibles are not emanated into the human soul directly from the agent intellect but rather are derived by individual thinkers from their experience of things of the world. Through the image-forming power the content of experience is presented to intellect in potency for abstraction or transference from the mode of intelligible in potency to a new mode of being as intelligible in act in the human intellect.

Two important ontological changes take place in the course of intellectual abstraction for al-Fārābī, one concerning the intelligible and one concerning the knowing human being. Regarding the first, al-Fārābī makes very clear the ontological status of the received intelligibles in act over and against the intelligibles in potency in things. He writes:

> When they become intelligibles in actuality, then their existence (*wujudu-hā*), insofar as they are intelligibles in actuality, is not the same as their existence insofar as they are forms in matters (*ṣuwar fī mawādda*). And their existence in themselves is not the same as their existence insofar as they are intelligibles in actuality.
>
> (al-Fārābī 1983: 16, 1973: 216)

That is, the formal content of the thing intelligible in potency comes to have a new ontological reality separate in being from the thing in the world. The second ontological change occurs to the human knower who is transformed or, better, who comes to actualization of full reality as intellect when the level of acquired intellect is attained (Taylor 2006).

In his *Political Regime* (*al-Siyāsa al-madaniyya*) al-Fārābī provides what has the appearance of being a different account but is likely a fuller account of the process of abstraction (see Vallat 2004: 207 ff.). There he writes:

> In regard to what the Agent Intellect provides to human beings there is similarity with what is the case for the heavenly bodies. For it provides to human beings first a power and a principle by which it achieves or by which human beings are able by means of their souls to achieve the rest of what remains of perfection for them. This principle is the first sciences and first intelligibles which come about in the rational part of the soul. For [the Agent Intellect] provides it these notions and intelligibles after it has come to be present in human beings and has made to come about in them first the sensing part of the soul and the desiderative part by which the two natures of desire and aversion belong to the soul.
>
> (al-Fārābī 1964: 71–2; see al-Fārābī 2012: 132–3)

The principle given by the agent intellect, which he explains as "first sciences and first intelligibles," refers to primary and common intelligible notions (e.g. that a whole is greater than its part and others) to which he also refers in his *The Perfect State* as needed for ultimate human fulfillment:

> The presence of the first intelligibles in man is his first perfection, but these intelligibles are supplied to him only in order to be used by him to reach his ultimate perfection, i.e. felicity. Felicity means that the human soul reaches a

> degree of perfection in existence where it is in no need of matter for its support, since it becomes one of the incorporeal things and one of the immaterial substances and remains in that state continuously for ever.
>
> (al-Fârâbî 1985: 204–7)

The power given by the agent intellect is the receptivity of the intellect in potency that makes abstraction of intelligibles possible. These two gifts or emanations to the human soul by the agent intellect enable philosophically and scientifically talented individuals trained in the dialectic and logic of Aristotle's *Organon* to form in themselves sets of intelligibles in act in virtue of which they are able to realize themselves fully as intellectual substances with the acquired intellect. When they have garnered all the intelligibles and no longer require bodily senses for the content of intellectual understanding (cf. Aristotle, *De Anima* 3.4), they leave the body behind and rise to the level of the agent intellect thereby attaining the afterlife (*al-ḥayā al-ākhira*), something not open in precisely this way to all human beings (al-Fârâbî 1983: 31).

Al-Fârâbî was quite familiar with Alexander's *De intellectu* (Geoffroy 2002) where the Arabic texts expressed the notion of abstraction as separation with forms of the synonymous verbs *farada* and *faṣala*. He was likely also familiar with the *Paraphase of the De Anima* by Themistius (d. ca. 390) and with the *De Anima*, both translated by Ishâq. The Arabic of the *De Anima* by Ishâq is not extant but, as Gutas has noted, the Arabic of the *Paraphrase* renders Aristotle's term for abstraction (*aphairesis*) by the Arabic *intaza'a* (Gutas 2012: 426–7), a term used by al-Fârâbî and later Ibn Sînâ. Al-Fârâbî and many later philosophers and translators of this tradition read Alexander's general abstractionist interpretation of Aristotle anachronistically back into the texts of Aristotle, developing it in greater detail and also in diverse ways with varying terminology.

Ibn Sînâ (d. 1037)

For Ibn Sînâ the natural world of human existence comes about through the emanative influence of celestial bodies and the agent intellect, the last in the cascading hierarchy of emanated intellects, souls and bodies that come forth eternally from the Necessary Being or God in accord with the Divine Will (see J. Janssens in the present volume). In the ontological framework of Ibn Sînâ all entities are ultimately dependent upon the Necessary Being's emanation since no other being, immaterial intellect or material composite, has existence in its own right and without reference to anything else outside of it. In the case of the agent intellect which has dominion over the natural world as "giver of forms" (Avicenna 1960: 2, 413.11; Arabic 2005: 337.16), when the material constituents are suitably arranged, an emanated essence comes to be instantiated in matter in the natural world as a determinate particular entity, a composite of form and matter. For Ibn Sînâ this is one of only two ways in which essences can exist, while the second way is in the intellect of a knower. Pure intellects are a unity and identity of what knows and what is known with the intelligible in act as something of its own essence. In the case of the agent intellect as well, all the intelligibles that it gives to the things of the world as forms composed with matter are pre-contained in its nature as intellect before it emanates them. However, for the human rational soul which comes into existence with a body to use for the end of developing intellectual understanding, this is the culmination of a process that comes about by means of body, senses and powers of the brain as well as rational powers of the soul and the involvement of the separate agent intellect in many steps and through time.

Like al-Fārābī before him, Ibn Sīnā sets out an account of the intellect relating to the powers of the human rational soul as four kinds of intellect. Nevertheless, the doctrine and the terms characterizing powers of intellect have very different meanings in his novel conception of the formation of human intellectual understanding. For Ibn Sīnā, analogous to its role as "giver of forms" to the natural world, the agent intellect (*al-'aql al-fa''āl*) in a certain very special way gives intelligibles in act to the rational soul, albeit only after the human soul has been suitably prepared. That preparation requires vigorous work on the part of the individual knower employing the primary principles provided to each in "the disposed intellect" (*al-'aql bi-l-malaka*). To describe the human power of intellect in the immediate process of intellectual understanding of essences, Ibn Sīnā uses the term "the acquired intellect" (*al-'aql mustafād*). And when the human being has come to fulfillment as intellectual knower of essences but is not presently exercising the intellect, he describes the intellect as actual intellect or intellect in act (*al-'aql bi-l-fi'l*). These powers work together with the preparatory external senses and internal powers of the brain, as part of a complex natural system which involves both abstraction (*tajrīd*) or separation of experienced particular essences in things of the world from their material contexts, and also an intellectualizing and confirming connection with the agent intellect where those essences exist in a prior way. Ibn Sīnā describes this writing:

> When the rational power regards the particulars which are in the imagination and the light of the agent intellect shines upon them in us … , they come to be abstracted (or: separate *mujarrada*) from matter and its concomitant properties and they are impressed on the rational soul, not as if the things themselves were transferred (*tantaqilu*) from the retentive imagination to the intellect in us and not as if the formal meaning (*al-ma'nā*) immersed in concomitant properties makes a likeness of the thing itself, for it is abstract (or: separate, *mujarrad*) in itself and in the consideration of its essence, but rather according to a formal meaning such that its study of it prepares the soul because the abstraction (*mujarrad*) emanates on it from the agent intellect.
>
> (Avicenna 1959: 235)

The account above has traditionally been understood to attribute the role of abstraction to the distinct and immaterial agent intellect as providing separate or abstract essences or intelligibles in act to the human intellect in a way described by Ibn Sīnā through the use of the metaphors of conjoining (*ittiṣāl*) and emanation (*fayḍ*) after the human rational soul has carried out suitable preparations through the use of external and internal sense powers. Some recent interpretations have tended to see less of a role for the agent intellect and to stress the activities of the human knower alone in bringing about abstraction and intellectual understanding. The preparatory efforts by the individual have even been described as empirical insofar as they are wholly founded on the contents of sense perception experience—though only if supplemented with human reflection and logical analyses and insight into syllogistic middle terms. While some recent accounts recognize an empiricism and keep a role for the agent intellect (Gutas 2013; Hasse 2013), another leaves out the role of the agent intellect entirely and finds parallels in the empiricism of John Locke (Gutas 2012). This latter, however, is severely problematic since Locke's empiricism and conception of abstraction—without any involvement of anything at all like the agent intellect—as well as his view on knowledge of real essences is very different from that of Aristotle in many ways. Foundational to their differences is that Locke denies real definitions and natural species, while for Aristotle these are central to his natural philosophy and metaphysics (Ayers 1981; Mackie 1976; Jones 2014).

For Aristotle intellectual understanding of essences adequate to meet the criteria for perfect scientific demonstration (Aristotle, *Post. An.* 1.2; cf. 1.4 and 2.19) cannot be achieved by empirical selective attention or imaginative generalization. The formation of intelligibles in act can be accomplished only through immaterial intellect's power to make an ontological change such that the essence in a material particular somehow comes to be an immaterial essence in an intellect. Further, the requirement of necessity (in the sense that something cannot be otherwise) for scientific knowledge prompted Aristotle to assert that the attainment of essences discussed in *De Anima* 3.4 requires an agent intellect in *De Anima* 3.5, something that is reflected in Ibn Sīnā's account of the agent intellect. Perhaps following a reading of the *Paraphrase of the De Anima* by Themistius (Taylor 2013: 31–3), Ibn Sīnā requires that what is garnered by the empirical method be confirmed in the prior existence of the forms of things in the agent intellect. One might describe this as a combination of an empirical epistemology with a distinct ontology of intelligibles (Hasse 2013), but it is more suitably characterized as a realistic essentialism ontologically grounded in the agent intellect, both as emanative cause of particular essences in the world and as primary locus of intelligibles in act apprehended by individual human intellects. While the essences in the intellects of individual human beings are not ontologically identical with those in the agent intellect, they cannot exist in the human intellect as intelligibles in act without an ontological link to those in the transcendent agent intellect. In this sense the full content of the intelligible in act does not naturally come to be in the soul without the preparation of empirical experience as a necessary albeit not sufficient condition; however, the intelligible in act as such comes to be in the human intellect only through the agent intellect. That is, the culmination of empirical efforts in knowledge is achieved not in those preparations but only in the ontological connection with the agent intellect which makes intellectual abstraction actual. Ibn Sīnā's denial of intellectual memory resulting from his view that human intellect can intellectually apprehend only one essence at a time, and only so long as it is actually connected with the agent intellect, is consonant with this view of the needed connection with the agent intellect.

As for al-Fārābī, so too for Ibn Sīnā, sensory experience and human reason are necessary conditions for knowledge, but these alone are not sufficient for the formation of demonstrative scientific knowledge. While al-Fārābī founded the process of abstraction of necessary and certain intelligibles in act on a receptive power given to human beings by the agent intellect, Ibn Sīnā grounded that process in the one agent intellect's connection with the human knower. To this extent the realism of intelligibles in act in Ibn Sīnā may owe something to the Arabic pseudonymous *Theology of Aristotle* (derived from the Arabic version of parts of the *Enneads* of Plotinus) and its modified account of emanated *Nous* or Intellect shared by all thinking beings (d'Ancona 2008: 64–6; but see Gutas 2012: 427–8).

Ibn Rushd (d. 1198)

Ibn Rushd sought to follow closely the thought of Aristotle in natural philosophy, metaphysics and other areas of philosophy and as a consequence set forth a world-view very different from that of al-Fārābī and Ibn Sīnā, though he studied the works of each of these thinkers and others from the Greek and Arabic traditions (Davidson 1992: 258 ff.; Taylor, introduction in Averroes 2009). Setting aside the role of agent intellect in the metaphysical constitution of the natural world, he embraced a conception of the universe as eternally in a steady structural state existing insofar as the unity and being of things are due to the eternal final and formal causality of the First Cause, something he called "creation" (*al-ikhtirāʿ* Averroes 1938–1952: 1497, 1985: 108). In this account there is no emanation of substantial forms from a separate agent intellect for the constitution of things; rather, the agent intellect and receptive material intellect are discussed only in regard to the explanation of human intellectual understanding, as was also the case for Aristotle himself. The views of Ibn Rushd evolved as he studied the work of Aristotle and his successors in greater depth in three distinctively different commentaries on the *De Anima*, the culmination of which was his *Long Commentary on the De Anima of Aristotle* which had its greatest impact in Latin translation in Europe from the early thirteenth century through the Renaissance (Akasoy and Giglioni 2013).

In his early *Short Commentary* (Averroes 1950, 1985) Ibn Rushd was under the influence of his study of Aristotle together with the work of Alexander and that of his Andalusian predecessor Ibn Bājja/Avempace (d. 1139) and set forth a novel view which also seems to be present in his *Commentary on the Parva Naturalia* of Aristotle of roughly the same period (Averroes 1972: 73 ff., 1961: 42 ff.). Here the "material" (i.e. receptive) intellect is a modal disposition of the human individual's imagination. When through sensation and internal powers of the brain the human imagination forms images of things, these are only potential intelligibles. But the agent intellect abstracts these and with its intelligibility actualizes the disposition bringing about intelligibles in act for the sake of human scientific knowing. Though the human imagination is a bodily power and as such cannot have immaterial intelligibles in act literally in it, it can have images that are now understood to represent intelligibles in act thanks to a change in its disposition due to the abstractive power of the agent intellect. While this might have been a promising start to a new approach to the issues, Ibn Rushd abandoned it in his later work.

Rejecting the earlier view, Ibn Rushd set forth a new account in his paraphrasing *Middle Commentary* (Averroes 2002) in part because he came to hold that the content of intellectual knowing must truly be intelligibles in act and so must have a "material" intellect, which is literally an ontologically immaterial subject. The requirements to be met here are (1) the subject must be a receptive power belonging to the individual bodily human knower and (2) the subject must be immaterial in order to be receptive of the intelligibles in act. Following the model of the medieval conception of immaterial celestial souls associated with the eternally moving celestial bodies, Ibn Rushd proposed that the agent intellect functions together with bodily human souls as form, agent and end in virtue of which dematerialized abstractions drawn from worldly experiences are brought about in the individual human being's immaterially existing receptive power of intellect. It should be noted, however, that this individual human "material" intellect is part of the human being and dependent on it for existence; hence, when the individual perishes, so too does its intellectual part.

In all three commentaries on the *De Anima* Ibn Rushd drew on the Arabic translation of the *Paraphrase of the De Anima* by Themistius (Taylor 2013) but for his *Long Commentary on the De Anima* (1186 C.E.) Ibn Rushd drew even more deeply on Themistius for important principles for the formation of innovative teaching on the material intellect and agent intellect as separately existing substances. The notion that there must be one common set of intelligibles for human intersubjective discourse and science was developed from remarks by Themistius (Themistius 1973: 188–9) as was the notion that the agent intellect must be operating somehow in the human soul (Taylor 2013). The former contributed to the assertion of one single material intellect as a substance shared by all human knowers; the latter contributed to Ibn Rushd's view that the material intellect and the agent intellect—respectively receptive subject of abstracted intelligibles in act and active efficient cause of abstraction—must be "in the soul" in some fashion. Ibn Rushd also drew on al-Fārābī for the consideration that the entirety of the content of human scientific concepts comes solely from experience of the world.

In this mature account Ibn Rushd holds that the human knower is the embodied individual making use of sensation, the internal powers of the brain, and conjunctions with the separately existing material intellect and agent intellect. The process of intellectual abstraction is as follows: the external five senses provide forms of sensed things of the world to the common sense which unifies these and produces a particular image in the imagination. That image is refined and denuded of extraneous considerations by the cogitative power and then impressed on memory. What is produced by these bodily powers is then presented to the agent intellect—sometimes called "the intellect in act"—for abstraction and impression onto the receptive material intellect. Ibn Rushd writes:

> For to abstract is nothing other than to make imagined intentions intelligible in act after they were [intelligible] in potency. But to understand is nothing other than to receive these intentions. For when we found the same thing, namely, the imagined intentions, is transferred in its being from one order into another, we said that this must be from an agent cause and a recipient cause. The recipient, however, is the material [intellect] and the agent is [the intellect] which brings [this] about.
>
> (Averroes 2009: 351–2, 1953: 439)

In doing so, the agent intellect transfers the intelligible in potency to a new modality and ontological status and actualizes the intelligible in act in the material intellect, an intelligible in act which is the same for every human knower who has gone through these steps in the process of garnering knowledge starting in sensation. The embodied human being who achieves this is said to have reached the level acquired intellect thanks to a conjoining (*ittiṣāl*) with the separate intellects, which bring about the abstraction in accord with the will of the human knower. As is the case for al-Fārābī and Ibn Sīnā, this attainment of knowledge as the apprehension of intelligibles in act constitutes human fulfillment and happiness, yet unlike those two thinkers Ibn Rushd has no philosophical doctrine of post mortem human existence (Taylor 1998, 2012).

Conclusion

The doctrine of intellectual abstraction of intelligibles in act for human understanding was first set out by Alexander of Aphrodisias as an interpretation of texts of Aristotle on the formation of scientific knowledge. For the Arabic philosophical tradition the general account of Alexander was attractive enough for it to be taken as genuinely that of Aristotle by philosophers as well as translators. Still, while the philosophers considered here held for intellectual abstraction with an important role for a separately existing agent intellect, each of them filled out the underdetermined account of abstraction provided by Alexander with unique philosophical accounts which they, like Alexander, read back into the texts of Aristotle.

Further Reading

Davidson, H. (1992) *Alfarabi, Avicenna, and Averroes, on Intellect. Their Cosmologies, Theories of the Active Intellect, and Theories of Human Intellect*, New York & Oxford: Oxford University Press.

Gutas, D. (2014) *Avicenna and the Aristotelian Tradition. Introduction to Reading Avicenna's Philosophical Works*, Leiden & Boston: Brill.

Ivry, A. (2012) "Arabic and Islamic Psychology and Philosophy of Mind," *The Stanford Encyclopedia of Philosophy*, E. N. Zalta (ed.), http://plato.stanford.edu/archives/sum2012/entries/arabic-islamic-mind/

Mueller, I. (1990) "Aristotle's Doctrine of Abstraction in the Commentators," in *Aristotle Transformed: The Ancient Commentators and Their Influence*, R. Sorabji (ed.), London: Duckworth.

Sirkel, R. (2011) "Alexander of Aphrodisias's Account of Universals and Its Problems," *Journal of the History of Philosophy* 49: 297–314.

References

Akasoy, A. & Giglioni, G. (2013) *Renaissance Averroism and its Aftermath: Arabic Philosophy in Early Modern Europe*, A. Akasoy & G. Giglioni (eds.), Dordrecht: Springer.

Alexander of Aphrodisias (1887) *Alexander of Aphrodisias. De Anima Liber Cum Mantissa*, I. Bruns (ed.), Berlin: George Reimer [Commentaria in Aristotelem Graeca, Suppl. II, pt. 1], pp. 106–13.

——. (1956) Finnegan, J., S.J. (ed.), in "Texte arabe du PERI NOU d'Alexandre d'Aphrodise," *Mélanges de l'Université Saint-Joseph* 33: 159–202.
——. (1971) *Commentaires sur Aristote perdus en grec et autres épîtres*, 'A. Badawi (ed.), Beirut: Dâr el-Mashriq.
——. (2004) *Alexander of Aphrodisias. Supplement to On the Soul*, R. W. Sharples (tr.), London: Duckworth.
al-Fārābī (1964) *Al-Fārābī's The Political Regime (al-Siyāsa al-Madaniyya also known as the Treatise on the Principles of Beings)*, F. M. Najjar (ed.), Beirut: Imprimerie Catholique.
——. (1973) "The Letter Concerning the Intellect," A. Hyman (tr.), in A. Hyman & J. J. Walsh (eds.), *Philosophy in the Middle Ages*, Indianapolis: Hackett Publishing Co., pp. 215–21.
——. (1983) *Alfarabi. Risalah fi al- 'aql*, M. Bouyges, S.J. (ed.), Beirut: Dar el-Machreq Sari.
——. (1985) *al-Farabi on the Perfect State. Abū Naṣr al-Fārābī's Mabādi' ārā' ahl al-madīna al-Fāḍila*, R. Walzer (ed. and tr.), Oxford: Clarendon Press.
——. (2007) "On the Intellect" in *Classical Arabic Philosophy*, J. McGinnis & D. C. Reisman (eds.), Indianapolis & Cambridge: Hackett Publishing, pp. 68–78.
——. (2012) *Le Livre du Régime Politique*, Ph. Vallat (tr.), Paris: Les Belles Lettres.
Aristotle (1956) *Aristotelis De Anima*, W. D. Ross (ed.), Oxford: Clarendon. (Scriptorum Classicorum Bibliotheca Oxoniensis/Oxford Classical Texts Series).
——. (1984) *Aristotle. The Complete Works*, 2 vols., J. Barnes (ed.), Princeton: Princeton University Press.
Averroes (1938–1952) Averroès, *Tafsīr mā ba'd aṭ-Ṭabī'at "Grand Commentaire" de la Métaphysique*, 3 vols., M. Bouyges (ed.), Beirut: Dar El-Machreq Éditeurs.
——. (1950) *Talkhīṣ Kitāb al-Nafs*, A. F. El-Ahwani (ed.), Cairo: Imprimerie Misr.
——. (1953) *Averroes Commentarium Magnum in Aristotelis De Anima Libros*, F. S. Crawford (ed.), Cambridge: The Medieval Academy of America.
——. (1961) *Averroes. Epitome of Parva Naturalia*, H. Blumberg (tr.), Cambridge: Medieval Academy of America.
——. (1972) *Abū al-Walīd Ibn Rushd. Talkhīs Kitāb al-Ḥiss wa-l-Maḥsūs*, H. Blumberg (ed.), Cambridge: Medieval Academy of America.
——. (1985) *Epitome de Anima*, S. Gómez Nogales (ed.), Madrid: Consejo Superior de Investigaciones Científicas.
——. (2002) *Averroes. Middle Commentary on Aristotle's De Anima. A Critical Edition of the Arabic Text with English Translation, Notes and Introduction*, A. L. Ivry (ed. and tr.), Provo, UT: Brigham Young University Press.
——. (2009) *Averroes (Ibn Rushd) of Cordoba. Long Commentary on the De Anima of Aristotle*, R. C. Taylor (tr.), New Haven & London: Yale University Press.
Avicenna (1959) *Avicenna's De Anima (Arabic Text) Being the Psychological Part of the Kitāb al-Shifā'*, F. Rahman (ed.), London: Oxford University Press.
——. (1960) *Ibn Sina. al-Shifā'. al-Illāhiyyāt*, 2 vols., G. C. Anawati & S. Zayed (eds.), Cairo: Organisation Générale des Imprimeries Gouvermentales.
——. (2005) *The Metaphysics of the Healing*, M. E. Marmura (tr.), Provo, UT: Brigham Young University Press.
Ayers, M. R. (1981) "Locke Versus Aristotle on Natural Kinds," *The Journal of Philosophy* 78, 5: 247–72.
Burnyeat, M. (2008) *Aristotle's Divine Mind*, Milwaukee: Marquette University Press.
Cleary, J. J. (1985) "On the Terminology of 'Abstraction' in Aristotle," *Phronesis* 30: 13–45.
d'Ancona, C. (2008) "Degrees of Abstraction in Avicenna. How to Combine Aristotle's *De anima* and the *Enneads*," in S. Knuuttila & P. Kärkkäinen (eds.), *Theories of Perception in Medieval and Early Modern Philosophy*, Dordrecht: Springer, pp. 47–71.

Davidson, H. (1992) *Alfarabi, Avicenna, and Averroes, on Intellect. Their Cosmologies, Theories of the Active Intellect, and Theories of Human Intellect*, New York & Oxford: Oxford University Press.
de Vaulx d'Arcy, G. (2010) "La *naqala*, étude du concept de transfert dans l'oeuvre d' al-Fārābī," *Arabic Sciences and Philosophy* 20: 125–76.
Geoffroy, M. (2002) "La tradition arabe du *Peri nou* d'Alexandre d'Aphrodise et les origines de la théorie farabienne des quatre degrés de l'intellect," in C. d'Ancona & G. Serra (eds.), *Aristotele e Alessandro di Afrodisia nella Tradizione Araba*, Padova: Il Poligrafo, pp. 191–231.
Gutas, D. (2012) "The Empiricism of Avicenna," *Oriens* 40: 391–436.
——. (2013) "Avicenna's Philosophical Project," in P. Adamson (ed.), *Interpreting Avicenna. Critical Essays*, Cambridge: Cambridge University Press, pp. 28–47.
Hasse, D. N. (2013) "Avicenna's Epistemological Optimism," in P. Adamson (ed.), *Interpreting Avicenna. Critical Essays*, Cambridge: Cambridge University Press, pp. 109–19.
Jones, J.-E. (2014) "Locke on Real Essence," *The Stanford Encyclopedia of Philosophy*, E. N. Zalta (ed.), http://plato.stanford.edu/archives/fall2014/entries/real-essence/
Mackie, J. L. (1976) *Problems from Locke*, Oxford: Clarendon Press.
Rashed, M. (2009) "On the Authorship of the Treatise *On the Hamonization of the Opinions of the Two Sages* Attributed to al-Fārābī," *Arabic Sciences and Philosophy* 19: 43–82.
Sharples, R. (1987) "Alexander of Aphrodisas: Scholasticism and Innovation," in *Aufstieg und Niedergang der römischen Welt*, vol. 2, Berlin & New York: De Gruyter, pp. 1176–243.
Taylor, R. C. (1998) "Personal Immortality in Averroes' Mature Philosophical Psychology," *Documenti e Studi sulla Traduzione Filosofica Medievale* 9: 87–110.
——. (2006) "Abstraction in al-Fārābī," *Proceedings of the American Catholic Philosophical Association* 80: 151–68.
——. (2012) "Averroes on the Ontology of the Human Soul," *Muslim World* 102: 580–96.
——. (2013) "Themistius and the development of Averroes' noetics," in R. L. Friedman & J.-M. Counet (eds.), *Medieval Perspectives on Aristotle's* De Anima, Louvain-la-Neuve/Louvain-Paris-Walpole: Editions de l'Institut Supérieur de Philosophie/Peeters, pp. 1–38.
Themistius (1973) *An Arabic Translation of Themistius' Commentary on Aristotle's De Anima*, M. C. Lyons (ed.), Columbia, South Carolina, & Oxford, England: Bruno Cassirer Publishers Ltd.
Tweedale, M. (1984) "Alexander of Aphrodisias' View on Universals," *Phronesis* 29: 279–303.
Vallat, Ph. (2004) *Al-Farabi et l'école d'Alexandrie. Des prémisses de al connaissance à la philosophie politique*, Paris: Vrin.
Wilson, A. B. (2014) "Locke's Externalism About Sensitive Knowledge," *British Journal for the History of Philosophy* 22: 425–45.

23
HUMAN KNOWLEDGE AND SEPARATE INTELLECT

Olga Lizzini

Introduction

Medieval Islamic theories of cognition generally posit as the principle of human rationality—itself described as a faculty and pure potency (*quwwa*)—an intellect (*'aql*) which is "separate" (*mufāriq*) from both matter and the human soul. This intellect is a descendant of the productive (*poietikos*) intellect in Aristotle's *De anima* (III, 5, 430a10–19), which is separate (*choristos*), impassible (*apathes*), unmixed (*amighes*) and, in its essence, act (*te ousia on energeia*). Exegetes of Late Antiquity (e.g. Alexander of Aphrodisias) had already compared it to the faculty that, in *De generatione animalium* (736b27–29), Aristotle describes as coming to the soul "from without" (*thurathen*). In addition to making use of this Aristotelian nucleus, Medieval Islamic theories of cognition elaborated the Neoplatonic elements they found particularly in the texts, often ascribed to Aristotle, of the Arabic Plotinus and Proclus: thus in al-Fārābī and Ibn Sīnā, for example—the two authors on whom this chapter is primarily focused—the transcendence ascribed to the separate intellect can be explained by the theory of emanation that is the foundation of their metaphysics.

Interpreting Aristotle

Roughly speaking, one can state that all the thinkers of classical Islam—with the exception of Ibn Rushd, who went so far as to separate even the intellect which is called "material" from the human soul (see R. C. Taylor in this title)—explain man's rational activity by means of the notion of a separate intellect that is always *in actu*, whereas human intellect is designed as a faculty that, from an initial state of absolute potency, proceeds to self-actualization through cognitive activity itself (Jolivet 2006). The Aristotelian productive intellect, "without which there is nothing that thinks" (*De anima*, 430a25), is interpreted not as a part of the human soul, but as a substance separate from it and hence "immortal and eternal." Human intellection—i.e. rationality, logical ability, knowledge, but also prophecy, which Arabic-speaking thinkers generally conceived as an extraordinary state of excellence of human cognitive faculties—is therefore often seen as the result of a contact, or more literally a "conjunction" (*ittiṣāl*) with this separate intellect. While the latter is rational and intellectual in an absolute sense, human intellect attains rationality and intellection through a gradual process which, although its description varies from author to author, always entails both the elaboration and simultaneous surpassing of experience and sense-related knowledge, and also connection or, more generally, communication with the separate intellect. It is this communication that allows the human intellect to attain a knowledge which is defined, in Aristotelian terms, as necessary and universal (*Posterior Analytics* I, 4–6). Thus, the separate and transcendent intellect takes on two essential meanings: it is "active" both because it always actualizes its intellection—it is always absolutely *in actu*—and because, by virtue of its own intellection, it makes human intellection actual. In so far as it is absolutely in act (*bi-l-fi'l*), the separate intellect is therefore "active" or "always active" (*fa''āl*) and "agent" (*fā'il*).

Immateriality and hence spirituality are the properties shared by the separate active intellect and the potential intellect. Aristotle had already defined the potential intellect as impassible (*apathes*; *De anima* 429a15), suggesting that it was reasonable to conceive it as unmixed with the body (*De anima* 429a24–25). In so far as it is absolutely potential, the possible intellect, however, is analogous to first matter, with which it shares absolute indetermination and the capacity to receive (and in Aristotelian terms even to be) *all* forms. Al-Fārābī, Ibn Sīnā and even Ibn Rushd (for whom, however, the potential intellect, while related to man, is not "of man" in a carefully defined way), in fact, interpret the absolute potential intellect in terms of materiality and, adopting a locution used by Alexander of Aphrodisias, call the intellect in potency (*al-'aql bi-l-quwwa*) "the material intellect" (*al-'aql al-hayūlānī*). Its ultimate perfection consists in being filled with all the forms it can actually receive, the same forms the "active" or "always active" intellect (*al-'aql al-fa''āl*) always thinks. Once it has attained its perfection, the human intellect becomes, in the vocabulary of Ibn Sīnā, an "intellectual" (*'aqlī*) world parallel to the real world: the ultimate perfection of the rational soul consists in becoming an intellectual world in which the form or the intelligible (*ma'qūl*) order of the whole bears the imprint of the good that is proper to it (Avicenna 1960: 425, 15–426, 4; cf. 428, 9–11; Avicenna 2005: 350; 352–53). At least two problems, which are interrelated, are implied by such a vision. First, it is clear that, despite being conceived in itself as a potency, the human intellect should also be identified as the subject of thought: in other words, it should be identifiable with the human being. Authors such as Ibn Sīnā, who ascribed potentiality to the human intellect, have the problem of defining it as a substance (*jawhar*) as well. Thus, turning again to Ibn Sīnā, the real name of the soul, as far as its substance is considered, is "intellect" (Avicenna 1952: 53, 11–13; Michot 1997: 241) and the identity of a human being is defined in essentially intellectual terms. This is illustrated by the so-called flying-man argument: let us imagine a man created whole in an instant, his sight veiled so that he cannot directly observe the external world and his body afloat in air or in a void, his limbs extended and not touching his body or one another. Now, if we ask what this man would be capable of knowing and asserting with certainty, we must answer that he would know his self as something that exists. No reference to the existence of any of his exterior or interior parts or anything external would be implied by this assertion. The self whose existence the flying man would assert is therefore not his body and its parts: the soul must be conceived as something that is not the body—nor in fact any body—and hence immaterial or intellectual (Avicenna 1959: 15, 16–17, 17; 255, 1–257, 17, 1957–1960: II, 343–45, 345–58, 1969: 140–144; Pines 1955; Marmura 1986; Hasse 2000; cf. Black 2008).

The two-fold and partly aporetic conception of the intellect as a faculty and a substance is reflected in what has been defined (Jolivet 1995) as the essential "diffraction," that is, dichotomy of the term, which is translated—first in Latin and then in other European languages—in a twofold manner: it is intellect (*intellectus*) as a faculty and intelligence (*intelligentia*) as a (separate) substance. In fact, the Arabic word *'aql* (like the Greek *nous*) has a dual reference: it indicates both a power or a faculty (*quwwa*: the same term used to indicate potency) and (problematically) a substance in the case of human beings, and a substance (always in act) in the world of separate intelligences: indeed, one should add to the separate intellect involved in human intellection the intelligences that are both involved in the pattern of emanation and in charge of celestial motion. The problem of defining the human being as the subject of thought is also, although in different terms, in Ibn Rushd. In his *Long Commentary on De anima*, he seems to conceive two subjects of thought: one is a principle of movement, the subject by virtue of which intelligibles are true and belong to each thinking human being; the other is a substratum of the intelligible, the subject by virtue of which intelligibles exist and the universal, eternal "material" intellect (Averroes 1953: 400, 2009: 316; lix–lxi).

Secondly, the position of the separate intellect as the cause of human intellection poses the fundamental problem of how to interpret the kind of causality it expresses. Is it an efficient causality? In that case, the human intellect is acted upon by the principle and cannot truly be considered an active element in the process of intellection (Rahman 1958; Davidson 1972, 1992; Taylor 1996). Or is it merely an exemplary cause? Then the human intellect would find in the divine separate intellect the model of an intellection that it would attain in an essentially autonomous way (abstraction could in fact be attributed to the human intellect; see Gutas 2001; Hasse 2001). Or is it, instead, a formal causality? This is how Ibn Rushd seems to solve the problem in his *Long Commentary on De anima*: if the material intellect is the first perfection of man, the agent intellect is a form in us (*ṣura fī-nā*; *forma in nobis* and *forma nobis*; e.g. Averroes 1953: 485, 500; Averroes 2009: 386, 399; Taylor 2005).

The solution clearly involves an interpretation of the philosophical system as a whole and cannot depend on the examination of epistemology alone. In the theories of emanation devised by al-Fārābī and Ibn Sīnā, for example, the idea of knowledge as a reception of forms, harking back to Aristotle (*De anima* 429a15; 429a28–29), leads to interpreting the cognitive process as a bestowal of intellectual forms (or intelligible impressions: *rusūm al-ma'qūlāt*, al-Fārābī 1985: 199), a bestowal from the separate active intellect to the potential, receptive human intellect. Exactly as first matter receives the forms of things, so the material (human) intellect would receive the intellectual forms—the intelligibles (*al-ma'qūlāt*)—that correspond to things when they are abstracted from their materiality. In at least one passage (Avicenna 1959:

247, 8), Ibn Sīnā speaks of "a principle which bestows intellect" (*al-mabda' al-wāhib li-l-'aql; principium dans intellectum*), a locution which is comparable to the rare *wāhib al-ṣuwar* (*dator formarum* in Latin) he uses in *Ilāhiyyāt* IX, 5 (Avicenna 1960: 413, 11, but cf. 411, 9, VI, 2, 265, 4) in an ontological sense. Both expressions seem to refer to the agent intellect, which is at once part and vehicle of the divine flow; they indicate "a third thing" (Avicenna 1960: 81, 14) that, while separate from the sublunary world and from the human soul, is responsible for the actualization of them both (Davidson 1972, 1992; Rahman 1958; cf. Hasse 2000, 2001). Moreover, unlike al-Fārābī, Ibn Sīnā views the separate agent intellect as the immediate principle of the forms that ontologically constitute the sublunary world. The identification of the agent intellect with the *dator formarum* was then made by al-Ghazālī and Ibn Rushd and, in their wake, by several medieval and modern authors. Some of them indicated it with the term *cholcodea*, borrowed from astronomy and in any case obscure (Porro 2006; Hasse 2011). The theory of cognition is therefore seen as related to both ontology and the philosophy of nature.

Another important element related to the idea of the separate intellect is the image of light. Aristotle had already associated the role of the agent intellect with that of light (*De anima* 430a15ff.). Alexander of Aphrodisias, having distinguished the active intellect from the human capacity of understanding, had identified that intelligence with the God of Lambda (*De anima* 89, 16–19), interpreting the metaphor of light as like the bright and powerful sun which radiates light. Themistius also uses the image of light to explain how forms are abstracted from material objects: the active intellect, which is something within the human soul (CAG 5.3. 103), both leads the potential human intellect to actuality and illuminates potential objects of thought, rendering them actually intelligible (CAG 5.3. 98–9; Davidson 1972: 123). The image of intellect as the sun or main source of light can thus be found in authors such as al-Fārābī, Ibn Sīnā and Ibn Rushd. Sometimes, but not always, this image betokens the theory of emanation. In fact, Ibn Sīnā uses this image to explain knowledge, conveying the idea of an emanation or a bestowal of forms—the agent intellect illuminates the human intellect (Avicenna 1959: 234, 14–236, 2; Avicenna 1985: 395–96; also Avicenna 1963); al-Fārābī inserts it in a more abstraction-oriented theory of cognition: the agent intellect has what Taylor defines as a "cooperating causality" which allows the human intellect to attain the power of abstraction and consequently the understanding of intelligibles (Taylor 2006).

In sum, the Arabic theories of intellect—although with different modulations (especially in the case of the theories of Ibn Bājja and Ibn Rushd, for which see R. C. Taylor's chapter in this title)—are essentially characterized by transcendent causality, which is ascribed to the agent intellect in a universe in which intellection and causation ultimately correspond: the Neoplatonic sources —already reinterpreted and transformed, probably within a monotheistic context (Endress 1973; Taylor 1986; d'Ancona 1995; Adamson 2003)—led Arabic thinkers to incorporate the function of active intellect into a context broader than that of epistemology. In fact, as should be clear, while the origin of the idea of a separate agent intellect must be attributed to Aristotle's *De anima*, its overall interpretation depends on Late Ancient and Neoplatonic exegeses of this work. It is on their authors—and particularly on Alexander of Aphrodisias, Plotinus in the *Ps.-Theology of Aristotle*, Proclus in the *Liber de Causis*,

Themistius and Philoponus—on whom the thinkers of Classical Islam depend. Late Ancient and Neoplatonic sources led Arabic authors to consider intellection within the framework of the theory of emanation and to connect the active or productive intellect of *De Anima* III, 5 with the cosmology of *Metaphysics* XII and *De caelo*, integrated with the cosmology of Ptolemy's work. For instance, the separate intellect is usually identified, as in Late Antiquity, with a divine or angelic entity, which is also significant as far as eschatology and the theory of revelation are concerned. Thus it is probably after the example of some Neoplatonic elaboration (al-Fārābī 1985: 363; Vallat 2004) that, in the so-called *Perfect State* and in *The Political Regime* or *Treatise on the Principles of Beings*, al-Fārābī identifies celestial intelligences, and among them the active intellect, with spiritual entities (*al-rūḥāniyyūn*), traditionally called "angels" (*al-malā'ika*), an identification that can also be found in Ibn Sīnā (e.g. *al-Ilāhiyyāt*, 9. 2, 10. 1, 10. 2, 10. 3; Avicenna 1960: 391, 12; 435, 7, 8; 442, 3, 13; 444, 18; 446, 1). In other words, Arabic theories of cognition, as has been noted, "integrate the active intellect and the human potential intellect into larger cosmic schemes" (Davidson 1992: 4) which explain not only knowledge, but also, more generally, the God–human relationship. The transcendent character ascribed to the agent intellect lends qualities to its conjunction with the potential human intellect that lie outside the field of epistemology. The very principles that explain the cognitive process also account for all the phenomena that express what is seen as the privileged contact of human beings with the celestial region: prophecy, eschatology, and angelology. Although the primary function of the active intellect is to explain truth and the universality of knowledge, it is relevant not only to the human intellect and its development in terms of knowledge (and in ethics and eschatology), but also to metaphysics, cosmology, and natural science. Furthermore, by reconciling the Neoplatonic theory of communication with the divine with what they considered to be the Aristotelian doctrine of nature, Arabic authors also explain some specific modes of imaginative knowledge: by making use of the notion of emanation or of the illuminating separate intellect together with the doctrine of *Parva naturalia*—in particular *De Sensu et sensibili*, *De memoria et reminiscentia*—in their elaborated Arabic version, in which explicit reference to a transcendent source of dreams and visions is made—they in fact explain inspirational dreams, visions and prophecy (Pines 1974; Ruffinengo 1997; Hansberger 2008, 2010; cf. Streetman 2008). The separate intellect is actually part of the divine or celestial sphere: for human beings the actualization of the intellect means not only the attainment of their personal perfection and hence true happiness, but also the entrance into a separate and consequently divine sphere of life. Ibn Sīnā, for example, calls the highest form of conjunction with the separate intellect, which accounts for both prophecy and the philosopher's exceptional knowledge, "sacred intellect" (*al-'aql al-qudsī*, Avicenna 1959: 248). The degrees of actualization of the human intellect (which differ markedly according to which of the various authors describes them) are thus significant in so far as they literally mark a *progression* leading human beings from the imperfect sublunary dimension, to which their lives belong, to the horizon of perfection—often described, once again in terms which evoke Aristotle's distinctions (see e.g. *Nicomachean Ethics*, 10, 7, 1177b30), as angelic or divine—to which they aspire. In Ibn Sīnā's vocabulary, the human interpretation of the world is intellectual (*'aqlī*) or rational (*nuṭqī*) in so far as it is comparable to that of the supernal world, and it is often described as mental (*ḏihnī*) to the extent that it is simply human. Whereas the intellect indicates human beings' participation in the divine, purely intellectual world, the mind (*ḏihn*) comprises not only the intellect but, thanks to the mediation of the imaginative and estimative faculties, the senses as well (Lizzini 2005).

The Philosophical Context

Arabic epistemological theories cannot be explained only on the basis of their sources. To the historical consideration—according to which any philosophical doctrine is, in this context, also an exegesis of the Aristotelian text, and, as such, part of a tradition—a fundamental theoretical consideration should be added: the idea of a separate and celestial intellect is in fact a guarantee of truth in the presence of the mutability of natural experience and the perishable character of man. The Aristotelian notion of knowledge, to which truth, necessity and universality are ascribed, implies a principle of absoluteness and universality that cannot coincide with knowledge gained through the senses. The requirements of Aristotelianism are reconciled with the Neoplatonic tenets that inspired Arabic theories of cognition and more generally Arabic philosophy: if reality is formal and intellectual, only intellect can truly know it. Therefore, the celestial intellectual world is at once the source and the best, indeed the perfect way of being and knowing. Or, as Ibn Sīnā states in his *Metaphysics*, the *Kitāb al-Ilāhiyyāt* (Avicenna 1960: IX, 5: 410, 14–17), in the celestial intelligences there is "the active designing [or design] of the forms" (*rasm al-ṣuwar ʻalā jihati al-tafʻīl*), the "project," one might say, of reality. Conversely, the knowledge that human beings can have of the forms that constitute the world is always a *passive* impression or design (*irtisām, rasm al-ṣuwar ʻalā jihati al-infiʻāl*). Even if it abstracts them from the senses, the human intellect *receives* the forms that correspond to the active thought of the celestial intelligences.

The basic lines of the Arabic theories of cognition are those of the Aristotelian tradition: sense experience is the first degree of knowledge, but it is also a degree that, if one is to achieve proper knowledge, must be surpassed. Sense experience gives access to knowledge; at the same time, since true and absolute knowledge is universal and intellectual, sense experience cannot be part of it. However, on the rise of elements of Greek thought, the Arabic philosophical tradition, starting with al-Fārābī, established some well-developed first principles that are conceived as a proper basis of knowledge. They take the form of rules (predicative elements to which one must assent: the principle of non-contradiction, for example, or the rules of geometry, such as that the whole is greater than the part), but also (in Ibn Sīnā) conceptual representations (existence, thing, necessity, and, in some texts, unity; *al-Ilāhiyyāt* I, 5; *R. fī aqsām al-ʻulūm al-ʻaqliyya*; Avicenna 1960: 30, 3–4; Avicenna 1908: 112, 13–15) and, rather problematically, they constitute the founding principles and the first actualizations of human knowledge. These principles, which can be defined *a priori*, are presented at times as innate, at times as the result of a first bestowal from the agent intellect, at still other times, ambiguously, as derived from experience (e.g. al-Fārābī 1985: 202, 6–204, 5, where the metaphor of light is used). Moreover, the very notion of them is aporetic: on the one hand, because they serve as the foundation for the system of knowledge, these principles should not be part of it; on the other, since they are presented as the first actualization of human intellect, they are, in fact, the first moment of knowledge. As a whole, the theory of first principles seems to respond to the requirements of the absolute universality and necessity of knowledge. In fact, behind Aristotle and the whole tradition of his commentators, first in Late Antiquity and then in the Medieval Arabic world, is the Platonic theory of forms, by means of which philosophy had first attempted to solve the problem of the irreducible diversity between the variety of the sensible world and the uniqueness of truth.

One should, finally, mention the distinction between theoretical and practical intellect. In fact, in keeping with Aristotle's theory (*De anima* 3. 10, 433a14 and ff.; *Nicomachean Ethics* 6. 1, 1139a12 and ff.), Arabic authors invest the human intellect with both practical and theoretical dimensions. By connecting the former to a kind of knowledge by means of which human beings intervene *in the world*, and the latter to knowledge *of the world* only, they ascribe first principles to the practical intellect and link the development of the human intellect to its conjunction with the separate intellect, in both practical and theoretical modes (Druart 1997; Lizzini 2009). The logical development of all this in theoretical and practical terms goes so far at times as to touch upon the celestial world. Ibn Sīnā, for example, connects celestial souls to the practical intellect and the intelligences to the theoretical dimension of knowledge (e.g. Avicenna 1960: 9.2, 387, 4–7).

Al-Kindī and the First Theories

The history of Arabic theories of cognition and their interpretation of the agent intellect begins with the Arabic elaboration of the Neoplatonic writings attributed to the so-called circle of al-Kindī. As some scholars have shown (Geoffroy 2002), it is in the first *mīmar* of the pseudo-Aristotelian *Theology*, which is about the soul (*Fī l-nafs*), that al-Kindī first and al-Fārābī later found the key to interpreting, respectively, the Aristotelian doctrine of the soul and the intellect, and the *Treatise on the Intellect (Peri nou)* by Alexander of Aphrodisias, which itself was an interpretation of Aristotle (al-Fārābī probably did not have direct access to the Aristotelian text). Al-Kindī was the first author to write a *Letter* or *Epistle on the Intellect* (*Risāla fī l-'aql*; Jolivet 1971; Endress 1980; Ruffinengo 1997); his is an exegetical text in which, after the example of Aristotle's *De anima* and the treatises of Late Antiquity, he develops the doctrine of the degrees of human knowledge: intellect in potency, acquired intellect (*al-'aql al-mustafād*) and intellect in act filled with the forms received from the separate intellect (Jolivet 1971: 50–73; Endress 1994: 197). Intellectual knowledge is presented as substantially distinct from sensible knowledge. In contradistinction to the idea of continuity between sensible and intellectual knowledge, al-Kindī defines the senses and the intellect as two radically different ways of knowing, just as radically different as are their objects. Sensible reality is the object of the senses. True knowledge, however, is that which deals with immutable and eternal reality, which is independent of the laws of generation and corruption (d'Ancona 1999; Adamson 2007). Translated into Latin twice (as *De intellectu* and *De ratione*), the text had a certain success in the European Latin world.

Al-Fārābī

The intellectual development outlined by al-Fārābī, who ascribes a central role to abstraction, is better organized and more explicitly involved in the dynamics of emanation than al-Kindī's. Although a psychological analysis can be found in his major works as well—e.g. *The Perfect State, The Philosophy of Aristotle*—the *Epistle on the intellect* (*R. fī l-'aql*), also known as the *Treatise on the meanings of the intellect* (*Maqāla fī ma'ānī al-'aql*), contains the clearest exposition. Here al-Fārābī's main focus is terminological: he intends to clarify how the term *'aql* is used and, consequently, how it should be understood. He presents not only strictly philosophical meanings—indeed, to a certain extent, his intent is to explain how the different philosophical uses of the term can be reconciled to each other—but also how the word is used in ordinary speech and rarefied theological language. Philosophically speaking, the meanings of *'aql* are categorized first according to the already mentioned distinction between practical and speculative intellect and, secondly, in relation to the various phases of development involved in the learning process. The intellect in potency (*al-'aql bi-l-quwwa*) is a part of the soul, or, more vaguely, a "thing" whose essence (*ḏāt*) is prepared or disposed (*mu'adda, musta'idda*) to abstract the forms of existing material things (al-Fārābī 1983: 12.6–8). Starting from a state of absolute potency, the intellect, as it responds to the stimuli supplied by experience, abstracts forms in so far as it is actualized by virtue of the action of the separate agent intellect, which can be identified with the tenth agent intelligence (see also al-Fārābī 1985: 203) and associated with the illuminative power of the sun (al-Fārābī 1985: 201).

The degree that—at least theoretically—corresponds to the first actualization and refinement of the human intellect is that of the intellect "in act," in which the intelligible forms of things constitute in act the object of intellection (al-Fārābī 1983: 15.3–10). In the so-called *Perfect State*, however, the first degree of the intellect is endued with the "first intelligibles": the first contents of truth, which al-Fārābī reduces for the most part to the principles of Euclidean geometry and Aristotelian logic (al-Fārābī 1985: 203–205). An essential element, however, arises from both of his descriptions: when they are actually realized in the soul, intelligibles have an existence (*wujūd*) that is neither the existence they had when they existed as forms in matter nor the existence to be ascribed to them in so far as they are themselves (al-Fārābī 1983: 16.6–8). The different ontological status attributed to forms as they are in the world and as intelligibles is relevant not only for the discussion about universals (and their existence *in re, post rem* and *ante rem*): the intellectual existence of intelligible forms highlights the role of the knowing subject. In fact, it is precisely the subject who plays a fundamental role in the explanation of the next degree of knowledge. The degree of acquired intellect (*al-'aql al-mustafād*) corresponds to the operation by which or the moment in which intelligibles, thanks to an act of reflection on the part of the subject, are understood to be identical to the subject who understands them (al-Fārābī 1983: 19, 6–20, 3) and who has, consequently, no need to look at the world in order to *know*. This subjective independence of the acquired status of knowledge explains, on the one hand, how the acquired intellect can express the status of the human intellect in the afterlife and, on the other, how its actuality is, in a sense, the realization in a human being of the agent intellect (Taylor 2006: 153–4).

Al-Fārābī's *Epistle*, at once a discussion of metaphysical cosmology (the separate intelligences), epistemology, and philosophical terminology (the real objects of investigation are the meanings—*ma'ānī*—of the term intellect), is based on Neoplatonic sources (Geoffroy 2002; d'Ancona 2008). At the same time, al-Fārābī adopts the Aristotelian idea of empiricism: the intellectual knowledge of separate substances is perfect, but abstractive knowledge—which is possible through the action of the separate agent intellect that activates human potential—is a necessary step in the quest for perfection. Al-Fārābī's *Epistle* also exerted some influence on the Latin world, not only in its Latin version, probably by Gundissalinus (Gilson 1929; Fidora 2003), but mainly through the *Long Commentary on the De Anima* by Ibn Rushd (Taylor 2006). An important element in al-Fārābī's theory of knowledge is imagination, which plays a special intermediate role between the senses and intellection. In *The Perfect State*, imagination makes possible a first abstraction and elaboration of sense data: it not only contributes to the formation of images for abstraction, it also explains the use of known intelligibles in the realm of sensible things (al-Fārābī 1985: 164–75). Moreover, human imaginative power represents an initial channel of communication with the divine world. Imagination is not limited to retaining and making use of a sense datum, at times combining it with other data, and even coming up with a new effect, different from their appearance in real life; it also imitates intellectual forms, endowing the essences of things with the form of sense impressions (al-Fārābī 1985: 211–27). Thus, according to al-Fārābī, prophecy can be considered as the perfection of imagination. The primacy of the intellect, however, remains intact: intellect is the only faculty capable of assessing the truth or falsity of imaginative representations and also how close they come to the original. In this respect, prophecy, restricted as it is to the imagination, is subordinate to the intellectual power of the philosopher, whose contact with the divine is on the rational level. Moreover, the absolute perfection of the human soul, as well as its true happiness, are to be found, according to al-Fārābī, in intellection—celestial life is, after all, intellectual—and even politics ultimately depends on the perfect intellection of the philosopher.

Ibn Sīnā

Ibn Sīnā's theory of cognition seems, even more than al-Fārābī's, to be suspended between Neoplatonism and Aristotelianism: although Ibn Sīnā insists on the Neoplatonic idea that intellection is the reception of and contact with the celestial dimension (*al-Nafs*; Avicenna 1959: 235, 7), he nevertheless assumes that he must explain the role of experience and sensation in terms of the Aristotelian tradition, taking into account, all the while, the definitions of the third book of the *De anima* (3.5). Hence man's intellect, considered in itself, is first of all potential and receptive. Its perfection, and therefore the ultimate perfection of the human being accessible to philosophers' souls in the afterlife, consists in receiving the forms of the entire universe and thus in becoming a separate intellect or an angel. The first elements of knowledge reside nevertheless in experience. In other words, knowledge proceeds by stages toward greater abstraction (*tajrīd*). This involves not only intellect, but also the various faculties of the soul that free the object of their perception from matter and its constraints (for intellectual abstraction: Avicenna 1959: 170, 188, 237).

Abstraction ensures both the universality and the truth of knowledge. Knowing means focusing on external reality, no longer in its changeable physical manifestations, but in its universal meanings (*ma'ānī*), i.e. the essences or forms of which it consists. Specifically, the gradation of human intellect—as laid out in the first *Treatise* of the *Book on the soul* (*al-Nafs*, I, 5; Avicenna 1959: 48–50)—begins with "absolute potency," then moves up to potency—which, being relatively near *act* as "possible" intellect, coincides with a first actualization—and ends with perfective potency (*al-quwwa al-kamāliyya*). Absolute potency is degree zero of intellectual knowledge and corresponds to "material intellect." The first degree of actualization coincides with the intellection of the first intelligibles, that is, of those notions, whether simple like concepts or complex like articulations of concepts that form the basis of all kinds of knowledge. At this degree of intellection, the human intellect is in a sense an intellect in act (*al-'aql bi-l fi'l*); it is, in fact, in act compared to the absolute potency of the previous state and is more properly *in habitu* (*bi-l-malaka*), because it already has a first form of knowledge. But the first real actualization of the human intellect arrives with perfective potency (*al-quwwa al-kamāliyya*), thanks to which the human intellect can be properly said to be "in act" (*al-'aql bi-l-fi'l*). But even in this state of actualization, the human intellect is not in act to the extent that it actually has intellection and grasps the forms and truth of things, but rather in that it is free to access intellection whenever it likes.

Intellection is the reception of forms, namely the conjunction with the agent principle, which, for Ibn Sīnā (as also for al-Fārābī), corresponds to the last heavenly intelligence. In other words, since it is basically receptive, the intellect "in act," if placed in relation to the next stage, may still in a way be called "intellect in potency" (*'aql bi-l-quwwa*). Ultimately, a state of true actuality can be attributed only to the intellect that actually knows, and Ibn Sīnā, harking back to the preceding exegetical tradition, calls it "acquired intellect" (*al-'aql al-mustafād*). This is the intelligible form that is present in the intellect and that the intellect considers to be in act, thus having intellection of it in act and having intellection of having intellection of it in act (Avicenna 1959: 50). Hence acquired intellect corresponds to the full actualization of the rational human soul; it is the state of the human intellect that, filled with the forms "received" from the separate intellect, is able to dwell on them consciously. Thus, while acquired intellect corresponds to the datum of intellection that is received and literally "acquired" from outside itself, it also expresses an exalted moment of the subject's activity of self-reflection, an element which was central in al-Fārābī's analysis as well. So the acquired intellect is not a fourth stage of the potency of the intellect but the moment of its full actualization. Therefore the cognitive dimension it represents has a fundamental function in Ibn Sīnā's anthropology as well as his eschatology: because it is a sign of the progressive perfectibility of the human soul, acquired intellect is in fact not only the complete actualization of human knowledge, but also the precondition, first, of man's true intellectual happiness, and, second, of his celestial intellectual life. For Ibn Sīnā, as for any Neoplatonic thinker, knowledge is the true way to communicate with the celestial world. To know is to draw on our own authentic intellectual dimension, which is also that of the divine world. In this sense, knowledge is also the main—if not the only—way to happiness (Avicenna 1960: 9, 7).

One of the most interesting elements of Ibn Sīnā's theory of knowledge—and one of the most important at the historical level—is the theory of the so-called "holy intellect" (*al-'aql al-qudsī*, see Avicenna 1959: 5, 6, or the "holy power," *al-quwwa al-qudsiyya*). As the ultimate perfection of the intellect (*in habitu*), and therefore the highest and most perfect degree of the human intellect, the holy intellect is essentially prophetic. It should be noted, however, that Ibn Sīnā does not thereby refer to a degree to be added to the gradation mentioned above, but to a quicker and readier way to achieve the maximum actualization of the human intellect, i.e. the intellect *in habitu*. The mind of a prophet is, indeed, directly connected to form, without the need of the mediation (i.e. preparation) normally represented by learning. In fact, while a human being usually actualizes his intellect only by means of a learning process (education and experience) that leads to the middle term and prepares the soul to receive the intelligible forms, in the exceptional case of prophets, reception occurs directly, without education, without experience. The "holy" intellect is, in other words, always ready (i.e. always already prepared or willing) to receive the intelligibles. But the doctrine of the holy intellect should not be understood as a theory that deals exclusively with prophecy. Ibn Sīnā explains not only the particular phenomenon of prophecy but, more generally, that of exceptional knowledge. The exceptionality of prophecy is included in the category of knowledge and integrated into anthropology (prophets are bracketed, in fact, with philosophers). Moreover, a key notion in interpreting the holy intellect is the Greek *eustochia*, the faculty that in Aristotle explains the extraordinary intuitive ability of certain people. The same exceptional knowledge that in prophets is defined as revelation is, in human beings who are endowed with *ḥads*, mere intuition, or immediate apprehension of the syllogism's middle term (Gutas 2001 and cf. 1988).

A critical point is the real role played by abstraction in a context that seems to be dominated by emanation and therefore reception of intelligible forms (Davidson 1972, 1992; Jabre 1984; Rahman 1958; Hasse 2000, 2001; McGinnis 2007). Actually, the idea of conjunction with the agent intellect reveals the aporetic character of Ibn Sīnā's theory of knowledge. On the one hand, sensible knowledge and experience play a significant role in preparing the intellect to receive forms: human theoretical intellect achieves its first actualization through the first abstraction of sensible knowledge; moreover, forms become increasingly abstract as one moves from the imaginative to the intellectual dimension (Avicenna 1985a: 220–2; Avicenna 1985b: 372–3). On the other hand, understanding seems to depend on the conjunction with the separate celestial intellect, as is evident in the case of the holy intellect and more generally with intuition, which is unrelated to any prior sensation, experience or education. In short, it is difficult to understand if intelligible forms are the result of an abstractive operation (*taǧrīd*). Perception, imagination and the estimative faculty capture a more or less abstract form or essence (Sebti 2005). The continuity between perception and intellection is, however, diminished by a fundamental difference between sensation and intellection: intellection grasps the core of the thing, while sensation stops at its outward appearance (Avicenna 1960: 8, 7, 369, 11–13). Intellection leads to a totally different dimension from that of sense-perception: it "sees," so to speak, essences and is realized by means of an act that depends on the higher dimension of the agent intellect, "the giver of intellect" that enlightens (*ishrāq*) the human mind as the sun does the eyes. As is evident, however, while intellection is nothing but conjunction with the separate intellect and reception of intellectual forms (*ṣuwar ʻaqliyya*), abstraction, instead, reveals a state of the intellectual or intellected forms "given" by the superior intelligence and "received" by the human intellect, rather than an operation of human intelligence. But is this interpretation—the traditional account—satisfactory? Certainly it fails to account for all the passages in which Ibn Sīnā indicates sensation and experience as a route to knowledge, also making explicit use of the term "abstraction" (*taǧrīd*: *Najāt* ed. Fakhry: 218, 6; *Ilāh*.: 5, 1, 205). Scholars have therefore advocated an alternative explanation, claiming a real role for abstraction and insisting on the philosophical evolution of Ibn Sīnā's thought (Gutas 2001; Hasse 2000, 2001). Dimitri Gutas, for example, finds in the mature period of Ibn Sīnā's philosophy (corresponding to such texts as the *Kitāb al-Ishārāt*, *al-Nafs al-nāṭiqa* and, at least in part, *Kitāb al-Mubāḥaṯāt*), a theory in which the separate intellect is not the efficient cause of human intellection, but a kind of condition or exemplary cause: according to this reading, separate intellect is a sort of place for intelligibles, which could be stored neither in the human body nor in the human intellect; thus, at the same time it is a guarantee for human intellection: we are able to think because there is a mind that thinks in act "and in this sense the thoughts emanate from it in us" (Gutas 2001: 29–30). Emanation must therefore be activated by human thought that passes through the different degrees of abstraction related to the various faculties of the human soul. Dag Nikolaus Hasse, who also insists on the evolution of Ibn Sīnā's thought, recognizes a real theory of abstraction in Ibn Sīnā, which is fully defined in the *Ishārāt*, the *Book of indications* (Hasse 2001: 64). Lastly, a new interpretation has been proposed by Jon McGinnis (2007): the subject of our scientific representations (the idea of a horse) does not match the pure essence of what we know (the horse), but adds to it the quantitative predicate of universality. According to McGinnis, this predicate (like other intellectual accidents such as being a predicate, etc.) is what the separate intellect emanates upon the human intellectual power. So human intellect "abstracts" the essence from the cognitive material offered by sense experience. Abstraction is a sort of selective attention that leads to the intellect's dwelling on the essence of the thing. The intellectual accidents without which true knowledge would be impossible (that is, the predicates of universality, particularity, etc.) derive from emanation: they are the "intellectualizing forms" (*al-ṣuwar al-ʻaqliyya*) bestowed by the Principle (for the intellection of non-existent things, see Black 1997; Michot 1985). All interpretations are based on Ibn Sīnā's texts and philosophical lexicon, which include both emanation and abstraction. In this sense, Ibn Sīnā's theory of knowledge cannot avoid the dichotomy and aporia that define it. Apart from the question of the historical development of the doctrine, abstraction reveals a difficulty that affects the whole Avicennian system: on the one hand, there is the fundamental principle of emanation; on the other, the appropriate preparation for it as well as its reception.

Conclusion

Aristotle's text—from which the Arabic epistemological doctrines are clearly derived—is difficult and to a certain extent ambiguous: the active intellect is the prerequisite of actualization of the intellect in potency, but the latter too is impassible. It can be reasonably stated that all the authors of the Arabic tradition derive the universality of knowledge from the separate intellect; the cognitive process is always conceived as a progression towards pure and abstract knowledge—and the term "intellect" itself is a keyword in describing the relationship between the human and celestial or divine dimensions; differences among the authors are related to the explanation of the process in its details and/or the role of the possible intellect and imagination and, of course, to the sources they use. The great vexed questions in Arabic epistemology are the result of its straddling the border between Aristotelianism and Neoplatonism; they involve both the definition of the human soul and subjectivity and man's relationship to experience and knowledge gained through the senses (abstraction, first intelligibles). With his doctrine of the "unique intellect," which he worked on throughout his life, Ibn Rushd attempted to resolve the ambiguity of Aristotle's text (see here R. C. Taylor's chapter in this book) and introduced new elements in the speculation about knowledge, the subject of knowledge and the *visio beatifica* (Taylor 2004, 2011; Jolivet 1991; Brenet 2003, 2011).

All Islamic Medieval theories of cognition are linked to the idea of the communication of truth and the specific anthropology it implies. This is evident, although also different, in the metaphysical-political theory of al-Fārābī, in Ibn Sīnā's theory of imaginative language and eschatology and in Ibn Rushd's theory of truth communication: only very few human beings, "demonstrative people" or philosophers, have innate dispositions that enable them to grasp the truth (*The Decisive Treatise* is in this respect a fundamental work: Taylor 2000; de Libera 2002).

Further Reading

Al-Fārābī (2012), *Epître sur l'Intellect*, Introduction, Traduction, et commentaires de Ph. Vallat, Paris: Les Belles Lettres.

Gutas, D. (2014) *Avicenna and the Aristotelian Tradition*, Leiden: Brill.

——. (2006) "Imagination and Transcendental Knowledge in Avicenna," in J. E. Montgomery (ed.), *Arabic Philosophy, Islamic Theology. From the Many to the One: Essays in Celebration of Richard M. Frank*, Leuven: Peeters, pp. 337–54.

Ivry, A. L. (1995) "Averroes' Middle and Long Commentaries on the De Anima," *Arabic Sciences and Philosophy* 5: 75–92.

——. (1997) "Averroes' Short Commentary on Aristotle's De anima," *Documenti e Studi Sulla Tradizione Filosofica Medievale* 8: 511–49.

——. (1999) "Averroes' Three Commentaries on De anima," in G. Endress & J. A. Aertsen (eds.), *Averroes and the Aristotelian Tradition*, Leiden: Brill, pp. 199–216.

Janssens, J. (2004) "Experience (*tajriba*) in Classical Arabic Philosophy (al-Fārābī and Avicenna)," *Quaestio* 4: 45–62.

References

Adamson, P. (2003) *The Arabic Plotinus*, London: Duckworth.

——. (2007) *Al-Kindi*, New York: Oxford University Press.

al-Fārābī (1983) *Risāla fī l-'aql*, M. Bouyges (ed.), Beirut: Dar el-Mashriq.
——. (1985) *Alfarabi on the Perfect State*, R. Walzer (ed. and tr.), Oxford: Clarendon Press.
Averroes (1953) *Averrois Cordubensis Commentarium Magnum in Aristotelis De Anima Libros*, F. S. Crawford (ed.), Cambridge, MA: Mediaeval Academy of America.
——. (2009) *Long Commentary on the De Anima of Aristotle*, R. C. Taylor (tr.), New Haven: Yale University Press.
Avicenna (1908) *Risāla fī aqsām al-'ulūm al-'aqliyya* in *Tis' Rasā'il fī l-ḥikma wa l-ṭabī'iyyāt*, Cairo: Maṭba'a hindiyya, pp. 104–18.
——. (1952) *Aḥwāl al-nafs*, F. A. al-Ahwānī (ed.), Cairo: al-Halaby and Co.
——. (1959) *Avicenna's* De Anima. *Being the Psychological Part of Kitāb al-Shifā'*, F. Rahman (ed.), London, New York & Toronto: Oxford University Press.
——. (1957–1960) *Kitāb al-Išārāt wa-l-Tanbīhāt li-Abī 'Alī ibn Sīnā ma'a šarḥ Naṣīr al-Dīn al-Ṭūsī*, vol. IV, S. Dunyā (ed.), Cairo: Dar- al-Ma'ārif (repr. 1985, 1994).
——. (1960) *Kitāb al-Ilāhiyyāt (La Métaphysique)*, vol. I, G. C. Anawati & S. Zāyid (eds.); vol. II, M. Y. Mousa, S. Dunya, & S. Zāyid (eds.), Cairo: Ministère de la Culture et de l'Orientation.
——. (1963) "On the Proof of Prophecies and the Interpretation of the Prophet's Symbols and Metaphors," M. E. Marmura (tr.), in R. Lerner & M. Mahdi (eds.), *Medieval Political Philosophy: A Sourcebook*, Canada: Collier Macmillan Limited, pp. 112–21.
——. (1969) *Epistola sulla vita futura (al-Risāla al-aḍḥawiyya fī l-ma'ād)*, F. Lucchetta (tr.), Padua: Antenore.
——. (1985a) *Kitāb al-najāt (The Salvation)*, M. Fakhry (ed.), Beirut: Dār al-afāq al-jadīdah.
——. (1985b) *Kitāb al-Naǧāt min al-ġaraq fī baḥr al-ḍalālāt (Salvation of the Immersion in the Sea of Errors)*, M. Dānišpažūh (ed.), Tehran: Dānišga.
——. (2005) *The Metaphysics of The Healing*, M. E. Marmura (tr.), Provo, UT: Brigham Young University Press.
Black, D. (1997) "Avicenna on the Ontological and Epistemic Status of Fictional Beings," *Documenti e studi sulla tradizione filosofica medievale* 8: 425–53.
——. (2008) "Avicenna on Self-Awareness and Knowing that One Knows," in S. Rahman, T. Hassan, & T. Street (eds.), *The Unity of Science in the Arabic Tradition*, Dordrecht: Springer, pp. 63–87.
Brenet, J-B. (2003) *Transferts du sujet. La noétique d'Averroès selon Jean de Jandun*, Paris: Vrin.
——. (2011) "S'unir à l'intellect, voir Dieu. Averroès et la doctrine de la jonction au coeur du thomisme," *Arabic Sciences and Philosophy* 21: 215–47.
d'Ancona, C. (1995) *Recherches sur le Liber de Causis*, Paris: Vrin.
——. (1999) "Aristotelian and Neoplatonic Elements in Kindī's Doctrine of Knowledge," *American Catholic Philosophical Quarterly* 73: 9–35.
——. (2008) "Degrees of Abstraction in Avicenna. How to Combine Aristotle's *De Anima* and the Enneads," in S. Knuuttila & P. Kärkkäinen (eds.), *Theories of Perception in Medieval and Early Modern Philosophy*, Amsterdam: Springer, pp. 47–71.
Davidson, H. A. (1972) "Alfarabi and Avicenna on the Active Intellect," *Viator* 3: 109–78.
——. (1992) *Alfarabi, Avicenna, Averroes on Intellect. Their cosmologies, theories of the Active Intellect, and Theories of Human Intellect*, Oxford: Oxford University Press.
de Libera, A. (2002) "Foi et raison. Philosophie et religion selon Averroès et Thomas d'Aquin," *Studi Medievali* 43: 833–56.
Druart, T-A. (1997) "Al-Farabi, Ethics, and First Intellegibles," *Documenti e Studi sulla Tradizione filosofica medievale* 8: 403–23.
Endress, G. (1973) *Proclus Arabus. Zwanzig Abschnitte aus der Institutio Theologica in arabischer Uebersetzung*, Beirut & Wiesbaden: Orient-Institut der deutschen morgenländischen Gesellschaft.
——. (1980) *Jean Jolivet: L'intellect selon Kindī (Rez.), Zeitschrift der deutschen morgenländischen Gesellschaft* 130: 422–35.

——. (1994) "Al-Kindi über die Wiedererinnerung der Seele," *Oriens* 34: 174–221.

Fidora, A. (2003) *Die Wissenschaftstheorie des Dominicus Gundissalinus: Voraussetzungen und Konsequenzen des zweiten Anfangs der aristotelischen Philosophie im 12. Jahrhundert*, Berlin: Akademie Verlag.

Geoffroy, M. (2002) *La tradition arabe du Peri nou d'Alexandre d'Aphrodise et les origines de la théorie farabienne des quatre degrés de l'intellect*, in C. d'Ancona & G. Serra, *Aristotele e Alessandro di Afrodisia nella Tradizione Araba*, Padua: Il Poligrafo, pp. 191–231.

Gilson, E. (1929) "Les sources gréco-arabes de l'augustinisme avicennisant," *Archives d'Histoire Doctrinale et Littéraire du Moyen Age* 4: 5–158.

Gutas, G. (1988) *Avicenna and the Aristotelian Tradition. Introduction to Reading Avicenna's Philosophical Works*, Leiden: Brill.

——. (2001) "Intuition and Thinking: The Evolving Structure of Avicenna's Epistemology," in R. Wisnovsky (ed.), *Aspects of Avicenna*, Princeton: Wiener, pp. 1–38.

Hansberger, R. (2008) "How Aristotle Came to Believe in God-given Dreams: The Arabic Version of De divinatione per somnum," in L. Marlow (ed.), *Dreaming Across Boundaries: The Interpretation of Dreams in Islamic Lands*, Washington/Cambridge, MA: Ilex Foundation/ Center for Hellenic Studies, pp. 50–77.

——. (2010) "Kitāb al-Ḥiss wa-l-maḥsūs: Aristotle's Parva Naturalia in Arabic Guise," in C. Grellard & P.-M. Morel (eds.), *Les Parva naturalia d'Aristote: Fortune antique et médiévale*, Paris: Publisher, pp. 143–62.

Hasse, D. (2000) *Avicenna's De anima in the Latin West. The Formation of a Peripatetic Philosophy of the Soul 1160–1300*, London/Turin: The Warburg Institute/Nino Aragno Editore.

——. (2001) *Avicenna on Abstraction*, in R. Wisnovsky (ed.), *Aspects of Avicenna*, Princeton: Wiener, pp. 39–72.

——. (2011) *Avicenna's Giver of Forms in Latin Philosophy Especially in the Works of Albertus Magnus*, in A. Bertolacci & D. Hasse (eds.), *The Arabic, Hebrew and Latin Reception of Avicenna's Metaphysics*, Berlin: De Gruyter, pp. 225–50.

Jabre, F. (1984) "Le sens de l'abstraction chez Avicenne," *Mélanges de l'Université St. Joseph* 50: 281–311.

Jolivet, J. (tr.) (1971) *L'Intellect selon Kindī*, Leiden: Brill.

——. (1991) *Averroès et le décentrement du sujet*, in *Le choc d'Averroès. Comment les philosophes arabes ont fai l'Europe*, Internationale de l'Imaginaire, 17/18, pp. 161–9.

——. (1995) *Intellect et intelligence. Note sur la tradition arabo-latine des XIIème et XIIIème siècles*, in J. Jolivet, *Philosophie médiévale arabe et latine*, Paris: Vrin, pp. 169–80 (already in S. H. Nasr (ed.), *Mélanges offerts à Henry Corbin*, Institute of Islamic Studies, McGill University, Tehran: Tehran Branch, 1977, pp. 681–702).

——. (2006) "Etapes dans l'histoire de l'Intellect agent," in J. Jolivet, *Perspectives médiévales et arabes*, Paris: Vrin, pp. 163–174 (already in A. Hasnawi, A. Elmarnai-Jamal & M. Aouad (eds.), *Perspectives arabes et médiévales sur la tradition scientifique et philosophique grecque. Actes du Colloque de la SIHSPAI*, Paris, 31 Mars - 3 Avril 1993, Leuven/Paris: Peeters – IMA, 1997).

Lizzini, O. (2005) "Intellectus, intelligentia, mens' *in Avicenna*," in E. Canone (ed.), *Per una storia del concetto di mente*, Rome & Florence: Lessico Intellettuale Europeo, Olschki, pp. 123–165.

——. (2009) "Vie active, vie contemplative et philosophie chez Avicenne," in C. Trottmann (ed.), *Vie active et vie contemplative au Moyen Age et au seuil de la Renaissance*, Rome: École Française de Rome, pp. 207–39.

Marmura, M. (1986) "Avicenna's 'Flying Man' in Context," *The Monist* 69: 383–95.

McGinnis, J. (2007) "Making Abstraction Less Abstract: The Logical, Psychological, and Metaphysical Dimensions of Avicenna's Theory of Abstraction," *Proceedings of the American Catholic Philosophical Association* 80: 169–83.

Michot, Y. (J.) (1985) "Avicenna's Letter on the disappearance of the vain intelligible forms after death," *Bulletin de philosophie médiévale* 27: 94–103.

——. (1997) "La Définition de l'âme, section I de l'Épître des états de l'âme," in A. De Libera, A. Elamrani-Jamal, & A. Galonnier (eds.), *Langages et Philosophie*. Hommage à Jean Jolivet, Paris: Vrin, pp. 239–56.

Pines, S. (1955) "La conception de la conscience de soi chez Avicenne et Abû-l-Barakât al-Baghdâdî," *Archives d'Histoire Doctrinale et Littéraire du Moyen Age* 21: 5–85 (repr. in *The Collected Works of Shlomo Pines. Studies in Abū'l-Barakāt al-Baghdādī Physics and Metaphysics*, I).

——. (1974) "The Arabic Recension of *Parva Naturalia* and the Philosophical Doctrine Concerning Veridical Dreams According to *al-Risala al-Manamiyya* and Other Sources," *Israel Oriental Studies* 4: 104–53.

Porro, P. (2006) Colcodea, in V. Melchiorre (ed.), *Enciclopedia Filosofica*, vol. III, Milan: Fondazione Centro Studi Filosofici di Gallarate/Bompiani, 2009–10.

Rahman, F. (1958) *Prophecy in Islam*, London: Allen & Unwin.

Ruffinengo, P. P. (1997) "Al-Kindi, *Trattato sull'intelletto. Trattato sul sogno e la visione*," *Medioevo* 23: 337–94.

Sebti, M. (2005) "Le statut ontologique de l'image dans la doctrine avicennienne de la perception," in *Arabic Sciences and Philosophy* 15: 109–40.

Streetman, W. C. (2008) "'If it were God who sent them ... ' Aristotle and al-Fārābī on Prophetic Vision," *Arabic Sciences and Philosophy* 18: 211–46.

Taylor, R. C. (1986) "The *Kalām fī mahd al-hayr* in the Islamic Philosophical Milieu," in J. Kraye et al. (eds.), *Pseudo-Aristotle in the Middle Ages*, London: The Warburg Institute, pp. 37–52.

——. (1996) "Davidson on al-Farabi, Avicenna and Averroes. A Critical Review," *Journal of Neoplatonic Studies* 5: 89–105.

——. (2000) "Truth Does Not Contradict Truth: Averroes and the Unity of Truth," *Topoi* 19: 3–16.

——. (2004) "Separate Material Intellect in Averroes' Mature Philosophy," in R. Arnzen & J. Thielmann (eds.), *Words, Texts and Concepts Cruising the Mediterranean Sea. Studies on the sources, contents and influences of Islamic civilization and Arabic philosophy and science, dedicated to Gerhard Endress on his sixty-fifth birthday*, Leuven: Peeters, pp. 289–309.

——. (2005) "The Agent intellect as 'form for us' and Averroes's Critique of al-Fārābī," *Proceedings of the Society for Medieval Logic and Metaphysics* 5: 18–32 (already in (2005), *Tópicos, Revista de Filosofía* 29: 29–51).

——. (2006) "Abstraction in al-Fārābī," *Proceedings of the American Catholic Philosophical Association* 80: 151–68.

——. (2011) "Averroes' Philosophical Conception of Separate Intellect and God," in A. Hasnawi (ed.), *La lumière de l'intellect: La pensée scientifique et philosophique d'Averroès dans son temps*, Leuven: Peeters, pp. 391–404.

Vallat, P. (2004) *Farabi et l'École d'Alexandrie, Des prémisses de la connaissance à la philosophie politique*, Paris: Vrin.

24
INTELLECT AND THE INTELLIGIBLE IN UNITY

Cécile Bonmariage

Introduction

What is it to know, how do we acquire knowledge, and more precisely, how do we obtain the kind of knowledge that reaches that which is not determined by the limitations of the material world, the kind of knowledge that is beyond conditions of time and place, allowing for universal judgments? And, in a system of thought where a higher level of reality than this material world is conceived, what kind of knowledge reaches this higher realm?

Arabic philosophy inherited the conceptual framework for its understanding of such questions and other epistemological issues from Greek philosophy. The opinions defended as well as the point of the debates are not always as clear as one would like in Greek and Hellenistic philosophy and, more often than not, the same holds for their Arabic version and further developments in the Arabo-Islamic cultural area. One of the points Arabic reading thinkers had to come to grips with is Aristotle's statement in his treatise *On the Soul* that in immaterial things, the knower and the known (or what "intelligizes" and what is "intelligized") are identical (*On the Soul* 430a3–5). This observation—seen through the lenses of its various understandings by later commentators and of its further developments in Neoplatonic texts such as those of Plotinus or Proclus (all of these known through more or less faithful translations and paraphrases, making the theories sometimes quite different from their Greek counterpart)—brought about many discussions in later Arabic philosophy, even if its ultimately Aristotelian origin was not always recognized as such.

This chapter focuses on the unity of intelligible and intellect as theorised by one of the major thinkers of post-classical Islamic philosophy, Mullā Ṣadrā (Ṣadr al-Dīn Shīrāzī, d. ca 1640), who, unlike some of his most eminent predecessors such as Ibn Sīnā, thought it appropriate to conceive the relationship between the knower and the known, the subject and the object of intellection, as a unification. What did he mean by this? What are the questions he aims at solving? And what problems does his position create? These are the questions we will explore in what follows.

Intellection as Unity

Unity as Identification

To understand Ṣadrā's thought it is necessary to grasp what he means by "unity" or "identification" (*ittiḥād*) when he maintains that in the act of intellection, the subject of intellective knowledge and the object of intellective knowledge come to unite or become one. How unity is here understood as identity seems clear from the following definition of the term: "Unification/being one, that is identity" (*al-ittiḥād ayy al-huwahuwa*; Ṣadr al-Dīn Shīrāzī 1981: 1, 67). Ṣadrā follows here Ibn Sīnā's understanding of the word in this context, as it appears in the *Metaphysics* of the *Shifā'* in a passage about God's knowledge: intellect "unites with its (object), so as to become in a way identical to that which it intellects" (Avicenna 1960: VIII.7, 369.12).

Thus for Ṣadrā to say that there is "unification/unity of the knower and the known" means that in the act of intellection, knower and known are one and the same. Why he holds this view and precisely what its sense is requires careful explanation. It is so because, Ṣadrā maintains, it is only as being actually known that what is known is an object of knowledge. The act of being of an intelligible form in act (that is, a form which is totally devoid of matter, location and position) and its being for that which intellects it are one and the same thing, and nothing else, since it has no other being than this very being: otherwise it would not be what it is, an actually intelligible form (Ṣadr al-Dīn Shīrāzī 1981: 3, 313–15).

Every act of intellection is a unification insofar as, for Ṣadrā, that which is intellected, while remaining the same in its essential meaning, exists in this act by the very existence (or act of being) of the knower. The simile Ṣadrā gives for what is happening here is the relationship between act of being and quiddity in particular beings as he understands it. Ṣadrā conceives all that is as sharing one fundamental reality: being. Everything that is, is primarily an act of being, one of the modes that manifest the highest degree of being in ever more multiplicity and deficiency as one gets farther from the source of all being. Several distinctions are made in order to preserve the transcendence of the First and the existence of the different levels of reality. But, what is of interest to us here is rather that Ṣadrā, in his position on the act of being as the only founded reality, considers the quiddities (understood in its strict meaning of that which answers the question "what is it?", "quid est?") as merely a way of expressing the specific aspect of perfection that each lower being is, its deficiency making it "this" and not "that" in the language of quiddities. What is real is the act of being, and quiddity is derived from it. The quiddities are not through another act of being but they are simply another point of view on things, when the mind considers reality. Quiddities are thus nothing but this particular act of being, with no other ground for their reality than this very act, and still they are "something" when looked at in their own level of reality.

What happens in intellection understood as unification is thus not, as detractors would have it, that by intellecting a cow, I would become ontologically identical with a cow, but rather, that the intelligible form I intellect in act exists, in the act of intellection, by my own act of being, meaning that "both beings are through one and the same act of being" (Ṣadr al-Dīn Shīrāzī 1981: 3, 326). It is thus not the case that one thing would become another or that both things would disappear and become a third one, but in the knower both are by one act of being.

The Identification Paradigm

The unification or identification paradigm goes even beyond intellection to encompass perception as such: "Every act of perception," says Ṣadrā, "is through unification/identification of the perceiver and that which is perceived" (Ṣadr al-Dīn Shīrāzī 1984: 585). What he means by this is simply that every form of perception is only a form for that which perceives it: "What is sensed in act is united in its being with the substance that perceives it in act" (Ṣadr al-Dīn Shīrāzī 1981: 3, 315). Or in other words, "the being of what is sensed insofar as it is sensed, is in itself its being for that which senses it, just as the being of the intelligible as intelligible is the fact that it is actualized for that which intellects it" (Ṣadr al-Dīn Shīrāzī 1981: 3, 299; 3: 313). This is to be understood in the following way: the very reality of a perceived form is to be that form, meaning, to be a form for that which perceives it. Thus, for example, the form that is perceived in the sensation one can have of a concrete thing in the material world outside of our mind is this sensible form that exists for us as opposed to the form of the material thing in itself, which cannot be sensed as such.

For sensation and imagination (that is, the perception of those forms that are disengaged from matter but whose perception is subject to conditions pertaining to the corporeal world, such as location and position), this is relatively easy to understand, since for Ṣadrā, between these forms and that which perceives them, the relationship is more one of creation than of reception: "With respect to what it perceives in imagination and sensation (*mudrakātu-hā al-khayyāliyya wa-l-ḥissiyya*) the soul is more similar to an agent and an originator than it is to a depository that would receive (them)" (Ṣadr al-Dīn Shīrāzī 1981: 1, 287). This is for Ṣadrā one of the signs that man is created in God's image: the soul, like God, creates its own world. These forms that exist by virtue of the soul are "shadows of the beings of the outside world, which emanate from the Creator" (Ṣadr al-Dīn Shīrāzī 1981: 1, 266). If this is the way perception is conceived, to think that what is perceived is by the act of being of the perceiver does not seem to be problematic in any way.

But for intellection, the matter is not quite the same, since Ṣadrā, like most philosophers in his tradition, holds that the principles of intellective thought are not present and actual in the soul as soul, and cannot be attained by experience: something else is needed to obtain universal knowledge. This distinction between the various kinds of perception is expressed in what follows the passage just quoted: "As for the soul's state with respect to the intellective forms among the founded species, it is through a pure illuminative connection (*iḍāfa*) that occurs for the soul with the intellective and luminous essences that are in the World of Origination" (Ṣadr al-Dīn Shīrāzī 1981: 1, 288). At this point there enters another crucial tenet of Ṣadrā's thought indispensable in order to grasp how he understands intellection: the affirmation of the existence of a world of Intelligible Forms, something like self-subsisting Platonic Forms. It is by connecting with this world that intellection is possible for human beings.

Intellection as Unity

Ṣadrā finds it better to think intellection (and perception) as unity for several reasons. First, were it otherwise, acquisition of knowledge would not bring about any change in the knower, but remain external to what the knower is. This would be the case if the acquisition of knowledge were conceived as the fact that an intelligible form occurs to the human intellect without any change in the intellect as such, something like the occurrence of something to something distinct from it or "the attainment by something of something distinct from it" (*ḥuṣūl amr mubayin li-amr mubayin*; Ṣadr al-Dīn Shīrāzī 1984: 584). But acquiring knowledge is not like acquiring "a house, goods, or children" (Ṣadr al-Dīn Shīrāzī 1981: 3, 319). Acquisition thus understood can at most increase the number of relations something has with what is distinct from it, but not bring any change in the thing itself. But this is not what knowledge does to the knower: to acquire knowledge is for the knower to become more perfect. A person who knows something is not the same as when that person did not know that thing, since now a mode of perfection belongs to the knower that did not before, or more precisely, exists through the knower.

But, more essentially, what Ṣadrā maintains here is linked with his metaphysics. We said earlier that Ṣadrā conceives all that is as sharing one fundamental reality: being. From the First principle of all that is, the Real, come to be a variety of beings at different levels of perfection, which are so many realms of manifestation of the perfections of being. Three main levels or planes of reality are defined: an intellective realm, an imaginative realm, and the physical realm of the beings of this material world.

The passage from sensible perception to intellection is not to be understood as a process whereby the knower remains the same while what is known becomes increasingly disengaged from material conditions. It is rather a journey through modes of being:

> In its perception of the universal intelligibles, the soul witnesses intellective essences that are disengaged [from matter] not [because] soul would have disengaged them or abstracted the intelligible from the sensible, as is commonly held by philosophers, but through the transfer of the soul from that which is sensed to the imaginative, then to the intelligible, a departure from this world to the other world, then to what is beyond them, and a journey from the world of bodies to the world of images, then to the world of intellects.
>
> (Ṣadr al-Din Shīrāzī 1981: 1, 289)

Epistemological perfection goes along with, or corresponds to, ontological perfection: one knows what is at our level of being, one can reach what is in our plane of reality. This explains one of the aspects of Ṣadrā's statement that knowledge is being or being is knowledge (Ṣadr al-Dīn Shīrāzī 1981: 3, 291). The perfection of a human being in the journey through different levels of reality is an intensification by which one becomes more fully or more intensively what one is: from a rational animal, able potentially to perceive universal intelligibles, the human being becomes one of the separate substances. This is for Ṣadrā one of the key examples of his theory of substantial movement and explains how human beings can be said to be corporeal in their coming to be, immaterial in their subsistence.

To reach the level of intellection is thus to reach a mode of being free from the limitations due to matter or place. At this point, the human soul comes to participate in the intelligible realm and unites with the world of Intellect, that is, for Ṣadrā, the Platonic Forms. "There is a luminous and intellective form in the World of the Intellect (i.e., the Platonic Forms) for the things (in the world of) generation," says Ṣadrā. And it is this form "that a human being meets when perceiving the universal intelligibles" (Ṣadr al-Dīn Shīrāzī 1981: 2, 68).

What should be understood by this seems to be that this contemplation of the Intellective Forms allows one to recognize in what one encounters in our world expressions of the same realities, albeit in another, lower, mode of existence defined by multiplicity and deficiency. The very principle of the intelligibility of this world is assured by the existence of the Immaterial and Intellective Forms of the World of the Intellect, which this world manifests at a lower level. Our reaching out to this World of Forms gives us the key of the intelligibility of this lower world.

But some texts seem to point to a slightly different understanding. These are texts where it is stated that because we reach the Intelligible World from our position in this lower world, the realities that comprise that World, while in themselves intellective individuals, appear to us as universal concepts susceptible of being said of several things (Ṣadr al-Dīn Shīrāzī 1981: 1, 289; 2, 68–9). This seems to imply that our conceptualization of the world, which is one aspect of intellective knowledge, is due to the fact that our reaching out to the Intelligible World is not as successful as it might be and that there might thus be a higher kind of intellective knowledge. But before embarking on an explanation of what this might imply, we first have to consider another aspect of intellection as unity, the unification that takes place in intellection between the knower and the Active Intellect, conceived as a unique entity pertaining to the Intelligible World.

Unification of the Knower and the Active Intellect

This aspect of intellection as unity, unlike that just explained, appears more as an extra piece, added to the picture because it is usually linked to the unity of the knower and the known. When Ṣadrā deals with this question, he generally introduces it as being said by the Ancients, and as such in need of a proper meaning (Ṣadr al-Dīn Shīrāzī 1981: 3, 335, 1999: 96). Some have raised doubts about the necessity of such a theory in Ṣadrā's understanding of intellection and think that his discussion of the topic shows an unresolved (and even unproblematized) tension between unification with the world of intelligible entities or the World of the Intellect on the one hand, and unification with the Active Intellect on the other (Kalin 2010: 30). What Ṣadrā says here seems thus more of a way to give a correct interpretation of the Ancients' claim than a deliberate endorsement of the theory.

More often than not, this does not appear to be such a significant problem, since the Active Intellect, considered as having in itself all intelligibles, is often said to be the Intellective World seen as one single reality. When Ṣadrā deals with the question more precisely, this is what he says: soul in its act of intellection can be said to unite with the agent Intellect insofar as it unites with it with respect to the intelligible that is intellected, since the form that is intellected by the soul cannot be other than the form that is in the Active Intellect (or in any other knower), as intelligible forms can only be one and the same. The distinction Ṣadrā draws between intellective unity (where a multiplicity of meaning does not impair the unity of being) and numerical unity allows him to sweep away the traditional question of a multiplication of the concept when several knowers know the same thing. Ṣadrā's answer to another famous question—namely, if soul unites with the Active Intellect, would it know everything, since in it are all intelligible forms?—is that it is only with respect to the intelligible it is intellecting that the soul unites with the Active Intellect.

Nowhere does Ṣadrā seem to consider this unification as implying or likely to imply a loss of individuality for the human soul that unites with the Active Intellect. Nor does he make any strong statement about a possible strict distinction between unification and conjunction. In the *Mafātīḥ*, Ṣadrā states that the ultimate perfection of the human soul is to have in itself the forms of everything, and to "unite with the universal Intellect" (Ṣadr al-Dīn Shīrāzī 1984: 586). Since unification does not mean a loss of individuality, and since it is understood as identification, one way of understanding what is said here is that what Ṣadrā means when he speaks about unification with the Active Intellect or the universal Intellect is the same as what he says when he speaks about the soul as becoming itself an intellective world or an Active Intellect (Ṣadr al-Dīn Shīrāzī 1984: 587, 1981: 1, 20).

However, one also finds a different discourse regarding the role of the Active Intellect in human intellection in texts where the Active Intellect is described as illuminating the human soul and the imaginative forms so as to make them intellect in act and intelligible in act respectively (Ṣadr al-Dīn Shīrāzī 1981: 9, 143); in yet other texts, the Active Intellect is said to be that which gives the principles of universal knowledge rather than the content of thought. That is, the Active Intellect would give *a priori* truths necessary for universal knowledge (such as "the whole is greater than its parts") and not actual content of thought. As Kalin showed, this last interpretation of the role of the Active Intellect is left hardly explained by Ṣadrā, and how to understand these statements is not yet quite resolved (Kalin 2010: 149, 158). In fact, what Ṣadrā says about intellection, and more broadly about epistemological issues, is often not as clear and straightforward as one would hope. There are clearly implicit distinctions behind the various and not always entirely compatible (at least at first sight) explanations Ṣadrā gives about what actually happens here.

Knowledge of Concepts vs. Knowledge of Things as They Are

This is one of several distinctions not always explicitly stated by Ṣadrā. It comes near but does not entirely coincide with the distinction between knowledge having to do with the present world and knowledge having to do with the higher realm of reality, each having a separate criterion of truth: the correspondence of concepts with the external world for the first and mystical experience for the second (Rezaee & Hashemi 2009). It has also to do with propositional knowledge in a predicative and logical environment and knowledge of things as they are, in a direct witnessing of their very reality.

It is stated as such in a passage where Ibn Sīnā is said to err whenever he has to go beyond the first kind of knowledge to reach the second: there is a difference between knowing "what is general and universal," i.e. concepts, and understanding "what existential ipseities (*huwiyya*) really are" (Ṣadr al-Dīn Shīrāzī 1981: 9, 109). The same distinction is explained as that between knowing through definitions and knowing reality itself. The example par excellence is that of being itself, when considered as a concept, which is predicated of quiddities in the mind, and when being is considered in what it really is, the basic foundation of what is real outside of the mind. Realities are not instantiations of the concept of being but acts of being in their own right, concrete entities with distinct effects, although these vary in the different levels of reality.

What was said earlier about the source of universal concepts as coming from the weakness of our reaching out to the World of the Intellect shows how this conceptual knowledge is viewed by Ṣadrā as unsatisfactory and linked to our present state in this world. But in fact, the ultimate source of both understanding of what is seems to be the same. To reach the second higher kind of knowledge means to witness the Intelligible Forms of the World of the Intellect in their being and ipseity, as acts of being and not as a content of sense. And to reach intelligible concepts is to reach these same Intelligible Forms in their own meaning and as universal concepts (Ṣadr al-Dīn Shīrāzī 1981: 3, 386; see also 1, 291, where it is said that Intellective Forms are singular/individual in themselves, universal in consideration of their quiddities, which are concepts taken absolutely, predicable to all the individuals of a species; and 9, 144 where natural universals are said to be names for intellective ipseities). In other passages, however, the distinction could be interpreted as one between the work of the mind in its apprehension of the external world and proper intellection (something like the distinction between the work of the *mens* and that of *intellectus*). These are texts where concepts in the mind (used in universal propositions) are said to derive from experience ultimately going back to sense data, something that does not seem to entirely fit with what Ṣadrā says elsewhere employing the language of abstraction: "The human soul has the power to abstract (*intaza'a*) the universal intelligibles from the concrete (things) in the external (world) and from the imaginative forms" (Ṣadr al-Dīn Shīrāzī 1981: 1, 324):

> We can take from the various individuals ... one single meaning that corresponds to each of the individuals, insofar as this abstract universal meaning can be said of each of them; for instance, you can abstract from various human individuals ... one single meaning that they all share, that is "human being" (taken) absolutely.
>
> (Ṣadr al-Din Shīrāzī 1981: 1, 272)

The conceptual knowledge thus attained through these mental forms is labeled "intellective knowledge" (Ṣadr al-Dīn Shīrāzī 1981: 6, 155), since it fulfills the conditions of being free from matter, space, and position.

Whatever the interpretation one may give of such passages, the other side of the distinction is clear: it consists of witnessing intellective realities in a face-to-face or presential mode of knowledge, a direct cognitive intuition of the reality faced, in an experience similar to that of self-knowledge. Here again, Ṣadrā returns to the difference between concept and reality, and distinguishes this experience of self-knowledge (where one knows oneself as unique and not subject to any participation of others), from the conceptual knowledge we can have of ourselves as a human being, with what this universal concept entails of sharing with other individuals of the human species (Ṣadr al-Dīn Shīrāzī 1981: 6, 155–6).

Conceptual knowledge does however provide an understanding of reality, and corresponds to what things really are: the truthfulness of the concept and its correspondence with the outside world is grounded in its source, which is the Intelligible realities of the World of Intellect. This is so at least for those intelligible forms other than our own mental constructions, that is, for "founded species" as was said in the passage of the *Asfār* quoted earlier (Ṣadr al-Dīn Shīrāzī 1981: 1, 288) as opposed to intelligible forms created by the mind without any reference to reality (like "associate of the Creator" or "non-being") but considered as intelligible and subject to correct universal judgments (Ṣadr al-Dīn Shīrāzī 1981: 1, 263–326 on mental existence). But this conceptual knowledge is not the highest way of grasping the reality of things.

To reach a direct intellective knowledge or intuitive intellection that goes beyond concepts is "the most perfect part of knowledge" (Ṣadr al-Dīn Shīrāzī 1981: 6, 164). It is this kind of knowledge that reaches the fundamentals of a genuine understanding of what really is, the basic tenets of a correct metaphysical comprehension of reality. This does not mean that we have to get rid of demonstrative knowledge. What it means rather—in a way Suhrawardī and Ishrāqī illuminationists after him would recognize as properly *ishrāqī* (see Suhrawardī 1999: §5 at the end and §279)—is that the primary premises of demonstration, if founded, can only be attained through direct contemplation of the realities of things, as they are in the higher level of reality, that of the World of the Intellect. It is only when built on such bases that knowledge can reach an understanding of what is that is not subject to doubt, even when considering a conceptual understanding of things. For Ṣadrā,

> to attain this is only possible through the power of unveiling (or, revelation, *mukāshafa*), associated with a strong power of rational study (*baḥth*) for the one who studies without having a perfect taste and a correct unveiling cannot reach the contemplation of the existential realities. The study and investigations of these people turn for the most part around universal concepts, and these are the subjects of their sciences, and not the existential entities. This is why whenever the course of their study gets them to such questions, they show only deficiency, stammering and scribble.
>
> (Ṣadr al-Din Shīrāzī 1981: 6, 239)

Ṣadrā uses not only the language of vision, contemplation, and presence, but also that of inspiration (*ilhām*), of opening or unveiling (*fatḥ*), and of bestowals (*mawāhib*). He often presents himself as having been granted such bestowals: it is by inspiration that he discovered the major points of his metaphysics such as the primacy of being as act (Ṣadr al-Dīn Shīrāzī 1981: 5, 181); it is by an "opening" bestowed to him from God that he figured out how to understand the unification of knower and known (Ṣadr al-Dīn Shīrāzī 1981: 3, 313).

There are thus two types of apprehension of reality, one better than the other, even though in a few texts, the lower one seems to be described as a way towards the second. This is evident in the following passage, about the most perfect soul, that endowed with a "sacred power" (*quwwa qudsiyya*) says Ṣadrā, following here Ibn Sīnā:

> It perceives the pure intellective (entities) as such, in their being and what they are in themselves, not from the point of view of their meaning and their universal quiddity. For to attain the realities of these intelligibles, and not universal knowledge [i.e., conceptual knowledge], is that which matters in (this) perception, even if the latter is also a way to reach this attainment, when the inner meaning of these (realities) is deeply rooted in the soul. This is why it is said that knowledge is the seed of vision.
>
> (Ṣadr al-Din Shīrāzī 1981: 3, 386)

To reach the realities of the World of Intellect in their meaning, as concepts, is one step; to see them in their being is one step further: "When knowledge attains the species and their statutes, rational enquiry (*al-naẓar al-baḥthī*) stops, and after it there is only presential contemplation of the intellective natures and of the separate forms" (Ṣadr al-Dīn Shīrāzī 1981: 5, 266).

Very few reach such a level of knowledge (and even the level of intellective knowledge as such). Most human beings live at the level of the sensible and imaginative worlds, and since existence and perception go side by side, most human beings perceive only what is in these levels of reality and have no other mode of knowledge than that pertaining to this sensible and imaginative realm. And even those who do reach intellective knowledge only rarely do so without any trace of or mixing with imagination, since human beings while in this world can only rarely reach a pure intellective knowledge (Ṣadr al-Dīn Shīrāzī 1981: 3, 460; 378–80). More often than not, even the most perfect human beings remain at the level of the "science that pertains to the soul" (*'ilm nafsānī*), something between the imaginative grasp of things (*khayyāl*) and simple intellect (*'aql basīṭ*) (Ṣadr al-Dīn Shīrāzī 1981: 3, 378).

But the goal of human perfection is nevertheless

> to perceive all of the existential realities and unite with them … . It is also in the nature of the human soul to become a simple intellect and an intellective knower, in whom resides the form of every intellective existent and the meaning of every physical being in a way higher than their mode of physical existence.
>
> (Ṣadr al-Din Shīrāzī 1999: 38–9; Kalin 2010: 282 and 1981: 3, 338–9; note the implicit distinction between the knowledge pertaining to this world and that of the world of the intellect expressed by the change in terms: "meaning" and "form")

It is this ability to know things as they are that differentiates human nature from all the realities of this world (Ṣadr al-Dīn Shīrāzī 1981: 9, 139). Another important peculiarity of human nature is that only human beings can exist in the different levels or modes of being while keeping their individuality, their "individual ipseity" as Ṣadrā has it, thus remaining individuals at each level of reality (Ṣadr al-Dīn Shīrāzī 1981: 9, 96–9, 194).

To reach intellective knowledge, and thus to unite with the Intelligible World, is not something that can be done only after death, except as Ṣadrā says, if by "death" the soul's departure from the world of nature is meant, since this is indispensable for every intellection (Ṣadr al-Dīn Shīrāzī 1981: 5, 303–4). While living in this world, and while partly still living in the physical realm and having to take care of ones body for instance, one can already access higher modes of knowledge and of realization of oneself. Such a human being, while still in this physical world, is yet already free from its limitations.

Being in This World

What is the role, if any, of sense data and of the mental work on what we get from our encounter with things in this world in the acquisition of knowledge in such a theory? It could well be assumed to be very little. This is not however the case. Ṣadrā insists on the necessity to start from the grasp of sensible forms and thus from sense data gathered in this world as a first step towards higher levels of knowledge. Against those who think that the best way to prepare oneself to obtain knowledge from a higher realm is to refrain from any confrontation with the world and to abstain from sensation as much as possible, Ṣadrā declares that this is wrong. The first step of acquisition of knowledge for human beings is by way of sensible perception: by seeing "what is common to things and by what they differ, knowledge and definitions arise, then arguments and demonstrations." These perceptions are like "wings for the human intellect by which it flies to the Higher Realm and the Lofty World" (Ṣadr al-Din Shīrāzī 2004: 1, 393–4). Ṣadrā warns his readers to be diligent in their quest for self-sufficiency through this body and its instruments lest they would be taken by surprise by death and remain eternally deficient (Ṣadr al-Dīn Shīrāzī 1981: 2, 81).

Ṣadrā and His Sources

In his defense of a conception of knowledge as unity, Ṣadrā presents his own views as a rediscovery of the true meaning of the theory held by the Ancients. On the various meanings of "intellect" (*'aql*), in a reading that sees them as pointing to the identification paradigm he himself supports, Ṣadrā quotes extensively al-Fārābī speaking about the Ancients (Ṣadr al-Dīn Shīrāzī 1981: 3, 421–7) or Alexander of Aphrodisias about Aristotle's distinction of three kinds of intellect, material, *in habitu*, and agent (Ṣadr al-Dīn Shīrāzī 1981: 3, 428–33, quoting without naming as his source the *De Intellectu*). But the number of quotations from the *Uthūlūjīya* (the so-called *Theology of Aristotle*) points to Ṣadrā's main source here. One example should suffice to show this: "When the intellective man casts his gaze on the intelligible things, he does not reach them until he and they become one and the same thing" (*Uthūlūjīya*, VIII, §163, G. Lewis tr., 1959: 403, quoted in Ṣadr al-Dīn Shīrāzī 1981: 3, 317; on epistemology in the *Theology*, see d'Ancona 1997).

But there are other sources for what Ṣadrā maintains: Suhrawardī and Ishrāqī, but also Akbarī thought, are all likely inspirations for Ṣadrā in the development of his epistemological views. This aspect is not however stressed here (as it is in his metaphysics for instance), even though one can find in Ṣadrā's texts a discussion of Suhrawardī's own understanding of knowledge by presence or of imagination.

It is against the background of Ibn Sīnā's epistemological positions that Ṣadrā states his own view. His claim that in the act of intellection, subject and object become one breaks with Ibn Sīnā's outright rejection of identity of knower and known in human knowing (as distinct from God's knowledge of things). Ibn Sīnā considers it utterly inconceivable to claim that the knower "becomes the intelligible form it intellects." In his discussion of the matter, he offers several arguments, all of them going back to the basic principle that, for him, it is not possible for one thing to become another while still remaining itself (Avicenna 1892: 178–9; see also 1959: 239; see McGinnis 2010: 139–42).

Ṣadrā gives a point-by-point answer to Ibn Sīnā's arguments against identification of knower and known and of knower and Active Intellect in the texts where he discusses intellection (Ṣadr al-Dīn Shīrāzī 1981: 3, 321–40, 1999: 80–92, 96–100). But his answer would not have convinced Ibn Sīnā and those who follow his views: the discrepancy between the two thinkers runs deeper and their divergence regarding intellection is but a symptom of a radically different conception of the basic principles of metaphysics (Bonmariage 2002).

Conclusion

Ṣadrā's epistemology is often complex and challenging. In his major opus, the *Asfār*, the texts where these questions are discussed are disseminated in several parts centered on very different questions, and often Ṣadrā's own views are presented in a dialogue with his predecessors and as a response to previous debates. His doctrine on the unity of intellect and intelligible requires subtle awareness and attention on the part of the reader, with the danger of constructing an overly harmonizing account of the complex theory here presented by Ṣadrā. Still, it seems fair to say in conclusion that, like his metaphysics, Ṣadrā's epistemology is concerned primarily with individual, singular, realities. But as the most ontologically founded realities are those pertaining to the Intelligible World, the highest level of knowledge is to reach the intelligible singular, the Intelligible Form, through something like an intuitive intellection. This enables the soul to grasp the intelligibility of the lower levels of reality and to recognize in each lower level the actualization of the intelligible.

The questions and ideas here discussed are not unfamiliar to philosophers versed in Western thought: the debates may not exactly be the same, but they still try to tackle similar problems.

Further Reading

Ha'iri Yazdi, M. (1992) *The Principles of Epistemology in Islamic Philosophy. Knowledge by Presence*, Albany: SUNY Press.

Jambet, C. (2006) *The Act of Being. The Philosophy of Revelation in Mullā Sadrā*, J. Fort (tr.), New York: Zone Books.

Kalin, I. (2010) *Knowledge in Later Islamic Philosophy: Mullā Ṣadrā on Existence, Intellect and Intuition*, New York: Oxford University Press.

Rahman, F. (1975) *The Philosophy of Mulla Sadra*, Albany: SUNY Press.

Rezaee, H. S. & Hashemi, M. M. (2009) "Knowledge as a mode of being: Mulla Sadra's theory of knowledge," *Sophia Perennis* 4: 19–44.

Rizvi, S. H. (2009) *Mullā Ṣadrā and Metaphysics. Modulation of Being*, London & New York: Routledge.

Safavi, G. (ed.) (2002) *Perception according to Mulla Sadra*, London: Salam-Azadeh Publication.

References

Avicenna (1892) *Kitāb al-Ishārāt wa-l-tanbīhāt*, J. Forget (ed.), Leiden: Brill.

——. (1959) *Shifā', Fī l-nafs (Avicenna's* De anima *(Arabic text): being the psychological part of* Kitāb al-Shifā'), F. Rahman (ed.), London & New York: Oxford University Press.

——. (1960) *al-Shifā': al-Ilāhiyyāt*, 2 vols., G. C. Anawati (ed.), Cairo: al-Hay'a al-'Āmma li-Shu'ūn al-Muṭābi' al-Amīrīya.

Bonmariage, C. (2002) "L'intellection comme identification. Mullā Ṣadrā vs. Avicenne," in J. Janssens & D. De Smet (eds.), *Avicenna and his Heritage*, Leuven: Leuven University Press, pp. 99–112.

d'Ancona, C. (1997) "Divine and human knowledge in the *Plotiniana Arabica*," in J. Cleary (ed.), *The Perennial Tradition of Neoplatonism*, Leuven: Leuven University Press, pp. 419–42.

Kalin, I. (2010) *Knowledge in Later Islamic Philosophy: Mullā Ṣadrā on Existence, Intellect and Intuition*, New York: Oxford University Press.

McGinnis, J. (2010) *Avicenna*, Oxford: Oxford University Press.

Rezaee, H. S. & Hashemi, M. M. (2009) "Knowledge as a mode of being: Mulla Sadra's theory of knowledge," *Sophia Perennis* 4: 19–44.

Ṣadr al-Dīn Shīrāzī (1981) *al-Ḥikma al-muta'āliya fī l-asfār al-'aqliyya al-arba'a*, 9 vols., Beirut: Dār Ihyā' al-turāth al- 'arabī.

——. (1984) *Mafātīḥ al-ghayb*, M. Khājavī (ed.), Tehran: Cultural Studies and Research Institute.

——. (1999) *R. fī ittiḥād al-'āqil wa-l-ma'qūl*, in H. Nājī Isfahānī (ed.), *Majmū'a-yi rasā'il-i falsafī-yi Ṣadr al-muta'allihīn*, Tehran: Intishārāt-i Ḥikmat, pp. 61–103; I. Kalin (tr.) (2010) "Treatise on the unification of the intellector and the intelligible," *Knowledge in Later Islamic Philosophy*, New York: Oxford University Press, pp. 256–86.

——. (2004) *Sharḥ Uṣūl al-Kāfī*, M. Khājavī (ed.), Tehran: Cultural Studies and Research Institute.

Suhrawardī (1999) *The Philosophy of Illumination*, J. Walbridge & H. Ziai (tr.), Provo, UT: Brigham Young University Press.

Part VI

ETHICS AND POLITICAL PHILOSOPHY

25
THE ETHICS AND METAPHYSICS OF DIVINE COMMAND THEORY

Mariam al-Attar

Introduction

Divine Command Theory (DCT) is a moral theory with definite metaphysical assumptions. It has never lacked adherents among the followers of the three Abrahamic traditions: Judaism, Christianity and Islam. Different aspects of the theory were emphasized by different authors and thus different labels were given to the same theory. George Hourani called it "theistic subjectivism" emphasizing the fact that it denies anything objective in the acts themselves which would make them good or bad (Hourani 1985: 15). It has also been labeled as "theological voluntarism," emphasizing the fact that, according to this theory, it is the divine free will—which is not subject to any reason or requirements—that establishes morality and renders any action good or evil by command and prohibition. The central assumption of this view, which we choose to call Divine Command Theory (DCT), is that God is absolutely free to command anything, and that entails both aspects emphasized by those who called it ethical voluntarism and theistic subjectivism. What is sometimes called Modified Divine Command Theory which presupposes the goodness, love or purposefulness of God is not really a Divine Command Theory, since the ultimate basis of morality will then lie in the purposes or in a certain conception of good and bad rather than the commands and the prohibitions themselves. A Divine Command Theory which supports its argument by claiming that God is identical to the property of goodness or rightness is properly speaking incoherent and unintelligible. "A Divine Command Theory worthy of the name says that to be right is to be commanded by God, and to be wrong is to be forbidden by God" (Tuggi 2005: 53). It seems that in Christianity, as in Islam, theologians have adhered to the theory in order to preserve God's free will and omnipotence, since "the view that God's will is subject to independent standards of right and wrong, good and evil, appears to compromise His omnipotence" (Wainwright 2005: 74). Hence, "the Divine Command Theory has traditionally been associated with a particular conception of God's nature, one which emphasises His absolute power and freedom, and consequently the unknowability of His will by human reason" (Chandler 1985: 238). Nevertheless some hold different views and uphold different versions and interpretations of the theory, and refer to it as a "Modified Divine Command Theory" (Adams 1981).

In Christian thought, the most prominent figures who argued for forms of DCT included Augustine (d. 430), John Scotus (d. 1308), William of Ockham (d. 1348), Martin Luther (d. 1546), Karl Barth (d. 1968), Emile Brunner (d. 1966) and finally the contemporary Divine Command Theorists such as Philip Quinn (d. 2004) and Robert Adams. Yet, though one contemporary philosopher holds that "the dominant theory of ethics is not Divine Command Theory. That honour goes to the Theory of Natural Law" (Rachels 2003: 53), others have interpreted Christian ethics, including that of Aquinas—the greatest of the natural law theorists—as endorsing DCT (Quinn 1990: 358).

In Islamic ethics the proponents of DCT are generally held to be the Ashʿarites, i.e. those who belonged to the Ashʿarī school of theology (*kalām*) or, more precisely, that field of study which is related to the fundamental principles of the Islamic religion. The school of *kalām*, named after Abu al-Ḥasan al-Ashʿarī (d. 324/935), prevailed in the Sunni Islam context from the eleventh century onward, although many Muslim scholars did not adhere to any of the *kalām* schools and some even condemned it altogether. Some contemporary scholars have also interpreted all Ashʿarite thought, including that of al-Juwaynī (d. 478/1085), Fakhr al-Dīn al-Rāzī (d. 606/1209) and Abū Ḥāmid al-Ghazālī (d. 505/1111)—the first to articulate the purposes of law theory *maqāṣid al-sharīʿa*—as endorsing ethical voluntarism (e.g. Hourani 1985: 140 and Leaman 1999).

This chapter focuses on DCT, its criticism and its development. In Islamic thought DCT and other metaethical theories and ethical theories of action are mainly expounded in those books that are traditionally classified under the field of study known as the fundamental principles of law (*uṣūl al-fiqh*) and the fundamental principles of religion (*uṣūl al-dīn*), another name given to theology (*kalām*), rather than the books written under philosophy (*falsafah*). The early Muslim scholars seem to have discussed the judgments of the actions of those people who have not received revelation and the judgments of actions before revelation. In this they must have noticed that if it is possible for human actions to be judged as good or evil apart from revelation then certainly what makes an action good or evil is something other than divine commands. The moral values of actions before the arrival of revelation were affirmed by most of the scholars and jurists, before al-Ashʿarī (Reinhart 1995: 25).

In Islam the issue was: did God command what is good because it is good or did something become good because God commanded it? Long before the advent of Islam, Socrates raised a parallel philosophical question in Plato's *Euthyphro*, which has been interpreted as a moral dilemma for a theist. For, if one answers the question by affirming that God commands what is good because it is good, then one undermines God's free will and omnipotence because it assumes that His will is restricted by a prior standard of good and evil; and if one answers that anything becomes good because God commands it, one undermines God's goodness and renders His will arbitrary. In Islamic thought the issue was discussed under the title "good and bad or evil" (*al-ḥusn wal-qubḥ*). The specific question was whether God or

His divine law (*sharī'a*) establishes morality or whether it only indicates it (*al-shar' muthabbit am mubayyin*). If divine law establishes morality then no good or evil can be perceived apart from what is commanded or prohibited by God, because no good and evil could have possibly existed before revelation or without revelation. If divine law establishes morality, then the ontological basis of morality fully depends on His absolute will and our knowledge of good and evil is only attainable through revelation. Thus moral ontology and moral epistemology would explicitly depend on divine commands. Al-Ash'arī seems to be the first to hold such a position. Before him the prevalent school of *kalām* was that of the Mu'tazila. Mu'tazilite scholars held different views about the nature of moral values, yet they all agreed that good and evil are known by reason.

Some early Mu'tazilites such as Abu al-Hudhayl al-'Allāf (d. 227/841) held that the moral values of actions are intrinsic properties of actions, some maintained that it is the state of the agent that determines the quality of the action, and others, mainly late Mu'tazilites such as 'Abd al-Jabbār al-Asadabādī (d. 415/1025), maintained that it is rather the state of the action itself which includes the consequences and the circumstances of the action that determines its moral value (al-Attar 2010: 123–35).

Al-Ash'arī's DCT

Initially, al-Ash'arī adhered to the Mu'tazilite school of *kalām*. When he was around forty years old, however, he came into disagreement with his Mu'tazilite master Abu 'Alī al-Jubbā'ī (d. 303/915) over various matters, including the issue of good and evil (*mas'alat al-ḥusn wal-qubḥ*). Other areas of disagreement included the question of whether the Qur'ān is created in time (*muḥdath*) or whether it is eternal (*qadīm*), the nature of divine attributes, divine justice, and free will of human beings.

Al-Ash'arī, according to the Ash'arite scholar al-Shahrastānī (d. 548/1153), held that "all knowledge is derived by reason (*al-'aql*), but obligation is established by revelation" (al-Shahrastānī, n.d.: 371). Al-Shahrastānī explains that this was held to deny rational obligation (*al-wujūb al-'aqlī*), not to deny the knowledge occurring by reason. Thus, knowing that something is good is separate from knowing that it is right or obligatory or recommended. In other words, ethical judgments are not grounded in value judgments. Knowledge of ethical judgments is explicitly derived from divine commands and prohibitions; therefore, value judgments will depend on ethical judgments and ethical judgments are divine judgments known from His commands and prohibitions. Therefore, knowledge of what is the case is known by reason, yet knowledge of what ought to be done is derived from divine commands. Al-Ash'arī absolutely rejected the early attempts of the Mu'tazilites to establish moral ontology. In that he might have been in a way justified, because the early Mu'tazilites believed that good and evil are objective qualities of things and actions. According to the Baghdādian theory (a branch of the Mu'tazilites), inflicting pain and injury must be evil by species, and correspondingly, pleasure and benefit must be good by species. Lying can only have the property of evilness and truth telling can only have the property of goodness just as fire can only produce heat and ice cooling. Moral values are causal determinants (*ma'ānī*) that necessitate the goodness or badness of actions just as redness or yellowness determine the color of an object. However, the late Baghdādian and the Baṣran Mu'tazilites abandoned this theory, and Abū Hāshim al-Jubbā'ī (d. 321/933), a contemporary of al-Ash'arī, introduced a different theory known as the theory of states (*al-aḥwāl*), which, according to him, is the notion that it is the state of the agent that determines the moral quality of the action. Thus, if something is perceived with aversion, it is considered evil (*qabīḥ*), and if it is perceived with attraction then it is considered good (*ḥasan*). Thus the same genus of action such as pain can sometimes be good and sometimes evil depending on whether it is performed for the benefit of the agent or not. For example, the pain of studying hard and the pain experienced when undergoing certain treatments or medications would be considered good, while pain inflicted without any perceived benefit would be considered evil. Such a theory could have also easily been rejected on the ground that it makes moral values subjective by having them dependant on the state of the agent.

Both the theory of causal determinants (*al-ma'ānī*) and the theory of states (*al-aḥwāl*) were introduced to understand divine attributes, as divine attributes were understood to be *ma'ānī* or *aḥwāl* according to the different schools of the Mu'tazilites. In understanding the nature of God and explaining His attributes the Mu'tazilites applied a methodological principle known as "the analogy of the invisible to the visible" (*qiyās al-ghā'ib 'ala al-shāhid*). The states (*aḥwāl*), unlike the determinant causes (*ma'ānī*), were not considered intrinsic properties of actions, but rather conditions, circumstances and consequences that determine the value of an action. Later, 'Abd al-Jabbār developed the theory of *aḥwāl* and clarified that it is the state of the action rather than the state of the agent that determines the moral quality of the action.

None of the above theories were accepted by al-Ash'arī or his followers, although the theory as articulated by 'Abd al-Jabbār does not seem to have been given enough consideration or criticism by the Ash'arites. For al-Ash'arī, the theory of *aḥwāl* would only mean that good and evil are subjective and that both depend on the individual who perceives them with aversion or attraction. Good and evil are certainly not qualified to provide the foundations for moral obligation. Thus, it is only the commandments and the prohibitions of the absolute being who is not subjected to pain and pleasure and who has no desires qualified to establish moral obligation. However, His commands and prohibitions are not related to His will, which is a rather difficult idea to grasp. We are told that some Ash'arites distinguished between divine creative will and His normative will since He might command something and will the opposite, which seems to be evident from the examples of people who were commanded to believe but in fact they became disbelievers. In order to preserve divine omnipotence some Ash'arites held that no one becomes a disbeliever against divine will, which certainly implies that God commands what He does not want to happen. The main reason given for the conversion of al-Ash'arī is related to the issue of divine will and divine justice. Most of the Mu'tazilites held that the principle of divine justice made it obligatory for God to do for people what was in their best interest. Al-Ash'arī is alleged to have asked Abu 'Alī al-Jubbā'ī about the likely fate of three brothers: a believer, an unbeliever and one who died as a child. Al-Jubbā'ī answered that the first would be rewarded, the second punished and the third neither rewarded nor punished. To the objection that God should have allowed the third to live so that he might have been rewarded, al-Jubbā'ī replied that God knew that had the child lived he would have become an unbeliever. Al-Ash'arī then objected by saying: why in that case did God not make the second brother die as a child in order to save him from Hell?

For al-Ash'arī, it seems that there is no convincing reason for God to will something over its opposite and no reason for Him to command something rather than the opposite. Al-Ash'arī even accepted the abhorrent implication of such position, which is that lying and other conduct that is generally considered wicked would have been good if God had declared them so (Hourani 1985: 123). From the above it is clear that al-Ash'arī's theory was a clear example of a proper Divine Command Theory, as understood today.

Criticisms of DCT

The Baṣran Mu'tazilites who belonged to the school of Abu Hāshim criticized the Ash'arite view and held that divine commands are not issued to change the facts of good and evil but to guide human conduct. "Law (*al-shar'*) does not change the facts" (al-Jabbār, vol. 6: 323). Divine law only indicates and does not establish morality. Any form of speech, whether a command or statement, does not change the moral quality of an act:

> Prohibitions indicate the depravation or corruption (*fasād*) of what is prohibited and His commands indicate the righteousness (*ṣalāḥ*) of what He commands. Both [command and prohibition] indicate the states of actions, not the fact that they necessitate (*yūjibāni*) the evilness of an action and the goodness of another.
>
> (al-Jabbār, vol. 6: 103)

Moreover good and evil cannot be established by commands and prohibitions. Since all Muslims, including the Ash'arites, believe that God is good although He is neither commanded nor prohibited:

> Those who say that good and evil are determined by commands and prohibitions would be bound to say that the acts of God are neither good nor evil, because He is neither commanded nor prohibited, which is contrary to what is anonymously accepted, and contradicts the religion.
>
> (al-Jabbār, vol. 6: 89)

Another criticism raised against DCT is that God is worshiped and thanked for His goodness. So, if He does not command what is good, then why would He deserve thanks and worship, "for how could He deserve thanks and worship for what is not good?" (al-Jabbār, vol. 6: 108). Also al-Jabbār stated that all people, regardless of their religion, share the basic knowledge of morality. If good and evil were known only through Scripture, then the rational human beings who do not believe in God would not have any knowledge of good and evil, which is certainly not the case; hence, good and evil are not only known through revelation, but through human reason. He says:

> If good and evil are known only through divine commands, then it would necessarily follow that the materialists (*al-dahriyya*) and others who believe in the pre-eternity of the world would not know or doubt, given their state [as atheists], the evil of injustice and other such evils. This is wrong because it is based on the view that they, despite their maturity of the intellect (*kamāl ʿuqūli-him*), do not know that which is clearly observed (*al-mudrakāt*).
>
> (al-Jabbār, vol. 6: 89)

One might wonder whether the proponents of DCT in Islam have presented any examples from the Qurʾān, which would support their theory. This might be a text that proves that God has commanded things that would have been considered evil if not commanded, or, in other words, a text that indicates certain divine commandments contradicts common morality, and thus would have no rationale behind being commanded. Yet it seems that no textual commandment has ever been perceived as contradicting common morality. Almost all Muslim scholars, whether Ashʿarites or Muʿtazilites, agreed on the view that the lawgiver issues commands and prohibitions for the best benefit of people, although most of the Ashʿarites explicitly rejected the view that God is obliged by virtue of His nature to command what is good for people. They must have been concerned about the divine free will and omnipotence which could have been compromised by holding Him bound to command certain things. Some contemporary divine command theorists coined the term "the immoralities of the patriarchs" which refers to certain incidents where God is perceived to have commanded what would, if not commanded, be perceived as immoral (Quinn 1990: 359). Among those immoralities applied by some philosophers in support of their theory, only the story of Abraham has a parallel in Islam. However, it seems that the story of Abraham or Ibrāhīm has never been invoked in support of DCT in Islam, not even by the strongest proponents of the theory.

ʿAbd al-Jabbār's understanding of the story of Ibrāhīm, as mentioned in the Qurʾān (37:101–110), seems to allow for the interpretation that the command to slaughter his son was never issued to Ibrāhīm but was merely a dream misunderstood by Ibrāhīm as a divine command. ʿAbd al-Jabbār says:

> We have shown that the sacrifice (*al-fidāʾ*) does not indicate that slaughter had been commanded … but when Ibrāhīm strongly suspected that he would be ordered to slaughter, and felt what all fathers would feel, God provided a substitute for what he expected would be a command. If God had really commanded him [to slaughter his son] He would not have eliminated the command, either by prevention, or by prohibition or by sacrifice.
>
> (al-Jabbār, vol. 6: 321)

ʿAbd al-Jabbār, the chief Muʿtazilite figure of the late tenth to early eleventh century, wrote a 20-volume book, *Summa on the Principles of Religion* (*Al-Mughnī*), where he expounded and developed various Mu'tazilite doctrines. He propounded a sophisticated theory of moral action that is mainly teleological in nature, although it incorporated some deontological rules which the Mu'tazilites considered to be necessarily known, like the evilness of lying and injustice.

Moral principles, such as the evilness of injustice and the obligation to return a deposit, constitute necessary ethical knowledge and are, according to 'Abd al-Jabbār, the basis for rational obligation (*taklīf 'aqlī*) (al-Jabbār, vol II: 298). He clearly distinguishes between rational obligation and religious obligation (*taklīf sam'ī*). The latter no doubt includes rituals and some dietary rules and only applies to those who know Islam and accept the religion, whereas the former applies to all rational human beings. Moreover, it is on the basis of the first one, i.e. rational obligation, that 'Abd al-Jabbār's ethical theory is established. Both kinds of obligation are considered to be assigned by God, yet 'Abd al-Jabbār, like Abū al-Hudhayl before him, believes in "obedience not directed toward God" that might be practiced by all people regardless of their religious beliefs. Performing rational obligations is considered by him a kind of worship, he stated:

> Rational worship (*al-'ibādāt al-'aqliya*), in order to be properly performed, does not require anything except to be performed in the right way. Approaching the One who has to be worshiped is not a condition for the validity of rational worship, but it is a condition for religious worship (*al-'ibādāt al-shar'iya*) [like praying and fasting].
>
> (al-Jabbār, vol. 4: 329)

All rational beings necessarily know the evil of lying and injustice, and the goodness of truth telling, of returning a deposit and of thanking a benefactor. These deontological rules are introduced within a teleological framework as has already been indicated, where good and evil are ultimately perceived as harm and benefit, respectively. The necessary moral knowledge of moral rules was disputed by the late Ash'arites, yet the teleological framework propounded by the Mu'tazilites was adopted, adapted and further developed by the late Ash'arite scholars. Harm (*mafsada*) and benefit (*manfa'a*) were the ultimate foundations of moral and legal judgments and it was agreed upon among almost all Muslim jurists that *maṣlaḥa*—which literally means advantage or benefit—is the ultimate foundation and the reason behind all commands and prohibitions. For something to be judged permissible, recommended or obligatory it has first to be good. According to the author of *al-Mu'tamad*, Abu al-Ḥusayn al-Baṣrī (d. 436/1044), the reason (*'illa*) of its goodness is its being beneficial. However, for a benefit to be good, according to the Baṣran Mu'tazilites, including Abu al-Ḥusayn, it should be void of any aspect of evil, such as lying, ignorance, not thanking a benefactor (*kufur ni'ma*), harming oneself, or harming others (al-Baṣrī: 315). Thus it is pure benefit that is intrinsically good. *Al-manfa'a* is what demands the action and justifies it (al-Baṣrī: 315). It is an end desired for itself, and thus it is intrinsically good, just as pleasure or happiness is a good in itself, and it has intrinsic, not instrumental, value. Thus it was considered the ultimate purpose of divine law.

'Abd al-Jabbar investigated the nature of values. For him the value of an action is not inherent in the action as held by some of the Baghdādian Mu'tazilites, nor by the state of the agent, i.e. feeling attraction or repulsion; rather, it is determined by the state of the action considering its circumstances and consequences. Pain and pleasure were familiar concepts in Muʿtazilite *kalām*. But instead of introducing something like the hedonistic calculus of Bentham by taking into consideration the extent of the pleasure and the intensity of the pleasure or even discriminating between high and low pleasures as did Mill, he recognized that what might be a source of joy and pleasure to someone might in the same time be the source of pain and sorrow to someone else. Therefore benefit (*manfaʿa*) can be defined in terms of pleasure, although as seen above it is pleasure without causing harm to oneself or the others and without being polluted with any aspects of evil doing such as lying or being ungrateful or unjust.

Divine Purposes Theory (*maqāṣid al-Sharīʿa*)

Until recently it has been believed, by most of the scholars who studied Ashʿarite moral thought, that all of them adhered to DCT in ethics. This was due to their declared position, since they insisted on holding to the Ashʿarite doctrine that the divine law establishes morality and to their occasionalist metaphysical framework. However, this has been disputed in some recently published literature. Their thought has been interpreted as endorsing soft Natural Law Theory, compared to the hard Natural Law Theory of the Muʿtazilites (Emon 2010).

Al-Ghazālī (d. 505/1111) held that *al-maṣlaḥa* originally means promoting a benefit (*manfaʿa*) or preventing a harm (*ḍarar*) (al-Ghazālī 1995: 258). But for al-Ghazālī this is not the true sense of *maṣlaḥa*, because such a conception of *maṣlaḥa* suffers from important weaknesses. First, people might prefer immediate benefit over long-term benefit. Second, they might prefer limited over universal benefit. Third, it might lead to a conflict of interests when different groups of people have different benefits. Al-Ghazālī offers an interesting example when he investigates the rightness or wrongness of torturing an individual accused of theft to make him confess. He says that Anas bin Malik accepted torture on the ground of *al-maṣlaḥa*, but al-Ghazālī rejects this vision, not on the basis of rejecting the doctrine of *maṣlaḥa*, but because this sort of *maṣlaḥa* contradicts another one, which is that of the tortured person. Al-Ghazālī says: "He might be innocent and not torturing the guilty is better than torturing the innocent" (al-Ghazālī 1995: 260). For him, not torturing a probably innocent man is far more important than returning any stolen thing, since preserving a human's life and dignity has priority over preserving one's property. Al-Ghazālī maintained that divine law has purposes and these consist in the preservation of the true *maṣlaḥa*. However, he explains that bringing benefit and repelling harm are human purposes (*maqāṣid al-khalq*). The true *maṣlaḥa* is preserving the purposes of divine law *maqāṣid al-sharīʿa*. He writes,

> What we mean by *maṣlaḥa* is maintaining the purposes of the law (*sharʿ*). The purposes of law concerning human beings are five: preservation of their religion, life, mind, progeny and property. Thus whatever entails preserving these principles (*uṣūl*) is *maṣlaḥa* and whatever destroys them is corruption (*mafsada*), and repelling it is *maṣlaḥa*.
>
> (al-Ghazālī 1995: 258)

Al-Ghazālī interprets all human purposes and intentions in a way that corresponds to the theory of psychological egoism, which is a descriptive theory that interprets human motivations as being egoistic and interprets all human actions in a way that fits the theory. Al-Ghazālī does not acknowledge the moral value of an action that is performed for altruistic reasons. According to him, even when one rescues an animal or a human being from death one does it out of sympathy and compassion, since one imagines oneself in that situation and finds it abhorrent not to be helped (al-Ghazālī 1994: 151). Even the intentions of the one who dies for a cause are considered by al-Ghazālī to be motivated by the desire to be remembered and praised (al-Ghazālī 1994: 154). No moral value can be attached to any action if not performed out of a desire to act in accordance with divine wishes. That, in a way, reminds us of Kant and his categorical imperative where the right action is that which is performed for the right reason, which is to do one's duty. However, unlike Kant, the late Ash'arites denied the existence of absolute moral rules. They maintained that lying is not always evil, since sometimes it is good when lying is necessary to save someone's life. Even the divine rules and commandments according to which we have to act are not absolute deontological rules simply because those are perceived to serve some purposes and those purposes are the universal necessities of human existence or purposes of divine law (*maqāṣid al-sharī'a*). Therefore, those latter are the things that have the intrinsic absolute values: life, religion, intellect, progeny and property. In the articulation of the purposes of the divine law the influence of 'Abd al-Jabbār may be detected. He stated, "If God had no purpose in assigning an obligation, then the assignment of the obligation would be irrational (*qabīh*)" (al-Jabbār, vol. II: 407). Further, since He is beyond harm and benefit, His purpose (*gharaḍu-hu*) must be for the benefit of the addressee (*al-mukallaf*) (al-Jabbār, vol. II: 410). Divine Command Theory advocated by al-Ash'arī and other Ash'arites scholars implies that "it is fundamentally and ultimately impossible to explain God's commands in terms of any purpose or end" (Frank 1983: 214). Al-Ghazālī and the late Ash'arites like Fakhr al-Dīn al-Rāzī maintained that divine regulations and the interests of man lie side by side or exist together, yet they did not admit of a causal relationship between them, that is, they did not say that the interests of man cause divine commands, since that must have been considered blasphemous.

The late Ash'arites were eager not only to establish a normative theory that is based on the *sharī'a*, but a theory that would provide us with a criterion for what is a true *maṣlaḥa*, or what needs to be preserved in order to safeguard humans' well-being. The Mu'tazilites established the foundations of a teleological moral theory and the late Ash'arites developed it into a theory which set the priorities that need to be observed when deriving moral judgments.

Conclusion

This chapter explored divine command theory in medieval Arabo-Islamic thought. It has been shown that al-Ash'arī was most probably the first one to explicitly hold that good and evil are only known through divine commands and prohbitions. The Mu'tazilite 'Abd al-Jabbār raised sound criticisms against the Ash'arite conception of good and evil and developed an understanding of moral values and moral judgement that is compatible with a teleological theory in ethics. This teleological aspect was incorporated in the late Ash'arite theory which can be called Divine Purposes Theory, rather than Divine Command Theory.

Further Reading

Hourani, G. F. (1971) *Islamic Rationalism. The Ethics of 'Abd al-Jabbār*, Oxford: Clarendon Press.

Opwis, F. (2010) *Maṣlaḥa and the Purposes of Law*, Leiden: Brill.

Reinhart, K. (1995) *Before Revelation: the Boundaries of Muslim Moral Thought*, New York: State University of New York.

Shihadeh, A. (2006) *The Teleological Ethics of Fakhr al-Dīn al-Rāzī*, Leiden: Brill.

References

Abd al-Jabbār (n.d.) *Mughnī, al-Irāda*, vol. 6, part 2, M. M. Qāsim (ed.), Cairo.

——. (n.d.) *Mughnī, Ru'yat al-Bārī*, vol. 4, M. M. Qāsim (ed.), Cairo.

——. (1965) *Mughnī, al-Taklīf*, vol. 11, M. 'A. al-Najjār & A. al-Najjār (eds.), Cairo.

Adams, R. M. (1981) "A Modified Divine Command Theory of Ethical Wrongness," in P. Helm (ed.), *Divine Command and Morality*, New York: Oxford University Press, pp. 83–108.

al-Attar, M. (2010) *Islamic Ethics, Divine Command Theory in Arabo-Islamic Thought*, London: Routledge.

al-Baṣrī, A. H. (n.d.) *al-Mu'tamad fī Uṣūl al-Fiqh*, vol. 2, Khalīl al-Mays (ed.), Beirut: Dār al-Kutub al-'Ilmiya.

al-Ghazālī (1994) *Al-Iqtiṣād fil-I'tiqād*, Damascus: Al-Hikma.

——. (1995) *Al-Mustasfa*, vol. 1, Beirut: Dar Sadir.

al-Shahrastānī, Muḥammad b. 'Abd al-Karīm (n.d.) *Nihāyat al-Iqdām fī 'Ilm al-Kalām*, A. Jayūm (ed.), Cairo: Maktabat al-Thaqāfa al-Dīniya.

Chandler, J. (1985) "Divine Command Theories and the Appeal to Love," *American Philosophical Quarterly* 22: 231–9.

Collins, J. (2003) "The Zeal of Phinehas: The Bible and the Legitimation of violence," *Journal of Biblical Literature* 122, 1: pp. 3–21.

Emon, A. M. (2010) *Islamic Natural Law Theories*, New York: Oxford University Press.

Frank, R. M. (1983) "Moral Obligation in Classical Muslim Theology," *Journal of Religious Ethics* 11: 204–223.

Hourani, G. F. (1985) *Reason and Tradition in Islamic Ethics*, United Kingdom: Cambridge University Press.

Leaman, O. (1999) "Ethics," in *A Brief Introduction to Islamic Philosophy*, USA: Blackwell, pp. 108–19.

Quinn, P. (1990) "The Recent Revival of Divine Command Ethics," *Philosophy and Phenomenological Research* 50: 345–65.

Rachels, J. (2003) *The Elements of Moral Philosophy*, New York: McGraw-Hill.

Regional Bureau for Arab States (2003) *United Nations Development Programme – The Arab Human Development Report*, Amman: National Press.

Reinhart, K. (1995) *Before Revelation: the Boundaries of Muslim Moral Thought*, New York: State University of New York.

Tuggi, D. (2005) "Necessity Control and the Divine Command Theory," *Sophia* 44, 1: 53–75.

Wainwright, W. J. (2005) *Religion and Morality*, United Kingdom: Ashgate.

26
FREEDOM AND DETERMINISM

Catarina Belo

Introduction

The work of medieval Islamic philosophers builds upon the theories and findings of Ancient Greek and Hellenistic philosophy, primarily the Aristotelian and the Neoplatonic traditions, but this commonly shared heritage alone would not account for the diversity of interests nor the originality of medieval Islamic philosophy, which in drawing on the past philosophical tradition seeks to clarify and solve contemporary theological and religious as well as philosophical problems.

The complex relationship between Islamic theology and philosophy has a fitting illustration in Ibn Rushd's (d. 1198) *Decisive Treatise on the Harmony of Religion and Philosophy* (Averroes, 2001). There he compares and contrasts the merits of both disciplines, ultimately ranking philosophy above *kalām* (speculative theology) and proposing that philosophers rather than theologians should have the final word on the exegesis of the Qur'ān and on the appropriate method of conveying its message to the majority of people, thereby implicitly but effectively proposing an end to Islamic speculative theology, which according to his project would be replaced by philosophy as an Islamic science.

Nevertheless, the impact of theology and, more broadly, Islamic religion in shaping the views of the Islamic philosophers, the *falāsifa*, should not be underestimated, and the issue of freedom and determinism is a case in point.

Theological Positions

Islamic theology, like other Islamic disciplines such as *fiqh* (jurisprudence), is based on the analysis of the Qur'ān and the *sunna*, which comprises written and oral traditions attributed to Muḥammad. Hence debates over whether human beings have free-will were originally based on Qur'ānic verses, some pointing to a divine omnipotence that includes the full control of human action, with others stressing that we earn our ultimate reward or punishment in the Hereafter in accordance with our deeds, with the underlying assumption of our responsibility and power to choose our actions, good or evil. In addition, this controversial issue features prominently in *ḥadīth* literature which narrates the deeds and sayings of Muḥammad. A recurrent theme in the Qur'ān is God's guiding or leading astray whom He will, including in matters of faith (Qur'ān 2:272, 6:125). In addition, we find in the Qur'ān mention of the fixed term for any person's death (Qur'ān 3:145), and God's eternal omniscience, whereby everything that comes to be is eternally inscribed in a book (Qur'ān 6:59). However, it also stresses a person's freedom to believe or reject Islam (Qur'ān 18:29).

The significance of the debate is evidenced by the fact that some of the earliest theological schools were named according to their position on the subject of predestination, and whether they favoured human free agency or God's omnipotence. This question came to be known in Arabic as *al-qaḍā' wa-l-qadar*, God's decree and determination, although occasionally *qadar* referred also to human power. God's predestination was considered as part of the extended Islamic creed, which contained six items—the belief in God, the angels, the prophets, the scriptures, the Last Day and *qadar* (Caspar 2007: 2)—found alongside the five pillars of Islam which, in addition to the *shahāda* (the profession of the creed), include the practical obligations incumbent on Muslims.

With regard to theological positions taken on the issue of *qadar* and theories of human action, an early group which defended free will came to be known as the *Qadarites*, for they rejected an all-embracing divine *qadar* that precluded human freedom, claiming instead that human beings have the power and free will to carry out their actions. One major figure associated with this group was al-Ḥasan al-Baṣrī (d. 728) whose renowned letter, known as the *Epistle* to the Caliph 'Abd al-Malik (d. 705), emphasizes human moral and religious freedom.

Other schools were formed on the basis of a well-defined position on the topic, such as the Jabarites, who defended divine omnipotence and the necessity, indeed compulsion, of human agency owing to God's decree. One exponent of this group, Jahm Ibn Ṣafwān (d. 746), even argued that man does not truly act (Watt 1948: 96).

Another famous early theological school was the Mu'tazilite, founded in the eighth century, who styled themselves as champions of God's justice and oneness. They argued that since God is just he cannot punish human beings for something they did not voluntarily choose to do and cannot hold them accountable for coerced actions, hence their emphasis on human freedom. On a number of issues the Mu'tazilites were considered rationalists by virtue of their emphasis on the logical consequences flowing from given principles. If God is just, one is to be accountable for one's actions, and one must logically be free in some actions, for it would not be just to punish for involuntary or coerced agency. The Mu'tazilites favoured a rationalistic reading of the Qur'ān that interpreted metaphorically the anthropomorphic descriptions of the Godhead. Some scholars have considered them to be the precursors of the Islamic philosophers, but the extent to which they were influenced by the ancient philosophical heritage remains to be determined. Ibn Rushd explicitly states his preference for the Mu'tazilite interpretation of religious texts over that of the Ash'arites (Averroes 2001: 26). And while the works of Aristotle and other Greek ethical texts, Platonic, Aristotelian or Stoic, were yet to be translated into Arabic when Mu'tazilism was founded in the first half of the eighth century C.E. by Wāṣil Ibn 'Atā' (d. 748), they would have influenced subsequent discussions of Islamic ethics (Fakhry 1991: 63, 67). Some scholars have emphasized the influence of Greek philosophy on Islamic theology (Wolfson 1976: 64–6), while others have downplayed it (Frank 1978: 2).

Other theologians, however, preferred to emphasize divine omnipotence, thereby excluding or downplaying human ability to choose a voluntary course of action without external compulsion or hindrance. The Mu'tazilite school became particularly influential in the first half of the ninth century and their views, such as the createdness of the Qur'ān, constituted state dogma during the reign of Caliph al-Ma'mūn (d. 833). However, more traditional voices were beginning to rise to prominence, for instance that of Ạhmad Ibn Ḥanbal (d. 855), who advocated a much more literal reading of the Qur'ān, including the passages where God is portrayed with human features, and who discouraged speculation on the meaning of the Qur'ān but instead emphasized an acceptance of its literal message without questioning. The Mu'tazilites continued to have their advocates and theologians for several centuries, but another group arose in opposition to them. The Ash'arites are named after al-Ash'arī (d. 935), a Mu'tazilite who abandoned the teachings of this group at the age of forty. The Ash'arites depart from these teachings on a number of points. One of the most striking issues that divides the schools is the freedom of human action in view of divine omnipotence. The Ash'arites stress God's omnipotence, based on the Qur'ānic verse to the effect that "God created you and what you do" (37:96), for them an unequivocal statement to the effect that nothing escapes God's all-embracing agency. This includes the creation of every substance and event but a solution was to be found in favour of the accountability of human action, without which the reward or punishment in the Hereafter would be meaningless—and in contravention to another divine attribute, God's justice. The Ash'arite solution consists in a subtle endeavour to reconcile these potentially opposite attributes. As the verse states, God is the creator of every action and every substance that exists—everything and every event. He creates these directly, without any intermediary or help, or what one would technically term secondary causes—secondary in relation to the first cause who is God Himself. This position defending God's direct agency came to be known as Islamic occasionalism. It states that everything is directly caused by God with the denial of any concurring or independent causes. In this sense, people do not create their actions since they are not their authors. This, however, does not detract from their responsibility and accountability on the Day of Judgment. They are accountable because they appropriate, by choice, their actions. God creates everything that exists, individual beings as well as any events or processes, including human actions. This would seem to make human agency predestined in such a way that it would not be liable to reward or punishment on the part of God. On this interpretation, human beings cannot be held accountable for their actions and there could be no justice or reward or punishment. However, human beings, according to the Ash'arites, choose the actions that have been created by God. Among all the actions created by God, humans choose the ones they perform. This is famous Ash'arite theory of "acquisition" (in Arabic "*kasb*" or "*iktisāb*"), which allows them to uphold at once God's attributes of omnipotence and justice. Not all scholars were convinced by these arguments, as we shall see, but it is important to set the background and show two main divergent positions within Islamic theology before analyzing the stances of the philosophers.

Philosophical Positions

Medieval Islamic philosophy was primarily influenced by Aristotle, the majority of whose works were translated into Arabic in the late eighth century and the early ninth century, in a historical phenomenon known as the Greek into Arabic translation movement, which involved state support from caliphs as well as a considerable philanthropic effort. The other major influence was Neoplatonism, introduced primarily but not solely through the spurious *Theology of Aristotle*, which was in fact a translation with adaptation of books IV, V and VI of *The Enneads* of Plotinus (d. 270). While the philosophers generally subscribe to certain general Aristotelian philosophical principles such as secondary causation, to the effect that God is not the sole agent of events in the world but delegates his power to celestial and earthly substances, the increasingly deterministic character of the Islamic theological schools does make a mark in Islamic philosophy, as we shall see. According to Aristotelian philosophy as developed by such commentators as Alexander of Aphrodisias (fl. ca. 200) the whole world depends on a first cause which is the first, unmoved mover, of the celestial spheres. These in turn are responsible for events on earth, the world of generation and corruption. In addition, earthly beings do have efficient powers of their own. For instance, Aristotelian philosophers, pagan and religious, agreed that fire has the power to burn certain substances. Consequently we do not find Muslim philosophers defending an Ash'arite position, which denied any true power of created substances. In addition to the efficacy of natural substances, human beings also have their proper agency characterized as voluntary, as opposed to natural or accidental agency. This distinction is made by Aristotle as well as the Muslim philosophers, such as Ibn Rushd and Ibn Sīnā (d. 1037), and is an important element of this debate.

Voluntary agency is more complex and multifaceted than natural agency. When fire approaches a combustible substance, and in the absence of such obstacles as humidity, it will necessarily burn that substance. Human agency is faced with many possible outcomes, unlike natural agency. In this sense, it is possible to defend natural or physical determinism, which would be in line with the belief in general laws of nature, while allowing for freedom of action on the part of human beings, a position termed as compatibilism in contemporary philosophy (McKenna 2009). The defence of secondary causality is thus not a necessary obstacle to upholding a compatibilist or even libertarian position which allows for human freedom. One could envisage, a possibility entertained by Kant in his antinomies of pure reason as laid out in the *Critique of Pure Reason* (Kant 1911), two possible causal chains, natural and voluntary or human, that are related but independent of each other. In this sense, it would be possible to defend a position that accepts determinism at the physical, natural level, while upholding freedom of human action. What is the position of medieval Islamic philosophers, and how does the influence of Aristotelianism and Neoplatonism make itself felt? Do they accept any kind of indeterminacy and freedom, at the natural or at the voluntary level?

The problem can be approached from different angles. For the medieval Muslim theologians the question of free will and predestination was grounded within the Qur'ān and involved, as we have seen, God's attributes on the one hand and human free will on the other, and more generally the articulation between human and divine agency. There were important implications at the level of the natural world, with the Ash'arites advocating what could be termed a kind of occasionalism or atomism, by stressing, unlike in ancient atomism, that everything has a fixed and necessary cause, God. However, the crux of the argument had an ethical, or rather, theological emphasis. In philosophy other disciplines of knowledge, such as metaphysics and physics, bear on the issue in addition to ethics.

Ibn Rushd famously credits Aristotle with the foundation of the three main philosophical disciplines: logic, physics and metaphysics. Concurrently, determinism or indeterminism can be found at all these levels, logical, physical and metaphysical. We will now look into the place of freedom or necessity in these various disciplines according to the foremost Islamic philosophers.

At the metaphysical level, one may stress that every existing thing is necessary or necessitated, such that it could not have been otherwise, or one may allow for a degree of contingency or possibility. At the natural or physical level, one may defend that actions, events and substances are strictly and necessarily determined by their causes so that there is nothing contingent about them. There is still the logical level to be considered. Logical determinism states that since all propositions, including those referring to future events, have a definite truth value, given that they are necessarily true or false, and therefore future events are already determined in the present. The debate over logical determinism is amply illustrated in book nine of Aristotle's *On Interpretation*. There, Aristotle offers us his famous example of a prospective sea battle. If a sea battle is to take place tomorrow, do our statements concerning the future hold a definite truth value? In other words, if the event signified by the statement "p," "a seabattle is to take place tomorrow," is now definitely true, does this not imply that the sea battle is predestined to happen?

One must look into these different levels in order to ascertain if medieval Islamic philosophers are determinists or not, and what kind of positions they advocate.

Logical, Metaphysical, and Physical Determinism

Al-Kindī (d. c. 866), considered to be the first Arab Muslim philosopher, was at the crossroads of an important scientific and social movement that has been dubbed by scholars the "Greek into Arabic" movement, and which consisted in the translation of important works of Greek and Hellenistic origin into Arabic, sometimes through the intermediary of Syriac. Al-Kindī, although not himself a translator since he did not know Greek, had his own circle of translators, and was thus acquainted with Aristotelian as well as Neoplatonic philosophy (through the *Theology of Aristotle*) and built this heritage into his own brand of philosophy, having composed many important treatises on issues ranging from metaphysics to mathematics through physics and astrology.

Where does he stand on the issue of human freedom and determinism? He did not write extensively on ethics and therefore not much on human agency, but his considerations on this issue are found in his works on metaphysics and other subjects. He represents a certain approach, typical among the philosophers, which combined strong Aristotelian and/or Neoplatonic influences with the conclusions of the various Islamic theological schools. He combined Aristotelian and Neoplatonic notions of causality and agency with reflections on the issue of *qadar*, usually leading to a deterministic outcome which reflected an influence of later (post-Muʿtazilite) Islamic theology.

Al-Kindī believes, like Aristotle, that elements such as fire and other natural substances have their own powers. Fire has the power to burn unless an obstacle, such as moisture, prevents its action. He also believes that actions are up to us, in the sense that our actions are not primarily caused by natural substances around us but by our will, thus distinguishing voluntary from natural agency. This would seem to indicate an affirmation of freedom on behalf of human beings, and their capability to act and be held responsible. Does this mean that they are free to choose their actions independently of external constraints? Al-Kindī places limitations on the freedom of human action. It is not just the case that we have limited options to choose from but also that our actions are conditioned, if not determined, by external factors. What could these conditioning factors be? Al-Kindī wrote on astrology, whose goal is to predict future events on the assumption that the heavenly bodies control every happening. To believe that we have free will boils down to an ignorance of external determining factors, such as the stars which control the elements which in turn determine our actions through our bodily mixtures. The stars in turn are controlled by God. So indirectly and through various causes, God is the ultimate determining cause of our actions, even if we may appear to act freely (al-Kindī 1974: 246–7). One might argue that this is a compatibilist position since it gives at least a semblance of freedom to the agent and ascribes him or her the power to act, but if that power ultimately comes entirely from God and our agency rests on the causes made available to us by God, then there is nothing truly autonomous in voluntary agency. On the question of *al-qaḍā' wal-l-qadar*, al-Kindī appears to have supported the idea of God's overall determination of events through his wisdom. When speaking of the first agent, God, al-Kindī also affirms that every agent other than God is only termed so metaphorically, for all power comes from God. This again supports the view that human beings are not autonomous in their agency, even though we have a power or faculty of will and choice, whereby we differ from animals who do not act on the basis of a rational faculty, which they lack.

Another major exponent of the medieval Islamic philosophical tradition, al-Fārābī (d. 950), integrates into his philosophy the Neoplatonic emanationist scheme which stipulates that from the One or God another intellect proceeds and so forth until we obtain ten emanated intellects with their corresponding spheres—with the exclusion of the last emanated intellect, the active intellect which has no sphere of its own. From the celestial world, composed of intellects and spheres, the sublunary world comes to be. This might lead one to think that al-Fārābī would be inclined to favour the kind of seminal determinism that we find in al-Kindī and which becomes explicit in Ibn Sīnā, another medieval Muslim Neoplatonist. However, he does accept the existence of possibility in the realm of existing things. Moreover, in his commentary on Aristotle's *On Interpretation* (al-Fārābī 1991), he accepts that we cannot assign definite truth or falsity to propositions that describe events which will happen in the future. And according to him, acts that result from deliberation include an aspect of possibility rather than necessity. To exclude the use of deliberation in human action he finds absurd, which means that possibility affects future affairs. The idea of predestination is thus rejected by al-Fārābī. Voluntary action which involves an element of contingency is thus contrasted by al-Fārābī to the regularity to be found in the celestial realm through the constant motion of the celestial spheres. The future too holds a degree of uncertainty. If something is contingent in the present it is also contingent in the future. He does not just deny that we have knowledge of future events, but entertains the possibility that things are in themselves indefinite. However, the question arises whether God knows the possible as possible or as necessary. The latter case would imply that the future is foreordained, but the former would call into question divine omniscience. Al-Fārābī argues that something can remain in the realm of possibility even if it is necessarily known. An action or event is possible if it involves free will and necessary if the causes necessarily lead to the effect. On his interpretation, God's foreknowledge of events does not detract from their possibility.

Ibn Sīnā (d. 1037), who wrote extensively on almost every aspect of philosophy—logic, physics and metaphysics—was conspicuously uninterested in ethics and in ethical problems, a lack of interest which can be indicative of an inclination towards determinism. For determinism, the view that everything is necessary or necessarily produced by its causes, can be particularly problematic in the way it denies a free will in human beings, leading to considerable ethical paradoxes. Determinism bears other unacceptable consequences for some theologians, e.g. if the strict chains of causes exclude miracles or direct divine intervention this would be a denial of God's own free will.

Ibn Sīnā does not appear to tackle logical determinism. What of his natural philosophy? How does he envisage the relation between cause and effect in nature and the production of phenomena in the physical world? We can find his position clearly stated in his *Physics of The Healing* (2009), in particular when elucidating the concept of "chance" and chance events, which is patterned on Aristotle's own analysis in his *Physics*. Some philosophers, Aristotle argues, have considered chance to be a cause in its own right, over and above the four causes he stipulates: formal, material, final and efficient. To illustrate these causes, we can say that in a table the shape and the wood are respectively the formal and the material causes, while the carpenter is the efficient cause or the agent, and the final cause is the purpose of the table, for instance, to write. For our purposes it is the efficient cause that is relevant. A determinist position would say that from given efficient causes a necessary effect comes to be. For instance, upon approaching wood, fire will necessarily burn it. Some philosophers, such as the Epicureans, have proposed a theory of clashes between atoms whereby the outcome of the clash or encounter between two objects or atoms is unpredictable and does not follow a regular pattern, thus detracting from a necessary causal chain.

Ibn Sīnā also speaks of clashes in nature and encounters between two objects; however, he considers the encounter and the resulting effect as necessary, that is, at least theoretically predictable. In general Ibn Sīnā defends the position that everything that happens does so according to determinate efficient causes. In other words, everything that happens in the world of nature—for instance, finding someone in the marketplace unexpectedly or the clash between two atoms—is determined by its preceding causes or antecedents. He provides examples such as going to the garden and finding a treasure. Some might term this a chance event, but he appears to side with the position of those who believe that the combination of the person's walking to the garden and digging to sow, and the existence of the treasure underneath the earth, determine that the treasure will be found by the digger, even though it is an unexpected happening. He does highlight the significance of intent in voluntary actions, for a person would not have gone out without an intention. So the voluntary aspect does have an important role to play, but the outcome is pre-determined.

Ibn Sīnā does distinguish natural causality between two natural objects or two animals (in other words, non-rational beings) and voluntary actions (those involving human beings who have a rational will). But whether a falling stone, with no rational purpose but merely falling owing to its own weight, fractures someone's head, or whether someone looks and finds a friend for a particular purpose, the outcome is equally certain, if one is in possession of all the information surrounding an event. The same applies to the formation of natural substances. If it rains on a terrain that has been sown with barley seeds, barley will eventually be produced. Our actions follow the same pattern as physical phenomena, so there is no scope for truly autonomous human free will. That is not to say that the intention or the final cause, natural or rational, is unimportant, as it does determine the outcome of actions, as we have seen, but there is nothing for Ibn Sīnā that arises spontaneously through two or more efficient causes, or that was not somehow contained in those causes. The concurrence of the various causes determines an event, whether natural or voluntary. So a human being is limited in his or her choices by natural causes and, as we shall see, by God's will. Voluntary and natural causes all go back to the first, ultimate cause, which is God.

This deterministic outlook is also observable in Ibn Sīnā's metaphysics, where he discusses causality from a more abstract perspective. Now not examining causality in nature, but the relation between existence and causality, he divides all existing things into those that are necessary in themselves (in effect only God) and those which are necessary through another (that is to say, things that exist through a cause and not through themselves, for example, the child through the parents, or the fire through friction). Also, things are divided into caused (everything that exists except God) and uncaused (only God). His metaphysics confirms His deterministic views—here physics and metaphysics are perfectly aligned to state that everything has definite causes and is conditioned and fully determined by them. But unlike Ash'arism, which denies secondary causality for fear that it detracts from God's omnipotence, in Ibn Sīnā's view all causes must be referred back to God, so in fact the chain of secondary causes serves to reinforce divine omnipotence. The link between this physical and metaphysical determinism becomes apparent in short treatises written on the subject of God's determination, or predestination (*qadar*), in which he advocates a strong predestinarian position. He explains how all the causes are subordinate to God in an ascending causal chain which accounts for every single existent and every single event. It is God who determines these causes (Belo 2007). There does not seem to be a possibility of free will and because Ibn Sīnā is not preoccupied with ethical questions it is not clear how this is articulated with the notion of a provident, just God. In reality, when discussing the issue of *qadar*, he cites a Hanbalite *ḥadīth* which does not question the fact of predestination (Avicenna 2000: 103–7). Every human being is predestined by God to be either saved or damned and we must not question or enquire into God's decisions. We find a tendency in Ibn Sīnā to combine a defence of certain Aristotelian elements, such as secondary causality, which are discussed from a physical and a metaphysical point of view, with an evident theological influence from those theologians who advocate predestination to the exclusion of free will. While he frames the question of chance within a philosophical mould and in reference to causality, the theological influences are undeniable.

Another thinker in the Ash'arite tradition who opposed the theories of the philosophers on many counts, as well as their less than literal reading of the Qur'ān, is al-Ghazālī. He objected to their conception of God as excessively impersonal and devoid of true will and omnipotence. Although not a philosopher, he was acquainted with the philosophy of Ibn Sīnā and adopted certain aspects of the Greek and Islamic philosophical tradition, including a preference for Aristotelian logic. On the question of divine power, he believes that God is the only creator and humans acquire their actions, so that there is no truly temporal power, but only God's power (McGinnis and Reisman 2007). According to al-Ghazālī, God creates all actions, including human actions to the exclusion of secondary or independent causes (al-Ghazālī 1962: 91). Moreover, God's power creates everything directly, without the need for an intermediary cause. Both the power and its effect are directly created by God (Marmura 2005: 301–2).

Another major figure in the panorama of medieval Islamic philosophy is Ibn Rushd who lived in twelfth-century Muslim Spain. As well as a famed jurist, judge and physician, he was well versed in the past philosophical literature ranging from Aristotle through Hellenistic philosophy to his immediate predecessors as Muslim philosophers, not only Ibn Sīnā, but the Andalusian philosopher Ibn Bājja and his own contemporary Ibn Ṭufayl. Ibn Rushd came to be known primarily as Aristotle's commentator since his various commentaries on the Stagirite's corpus were among the works that were first translated into Latin and Hebrew only a few decades after his death, but he developed a philosophy of his own as well as his own brand of Aristotelianism. A philosophical current loosely based on his theories was adopted in the medieval Christian world and came to be known as Latin Averroism.

In his logical works, particularly in commenting on Aristotle's *On Interpretation* (Averroes 1983), he acknowledges the undeniable fact of human deliberation, the power of voluntary choosing our course of action, which would hint at an admission of human free will. He also states that our choices do determine the future. This is consonant with his reflections in his commentary on Aristotle's *Nicomachean Ethics*. In other fields, such as physics and metaphysics, his position is closer to that of Ibn Sīnā.

Unlike Ibn Sīnā, who conceives of a strict and necessary link between efficient cause and effect, Ibn Rushd places the stress on the final cause in physical processes, to the point of denying efficient causation in the celestial realm. In other words, every substance that is formed and any event that occurs in the natural world comes to be from its efficient, preceding causes, but more so because of its purpose. Therefore a tree comes to be from its seed, but more properly in order to give fruit or to provide shade. Thus one can argue that generally things act by virtue of their intrinsic goals and forms, not so much because they are compelled by something to act or to produce their effects in a determinate way. However, he also defends the position that everything in the natural world has a necessary determining efficient cause, thereby excluding the possibility of spontaneous events.

Ibn Rushd was a critic of Ibn Sīnā, not least in his understanding of necessity and contingency, for he displays no strong metaphysical modal determinism as does Ibn Sīnā. Unlike the latter's division of all beings into possible and necessary, Ibn Rushd thinks of metaphysical necessity much like Aristotle. Some beings are necessary because they are eternal. He also considers the (1) necessity of that which cannot be otherwise, the necessary (2) as that which is conditioned by its cause, (3) as necessary condition, and (4) as coercion. But he does not present us with a metaphysically determined universe as does Ibn Sīnā.

However, when seeking to settle theological debates in a work that addresses the theologians of Islam, *Unveiling of the Ways of [finding] proofs concerning the beliefs of the religious community* (*Kashf 'an manāhij al-adilla fi 'aqā'id al-milla*) (Averroes 1998), he seeks to solve the problem posed by theologians. While defending, against the Ash'arites, the notion of human (and so secondary) causality, he admits that this is effectively conditioned by external causes and ultimately by divine agency, so as to deny the full autonomy of human actions. However, this is a work of dialectical theology and Ibn Rushd warns in his *Incoherence of the Incoherence* (a work he identifies as dialectical) that his own views are found in his demonstrative philosophical writings, meaning his philosophical commentaries and related materials (Averroes 1969: 257–8).

One important philosopher-theologian who tackled the question of human agency and the status of human actions is Fakhr al-Dīn al-Rāzī (d. 1209). He endorsed some aspects of Ibn Sīnā's philosophy alongside Ash'arite theology and opposed Mu'tazilite arguments to the effect that human beings are free in their actions. Al-Rāzī argues that the combination of human motivation and power to effect an action effectively determines its outcome (Shihadeh 2006). The action stems from an individual human will, but the motive is occasioned by God. All elements that determine the action are ultimately originated by God, so there is only a semblance of free will on the part of the human agent because he or she is conscious of his or her acts. For al-Rāzī, action ensues when human power and motivation combine, necessarily producing an action. Human power is not an accident as it is for al-Ash'arī, and neither does he accept the theory of acquisition but this does not detract from his defence of determinism for human agency. This analysis results also from an admission of God's eternal foreknowledge of all events, with its logical consequences. Even though voluntary actions are much more complex than natural processes, as they involve human will, they are determined, indeed necessitated, by God. And thus al-Rāzī defends that human acts are determined, even compelled, by God.

Conclusion

The issue of God's determination of events was the subject of much debate since the inception of Islam and in particular with the formation of the various theological schools, some of which were named after their position on this issue. Some Islamic scholars have remarked on the existence of a belief in destiny (*al-dahr*) in pre-Islamic poetry which was absent from the Qur'ān, where instead God determines events and men are responsible for their actions. In theology, libertarian positions were initially favoured but the stress of God's predestination of events became increasingly more prominent. This development seems to have had an impact on Islamic philosophy too. In addition to their belief and defence of divine omnipotence, in line with the medieval theologians, the philosophers employ certain aspects of the Greek philosophical tradition to buttress their claims for the defence of divine omnipotence. We therefore find a reluctance to expand on the issue of human free will and a predominance of determinist positions among medieval Muslim philosophers.

Further Reading

Adamson, P. (2002) *The Arabic Plotinus: A Philosophical Study of the* 'Theology of Aristotle,' London: Duckworth.

——. (2007) *Al-Kindī*, Oxford: Oxford University Press.

Alfarabi (1985) *Al-Farabi on the Perfect State: Abū Naṣr al-Fārābī's Mabādī' Arā' Ahl al-Madīnah al-Faḍīlah*, R. Walzer (ed. and tr.), New York: Oxford University Press.

Averroes (2001) *Faith and Reason in Islam, Averroes' Exposition of Religious Arguments*, I. Najjar (tr.), Oxford: Oneworld.

Avicenna (2005) *The Metaphysics of The Healing*, M. E. Marmura (tr.), Provo, UT: Brigham University Press.

Frank, R. M. (1994) *Al-Ghazali and the Ash'arite School*, Durham & London: Duke University Press.

Gimaret, D. (1980) *Théories de l'acte humain en théologie musulmane*, Paris: Vrin.

——. (1990) *La doctrine d'al-Ash'ari*, Paris: Éditions du Cerf.

Sorabji, R. (1980) *Necessity, Cause and Blame*, London: Duckworth.

Wisnovsky, R. (2003) *Avicenna's Metaphysics in Context*, Ithaca: Cornell University Press.

References

al-Fārābī (1991) *al-Farabi's Commentary and Short Treatise on Aristotle's* De Interpretatione, F. W. Zimmermann (tr.), Oxford: Oxford University Press.

al-Ghazālī (1962) *Al-iqtiṣād fi-l-i'tiqād*, I. A. Chubuqchi & H. Atay (eds.), Ankara: Nur Matbaasi.

al-Kindī (1974) *De radiis*, M-T. D'Alverny & F. Hudry (eds.), *Archives d'histoire doctrinale et littéraire du moyen âge* 61: 139–260.

Aristotle (1995) *The Complete Works of Aristotle*, 2 vols., J. Barnes (ed.), Princeton: Princeton University Press.

Averroes (1969) *Averroes' Tahafut al-Tahafut (Incoherence of the Incoherence)*, S. van Den Bergh (tr.), London: Luzac & Co.

——. (1983) *Averroes' Middle Commentaries on Aristotle's Categories and De interpretatione*, C. E. Butterworth (tr.), Princeton: Princeton University Press.

——. (1998) *Kashf 'an manāhij al-adilla fi 'aqā'id al-milla*, M. 'A. al-Jābirī (ed.), Beirut: al-Ṭab'at al-ūlā.

——. (2001) *Decisive Treatise and Epistle Dedicatory*, C. E. Butterworth (tr.), Provo, UT: Brigham University Press.

Avicenna (2000) *Lettre au Vizir Abū Sa'd*, Y. Michot (ed. and tr.), Beirut: Albouraq.

——. (2009) *The Physics of The Healing*, J. McGinnis (tr.), Provo, UT: Brigham Young University Press.

Belo, C. (2007) *Chance and Determinism in Avicenna and Averroes*, Leiden: Brill.

Caspar, R. (2007) *Islamic Theology*, vol. II, *Doctrines*, Rome: Pontificio Istituto di Studi Arabi e d'Islamistica.

Fakhry, M. (1991) *Ethical Theories in Islam*, Leiden: Brill.

Frank, R. M. (1978) *Beings and Their Attributes. The Teaching of the Basrian School of the Mu'tazila in the Classical Period*, Albany: State University of New York Press.

Kant, I. (1911) *Kant's Gesammelte Schriften*, Berlin: Koeniglich Preussischen Akademie der Wissenschaften.

Marmura, M. E. (2005) "Ghazali's Chapter on Divine Power in the Iqtisad," in *Probing in Islamic Philosophy: Studies in the Philosophies of Ibn Sina, al-Ghazali and Other Major Muslim Thinkers*, State University of New York at Binghampton: Global Academic Publishing/Binghampton University, pp. 301–34.

McGinnis, J. & Reisman, D. (eds. and tr.) (2007) *Classical Islamic Philosophy, An Anthology of Sources*, Indianapolis: Hackett Publishing Company.

McKenna, M. (2009) "Compatibilism," in the *Stanford Encyclopedia of Philosophy*, http://plato.stanford.edu/entries/compatibilism

Shihadeh, A. (2006) *The Teleological Ethics of Fakhr al-Dīn al-Rāzī*, Leiden: Brill.

Watt, W. M. (1948) *Free Will and Predestination in Early Islam*, London: Luzac & Co.

Wolfson, H. A. (1976) *The Philosophy of Kalam*, Cambridge: Harvard University Press.

27
PRINCIPLES OF THE PHILOSOPHY OF STATE

Philippe Vallat

Introduction

To talk about political philosophy in Islam, or Islamicate Civilization, might amount to talking about Abū Naṣr al-Fārābī, a Persian philosopher whose life is largely unknown, yet who singles himself out in the history of Arabic-Islamic philosophy as having envisioned politics as a central part of philosophy as well as a subject worthy of attention in itself. In order to summarize his political doctrine, one must focus on what al-Fārābī considered the unique goal of politics and the main means of achieving it. The literary aspects of al-Fārābī's concrete political project and just what it meant for a writer in fourth-century Islamic society (tenth-century C.E.) to provide his contemporaries with a thoroughly philosophical form of politics have not been given enough weight. While still a disputed question among modern scholars, it is arguable that al-Fārābī's three main political writings—the *Perfect City-State*, the *Political Aphorisms*, and the *Political Regime* or *Governance*, all written or completed after he left Baghdad in 942 and settled in Damascus in the last decade of his life—form a set, the practical intention of which was not only theoretical, but also performative. These three writings, especially the first, were supposed to fulfill the first condition for the perfect city to become a reality, this condition being the recruitment of its philosophers.

In the broader context of philosophy, al-Fārābī introduced new insights founded on epistemological principles that structured his approaches to metaphysics and language, natural philosophy and cosmology and political philosophy. In the latter he introduced an approach founded on select writings of Plato and Aristotle that at once (1) explicated the precise role of religion in society from the stance of the philosopher, and also (2) provided a penetrating analysis into issues of language, meaning and metaphysics. In what follows I focus on these two topics which constitute areas of lasting philosophical contributions in the tradition as well as in contemporary political philosophy.

Philosophical Soteriology and Religion

In the curriculum of philosophical studies, politics comes last. In order to be properly understood and studied, politics requires that the philosopher apprentice has already gone over the different disciplines which together form philosophy. This is the only way to assess the purpose of human life and, at the same time, the way in which human nature defines itself. Without a clear definition of humanity, there can be no politics, only theories blind to the right definition of human nature. Bringing to life such theories could only result in failure. Thus al-Fārābī held that religions that negate human free will in any way or conceive of God as the common cause of good and evil can only drive humanity to its fall.

But what is the destination of human beings? His inquiry is carried out in stages. The study of logic comes first as a safeguard against false opinions and as the indispensable tool for any further study. Then comes physics, which is the study of what human beings share in with the substances of the physical world and what distinguishes them from higher kinds of beings, i.e. the celestial bodies. Then comes metaphysics, which reveals the specific difference of the human species, what makes it unique among all other species of beings, whether material, celestial or immaterial. This curriculum, mostly inherited from the Neoplatonists of Alexandria through various channels, provides the philosopher with the means for elaborating the idea that human beings not only possess a physical hylomorphic constitution common to all material substances, but also a disposition—a mere enmattered disposition at first (*hay'a fī mādda*)—to think beyond nature. In al-Fārābī's understanding of human nature, we are both material through our natural constitution and potentially immaterial if and only if we succeed in achieving the purpose for which we first came to be. Between the immaterial and the material we stand either as a gap, if we fail to be our fullest selves, or as a bridge, if we succeed.

To be human is not given as an inalienable advantage received at birth. We must become human, which means perfectly human; for any substance must achieve the most perfect act in order to become what it ought to be, the possibility of which is inscribed in its very nature (*fiṭra*). Nature is always a process of success or a failure and never a stable state. But nature does not do anything in vain. There is a natural reason why we are thinking beings and not irrational animals. Hence, in order to become *truly* human, each human being must be given the opportunity to become *perfectly* human. According to al-Fārābī, the only way to make this possible is to provide everyone with the appropriate form of philosophical teaching, because becoming human is to act in accordance with what makes us unique among all natural species. And this is the capacity to think rightly, a capacity that only truth, that is, demonstrative philosophy, can properly channel and lead to its end. But peoples are different through their particular natural traits and cultures. Truth, remaining essentially the same, must therefore take on the appropriate shape to fit each people. Theoretically, there can be as many inflections of such a true philosophical teaching as there are peoples on earth apt to be taught.

A question that al-Fārābī did not address directly, but which is nevertheless striking, is why it is not sufficient, after all, to be born human and live the way we wish to live? His answer is that living without taking any notice or care of what our nature binds us to become can only end in the death of our soul. Not achieving the purpose for the sake of which we human beings came to be inevitably results in the withering of our soul as our body dies. Al-Fārābī does not believe human souls are immortal *per se* in virtue of their initial natures. Rather, he thinks they can become immortal given specific conditions. Immortality here means that souls become immaterial at the moment when they no longer depend for their subsistence on the physical matter on which they first function as forms of bodies. The soul that achieves its life course successfully becomes self-subsisting and eternal. Failing that, both the soul and its body are forever annihilated. Each of our life choices confronts us with these simple alternatives: either life eternal or death eternal.

For al-Fārābī philosophy consists in all that is really human in our knowledge because it is true. Truth is the appropriateness of a certain content of knowledge to the specific intellectual acts and ethical decisions whereby we coincide with our natural destination. If not impaired by damaging false opinions and bad habits, any mind which comes into contact with truth is induced to think in accordance with his/her human nature and to act accordingly. This is why truth makes human beings what they are beckoned to become and why it makes them felicitous, blessed. It is truth, then, that makes happiness possible. And happiness is synonymous with immortality. Consequently, there can be no immortality without a true philosophy.

Knowing this, we also know what the purpose of politics is: to gather together all the social and material conditions to be fulfilled in order for everyone in a given place to receive this appropriate, salvific teaching, and thus to be rescued from otherwise inescapable annihilation. But not everyone is a philosopher since philosophy as an intellectual discipline surely suits only minds suitably disposed for it. Then how can philosophy be taught to everyone?

In al-Fārābī's view philosophy may become a sort of religion, but only on the condition that it does not lose its rational structure. This rational structure can be mirrored in the way symbolic forms such as laws and cultural productions are co-ordained to form a consistent set of *endoxic* tenets. Properly understood, religion is the likeness of demonstrative knowledge reflected in people's minds as true (albeit mere) *opinions*. This *endoxic* likeness of philosophical truth, however, is not a likeness though it contains everything needed in order for the non-philosophers' minds to be perfected within their own respective order. Religious tenets or dogmas, then, must be philosophically grounded in such a way that only a real philosopher can found a truthful religion by encapsulating his knowledge in such a form that it may trigger in the common mind a kind of response tantamount to philosophical certainty. As well as any other sound kind of knowledge, religion is a kind of syllogistic reasoning, partly implicit or unnoticed as such, but no less syllogistic or rational in its core than philosophy itself. Provided that its dogmas have been defined by the philosopher, theology is an imitative copy of philosophy. If within a given religion all the tenets are opinions (*endoxa*) congruent with philosophical truths, then the theologian is at his own level a true philosopher. And what is true of the theologian is also true of simple believers at their level. Thus, the aim of religion as a form of knowledge is the same as that of philosophy: to help people use their rational capacities at their best. In this way the rational soul, which makes an individual human, will actualize its proper end whereby it will attain happiness and immortality by becoming a self-subsisting substance.

What we have seen in al-Fārābī so far explains only partly the necessity of politics: non-philosophers cannot be saved if they remain ignorant of the supernatural destination ingrained in their nature as a potentiality meant to be voluntarily actualized.

A regime whose civic religion is grounded in philosophy is the way to provide its citizens with the knowledge they need. The perfect city-state imagined by al-Fārābī is like a school where the philosopher teaches, by different means, natural born philosophers as well as non-philosophers the way to save their souls not only by pedagogy and incentive, but sometimes by compulsion too. So considered, politics is by definition thoroughly soteriological. But why should the philosopher weary himself with others' salvation? Is it not enough for him to enjoy happiness on his own? The reason why al-Fārābī's answer is clearly "no" is found in the structure of knowledge that defines philosophers. If only philosophers can rule, this is not because what defines them is their knowledge of material and immaterial substances only—even if this in itself is enough to lead them to happiness—but because, in addition to this theoretical knowledge, they also possess the practical knowledge of all the conditions by which their theoretical or contemplative philosophy can be made useful to all mankind. Consequently, one who fails to equip oneself with the corresponding practical arts is half a philosopher and half an impostor. After what he says about those failed philosophers, it seems al-Fārābī regarded them as the living proofs of the difference existing between a real wise person who is by definition a virtuous soul and a contemplative mind and an abstract-minded person who most of the time is a wicked person whose knowledge serves only as a social posture—philosophers were famous in tenth-century society—and as a conceptual vindication of his wickedness. The first becomes what is known. This philosopher is divine in a true sense. The second, failing to live as the first, finally comes to think in accord with the life lived. This soul, by nature foreign to philosophy, was incapable in the first place to assimilate it, or was only capable of it as a superficial adornment of vices. This description is found both briefly in the *Attainment to Happiness* (1992: 191–5, tr.: 48–9), and, more at length, at the end of the *Political Regime* (1993: 104–7; French transl.: 222–32).

Thus politics, if genuinely founded on a true philosophy, proceeds from the highest theoretical virtue, happiness, which is by nature a virtue to be shared by all. And only someone who possesses something is able to share it. The philosopher is perfect only if personally he/she is the embodiment of contemplative knowledge and is able to bring about such perfection politically. As for happiness, it can be called the ideal common good, because it is for all to share without being divided or diminished in the process. Everyone in the city should partake in it as much as his/her natural ability (*fiṭra*) allows him/her. The justice at work in al-Fārābī's perfect city-state is then both distributive and hierarchical.

Language, Meaning, and Metaphysics

When al-Fārābī states that a religion (*milla*) in its twofold dimension of orthodoxy and orthopraxy must be in the likeness of philosophy (*sabīha bi-l-falsafa*) in its twofold dimension of contemplation and practice, he means that philosophers need to take hold of the vernacular. Language can be the vehicle of three things: truth, error and verisimilitude. Truth pertains to demonstrative philosophy. Errors, in his opinion, are the common share of all historical religions which have been founded on corrupted forms of philosophy and whose members remain unaware of this. Verisimilitude, in turn, is what the philosopher needs in order to be understood by a community, that is, to provide it with a teaching appropriate to the rational abilities of its members.

Al-Fārābī's apparent starting point is the idea that "The perfect *milla* (religion) resembles philosophy" (1986b: 46, 22). In fact, this idea is itself based on the following principle. There are three main ways for the mind to submit to any true proposition, what al-Fārābī calls *inqiyād*. The mind can have an *intellectual understanding* (*taṣawwur* or *ʿaql*) of the truth of a proposition and assent to it (*taṣdīq*). Without knowing the reason why something is true (the minor premise of the demonstrative syllogism that proves it), it can have a *right opinion* (*ṣawāb al-raʾy*) about it, grounded on probable premises, and adhere to it. The mind can *believe* that something is true through a mental image (*ḫayāl* or *miṯāl*) of its truth. This scheme is the pattern after which all human beings are hierarchized in al-Fārābī's perfect city-state. Intellectual understanding, synonymous with contemplative certainty, metaphysics, and demonstrative knowledge, is what characterizes philosophical minds. Right opinions, which correspond to dialectics, are what define the kind of knowledge accessible to the ancillary orders of the city: mainly the people in charge of the language (rhetors, poets-musicians), the mathematicians (arithmeticians, geometers and musicians) and the theologians as religious dialecticians. Belief (*iqnāʿ* or *īmān*) characterizes all the other natural kinds of citizens who are to be addressed rhetorically or poetically (farmers, merchants and soldiers).

The important point here is that philosophical poetry and rhetoric do not convey a lesser sort of knowledge than demonstration. In fact, provided that the philosopher-king defines the content, their value is only measured by their appropriateness to, and effectual power upon, the kind of minds for which they are meant. Al-Fārābī sometimes uses the same term, *ʿilm* ("science"), to denote the content of knowledge of both philosophers and non-philosophers. What certain demonstration is to philosophers, poetry is to ordinary minds: science (al-Fārābī 1992: §56, 185; English tr. 44, l. 16). What is eminently present in the philosopher's demonstrative science is analogically present in the science of ordinary minds.

Al-Fārābī is here drawing partially upon a principle found both in Aristotle and in Alexander of Aphrodisias (*De anima* 89:7–8; *In Met.* 246:11–12): what possesses a thing eminently is the cause for others to possess it secondarily. For example (*Politics* I, 13, 1260b 15 *ss.*), the virtuous master is the cause of virtue in his slave; and order is eminently present in the general as the cause of order in the army (*Met.*, Λ 10, 1075a 15; cf. α 1, 993b 24–6).

Only thus can the ultimate sentence of al-Fārābī's *Philosophy of Aristotle* be understood: "Therefore it is utterly necessary that philosophy comes to actually exist in *every man's soul* in the mode possible to him" (1961: 133; English tr. 130). Given that this knowledge is supposed to confer immortality on those who receive it, which explains its necessity, this cannot mean only "some" philosophy or a popular form of philosophy, but philosophy in its most proper sense: metaphysics. Thus, each individual should be given the opportunity to assimilate metaphysics, "in a mode possible to him," which means in accordance to his nature or "analogically."

The novel tenet that beliefs (rhetoric and poetics) and opinions (dialectics) can convey the same content of knowledge as demonstrative philosophy does, is the way al-Fārābī merged into one seemingly consistent theory two different sets of ideas respectively found in *Republic* VI, 509d–511e, where Plato exposes the mathematic reason behind the Myth of the Cave, and in Aristotle's *Organon* which the Greek philosophers of Alexandria divided into five syllogistic arts (Boggess 1970: 89; cf. Vallat 2004: 189–90). More specifically, when al-Fārābī asserts, for instance, in the *Book of Religion* (1986b: 46, 17–18), that religion's content is either truth itself or what resembles it (cf. Aristotle, *Rhetoric* I, 1, 1355a, 14–15, Arabic, 1979: 7, 6–7), what he means is not that dialectics, rhetoric and poetics directly resemble philosophy, but rather the resemblance is found in the opinions they employed as premises to convey philosophical truth. The verisimilitude is to be found in the *endoxa* (opinions) *qua* premises. For example, a philosophical proposition expressed in a poetic or rhetorical form, even if it does not exhibit the three terms of which all syllogisms are composed in order to be valid, must comply with this threefold structure implicitly, with its two premises and conclusion. This means that the philosophical religion created through Aristotle's logical arts requires an extremely exacting *techne*. This is why al-Fārābī sometimes speaks of a "scientific" or even "speculative" form of rhetoric. This has nothing to do with "revelation" or "inspiration" (*ilhām*), the very existence of which is denied by al-Fārābī (1987: 82: 1–8).

Even more technical in the grounding of his view are the criteria for the choice of the vocabulary to be employed in such arts. Al-Fārābī applied to this question the theory of the *analogia entis* (the analogy of being) which he is the first to have elaborated, some two centuries before Thomas Aquinas. His idea is that the hierarchical structure of Being appeared to human minds not only through ingrained notions in the first principles of any reasoning and the threefold structure of any valid reasoning in syllogism, but also through the main grammatical and morphologic divisions of the vocabulary we use to interpret and understand the world and its phenomena. Language, because it has been created by philosophical minds, is supposed to reflect something true about reality. Like the syllogistic arts, this ontological grammar received a privileged place in al-Fārābī's theory of the perfect religion. In fact, he postulates the existence of a structure immanent both to the thought and language which is universal because it is transposable from one language to another and identical with the structure of reality. The first theoretical task of the founder of a philosophical religion is thus to master the semantic *modus operandi* of three classes of nouns or adjectives, synonyms, homonyms, paronyms, so as to assess the way they act on people's minds. Then, given the respective ways they do act upon people's minds, the founder must syllogistically intertwine them so they form discourses, poetry or prose, in order that, at the end, metaphysics can be conveyed in a persuasive manner through non-philosophical forms of speech to all the citizens. In this theory of language and ontology, the stroke of genius is the identification of the Platonic analogy (*Timaeus* 31c), composed of three terms (A is to B, what B is to C) with the Aristotelian syllogistic with its three terms: the major premise, the minor and the conclusion. The kind of religious syllogisms al-Fārābī had in mind are those which are able to bring together two subjects—for instance, human beings and an immaterial reality—through a common homonymous predicate called *sabīh*—B in Plato's analogy—which is successively said of both in each one of the two premises. This term *sabīh* means both what is common to two beings that are said to resemble each other in some way and the geometric mean between two numbers in the Euclidean definition of analogy. As for Plato, al-Fārābī describes the former's analogy in the *Timaeus* as the most perfect way to conceive of the unity and the continuity (*sunecheia*) that exist between the different realms the universe is made of, from the Ideas to their imitative material instantiations. In other terms, this analogy is supposed to show how the material realm partakes of immutability through its link with the immutable Ideas. As for al-Fārābī's religious syllogistic, it is meant to depict to peoples' minds that they live in a universe within which the human political order is congruent with the structure of the All through its own hierarchical organization. Only through the forming of hierarchy within itself can the city be connected with the ultimate cause of all things, just as the intellect is connected (cf. *ittiṣāl*) to its ultimate cause through a methodical assimilation of the hierarchical set of sciences, viz. the philosophical curriculum.

Accordingly, one could label al-Fārābī's theory as a syllogistic transposition of a thoroughly Neoplatonic metaphysics to political and religious matters—and with this specification it perfectly fits the framework of the doctrines studied by D. O'Meara in his *Platonopolis* (2003).

Conclusion

For al-Fārābī the first task of the philosopher consists not in creating a philosophical regime *ex nihilo*, but in shaping pre-existing popular opinions to bring them closer to what resembles the truth so that they can finally form a set of consistent philosophical opinions. In order to do so, the philosopher must assess the degree of truth of opinions generally accepted in the society he/she lives in. These opinions are his/her starting point, the matter he/she has to mold, in order to convert society to philosophy. Verisimilitude is then the key to conquer the souls, which in turn is the first condition to bring about a philosophical regime. Thus, language as the vehicle of verisimilitude should be seized by philosophers if they want to succeed in their attempt to win over souls. This is why al-Fārābī composed his *Book of Particles*, an in-depth technical inquiry into the capacity of Arabic to convey Greek philosophical notions. A large part of it is devoted to a detailed description of the various possible cases of conflictual relations between philosophy and already existing religions, these religions being considered as sets of concurrent opinions. As he emphasized in the postscript of his *Perfect City-State*, called *Summary of the Perfect City-State*, and also in his *Political Aphorisms*, a detailed knowledge of existing religions is the condition for the philosopher to ascertain the most appropriate means to divert peoples' minds from error to truth. His *Book of Particles* was intended for already trained philosophers and future rulers. But who exactly were these figures from whom al-Fārābī expected that they could take hold of Arabic and thereby change the general opinions of society, these thinkers who, in his city-state, are only second to philosophers (1971: 65)? The answer, found in his political writings, is the secretaries of chancellery (*kuttāb*) who formed the elite of the Imperial model of administration. So far as we know they shared with him a common background: most of them were neither of Arab descent nor had any particular predisposition towards Islamic sciences, but rather for Iranian or Hellenist lore and Aristotelian philosophy (Heck 2002: 41 and Vallat 2012a).

Of his overarching political project—which intended taking hold of a small city-state, not as unrealistic a plan as it may now seem to us—nothing quite comparable survives in later Arabic philosophy. However, all later Arabic philosophers inherited from al-Fárábī, in one form or another, his theory of the correspondence of the different logical disciplines to the various rational abilities of those to whom the philosopher must make himself understood while safe-keeping *falsafa* (Hellenizing philosophy).

Further Reading

Crone, P. (2004) "Al-Fárābī's Imperfect Constitutions," *Mélanges de l'Université Saint-Joseph* 57: 191–228.

Gutas, D. (2004) "The Meaning of *madanī* in al-Fárābī's 'Political' Philosophy," *Mélanges de l'Université Saint-Joseph* 57: 259–82.

Mahdi, M. (1975) "Remarks on Alfarabi's Attainment of Happiness," in G. F. Hourani (ed.), *Essays on Islamic Philosophy and Science*, Albany, New York: State University of New York Press, pp. 47–66.

——. (1990) "Al-Fárābī's Imperfect State," *Journal of the American Oriental Society* 110, 4: 691–726.

McGinnis, J. & Reisman, D. (2007) *Classical Arabic Philosophy: An Anthology of Sources*, Indianapolis & Cambridge: Hackett Publishing.

References

al-Fárābī (1961) *Al-Farabi's Philosophy of Aristotle*, M. Mahdi (ed.), Beirut: Dar Majallat Shi'r; Mahdi, M. (tr.) (1962) *Alfarabi: Philosophy of Plato and Aristotle*, USA: The Free Press of Glencoe, pp. 59–130.

——. (1971) *Alfarabi's Fuṣūl Muntaza'a (Selected Aphorisms)*, F. M. Najjar (ed.), Beirut: Dar El-Mashreq; Butterworth, C. E. (tr.) (2001) *The Political Writings, Selected Aphorisms and other Texts*, Ithaca & London: Cornell University Press, pp. 11–67.

——. (1985) *Alfarabi on the Perfect State*, R. Walzer (tr.), Oxford: Clarendon Press.

——. (1986a) *Summary of the Perfect City-State, Fuṣūl mabādi' ārā' ahl al-madīna al-fāḍila* in *Alfarabi's Book of Religion and Related Texts*, M. Mahdi (ed.), Beirut: Dar El-Mashreq, pp. 79–86.

——. (1986b) *Book of Religion*, in M. Mahdi (ed.), *Alfarabi's Book of Religion and Related Texts*, Beirut: Dar El-Mashreq, pp. 41–66; C. E. Butterworth (tr.) (2001) *The Political Writings, Selected Aphorisms and other Texts*, Ithaca & London: Cornell University Press, pp. 85–113.

——. (1987) *On Demonstration, Kitāb al-burhān*, in M. Fakhry (ed.), *Al-manṭiq 'inda al-Fārābī*, Beirut: Dar El-Mashreq, pp. 19–96.

——. (1990) *Book of Particles, Alfarabi's Book of Letters*, M. Mahdi (ed.), Beirut: Dar El-Mashreq.

——. (1992) *Attainment of Happiness, Kitāb taḥṣīl al-sa'āda* in al-Yasin (ed.), *Al-Fārābī, The Philosophical Works*, Beirut: Dar al-Manahel; English translation (*Taḥṣīl al-sa'āda*, ed. Hyderabad, 1345 A.H.): Mahdi, M. (tr.) (1962) *Alfarabi: Philosophy of Plato and Aristotle*, USA: The Free Press of Glencoe, pp. 13–50.

——. (1993) *Political Regime* (or *Governance*), *Al-Fārābī's The Political Regime*, F. M. Najjar (ed.), Beirut: Dar El-Mashreq; J. McGinnis & D. Reisman (tr.) (2007), *Classical Arabic Philosophy: An Anthology of Sources*, Indianapolis & Cambridge: Hackett Publishing, pp. 81–102; for complete French translation, see Vallat (2012b).

——. (1998) "Le Sommaire du livre des 'Lois' de Platon," T-A. Druart (ed.), *Bulletin d'Études Orientales* 50: 109–55.
Aristotle (1979) *Rhetoric, Arisṭūṭālīs, Al-ḫaṭāba*, ʿA. al-Raḥmān Badawī (ed.), Beirut-Koweit: Dār al-qalam-Wikālat al-maṭbūʿāt.
Boggess, W. F. (1970) "Alfarabi and the Rhetoric: The Cave Revisited," *Phronesis* 15: 86–90.
Butterworth, C. E. (2001): *Alfarabi, The Political Writings*, Ithaca & London: Cornell University Press.
Heck, P. (2002) "The Hierarchy of Knowledge in Islamic Civilization," *Arabica* 49, 1: 27–54.
Mahdi, M. (1962) *Alfarabi's philosophy of Plato and Aristotle*, New York: The Free Press of Glencoe.
O'Meara, D. (2003) *Platonopolis: Platonic Political Philosophy in Late Antiquity*, Oxford: Oxford University Press.
Vallat, P. (2004) *Farabi et l'École d'Alexandrie, Des prémisses de la connaissance à la philosophie politique*, Paris: Vrin.
——. (tr.) (2012a) *Abū Naṣr al-Fārābī, L'Épître sur l'intellect*, Paris: Les Belles Lettres.
——. (tr.) (2012b) *Abū Naṣr al-Fārābī, Le Livre du régime politique*, Paris: Les Belles Lettres.

28
NATURAL AND REVEALED RELIGION

Nadja Germann

Introduction

If by "religion" we refer to a doctrine regarded by its adherents as imparting true and authoritative knowledge about the world's efficient, formal, and final causes, then certainly philosophy, and particularly metaphysics, deals with problems belonging to the realm of religion. If we want it furthermore to refer to a doctrine demanding of its adherents accordance with certain moral standards, often including specific rituals and practices, then the connection with philosophy becomes less obvious. For although I might be a keen metaphysician, I may not necessarily feel compelled to behave or organize my everyday life in a particular way. The question thus arises of whether philosophy in and of itself, beyond its avowed interest in the world's efficient, formal, and final causes, has direct *practical* implications inducing the philosopher to live her life in a certain, which is to say, morally relevant way. At first sight, my own example seems to offer an unequivocal and negative answer to this question. However, reality is more complicated, as a brief glance into the history of philosophy shows. For, obviously, there are philosophers who believe that theoretical knowledge has (and must have) a bearing on the conduct of one's life, one of the most famous examples being Socrates. To live the "examined life," he suggests in the *Apology* (28b), entails not only the search for truth, but simultaneously requires the habit of constantly reassessing whether or not one "is acting like a good or a bad man." Accordingly, it seems rather to be a matter of which kind of philosophy one endorses whether or not one believes that insight into the truth has implications for how one ought to live, i.e. whether or not philosophy turns out to be some sort of natural religion. (In this paper, I will use "natural theology" as an equivalent of "metaphysics/theology"; "natural ethics" to refer to the practical implications of natural theology; and "natural religion" as an umbrella term embracing these two aspects.)

This leads us to the first question to be addressed here, namely, whether there are philosophers in the Arabic-Islamic world whose philosophies possess the character of natural religion. While I argue that this is indeed the case, it should be noted that my focus is on the classical era of Islamic philosophy, especially the tenth through twelfth centuries, and hence on the formative period of pre-modern Islamic intellectual culture. This is not only the most accessible phase of Islamic intellectual history given the current state of research, it is also considered one of the most vibrant epochs, excelling both by virtue of its diversity and by the sophistication of its scholarly debates. To be sure, this choice impacts the present discussion, insofar as it entails the omission of certain later developments in philosophy, particularly in the field of epistemology (e.g. Suhrawardī and the rise of illumination theory). Nonetheless, this concentration also has the advantage of bringing to the fore some essential features which set the course for the relationship between natural and revealed religion in the Islamic world directly from the outset.

Inspired by his Neoplatonic predecessors, the "first philosopher of the Arabs," al-Kindī (d. 870), already interpreted metaphysics as natural theology (e.g. al-Kindī 1974: 55–6; cf. Adamson 2011). Despite the "Aristotelian turn" in subsequent decades and substantial adjustments of the concept of metaphysics, natural theology, i.e. inquiry into "the world's efficient, formal, and final causes," remained an integral part of it, with the effect that metaphysics was often referred to as *ilāhiyyāt* ("divine science"). From about the time of al-Fārābī (d. 950) onwards, natural theology was usually supplemented by a natural ethics. In this regard, drawing primarily from Plato's *Republic*, classical Islamic philosophers insisted that insight into the truth does imply certain practical consequences. There are, accordingly, several aspects, specific for natural religion in the early Arabic-Islamic world, which we must study in particular. These concern: (1) knowledge about God and His creation and the means by which it can be acquired; (2) an anthropology and eschatology according to which happiness is the ultimate human goal, whose perfection, however, can only be fully attained in the afterlife; and (3) natural ethics, inasmuch as comprehension of (1) and (2) reveals that in order to attain happiness, a certain way of life is required. These three aspects are also dealt with in the Islamic religious sciences, first and foremost, theology (*kalām*). Therefore, we shall briefly examine the relation between natural and revealed religion, not only from the perspective of the philosophers, but also from the theologians' viewpoint. In order to cover these issues and reveal their intricate interrelations, I shall proceed as follows. Even though I will not "here undertake a mere flight of fancy," I shall use a certain "document as a map" (Kant 1786: 49.109), namely, Ibn Ṭufayl's *Ḥayy ibn Yaqẓān*, a philosophical novel which—for our purposes—stands out, as it circles precisely around the problem of natural versus revealed religion and carefully discusses core philosophical and theological positions defended throughout the classical era.

The Roadmap: Ibn Ṭufayl

In his novel, Ibn Ṭufayl (d. 1185) tells the fictitious story of a boy called Ḥayy growing up the only human being on a lonely island (Mallet 2011; Conrad 1996). With its peculiar *dramatis personae*—Ḥayy, the autodidactic philosopher, Absāl and Salāmān, the representatives of two different theological schools, and their interaction—the tale can be read as a parable displaying and pondering the chief competing approaches current in Ibn Ṭufayl's time to the question of how to attain ultimate happiness. Hence, despite its fictitious character, it provides an excellent insight into the historical positions prevailing around the dusk of the classical era. With respect to our topic, the story can be broken down into six stations:

i Knowledge. While developing into an adult, Ḥayy acquires an increasingly comprehensive knowledge about the world and its constitution, all on his own. Eventually he reaches the point where he masters all the traditional philosophical sciences, including metaphysics, although he never had a teacher and, for lack of company, never learned to speak.

ii Happiness. At this stage, the novel takes an interesting turn. Having discovered the existence of God, Ḥayy understands that "to preserve constant awareness of Him is to know joy without lapse, unending bliss, infinite rapture and delight" (Ibn Ṭufayl 1972: 137). From this he concludes that it is his final goal to strive for this awareness and bliss. However, "[s]eeing that [ultimate] happiness [sc. in the afterlife] meant constant actual experience of the Necessarily Existent [i.e. God] ... so that when death came it would find him rapt in ecstasy" (Ibn Ṭufayl 1972: 138), he recognizes that his newly discovered final goal entails practical consequences; he comprehends that he must conduct his life in a way that would bring him as close as possible to constant experience of God.

iii Practical Implications. Due to the fact that he is a compound being, Ḥayy reasons, his duties "fall under three heads" (Ibn Ṭufayl 1972: 142). For one, owing to the corporeality he shares with any other animal, he has to take in food and protect himself against the weather in order to keep himself alive. The second sort of activity, by contrast, is based on an imitation of the heavenly bodies, their uninterrupted circular movement along their trajectories, an exercise which Ḥayy believes is crucial as preparation for the duties of the third stage. These latter, finally, consist in concentration on God Himself, resulting in the attainment of "the pure beatific experience" which was, after all, the "supreme goal" of his endeavors (Ibn Ṭufayl 1972: 143).

iv Diet and Rites. Given this goal, Ḥayy infers that regarding the first kind of duties he must carefully control his bodily requirements and "set himself [limits] he would not overstep" (Ibn Ṭufayl 1972: 144). These "limits" turn out to be rules concerning, for example, the amount and kind of food he might take in, the way he disposes of waste, the clothing he can wear, and the features of his dwelling. Similarly detailed are the exercises Ḥayy assigns himself for the fulfillment of the second type of duties, such as taking care of plants and animals, keeping himself clean, performing circular movements either around the island or his shack or his own axis (Ibn Ṭufayl 1972: 145–7). Interestingly, as previous research has already noted, these rules share a close affinity with Sufi practices, geared—just like Ḥayy's activities—to reaching the stage of actual awareness of God.

v Revealed Religion. At this point, Ibn Ṭufayl's tale takes yet another twist, in a direction likewise important for our purposes. For now our hero encounters other human beings, one of whom, Absāl, happens to disembark on Ḥayy's island. Absāl grew up on a neighboring island, inhabited by a people adhering to a revealed religion reminiscent of Islam. Together with a close friend, Salāmān, he immersed himself into the study of the religion's holy Scripture. Yet, whereas Absāl believed that this Scripture embraces many hidden meanings and requires interpretation, his friend held to its literal reading and the faithful observance of its rituals. Eventually, Absāl decided to retreat from society to focus exclusively on the contemplation of God, which is why he travels to Ḥayy's island (Ibn Ṭufayl 1972: 156–7).

vi Communicability. The two encounter one another, Absāl teaches Ḥayy to speak, and Ḥayy explains all his insights to Absāl. The latter is amazed to find that not only are Ḥayy's truths in neat accordance with his own religion's Scripture, but that they even explain many of its hidden meanings. When Ḥayy realizes that he could help Absāl's people to better understand their religion, he insists on moving to Absāl's island to teach his friends. However, this enterprise ends in complete failure: Absāl's friends become angry with him and reject his teachings, so the two decide to return to Ḥayy's island once more, and remain there in order to contemplate God (Ibn Ṭufayl 1972: 157–65).

Having laid out our "roadmap," we shall first study the chief philosophical positions considered by Ṭufayl, including their respective concepts of natural religion and attitudes towards revelation, before shifting to the theological and Sufi perspectives.

The Model: al-Fārābī

The figure most closely connected with the concept of natural religion in Ibn Ṭufayl's novel is Ḥayy himself. He gradually grows into a "knower," rather than a "believer" of the existence of God, the kind of existence He gave the universe, and the happiness resulting from contemplating Him. Ḥayy's natural religion comprises a full-fledged theology, anthropology, eschatology, and ethics (the latter of a very ritual nature). With a few exceptions (on which more below), Ibn Ṭufayl shaped his Ḥayy according to a certain model, originating with al-Fārābī (d. 950), whose writings became the chief point of reference for any later philosopher throughout the classical period on the topics of natural religion and political philosophy (Vallat 2011; Mahdi 2001). For our purposes, some chief aspects of al-Fārābī's concept of science, theory of knowledge, and political thought need to be mentioned.

For al-Fārābī, as for his late-ancient predecessors, "philosophy" is a collective term referring to the sum total of the scientific disciplines. According to al-Fārābī, however, this aggregate possesses a particular makeup: the various sciences depend upon one another and thus cohere in a hierarchical structure. Moreover, this structure neatly corresponds to the process of learning and understanding, leading from the most accessible and simple to the most remote and complicated things. On this account, the novice begins her studies with logic—the propaedeutic tool necessary for the study of any discipline whatsoever—continues with the mathematical and then the natural sciences—i.e. the investigation of "real" things—and arrives at metaphysics, where she examines the principles of reality, before she finally delves into practical philosophy, which is based on the theoretical sciences (al-Fārābī 1968; al-Fārābī 2001: 1.10–12: 18–20). It should be noted that Ḥayy, while teaching himself, followed closely this pattern (Germann 2008: 279–80; Schaerer 2004: xlvii–xlviii).

In order to elucidate the connection al-Fārābī sees between practical and theoretical philosophy, a short glance into his *The Attainment of Happiness* is instructive. At the beginning of this treatise, al-Fārābī intimates that

> [t]he human things through which nations and citizens of cities attain earthly happiness in this life and supreme happiness in the life beyond are of four kinds: theoretical virtues, deliberative virtues, moral virtues, and practical arts.
> (al-Fārābī 2001: 1.1: 13)

While "theoretical virtues" is just another name for the theoretical sciences, with "deliberative virtues" al-Fārābī refers to the various methods which must be applied in order to acquire knowledge in the sciences in a way that accords with the demands of the topics in question (al-Fārābī 2001: 1.3–4, 13–15). Provided one carefully applies these methods and studies the theoretical sciences in the indicated order, at one point

> the inquirer will have sighted another genus of things, different from the metaphysical [which is the culmination point of the theoretical sciences]. It is incumbent on man to investigate what is included in this genus: that is, the things that realize for man his objective.
> (al-Fārābī 2001: 1.18: 22)

This objective, now, consists in attaining "the ultimate perfection," which is as such the prerequisite for human beings to achieve the aforementioned supreme happiness (first quote). And this, according to al-Fārābī, is precisely where practical philosophy comes into play. For on his account, man

> cannot labor toward this perfection except by exploiting a large number of natural beings and until he manipulates them.
> (al-Fārābī 2001: 1.18: 23)

These three passages present a highly compressed account of al-Fārābī's natural religion. Developing a distinctive blend of Aristotle and Plato, al-Fārābī defines natural religion as an enterprise whose final goal consists in the attainment of supreme happiness in the afterlife. In order for human beings to reach this goal, two things are requisite. First, reminiscent of *Nicomachean Ethics* X, they must acquire comprehensive knowledge of the theoretical sciences, including natural theology. Second, in line with the *Republic*, they must establish what al-Fārābī refers to as the "virtuous city." To facilitate a better understanding of this second aspect, let us remain briefly with the third quotation. As this reference to human perfection reveals, man is a social being not simply because of the advantages company with other human beings offers, for example, for procreation or cooperation. Rather, society and the formation of political entities are necessary because "an isolated individual cannot achieve all the perfections by himself" (al-Fārābī 2001: 1.18: 23; cf., similarly, Miskawayh 1968: 1: 14). Therefore, concludes al-Fārābī, one must finally learn and apply the "science of man and political science," a science "that investigates [the] intellectual principles and the acts and states of character with which man labors toward this perfection" (al-Fārābī 2001:

1.18: 23). In short, the formation of morality is the second necessary condition for the attainment of happiness, in addition to perfection in the sciences (cf. also Miskawayh 1968: 2: 37).

A First Comparison: Philosophical Perspectives

Against this background, it becomes obvious that the entire first part of *Ḥayy ibn Yaqẓān* (station i of our "roadmap")—the acquisition of knowledge up to the point where Ḥayy masters metaphysics—is constructed along the lines of al-Fārābī's concept of theoretical perfection as laid out in the *Attainment*. Both accounts indicate that the theoretical sciences embrace a comprehensive knowledge of everything there is, stretching from the most minuscule kind of being on earth to the first principle or God. Moreover, as both texts unanimously insist, this knowledge, including metaphysics or natural theology, can be acquired by means of reason alone, without the need for divine revelation. *Ḥayy ibn Yaqẓān* highlights this aspect in particular, given that Ḥayy learns all these things "simply" by persistent inquiry, even without teachers or books. In the light of al-Fārābī's theory of intellect, Ḥayy thus represents a particularly gifted human being, one of the rare philosopher-prophets (on which more below), but nonetheless a *human* being applying *human* reason. It appears that classical Islamic philosophers are in agreement in their conviction *that* philosophy is an all-embracing knowledge, includes natural theology, and is attainable through pure natural reason (cf., e.g. Miskawayh 1968: 1: 12–14; Avicenna 2005: 9.7.11: 350, particularly in view of his theory of knowledge as laid out in Book 5 of his psychology of *The Healing*). Dissent, however, emerges both with regard to the presumed practical implications and the assessment of the relationship with revealed religion.

As for the practical implications (station ii), the comparison between Ibn Ṭufayl and his model, al-Fārābī, reveals several peculiarities. As mentioned above, al-Fārābī is convinced that both the formation of the intellect (theoretical knowledge) and the enhancement of the virtues (practical philosophy) are required for the attainment of happiness. The final goal of politics, hence, consists in governing the city in a way which encourages every citizen to strive for perfection, according to their capacities. For this is the precondition under which at least a few people—philosophers, who are sufficiently endowed to reach both intellectual and moral perfection—can fully develop their intellects and virtues and thus attain supreme happiness. Consequently, the ruler is preferably a philosopher-prophet, a particularly skilled philosopher who—just like Ḥayy in Ibn Ṭufayl's novel—is capable of acquiring an all-embracing knowledge of all the philosophical sciences (re. prophecy, see also al-Fārābī 1985: 14.9: 223–4 and 15.7–8: 239–43, 15.10–11: 245–7). Due to this knowledge, the ruler will understand how best to govern the city: how most effectively to support the inhabitants to pursue their individual perfections, which laws to decree in order to elicit moral behavior, and how to organize the city so that everyone can contribute to its well-being in proportion to their abilities. In short, the practical implications al-Fārābī finds entailed in what he considers to be a correct understanding of the world's constitution and human nature, turn out to closely resemble the political teachings of Plato's *Republic* (e.g. al-Fārābī 2001: 3.34–41). Even though he underscores that the citizens of the virtuous city must each develop their moral character, his focus is on the political level. There is nothing approaching Ḥayy's carefully designed rules for proper behavior toward plants, animals, and oneself (station iii); instead of worship and meditation of God, al-Fārābī recommends education of citizens in view of their service to the public welfare (particularly, al-Fārābī 2001: 3.38: 34–5).

The discrepancies between al-Fārābī and Ibn Ṭufayl increase further when one compares their respective positions on the relation of natural and revealed religion (station iv). On this topic, al-Fārābī has probably the most extreme stance of all the classical authors. To him, essentially, the truth can be known and happiness achieved through natural reason alone; the previously mentioned philosopher-prophet, deemed to be the perfect ruler, would be the best example of this. However, al-Fārābī is well aware that not all human beings possess such strong natural endowments. It is for this sole reason that, even in al-Fārābī's perfect state, there is a need for revelation and revealed religion (particularly, al-Fārābī 2001: 4.59: 47; broader context, 4: 41–50). Given that a majority of people are not able to attain a full grasp of all that can be known, given further that most people do not arrive beyond a basic understanding of only a limited number of topics, their education must have an appropriate character. They must be taught in a way they can follow and to a degree they can handle without slipping into error and confusion (cf. al-Fārābī 1968: 27–91).

At this point, the prophetic skills of the ruler and the purpose of revealed religion come into play: revealed Scriptures like the Qur'ān are, so to speak, textbooks for the instruction of the masses. They talk about the same truths a scholar can discover by means of scientific inquiry, and about the same practical demands such a scholar may deduce from her discoveries, only they apply simplified methods. For one, they use metaphors and similar stylistic figures where the theoretical explanation of the underlying truth would be too complicated for the majority. In addition, revealed Scriptures offer clear-cut rules and handy guidelines aimed at the betterment of people's morality by virtue of habituation. The prophetic gift of al-Fārābī's philosopher-prophet consists in the ability to break the truth down into metaphorical language and straightforward moral commandments, thus making it digestible for the masses, without however voiding it of its true content. Revelation, therefore, boils down to an act of translation, performed by a human being (for instance, al-Fārābī 2001: 4.55–56: 44–46; cf. also Avicenna 2005: 10.2.4–7: 365–67).

Ibn Ṭufayl was obviously well acquainted with al-Fārābī's bold position regarding the relation between natural and revealed religion, and he makes it the object of a critical evaluation. We already noticed that, having reached the culmination point of the theoretical sciences, i.e. natural theology, Ibn Ṭufayl has his hero Ḥayy depart from al-Fārābī's pattern. The practical consequences Ḥayy draws from his theoretical insights differ significantly, belonging to the devoutness of Sufism rather than political philosophy inspired by Plato. Nonetheless, al-Fārābī's theory of educating the people of the perfect city as devised by its ruler reappears on the scene (station vi): Ḥayy, predisposed due to his natural endowments and knowledge to be the Fārābian ruler, begins teaching the people of the neighboring island. Notably, his subject matter is their revealed truth as transmitted by their religion's founding prophet. Ḥayy's motivation to do so resulted from his consternation about the nature of their revelation (station v):

> First, why did this prophet rely for the most part on symbols to portray the divine world allowing mankind to fall into the grave error of conceiving the Truth corporeally ... ? Second, why did he confine himself to these particular rituals ... and allow ... men ... to busy themselves with inane pastimes ... ?
>
> (Ibn Ṭufayl 1972: 161.146)

In short, Ḥayy notices the same features of revealed religion al-Fārābī had ascribed to it, but has not yet understood their reason. Through his teaching experience, however, this changes, and Ḥayy acknowledges the prophet's wisdom in educating in this way. Now in unison with al-Fārābī, Ibn Ṭufayl accepts the necessity of different methods of teaching according to differing degrees of mental capacity. The method suited to the masses is revealed religion, just as al-Fārābī had said. At this stage, however, the story once again departs from the Fārābian pattern. Instead of remaining on Absāl's island, adjusting, and continuing the work of the religion's founder (cf. al-Fārābī 2001: 3.47: 40), Ḥayy decides to retreat and spend the rest of his life in ascetic isolation, which is to say, according to the rules he had given himself prior to his encounter with Absāl.

The Solitary Alternative: Ibn Bājja

With this move, Ibn Ṭufayl zooms in on another position and carefully integrates it into his balance: the position developed by Ibn Bājja (d. 1138) in his *The Governance of the Solitary*, which in itself is already a specific reply to al-Fārābī's practical philosophy (Geoffroy 2011; Harvey 1992). While al-Fārābī's political writings may be described as idealistic—developing a certain ideal, namely, of the virtuous city, without bothering whether an instantiation of this ideal actually exists—Ibn Bājja's *Governance* takes a realistic, but at the same time fairly pessimistic starting point. With reference to the features of a Fārābian virtuous city, he dryly remarks:

> All the ways of life that exist now or have existed before ... are mixtures ... , and for the most part we find them to be mixtures of the four (imperfect) ways of life.
>
> (Ibn Bājja 1963: 1.4: 127–28; cf. al-Fārābī 1985: 15.15–19: 253–259)

As a matter of fact, Ibn Bājja gives one to understand cities *are* imperfect. Therefore, his *Governance* is directed towards those few individuals who nonetheless strive for happiness, which can only be "the happiness of an isolated individual"; accordingly, the "only right governance (possible in these cities) is the governance of an isolated individual" (Ibn Bājja 1963: 1.4: 128) and this is precisely the subject matter of his treatise. In contrast to al-Fārābī, Ibn Bājja rejects the idea that each citizen with her actions attempts (or ought to attempt) to serve the city. While this is true for the virtuous city, he counters, in the imperfect city one's ultimate goal is the attainment of individual happiness. In this regard, Ibn Ṭufayl obviously sides with Ibn Bājja and likewise endorses the idea of achieving happiness independent of the political community (cf. Miskawayh 1968: 1: 25–6). For this is precisely the step his hero takes having failed to educate Absál's friends, much as his self-imposed obligations are duties related to the care of one's individual refinement, not the improvement of a community.

As an explanation of how to live one's life in order to reach the ultimate goal of happiness, Ibn Bájja suggests that

> [t]he ends that the solitary individual establishes for himself are three: his corporeal form, his particular spiritual form, or his universal spiritual form.
> (Ibn Bájja 1963: 12.1: 129)

This distinction reminds us of the three kinds of activities Ḥayy discovers for himself (station iv) and at the same time indicates that Ibn Bájja's subsequent explanation likely served as a model for Ibn Ṭufayl. While the "corporeal form" refers to those aspects related to a human's vegetative power (e.g. nourishment), the "particular spiritual form" concerns moral virtues which, according to the Aristotelian tradition, are located in the sensible faculty of the soul (cf. Miskawayh 1968: 1: 14–15). However, this stage is only preparatory for the highest level, the human "universal spiritual form"; this last corresponds to the human rational faculty and hence refers to intellectual acts, thus conjuring up the Fárábian motive of acquiring knowledge as the precondition for supreme happiness. As Ibn Bájja concludes:

> the philosopher [i.e. the one who strives for happiness] must perform numerous (particular) spiritual acts—but not for their own sake—and perform all the intellectual acts for their own sake: the corporeal acts enable him to exist as a human, the (particular) spiritual acts render him more noble, and the intellectual [i.e. universal spiritual] acts render him divine and virtuous.
> (Ibn Bájja 1963: 13.2: 131)

Even though Ibn Ṭufayl obviously adopts the general matrix of his predecessor, there are notable differences. The first concerns the second stage, i.e. the particular spiritual forms. While Ibn Bájja translates this into magnanimity and high-mindedness and thus remains strictly within an Aristotelian framework (cf. *Nicomachean Ethics*, particularly IV.4–10; cf. also Miskawayh's list of cardinal virtues, Miskawayh 1968: 1: 23–5), Ibn Ṭufayl cites Sufi practices, such as the famous circling. Second, on Ibn Bájja's account, the solitary "achieves the final end … when he intellects simple essential intellects," for then he "becomes one of these intellects" and can be called "divine" (Ibn Bájja 1963: 13.2: 132; on various conceptions of afterlife, cf. al-Fárábī 1985: 17: 259–77; Miskawayh 1968: 2: 61–4; Avicenna 2005: 9.7: 347–57). This, however, is the stage Ḥayy had already achieved *before* he understood that there would be yet a higher level, the sole to impart true happiness—that of awareness and experience. Hence, whereas Ibn Bájja, once again, remains faithful to the Aristotelian theory of cognition, Ibn Ṭufayl transcends this pattern and thus degrades it to a preliminary rank. True happiness is not only deferred to the afterlife—a view most of his Peripatetic colleagues would share (cf., e.g., Avicenna 2005: 10.3.5: 369)—but also limited to a mental state stretching *beyond* mere theoretical understanding.

While these are the chief philosophical positions discussed throughout the novel, there is one more party involved in Ibn Ṭufayl's choir of the various concepts of happiness and religion, and this is theology, the guardian of revealed religion. Hence, before we can conclude with a final evaluation of the relation between natural and revealed religion, a digression into the major theological schools evoked by Ibn Ṭufayl is in order.

From a Different Angle: Theological Perspectives

While we already referred to Sufism on a number of occasions, there are two further religious groups represented, embodied by Absāl and his friend Salāmān, respectively (station v). Their chief controversy concerned the question of how to study the revealed Scripture:

> Absāl, for his part, was the more deeply concerned with getting down to the heart of things, the more eager to discover spiritual values, and the more ready to attempt a more or less allegorical interpretation. Salāmān, on the other hand, was more anxious to preserve the literal and less prone to seek subtle intensions.
> (Ibn Ṭufayl 1972: 156.136–7)

Obviously, these two figures are designed to highlight the well-known chasm between the so-called traditionalists—principally, the Ḥanbalite and Ẓāhirite law schools—and those inner-Islamic trends open to the application of logical reasoning practiced by speculative theology (*kalām*)—chiefly, Ashʿarism, which was widely accepted in the Shāfiʿite and Mālikite law schools (Schacht 2011). However, the significance of the controversy as displayed in *Ḥayy ibn Yaqẓān* is not limited to the problem of whether to interpret Scripture literally or allegorically; it moreover impacts our topic in that both positions imply particular stances regarding the conceivability from a theological perspective of something like natural religion.

For a traditionalist in the wake of Ibn Ḥanbal and al-Ẓāhirī (d. 883), revelation is not just an important component, it is the unique way for human beings to learn about their creator and their moral obligations towards Him as well as one another. Consequently, extreme traditionalists would not only reject the claims of philosophers maintaining that they too had access to the truth, namely, by virtue of natural reason; they would (and did) criticize even those of their own colleagues who engaged in *kalām*, a futile enterprise to hard-core traditionalists. By contrast, for theologians adhering to the Sunni mainstream, Ashʿarism, the situation was much more complicated. To be sure, they would also insist that revelation was necessary; at the same time, however, they would admit that certain truths can be known through rational inquiry, for example, that God exists; that He is the first cause of everything; or that He is eternal, almighty, omniscient, etc. The practitioner of a natural religion, however, cannot discover the specifics of the revelation, such as the true nature of the afterlife (paradise and hell); the bodily resurrection; or the concrete moral obligations and ritual practices imposed on human beings by God (Frank 2007; re a much more complex position in Ashʿarite *kalām*, see al-Ghazālī, e.g. 1997: 3).

Consequently, any theologian in the classical period would reject al-Fārābī's theory according to which the only reliable path to cognition of the truth and all its practical implications is philosophy, while revelation is simply a watered-down translation of this truth into folksy metaphors, tales, and regulations by an especially gifted human being. Quite to the contrary, it is precisely these descriptions and commandments that God Himself chose to divulge and not some abstract universal truth which might be concealed in any other religion as well and discovered by unaided reason. From a theological angle, dogmatic positions are not just arbitrary and hence negotiable, nor are religious morality and rites. It is *exactly* these specifics which constitute the *raison d'être* of a particular religion with its unique instructions and decrees. As a consequence, the view of al-Fārābī and his followers is untenable for any religious scholar whatsoever. However, there is yet something else, more profound at stake which I believe is the crux of the relationship between natural and revealed religion in classical Islamic culture. As the comparison with Ashʿarism shows, there is an irreconcilable and ultimately insurmountable contradiction between the approach of natural religion and that of revealed religion, reaching as deep down as the level of absolute presuppositions (for this concept see Collingwood 1940: 3–77, particularly 34–48; also Collingwood 1939, particularly 29–43, 65–7): the very notion of God itself.

Philosophers since the age of al-Fārābī believed in a God who—like the Neoplatonic One or First Cause—brought everything into existence due to the necessity of His own essence. Through a process styled along the lines of emanation theory, His original efficient causality transitioned into secondary causality penetrating the entire universe and determining any being or event. On this basis, the philosophers could indeed agree with the theologians and maintain that God is almighty and the one true agent. However, this agreement is the result of a purely equivocal use of the terms "God," "almightiness," and "agency." According to the theologians, God does not just "overflow," He actively operates. "Power," to them, means the ability to intervene at any given time with any given event. "Creation" is the voluntary, actual bringing forth of something. Likewise is "revelation" the active promulgation of something by God and *not* the translation of some abstract scientific truth into metaphorical language by a particularly bright human being. Just like creation itself is described in the Qurʾān as God's addressing things, revelation is God's literally speaking to humanity, His prophet merely being His medium. With these striking conceptual contradictions, the two accounts—the philosophical and the theological—end up being utterly incommensurable.

Returning with this background one last time to Ibn Ṭufayl's novel, it is striking to note that Absāl is not taken aback by Ḥayy's account of his insights about God. Instead, he is happy to recognize the same truths as those enclosed in his religion, just as Ḥayy was glad to find the harmony of Absāl's beliefs with his own discoveries. While this at first glance might surprise, closer analysis shows that Ibn Ṭufayl obviously believed there is an avenue to bridge the gap between natural and revealed religion. According to him, this *via media* resides in Sufism (cf. Lewisohn et al. 2011; Daiber 2011). Even though they use different paths—Ḥayy his natural reason, Absāl his Scripture—both come to believe that ultimate happiness consists in the uninterrupted awareness of God, accompanied by the pinnacle of joy. Unanimously, they hold that this immediate experience of God is a mode of cognition which transcends the indirect knowledge provided by theoretical inquiry. The Sufi methods they apply in the quest for this goal serve the very same purpose: the purification of the soul and its preparation for the desired experience.

As such, Ibn Ṭufayl's Sufistic take on natural religion aspires to transcend and unify both philosophy and revealed religion. As attractive as this idea might appear on the surface, however, it is doomed to failure. From any theological perspective whatsoever, this kind of "universalized Sufism" has the same flaw as the majority of philosophical positions: it divests religion of its specifics. Hence, for a theologian, Ibn Ṭufayl falls into the same "universal truth trap" as al-Fārābī and his fellow philosophers. For a Fārābian Peripatetic, in turn, Ibn Ṭufayl's position is shaky due primarily to its contradiction with standard epistemology. In contrast with later periods of Islamic thought, classical philosophers by and large reject a mystical kind of knowledge through awareness as distinct from and superior to the theoretical knowledge of the sciences. Only with the rise of illuminationism and the explicit integration of an experiential moment (Marcotte 2008; Walbridge 2005) did this paradigm change—but that is another story.

Conclusion

On the basis of our study, the chief features of natural religion and its relation to revealed religion in classical Islamic culture can be summarized as follows: natural religion unswervingly centers on the idea that a human's ultimate goal consists in the attainment of happiness. Natural ethics, therefore, is the result of the insight of how to reach this happiness whose supreme form is considered to be accessible only in the afterlife. While the character of this practical component varies from philosopher to philosopher, all unanimously hold that a necessary condition to attain the final goal is the acquisition of knowledge according to the Aristotelian curriculum. However, since natural theology counts as one of the branches of philosophy, this has the remarkable effect that the practitioner of natural religion is expected to *know* rather than *believe* the "natural dogmas."

The content of the ethical requirements depends on what philosophers consider human perfection to consist in. Since al-Fārābī maintains that it presupposes the perfect city, political virtues star. Ibn Bājja, by contrast, rejects this idea and suggests that acquiring knowledge and, hence, *doing* science are imperative. Ibn Ṭufayl, though siding with Ibn Bājja and due to his specific take on what it means to know, supports specific dietary and ritual prescriptions. Notwithstanding these discrepancies, it is noteworthy that, contrary to revealed religion, ethical requirements play only an instrumental role in natural religion. Whereas all-embracing knowledge or sustained awareness *as such* brings about happiness, the formation of one's character or the performance of right actions only *prepare* one for this to occur—either by providing the necessary circumstances (virtuous city) or by preparing oneself (purification of the soul). An Islamic theologian, by contrast, would insist that the practice of religious rites and worship of God are more than just means to an end: even though they are a sine qua non with respect to the afterlife, they are *also* decreed for their own sake.

Two final points of discord concern the philosophers' disregard for the specific contents of revealed religion. From a philosophical perspective, the teachings of revelation are metaphors and symbols serving the sole function of leading the believer to the enclosed truth. Hence, they are—just like the aforementioned rites—nothing more than means to achieve a certain end and, as such, only as valuable as they are effective. The chief stumbling block in the relation of natural and revealed religion, however, is the equivocity of core concepts, such as God, agency, and volition. As discussed above, a philosopher can neither accept a theologian's position in this regard nor the other way round. It is primarily for these reasons that in classical Islamic culture natural and revealed religion—despite so many shared concerns, closely linked discussions, and joint methods—are ultimately irreconcilable.

Further Reading

Griffel, F. (2009) *Al-Ghazālī's Philosophical Theology*, Oxford & New York: Oxford University Press, particularly pp. 97–122.

Winter, T. (ed.) (2008) *The Cambridge Companion to Classical Islamic Theology*, Cambridge: Cambridge University Press (particularly Y. Michot, "Revelation," pp. 180–96; W. C. Chittick, "Worship," pp. 218–36).

Wisnovsky, R. (2010) "Philosophy and Theology: Islam," in R. Pasnau (ed.), *The Cambridge History of Medieval Philosophy*, vol. 2, Cambridge: Cambridge University Press, pp. 698–706.

References

Adamson, P. (2011) "Al-Kindi," in E. N. Zalta (ed.), *The Stanford Encyclopedia of Philosophy*, http://plato.stanford.edu/archives/spr2011/entries/al-kindi/

al-Fārābī (1968) *Enumeration of the Sciences: Iḥṣā' al-'ulūm*, 'U. Amīn (ed.), Cairo: Maktaba al-Anjlū al-miṣriyya.

——. (1985) *Al-Farabi on the Perfect State: Mabādi' Ārā Ahl al-Madīna al-Fāḍila*, R. Walzer (ed. and tr.), Oxford: Clarendon Press.

——. (2001) *The Attainment of Happiness*, M. Mahdi (tr.), *Philosophy of Plato and Aristotle, Part I*, Ithaca: Cornell University Press, pp. 13–50.

al-Ghazālī (1997) *The Incoherence of the Philosophers*, M. E. Marmura (tr.), Provo, UT: Brigham Young University Press.

al-Kindī (1974) *Al-Kindī's Metaphysics: A Translation of Ya'qūb ibn Isḥāq al-Kindī's Treatise "On First Philosophy" (fī al-Falsafah al-Ūlā)*, A. L. Ivry (tr.), Albany: State University of New York Press.

Avicenna (2005) *The Metaphysics of The Healing*, M. E. Marmura (tr.), Provo, UT: Brigham Young University Press.

Collingwood, R. G. (1939) *An Autobiography*, Oxford: Oxford University Press.

——. (1940) *An Essay on Metaphysics*, Oxford: The Clarendon Press.

Conrad, L. I. (1996) *The World of Ibn Ṭufayl: Interdisciplinary Perspectives on Ḥayy Ibn Yaqẓān*, Leiden: Brill.

Daiber, H. (2011) "Sa'āda," in P. Bearman et al. (eds.), *Encyclopaedia of Islam*: Brill Online, http://www.brillonline.nl/subscriber/entry?entry=islam_SIM-6361

Frank, R. M. (2007) "Elements in the Development of the Teaching of al-Ash'arī," in D. Gutas (ed.), *Early Islamic Theology: The Mu'tazilites and al-Ash'arī. Texts and Studies on the Development and History of Kalām*, vol. II, Aldershot—Burlington: Ashgate, Article VI (first in *Le Muséon* 104, Louvain, 1991), pp. 141–90.

Geoffroy, M. (2011) "Ibn Bājja, Abū Bakr ibn al-Sā'igh," in H. Lagerlund (ed.), *Encyclopedia of Medieval Philosophy: Philosophy Between 500 and 1500*, Dordrecht: Springer, pp. 483–6.

Germann, N. (2008) "Philosophizing Without Philosophy? On the Concept of Philosophy in Ibn Ṭufayl's *Ḥayy Ibn Yaqẓān*," *Recherches de Théologie et Philosophie Médiévales* 75: 97–127.

Harvey, S. (1992) "The Place of the Philosopher in the City According to Ibn Bájjah," in C. E. Butterworth (ed.), *Political Aspects of Islamic Philosophy: Essays in Honor of M. Mahdi*, Cambridge: Harvard University Press, pp. 199–233.

Ibn Bájja (1963) *The Governance of the Solitary*, in R. Lerner & M. Mahdi (eds.), *Medieval Political Philosophy: A Sourcebook*, Ithaca, New York: Cornell University Press, pp. 122–34.

Ibn Ṭufayl (1972) *Ibn Ṭufayl's Ḥayy Ibn Yaqẓān: A Philosophical Tale*, L. E. Goodman (tr.), New York: Twayne.

Kant, I. (1786) "Speculative Beginning of Human History," in *Perpetual Peace and Other Essays on Politics, History, and Morals*, T. Humphrey (tr.), Indianapolis: Hackett (1983), pp. 49–60.

Lewisohn, L. et al. (2011) "Taṣawwuf," in P. Bearman et al. (eds.), *Encyclopaedia of Islam*: Brill Online, http://www.brillonline.nl/subscriber/entry?entry=islam_COM-1188

Mahdi, M. (2001) *Alfarabi and the Foundation of Islamic Political Philosophy*, Chicago: Chicago University Press.

Mallet, D. (2011) "Ibn Ṭufayl, Abú Bakr (Abubacer)," in H. Lagerlund (ed.), *Encyclopedia of Medieval Philosophy: Philosophy Between 500 and 1500*, Dordrecht: Springer, pp. 531–3.

Marcotte, R. (2008) "Suhrawardi," in E. N. Zalta (ed.), *The Stanford Encyclopedia of Philosophy*, http://plato.stanford.edu/archives/fall2008/entries/suhrawardi/

Miskawayh (1968) *The Refinement of Character*, C. K. Zurayk (tr.), Beirut: The American University of Beirut.

Schacht, J. (2011) "Fiḳh," in P. Bearman et al. (eds.), *Encyclopaedia of Islam*: Brill Online, http://www.brillonline.nl/subscriber/entry?entry=islam_SIM-2365

Schaerer, P. O. (2004) "Einleitung," in *Der Philosoph als Autodidakt: ein philosophischer Inselroman*, P.O. Schaerer (tr.), Hamburg: Meiner, pp. xi–lxxxvi.

Vallat, P. (2011) "al-Fárábī, Abú Naṣr," in H. Lagerlund (ed.), *Encyclopedia of Medieval Philosophy: Philosophy Between 500 and 1500*, Dordrecht: Springer, pp. 345–52.

Walbridge, J. (2005) "Suhrawardī and Illuminationism," in P. Adamson & R. C. Taylor (eds.), *The Cambridge Companion to Arabic Philosophy*, Cambridge: Cambridge University Press, pp. 201–23.

29
LAW AND SOCIETY

Steven Harvey

Introduction

The medieval Islamic philosophers did not have access to Aristotle's *Politics*. Whether this was by design or not, it was the one of the few major works of the Aristotelian corpus that was not translated into Arabic. In its stead, al-Fārābī (d. 950), the inaugurator of the tradition of Aristotelian philosophy in Islam, and his followers turned to Plato's *Republic* and *Laws*—two works that were available in Arabic, or at least summaries of them. From Plato they learned *inter alia* about the place of the philosopher in the city, the distinction between the few and the many and the proper ways of educating each of them, the purpose of law, and the importance of religion for the well-being of society. They learned from Aristotle's *Nicomachean Ethics* that human beings are political by nature and that to achieve that end, a human being must live with others in society. They also learned from Aristotle that a human being's end is to attain happiness, and that the purpose of the city is to make possible the attainment of happiness for its citizens to the extent that is possible for each of them.

But why should learned Muslims need to turn to ancient pagan philosophers to learn about topics such as ethics, the nature and purpose of law, and the ultimate happiness of humans? Does not Islam provide sufficient guidance on these important matters? In actuality, the Islamic Aristotelians were intrigued and very interested in the political teachings of Plato and Aristotle. These teachings helped them to understand their own religion and to interpret their divine Law, the Qur'ān. Plato and Aristotle made clear to them how to distinguish true happiness from what was mistakenly believed to be happiness and pointed them in the direction of human perfection. As we will see, these philosophers did not read the ancients through the tinted glasses of Islamic theology. They were informed logicians and had mastered Aristotelian natural science and metaphysics. They sought to understand the relation between the teachings of religion and those of philosophy, and where possible to harmonize the two. For them, political philosophy—which, following Aristotle, comprised ethics (the governance of oneself), economics (the governance of one's household), and politics (the governance of the city)—had a special place in the enumeration of the sciences: it followed and thus could be studied only after one had first studied metaphysics. This implies, as Muhsin Mahdi has pointed out, that "the understanding of political science has to be based on the conclusions arrived at in metaphysics" (Lerner and Mahdi 1963: 98). The implications of this teaching for the Islamic philosophers will be discussed below.

Al-Fārābī, who is rightly regarded as the true founder of political philosophy in Islam, wrote many works on this discipline. While these writings have different aims and contain different teachings, there are certain fundamental points that are explicit or assumed in all of them. The most basic is that human beings are political by nature: it is their nature to live in society. Al-Fārābī spells this out in several of his writings. In his *Political Regime* (*al-Siyāsa al-madaniyya*) he writes that human beings belong to a species of animals that cannot accomplish their necessary affairs or achieve their best state, except through the association of many groups of them in a single place. The smallest such perfect association is that of the city (Lerner & Mahdi 1963: 32). In the *Principles of the Opinions of the Inhabitants of the Virtuous City* (*Mabādi' ārā' ahl al-madīna al-fāḍila*) he explains that a human being by nature needs many things for sustenance and to achieve highest perfection, and one cannot provide all these things by oneself. One needs others to supply each of the things that one cannot provide by oneself. Human beings thus by nature come together in associations in order to supply each other with what they need to subsist and to attain their end as human beings. Al-Fārābī makes clear that one's supreme good and highest perfection cannot be attained in an association smaller than a city (al-Fārābī 1985: 228–31).

This need for the city is further explained by Ibn Sīnā (d. 1037) at the end of his magnum opus, *The Healing* (*al-Shifā'*). Human beings differ from other animals in that they cannot live a proper life when isolated as a single individual, managing one's own affairs. Human beings need each other so they can be provided with their basic needs. Ibn Sīnā explains that one provides another with vegetables, and the other bakes bread for the other; one sews for the other, and the other provides that one with the sewing needles. Through this division of labor, people coming together in an association can provide each other with all they need. For this reason, human beings must necessarily come together in associations and preferably, if they can, in cities. Their very existence and survival depends on it. But these mutual relations and transactions must have laws and justice. There is thus a need also for a giver of law and a dispenser of justice, for people cannot decide for themselves what is just and fair in their dealings with others because they will invariably consider their own interests and disagreements will occur (Avicenna 2005: 364–5).

This human need for others is also emphasized by Ibn Rushd (d. 1198) at the beginning of his commentary on Plato's *Republic*, and he too cites verbatim Aristotle's dictum that human beings are political by nature. He explains that human beings must join together in an association, not only to attain the theoretical and moral virtues needed for human perfection, which cannot be acquired without the help of others, but even for their very subsistence. One human being alone cannot secure all basic needs. In this connection Ibn Rushd emphasizes the advantages of the division of labor. One who chooses an art in youth and constantly practices it for a long time will become much better at it than if it were simply one of many things that a person does. In this way, division of labor is not only necessary, but works out the best. Ibn Rushd explains that this is the very justice that Plato uncovers in the *Republic*. It is nothing more than each individual in the city doing the work that is that individual's by nature in the best way that one possibly can (Averroes 1974: 5–7).

The Place of Religion in the City

From these and similar accounts, we can see that the leading Islamic philosophers were quite familiar with fundamental political teachings of Plato and Aristotle, and appreciated the need of human beings to join together and live in cities. Society is crucial for our subsistence, for living the good life, and for the attainment of perfection. But where does religion come in? Is it really needed? These questions concerning the appearance of religion and its place in the city are addressed by Al-Fārābī directly in one of his most philosophic works, the *Book of Letters* (*Kitāb al-ḥurūf*). The central section of this book is devoted to the origin and development of language—how people begin to speak and express themselves from the first sounds, letters, and words to simple utterances and sentences. He then discusses the emergence of the syllogistic arts from crude syllogisms to the framing of formal demonstrative proofs. These chapters on the origin of language (Chapters 20–23) are sandwiched between chapters on religion and philosophy that treat the origin of religion and its relation to philosophy (Chapters 19 and 24). The second sentence of Chapter 19 reads: "If religion is assumed to be human, then it follows philosophy in time" (al-Fārābī 1969b: 131). For al-Fārābī, the purpose of religion is to teach the multitude the theoretical and practical things discovered in philosophy in such ways that it becomes easy for them to understand them, either through persuasion or imagining or both together, for there is no other way to teach the multitude these things apart from persuasion and the use of images. Al-Fārābī in his *Attainment of Happiness* (*Taḥṣīl al-sa'āda*) similarly writes that philosophy is prior to religion in time, that religion is an imitation of philosophy, and that "in everything of which philosophy gives an account based on intellectual perception, religion gives an account based on imagination" (al-Fārābī 1969: 44–5). In Chapter 24 of the *Book of Letters*, the last chapter of this section, al-Fārābī continues the discussion of religion and philosophy, and distinguishes the correct religion of the utmost excellence from a corrupt religion. Correct religion comes after and depends upon the certainty provided by philosophy that is based upon demonstrative proofs; corrupt religion comes after and is dependent upon false opinions and rhetorical and sophistical arguments, that is, philosophy based on opinion, which is thought to be philosophy, but in truth is not. He also discusses the differences and similitudes between the truths of philosophy and the truth of religion, and the harm that religion can cause to philosophy and its adherents.

Al-Fārābī defines religion in his *Book of Religion* (*Kitāb al-milla*) as "opinions and actions, determined and restricted with stipulations and prescribed for a community by their first ruler" (al-Fārābī 2001: 93). If this first ruler has learned the truths through demonstration and is virtuous, the goal will be to obtain true happiness for the ruler and for those under that rule. The religion the ruler will establish will be a "virtuous religion." The problem with this philosophic religion, even the virtuous one that makes possible the happiness of its believers, is that it is not divine religion in the sense that Muslims and Jews, for example, generally understand the term. Al-Fārābī tries to avoid this problem here by speaking of the *sharī'a* and writing that the first ruler determines the opinions and actions by means of divine revelation (*al-waḥy min allāh*) (al-Fārābī 2001: 94–6). The nature of this divine revelation is intentionally, it seems, not spelled out. Al-Fārābī begins to discuss the need for this religion in his *Book of Letters* as a necessary consequent of the perfection of philosophy. At some point, after human beings have developed language and logic and studied the sciences in their proper order, theoretical and general practical philosophy will be perfected. At that point, philosophy becomes something that ought to be studied and learned, but cannot be further advanced, as it has already been perfected. The goal of the philosophers becomes to teach the demonstrated truths of philosophy to the few via demonstration, and to the many via rhetorical and other non-demonstrative methods. The first ruler does this by (1) setting down laws and (2) teaching the multitude the theoretical objects (or images of them) that the ruler has learned through demonstration and the practical objects discovered through practical wisdom. Al-Fārābī concludes that if laws dealing with these theoretical and practical objects are set down properly and through the appropriate methods, then a "religion will come about through which the multitude is taught, its character is formed, and it is made to do everything with which to gain happiness" (al-Fārābī 1969b: 152).

In this way, philosophic religion arises. Yet until the last lines of al-Fārābī's account, it was not at all apparent that he was describing the emergence of religion. Rather it seemed that he was giving an account of something like the beginnings of a virtuous city, whose lawgiver is a true philosopher. Interestingly, the thirteenth-century Hebrew popularizer and paraphraser of al-Fārābī, Shem-Ṭov ibn Falaquera, reproduces the first part of his discussion, but leaves out precisely the lines that follow that speak of the emergence of religion. In general, Falaquera omits al-Fārābī's statements on the relation between philosophy and religion. It seems as if Falaquera wanted no part of philosophic religion, but was very interested in al-Fārābī's account of how the philosopher comes to be a lawgiver. This impression is borne out by Falaquera's slightly abridged translation of the section that immediately follows the lines just cited. Here Falaquera translates the term *milla* (religion) with *nimmus* (*nomos* or human law) each of the six times it appears in this section (Falaquera 1902: 30–1). Thus, instead of al-Fārābī's discussion of philosophic religious law, Falaquera gives us a discussion of philosophic civil law. In this way Falaquera turns al-Fārābī's account of the origin of philosophic religion into a discussion of the origin of perhaps the virtuous city.

For al-Fārābī then, while society is indeed necessary for our subsistence, for living the good life, and for the attainment of perfection, these goals are best served through a religious society, whose laws and beliefs are established by a philosopher lawgiver. This notion of the importance of religion for the well-being of society is found as well in al-Fārābī's *Summary of the Laws*, and likely derives for him from Plato's *Laws*, even though al-Fārābī, by his own account, did not have *Laws* X. A good illustration of this is al-Fārābī's summary of *Laws* VIII and its discussion of festivals. This discussion forces us to reflect on the centrality of the festivals for the well-being of the city and thus explains why they ought to be considered so carefully by the legislator.

Al-Fārābī states that Plato subtly revealed a "wonderful advantage of festivals other than the advantage alluded to in the beginning of the book, namely, exalting the gods and restoring their renown. For exalting and esteeming the gods exalts the traditions and the laws" (al-Fārābī 1998: 147). Al-Fārābī thus ties the discussion of festivals in Book VIII to the earlier discussion in Book II (653d), where the festivals' purpose is seen as providing needed rest from the labors of life, and also to an earlier one in Book I (637b–e), wherein, according to al-Fārābī's account, the rules concerning festivals in earlier laws are mentioned and judged "extremely right" in the way they provide an outlet for the pleasures to which all human beings are naturally inclined, and render them divine (al-Fārābī 1998: 127; Lerner & Mahdi 1963: 88). Later he explains that had the lawgiver prohibited pleasures completely, his law would not have been followed as human beings are naturally inclined to pleasures. Instead he wisely appointed the festivals as times during which human beings could legally pursue certain pleasures (al-Fārābī 1998: 130; Lerner & Mahdi 1963: 91). Thus, for al-Fārābī, Plato in the early books of the *Laws* assigns to the festivals important political functions, but the one in Book VIII, not previously mentioned, is a wonderful one, namely that the festivals exalt the gods. It is wonderful because, as mentioned, "exalting and esteeming the gods exalts the traditions and the laws." Those who believe and exalt the gods are more likely to respect and obey the laws. In other words, the well-being of the city may be achieved through strengthening the people's belief in the gods. While al-Fārābī underscores the political importance of proper belief in the gods, he apparently saw no need as commentator on Plato's *Laws* to Islamize the text by speaking of a single God instead of gods.

The importance of religious legislation for the good of the city is presented in a monotheistic context in Ibn Sīnā's account of political science at the very end of his *Healing*. Significantly, the subjects of this last treatise of the *Healing* include not only rulers, succession of rulers, legislators, laws, and the virtuous city, as one would expect, but also topics such as prophecy and prophets, divine law, prayer, and the afterlife. This is not surprising, for according to Ibn Sīnā's classification of the sciences, political science is the science that deals with prophecy and divine law (Lerner & Mahdi 1963: 97). This treatise is thus most useful for discerning Ibn Sīnā's opinions on the place of religion within the city. As stated above, for Ibn Sīnā, human beings' relations with one another require laws and thus a lawgiver. In Ibn Sīnā's account, this lawgiver is a divinely appointed prophet, who lays down the laws "by permission of God, the Exalted, by His command, inspiration, and the *descent of His Holy Spirit* (Qur'ān 16:102) on him." Ibn Sīnā does not explicitly say why the lawgiver must be a prophet, but the need for the religious underpinnings of the law emerges from his discussion. At the outset the prophet-lawgiver must make known that God exists, that He is one, omnipotent, all-knowing, and that an afterworld of bliss awaits those who obey Him and an afterworld of misery for those who do not. This is important to persuade the many to follow the Law established by the prophet through divine inspiration. Ibn Sīnā warns that one should not go into details regarding basic truths, for example, that God is incorporeal and in what consists the nature of his unity, for that would only confuse the many with things they cannot grasp and this could lead to false beliefs which in turn could stand in the way of the performance of their political duties (Avicenna 2005: 365–6).

Ibn Sīnā also stresses that the prophet-lawgiver must consider how the laws may be preserved and obeyed from generation to generation, and this requires that human beings must continue to have knowledge of God and the resurrection. This is best achieved through the repetition at specified times of certain acts, such as prayer and fasting, that bring God and the afterlife to mind. Other acts such as holy war (*jihād*) and pilgrimage (*ḥajj*) help strengthen and spread the Law. But it is the repeated worship of God with proper postures and frame of mind that will best bring about remembrance of God and the afterlife, turn souls away from their bodies, and purify them. Ibn Sīnā adds that "in this way, the adherence to the statutes and the laws will continue" (Avicenna 2005: 367–9). In short, belief in God and the afterlife is good for the city, for it ensures that the laws put forth by the lawgiver will be followed. In his *Treatise on the Quiddity of Prayer*, Ibn Sīnā refers to this worship as the outward prayer or normative prayer (*al-ṣalāt*), and distinguishes it from the inward or true prayer, which is not connected with the body, but with the rational soul. He defines this intellectual worship as "the [intellectual] viewing [that is, contemplation] of the Truth [that is, God] with a pure heart and a soul freed and purified of desires." He explains:

> When the lawgiver saw that the intellect enjoins the true pure prayer upon the rational soul—and it is the cognition and knowledge of God the Exalted, he prescribed prayer for the body as a sign [of this true] prayer. … The lawgiver [Muḥammad] knew that all men do not ascend the ranks of the intellect and hence need direction and ceremonial bodily training to counter their natural inclinations.
>
> (Avicenna 1894: 36–7, 1951: 56–7)

In other words, the true or inward prayer is pure contemplation, and has nothing to do with speech or bodily postures. It is the prayer of the few. Normative or outward prayer is for the multitude, who are incapable of true prayer. The lawgiver enjoins it as a kind of training of character to combat natural human inclinations and passions. In short, for Ibn Sīnā, the lawgiver prescribes normative or outward prayer for political purposes: to bring about and preserve a law-abiding society that aims at the well-being of all its inhabitants. It is telling that Ibn Sīnā saw no need to even mention the inward or true prayer in his political writings, particularly in light of his teaching that one ought not to reveal that one has knowledge one is hiding from the multitude (Avicenna 2005: 366).

The importance of religious belief for the well-being of society is clearly articulated by Ibn Rushd, the last of the great Islamic Aristotelians, in his brief response in the *Incoherence of the Incoherence* (*Tahāfut al-tahāfut*) to al-Ghazālī's charge that the Islamic philosophers deny resurrection. His defense is quite simply that no true philosopher would deny this principle, but his explanation why this is so is one of the most remarkable passages in the entire Averroean corpus. He writes:

> Philosophers in particular, as is only natural, regard this doctrine as most important and believe in it most, and the reason is that it is conducive to an order amongst men on which man's being, as man, depends and through which he can attain the greatest happiness proper to him, for it is a necessity for the existence of the moral and speculative virtues and of the practical sciences in man. … In short, the philosophers believe that religious laws are necessary political arts, the principles of which are taken from natural reason and inspiration, especially in what is common to all religions. … The philosophers further hold that one must not object (…) to any of the general religious principles … for instance, bliss in the beyond and its possibility; for

> all religions agree in the acceptance of another existence after death, although they differ in the description of this existence. ... It belongs to the necessary excellence of a man of learning that he should not despise the doctrines in which he has been brought up ... and that if he expresses a doubt concerning the religious principles in which he has been brought up ... he merits more than anyone else that the term unbeliever be applied to him, and he is liable to the penalty for unbelief.
>
> (Averroes 1954: 359–61)

No philosopher then would deny the resurrection of the dead because they realize the central importance of this teaching for the political well-being of the city. Of course, not to deny the doctrine and to believe in its political importance is not necessarily the same as actually believing in its details.

Laws Conducive to the Well-Being of the City

The Islamic philosophers also discussed other sorts of laws that are needed in the city. There are, for example, interesting well-thought-out discussions of such laws in al-Fārābī's *Summary of Plato's Laws* and Ibn Rushd's *Commentary on the Republic*.

Ibn Sīnā also discusses certain civil laws that are needed, in the continuation of the section of the *Healing* discussed above. The discussion is not at all intended to be comprehensive, but highlights laws conducive to the well-being of the city. For example, idleness and unemployment must be prohibited, and every one—unless he is ill or physically incapable—must work for a livelihood. This directive explicitly excludes well-known professions such as gambling, usury, and thievery. The city must have its own funds for the "exigencies of the common good," for paying its leaders, and supporting those who are not physically capable of working. These funds may come from taxation, punishment fines, and war booty. Also marriage must be strongly encouraged for it is the "pillar on which the city stands," divorce discouraged, and fornication and sodomy prohibited. Marriage is a fundamental concern of society because *inter alia* it leads to the propagation of the species, the proper upbringing of children, the orderly transfer of inheritances, and the emergence of love, which is a major factor in the well-being of society. For Ibn Sīnā, this true love comes about only after long association. The proper upbringing of children should also be legislated by the lawgiver, along with honor for one's parents.

Ibn Sīnā is also greatly concerned with the character traits of the ruler, and the laws needed to bring about a smooth transfer of power and authority to a fitting successor and to prevent wrongful usurpation of office. As regards transactions among human beings, the lawgiver must prescribe laws that prevent treachery and injustice in such dealings. Indeed he should legislate that people should help protect each other's lives and properties to the extent that in so doing they do not harm their own. It may be observed that Ibn Sīnā requires of the lawgiver to promulgate other laws that do not simply establish justice, order, and security in the city, but also build the moral character of its citizens. This is important not only for the perfection of the individual person, but also for the success and survival of the city.

Nonetheless, despite these civil laws and despite the religious foundation of the city, suitable punishments must be imposed to prevent disobedience to the laws. Ibn Sīnā explains "for not everyone is restrained from violating the law because of what he fears of the afterlife" (Avicenna 2005: 370–8).

The Place of the Philosopher in the City and the Virtuous Regime

It was stated above that the Islamic Aristotelians learned from Plato about the place of the philosopher in the city. Al-Fārābī, as has been shown, explicitly identified the prophet-lawgiver with the philosopher. This identification of the prophet-lawgiver with the philosopher seems implied in the discussion above in Ibn Sīnā's *Healing*, as well as in the writings of other Islamic Aristotelians. In the *Attainment of Happiness*, al-Fārābī explained that "Philosopher, Supreme Ruler, Prince, Legislator, and Imam" signify a single idea (al-Fārābī 1969: 58, 47). Ibn Rushd followed him in this in the *Commentary on the Republic* (Averroes 1974: 72). For them, the first ruler and lawgiver ought to be a philosopher, and—following Plato—so ought the subsequent rulers.

For the Islamic philosophers, there are many kinds of regimes, but only a single virtuous regime. Al-Fārābī explains that these various kinds of regimes reflect the various notions of highest happiness that people have, e.g. that happiness derives from wealth or sensual pleasure or honor or domination. The supreme ruler without qualification is the philosopher, the one who has mastered the sciences and every kind of knowledge, and can distinguish true happiness from what is commonly thought or imagined to be happiness. Because he knows what true happiness is, he is the one who must govern the inhabitants of the virtuous city and lead each of them to that true happiness and knowledge of truth that each is capable of attaining (Lerner & Mahdi 1963: 35–43). Now, Ibn Bājja (d. 1138) was the first major proponent of the school of Islamic Aristotelianism in the West, and he too knew well and followed the political teachings of Plato. But while he valued the virtuous regime as much as al-Fārābī, he believed it could not be realized in his time or in the foreseeable future. Any attempt on the part of the philosopher to do so was destined to be futile. Ibn Bājja thus wrote his book the *Governance of the Solitary* (*Tadbīr al-mutawaḥḥid*) to provide guidance for the solitary individual living in an inevitably imperfect city, and to explain that true happiness, which is intellectual, can be achieved by him even in such a city if he devotes himself to developing his intellect, while dealing with the multitude only to the extent necessary, that is, for indispensable matters such as purchasing food and clothing.

It should be noted that Ibn Bājja did not encourage the solitary individual seeking intellectual happiness to abandon completely the inevitably imperfect society, but to live within it, for he too recognized that a human being is a political animal and is better off even in an unvirtuous city than fending for oneself (Harvey 1992: 224–33). Ibn Rushd, who certainly appreciated the philosopher's active participation in the city, agreed with Ibn Bājja that when the "true philosopher" grows up in such imperfect cities, he should turn to isolation and live the life of the solitary (Averroes 1974: 78). The philosopher need not concern himself with reforming the opinions of the multitude and trying to bring about the virtuous regime because of the grave dangers inherent in trying to bring about such a change and the very minute chances of success.

Ibn Ṭufayl (d. 1185) lived in al-Andalus between Ibn Bājja and Ibn Rushd and was part of the same philosophic tradition. His philosophic novella, *Ḥayy ibn Yaqẓān*, tells the story of Ḥayy, an autodidact on a deserted paradise island, who comes to learn all things or almost all things through the use of reason alone. Through observation, experimentation, and logical deduction he uncovers the natural sciences and metaphysics, but does not know political science, for there are no other people on the island on which he has spent his entire life. One day, a man arrives on the island from an island close by in search of solitude so he can devote his life to the contemplation and worship of God. This man is a follower of the religion of his island, a religion that imitates "all the true beings through parables that present images of those things." After he teaches Ḥayy language, he tells him the details of his religion, a religion reminiscent of Islam. Ḥayy at once understands that the founder of this religion was "truthful in his description ... and a messenger from God," for the beliefs represent the truths he has come to know on his own. What he cannot understand is why the founder used parables and images of the truth and thereby concealed the true essence of things, e.g. that God is incorporeal. Ḥayy persuades the man to return with him to his island where he speaks with the best and most intelligent of its inhabitants. He tries to uncover for them the meaning of the parables and the truths as they are, but fails completely and comes to learn that the best hope for these people is to continue to believe in the parables and images of the truth set forth by the founder of the religion. Ḥayy and his friend return to the paradise island, where they spend the rest of their lives in the contemplation and worship of God. On the surface it may seem that Ibn Ṭufayl, following Ibn Bājja, argued for the life of the solitary, but they are really describing different situations. Ibn Bājja advises the solitary existence within the imperfect city. Human beings are political animals and must live with other people in the city for meeting basic needs. By limiting his contact with the ignorant multitude to necessary transactions, the philosopher can pursue intellectual happiness alone. Ibn Ṭufayl describes a different kind of society, where a wise prophet lawgiver prescribed beliefs and actions that allow human beings to live together securely and that present worthy images of God and other fundaments of religion that make possible the happiness for which each person is capable. This lawgiver is similar to Ibn Sīnā's and, indeed, both thinkers may be describing Islam or a religion close to it. Ḥayy learns that the lawgiver was wise not to unveil the pure truth, and that it would be a dangerous mistake to make known—as Ḥayy tried unsuccessfully to do—anything more about the truths than what the lawgiver had written. Yet Ḥayy and his new friend see no reason to stay in the city, whether as active participants or as solitary inhabitants, and choose instead to return to Ḥayy's island to live their lives outside of society in contemplative bliss (Lerner & Mahdi 1963: 153–62). But how literally ought one to take Ibn Ṭufayl's philosophic tale? And how seriously ought one to take the apolitical teachings of Ibn Bājja and Ibn Ṭufayl regarding the solitary life? After all, *Ḥayy ibn Yaqẓān* with its wondrous island is just a fantasy, and both Ibn Bājja and Ibn Ṭufayl, like Ibn Rushd and other philosophers, chose to live their lives as active participants in the city, connected in different ways to its ruler.

Conclusion

The Islamic philosophers of al-Fārābī's school of Aristotelian philosophy and Plato's political philosophy were all interested in society and the different kinds of cities. The focal subject of politics for these philosophers was happiness, no doubt influenced by Aristotle's discussions of *eudaimonía* in the first and last books of the *Nicomachean Ethics*. The lawgiver and the ruler must each know what true happiness is and how to distinguish it from imagined or false happiness, for their task is to make possible the highest happiness for each of the inhabitants of the city in accordance with the inhabitant's capacities. As Muslims and philosophers living under Islamic rule, the Islamic philosophers investigated how revealed religions—Islam, in particular—and thus the religious state differed from and improved upon the best models of the city described by the Greek philosophers. Their discussions were far from parochial and thoroughly philosophic. Why must people come together in societies? What is the purpose of the city? What kinds of laws are needed to achieve these goals? Following Plato they fully appreciated the role of religion in the city. And like Plato, they gave special consideration to the role of the philosopher in the city and the philosopher's often precarious position therein. Significantly, these inquiries did not take place and could not be studied until one had first learned the natural and divine sciences. We are led to believe that one cannot come to understand properly man's governance of the city until one first understands God's governance of the world. The philosopher, after mastering the sciences, must return to the cave, as it were, to help his fellow man in the noblest act of *imitatio dei*.

Further Reading

Butterworth, C. E. (1992) *The Political Aspects of Islamic Philosophy*, Cambridge: Harvard University Press.

Galston, M. (1990) *Politics and Excellence: The Political Philosophy of Alfarabi*, Princeton: Princeton University Press.

Harvey, S. (2002) "Falaquera's Alfarabi: An Example of the Judaization of the Islamic *Falāsifah*," *Trumah: Zeitschrift der Hochschule für Jüdische Studien Heidelberg* 12: 97–112.

Mahdi, M. S. (2001) *Alfarabi and the Foundation of Islamic Political Philosophy*, Chicago: University of Chicago Press.

References

al-Fārābī (1969) *Alfarabi's Philosophy of Plato and Aristotle*, M. Mahdi (tr.), Ithaca, New York: Cornell University Press.

——. (1969b) *Kitāb al-ḥurūf*, M. Mahdi (ed.), Beirut: Dar el-Mashreq.

——. (1985) *Alfarabi on the Perfect State*, R. Walzer (ed. and tr.), Oxford: Clarendon Press.

——. (1998) "Le sommaire du livre des 'Lois' de Platon," T-A. Druart (ed.), *Bulletin d'études orientales* 50: 109–55.

——. (2001) *Alfarabi, The Political Writings: "Selected Aphorisms" and Other Texts*, C. E. Butterworth (tr.), Ithaca, New York: Cornell University Press.

Averroes (1954) *Tahāfut al-tahāfut (The Incoherence of the Incoherence)*, S. Van den Bergh (tr.), London: Luzac.
——. (1974) *Averroes on Plato's* Republic, R. Lerner (tr.), Ithaca, New York: Cornell University Press.
Avicenna (1894) *Traités mystiques d'Avicenne*, M. A. F. Mehren (ed.), Leiden: Brill.
——. (1951) *Avicenna on Theology*, A. J. Arberry (tr.), London: J. Murray.
——. (2005) *The Metaphysics of the Healing*, M. E. Marmura (tr.), Provo, UT: Brigham Young University Press.
Falaquera (1902) *Reshit Ḥokhmah*, M. David (ed.), Berlin: M. Poppelauer.
Harvey, S. (1992) "The Place of the Philosopher in the City according to Ibn Bājjah," in C. E. Butterworth (ed.), *The Political Aspects of Islamic Philosophy*, Cambridge: Harvard University Press, pp. 199–233.
Lerner, R. & Mahdi, M. (eds.) (1963) *Medieval Political Philosophy: A Sourcebook*, Glencoe, IL: The Free Press.

30
THE ETHICAL TREATMENT OF ANIMALS

Peter Adamson

Introduction

There are a number of philosophical themes—for instance, divine attributes, theories of intellect, or the eternity of the world—that leap to mind in connection with philosophy in the Islamic world. The ethical treatment of animals is not one of them. Indeed one might suppose that this is a distinctively contemporary topic, that we have only recently started to include the welfare of non-human animals within the scope of our moral, and philosophical, concern. In this chapter, though, I hope to show that Muslim philosophers of the classical era had interesting things to say about how we should treat animals. (For simplicity I use the word "animals" throughout to refer to non-human animals.) In fact, antique philosophers had already explored the issue at length (Sorabji 1993; Osborne 2007). Epicureans and Stoics had given arguments to show why it is not unjust to kill and eat animals, arguments that were rebutted by Porphyry. In *On Abstinence from Animal Food* (Clark 2000), Porphyry followed the early Imperial Platonist Plutarch in pointing to the fact that animals display a capacity for reasoning and language. This undercut Stoic arguments that justified the killing of animals on the grounds of their irrationality.

On the other hand, the relevant works of Porphyry and Plutarch were not translated into Arabic (on Porphyry in Arabic see Adamson 2007). Positive attitudes towards animal welfare in Arabic philosophical literature were not, it would seem, derived from the ancient philosophical tradition. Somewhat more important, as we will see, was the ancient *medical* tradition. But the really crucial impetus came from the Qur'ān and the teachings of the Prophet collected as *ḥadīth* (Benkheira 2005; Foltz 2006). For instance, we find in the Qur'ān, "no creature is there crawling on the earth, no bird flying with its wings, but they are nations like unto yourselves. We have neglected nothing in the Book; then to their Lord they shall be mustered" (Qur'ān 6:38). This suggests both that God exercises providence over animals and that He will give them some kind of dispensation in the hereafter, an idea developed by Mu'tazilite theologians (Heemskerk 2000). The *ḥadīth* meanwhile record that Muḥammad showed benevolence to animals, for instance by chastizing his wife 'Ā'isha for overburdening a camel, criticizing blood sports, and even saying that charity towards animals as well as humans will be rewarded by God (Foltz 2006: 19–20). A further spur to reflection on the status of animals was the literary tradition. Philosophers drew on animal fables like *Kalila and Dimna*, an Indian work translated into Arabic in the second/eighth century.

An outstanding early example of the theme in Arabic literature is the enormous *Book of Animals* by al-Jāḥiẓ, the greatest practicioner of Arabic belles-lettres (*adab*) in the third/ninth century, at the high-water mark of the ʿAbbāsid caliphate. Al-Jāḥiẓ already serves to unify the strands of thinking about animals just identified: he was not only a refined author, but also steeped in Muʿtazilite *kalām* and reasonably well informed about Hellenic philosophical ideas. Here though we will be looking at three more philosophical discussions of animals. First we will discuss the doctor and controversialist Abū Bakr al-Rāzī (d. 313/925). He argues explicitly that we have an ethical obligation to treat animals well. Next we will turn our attention to Ikhwān al-Ṣafāʾ ("the Brethren of Purity") and their most famous epistle, in which they imagine a debate between humankind and the animals, regarding the question of whether animals should continue to be enslaved and oppressed by humans. Finally, we will look at *Ḥayy ibn Yaqẓān* by Ibn Ṭufayl (d. 581/1185–1186), which features a self-taught philosopher who adopts a remarkably animal-friendly lifestyle.

These three texts will reveal that attitudes towards the treatment of animals were intimately related with conceptions of divine providence. In this the Islamic sources differ from not only the modern debate, but also the ancient tradition. In antiquity, the key question was whether or not animals share rationality with humans. The Stoics said that because animals are irrational they have no moral standing, being insufficiently akin (*oikeion*) to humans. Among our three authors, by contrast, it is al-Rāzī and Ibn Ṭufayl who recommend treating animals well, despite believing that animals are inferior to humans. Their humane attitude is not based on any kinship or parity between animalkind and humankind. The Ikhwān, meanwhile, do explore the possibility that animals are equal to (or even superior to) humans. Yet they ultimately reach a less animal-friendly conclusion than al-Rāzī and Ibn Ṭufayl. As we will see, however, they likewise consider divine providence pivotal in discerning the appropriate way to treat animals.

Al-Rāzī

I have mentioned that the ancient medical tradition gave readers in the Islamic world good reason to see commonalities between animals and humans. This is primarily because of anatomy. Although human dissection (and possibly vivisection) was performed in Hellenistic Alexandria, Galen had demonstrated that the brain, and not the heart, is the seat of the "ruling faculty" (*hegemonikon*) by dissecting animals such as pigs. (He remarks that they are a good choice because they squeal loudly, which makes the effect more impressive when one cuts the nerve to their vocal cords.) The tacit assumption is that what is true of pigs should apply to humans also. Following suit, al-Rāzī too experimented with animals, for instance by testing the effects of mercury on an ape (Pormann 2008). In works like his *Medical Introduction* (al-Rāzī

1979), he applies points about anatomy and organic functions to animals and humans jointly. The same applies to what al-Rāzī calls "psychological" (*nafsānī*) powers. In the Islamic tradition the most famous example along these lines appears in Ibn Sīnā's discussion of the estimative faculty (*wahm*). This power, shared by both higher animals and humans, is illustrated by Ibn Sīnā with the example of a sheep perceiving hostility in a wolf. There is a link here to Galenic anatomy, since Ibn Sīnā locates this and other "internal senses" in ventricles of the brain.

Al-Rāzī anticipates Ibn Sīnā by ascribing most psychological functions to both animals and humans. Starting at the bottom we have the "natural" power seated in the liver, which handles nutrition (to be specific, the liver has the function of turning food into blood). The "animal" (*ḥayawānī*) powers are the vital functions seated in the heart, which is the source of life and provides vital *pneuma* for the rest of the body. The brain, which contains a finer type of *pneuma*, is the instrument for the three so-called "governing" or "psychological" functions—imagination (*takhayyul*), thought (*fikra*), memory (*dhikr*)—and also voluntary motion and sensation. Although the vital functions in the heart are specifically designated as "animal" powers, it is clear that many if not all animals will have some of the brain-centered functions, such as sensation and voluntary motion. Although one might wonder about the "governing" functions, we know that al-Rāzī ascribed even "thought" (*fikra* or *fikr*, also called *rawiyya*) to animals. This emerges from a fascinating passage in his catalogue of errors found in Galen, *Doubts About Galen* (al-Rāzī 1993: 26–7). He castigates Galen for denying that animals are rational, giving the evocative counter-example of a mouse that gets oil out of a bottle by dipping its tail into the bottle and then licking it.

Nonetheless, it would seem (Adamson 2012, against Druart 1996) that al-Rāzī draws a sharp distinction between animals and humans, on the basis that humans possess "reason" (*nuṭq*) and above all "intellect" (*ʿaql*). Indeed, the beginning of his ethical treatise *The Spiritual Medicine* identifies intellect as the distinctive feature of mankind. "Through it," he says, "we are better than the irrational animal (*al-ḥayawān ghayr al-nāṭiq*), so that we rule and control them, subjecting them to us and directing them in ways conducive to our advantage as well as theirs" (al-Rāzī 1939: 18). He would have at least two reasons for insisting on the primacy of intellect and reason. First, already within the bodily life, intellect and reason enable humans to resist their drives and desires, so as to refrain from food, drink or sex when these are judged to be harmful in the longer run (al-Rāzī 1939: 22). Second, within his notorious cosmological theory, al-Rāzī claims that the physical universe is the product of a foolish involvement of soul with matter. It is only through the divine gift of intellect that the soul is able to free itself to "live in its own world" using reason (al-Rāzī 1939: 30). When he remarks that animal souls cannot free themselves from matter (al-Rāzī 1939: 105), his rationale must be that animals are incapable of reason and intellect.

Thus, despite the features that animals share with humans, al-Rāzī seems to be firmly committed to the idea that humans are superior to animals—at least when the humans in question are virtuous. I add this caveat because he says that some humans act in a "bestial" fashion, giving into their desires without rational reflection (al-Rāzī 1939: 56, 73), while some are even worse than beasts because they indulge in unnatural pleasures (al-Rāzī 1939: 24–7, cf. 29, 39, 77). Animals are incapable of restraining their desires, but they lack immoderate desires, as we can see from the fact that they eat only what they need and no more. Still, as a species humans have psychological capacities that make them better than animals, and this for al-Rāzī justifies the human "subjugation" of animals. He also finds it acceptable to slaughter and eat animals "in accordance with need" (al-Rāzī 1939: 105), and even judges that a human would be justified in riding a horse to death in order to escape an enemy and save his own life (al-Rāzī 1939: 104).

Nonetheless, al-Rāzī should be recognized as a notable advocate for the humane treatment of animals. In his brief work *The Philosophical Life*, he sets out his general ethical outlook in response to certain unnamed critics of his own lifestyle. He defends his own life of moderation over asceticism, and speaks out against the behavior of religious adepts who deliberately harm themselves (e.g. self-immolation among Hindus and voluntary castration among Manicheans). He also devotes considerable space to the requirement that we avoid harming animals unless absolutely necessary. In fact, the points just mentioned—a human riding a steed to death to save himself, and moderate consumption of meat—are presented as exceptions to this general rule. The rule stems from a more fundamental tenet of al-Rāzī's ethics:

> We say that, in light of the principle we put down—namely that our Lord and Master is concerned for us, watches over us and is merciful to us—it follows that He also hates for us to suffer pain, and that all the pain we do suffer which is not our fault or due to our choices but is by nature, is something necessary and unavoidable. From this it necessarily follows that we must cause no pain at all to anything capable of sensation, unless it is deserved, or unless by this pain we can prevent another which is worse.
>
> (al-Rāzī 1939: 103)

This same principle underlies both the prohibition against self-harm and the prohibition against harming animals needlessly. It is also invoked to permit the extermination of beasts of prey and dangerous creatures like snakes. Such predators harm other animals, so killing them yields a net reduction in suffering. Also, al-Rāzī adds, once they are killed their souls may pass into better bodies. This passage provoked later authors to ascribe a doctrine of transmigration to al-Rāzī (Walker 1991), though there seems to be no basis for assuming that he countenances the reincarnation of animals as humans or vice-versa (Adamson 2012).

Though the point about transmigration may strike us as bizarre, al-Rāzī's focus on minimizing animal suffering would be very much at home in modern discussions of animal ethics. But we should notice that he does not, as a modern-day consequentialist might do, take it as a fundamental ethical principle that suffering is a bad thing that we should strive to eliminate. Rather, al-Rāzī wants us to seek "likeness to God," a Platonic idea cited in *The Philosophical Life* (al-Rāzī 1939: 108, cf. Plato, *Theaetetus* 176b). We should strive to avoid inflicting pain on ourselves or any other creature that can suffer, not because suffering is intrinsically bad, but because God is merciful and hates for anything to suffer. (Of course, one might wonder why God hates suffering, and how we know that He does. Perhaps ultimately the view does implicitly rest on the intuition that suffering is intrinsically bad. But this is not the rationale presented here.) For al-Rāzī, the imperative to treat animals humanely does not arise from their similarity to us—except insofar as the capacity for suffering is itself shared with us. One might even infer that it is not in spite of animals' inferiority to us that we should show them benevolence, but rather *because* of their inferiority to us. We are more powerful and wise than they are, just as God is more powerful and wise than we. Given that He shows us mercy and benevolence, we should imitate Him by showing providential mercy towards animals. This line of thought will however emerge more explicitly in the fable of Ibn Ṭufayl.

Ikhwān al-Ṣafā'

For a very different treatment of animal ethics, we may turn to the *Epistles* of Ikhwān al-Ṣafā', a group of rather mysterious philosophers in the tenth century (Netton 1991; El-Bizri 2009). Sometimes referred to as a philosophical "encyclopedia," the epistles cover more or less every area of philosophy and science, including zoology. This is the topic of the 22nd Epistle, which is the most celebrated of the entire collection (Goodman & McGregor 2009, hereafter cited by English/Arabic page numbers). It begins with an overview of the subject at hand but then confounds our expectation that we will be given a discursive treatment of zoology. Instead, the Ikhwān launch into an extensive fable or parable, set on an island ruled by the king of the *jinn* (comparable to the daemons of antiquity). Because the *jinn* are neither human nor animal, their king is an impartial judge in a trial that will determine how humankind ought to treat animals. The trial is initiated by the complaints of the animals, who protest at the fact that they are oppressed by humans, treated as slaves (as in the case of beasts of burden) or harvested as food. In a spectacularly inventive series of chapters, the Ikhwān imagine the various kinds of animals (e.g. birds, beasts of prey, and even insects) consulting amongst themselves as to the most effective arguments to present to the king. We are also shown the trial itself, as representatives of humanity argue that they do have the right to enslave animals.

The central question of the trial is whether animals are in any respect inferior to humans. Thus the Ikhwān depict the animals arguing that they partake of every apparent advantage possessed by humans, and are in some respects in fact superior. For instance the animals point out that unlike humans, they never rebel against God (250/197) or engage in sin (256/205). Rather, they claim to be devout monotheists and even Muslims (301–2/261–3). Nor are they riven by strife, like humans with their disparate religious and philosophical sects. The animals adhere to a single "teaching" (*madhhab*) which recognizes one Lord (287/246–7). Not only are the animals presented as uniformly pious religious believers, but they are said to live in politically arranged societies, with leaders singled out for each type of creature (e.g. the lion for the predators). At one point the animals even discourse on the characteristics of the ideal king (153/90–1). Of course, it is not clear how seriously we should take all this. The occasion for the fable may be the question of how animals should be treated, but its apparent purpose, apart of course from the refined entertainment it offers, is to critique human foibles and shortcomings and not to defend a theory of animal ethics.

This goes some way, but not I think all the way, towards resolving a fundamental difficulty with the epistle, namely the flagrant contradictions between the introductory section and the fable itself. In the introduction, the inferiority of animals is taken to be all but obvious. The very first page tells us that animals occupy a place in the hierarchy of nature between that of plants and humans: "the end of the order of animals is in contact with (*muttaṣila*) the beginning of the order of humans, and the end of the order of humans is in contact with the beginning of the order of angels" (63/4). The talk of "contact" or "continuity" here suggests that the highest animals are all but indistinguishable from the more inferior humans. But the Ikhwān go on to cite the traditional reason for sharply distinguishing animalkind from humankind: humans possess reason (*nāṭiq*) and discernment (*tamyīz*), whereas animals do not (65/5). They give a further argument based on the premise that God created animals before He created humans. From this one can infer that animals must exist for the sake of man. For it is a "first principle of the intellect in need of no proof" that "whenever one thing is for the sake of another, its existence is prior" (68/8).

This point provides a good example of the tensions between the introduction and the fable. Within the fable, the idea that animals pre-existed humans reappears, but is placed in the mouth of the mule who speaks first on behalf of the animals before the king of the *jinn* (106/45). The mule does not however infer that animals are for the sake of humans, but rather complains that animals lived peacefully until humans came along. Similarly, the fable frequently contradicts the claim that animals are ranked below humans because they lack distinctively human cognitive faculties. To begin with language, at one point the *jinn* say that in the name of fairness, they should ignore the animals' lack of eloquence and clarity in speech (*faṣāḥa* and *bayyān*, 142/79–80), something the animals also fret about as a potential weakness in the debate (149/86–7). But this same trait of eloquence (*faṣāḥa*) is elsewhere ascribed to the nightingale (172/112), the frog (186/126), the bee (247/190), and the cricket (301/261–2). Many kinds of animals also claim to offer "acclamations of God" (*tasbīḥ*) in the songs and other sounds that they make, though humans "do not understand" (302/263; cf. Qur'an 24: 41, 21: 79, 34: 10, 38: 19; Foltz 2006: 20).

One might be tempted to dismiss this as a trivial fictional device (Goodman & McGregor 2009: 149 n.150), given that the fable of course needs to pretend that animals can talk for the sake of its narrative. But animals are also said to partake of a range of rational faculties. For instance:

> 150/87: Every kind (*jins*) of [animal] has an excellence not possessed by the others, and varieties of discernment (*tamyīz*), opinion (*ra'y*), mind (*ṣawāb*), eloquence (*faṣāḥa*), clarity (*bayyān*), insight (*naẓar*) and proofs (*ḥujaj*).
>
> 243/184: We [insects] too have knowledge (*ma'rifa*), discernment (*tamyīz*), thinking (*fikr*), reflection (*rawiyya*) and governance (*siyāsa*), more refined and subtle, better considered (*aḥkam*) and more perfect than theirs.

Admittedly, the key terms "rationality" and "intellect" (*'aql*) do not feature in these lists (to which one could add similar passages at 244–5/187 and 247/190). But the Ikhwān are going at least as far as the rather open-minded al-Rāzī had gone, by ascribing such capacities as "thought" and "discernment" to animals. It is worth re-emphasizing the direct contradiction with the introduction to Epistle 22, which as we saw denies that animals have discernment (*tamyīz*). I believe the Ikhwān are not just getting carried away with their literary tour de force, given that they supply detailed and convincing reasons to ascribe these higher faculties to animals—referring, for instance, to the social structures we find among insects.

A philosophically minded reader might conclude with disappointment that the Ikhwān have simply failed to take seriously the empirical observations named in the fable. When they give their (presumably sincere) assessment of animals in the introduction, they do not notice that the points raised on behalf of animals in the fable seriously undermine that assessment. This may contain a grain of truth, and, of course, given the collective authorship of the *Epistles*, one cannot even assume that the introduction and the fable were written by the same person or persons. But a more important point is this: the Ikhwān are not in the same dialectical situation as, say, Porphyry in his attack on the Stoics. The question of whether animals are equal to, or even superior to, humans is not raised in order to decide whether animals have enough in common with us to fall within our ethical purview. Rather, the debate in the fable concerns the design of divine providence. The question of how animals compare to humans (in respect of cognition or anything else) arises only because animal inferiority would imply that God has favored humans above animals.

This is clear from the very beginning of the debate. When the mule begins to mount (pun intended) the case for the animals, he admits that God intended that animals should provide benefit to humans. But He wanted humans to care for animals and not oppress them: "God's subjugation of animals to humans was for the sake of benefitting [humans] or to keep [humans] from harm ... not in order that they be our masters and we their slaves" (106/44–5). When the animals lay claim to their range of cognitive capacities, this is only one example of the many blessings God has bestowed upon animals. It serves the same purpose in the argument as the useful innate weaponry of animal bodies (190/131, 297/256–7), or the animal instincts that are the result of divine "inspiration" (278/234). The point of all this is to insist on what is implied in Qurʾānic verses such as "no creature is there crawling on the earth, but its provision rests on God" (Qurʾān 11:6, cited at 105/59), namely that animals too are included within the mercy and care of divine providence. For the same reason the animals insist that verses that subordinate animals to humans (several are cited at 104/43) only indicate that animals should benefit the humans, rather than licensing the humans to oppress and abuse them.

The centrality of providence in the epistle also explains the rather jarring conclusion of the fable. The humans have failed to sway the king by pointing out that they may reach paradise, whereas animals do not—something that, incidentally, Muʿtazilite theologians would have denied. After all, the animals retort, humans can also be punished in the afterlife, something animals are free of (311/275). But then the humans prevail with a decisive point: humans can count among their number saintly figures who display a piety and virtue beyond what can be found in any animal (313/277–8). After an uncharacteristically brief passage in praise of such holy men, the fable ends. Tellingly, the equally brief conclusion to the epistle placed after the fable alludes again to the saints, asking God to help the reader as He has helped these outstanding individuals—"for He is capable of whatever He wishes" (315/279).

These concluding sections of the epistle may seem rather abrupt, but they cohere fully with the implicit terms of the debate between animals and mankind. If mankind can show that God favors them more highly than he favors animals, then this will establish their higher status in the order of creation. Still, it is worth noting that the Ikhwān do not explicitly say that this justifies enslavement and abuse of animals by humans. The intended effect of the fable may well be for the reader to realize that such treatment of animals is unjustifiable. But this is not stated explicitly and is certainly not the main point. More important is to show that humans do occupy a special place in God's providence. The existence of saints establishes this. Their outstanding virtue lifts the human species as a whole above the animal realm. On the other hand, this is consistent with the possibility that some, perhaps most, humans are no better than animals (a point we saw already in al-Rāzī, and made in the fable at e.g. 155/92–93 where the lion says that warlike humans have "souls of predatory beasts").

Ibn Ṭufayl

Another island fantasy that contains interesting remarks about animal ethics is the "philosophical novel" *Ḥayy Ibn Yaqẓān*, by the Andalusian thinker Ibn Ṭufayl (cited by page number from the Gauthier/Nader editions; for an English translation see Khalidi 2005). The eponymous hero grows up alone on a desert island and becomes a self-taught philosopher. Animals loom large in his physical and intellectual development. As a baby, he survives only because he is nurtured by a doe, who is described by Ibn Ṭufayl as showing the infant "kindness and compassion" (*rifq* and *raḥma*) and even building him a bed out of feathers (27/33). Ḥayy reciprocates to the extent that he is heartbroken upon the doe's death. Perhaps not all of us would react to such heartbreak by examining our mother's own heart, as Ḥayy does in a session of impromptu anatomical dissection (31/35). As with Galen and al-Rāzī, we may note that Ḥayy is allowed to draw inferences about human anatomy from animal anatomy (the point is especially clear at 39/42, where vital heat in animals is explicitly compared to the heat in Ḥayy's own chest).

Yet despite his anatomical similarity to animals and his emotional connection with the doe, Ḥayy spends little time thinking that he is on an equal footing with the animals on the island. In fact he at first takes himself to be inferior to them, since he is not equipped with their natural covering and weapons. He does meditate on the unity of animalkind, seeing all animals as united by their possession of "spirit" or *pneuma* (*rūḥ*) that is parceled out to them like a liquid poured into many vessels (45/46–7). Plants are, surprisingly, presented as something like defective animals (Kukkonen 2011: 204 n.40), but there is a clear line demarcating plants and animals on the usual Aristotelian basis of the latter's capacity for sensation and self-motion (54/52). Of course Ḥayy can likewise engage in sensation and self-motion, and in one remarkable passage he is said to eliminate any feeling of alienation from animals by imitating their calls (28/33).

Soon though, Ḥayy comes to distinguish himself from the animals just as sharply as he has distinguished animals from plants. Whereas animals spend their entire lives seeking nothing but nourishment and the satisfaction of base physical desires (77/69), Ḥayy is able to contemplate the Necessary Existent, God. As Ibn Ṭufayl has put it earlier in the work, both animals and humans reflect light shed from the Necessary

Existent, but humans reflect more light than animals are able to (23–4/30). Admittedly, this differentiates animals only from those humans who have managed to achieve contemplation. Humans who fail to do so remain on a bestial level, with dire consequences for their chance at an afterlife. After all, they have used only their bodily powers, which "disappear along with the body … . This is the case of all non-rational beasts (*al-bahā'im ghayr al-nāṭiqa*), whether they are in human form or not" (75/67–8).

Ibn Ṭufayl's broadly traditional ideas about animal psychology do not prepare us for a passage where Ḥayy converts to a life devoted to caring for the animals, and even plants, on the island (83/73ff.). In fact he goes through two distinct phases in his attitudes towards other living things. The first is reached when Ḥayy is considering how to nourish himself. This basic, physical need, and his susceptibility to generation and corruption, make him akin to the animals (83/73). He thus has a first "purpose" (*gharaḍ*), which is simply to keep his body alive. But Ḥayy realizes that it would be wrong for him to inflict harm on another living thing in order to pursue his own survival:

> 86/75: All these bodies [plants and animals] were the act of this Necessary Existent—and it was clear to him that he would become happy by nearing it and seeking likeness to it. Inevitably, if he sought nourishment from them, he would cut them off from their perfection and prevent them from the ultimate end they were pursuing. This would be putting an obstacle in the way of the act of the Agent, an obstacle opposed to the nearness and likeness he was seeking. So he realized it would be right for him, if it were possible, to abstain from nourishment entirely. But this was not possible, given that there was no way to do it without destroying his body, which would constitute a greater obstacle to the Agent than the first, since he was nobler than those other things.

In consequence, Ḥayy becomes what we would now call a "fruitarian," eating no meat and partaking of plants only in such a way that the plants may survive (87/76).

To this point he has come to accept an ethical precept familiar from al-Rāzī: harm no living thing unless absolutely necessary. And like al-Rāzī, he bases this precept on God's intentions. He is trying to avoid "putting an obstacle in the way of the act of the Agent." There is a significant difference though, insofar as Ḥayy does not think in terms of minimizing suffering (a theme that al-Rāzī probably adopted from the Mu'tazila). Rather, he tries not to stop anything from flourishing. This is why Ḥayy, unlike al-Rāzī, extends the range of his care to plants. Here one might ask why he should not go even further, and consider what God intends for inanimate objects too. After all, such objects do have final ends: the four elements strive to reach their natural places. Perhaps the answer to this question is simply that such things cannot really *flourish*, since as non-organisms they have no internal principle allowing them to develop towards greater perfection. And certainly, it would be wrong to try to free elemental bodies from plant and animal bodies so that they can move towards their natural places. After all plants and animals are more noble than the elements, just as a human is nobler than they are. So it would make no sense to destroy a plant to free the earth in it to move downward, any more than it would make sense for a human to starve himself to avoid bothering plants. In any case the question does not arise here, since the passage concerns only things from which Ḥayy can receive sustenance.

Ibn Ṭufayl next discusses a second, more exalted purpose pursued by Ḥayy, predicated on the similarity he notices between himself and the celestial bodies (81/72). Unlike animals, but like the heavens, Ḥayy has a perfectly balanced spirit. But how should he more perfectly imitate the heavens? Part of the answer is for Ḥayy to imitate their physical characteristics. He keeps his body clean, and moves like them, traveling around the island in circles and spinning until he is dizzy. (This is presumably meant to evoke religious rituals in Islam concerning purification and induced dizziness.) Furthermore, because the celestial movers are contemplating God, Ḥayy tries to concentrate on the Necessary Existent and to block out sensory stimulation. More relevant, for our purposes, is that Ḥayy is convinced that the celestial bodies are the instruments of divine providence. Ibn Ṭufayl has already observed, perhaps thinking of Galen's *De Usu Partium*, that God's generosity is proved by the useful organs given to animals (70/64, citing Qur'ān 20:50): "Our Lord is He who gave everything its creation (or nature: *khulq*), then guided it." So again, it is God's intentions that are uppermost in Ḥayy's mind when he begins actively to care for the living things around him. He roves the island looking for animals in need of help, by removing thorns from their paws or bringing them food. He even waters plants and makes sure that they are getting enough sunlight (89/77–8).

Although it is clear that this behavior is all intended to aid God's providential activity, it is equally clear that Ḥayy's ecological benevolence is an imitation of the heavens, and *not* of God. In fact, when Ḥayy passes on to a still more ambitious third objective, which is the emulation of God Himself, he leaves behind his interest in plants and animals. Along with physical motion, his care for other organisms belongs to the "corporeal attributes" (*ṣifāt al-ajsām*). It thus has no place in a life lived in imitation of an incorporeal God (92–3/80). In his treatment of the second objective of imitating the heavens, Ibn Ṭufayl is drawing on a theory familiar to him from Ibn Sīnā—though it goes back further through the tradition, all the way to al-Kindī. According to this theory, the four elements in the sublunary world are fashioned into more complex substances by heavenly influence. On the other hand, Ibn Ṭufayl gives God a more direct role than we find in al-Kindī or Ibn Sīnā. The heavens' role is straightforwardly physical and consists of providing heat, cooling, and so on; these physical manipulations "prepare [things in the sublunary world] for the emanation of spiritual forms from the necessarily existing Agent" (88/77).

Given this providential cosmic scheme, one might find it odd that Ḥayy does not trust God's providence to take care of itself without any help from humans. If an animal has a thorn in its paw, why not trust that this is part of the divine plan and leave well enough alone? At the risk of reading too much into the passage, the answer seems to be that Ibn Ṭufayl understands God's providence to apply to each *individual* plant and animal. God has an interest in each individual's reaching its final cause. This fits well with the idea just mentioned—that God directly bestows form on every individual, rather than delegating this task to a celestial intellect. Thus Ḥayy not only avoids interfering harmfully with living individuals (by eating them for instance), but also sets out to interfere positively when he can be helpful. The implicit conception of providence contrasts starkly with that of Ibn Sīnā. He infamously holds that God does not even have knowledge of particulars, except insofar as they fall under universal species (Adamson 2005), and also believes that the active intellect and not God is the "giver of forms." Ibn Ṭufayl's position of providence may also be contrasted with what we saw in the Ikhwān. They invoke providence only to explain the traits bestowed on each animal species, and to settle the question of how animals in general should relate to the human species. Nonetheless, Ibn Ṭufayl's treatment of animal ethics broadly fits the pattern we have already observed in al-Rāzī and the Ikhwān.

Conclusion

All three, al-Rāzī, the Ikhwān, and Ibn Ṭufayl, raise the question of how humans relate to animals. They give a range of responses to this question. Al-Rāzī seems to be the most positive about animal capacities. The Ikhwān concede even more than al-Rāzī in this direction within the problematic context of their fable, but arguably their more considered view is the traditional one expressed in the introduction to Epistle 22. Ibn Ṭufayl, meanwhile, barely budges from the standard Aristotelian understanding of "irrational beasts," apart from a sentimental line or two about the mother doe. Interesting though this variation may be, it plays little role in shaping the philosophers' animal ethics. Instead, all three tell us to treat animals as God treats them, and us: with mercy and justice. It is telling that, of the three, Ibn Ṭufayl grants least to animals in terms of cognitive capacities, but goes furthest in the direction of imagining a comprehensive and radical ecological ethical regime. Admittedly, this regime is trumped by his character's desire to imitate God Himself, something we might compare to the way that human saints trump all other considerations in the epistle of the Ikhwān. Still, these Muslim thinkers developed innovative views on the ethical treatment of animals, views based not on what we share with animals, but on an understanding of God as a Creator who shows benevolence to all creation.

Acknowledgement

The author would like to thank the Leverhulme Trust for its support of this research, and participants in a June 2012 workshop on medieval philosophy held at the British Academy for their helpful comments.

Further Reading

Adamson, P. (2012) "Abū Bakr al-Rāzī on Animals," *Archiv für Geschichte der Philosophie* 94: 249–73.

Druat, T-A. (1996) "Al-Razi's Conception of the Soul: Psychological Background to His Ethics," *Medieval Philosophy and Theology* 5: 245–63.

El-Bizri, N. (ed.) (2009) *The Epistles of the Brethren of Purity. Ikhwān al-Ṣafā' and their Rasa'il: an Introduction*, Oxford: Oxford University Press.

Foltz, R. C. (2006) *Animals in Islamic Tradition and Muslim Cultures*, Oxford: Oneworld.
Goodman, L. E. & McGregor, R. (tr.) (2009) *The Case of the Animals Versus Man Before the King of the Jinn*, Oxford: Oxford University Press.
Kukkonen, T. (2011) "Heart, Spirit, Form, Substance: Ibn Ṭufayl's Psychology," in P. Adamson (ed.), *In the Age of Averroes: Arabic Philosophy in the Sixth/Twelfth Century*, London: Warburg, pp. 195–214.

References

Adamson, P. (2005) "On Knowledge of Particulars," *Proceedings of the Aristotelian Society* 105: 273–94.
——. (2007) "*Porphyrius Arabus* on Nature and Art: 463F Smith in Context," in G. Karamanolis & A. Sheppard (eds.), *Studies on Porphyry*, London: Institute of Classical Studies, pp. 141–63.
——. (2012) "Abū Bakr al-Rāzī on Animals," *Archiv für Geschichte der Philosophie* 94: 249–73.
al-Rāzī (1939) *Rasā'il falsafiyya (Philosophical Epistles)*, P. Kraus (ed.), Cairo: Paul Barbey.
——. (1979) *Libro de la introducción dal arte de la medicina o 'Isagoge,'* M. Vázquez de Benito (ed. and tr.), Salamanca: Universidad Salamanca.
——. (1993) *Kitāb al-Shukūk 'alā Jālīnūs (Doubts About Galen)*, M. Mohaghegh (ed.), Tehran: Society for the Appreciation of Cultural Works and Dignitaries.
Benkheira, M. H. (2005) *L'animal en islam*, Paris: Indes Savantes.
Clark, G. (2000) *Porphyry: On Abstinence from Killing Animals*, London: Duckworth.
Druat, T-A. (1996) "Al-Razi's Conception of the Soul: Psychological Background to his Ethics," *Medieval Philosophy and Theology* 5: 245–63.
El-Bizri, N. (ed.) (2009) *The Epistles of the Brethren of Purity. Ikhwān al-Ṣafā' and their Rasa'il: an Introduction*, Oxford: Oxford University Press.
Foltz, R. C. (2006) *Animals in Islamic tradition and Muslim cultures*, Oxford: Oneworld.
Goodman, L. E. & McGregor, R. (tr.) (2009) *The Case of the Animals Versus Man Before the King of the Jinn*, Oxford: Oxford University Press.
Heemskerk, M. T. (2000) *Suffering in the Mu'tazilite Theology: 'Abd al-Jabbār's Teaching on Pain and Divine Justice*, Leiden: Brill.
Ibn Ṭufayl (1900) *Hayy ben Yaqdhân*, L. Gauthier (ed. and tr.), Algiers: Imprimerie Orientale.
——. (1993) *Ḥayy Ibn Yaqẓān*, A. N. Nader (ed.), Beirut: Dār al-Mashriq.
Khalidi, M. A. (ed. and tr.) (2005) *Medieval Islamic Philosophical Writings*, Cambridge: Cambridge University Press.
Kukkonen, T. (2008) "No Man Is an Island: Nature and Neo-Platonic Ethics in *Ḥayy Ibn Yaqẓān*," *Journal of the History of Philosophy* 46: 185–204.
——. (2014) *Ibn Tufayl: Living the Life of Reason*, London: Oneworld.
Netton, I. R. (1991) *Muslim Neoplatonists: an Introduction to the Thought of the Brethren of Purity*, Edinburgh: Edinburgh University Press.
Osborne, C. (2007) *Dumb Beasts and Dead Philosophers: Humanity and the Humane in Ancient Philosophy and Literature*, Oxford: Oxford University Press.
Pormann, P. E. (2008) "Medical Methodology and Hospital Practice: the Case of Fourth-/Tenth-Century Baghdad," in P. Adamson (ed.), *In the Age of al-Fārābī: Arabic Philosophy in the Fourth/Tenth Century*, London: Warburg Institute, pp. 95–118.
Sorabji, R. (1993) *Animal Minds and Human Morals: the Origins of the Western Debate*, Ithaca: Cornell University Press.
Walker, P. E. (1991) "The Doctrine of Metempsychosis in Islam," in W. B. Hallaq & D. P. Little (eds.), *Islamic Studies Presented to Charles J. Adams*, Leiden: Brill, pp. 219–38.

Part VII

PHILOSOPHY, RELIGION, AND MYSTICISM

31
PHILOSOPHY AND PROPHECY

Frank Griffel

Introduction

Islam is a revealed religion and for Muslims it began when Muḥammad received his first revelation some time around 610 C.E. in a cave outside of Mecca. Islamic tradition tells us that Muḥammad obtained his revelations either directly from God or through the mediation of the archangel Gabriel (Madigan 2004). Subsequently, Islamic thinkers developed different theories of how the process of revelation unfolds and what happened in the interplay between God, Gabriel, and Muḥammad. Such theories would also cover earlier messengers (singl. *rasūl*) such as Moses or Abraham, who are believed to have received revelations similar to the Qur'ān. Finally, there were also the smaller prophets to be considered, whom God had sent to warn different people. These had not produced revelations in the form of a text, yet still had the ability to foretell future events—i.e. divination—or to accurately predict the punishment of people who would neglect to heed God's warnings. All these phenomena were understood as expressions of prophecy. Authors within the movement of *falsafa* developed theories that would explain prophecy (*nubuwwa*) and the process of receiving revelation (*waḥy*) as part of the normal course in this world. Although a rare event in human history, prophecy was not understood as something extraordinary or even superhuman. It was considered a regular part of the way God created this world and therefore something we would call a natural phenomenon. Islamic philosophical explanations of prophecy should be considered "scientific" in the sense that they give rational explanations for various phenomena called prophecy, explanations that were seamlessly embedded in the physical, metaphysical, and psychological theories held by these thinkers.

Psychology here means "theories of the soul" or "explanation of processes within the soul" and has little to do with the modern sense of that word. Prophecy and receiving revelation were regarded as processes that happen within the human soul. They were, of course, not the kind of process that every human could perform. Yet for *falāsifa*—and subsequently also for many theologians who adopted the philosophical explanation—prophecy was a faculty (*quwwa*) of the prophet and thus embedded in his soul. More precisely, it was a combination of several faculties.

Aristotle's Psychology and the Corrupted Arabic Version of the *Parva Naturalia*

Psychological theories in *falsafa* were expressed in works that take their subject matter and much of their inspiration from Aristotle's (384–322 B.C.E.) book *On the Soul* (also referred to as *De anima*). It is interesting that Aristotle in his *On the Soul* does not mention prophecy or divination. In fact, Aristotle himself did not believe that people could foretell the future or receive messages from the gods. In some of his smaller writings on the subject of dreams and related psychological events, writings that became known as *Parva Naturalia*, Aristotle denies that dreams have a supernatural origin and that a dreamer can foresee events in the future. Aristotle did not deny that people experience veridical dreams, something we today refer to as *dejà-vu* experiences, where people dream of events that later take place in reality. He, however, explained this as pure coincidence or as cases where the dream is the cause of the event it predicts and prompts a human to act unconsciously towards its fulfillment. Dreams do not come from a god but are natural events in the human faculty of imagination (Aristotle 1957: 374–85). In a short work *On Dreams* that is part of the *Parva Naturalia*, Aristotle clarifies how dreams can reflect certain physiological processes that happen while a human sleeps. Other dreams are the residue of earlier perceptions in our sense organs and they are too subtle to be noticed except when we are asleep. They are like the spots we see after we look into a bright light (Aristotle 1957: 348–74). Aristotle did not believe in divination or clairvoyance and regarded people who pretended to have knowledge about the future as charlatans.

When Aristotle's *Parva Naturalia* was translated into Arabic during the ninth century, his denial of any divine or supernatural involvement in human dreams was turned into its opposite. It appears that a philosophical scholar of the ninth century, who may have been the unknown translator of Aristotle's *Parva Naturalia*, had both the Arabic translation of this text as well as the Arabic version of Book IV from Plotinus's *Enneads* in front of him and, for reasons that we can only speculate about, conflated passages from these two texts to one which circulated as the Arabic version of Aristotle's *Parva Naturalia* (Hansberger 2011: 73–80). In conscious opposition to Aristotle, the Neoplatonic philosopher Plotinus (d. 270 C.E.) had argued that dreams may indeed foretell the future. In their "spiritual faculties," humans may receive pure intelligibles from the celestial intellect and this process may convey information about events that will happen in the future. The Arabic text that purports to be an Arabic translation of Aristotle's *Parva Naturalia* contains elements from Plotinus's and from Aristotle's texts on dreams. It teaches, for instance, that dreams are the residue of earlier perceptions, as Aristotle did, and that veridical dreams are caused by God through the mediation of a celestial intellect, as Plotinus did (Hansberger 2008).

This Arabic text that pretends to be by Aristotle draws on post-Aristotelian metaphysical and psychological theories and identifies, for instance, a celestial intellect as source of veridical dreams whereas Aristotle neither commits himself to the existence of such celestial intellects nor assigns to them any role in psychological or cosmological processes. Such intellects are, however, a hallmark of an understanding of Aristotle that formed in late antiquity and that aimed at reconciling his teachings with those of Plato. The tampering with the text of Aristotle during the earliest

Arabic reception of the *Parva Naturalia* is a rare and drastic illustration of the fact that when Arabic philosophers received Aristotle, they did so through the lens of the tradition of late antique commentators on Aristotle, some of them Neoplatonists. Alexander of Aphrodisias, for instance, was an important commentator on the works of Aristotle who worked at the turn of the third century C.E. While he was not a Neoplatonist, others such as Plotinus, Porphyry (d. ca. 304), and Proclus (d. 485) were and they were powerfully influential on the understanding of the texts of Aristotle (d'Ancona 2009). They aimed at reconciling Aristotle's text in *On the Soul*, for instance, with the Platonic teaching that our knowledge consists of ideas and intellectual forms received from the higher realm of nous or "the intellect," something also found in the *Paraphrase of the De Anima* by the Aristotelian commentator Themistius (d. 388), who followed teachings of the Neoplatonists in philosophical psychology.

Aristotle had written that cognition and thinking are processes where both active and passive components are present. The passive, says Aristotle, is mind, which "becomes all things," meaning it has the potential to "become" every idea (Aristotle 1957: 171). Aristotle also writes that the passive part is similar to prime matter (*hylé*), which can also become all things. Commentators such as Alexander of Aphrodisias interpreted this to mean that the process of understanding is a combination of form and matter, where the individual human's "material intellect" comes to attain universals through the active element, the "active intellect." This active intellect was understood to be just one, shared by all humans, a separate, immaterial object that exists in the heavens. It is the repository of all forms and concepts, that is, all the "universals" humans would need in their actual thinking. Like light, the active intellect shines upon the individual objects of knowledge that we perceive with our senses and allows our individual material intellect to abstract universal qualities from those perceived objects. The late antique Greek commentators regarded the acquisition of theoretical knowledge as a process where the individual human material intellect receives the universal concepts thanks to the involvement of the celestial active intellect.

Al-Kindī on Prophecy

When in the ninth century, Aristotle's *On the Soul* together with the commentaries of Alexander and Themistius as well as portions of the *Enneads* of Plotinus and some works of Proclus were translated into Arabic, these texts shaped the way Arabic philosophers thought about the human soul and the intellects. A number of works by Plotinus and Proclus circulated in Arabic under the name of Aristotle, most importantly the pseudo-Aristotelian *Theology*, and together with the mangled translation of the *Parva Naturalia* they gave an inaccurate impression of what Aristotle taught on matters of the soul, dreams, and divinity. Already a few decades before Aristotle's *On the Soul* became available, al-Kindī (d. after 870) had written about prophecy and sided with the Neoplatonists. In his work *On Sleep and Dream Visions*, which seems to follow the modified text of Aristotle's *Parva Naturalia* with its elements from Plotinus, al-Kindī teaches that some humans have the capacity to perceive future events in their dreams (al-Kindī 2012: 124–133). This theory is based on Aristotle's position that in sleep the soul is still active and awake, while many other activities that usually distract the soul, most importantly sense perception, are not taking place. The soul thus can come to itself and find within itself a kind of knowledge that also exists while awake but is usually only perceived while asleep. Following the text of the Arabic *Parva Naturalia*, al-Kindī teaches that the soul may tell of future events while we are asleep (Adamson 2007: 135–43). If the human soul "is purified, cleaned, and polished ... the forms of knowledge about all things appear in it," and in the time of slumber, when it abandons the use of the senses, it finds this knowledge within itself (al-Kindī 2012: 115). These dreams may be of varying accuracy depending on, it seems, how receptive one's organs are. In a less than optimal receptive state the human may see future events not as they will be but merely as a symbol (*ramz*). A dream of flying could, for instance, symbolize a journey (al-Kindī 2012: 129). Already in al-Kindī there is an aspect that will later become very important. The souls of those people who receive divination and prophecy must, in addition to having organs able to receive the dreams well, be pure and well prepared. The soul must have "attained a full degree of purity" (al-Kindī 2012: 116).

Al-Kindī does not explain why the human soul is able to foretell the future, nor does he in any way tackle the much more complex phenomenon of a revelation that produces texts such as the Qur'ān. This next step is undertaken by al-Fārābī (d. 950–951). In contrast to al-Kindī, al-Fārābī knew about Aristotle's teachings in *On the Soul* and he had some important late antique commentaries at hand. His theories of prophecy are rooted in the epistemological tradition of the distinction between the "active intellect" (*al-ʿaql al-faʿʿāl*) that in some fashion causes all thought and the "passive intellect" (*al-ʿaql al-munfaʿil*) of the individual human that receives universal concepts from the celestial active intellect.

Al-Fārābī on Prophecy

Al-Fārābī identifies the active intellect with the tenth intellect that governs the sub-lunar sphere, i.e. everything on earth. The *falāsifa* understood the numerous Qur'ānic allusions to the angels in the heavens as references to the various intellects of the heavenly spheres. The "angels," i.e. the intellects of the heavenly spheres, act on behalf of God as intermediaries in His creation. In al-Fārābī the active intellect has a number of important functions, one of them is giving human souls the power that allows them to abstract intelligibles, i.e. universal concepts, from the things that they perceive with their senses. The active intellect is, thus, that which makes thinking possible. The active intellect is also the efficient cause of everything that happens on earth and it is the final cause for all the beings there. This means that all creatures in the sub-lunar sphere, particularly humans, strive to resemble the active intellect as perfectly as possible. This Aristotelian concept that the development and functioning of every organism is driven by entelechy, i.e. by a striving toward the full realization of its potential, had a firm hold on the philosophical tradition of the *falāsifa*. For humans, entelechy means that they endeavor to reach perfection in that faculty that distinguishes them from all other animals, i.e. thinking. For al-Fārābī this happens as humans acquire more and more universal ideas (i.e. "intelligibles," *maʿqūlāt*) by abstracting them from sense perceptions (Taylor 2006).

Given that the active intellect contains all universal concepts and ideas and can be understood as pure thought, humans strive to acquire as much of those universal ideas as possible. They try to develop their rational capacity to the extent that their individual material intellects will resemble the active intellect as much as possible. Doing so, the individual human intellect advances through different stages until it reaches a level that al-Fārābī calls the "acquired intellect" (*al-'aql al-mustafād*). This is the highest stage of human perfections where the human intellect becomes almost identical to the content of the active intellect. It is reached when the human masters "all or most" intelligible thought (al-Fārābī 1967: 217). Al-Fārābī calls this stage the "conjunction with the active intellect," when the active intellect enters into the human. Only very few humans can reach this stage and these are the best of the philosophers. After describing this stage, al-Fārābī continues:

> When this occurs in both parts of his rational faculty, namely the theoretical and the practical rational faculties, and also in his imaginative faculty, then it is this man who is granted divine revelation (*yūḥī ilayhi*). God Almighty grants him revelation through the mediation of the active intellect, so that the emanation from God Exalted to the active intellect is passed on to his passive intellect through the mediation of the acquired intellect, and then to his imaginative faculty.
>
> (al-Fārābī 1985: 244–5)

The perfect human, who has reached the stage of conjunction with the active intellect, receives divine revelation in the form of universal ideas from the active intellect via the mediation of his acquired intellect. That revelation (*waḥy*), however, is immediately passed on to the imaginative faculty (*quwwa mutakhayyila*) where it produces the kind of prophecy that we know from the text of the Qur'ān. The imaginative faculty is part of the human soul and located in the heart. It is immediately below the rational faculty, yet it also contains sense perceptions and impressions even at times when the objects of that perception are no longer present. The imaginative faculty is particularly active while the body is asleep and while it is not occupied with the actual perception of objects. According to al-Fārābī this imaginative faculty is responsible for our dreams. Mostly, the imaginative faculty receives revelation while the body is asleep. In rare cases, however, that may also happen in the waking state. When the imaginative faculty is powerful and developed to perfection, and when it is not overpowered by sense perception or attending to the rational faculty, "then its state in waking life … is like its state during sleep when it is relieved of these two activities." It then represents the emanations received from the active intellect "as visible objects of sense perception that imitate (*yuḥākī*) that which comes from the active intellect" (al-Fārābī 1985: 222–3). The imaginative faculty of the prophet thus transforms the rational and universal knowledge received from the active intellect into representations that express the purely rational universals by means of examples, parables, or metaphors. The imaginative faculty cannot help but recast what it receives in figurative images (Davidson 1992: 58–63).

While this is the highest level of prophecy, lower levels may affect people who have a less than perfect imaginative faculty and who may not have reached the level of the acquired intellect. These people receive revelation only in sleep and in ways that the imaginative faculty represents distant or future events as if they were happening here and now. Still, even the lower level includes the figurative representation of theoretical truths. Al-Fārābī does not call this "revelation" (*waḥy*) but merely "prophecy" (*nubuwwa*), and the higher of these two levels is incomparably more superior to the lower (al-Fārābī 1961: 75, 167).

It is clear that while the lower level of prophecy largely follows along the lines of what al-Kindī had already established on this subject, the higher level accounts for precisely the kind of prophecy that the earliest generation of Muslims had witnessed in the actions of the Prophet Muḥammad. Muḥammad and earlier messengers, such as Moses and Abraham, had reached a level of prophecy that far outstretched the mere foretelling and warning of future events or producing insights about past events. When verse 2:97 of the Qur'ān says that the archangel Gabriel "brings down" (*nazzala*) revelation to Muḥammad's heart, the *falāsifa* understood it as a reference to the most important of the heavenly "angels," i.e. the active intellect, which is the immediate cause of the revelation in the prophets' souls. In addition, it was well established that Muḥammad not only received his revelations while asleep but also in his waking hours. Finally, al-Fārābī's theory of prophecy explains characteristics of any revealed religion, according to a Muslim understanding of revealed religion. The Qur'ān and the earlier revelations are not cast as theoretical epistles that employ rational arguments, but they are full of figurative language, parables, metaphors, and visual descriptions of past or future events. Al-Fārābī's theory explains how a divine message, which according to the philosophers can only come in the form of universals, is expressed in the form of a book that appeals more to the common folk than to the philosopher. It is clear that in al-Fārābī we find a distinctly Muslim development of earlier philosophical theories about prophecy that aims at answering questions and solving philosophical problems which were posed by the historical circumstances of Muḥammad's prophecy and the revelation he brought.

For al-Fārābī, reaching the highest level of prophecy requires the development of an acquired intellect and the conjunction with the active intellect. Muḥammad, Moses, and Abraham were, according to al-Fārābī, not only messengers of God but also philosophers who had mastered all the theoretical sciences. They were also founders of political communities and each of them had brought a religious law that formed the legal foundation of the state they created. The prophets' most important achievement is, according to al-Fārābī, their ability to cast theoretical knowledge in a figurative and metaphorical language that most people can understand. The only person fully qualified to govern a virtuous state is such a philosopher-prophet (al-Fārābī 1985: 244–7). Only he is able to hold authority over the ordinary people and the elite alike and to pass just legislation.

This latter aspect of al-Fārābī's teaching on prophecy forms his political philosophy (Marmura 1979), and it can be understood as an Islamization of Plato's concept of a philosopher-king from his *Republic*. The perfect ruler appears in al-Fārābī as a law-giving prophet-philosopher-king whose prime interest is to increase the knowledge and the virtue of his subjects. Revealed religion plays an important part in that project. While the intellectual elite of the perfect state needs no instruction in theoretical or practical matters, all others rely on revealed religion to achieve some kind of training in metaphysics and ethics: "Since it is difficult for the public (*al-jumhūr*) to understand these things in themselves and the way they exist, instructing them about these things is sought by other ways—and those are the ways of representation [or imitation]" (al-Fārābī 2011: 45). Revealed religion is the most effective of those imitations. It is an imitation of philosophy, which also means there is no conflict between philosophy and religion. Still, while the true prophet is also a philosopher, only very few philosophers have the talent and ability to be astute statesmen and to direct the multitude by means of persuasive figurative speech and exemplary deeds.

In all this, al-Fārābī never mentions the name of Muḥammad, the religion of Islam, or the Islamic caliphate created by Muḥammad's companions. While al-Fārābī's theory of prophecy aims to explain all revealed religion, his identification of the prophet with the ideal ruler of the best state also legitimizes Muḥammad's activities as statesman and lawgiver. Al-Fārābī's political theory may be meant to describe the situation among the first generation of Muslims, but there is also a utopian aspect in it that applies to the Islamic state of his time. Al-Fārābī describes the political situation in the 'Abbāsid caliphate of the tenth century as a state where the theoretical opinions of the people are defective, yet where their actions are virtuous. Once the prophet-philosopher—that is Muḥammad—has revealed the law and established the virtuous state, he has been succeeded by rulers who are neither prophets nor philosophers, but who follow his example (sunna), adhere to the law, and by the use of analogical reasoning adopt it to new circumstances. The law that goes back to the prophet-philosopher still guarantees virtuous actions even if people hold utterly corrupt opinions. It would be better, of course, if the actions were virtuous and the theoretical opinions correct (Crone 2003). Al-Fārābī did not think that reaching such a state—maybe through a religiously led revolution—was impossible at his time. Later *falāsifa* like Ibn Bājja (d. 1138) would be more pessimistic and would regard the society they lived in as corrupt both in actions and in opinions (Ibn Bājja 1963).

Ibn Sīnā on Prophecy

Islamic philosophers after al-Fārābī accepted his distinction between prophecy (*nubuwwa*) and revelation (*waḥy*) with the first roughly described as clairvoyance and divination, and the second as a higher capacity where the prophet receives a universal truth from a celestial intellect and represents it in figurative language. At the turn of the eleventh century, Ibn Sīnā (d. 1037) significantly expands al-Fārābī's explanation of prophecy and creates what will become the most elaborate theory on this subject that influenced many Muslim theologians and Sufis. Like al-Fārābī, he aims at explaining the kind of prophecy that brought about Islam as well as all other types of divination like clairvoyance or the experience of what we would call *déjà-vu*. Ibn Sīnā also addresses the question of the miracles performed by prophets and holy men, a subject that al-Fārābī, for instance, had not touched upon.

Like al-Fārābī, Ibn Sīnā sees two different processes at work that may affect different people or also affect a single person all at once. Al-Fārābī's capacity of "prophecy" falls in Ibn Sīnā into the category of "imaginative revelation" (Rahman 1958: 36). Like al-Fārābī, Ibn Sīnā recognizes knowledge that results when an emanation from one of the celestial beings—for Ibn Sīnā it needs to be a celestial soul—acts upon the human faculty of imagination. Such an emanation produces prophecy in the sense of knowledge of future or distant events. The celestial souls contain such knowledge and can reveal it to the imaginative faculty (*quwwa mutakhayyila*) of the human. Part of both al-Fārābī's and Ibn Sīnā's theories of prophecy is that the celestial beings—which are understood to be the Qurʾānic angels—have a foreknowledge of events that happen in the sub-lunar world. The disposition for these events passes from the cosmological higher being to the lower until it finally reaches the earth. In the process of imaginative revelation, prophets get a glimpse of the foreknowledge contained within the celestial souls. The imaginative faculty of the human enters in "conjunction with the world of sovereignty" (*ittiṣāl bi-l-malakūt*), meaning the souls of the celestial spheres. Such imaginative revelation is for Ibn Sīnā a natural phenomenon that differs in strength depending on the power of the human's faculty of imagination. In most people it manifests itself as an occasional vision of a future event in a dream that might later cause the experience of *déjà-vu*. Only extraordinary strong souls are able to cut out the distracting influence of their external senses and can experience imaginative revelation in their waking state when it may produce clairvoyance or divination. Prophets lack the impeding forces that in the case of ordinary people suppress visions while they are awake and have sense experience. Therefore, prophets receive in their waking hours visions that less gifted people at best receive in their sleep (Ibn Sīnā 1959: 173). At the top of the spectrum stands a phenomenon that Ibn Sīnā calls the "holy spirit" (*al-rūḥ al-qudsī*), where a high degree of imaginative revelation is combined with an optimal disposition for the second channel of prophecy in Ibn Sīnā: intellectual revelation.

Ibn Sīnā recognizes the possibility of attaining instantaneous theoretical knowledge without following procedures for the acquisition of this knowledge. Al-Fārābī had rejected such a possibility since for him a prophet first had to become a philosopher through assiduous learning. In Ibn Sīnā, the prophet can also receive intellectual revelation, which is the capacity to find the link that combines two independent propositions into a compelling rational argument. These propositions then become premises in a correct argument, a so-called syllogism. Intellectual insight is thus the capacity to hit on the middle term of a syllogism. Ibn Sīnā calls this capacity *ḥads*, which may be translated as "quick wit," or "intuition." The moment we exercise this capacity and hit on the middle term of a syllogism we have the flash of a connection with the active intellect. We more or less receive the middle term from the active intellect. Some people have a talent to find middle terms, while others are slow at this. Philosophers usually have a higher degree of *ḥads* than ordinary people. Like in the case of imaginative revelation, every human has a share in this capacity—and many have only a very small one—yet at the higher end of the spectrum it becomes part of prophecy. Ibn Sīnā argues that because there are people who have next to no ability to find such middle terms—meaning, because there are people who are very, very slow at learning—there must be people at the upper range who are "burning with insights, that is, with the reception from the active intellect." The universal concepts in the active intellect regarding every object of knowledge are imprinted on these humans "instantaneously or almost so." Again, reaching such a stage requires purity and training: "It is possible that there is a person amongst humans whose soul has been rendered so powerful through extreme purity and intense contact with intellectual principles that he blazes with *ḥads*." This person receives instantaneous scientific knowledge without having to expend any effort in learning to formulate arguments. People at this stage experience a conjunction with the active intellect; they possess a "holy spirit" or "holy intellect" (*'aql qudsī*, Ibn Sīnā 1952: 35–7).

If such a strong power of intuition is combined with an equally strong imaginative faculty, then the effects of the "holy spirit" (*al-rūḥ al-qudsī*) emanate onto the person's imaginative faculty. These effects are depicted in images that can be perceived by the senses. In other words, the person who combines imaginative with intellectual revelation is able to recast theoretical knowledge that he or she has received through conjunction with the active intellect as figurative images. These people are the prophets who receive revelation (*waḥy*).

In addition to receiving knowledge from the heavenly realm through the two channels of intellect and imagination there is a third property (*khāṣṣa*) of prophets that distinguishes them from other people. Prophets have the ability to perform miracles by virtue of an exceptionally powerful "practical faculty of the soul" (*quwwa nafsiyya 'amaliyya*). Since all souls have the capacity to effect physical changes in our own bodies, the extraordinary powers of the prophets' souls have the capacity to bring about changes in natural objects outside of their own bodies. Prophets have the capacity to cause storms, let rain fall, cause earthquakes, or cause people to sink into the ground, but they are not capable of changing a piece of wood into an animal or of splitting the moon (Ibn Sīnā 1959: 199–201).

Prophecy in Ibn Sīnā thus consists of three elements: strong imaginative revelation, intellectual revelation, and a powerful practical faculty of the soul. These properties are not unique to prophets, indeed all people share in them to some degree. Through purity and training humans can increase the strength of these faculties in their souls. Revelation of the kind received by Muḥammad, however, requires the utmost degree of all three of these properties. The true prophet is for Ibn Sīnā also a philosopher. He may not have devoted as much time to learning as the philosopher has, but his power of intuition puts his theoretical insight at par with the most advanced among them. Both of them achieve the conjunction with the active intellect. Yet where the philosopher may teach his insights only to those who practice philosophy, the prophet can convey them in a figurative language and thus make them accessible to all people.

His ability to convey theoretical insights to the masses of the people makes the prophet the best of all rulers, and in his political philosophy Ibn Sīnā follows al-Fārābī closely. The prophet is the best of all lawgivers because if we compare his law with that of the laws passed by monarchic or even democratic states, we find that people have the strongest motivation to follow the prophet's law. They follow this law because they aim at reward in the afterlife, and they avoid transgression because they fear punishment both in this world as well as in the next. Unlike al-Fārābī, who never explicitly refers to the prophet of Islam, Ibn Sīnā leaves no doubt that Muḥammad has fulfilled all requirements of what a prophet should do and what he should convey in his revelation and as a lawgiver in order to create the most benefits for God's creation (Ibn Sīnā 2005: 365–78). In his philosophical psychology and his prophetology, Ibn Sīnā gives a distinctly Islamic expression to a theory that has its earliest roots in the Neoplatonic understanding of Aristotle and the mangled text of the Arabic *Parva Naturalia*. For Ibn Sīnā Islam is "the true religion which was brought to us by our Prophet, our lord, and our master, Muḥammad—God's prayer be on him and his family" (Ibn Sīnā 2005: 347–8). Whereas al-Fārābī gave a universal account of revealed religion as it is understood by Islam, Ibn Sīnā gives a specifically Islamic explanation that will have an enormous influence on almost all later Muslim thinking.

Al-Ghazālī on Prophecy

Ibn Sīnā's prophetology was embraced even by thinkers who harshly criticized other teachings of *falsafa*, such as their metaphysics and who rejected Ibn Sīnā's views on God as an expression of a merely impersonal creator who acts without choosing between alternatives, solely out of the necessity of His divine nature. The first Muslim theologian to adopt Ibn Sīnā's teachings on prophecy was al-Ghazālī (d. 1111). He is best known for his critique of Ibn Sīnā's metaphysics in his *Incoherence of the Philosophers* (*Tahāfut al-falāsifa*). None of the 20 teachings that al-Ghazālī discusses—and often dismisses—in that book goes to the heart of Ibn Sīnā's psychology. Al-Ghazālī tells us in his autobiography *Deliverance from Error* (*al-Munqidh min al-ḍalāl*) that for a long time he was undecided between the psychology of the *falāsifa* and that of his predecessors in *kalām*. At one point, however, it became clear to al-Ghazālī that the psychology of the *falāsifa*, which he identified with that of the Sufis, is the true one (al-Ghazālī 2000: 87).

Rather than adapting, al-Ghazālī appropriates Ibn Sīnā's teachings on prophecy and he rejects some elements and transforms others to better serve the requirements of his own theological agenda. First, al-Ghazālī severely criticizes the *falāsifa*'s position that prophets only teach the masses while philosophers are not in need of divine revelation. While al-Ghazālī accepts the position that prophets convey their message in figurative terms, he also insists that this message goes far beyond what humans can acquire through other sources of knowledge. No rational argument, for instance, can tell us anything about what will happen in the afterlife. The prophets' revelations are full of original information that humans cannot acquire through the practice of their reason. Revelation, therefore, is not just an imitation (*muḥākāt*) of philosophy as al-Fārābī and Ibn Sīnā have taught. All humans, including the philosophers, must learn from the prophets' revelations and study them closely. Al-Ghazālī alters the philosophical theories about prophecy in such a way that prophets now receive knowledge that goes beyond the rational faculties of the human intellect. Equally, he rejects the view that the benefits of prophecy are limited to their political activities of creating states and bringing laws. While these are important elements of the prophets' actions, they are only a small part of the numerous benefits prophets bring to humanity.

Ibn Sīnā's three properties of prophecy appear in many passages of al-Ghazālī's theological works (al-Akiti 2004). Never, however, does he mention the source from where he took these ideas. When he expresses these teachings, al-Ghazālī does not use the technical terminology of the *falāsifa* but rather words and concepts that are familiar to Muslim theologians and Sufis. One such passage is a central chapter on

"The True Nature of Prophecy" in al-Ghazālī's widely read autobiography *Deliverance from Error*. After giving a rough sketch of how humans acquire knowledge—a sketch that follows closely along the lines of Ibn Sīnā's psychology—al-Ghazālī presents an explanation of how prophets receive imaginative revelation (in Ibn Sīnā's sense) from the celestial souls. He avoids the terminology of Ibn Sīnā and casts his theory in a language that introduces some philosophical terms into the accepted parlance of Muslim theology and Sufism. In this passage, al-Ghazālī also stresses that prophecy reaches to insights otherwise unattainable to the human intellect:

> Beyond rationality there is another stage, where another eye is opened that looks into what is unknown and what will happen in the future and other things from which rationality is far removed. ... God most high has made this understandable to man by giving him a sample of the prophets' property, and that is sleep. For the sleeper perceives what will happen in the (otherwise) unknown future either clearly or in the guise of an example whose meaning is disclosed by dream-interpretation.
>
> Just as rationality is one of the stages of the human in which he acquires an eye by which he sees various kinds of universals ... , so is prophecy an expression signifying a stage in which the prophet acquires an eye that has a light wherein the unknown and other phenomena, which the intellect cannot perceive, become visible.
>
> (al-Ghazālī 2000: 84)

Shortly after this, al-Ghazālī introduces Ibn Sīnā's intellectual revelation in a language that does not mention technical details such as the active intellect as its source. Al-Ghazālī calls this property of the prophets "divine inspiration" (*ilhām ilāhī*). It is a way to acquire theoretical knowledge without the help of a teacher and without pursuing empirical experience (*tajriba*). Inspiration (*ilhām*) is described similarly to Ibn Sīnā's *ḥads*. Yet whereas in Ibn Sīnā *ḥads* is a rational method of acquiring theoretical knowledge that all humans can use, here in al-Ghazālī inspiration is a way to perceive theoretical knowledge that cannot be acquired by any other means, not even by the rational faculties of the soul. Inspiration (*ilhām*) is a super-rational faculty that only a few selected humans have. These are prophets, first of all, but also the "friends of God" (*awliyā'*) who are considered Sufi masters.

For al-Ghazālī the inspiration of prophets—meaning their intellectual revelation through their strong *ḥads*—accounts for much of the knowledge that is current among humans. Al-Ghazālī teaches that medical knowledge, such as which medicine cures which disease, or astronomical knowledge about the size of the planets, for instance, cannot be achieved by means of the intellect or through experiments. Rather, it had once been revealed to earlier prophets from where physicians and astronomers have adopted it. For al-Ghazālī, prophecy is responsible for the human acquisition of a whole body of theoretical knowledge that the human intellect cannot arrive at.

Al-Ghazālī, however, was only the first Muslim theologian of a long line who would appropriate Ibn Sīnā's prophetology. What attracted these theologians—and among them many Sufis—to Ibn Sīnā's psychology was the comprehensive way with which it approaches phenomena like clairvoyance, divination, and prophecy. All these are different degrees of strength of a single human faculty, namely the faculty of imagination (*quwwa mutakhayyila*). For Sufis, for instance, this opened up a way to explain the extraordinary insight achieved by those who have purified their souls and cleansed their hearts from the stains of bodily desires, immorality, and vice. If Ibn Sīnā teaches that purity and training can lead to a strengthening of the imaginative faculty, he also explains why an ascetic Sufi may have a deeper insight into the secrets of religion than one of the most learned among the rationalist theologians.

Ibn Sīnā's prophetology provided a congruent explanation of prophecy that satisfied the requirements of the scientific discourse of the day. It regarded prophecy not as a supernatural phenomenon but one that is rooted in the way God created the human soul. Al-Ghazālī shows how these teachings could be adopted to explain the superior insights of ascetics and "friends of God" (*awliyā'*), i.e. Sufi saints. These were often said to be able to predict the future and have other kinds of clairvoyance (*kahāna*). They were also said to perform wondrous deeds (*karāmāt*) that border on miracles. According to Ibn Sīnā, the human soul's practical faculty and its readiness to receive insights increases with its purity. The practical faculty can become so strong that it might affect organisms and natural processes outside of its own body but still within its vicinity. Ibn Sīnā offered a welcome explanation of convictions held by many Sufi Muslims.

Conclusion

In the period after al-Ghazālī, many Sufi authors and many rationalist theologians were drawn to Ibn Sīnā's psychology and applied it in their works. Not always were they aware that the ideas they found in al-Ghazālī or in such prominent Sufis like Ibn 'Arabī (d. 1240) had their roots in the writings of the *falāsifa*. Once they had found a way into the Muslim religious discourse, these ideas often shed their philosophical context and began a life of their own. This is particularly true in Sufism where the initial connection to Ibn Sīnā is almost immediately lost. Key doctrines such as the widespread assumption of a state of "dissolution" (*fanā'*) of the individual Sufi and his or her ascent or union with the transcendent realm, Ibn 'Arabī's teachings on the perfect man (*al-insān al-kāmil*), or Jalāl al-Dīn Rūmī's (d. 1273) conviction that the distinguished Sufi (*walīy*) can receive revelation (*waḥy*) and produce poetry that is on par with the Qur'ān (Rūmī 1925–1940, 3: 244–5, 4: 239–40), are unthinkable without the earlier philosophical concept of a conjunction with the active intellect. By proposing that prophecy is due to the extraordinary strong presence of faculties that exist in every human, the philosophical concept of prophecy brought down epistemological boundaries between the Prophet and his most pious followers. In Sufism this led to the construction of ever-closer affinities between the Sufi saint and the Prophet.

Note

This chapter is a revised version of my 2009 contribution "Muslim Philosopher's Rationalist Explanation of Muḥammad's Prophecy," in J. E. Brockopp (ed.), *Cambridge Companion of Muḥammad*, Cambridge: Cambridge University Press, pp. 158–79.

Further Reading

Butterworth, C. E. (ed.) (2000) *The Political Aspects of Islamic Philosophy*, Cambridge: Harvard University Press.

Davidson, H. A. (1992) *Alfarabi, Avicenna, and Averroes, On Intellect. Their Cosmologies, Theories of the Active Intellect, and Theories of Human Intellect*, New York: Oxford University Press.

Rahman, F. (1958) *Prophecy in Islam: Philosophy and Orthodoxy*, London: Allen and Unwin.

References

Adamson, P. (2007) *Al-Kindī*, New York: Oxford University Press.

al-Akiti, M. A. (2004) "The Three Properties of Prophethood in Certain Works of Avicenna and al-Ġazālī," in J. McGinnis (ed.), *Interpreting Avicenna. Science and Philosophy in Medieval Islam*, Leiden: Brill, pp. 189–212.

al-Fārābī (1961) *Fuṣūl al-madānī / Aphorisms of the Statesman*, D. M. Dunlop (ed. and tr.), Cambridge: Cambridge University Press.

——. (1963) "The Political Regime," in J. Perens & J. C. Macfarland (eds.), *Medieval Political Philosophy: A Sourcebook*, Ithaca: Cornell University Press, pp. 36–55.

——. (1967) "Epistle on the Intellect," in A. Hyman & J. J. Walsh (eds.), *Philosophy of the Middle Ages: The Christian, Islamic and Jewish Traditions*, New York: Harper & Row, pp. 215–21.

——. (1985) *On the Perfect State: Abū Naṣr al-Fārābī's Mabādi' ārā' ahl al-madīna al-fāḍila*, R. Walzer (ed.), Oxford: Clarendon Press.

al-Ghazālī (2000) *Deliverance from Error. Five Key Texts Including His Spiritual Autobiography*, al-Munqidh min al-Dalal, R. J. McCarthy (tr.), Louisville, KY: Fons Vitae.

al-Kindī (2012) *The Philosophical Works of al-Kindī*, P. Adamson & P. Pormann (trans.), Karachi: Oxford University Press.

Aristotle (1957) *On the Soul. Parva Naturalia. On Breath*, W. S. Hett (ed.), Cambridge: Harvard University Press.

Crone, P. (2003) "What Was al-Fārābī's 'Imamic' Constitution," *Arabica* 50: 306–21.

d'Ancona, C. (2009) "Greek Sources in Arabic and Islamic Philosophy," in E. N. Zalta (ed.), *The Stanford Encyclopedia of Philosophy*, http://plato.stanford.edu/entries/arabic-islamic-greek/

Davidson, H. A. (1992) *Alfarabi, Avicenna, and Averroes, On Intellect. Their Cosmologies, Theories of the Active Intellect, and Theories of Human Intellect*, New York: Oxford University Press.

Hansberger, R. (2008) "How Aristotle Came to Believe in God-given Dreams: The Arabic Version of De divination per somnum," in L. Marlow (ed.), *Dreaming Across Boundaries: The Interpretation of Dreams in Islamic Lands*, Boston: Ilex, pp. 50–75.

——. (2011) "Plotinus Arabus Rides Again," *Arabic Sciences and Philosophy* 21: 57–84.

Ibn Bājja (1963) "The Governance of the Solitary," in J. Perens & J. C. Macfarland (eds.), *Medieval Political Philosophy: A Sourcebook*, Ithaca: Cornell University Press, pp. 97–104.

Ibn Sīnā (1952) *Avicenna's Psychology: An English translation of Kitāb al-Najāt*, Book II, Chapter VI, F. Rahman (tr.), London: Oxford University Press.

——. (1959) *Avicenna's De Anima (Arabic Text) Being the Psychological Part of Kitāb al-Shifā'*, F. Rahman (ed.), London: Oxford University Press.

——. (2005) *The Metaphysics of The Healing*, M. E. Marmura (tr.), Provo, UT: Brigham Young University Press.

Madigan, D. A. (2004) "Revelation and Inspiration," in J. D. McAuliffe (ed.), *Encyclopaedia of the Qur'an*, vol. 4, Leiden: Brill, pp. 437–48.

Marmura, M. E. (1979) "The Philosopher and Society: Some Medieval Arabic Discussions," *Arab Studies Quarterly* 1: 309–23.
Rahman, F. (1958) *Prophecy in Islam: Philosophy and Orthodoxy*, London: Allen & Unwin.
Rúmī, Jalál al-Dīn (1925–40) *The Mathnawí of Jalálu'ddín Rúmí*, 8 vols., R. A. Nicholson (ed. and tr.), London/Leiden: Luzac & Co./Brill.
Taylor, R. C. (2006) "Abstraction in al-Fârâbî," *Proceedings of the American Catholic Philosophical Association* 80: 151–618.

32
PHILOSOPHICAL SUFISM

Mohammed Rustom

Introduction

It is often assumed that "philosophy" and "mysticism" are mutually exclusive. Of course, this all depends on how we define our terms, which is not something I will attempt to do here. In medieval Islam, the philosophy/mysticism dichotomy becomes even more problematic, since these are not necessarily watertight categories to begin with. This is why such a philosophical giant as Ibn Sīnā (d. 428/1037) wrote favorably about mysticism (Avicenna 1996), and why the influential philosopher and founder of the school of Illumination Shihāb al-Dīn Suhrawardī (d. 587/1191) openly espoused mysticism in both theory and practice (Aminrazavi 1997: 58–120). We even find a number of well-known figures in the Islamic mystical tradition (commonly referred to as "Sufism") whose approach to things was "philosophical," but who had little interest in the actual discipline of philosophy (Mayer 2008: 276–7). There are also Muslim mystics or Sufis who had a good grounding in philosophy proper, and some of whose works bear witness to a sort of wedding between philosophy and mysticism. The most eminent early examples of this tendency are to be found in the works of Abū Ḥāmid al-Ghazālī (d. 505/1111) (al-Ghazālī 1998) and the pivotal figure 'Ayn al-Quḍāt Hamadānī (d. 525/1131) (Izutsu 1994: 98–140).

Given all of these possibilities, which are symptomatic of a variety of other permutations and tendencies, it is understandable that some may view the phrase "philosophical Sufism" as a vague term or concept (Akasoy 2011: 248). Since it is beyond the parameters of this article to present what makes for good "philosophical Sufism" by providing examples from a wide variety of Islamic texts, authors, and intellectual traditions, I shall focus my presentation on what in Persianate Islam has traditionally been referred to as "theoretical gnosis" (*'irfān-i naẓarī*). This term refers to a specific intellectual explication of Sufi doctrine and praxis that came to the fore in the seventh/thirteenth century by-and-large due to the influence of the Andalusian mystic Ibn 'Arabī (d. 638/1240), a figure whose medieval Christian counterpart is Meister Eckhart (d. 1328) (Dobie 2010). An increasingly systematic and more philosophical understanding of Ibn 'Arabī's teachings (some fundamental to his worldview and others not) eventually came to take centre stage in the writings of his followers. The term "school of Ibn 'Arabī" thus describes a particular approach—largely colored by the thought of Ibn 'Arabī himself—to the major philosophical and religious issues which confronted medieval Islamic thought.

There are specifically two reasons why limiting our discussion of philosophical Sufism to the school of Ibn ʿArabī particularly recommends itself. First, the writings of this school, represented by a plethora of figures, has shaped the intellectual contours of Islamic civilization from North Africa to Malaysia for well over five centuries (Nasr 2005). This stands in stark contrast to the writings of those Sufi figures who incorporated philosophy into their works but whose sphere of influence was ultimately confined to a particular textual tradition, region, or historical period.

Second, the central concern of the school of Ibn ʿArabī is with being or *wujūd*, which is also the central concern of Islamic philosophy. Members of the school of Ibn ʿArabī did not invent an entirely new philosophical vocabulary to explain their teachings. Many of the technical terms and concepts with which they were working had been bequeathed from the well-developed traditions of Islamic philosophy and theology. Owing to the manner in which the main concerns of Islamic philosophy would take centre stage in Muslim theological texts from Ibn Sīnā onward (Wisnovsky 2004), Ibn ʿArabī himself became conversant in philosophical arguments not by way of the Islamic philosophical tradition, but through his educational background in general (Rosenthal 1988: 21) and the discipline of "philosophical theology" in particular (see Addas 1993: 102–10).

At the same time, some of the key "members" of the school of Ibn ʿArabī, such as his foremost disciple and step-son Ṣadr al-Dīn al-Qūnawī (d. 673/1274), were well-versed in the discipline of philosophy. Qūnawī initiated a correspondence with the polymath Naṣīr al-Dīn Ṭūsī (d. 672/1274) after having read Ibn Sīnā's *Remarks and Admonitions* (*al-Ishārāt wa-l-tanbīhāt*) along with Ṭūsī's commentary (Chittick 1981; Schubert 1995). We also have, in Qūnawī's own handwriting, his personal copy of Suhrawardī's *Philosophy of Illumination* (*Ḥikmat al-ishrāq*), as well as a set of glosses on Ibn Sīnā's *Remarks and Admonitions* by the Ashʿarite theologian/philosopher Fakhr al-Dīn al-Rāzī (d. 606/1210) (Chittick 1978: 51). All of this tells us that Qūnawī took the Peripatetic and Illuminationist strands of Islamic philosophy, which were the mainstream philosophical traditions current in his day, very seriously.

A phrase commonly used as a convenient label to "explain" the teachings of the school of Ibn ʿArabī is the term *waḥdat al-wujūd*, or the "Oneness of Being" (see Chittick 2012: Chapter 8 and Landolt 2005: 119–25, 245–300). The Oneness of Being has often been blithely characterized as some form of pantheism (rejected in Rustom 2006: 64–7). And not a few scholars have also sought to explain it as a type of "monism," a reductive and vague term that does not come close to conveying the stress the school of Ibn ʿArabī places upon "multiplicity," "otherness," and "relationality." From this perspective, the term "Oneness of Being" is itself problematic (Morris 1986: 544–5, n. 21), which is perhaps one reason why Ibn ʿArabī's own students and their followers did not employ it in any clearly discernible technical sense as a blanket expression to explain their worldview. In fact, it is well-known that Ibn ʿArabī did not use this expression himself. When it does become a technical term some three decades after his death, it is likely introduced by Ibn Sabʿīn (d. 669/1270) (Chittick 2012: 81; Cornell 2007: 34ff.), a figure who may have been influenced by Ibn ʿArabī, but who cannot strictly speaking be called a "member" of his school. Yet in very broad outlines, we can say that the Oneness of Being generally summarizes the philosophical outlook of the school of Ibn ʿArabī.

In what follows, I present the writings of the school of Ibn 'Arabī in a unified perspective, despite a wide range of opinions amongst its adherents and a somewhat fluid technical lexicon from author to author. This makes it possible to paint a picture of the main features of this school in fairly broad strokes. In order to do justice to the worldview of the school of Ibn 'Arabī, I weave into this presentation two of the main vehicles through which it tackles the central problems of philosophy: the philosophical and the mythic. By the former I mean that approach which is colored by the mainstream and largely abstract discourse of Islamic philosophy and philosophical theology. By the latter I mean the concrete portrayal of the same philosophical concepts, but in the language of myth, dogma, and religious symbolism.

Ontology

It was already mentioned that many of the philosophical and theological expressions used by Ibn 'Arabī were stock phrases in his day. One term he often employs when speaking of God is the "Necessary Being" (*wājib al-wujūd*) (Ibn 'Arabī 1968: 1:291), a technical term that became standard fare in texts of Islamic thought from the time of Ibn Sīnā onwards. Unlike God, whose being cannot not be, that which exists and whose existence depends upon Him is referred to as "contingent being" (*mumkin al-wujūd*), another well-known term bequeathed by Ibn Sīnā. Thus, all that we can inquire into is either Necessary Being—namely, God—or contingent being—namely, everything in existence apart from God. Since God is the source of all things that exist, His being is the most apparent and pervasive. This is because all other instantiations of being, all other existents, must necessarily be subsumed under the wider category of His being, which itself escapes all definition, since the moment we attempt to explain it, we can only do so with reference to one of its particular modes and instances.

Being, therefore, cannot be defined, nor can its "reality" be grasped in any fashion whatsoever. This explains why one of the principal members of the school of Ibn 'Arabī, Dāwūd al-Qayṣarī (d. 751/1350), speaks of being as the most general of things and the most apparent of them as well, as it is a self-evident reality, while at the same time remaining the "most hidden of all things in its quiddity and reality" (al-Qayṣarī 2002: 1:14), a "description" echoed by the famous philosopher Mullā Ṣadrā (d. 1050/1640) some three centuries later. At the same time, being "becomes absolute and delimited, universal and particular, general and specific, one and many without acquiring change in its essence and reality" (al-Qayṣarī 2002: 1:13).

Yet Ibn 'Arabī and his followers are not content to analyze the nature of being in purely philosophical terms. They want to explain the nature of things with reference to God as a concrete reality, which is why they normally take the usual philosophical categories of necessary and contingent being and graft them onto the plane of theology or religion proper. Thus, to call God the Necessary Being in philosophical terms is to speak of what is known in Islamic theology as the Divine Essence (*dhāt*). Another common name for the Divine Essence in the writings of the school of Ibn 'Arabī is the "Essence of Exclusive Oneness" (*al-dhāt al-aḥadiyya*) (Ibn 'Arabī 1946: 90–4). 'Abd al-Razzāq al-Kāshānī (d. 730/1330), another key figure in the school of Ibn 'Arabī, puts it this way: "The Reality called the Essence of Exclusive Oneness in its true nature is nothing other than being, pure and simple, insofar as it is being" (cited in Izutsu 1984: 25, tr. mod.). Like the Necessary Being, the Divine Essence also does not have a quiddity (*māhiyya*) (Chittick 1989: 80–1), and is completely indeterminate in every respect. Since it is completely simple, unqualified, and unqualifiable, it contains no multiplicity in its reality. This is why Maḥmūd Shabistarī (d. 740/1339) says the following in his famous Persian poem on Sufi metaphysics, the *Rosegarden of Mystery* (*Gulshan-i rāz*):

> In God's Presence there is no duality—
> in that Presence there is no "I," "we," or "you."
> "I," "we," "you," and "it," are one thing,
> for in Oneness, there are no distinctions at all.
>
> (Shabistarī 1976: lines 116–17)

Now, if the Divine Essence is pure simplicity, how does multiplicity emerge from It without introducing change into Its nature? In other words, how do instantiations of being emerge from being without any alteration taking place in the fundamental reality of being itself? Ibn 'Arabī points out that "contingent being" is what stands between being as such and nonexistence as such. For Ibn 'Arabī, contingent being is colored by non-being on account of its contingency. It does possess a type of existence, but an existence which is purely relational (Ibn 'Arabī 1968: 3:193). That is to say, contingent things stand in an intermediate position between being and non-being. With respect to being, they are nothing. But with respect to non-being, they are real. Their intermediate status thus guarantees that contingent things have existence, but only in a relative manner. In order to understand how contingent things take on a relative type of existence (but also remain relatively nonexistent), we must turn to a concept which lies at the heart of the metaphysics of the school of Ibn 'Arabī, namely the "immutable entities" (*al-a'yān al-thābita*).

According to Ibn 'Arabī's own testimony, he borrows the term "immutable entities" from the Mu'tazilites (Afifi 1969; Chittick 1989: 204), an important early Islamic theological school which fell into obscurity by the sixth/twelfth century only to be resuscitated in the wake of the modernist movement in Egypt in the late thirteenth/nineteenth century. The "immutable entities" are the latent possibilities which inhere in the very structure of being itself. Or, to use the language of the school of Ibn 'Arabī, they are nothing but the objects of knowledge forever fixed in God's "mind."

Upon close inspection, the immutable entities turn out to be nothing more than the quiddities (*mahiyyāt*) of Islamic theology and philosophy, a point that is made explicit by a number of Ibn 'Arabī's followers (see, for example, al-Qayṣarī 2002: 1: 45, reproduced in Jāmī 1977: 42; see also Mullā Ṣadrā 1964: 35). A quiddity is defined as that by virtue of which a thing is what it is, or its "what-it-is-ness." In other words, the quiddity of horse is horseness, the quiddity of book is bookness, etc. When we look at a particular horse shorn of its accidents, it is still characterized by the quiddity of horseness, but by virtue of being a particular horse, it is not any other horse, and thus is unique in terms of its particular "what-it-is-ness." An immutable entity, likewise, when brought into existence, is a particular instantiated object of God's knowledge which is completely unique in its "what-it-is-ness" apart from anything else. Since "existentiation" (*ījād*) refers to the manner in which things come to "be" in concrete existence, I will henceforth refer to the instantiations of the immutable entities by this technical philosophical term.

What does not change in the "what-it-is-ness" of an immutable entity, whether or not God brings it into concrete "existence," is its status of "immutability" as a contingent, and, hence, relatively nonexistent thing, despite the fact that it has a relative reality when it is brought into actual existence (Rustom 2006: 58–9). Members of the school of Ibn 'Arabī were therefore concerned with the immutable entities because they provided them with a way of accounting for the relative non-reality of everything other than God on the one hand, and their relative reality on the other.

Theology

It has already been said that the immutable entities, as quiddities, are (1) objects of God's knowledge and (2) relatively "nonexistent" in their reality even if they have a relative reality when brought into concrete existence. But the immutable entities have another important function which is related to (2): they also act as particularized loci through which being can become manifest. Thus, when God existentiates an immutable entity, it acts as a receptacle for the "reception" of being. When infused with being, an immutable entity is only capable of receiving a particular mode of it, since its reception of being is conditioned by its own particular "what-it-is-ness."

A more concrete way of expressing this point is to say that the immutable entities are the means through which God contemplates the objects of His knowledge—which form a part of His self-knowledge—in a purely externalized manner. When an immutable entity is existentiated, it acts as a locus of God's manifestation (*maẓhar*). This is on account of the fact that externalized existence is only possible by virtue of God's manifestation in the forms of the immutable entities (Ibn 'Arabī 1946: 81). And, although all objects of God's knowledge, all quiddities, are "immutable entities," it is only those that are existentiated which can act as receptacles through which God contemplates Himself. Each immutable entity that is brought into existence is unique unto itself on account of its particular ability to receive God's manifestation, which the school of Ibn 'Arabī refers to as its "preparedness" (*isti'dād*). Thus, because the immutable entities are specific objects of God's knowledge, His knowledge of them is His knowledge of Himself, but in a particular, delimited fashion (I will return to the concept of God's self-knowledge below).

Members of the school of Ibn 'Arabī maintain that the immutable entities, in their state as existentialized loci of God's manifestation, can only provide them with a means to explain how the cosmos is nothing other than an unfolding of God's self-knowledge when the role of God's names are brought into the discussion. Strictly speaking, the divine names do not have a direct philosophical equivalent, rooted as they are in the discipline of Islamic theology (Rustom 2012: Chapter 3).

For medieval Jewish, Christian, and Islamic thought, the nature of God's names is a common and vexing problem. How can we say, as Scripture does, that God has names which assign a type of "personality" to Him, although He is entirely unlike anything we can know? One common way of speaking of the divine names in classical Islamic theology was to say that they inhered somehow in God's Essence (*qā'ima bi-dhātihi*), but not in a way that gave them independent ontological status such that they could be said to be superadded to It. For many medieval Muslim theologians, the objective ontological status of the divine names was therefore a given, even if their modality could not be easily understood or explained. Ibn 'Arabī rejects this common type of picture of the divine names. He says that the divine names do not "inhere" in God's Essence in any fashion since they are not actually ontological entities. Rather, they are, technically speaking, relationships (*nisab*) (Ibn 'Arabī 1968: 4:294) between what we can call the manifest face of the Essence of Exclusive Oneness and the loci of manifestation, that is, the existentiated immutable entities which "receive" particular modes of being or God's manifestation. In the writings of the school of Ibn 'Arabī, that face of the Essence of Exclusive Oneness that becomes manifest and thus reveals It is often referred to as the "Essence of Inclusive Oneness" (*al-dhāt al-wāḥidiyya*).

We speak of the Divine Essence or the Essence of Exclusive Oneness as having a manifest face in juxtaposition to Its non-manifest face, which always remains utterly unknown and hidden to everything other than It. Thus, the manifest face of the Essence of Exclusive Oneness is that aspect of the Divinity that enters into the realm of relativity. This means that what we normally call "God" is not, for the school of Ibn 'Arabī, God *qua* God at the level of the Essence of Exclusive Oneness. Rather, the term "God" as commonly understood in religion and philosophy is that face of the Essence of Exclusive Oneness that is turned to the cosmos, namely the Essence of Inclusive Oneness.

When the Essence of Exclusive Oneness existentiates the immutable entities, It manifests Itself to them in accordance with their own natures, as has already been mentioned. What come about through the concretization of the immutable entities are the divine names; that is, the relationships that obtain on account of the Essence of Exclusive Oneness's manifestation to the immutable entities, thereby bringing them out of a state of non-externalized contingency into a state of externalized contingency, or, put differently, from a state of relative nonexistence into a state of relative existence. Indeed, if it were not for these relationships, God as apprehensible would not be "God" (Ibn 'Arabī 1946: 81). Notice also how carefully the terms are cast, such that neither the names nor the immutable entities are given absolute ontological status. At the same time, their relative reality assumes that they do take on some mode of existence.

By virtue of the fact that the divine names come about as a result of the Essence of Exclusive Oneness's manifestation, they are singularly responsible for making Its relationship to the cosmos known. Since the entire cosmos is nothing other than a conglomeration of the divine names as displayed through the existentiated immutable entities, each thing in the cosmic order points to the divine names, and, by extension, the divine qualities to which the names refer. One way to frame this picture is to say that the Essence of Exclusive Oneness is made manifest in the garment of the divine names and qualities (al-Qayṣarī 2002: 1:17; Chittick 1989: 85). Thus, all things in the cosmos reveal an aspect of the Essence of Exclusive Oneness by "naming" or pointing to aspects of Its manifest face, that is, the Essence of Inclusive Oneness. At the same time, the multiplicity of the Essence of Exclusive Oneness's manifestations does not imply any plurality in Its nature (al-Qayṣarī 2002: 1:16).

Because the names are nonexistent entities, we cannot speak of any kind of multiplicity. Thus, the Essence of Exclusive Oneness is made manifest by that which is paradoxically nonexistent on the one hand, but which has existence in a relative sense on the other. This explains why Fakhr al-Dīn 'Irāqī (d. 688/1289) says that the divine names do not compromise God's Unity (at the level of the Essence of Exclusive Oneness) in any fashion, just as the waves of the sea do not make the sea a multiplicity. Rather, the waves, insofar as they are waves, are real, but since they belong to the sea and will inevitably ebb back into it, they do not have their own independent and abiding ontological status: "Many and disparate waves do not make the sea a multiplicity; no more do the names make the Named more than one" ('Irāqī 1982: 78, tr. mod.).

Cosmology and Anthropology

We have thus far been using the term "manifestation" (*ẓuhūr*) to denote the manner in which the Essence of Exclusive Oneness turns to the cosmos; that is, how God *qua* Divine Essence reveals Itself. This term has a number of technical equivalents in the writings of the school of Ibn 'Arabī, one of which is the less common word *fayḍ* or "emanation" (al-Qayṣarī 2002: 1:45), an expression that was particularly common in earlier Islamic Neoplatonism. However, two other expressions that become key in the writings of the school of Ibn 'Arabī, and which denote the same idea as "manifestation" and "emanation," are "entification" and "self-disclosure." The word "entification" (*ta'ayyun*) is to be found in Ibn 'Arabī's writings, but assumes no technical significance in them (Chittick 1989: 83). It likely becomes a key term from Qūnawī onwards. For our purposes here, we will leave the words "manifestation" and "entification" aside and focus on the term "self-disclosure," since the structurally mythic ideas associated with the cosmology and anthropology of the school of Ibn 'Arabī are best presented with reference to it.

The term "self-disclosure" (*tajallī*, derived from 7:148 of the Qur'ān) is etymologically related to the idea of "illumination." Since God is identified with light in the Qur'ān (24:35) and in the sayings of the Prophet Muḥammad, it became commonplace to speak of Him as being light, a fundamental insight out of which Suhrawardī develops his philosophy. Thus, "self-disclosure" is a reflexive verbal noun which conveys the sense of God (*qua* Essence of Exclusive Oneness) disclosing Himself to Himself by displaying the intensity of His being/light to the "dark" and "contingent" immutable entities, that is, the objects of His knowledge. This bears some striking resemblances to the treatment of God's theophany that we find in John Scotus Eriugena (d. 877), who translated and was influenced by the Neoplatonist works of pseudo-Dionysius (Carabine 2000: Chapter 4; Sells 1994: Chapter 2).

The common imagery of the sun and its rays is particularly apt here, which is why it is often used to explain the relationship between God and the cosmos: although the sun is one, it has many rays which reveal aspects of the sun but which do not detract from its nature in any manner whatsoever, and which cannot be said to exist independent of it. Just as the rays of the sun illuminate the earth, so too do God's self-disclosures illuminate the cosmic order, revealing the presence of the divine Sun in each thing.

The significance of the term "self-disclosure" is made clear when we look to one of the Prophetic sayings which the school of Ibn 'Arabī commonly draws upon in order to explain why and how God brought about the cosmos, thus addressing the metaphysical problem, "Why is there something rather than nothing?" This report, referred to as a sacred tradition (*ḥadīth qudsī*), says that God was a Hidden Treasure who loved to be known, and, as a result of this desire to be known, He created the cosmos and all that is in it (*khalq*). We are told by Sa'īd al-Dīn Farghānī (d. 699/1300) (Farghānī 2007: 1:18–19) that this desire on God's part to want to be known was a "fundamental inclination," deeply rooted in His nature to gain a type of objectivized knowledge of Himself, since before creating the cosmos He only had a subjective knowledge of Himself. The cosmos thus becomes an objectivized reflection of God's self-knowledge in which God *qua* Essence of Exclusive Oneness can witness Himself *qua* Essence of Inclusive Oneness (Farghānī 2007: 1:21). The jewels contained in this Hidden Treasure are nothing other than the immutable entities. The existentiation of these entities would thus present to God an externalized aspect of His self-knowledge, which would not have been a possibility had He not existentiated them.

This desire for self-knowledge on the part of God is described as a type of "distress" on account of the immutable entities, though in other contexts Ibn 'Arabī also attributes this distress to the divine names. The immutable entities, as latent and non-existent objects of God's knowledge, "sought" their own existentation in the realm of relativity since they did not have existence in their state of fixity and non-existentiation. It is important to note in this context that the Arabic word *wujūd* (from the same root as existentiation, *ījād*) does not only mean "being," but also "finding." The account of the Hidden Treasure thus means that God *qua* being sought objectivized knowledge of Himself through the very objects of His own self-knowledge, and thus brought some of the objects of His knowledge into a relative state of "being" so that He could "find" Himself in them.

One of the key cosmological themes which punctuates the thought of the school of Ibn 'Arabī is a concept which also derives from a Prophetic saying, namely the Breath of the All-Merciful (*nafas al-raḥmān*) (Chittick 1989: 127–34; Corbin 1969: 115–16 et passim). In order to grant relief to the distress of the immutable entities, we are told, God "breathed out" or "exhaled" (Ibn 'Arabī 1946: 112), thereby granting relief and hence mercy to the constriction within His self. This means that the underlying stuff of the cosmos is mercy, since it is the result of the Breath of the All-Merciful. From another perspective, the constriction within the divine self is, as we have seen, the result of a desire on the part of the Divine (*qua* Essence of Exclusive Oneness) to see Himself (*qua* Essence of Inclusive Oneness), which is tantamount to God objectivizing His love for Himself. It is for this reason that Ibn 'Arabī describes the Breath of the All-Merciful as that which allows for God's self-love to come about: "The Breath of the All-Merciful made the cosmos manifest in order to release the property of love and relieve what the Lover found in Himself" (cited in Chittick

1989: 131). The love that motivated the All-Merciful to release His breath is, in the final analysis, the Hidden Treasure's desire to be "known," which is motivated by a fundamental self-love. We can speak of "desire" on the part of God *qua* Essence of Exclusive Oneness because of Its all-possibility, one mode of which is desire, and hence "self-negation."

In more philosophical terms, we can say that the breath is nothing other than the very externalization of the quiddities, which emerge within and by virtue of being. This explains why the school of Ibn 'Arabī explicitly identifies the Breath of the All-Merciful with what is known as "expansive being" (*al-wujūd al-munbasiṭ*) (al-Qūnawī 1969: 193). And since the "Breath of the All-Merciful" is to religious language what "being" is to philosophical language, the root of existence is nothing but mercy. Thus, since all things have come about through mercy, are engulfed in mercy, and are themselves instantiations of mercy, they experience nothing but mercy. Just as the breath marks the beginning in which the cosmos and its contents came about, so too is the end marked by the All-Merciful "inhaling" the objects of His self-knowledge; that is, when the quiddities return from their mode of relative existence to their original state of relative nonexistence. One of the implications of this position is that in their posthumous state, all people will eventually end up in mercy. Ibn 'Arabī defends this soteriological position on these grounds, as does Mullā Ṣadrā, who in many ways is a "member" of the school of Ibn 'Arabī (Rustom 2012: Chapters 6 and 7).

The question of God's originating the cosmos as a result of His seeking self-knowledge finds its perfect analogue in the human quest to seek self-knowledge. The school of Ibn 'Arabī's treatment of the idea of self-knowledge is informed by a well-known Prophetic saying, "He who knows himself, knows his Lord." Since human existence is nothing other than a delimited mode of God's being—that is, since the very substance of the human state is nothing but the self-disclosure of God—the act of gaining self-knowledge on the part of the human subject results in coming to know God in a more concrete and real way. From another perspective, it is God who comes to know Himself through the knowing human self. Mullā Ṣadrā thus identifies the human need to gain self-knowledge as being configured in the very nature of being. The key to gaining access to self-knowledge, which lies at the heart of Sufi praxis, is the remembrance of God (*dhikr*). By remembering God, one comes to know one's true self, since one returns to what one has always been:

> Since forgetfulness of God is the cause of forgetfulness of self, remembering the self will necessitate God's remembering the self, and God's remembering the self will itself necessitate the self's remembering itself: *Remember Me and I will remember you* [Qur'ān 2:152]. God's remembering the self is identical with the self's existence (*wujūd*), since God's knowledge is presential (*ḥuḍūrī*) with all things. Thus, he who does not have knowledge of self, his self does not have existence, since the self's existence is identical with light (*nūr*), presence (*ḥuḍūr*), and perception (*shu'ūr*).
>
> (Mullā Ṣadrā 1961: 14)

By virtue of the fact that one becomes more real and characterized by being, presence, and light the more one remembers God, and thus increases in self-knowledge, he who knows his self most will also come to know God most, since it is through him that God will come to know His objectivized self. This type of self-knowledge is actualized by the "Perfect Human" (*al-insān al-kāmil*), a term Ibn 'Arabī and others use to refer to anyone who has achieved self-realization.

In the school of Ibn 'Arabī there is an important cosmological doctrine that seems to have first been introduced by Qūnawī, referred to as the "Five Divine Presences" (*al-ḥaḍrāt al-ilāhiyya al-khams*). According to this teaching, God's Presence, which accounts for all that there "is," is "there" in five different modes. The first of these is uncreated (the divine Presence); the next three are created (the spiritual, imaginal, and the sensory); and the last (the human) takes in the previous four Presences (Chittick 1982: 124). Earlier members of the school of Ibn 'Arabī do not usually associate the first Presence with God *qua* Essence of Exclusive Oneness (Chittick 1982: 122; cf. the poem cited by Shabistarī above). Thus, above and beyond the first Presence we have God as He is to Himself, which corresponds to the Essence of Exclusive Oneness or what Mu'ayyid al-Dīn Jandī (d. ca. 700/1300) calls the "Non-Entified Essence" (Jandī 1982: 707). The first Presence corresponds to the level of the first delimitation of God, namely the Essence of Inclusive Oneness or what is known as the "First Entification," which corresponds to what we normally refer to as "God," i.e. the divinity that can be known. In general, other names for the second Presence, the spiritual world, can be the "Muḥammadan Spirit," "Highest Pen," "First Intellect," and "Divine Spirit" (Jīlī 2000: 153). The third Presence corresponds to a plane of existence that stands between the spiritual and the corporeal worlds, what is technically known as the "world of imagination" (*'ālam al-khayāl*) (Chittick 1989: 115–18). The fourth Presence is the corporeal world, or the world of matter. And the fifth Presence is the Perfect Human. The Perfect Human takes in all the other Presences because his Presence brings together all of the divine names in which God reveals Himself.

In the first Presence, God *qua* Essence of Inclusive Oneness contains all of the other Presences below it but in undifferentiated fashion (*mujmal*). As being becomes individuated within each Presence, it begins to become more differentiated (*mufaṣṣal*) and hence the relationships that begin to emerge between the Essence of Exclusive Oneness and the loci of God's self-disclosure begin to multiply. The multiplicity of relationships therefore means that the divine names become more widespread within each Presence. By the time we reach the fifth Presence, the Perfect Human, we have what was there in all of the Presences before it, but in completely differentiated form. This is why the Perfect Human is said to be a transcript (*nuskha*) of the cosmos (al-Qūnawī 1969: 106) and the locus for the disclosure of the divine name "Allāh" (Chittick 2012: 144–7). Unlike all of the other divine names which denote specific aspects of the Essence of Inclusive Oneness, the name Allāh is technically known as an all-gathering name (*ism jāmi'*), since it brings together all of the other divine names present in the cosmos. Since the Perfect Human embodies the all-gathering name "Allāh," his Presence is the most all-gathering Presence. The Perfect Human is therefore the mirror image of God (*qua* Essence of Inclusive Oneness), and is described as being a Presence unto himself since he manifests, in being's deployed and differentiated state, the fullness of being, and, hence, the fullness of God's objectivized self-knowledge.

If being in its undifferentiated state contains every perfection, goodness, and beauty in potentiality, then the same holds true for its differentiated state, the Perfect Human, who contains every perfection, goodness, and beauty in actuality. It is for this reason that the Chinese Sufi figure Liu Zhi (b. ca. 1081/1670) describes the Perfect Human, who in Chinese is called "The Human Ultimate," as "the great completion equipped with every beauty" (cited in Murata et al. 2009: 135). In accordance with the well-known Prophetic saying, "God is beautiful, and He loves beauty," the school of Ibn 'Arabī, much like Plotinus (d. 270) (Hadot 1993: 64–73), maintains that the full actualization of the human state is nothing other than to live a life of virtue and beauty. Since the Perfect Human best embodies the differentiated nature of being, thus acting as a mirror in which God *qua* Essence of Exclusive Oneness can witness Himself *qua* Essence of Inclusive Oneness, He looks upon the Perfect Human and sees a crystalline reflection of the objects of His love: the beautiful jewels contained within the Hidden Treasure.

Conclusion

Analyzing the teachings of the school of Ibn 'Arabī in a unified perspective, it becomes clear that their emphasis upon mythic formulations is largely a means by which they can present well-known philosophical concepts in an accessible and concrete fashion. This is not, however, an endorsement of the simplistic view which maintains that religious symbolism or mysticism is merely philosophy "clothed up" and made accessible to non-philosophers. In fact, through an engagement with both mysticism and philosophy, Ibn 'Arabī and his followers would also like to suggest that philosophical language is, in so many ways, itself a symbolic representation of religious or mystical truths. Nevertheless, their perspective forms a unique hybrid of both philosophy and mysticism in a particular technical language, largely informed by the view that, from one vantage point, philosophy and mysticism are two sides of the same coin.

Further Reading

al-Qayṣarī, Dāwūd (2012) *The Foundations of Islamic Mysticism: Qayṣarī's Introduction to Ibn 'Arabī's Fuṣūṣ al-ḥikam*, M. Ali (tr.), Milton Keynes: Spiritual Alchemy Press.

Chittick, W. (2001) *The Heart of Islamic Philosophy: The Quest for Self-Knowledge in the Writings of Afḍal al-Dīn Kāshānī*, New York: Oxford University Press.

Dagli, C. (2015) *Ibn al-'Arabī and Islamic Intellectual Culture: From Mysticism to Philosophy*, New York: Routledge.

Ibn al-'Arabī (2004) *The Ringstones of Wisdom*, C. Dagli (tr.), Chicago: Kazi.

Jāmī, 'Abd al-Raḥmān (1979) *The Precious Pearl*, N. Heer (tr.), Albany: State University of New York Press.

Kalin, I. (2010) *Knowledge in Later Islamic Philosophy: Mullā Ṣadrā on Existence, Intellect and Intuition*, New York: Oxford University Press.

Murata, S. (2000) *Chinese Gleams of Sufi Light: Wang Tai-yü's Great Learning of the Pure and Real and Liu Chih's Displaying the Concealment of the Real Realm*, Albany: State University of New York Press.

Nasr, S. H. & Aminrazavi, M. (eds.) (2012) *An Anthology of Philosophy in Persia*, vol. 4, London: I. B. Tauris in association with The Institute of Ismaili Studies.

Todd, R. (2014) *The Sufi Doctrine of Man: Ṣadr al-Dīn al-Qūnawī's Metaphysical Anthropology*, Leiden: Brill.

References

Addas, C. (1993) *Quest for the Red Sulphur: The Life of Ibn 'Arabī*, P. Kingsley (tr.), Cambridge: Islamic Texts Society.

Afifi, A. E. (1969) "al-A'yān al-thābita fī madhhab Ibn al-'Arabī wa-l-ma'dūmāt fī madhhab al-Mu'tazila," in I. Madkour (ed.), *al-Kitāb al-Tadhkārī: Muḥyī al-Dīn Ibn al-'Arabī*, Cairo: Dār al-Kitāb al-'Arabī.

Akasoy, A. (2011) "What is Philosophical Sufism?," in P. Adamson (ed.), *In the Age of Averroes*, London: Warburg Institute, pp. 229–49.

al-Ghazālī, Abū Ḥāmid (1998) *The Niche of Lights*, D. Buchman (tr.), Provo, UT: Brigham Young University Press.

al-Qayṣarī, Dāwūd (2002) *Maṭla' khuṣūṣ al-kalim fī ma'ānī Fuṣūṣ al-ḥikam (Sharḥ Fuṣūṣ al-ḥikam)*, Qum: Anwār al-Hudā.

al-Qūnawī, Ṣadr al-Dīn (1969) *al-Tafsīr al-ṣūfī li-l-Qur'ān (I'jāz al-bayān fī ta'wīl umm al-Qur'ān)*, 'A. A. 'Aṭā' (ed.), Cairo: Dār al-Kutub al-Ḥadītha.

Aminrazavi, M. (1997) *Suhrawardī and the School of Illumination*, Surrey: Curzon.

Avicenna (1996) *Ibn Sīnā on Mysticism: Remarks and Admonitions, Part 4*, S. Inati (tr.), London: Kegan Paul.

Carabine, D. (2000) *John Scottus Eriugena*, New York: Oxford University Press.

Chittick, W. (1978) "The Last Will and Testament of Ibn al-'Arabī's Foremost Disciple and Some Notes on its Author," *Sophia Perennis* 4: 43–58.

——. (1981) "Mysticism vs. Philosophy in Earlier Islamic History: The al-Ṭūsī, al-Qūnawī Correspondence," *Religious Studies* 17: 87–104.

——. (1982) "The Five Divine Presences: From al-Qūnawī to al-Qayṣarī," *Muslim World* 72: 107–28.

——. (1989) *The Sufi Path of Knowledge: Ibn al-'Arabī's Metaphysics of Imagination*, Albany: State University of New York Press.

——. (1996) "The School of Ibn 'Arabī," in S. H. Nasr & O. Leaman (eds.), *History of Islamic Philosophy*, New York: Routledge, vol 1, pp. 510–23.

——. (2012) *In Search of the Lost Heart: Explorations in Islamic Thought*, M. Rustom, A. Khalil, & K. Murata (eds.), Albany: State University of New York Press.

Corbin, H. (1969) *Creative Imagination in the Ṣūfism of Ibn 'Arabī*, R. Manheim (tr.), Princeton: Princeton University Press.

Cornell, V. (2007) "The All-Comprehensive Circle (*al-iḥāṭa*): Soul, Intellect, and the Oneness of Existence in the Doctrine of Ibn Sab'īn," in A. Shihadeh (ed.), *Sufism and Theology*, Edinburgh: Edinburgh University Press, pp. 31–48.

Dobie, R. (2010) *Logos and Revelation: Ibn 'Arabi, Meister Eckhart, and Mystical Hermeneutics*, Washington: Catholic University of America Press.

Farghānī, Sa'īd al-Dīn (2007) *Muntahā al-madārik fī sharḥ Tā'iyyat Ibn al-Fāriḍ*, 'Ā. I. al-Kayyālī (ed.), Beirut: Dār al-Kutub al-'Ilmiyya.

Hadot, P. (1993) *Plotinus or The Simplicity of Vision*, M. Chase (tr.), Chicago: University of Chicago Press.

Ibn 'Arabī (1946) *Fuṣūṣ al-ḥikam*, A. E. Afifi (ed.), Cairo: Dār Iḥyā' al-Kutub al-'Arabiyya.

——. (1968) *al-Futūḥāt al-makkiyya*, Beirut: Dār Ṣādir.

'Irāqī, Fakhr al-Dīn (1982) *Divine Flashes*, W. Chittick & P. Wilson (tr.), New York: Paulist Press.

Izutsu, T. (1984) *Sufism and Taoism: A Comparative Study of Key Philosophical Concepts*, Berkeley: University of California Press.

——. (1994) *Creation and the Timeless Order of Things: Essays in Islamic Mystical Philosophy*, Ashland: White Cloud Press.

Jāmī, 'Abd al-Raḥmān (1977) *Naqd al-nuṣūṣ fī sharḥ Naqsh al-fuṣūṣ*, W. Chittick (ed.), Tehran: Imperial Iranian Academy of Philosophy.

Jandī, Mu'ayyid al-Dīn (1982) *Sharḥ Fuṣūṣ al-ḥikam*, S. J. Áshtiyānī (ed.), Mashhad: Dánishgáh-i Mashhad.

Jīlī, 'Abd al-Karīm (2000) *al-Insān al-kāmil*, Beirut: Mu'assasat al-Tárīkh al-'Arabī.

Landolt, H. (2005) *Recherches en spiritualité iranienne*, Tehran: Insitut français de recherche en Iran.

Mayer, T. (2008) "Theology and Sufism," in T. Winter (ed.), *The Cambridge Companion to Classical Islamic Theology*, Cambridge: Cambridge University Press, pp. 258–87.

Morris, J. (1986) "Ibn 'Arabī and His Interpreters (Part I)," *Journal of the American Oriental Society* 106: 539–51.

Mullā Ṣadrā (1961) *Risāla-yi sih aṣl*, S. H. Nasr (ed.), Tehran: University of Tehran Press.

——. (1964) *Kitāb al-Mashā'ir*, H. Corbin (ed. and tr.), Tehran: Département d'iranologie de l'Institut franco-iranien.

Murata, S., Chittick, W., & Weiming, T. (2009) *The Sage Learning of Liu Zhi: Islamic Thought in Confucian Terms*, Cambridge, MA: Harvard University Asia Center.

Nasr, S. H. (2005) "Theoretical Gnosis and Doctrinal Sufism and their Significance Today," *Transcendent Philosophy* 6: 1–36.

Rosenthal, F. (1988) "Ibn 'Arabī between 'Philosophy' and 'Mysticism'," *Oriens* 31: 1–35.

Rustom, M. (2006) "Is Ibn al-'Arabī's Ontology Pantheistic?," *Journal of Islamic Philosophy* 2: 53–67.

——. (2012) *The Triumph of Mercy: Philosophy and Scripture in Mullā Ṣadrā*, Albany: State University of New York Press.

Schubert, G. (ed.) (1995) *Annäherungen: Der mystisch-philosophische Briefwechsel zwischen Ṣadr ud-Dīn-i Qónawī und Naṣīr ud-Dīn-i Ṭūsī*, Beirut: Franz Steiner.

Sells, M. (1994) *Mystical Languages of Unsaying*, Chicago: University of Chicago Press.

Shabistarī, Maḥmūd (1976) *Gulshan-i rāz*, J. Nurbakhsh (ed.), Tehran: Intishárát-i Khánaqáh-i Ni'mat Alláhī.

Wisnovsky, R. (2004) "One Aspect of the Avicennian Turn in Sunnī Theology," *Arabic Sciences and Philosophy* 14: 64–100.

33
RELIGIOUS READINGS OF PHILOSOPHY

Ayman Shihadeh

Introduction

In early Islamic culture, the theological and philosophical traditions developed largely independently of each other. As the branch of religious thought concerned with the establishment and exposition of doctrine, theology was very much an indigenous discipline guided chiefly by the teachings of scripture, though it was also influenced in various ways by pre-Islamic intellectual trends that were current in the late-antique Near East. Within the theological tradition, there was a broad and diverse spectrum of outlooks ranging from the highly rationalist, whereby faith had to be founded in reason, to the relatively fideistic, according to which faith should rest to some extent on the authority of scripture or some charismatic individuals. Philosophy (*falsafa*), on the other hand, was the continuation of the ancient philosophical tradition and in essence had no particular religious affiliations. Muslims, Christians, Jews and pagans contributed to the transmission and development of philosophy in medieval Arabic culture.

The two disciplines, however, overlapped considerably in their subject matter. Both, for instance, dealt with cosmology, cosmogony, epistemology, anthropology, ethics, soteriology, and eschatology. So it was natural that the relation between philosophers and theologians was one of mutual antagonism, though in practice this often manifested in the two sides ignoring each other, especially because they occupied distinct and mostly separate social spheres.

Gradually the interaction between the two disciplines increased, mainly under the influence of three key figures. Ibn Sīnā (d. 1037) developed a hugely influential philosophical system that in various ways captured the interest of many theologians. Some decades later, al-Ghazālī (d. 1111) defended theology by delivering a robust criticism of Avicennian philosophy, while advocating an open, though critical, attitude towards philosophy. Fakhr al-Dīn al-Rāzī (d. 1210) then developed the definitive synthesis of philosophical theology which led to the rise of neo-Ash'arism. Notwithstanding this development, many later theologians continued to adhere to more traditional theological doctrines and outlooks, and to view philosophy as a heresy whose misguided exponents preferred to acquire their beliefs from the conjecture of ancient pagans than to accept the infallible divine guidance offered in revelation.

In this chapter, we shall examine two representative theological approaches to philosophy, one pre-Avicennian, the other post-Avicennian. As the later, more philosophical strands of theology are dealt with elsewhere in this volume, we shall concentrate here on criticisms that theologians directed at the philosophers, rather than on their influence by their ideas.

Before Ibn Sīnā

Pre-Avicennian philosophers were widely perceived by contemporaneous theologians as the followers of a pre-Islamic belief system founded by ancient Greek pagans, most notably Plato and Aristotle. They were associated with the denial of revealed religions (*jaḥd al-sharā'i'*) as well as a small number of heterodox metaphysical and physical doctrines. With the exception of the individual efforts of a small number of early theologians to look more closely at the teachings of a particular philosopher, or to debate personally with one, classical theological sources generally exhibit little familiarity or direct engagement with the teachings and sources of the philosophical tradition. This is confirmed by the late-eleventh-century theologian al-Ghazālī, who writes on his predecessors:

> Of the teachings of the [philosophers], the books of the theologians, in places where they attempt to respond to them, only contain convoluted and sketchy fragments, which are clearly contradictory and defective, and which would not convince even a sound-minded common person, let alone those who claim mastery of intricate sciences. So I realised that refuting a doctrine without having understood it profoundly is nothing more than taking a shot in the dark.
> (*Munqidh*, 18)

Having been educated in the traditional religious disciplines and the Arabic language, theologians had little taste for the philosophers' foreign and, in their view, terribly ostentatious argot. One Mu'tazilite author, for instance, identifies the 'exponents of the doctrine of the *hyle*' (*aṣḥāb al-hayūlā*) as 'a group who hold that matter is pre-eternal and its compositions generated in time, and they refer to that using an array of bombastic expressions, such as 'element' (*usṭuquṣ*), 'prime matter,' 'matter' (*ṭīna*), 'element' (*'unṣur*), 'hyle,' etc. (Mānkdīm, *Sharḥ*, 111).

In the earlier theological sources, the philosophers are often referred to with vague designations: "the naturalists" (*ṭabā'i'iyyūn*) or "the exponents of the doctrine of the natures" (*aṣḥāb al-ṭabā'i'*), i.e. the notion that matter consists of four natures: hot, cold, moist and dry. They are characterised as advocates of a small selection of doctrines, which are discussed only to be refuted, particularly hylomorphism, the pre-eternity of the world, the notion that God is an involuntary cause, and, occasionally, metempsychosis. These earlier accounts of the philosophers' teachings appear highly selective, exiguous and essentially monologic (rather than dialogic). The theologians reported and addressed only a handful of views which, though connected to each other, were largely divorced from their original cosmological and epistemological contexts. In general, the broader theories to which these views belonged and the evidence and proofs that the philosophers adduced for them were absent, which rendered them unjustified and arbitrary. The manner in which these views were selected and presented shows that the theologians were less interested in what the philosophers actually taught than in the ways in which some of these teachings could pose hypothetical challenges to the theologians' own cosmology. In this early period, after all, philosophy was still not perceived as a real threat and could be treated in a cursory manner.

Let us consider the representative discussion included by the Ash'arite theologian al-Bâqillânī (d. 1013) in a medium-sized theological compendium. After proving that the world is created *ex nihilo* and that the Creator exists and has certain attributes, he considers questions concerning the nature of the creative act that brought the world into being (*Tamhīd*, 22–33). He argues that God's acts are voluntary, and neither motivated nor compelled (the competing Mu'tazilite school, by contrast, holding that God's acts are motivated but not compelled). This is followed by a refutation of alternative cosmologies taught in several non-Islamic belief systems. The first discussed are the so-called exponents of the theory of the natures (*Tamhīd*, 34–47).

Their overall thesis is that things and occurrences in the world are engendered by natural causes, which leaves no room for the creative activity of a voluntary divine being. To *kalām* theologians, these natural causes were in some respects analogous to their own concept of "necessitating cause" (*'illa mūjiba*): an accident that inheres in an atom and engenders an effect. (According to earlier *kalām* atomism, the world consists of homogeneous indivisible atoms, which are qualified by different classes of accidents that inhere in them.) And in fact, as we shall see, what al-Bâqillânī and other theologians tend to do in discussing the philosophers' concept of natural causality is to reduce it to their own concept of causation, despite the major differences between the two. For instance, Ash'arites hold that an individual quantum of a specific type of cause can only produce an individual quantum of a specific simple effect, which does not vary according to any other factors that accompany the occurrence. An effect, furthermore, can only occur in the same atom that serves as the substratum in which the cause inheres, never in a different atom.

The first main claim of this group that al-Bâqillânī considers is that the producer of the world is a "nature," by which he seems to mean an involuntary cause (rather than one of the four natures). He proceeds to confute this suggestion by setting up the following simple disjunction: If we postulate that the world was produced by such a cause, the latter would be either non-existent, in which case it would not be a cause for anything, or existent. If the cause exists, then it is either pre-eternal or created in time. It cannot be pre-eternal. For otherwise the series of its generated effects too would be pre-eternal; however, the world is created in time (as was argued earlier in the same book, 22–3). If, on the other hand, the cause is created, then it must have been brought into being either by another natural cause, which would lead to the infinite regress of natural causes, or by a different type of producer, which has to be conceded.

Al-Bâqillânī then turns to the theories of hylomorphism and natural causality—that the world consists of a mixture of the four natures and that each nature has specific activities—which clash with the atomism and occasionalism of classical Ash'arism (on which see Perler & Rudolph 2000). Providing extremely little detail on the philosophical views in question, he proceeds to disprove them using several arguments, of which the following are examples.

The first argument is this. When one nature (say, hot or moist) present in an object is followed by its contrary (cold or dry, respectively), the former will cease to exist and will be replaced by the latter, which comes into being. The body per se remains unchanged. Therefore, these natures are in fact none other than pairs of contrary accidents that inhere in atoms, and are generated in time from nothing and then return to nothing. It follows that they are neither pre-eternal themselves, nor, al-Bāqillānī adds vaguely, somehow parts of a pre-eternal hotness, coldness, moistness or dryness, as a generated thing cannot be part of a pre-eternal thing.

Another argument is that if occurrences in this world are engendered by involuntary natural causes, then these causes should produce uniform and unvarying effects. So in the availability of unlimited supplies of water and nourishment, individual animals and plants would continue to grow *ad infinitum*. However, that excessive watering and fertilisation will in fact destroy crops indicates that these substances do not engender any effects by any intrinsic properties of their own.

Perhaps the most interesting argument al-Bāqillānī puts forth targets the claim that, based on our sensory observation, the causal nexus between burning and the heat present in fire, and between intoxication and the properties of alcohol, is plainly evident and hence requires no proof. Not so, he responds. What we actually observe is only the concomitance of two occurrences: a certain change in the state of the body (respectively, intoxication or burning) with the drinking of alcohol, or with the object's coming into contact with fire. That is the extent of our knowledge. As to the identity of the producer of the new state, this is not immediately discernible to us, but only knowable through complicated investigation. This is confirmed by the fact that conflicting claims have actually been made concerning the identity of the producer: some, like the author, assert that it is a pre-eternal voluntary Creator, others that it is an accident, and yet others that it is the nature inherent in the fire. Al-Bāqillānī argues at some length that, in the presence of such differences of opinion, no one is entitled to claim that their own view, to the exclusion of all other views, is self-evident. Al-Ghazālī later advances a more developed version of this criticism of natural causality in his *Incoherence of the Philosophers* (al-Ghazālī 1927: 170 ff.).

Post-Avicennian Approach

Relations between philosophy and theology underwent a huge transformation under the influence of Ibn Sīnā. Not only did he develop a highly compelling philosophical system, he also theorised within that system various typically theological subjects such as prophecy, revelation, miracles, the afterlife and theodicy. In some discussions, he consciously employed characteristically Islamic (and, significantly, non-sectarian) religious and cultural language and concepts, most famously in the *Pointers and Reminders* (*al-Ishārāt wa-l-tanbīhāt*) in which he set out a philosophical soteriology using a Sufi register. Although the trend to theorise religious and soteriological concepts had already started from late antiquity, earlier Arabic philosophers who partook in this trend, including the Brethren of Purity and al-Fārābī, all failed to capture the interest and attention of religious scholars the way Ibn Sīnā did. By the end of the eleventh century, there were rumblings that philosophy was spreading and beginning to pose a real threat to orthodoxy.

The riposte came in the shape of the momentous criticism directed at Avicennian philosophy by the famous late-eleventh-century jurist and theologian al-Ghazālī, a *tour de force* that set the tone for the later theological interchange with philosophy. Yet as well as being a critic of philosophy, al-Ghazālī was to a great extent also responsible for setting into motion a process that led to the rise of a tradition of philosophical theology that continued into the modern period. He took on board a range of Avicennian doctrines, but more importantly, as we shall see, promoted a discriminating attitude towards philosophy that allowed later theologians to engage much more liberally with the subject. Towards the end of the twelfth century, Fakhr al-Dīn al-Rāzī developed the definitive synthesis of philosophical theology, which determined the broad outlines of the later neo-Ash'arite tradition (Shihadeh 2005). In what follows, we shall concentrate on al-Ghazālī's criticism, as it was historically influential and in some important respects exemplified the tension that a prophetic monotheism will inevitably encounter in the Neo-Platonised Aristotelianism that was dominant in the Arabic philosophical tradition.

Lamenting his predecessors' derisory portrayals of the philosophers' teachings, al-Ghazālī sets out, first of all, to study their works first-hand. A sound criticism, he emphasised, must be based on a proper and in-depth understanding of the views criticised. He distinguishes three "types" of philosophers (*Munqidh*, 19–20). First, the Physicalists (*dahriyya*), whom he describes as an extinct group of ancient philosophers who denied the existence of the Creator and maintained that the world is pre-eternal and self-sustaining. Second, the Naturalists (*ṭabī'iyyūn*), who affirmed the existence of the Creator, but nonetheless proposed an entirely physicalist account of human nature, hence denying the existence of an immaterial soul and the afterlife. Al-Ghazālī appears to believe that this group too was extinct. Third, the Theists (*ilāhiyyūn*), a "later" group of philosophers, including Socrates, Plato and most importantly Aristotle, who, we are told, refuted the views of the previous two groups and developed a comparatively mature and refined set of teachings. Aristotle's philosophy was then taken on board and transmitted by al-Fārābī and Ibn Sīnā. Though al-Ghazālī considers all three groups to be unbelievers, the last clearly deserves this verdict on fewer counts. They are also the only group of philosophers whose views deserve and need to be addressed, as the first two, according to al-Ghazālī, are obsolete and had already been dealt with by the third. By effectively redirecting much of the earlier anti-philosophical sentiment towards the two extinct groups, he not only presents Aristotelianism as the least-bad school of philosophy, but also paves the way for his view that it has much good to offer theology.

Al-Ghazālī thus concentrates on the teachings of the third group, particularly the philosophy of Ibn Sīnā, which he considers to be the most developed and relevant incarnation of Aristotelianism. In *The Doctrines of the Philosophers* (*Maqāṣid al-falāsifa*), he offers a concise and lucid summa of Avicennian philosophy, which targets a non-philosophical readership and is intended primarily as a companion to his better-known work *The Incoherence of the Philosophers* (*Tahāfut al-falāsifa*). The *Doctrines* should be seen, and indeed is presented by its author, essentially as a heresiographical text that offers a neutral report of the teachings of one school of thought. Its task was to facilitate a better-informed critical engagement with philosophy, such that certain views could be disproved using sound arguments, and other views accepted.

Like earlier theological sources, al-Ghazālī's *Incoherence* targets a range of metaphysical and physical philosophical doctrines that overlap in their subject-matter with religious doctrines. Most of the 20 discussions that comprise the book fall under two main categories. First, some discussions refute certain doctrines that conflict with widely held, Qur'ān-based Islamic beliefs, though in a small number of cases (for instance, discussion 6) the doctrine criticised clashes specifically with the teachings of the Ash'arite school to which al-Ghazālī belonged. The first two discussions, for instance, disprove the doctrines that the world is eternal, respectively, in the past and into the future, in defence of the generally accepted theological doctrines that the world was created in time, that its existence may come to an end, and that the occurrence of both events is directly dependent on God's power and will. Ibn Sīnā's doctrine that the First Cause knows only universals, to the exclusion of particular things, is also attacked in defence of the Qur'ānic conception of an omniscient God. So is his doctrine that only the immaterial rational soul survives the death of the human body and that the latter cannot conceivably be restored, which contradicts explicit Qur'ānic depictions of bodily resurrection.

Another group of discussions in the *Incoherence* only seeks to show that the philosophers fail to back certain doctrines with sound proofs, or that either these doctrines or their proofs contradict other views of theirs, even though the doctrines themselves are more or less in agreement with widely accepted religious tenets. This tactic is meant to substantiate further that rather than being based on sound evidence and critical thinking, in accordance with the principles enshrined in the philosophers' own theory of demonstration, these views are in fact arbitrary and received uncritically from past tradition. Al-Ghazālī argues, for instance, that they fail to prove the existence of the First Cause, that He is immaterial, and that He knows Himself.

At the end of his book, al-Ghazālī concludes that the philosophers should be deemed unbelievers on account of three doctrines of theirs: that the world is pre-eternal, that God does not know particular things, and that human bodies will not be restored and resurrected (al-Ghazālī 1927: 376–7). Other philosophical doctrines may be erroneous, but do not warrant the same harsh judgement considering, as he points out, that cognate doctrines were espoused by theological schools and sects within the fold of Islam. The last point is not an argument from historical contingency, but in fact rests on the assumption that even unorthodox Muslim theologians will recognise the authority of revelation and attempt to harmonise their beliefs with its statements, if need be by interpreting the latter figuratively. By contrast,

> These three doctrines do not agree with Islam in any respect. The one who believes them believes that prophets utter falsehoods and that they said whatever they have said in order to [promote common] utility by offering images (*tamthīl*) to the multitudes of people and by seeking to make them understand. This view amounts unequivocally to unbelief and has never been espoused by any Islamic sects.
>
> (al-Ghazālī 1927: 376)

For al-Ghazālī, therefore, the philosophers are branded as unbelievers not simply because they espouse three doctrines that happen to clash with the teachings of scripture, but first and foremost on account of what, from the theological viewpoint, is a more fundamental and potentially more global and far-reaching offence: the view that revelation employs images to explain certain things to common people and thus should not be taken at face value. It is precisely this view that allows the philosophers to make light of the teachings of scripture so as to contradict them so brazenly, and that al-Ghazālī is most worried about, as he perceives in it a threat to the very epistemological and soteriological foundations of religion. Let us consider this point of conflict more closely, starting with the theologians' views on the epistemological status of prophecy and then turning to their reception of Ibn Sīnā's theory of prophecy and revelation.

Theologians, of course, differ widely on the relative scope and application of so-called rational evidence (that is, discursive proofs grounded ultimately in self-evident items of knowledge) and revealed evidence, extracted mainly from the Qur'ān and the teachings of the Prophet. The two sources were referred to metaphorically as "seeing" (*naẓar*) and "hearing" (*sam'*), respectively. All theologians agreed, however, on the following two main points.

First, no matter how much or little knowledge it can provide, reason has limitations. There are areas in theology in which our minds can inform us only whether a thing is conceivable, but not whether or not it actually is, or will be. The main case in point is eschatology. Most Sunni theologians concede that resurrection, the existence of heaven and hell, and the experiences that humans will go through in the afterlife can only be learnt from scripture. For this reason, these subjects are discussed in theological texts under the heading "Doctrines known on the authority of tradition" (*sam'iyyāt*).

Second, though there may be cases of *prima facie* contradiction between the sound findings of reason and the contents of scripture, all are demonstrably semantic. Two major examples are scriptural anthropomorphisms and statements that imply either human autonomy or predeterminism, which *kalām* theologians often felt able to harmonise with their school doctrine. No instances of genuine contradiction are ever admitted, especially in cases where the teachings of the Qur'ān are unambiguous and reinforced by scholarly consensus, such as God's omniscience and various eschatological doctrines. So although, in theory, the mind in large areas of theology may (often, must) operate independently of revelation, in practice the "findings" of theological rational enquiry were always in keeping with the fundamental tenets of scripture. From the theologians' point of view, this agreement was unsurprising, as it confirmed that both reason and revelation were genuine, though independent, sources of knowledge.

Ibn Sīnā understands the nature, function and epistemological status of revelation very differently (Avicenna 1959, 1984; Marmura 1964; Michot 1986; Davidson 1992; Hasse 2000; Gutas 2006). The prophet, in his view, is a unique individual with certain highly developed psychological capacities, in particular the intellective, imaginative and motive capacities. He is, first of all, possessed of an intense capacity for intuition, which enables him to receive the secondary intelligibles from the active intellect almost instantaneously and without need for cogitation, which is the process that most other people, including philosophers, need to employ to become prepared to obtain knowledge. This intellective capacity allows the prophet to understand reality despite having no philosophical learning. The prophet also has a developed imaginative faculty which, under the influence of his intellective capacity, presents the intelligibles he receives in the form of visible apparitions and audible messages. These provide some of the substance of the revealed text and message that he conveys to others. His motive faculty is so developed that he influences objects other than his own body, thus producing miracles to prove his veracity.

According to Ibn Sīnā, the prophet must not divulge the knowledge that he receives to the public, as the absolute majority of people are unable to understand it and cannot be motivated by abstract metaphysical and ethical notions to lead good lives. The prophet's theological teachings, rather, should be devised in such a way as to employ tangible images that, if taken literally, can engender assent and awe within ordinary people. They are not intended to provide them with any amount of genuine knowledge, but primarily to curb their natural tendency to evil and to establish social order. God is thus depicted, in anthropomorphic terms, as a majestic heavenly personal being who knows and controls everything directly. And the afterlife is depicted using vivid physical imagery that people can relate to.

For several reasons, this theory of prophecy encountered much opposition among post-Avicennian theologians. First of all, although it confirms the high status and uniqueness of prophets, the Avicennian theory of prophecy reduces it to a purely psychological, and hence natural, phenomenon (Marmura 1964). Rather than being elected and ordained into his prophetic mission directly by God, who then proceeds to provide him with revelation and guidance, the Avicennian prophet is a superhuman being, who is naturally endowed by virtue of his rare bodily composition with superlative psychological faculties, and who may even have cultivated these capacities further in himself by his own efforts. The intellectual and imaginative revelations he receives are not handed exclusively to him by God, but are available for suitably-equipped persons to tap into. And the miraculous acts he performs do not really break any natural laws by divine intervention, but are perfectly natural occurrences that any suitably-equipped individual could perform.

The theologian Ibn Taymiyya (d. 1328), for instance, attacks Ibn Sīnā's prophetology on the grounds that it affords the prophet no special properties beyond natural human capacities (Ibn Taymiyya 2000: 695–703). Even an unbeliever, he argues, who dedicates himself to learning and worship may develop an aptitude for intuition comparable to that which Ibn Sīnā considers to be one of the properties of prophethood. Likewise, the visions that a prophet is said to perceive in wakefulness—a property that Ibn Sīnā attributes to the prophet's developed imaginative faculty—can also be experienced by magicians and the insane. Magicians are furthermore able to perform miraculous acts comparable to prophetic miracles on account of their developed motive faculty. The only difference that Ibn Sīnā makes between prophets and magicians, Ibn Taymiyya writes, is that the former teach virtue while the latter use their abilities for evil. Ibn Sīnā and later philosophers, he adds, believed that prophethood can be acquired, and he gives al-Suhrawardī (d. 1191) and Ibn Sab'īn (d. ca. 1270) as two figures who strove to become prophets themselves (cf. Ibn Taymiyya 1991: 1, 318).

Another major problem that theologians encounter in Ibn Sīnā's theory of prophecy concerned his view that the prophetic message addresses the general public using imagery that often does not correspond to reality, in order to serve an ethical and socio-political objective. To al-Ghazālī, reducing the contents of revelation to mere imaginations (*takhyīl, tamthīl*) amounts to accusing the prophets of lying. Commenting on scriptural depictions of the devil and the *jinn* as animate beings and the philosophers' denial of the existence of such beings and view that any occurrences ascribed to them have in fact purely natural explanations, he writes:

> Whenever they find anything in religion that suits them they accept it, but when they find something that contradicts their reasoning they claim that it consists of images devised by the prophets, who are obliged to descend to the level of the common people [to address them] often having to depict a thing in a way that does not correspond to its reality. They interpret whatever does not agree with their reasoning in this way. They thus went to the extreme in their rationalism, to the extent that they ascribed lying for the sake of common utility (*al-kadhib li-ajl al-maṣlaḥa*) to the prophets.
>
> (al-Ghazālī 1940: 7)

In the same way, al-Ghazālī assesses the philosophers' views on the nature of the afterlife, which he considers one of the major "principles of religion" (*uṣūl al-dīn al-muhimma*). He argues that they should be deemed unbelievers on account of their denial that bodies would be resurrected and would then experience the forms of physical reward and punishment depicted in scripture, because this would render the prophets liars (al-Ghazālī 1961: 142–3; 1964: 151–5; Griffel 2004: 113 ff.). The same is true of their denial that God knows particular things, including individual human beings, as taught in the Qur'ān. He writes,

> They say, 'The moral wellbeing (*ṣalāḥ*) of people hinges on their believing that bodies will be resurrected, as their minds are too deficient to grasp the notion that only the mind survives in the hereafter. Their moral wellbeing also lies in that they believe that God, exalted, knows all that happens to them and watches them, in order to produce desire and fear in their hearts. So it is permissible for the Messenger, peace be upon him, to teach them these things. However, one who serves the interest of another person, and who says what serves his interest though what he says does not correspond to the truth, is not a liar.' This view is certainly false, because it begins by an unequivocal affirmation that [the Prophet] lied, and then proceeds to find an excuse to explain why he lied.
>
> (al-Ghazālī 1961: 142–3)

Lying is a vice (*radhīla*), to which no prophet can conceivably resort. For it is perfectly possible, he maintains, both to tell the truth and, at the same time, to further the moral wellbeing of the public.

Al-Ghazālī felt that Ibn Sīnā's theory of prophecy posed a real threat to religion, one that he considered akin to the threat posed by antinomian strands of Sufism (al-Ghazālī 1969: 47–8). Some people who become exposed to this theory will feel that they fall under neither the category of common people (*'awāmm*) whom, according to Ibn Sīnā, revelation seeks to tame by means of imaginary sticks and carrots, nor that of the philosophers so as to lead a philosophical way of life. So they simply abandon religious practice altogether. Some, he adds, would pray and perform various religious practices, but show laxity in others on the grounds that they understand the true purpose of religious practices and hence know when it is harmless or even beneficial to break them. Wine is religiously prohibited, they would say, only because it promotes social discord, but can safely be consumed by the wise and virtuous philosopher as it sharpens the mind.

It is first and foremost for their views on religion and prophecy that al-Ghazālī takes an antagonistic stance towards the philosophers. Some religious thinkers concluded that philosophy was irreconcilably inimical to religion. The Sufi Shihāb al-Dīn al-Suhrawardī (d. 1234) (not to be confused with his aforementioned namesake), for instance, writes a book entitled *The Infamies of the Greeks Exposed and the Counsels of Faith Embraced* (*Kashf al-faḍā'iḥ al-yūnāniyya wa-rashf al-naṣā'iḥ al-īmāniyya*), in which he emphasises that the teachings of the divinely-revealed Qur'ān and the prophetic Sunna ought to be followed to the exclusion of the heretical innovations of the pagan philosophers, which contrarily have a satanic origin (al-Suhrawardī 1999: 91). In his diatribe against the philosophers, he cites various depictions of heaven in the Qur'ān and the Ḥadīth and attacks those who claim that such depictions are images merely intended for the weak minds of the common people, and who affirm "spiritual" happiness in the afterlife and deny bodily rewards (al-Suhrawardī 1999: 203 ff.).

Conclusion

For some theologians, Aristotelian philosophy had much to offer, but only if its points of conflict with orthodox theology are addressed. Under al-Ghazālī's influence, most later theologians who borrowed extensively from Ibn Sīnā and other philosophers opposed the three doctrines for which he condemned them as unbelievers. A century after him, the highly-Avicennised philosophical theologian and Qur'ān exegete, Fakhr al-Dīn al-Rāzī, who had a huge influence on later theology, ignores Ibn Sīnā's views on the epistemological status of scripture, and reinforces the view that prophets provide otherwise inaccessible knowledge and that contradictions between reason and revelation are semantic and not real.

Further Reading

Eichner, H. (2007) "Dissolving the Unity of *Metaphysics*: From Fakhr al-Dīn al-Rāzī to Mullā Ṣadrā al-Shīrāzī," *Medioevo* 32: 139–97.

Endress, G. (1990) "The Defense of Reason: The Plea for Philosophy in the Religious Community," *Zeitschrift für Geschichte der Arabisch-Islamischen Wissenschaften* 6: 1–49.

Griffel, F. (2009) *Al-Ghazālī's Philosophical Theology*, New York: Oxford University Press.

Marmura, M. (2005) *Probing in Islamic Philosophy*, Binghamton, New York: Global Academic Publishing, Binghamton University.

Shihadeh, A. (2006) *The Teleological Ethics of Fakhr al-Dīn al-Rāzī*, Leiden and Boston: E.J. Brill.

References

al-Bāqillānī, Muḥammad ibn al-Ṭayyib (1957) *Al-Tamhīd*, R. McCarthy (ed.), Beirut: Librairie Orientale.

al-Ghazālī, Abū Ḥāmid (1927) *Tahāfut al-falāsifa* [*Algazel Tahafot al-falasifat*], M. Bouyges (ed.), Beirut: Imprimerie Catholique.

——. (1936) *Maqāṣid al-falāsifa*, 3 vols. in one, M. al-Kurdī (ed.), Cairo: al-Maṭba'a al-Maḥmūdiyya al-Tijāriyya.

——. (1940) *Qānūn al-ta'wīl*, M. al-Kawtharī (ed.), Cairo: Maṭba'at al-Anwār.

——. (1961) *Fayṣal al-tafriqa bayna l-Islām wa-l-zandaqa*, S. Dunyā (ed.), Cairo: 'Īsā al-Bābī al-Ḥalabī.

——. (1964) *Faḍā'iḥ al-bāṭiniyya*, 'A. Badawī (ed.), Cairo: Al-Dār al-Qawmiyya.

——. (1969) *Al-Munqidh min al-ḍalāl*, F. Jabre (ed.), Beirut: Commission libanaise pour la traduction des chefs-d'œuvre.

al-Suhrawardī, Shihāb al-Dīn (1999) *Kashf al-faḍā'iḥ al-yūnāniyya wa-rashf al-naṣā'iḥ al-īmāniyya*, 'A. Y. al-Mannā'ī (ed.), Cairo: Dār al-Salām.

Avicenna (1959) *Shifā', al-Ṭabī'iyyāt, Kitāb al-Nafs* (published as *Avicenna's De Anima (Arabic Text): Being the Psychological Part of Kitāb al-Shifā'*), F. Rahman (ed.), London: Oxford University Press.

——. (1984) *Al-Aḍḥawiyya fī l-ma'ād*, Ḥ. 'Āṣī (ed.), Beirut: al-Mu'assasa al-Jāmi'iyya li-l Dirāsāt wa-l-Nashr wa-l-Tawzī'.

Davidson, H. A. (1992) *Al-farabi, Avicenna, and Averroes, On Intellect. Their Cosmologies, Theories of the Active Intellect, and Theories of Human Intellect*, New York: Oxford University Press.

Fakhry, M. (1958) *Islamic Occasionalism and its Critique by Averroës and Aquinas*, London: Allen & Unwin.

Griffel, F. (2004) "Al-Ġazālī's Concept of Prophecy: The Introduction of Avicennan Psychology into Aš'arite Theology," *Arabic Sciences and Philosophy* 14: 101–44.

Gutas, D. (2006) "Imagination and Transcendental Knowledge in Avicenna," in J. Montgomery (ed.), *Arabic Theology, Arabic Philosophy: From the Many to the One: Essays in Celebration of Richard M. Frank*, Leuven: Peeters, pp. 337–54.

Hasse, D. (2000) *Avicenna's De Anima in the Latin West: The Formation of a Peripatetic Philosophy of the Soul 1160–1300*, London/Turin: The Warburg Institute/Nino Aragno Editore.

Ibn Taymiyya, Taqī al-Dīn (1991) *Dar' ta'āruḍ al-'aql wa-l-naql*, 11 vols., M. R. Sālim (ed.), Riyadh: Muḥammad ibn Sa'ūd University.

——. (2000) *Al-Nubuwwāt*, 'A. al-Ṭawyān (ed.), Riyadh: Maktabat Aḍwā' al-Salaf.

Mānkdīm Shashdīw (1965) *Sharḥ al-uṣūl al-khamsa*, 'a. 'Uthmān (ed.), Cairo: Maktabat Wahba.

Marmura, M. (1964) "Avicenna's Theory of Prophecy in the Light of Ash'arite Theology," in W. McCullough (ed.), *The Seed of Wisdom: Essays in Honour of T. J. Meek*, Toronto: University of Toronto Press, pp. 159–78.

Michot, Y. (1986) *La Destinée de l'homme selon Avicenne: Le retour à Dieu (*ma'ād*) et l'imagination*. Louvain: Peeters.

Perler, D. & Rudolph, U. (2000) *Occasionalismus. Theorien der Kausalität im arabischislamischen und im europäischen Denken*, Göttingen: Vandenhoeck & Ruprecht.

Shihadeh, A. (2005) "From al-Ghazālī to al-Rāzī: 6th/12th Century Developments in Muslim Philosophical Theology," *Arabic Sciences and Philosophy* 15, 1: 141–79.

INDEX